THE HANDBOOK OF INTERNATIONAL MARKET RESEARCH TECHNIQUES

THE MARKET RESEARCH SOCIETY

The Market Research Society (MRS) is the world's largest international membership organisation for professional research practitioners. It serves over 8,000 members in more than 50 countries. All members are required to comply with the MRS Code of Conduct.

Tel: 020 7490 4911
Fax: 020 7490 0608
Web site: www.mrs.org.uk

THE HANDBOOK OF INTERNATIONAL MARKET RESEARCH TECHNIQUES

SECOND EDITION

EDITED BY

ROBIN J BIRN

KOGAN PAGE

First published as *A Handbook of Market Research Techniques* in 1990
Second edition 2000

Kogan Page Limited
120 Pentonville Road
London
N1 9JN
UK

Kogan Page Limited
163 Central Avenue, Suite 2
Dover
NH 03820
USA

© Robin Birn, Paul Hague and Phyllis Vangelder, 1990
© Robin Birn and named authors, 2000

British Library Cataloguing in Publication Data

A CIP record for this book is available from the British Library.

ISBN 0 7494 2616 0

Typeset by JS Typesetting, Wellingborough, Northamptonshire
Printed and bound by Creative Print and Design (Wales) Ebbw Vale

Contents

Part 2 Qualitative Techniques

Part 3 New Product Development

Section 3 Communications, Advertising and Media   **343**
Introduction   345

Section 4 Analysis and Modelling   **405**
Introduction   407

Section 5 Presenting Results   **537**
Introduction   539

The Editor

Robin Birn has been a marketing and market research practitioner for over 21 years, working in the leisure, travel, tourism, automotive, industrial, financial services, professional services, publishing and training sectors.

In 1985 Robin set up Strategy, Research & Action Ltd and decided to develop marketing information services for the map, atlas and travel guide sector. Now Strategy, Research & Action Ltd is the largest international marketing research company for the map, atlas and travel guide sector and other sectors of the book industry such as the academic and professional sector. Robin is also a registered trainer in marketing and marketing information in the book sector. Strategy, Research & Action Ltd is also the leading international research company for the food casing sector, particularly collagen sausage casings.

He is author of the books *Effective Use of Market Research*, Kogan Page, 1990, third edition 1999, and *Using Research to Grow Your Business*, Pitmans, 1994; and co-editor of *A Handbook of Market Research Techniques*, Kogan Page, 1990, and *Marketing for Publishers*, Routledge, 1997.

In July 1998, he was appointed one of the few Fellows of the Market Research Society. In the past Robin was also appointed to the Council of the Market Research Society and has been vice-chairman of the Society and chairman of membership development. He is a graduate, full member of the Chartered Institute of Marketing and a former member of the Global Marketing Council of the American Marketing Association. He was a founder and first year board member of the European Board of the International Map Trade Association.

Robin is a US/UK dual citizen.

Contributors

James R Adams spent most of his early career in advertising agencies. As Director of Media and Research at BBDO London he was involved in considerable international research. He has contributed numerous papers to trade publications, and several chapters to management books. He wrote *Media Planning*, the first edition of which was published as an IPA textbook. Since forming James R Adams & Associates in 1975 he has worked across a variety of product groups, and prominent among his activities has been the Adams Residential Property Index.

Ken Baker formed his own company, Ken Baker Associates, in 1987 after spending many years as Chief Statistician at the British Market Research Bureau (BMRB). He has written several articles on innovatory techniques for marketing and market research on subjects such as the application of geodemographic systems, and is Chairman of the Market Research Development Foundation (MRDF) working party on data fusion.

Peter Bartram is President of the City Research Group (acquired in 1998 by the leading US research company NFO Worldwide) and Chairman of its affiliates Applied Research and Communications and IQ Research. Following graduation from Cambridge, he worked for NOP, the Thomson Organization, and Louis Harris and Associates in London, New York and Los Angeles. In addition to his broad international experience as a research practitioner, he has been a European Marketing Director at American Express, and was Chairman of the UK Market Research Society (MRS) 1989/90, of which he is now a Fellow.

Chris Blamires is Managing Director of AIM Market Research Ltd and a partner in The Decision Modelling Consultancy. He has chaired, and spoken at, a wide range of international seminars on the role of multivariate analysis in market research, including applications of the more complex segmentation techniques.

A key ongoing interest is in the role of new technology in market research, from an early paper on probably the first ever documented application of artificial intelligence techniques to CAPI-based conjoint studies ('Micros and modelling: putting a new slant on established techniques', 1982), via CAPI use in pricing research ('Trade-off pricing research', 1988), to international applications of disk-by-mail technology ('Electronic data capture: taking advantage of a new era', 1997).

Chris has published extensively on cluster analysis and brand mapping, pricing research and market modelling, and has presented papers on these subjects world-wide. These include 'Micro-behavioural modelling as an aid to retailer strategic planning' (co-author, Best MRS Conference Paper Award, 1981), and 'Pricing research techniques: a review and a new approach' (MRS Silver Award 1982), reprinted in the 1997 50th Anniversary *Journal of the Market Research Society*'s Milestones in Market Research. His papers on pricing research form part of the MRS Diploma syllabus.

W G Blyth is Director of Research at AGB Market Information. Prior to joining AGB in 1982 he was Technical Director of MIL Research Ltd, and Company Statistician at BMRB, which he joined in 1970. He is a former chairman of the MRS and has written widely on market research. His responsibilities at AGB include control of the research aspects of panel services. He has spent the last three years on the development of AGB's electronic data collection service – AGB Superpanel.

Dr Stephan Buck is a main board director of AGB Research, having joined the company shortly after its formation and being associated with its growth to become the largest market research company in Europe. He has specialized in the theory and practice of research in a number of sectors including television, and has been responsible for the development, home and abroad, of innovative techniques in these areas. Dr Buck is co-editor of the *Journal of the Market Research Society* and author of many papers and articles, some of which are considered the standards in their field.

Steffen Conway, who passed away in May 2000, had been Deputy Chairman of INRA UK Ltd (formally Research and Auditing Services Ltd), and a chartered statistician by training (a BSc in mathematics and physics, he completed the examinations of the Institute of Statisticians). He was also a Fellow of the Market Research Society. His research career started in 1968 as Assistant Statistician with Marplan. In 1971 he became Research Executive there, moving to NOP in 1973, then to England Gross Associates in 1978 and on to Survey Research Associates in 1981 where he became a director and subsequently Deputy Managing Director before moving to RAS. He had spoken several times at the Market Research Society Conference on statistical issues as well as on research case studies and on fieldwork matters. Between 1990 and 1996 he served on various industry councils: MRS Conference Chairman in 1994 and 1995; Honorary Secretary and Treasurer of the Market Research Society between 1994 and 1996; and on the councils of the Interviewer Quality Control Scheme and the Association of Market Survey Organizations.

Bill Dunning BA MSc is Managing Director of Scantel International Ltd, a market research company specializing in new product development, new design and colour research both in the UK and internationally. His career in market research began in the 1970s after four years in product management. Mr Dunning has been Chairman of the northern region of the MRS. He has presented papers on the subject of design and colour research and is a regular speaker on this subject. Currently, he is Chairman of The Marketing Society for the north-west region.

Mary J Goodyear became involved with market research in 1962. She joined a specialist qualitative research company, Market Behaviour Ltd, in 1965 and subsequently became Chief Executive. She has been involved in many different areas of research in both the industrialized and the developing world, and has written articles and given numerous papers at MRS, American Marketing Association and European Society for Opinion and Marketing Research (ESOMAR) seminars. She has worked with a broad spectrum of research methodologies, from small tactical surveys in advertising creative development, to very large multi-country strategic studies. In 1984 and 1986 she planned and carried out two large-scale sociological surveys, 'AdAfrica' – a study of West Africans' response to advertising – and, latterly, 'The Arab as consumer' – a study of Gulf Arabs and how they are responding to their newly consumerized society.

Paul Harris is currently a director and the chief statistician of NOP Research Ltd, a position he has held for the past 24 years. He was formerly with the Market Research Department of the Electricity Council and before that with the Central Electricity Generating Board, working on power station statistics. His interests include the application of multivariate statistical methods to market research data and the use of computers in statistical analysis. Among his published works is a Market Research Society Silver Medal paper on the effects of clustering on random sample surveys. He lectures widely on various topics for the MRS and other bodies.

Stephen Howard joined SIA as a statistical consultant specializing in forecasting applications. Later he worked for Taylor Nelson Market Research, developing software for continuous tracking models. In 1987 he joined Forvus Computer Services where he has developed software for the data management, analysis and forecasting of time series data. He is now systems manager responsible for VAX computing services and UNIX development.

Peter Jackling is Managing Director of Independent Data Analysis Ltd and of the leading software company Merlinco. He has spent his entire 25-year career in the applications of computers in market research survey data capture and processing. Although mainly working in specialist survey analysis bureaux and software companies, he spent two years at AGB on IT strategy development, and designed and implemented all technical aspects of Superpanel. A past Vice-Chairman of the Market Research Society, and recently elected as a Fellow of the MRS, Peter is now Vice-Chairman of the British Market Research Association.

Peter Jackson's work in market research now spans four decades (though not 40 years). After spending time at the LSE in the 1960s, he worked for a number of consumer and industrial marketing companies. In 1973 he joined Paul Hague at Business and Market Research, since when he has been involved in the many types of market research carried out by the company. He has spent all his working life in market research and for most of this time as a director of Business and Market Research. He is now a consultant to research companies, principally in the field of quality management. He is also secretary of the Market Research Quality Standards Association (MRQSA). His publications include several books on market research and quality management and some of these have been translated and published in several languages.

Tony Lees had been Consumer Omnibus Research Director at the NOP Research Group. Having joined NOP in 1970, Tony has been involved with NOP's omnibus surveys for 25 years and was appointed Omnibus Director in 1986.

Dr Barry Leventhal is Vice-Chairman of Berry Consulting and has been their Research and Statistics Director since 1991.

He joined Pinpoint Analysis in 1987 where he was Chief Statistician from 1987–91. There he oversaw product development and statistical consulting on all aspects of geodemographics and census analysis. Previously he worked at AGB for 10 years where he was primarily concerned with the collection and analysis of consumer panel data.

He is a Fellow of the Royal Statistical Society, a Fellow of the Market Research Society and Chairman of the MRS Census Interest Group. A frequent speaker at marketing conferences, his publications include papers on geodemographics and applications of statistical techniques to database marketing.

Derek Martin is currently Chairman of the Martin Hamblin group of companies and of its specialist company Sensory Research Laboratories. He founded Martin Hamblin some 20 years ago and developed an interest in sensory research during the 1970s. He is particularly involved in work to utilize the disciplines of sensory analysis in marketing fields, both in the UK and internationally.

Terry McCarthy joined the then independent retail research company Stats MR straight from university in 1969. Between 1972 and 1975, he gained wide practical experience of differing research techniques by working for Market Research Africa in Johannesburg and the Australian Wool Board in Sydney. Returning to England in 1975, he rejoined Stats MR, joining the board of the company after it became part of the ACNielsen group in 1986. Since then, Terry has specialized in work for the leisure industries – mainly drinks (alcoholic) and travel – and in 1985 he set up the independent monitor of retail booking trends for the holiday industry. He often speaks and otherwise actively participates at seminars and international industry conferences, as well as providing regular contributions to both the trade and national media.

As an active member of the MRS, particularly in the regional structure, Terry was Chairman of the West Midlands branch for many years.

Erhard Meier joined Research Services Ltd in London in 1972 where he gained experience in consumer, social and international research before specializing in media research. Since 1977 he has been the executive responsible for servicing the JICNARS contract for the UK National Readership Surveys. His present position is Managing Director of RSL Media, a division of Research Services Ltd.

Peter Menneer is an independent broadcast researching consultant. He was Head of Broadcasting Research at the BBC from 1979 to 1992. His earlier career had been within research companies: BMRB 1960–77 (appointed a director in 1974), and as a joint managing director of RSMB 1977–79.

He is the author of *Towards Global Guidelines for Television Audience Measurement* (GGTAM–EBU, 1999) on behalf of the International Audience Research Methods Group, and the equivalent for radio (EBU, 1997). He has acted as technical adviser to joint in industry committees in a number of countries – including Denmark, Israel, Hungary, Romania and Russia – to help them develop their national audience measurement systems for TV and radio.

He is the founder and co-ordinator of the International Radiometer Evaluation Group.

Rory Morgan joined RBL (now Research International) in 1972. Since then, he has worked in a number of consumer groups covering a wide range of product areas, both in the UK and internationally. This involved him in spending a period of secondment to the research subsidiary in East Africa. He was group head of a consumer group within RBL, with special responsibility for the development of computer modelling techniques and similar areas, in which field he has delivered a number of papers both in Europe and North America. Subsequently, Mr Morgan has been appointed to the board of Research International UK as Technical and Development Director with the inventory role of developing and supporting advanced research techniques, in particular computer applications. As such, he is currently Managing Director of the Technical Systems division of Research International.

Peter Mouncey worked for the AA from 1971–2000 and was appointed to a new role as General Manager, customer relationship information strategy, after a number of years as General Manager, group marketing services.

An ex-chairman of both the Market Research Society and the Association of Users of Research Agencies (AURA) and an ex-member of the IDM Council, he has presented many papers on research and database marketing techniques and similar over the years and is on the editorial board of the *Journal of the Market Research Society* and *New Marketing Directions*, the journal of the IDM.

He has been Chairman of the Research Development Foundation of the market research industry and a visiting Fellow at Cranfield University.

Roy Norton was originally involved in statistical and forecasting methods before moving into mainstream market research. Following positions in both a market research agency and pharmaceutical companies, he joined Taylor Nelson to develop tracking and audit business in the medical area. He is now Chairman of the Medical Division and also the director responsible for the development of continuous database business for the Taylor Nelson Research Group.

Ellen Robertson is a founding partner of Analytica Research Consultants. Previously she was a director of Research and Auditing Services Ltd where she set up their full service division, Coefficient Research for Marketing. Her earlier marketing and research experience was gained with Beecham Products and Metal Box plc. She has been a visiting lecturer at universities in the USA and the UK. She is a full member of the MRS and has contributed to their publications and conferences.

Sue Robson is currently Managing Director of The Qualitative Consultancy. Her early market research experience was gained at the British Market Research Bureau. In 1972 Sue joined Market Behaviour Ltd and specialized in qualitative research. She then worked in new product development before returning to Market Behaviour Ltd. She was appointed to the board in 1978 and became managing director in 1981. In 1982 she set up The Qualitative Consultancy and since 1974 has regularly lectured and convened MRS courses on qualitative research. In collaboration with Angela Foster, she has developed tailor-made packages of qualitative research training for large companies and advertising agencies. In 1988 she won the David Winton award for best technical paper at the MRS Conference. She has served on the council of the MRS.

Peter Sampson is a psychologist who has worked in advertising and market research for over 30 years. He is equally at home with qualitative and quantitative methods and has written and lectured extensively in the area of simulated test marketing. As Managing Director of Burke Marketing Research Group, he launched BASES – the Burke Advanced Sales Estimating System – in the UK in 1980.

Tony Schlaeppi is CRL's Chief Executive and runs their advertising, packaging and design research group. He joined the London Press Exchange Advertising Agency in the 1950s as a media buyer, became one of the first 'planners' and was a founder director of two of their associated research companies. One of these – Telpex Ltd – pioneered pack testing equipment and research structures. He has published papers on poster design, advertising research and pack testing.

Professor Michael Thomas is the current President of the Market Research Society. He was Chairman of the Chartered Institute of Marketing in 1995, and is a chartered marketer. He worked for the Metal Box plc as a market researcher, and then began his academic career teaching postgraduate courses in the School of Management, Syracuse University. He was subsequently Senior Lecturer at Lancaster University, and Professor of Marketing at Strathclyde University. He has held visiting professorships at Georgetown University, Temple University, the University of Tennessee, Stockholm School of Economics, University of Karlstad and the Helsinki School of Economics. His books have been translated into Polish, Romanian and Portuguese. He edits the journal *Marketing Intelligence and Planning*. He was awarded the Order of Merit of the Republic of Poland for his contribution to the transformation of Poland post-1989, and founded the Gdansk Managers Training Foundation, now regarded as one of the top three business schools in Poland.

David Walker is International Director (New Media) at Research International Group. He has been with Research International for five years, having previously worked at Benchmark Research, a specialist IT and business-to-business research agency. Since joining RI, David has focused on work in telecommunications and, in particular, new media. His new media work has included many projects examining the effective use of the media and examining new concepts and developments. He has also been involved in developing these media as a means of conducting research. David has been at the forefront of RI's use of online research techniques and has been quoted widely on the topic in the research and marketing press. He has twice given papers at ESOMAR conferences and has a wide range of experience in all quantitative and qualitative online methodologies.

Janet Weitz is founder and Chairman of FDS Market Research Group Limited, one of the UK's top 20 agencies. She was one of the pioneers of computer-assisted telephone interviewing (CATI) and set up and chaired the first MRS Telephone Research Sub-Committee.

Kate Willis is an independent marketing and qualitative research consultant, specializing in financial, social and advertising research both in the UK and internationally. She has worked at three major research agencies, including The Research Business International, where she was a founder member and director, in charge of the Corporate and Financial Unit for a number of years. Her qualitative research experience and interests are broad-ranging, encompassing an enormous range of audiences although she is particularly interested in staff and customer service/ satisfaction research, a subject on which she has presented a number of papers at MRS and ESOMAR conferences.

Alan Wolfe has been Marketing Services Director of Primary Contact, and a consultant on strategic marketing for their parent company, the Ogilvy Group. He has 35 years' experience of a wide range of markets and techniques, including market research as Assistant to the Research Manager at Rowntree-Mackintosh, Research Group Head at Ogilvy & Mather and Director of RSGB. He has been Honorary Visiting Research Fellow at Bradford University, a full member of the MRS and IMRA and Fellow of five other professional bodies.

Foreword

Professor Michael J Thomas, OM (Poland), MBA, FRSA, FCIM, President of the Market Research Society, Chartered Marketer

It is almost 10 years since *A Handbook of Market Research Techniques* was published, and the revisions in this new edition reflect two things. One is that there has been a continuous development of the techniques of market research over the decade. Some aspiring PhD student may wish to do a textual analysis of the two editions to demonstrate the fact, but the editor will tell you that all of the 1990 edition authors have continued to toil in their chosen fields and specialisms, and that updating has been a fairly natural act, and that all the usual suspects are still around.

The other thing that this volume reflects is the growing stature of the market research profession. The skills and inventiveness of the people working in the profession have all contributed to the developments of the past decade. In the Age of Information, these people may have found their place in the sun. We are surrounded by information, perhaps deluged by it. But is it all any good? Is it trustworthy? Is it a goldmine or a septic tank? We exist in a rapidly changing environment – the changing consumer environment; the changing business environment, more global than local; and the changing technological environment.

Many of these changes are both stimulating and for the greater good; many other changes are negative, threatening, insidious, or all three. We need to understand these changes, and data is the vehicle for recording them, analysis the means for understanding and interpreting the data.

The market research profession in the United Kingdom rightly claims world leadership – in objectivity, accuracy and integrity. This handbook reflects that professionalism, professionalism nurtured and protected by the Market Research Society, of which I have the honour of being the

President. I trust that this new edition will be as useful and as well used as its predecessor.

Preface

Robin J Birn

Techniques are skills applied to a particular task. Market research is a practical subject and so the techniques become clearer and are sharpened by actually doing them. But they are constantly developing and changing. This new edition of the book provides a short cut to obtaining that experience, as each contribution has been written and updated by one of the industry's leading market research practitioners. What is said has been tried and tested – and it really works! And there are new contributions too.

This book is for all levels of researchers. The first edition has been widely used by students studying in universities and colleges and by professionals developing their qualifications. On basic subjects, such as planning a survey or designing a questionnaire, the researcher will find considerable help in Section 1. Both the novice and experienced practitioner may wish to dip into Section 2 to find out how best to collect the data. Those with an interest in communications, the media and now in this edition the Internet will turn to Section 3. Once the researcher has assembled the data, Section 4 of the book will show how to analyse it, while expertise in presenting the data will be gleaned from Section 5.

It is unlikely that the book will be read from cover to cover (though any person with such fortitude will be able to share the knowledge of the leading experts on all the techniques available to market researchers). It is more likely that the reader will use the book to gain knowledge in a particular field. I refer to it myself about once a month.

The next few paragraphs provide an overview of the techniques that are covered in the book.

TECHNIQUES OF MARKET RESEARCH

Preparation

- **Planning market research surveys** Lurking behind most surveys is a problem that needs solving. At the outset of the study it is the researcher's job to determine what the problem is and show how it can be solved. The researcher must develop skills in taking a brief from the 'problem owner' and translating it into a 'proposal' for carrying out the study. In the proposal the researcher states the objectives of the study, the methods that will be used to meet the objectives, the timing, the composition of the research team and the cost.
- **Desk research** There is no point in reinventing the wheel. If data exist, they should be used and not collected afresh. Desk research is the collection, sifting and interpretation of published data. It plays a part in most surveys, even if only to use the known breakdown of the population to guide the selection of a quota sample. Elsewhere it may involve the researcher in delving in the library or searching online databases for information on market size and structure.
- **Standards and methods** Standards have had an increasing impact on the practice of market research. Standards do not define good methods, but they encourage quality. They are intended to be implemented at an organizational level, rather than being a matter for individual practitioners – but they need to be followed by practitioners in an organization.
- **Sampling and statistics** Sampling is a worry for most researchers who are new to the business. Understanding the rudiments of random sampling is necessary, even though in most day-to-day surveys the researcher may learn to trust a quota sample of 300 interviews spread across five cities. Without an appreciation of why and how different samples are selected, the researcher cannot claim to be undertaking a valid, scientific piece of work.
- **Questionnaire design** Good market research is about asking the right people the right questions – not much more, not much less. We all ask questions in our daily life. We all fill in forms, and are critical of them. In theory, questionnaire design should be easy and yet it is one of the most difficult tasks to get right. Designing questions that draw out accurate information from everyone, that can be completed easily by the interviewer, that flow well and leave respondents feeling they have contributed something worth while, should be the aim of all researchers.
- **Geodemographics** Time was when survey samples were selected from a representative quota of the population based on sex, social class and age. Over the last 20 years the technique has made it possible to link the characteristics of people with the neighbourhoods in which they

live. This has become a powerful tool in allowing researchers to infer certain types of behaviour through knowing the geography of their homes. Geodemographics gave sampling a new lease of life. Plans for the 2001 census will give the techniques further development opportunities.

■ **Quantitative research over the Internet** The Internet has become a collection of virtual communities, all focused on sharing information. For some organizations the Internet may be no more than a marketing or promotional tool. Others will benefit from operating and distributing their services over the Internet. Market research is a service that will find the Internet providing a new method of collecting and distributing information. As a result, Web and e-mail questionnaires can be useful tools to researchers.

Data collection

■ **Quantitative research** Quantitative research supplies a number to anything that can be measured. And there is a large body of researchers who argue that measurement can be applied to anything. Quantitative research produces 'hard' data that can be defended or challenged and is more than just opinion. It is based on sizeable surveys, in the main, using samples of upwards of 200 people. However, the well-rounded researcher does not see quantitative research as a technique that can stand alone. It is often appropriate to gauge people's opinions first, using qualitative techniques, before determining exactly what should be measured.

■ **Face-to-face interviewing** The market research industry has been built around face-to-face interviewing – in the street and in the home. It is still the bedrock of many studies, as it allows the interviewer to use personal skills to elicit the information, show visual aids, smooth the interview and gain deeper insights. CAPI – computer-aided personal interviewing – has given the traditional technique technological advancement and efficiencies.

■ **Telephone interviewing** The telephone rose in popularity in the 1980s as a market research tool, as it allows interviews to be carried out speedily and under close supervision through central control. Now that almost all households have a telephone, this means of contact allows the researcher easily to sample households anywhere in the country. It is not necessarily a cheap method, costing approximately the same as a street interview. CATI – computer-aided telephone interviewing – has given the technique to increase quality and provide more detail in the interviews.

■ **Postal surveys** There is a certain prejudice about the use of postal surveys, but this is because they are frequently used in the wrong circumstances. They produce excellent results when there is a strong relationship between the respondent and the company carrying out the research. They are suited to testing opinion and sensitive subjects, and work best with closed questions. Case studies have been developed to show which approaches work best for maximizing responses.

■ **Omnibus research** Omnibus studies are targeted at certain groups of respondents and run at regular intervals. They provide the facility for buying space for a limited number of questions in a large interview programme. Because the cost of the interviewing and analysis is shared among the people contributing questions to the omnibus, it is an efficient means of collecting data. This is a technique that has seen an ever-expanding range of omnibus services covering all manner of target groups.

■ **Panels and diaries** A panel differs from an omnibus study in that it is a survey of the same people each time (although in practice it is not always the same people all the time as people drop out and need replacing, but care is taken to replace panel members with relevant demographic characteristics). The questions asked of the panel are consistent so that results can be tracked over time. This provides reliable trend data on purchasing or viewing habits. Panels that exist all over the world are usually sponsored by large media or consumer goods companies wanting to keep a check on movements in their target markets. The panel members keep records of their purchases and activities in diaries.

■ **Retail audits** As the name suggests, retail audits take place at the shop or store. Through checking the stock turnover at retailers', the audit companies produce accurate figures on the market shares of a wide range of consumer goods. The results are used by the subscribers to the audits to monitor changes in brand shares and the distribution routes through which their goods are sold.

■ **EPOS** EPOS or electronic point of sale is carried out by scanning the bar codes at the check-out. This allows researchers to measure quickly and accurately which goods have been sold and at what prices. EPOS is an extension of the retail audit. It is an excellent means of tracking product data as well as furnishing researchers with a basis for much predictive modelling.

■ **Qualitative research** In many studies researchers want to obtain a deep understanding of why and how something is happening. The qualitative researcher works with small samples of people, sometimes one to one, sometimes in small groups. These are less like interviews and more in the nature of conversations or discussions. They are long and unstructured and require considerable skill to draw out relevant information. Qualitative research can produce rich data, probing into people's unconscious attitudes and needs. Because the samples are small, there is no attempt to measure responses.

- **In-depth interviews** Using open-ended and unstructured interview guides, the researcher carries out in-depth interviews to 'get beneath' the superficial responses. The in-depth interview permits the researcher to be flexible in the order and style of questioning so that avenues of interest and relevance to a particular respondent can be explored.
- **Group discussions** In a group discussion (or focus group) between five and nine people are led into an exchange of views by the researcher (called the moderator). The interactions between people flush out views that would not otherwise be raised in one-to-one interviewing. The group discussion is a widely employed technique for researching new concepts and guiding creative teams in advertising agencies. Groups yield rich information but they require experienced researchers to hold them together and obtain true responses and not just the 'party line'.
- **Hall tests** There are many occasions in market research when it is necessary to have people look at or taste a product. For all sorts of reasons it may not be possible for this to take place in consumers' homes. When this is the case, hall tests are set up. Target consumers are 'recruited' from busy streets and invited to a nearby hall where the test takes place.
- **Sensory evaluation** Sensory evaluation is a tool to help the technical research and development teams design better products. It focuses on a small number of aspects of a product such as the materials that are used, their quality, the shape of the product and its performance in use. Data can be mapped to show where the product stands against consumer preferences and in comparison with the competition. Because the evaluation considers a number of variables, this type of new product research benefits greatly from multivariate analysis.

Communications, advertising, media and the Internet

- **Advertising research** Advertising research employs both quantitative and qualitative techniques. Large-scale samples are used for this purpose. Backing up the quantitative studies are group discussions or in-depth interviews, which test the adverts or give creative teams in advertising agencies ideas for campaigns.
- **Researching TV and radio** Broadcasting nowadays is a highly competitive business. The transaction from analogue to digital transmissions is revolutionizing the structure of broadcasting. Competition for audiences has been good for the business of audience researchers. The audience researcher can contribute his or her professional skills to identify the talent appropriate to the station, its deployment and

promotion. But the chapter (Chapter 21) shows that the researcher will need to deploy a wide range of research tools.

■ **Peoplemeters** In the past television viewing was recorded in diaries by panels of people in their homes. This method worked well when homes had just one television set and the family sat watching it together. Today television viewing is complicated by the many sets in homes and the use of video recorders. Peoplemeters overcome these problems. They are electronic devices that monitor all the sets in the home – and the viewing on video recorders.

■ **Packaging research** Packaging is an integral part of the products we buy. It plays an important functional role in protecting the product and it carries visual information that describes the contents as well as inviting consumers to buy. Packaging research is used to determine how well current or new packs actually work. In many cases straightforward questioning in the home or in hall tests will find out people's attitudes to packs. However, other techniques such as tachistoscopes are available to show how rapidly the visual information on the pack is absorbed.

Analysis and modelling

■ **Analysing data** Data on their own have no value. It is the implications of data that really matter. This means that researchers have a responsibility to screen out only the data relevant to the objectives of the study and simplify them so that the user can quickly and easily see a pattern. The data must be presented in a form that the reader can understand and, it is hoped, they will lead naturally to a conclusion and recommendation.

■ **Modelling** Computers have enabled researchers to get more out of their data than ever before. Programs now exist for testing the prices that people will pay for a product. They can show the degree to which consumers will trade off some feature such as quality or design for price. Simulated test markets can be set up. Missing data can be inferred by 'fusing' together sets of data. Data can be analysed to map or segment consumers to show their different characteristics or attitudes to brands. And the models can be used to forecast a course of action.

Presentation

■ **Presentation and report writing** The final output of the researcher's efforts is the presentation of the work. Presentations are the 'day of reckoning' for researchers, a chance to make a mark for better or worse. Good presentations have a clear objective. They are short but to the point with little time spent describing the method and more time spent on the findings and conclusions. The use of visual aids to communicate the data through charts and diagrams has become sophisticated with the use of PowerPoint. While the personal presentation has impact, it is nevertheless ephemeral. The written report is more enduring and may be read over a long period of time. It is worth getting it right! The same rules apply as with presentations. The audience must be kept in mind and the writing style should quickly and clearly communicate the points, leading logically to the conclusions and recommendations.

KNOWLEDGE DISTINGUISHES SUCCESSFUL COMPANIES

The risks faced by businesses today have never been greater. Competition is fierce at every level of the market. Small businesses are likely to be funded by a family's life savings or expensive borrowing. The cost of failure can be very high for the entrepreneur and his or her associates. Large businesses face the same risks except that there are more noughts on the figures. The cost of failure for the large business may mean redundancies, scrapped plant and dire financial losses.

Success and failure in business is a consequence of making the right or wrong decisions. The right decisions are easy with hindsight, much more difficult when the conditions are unknown. It is a relatively simple matter to plan the production resources and estimate the financial requirement for a business. And yet both these plans must be based on understanding the needs of the market, and whether customers buy the products and then become repeat buyers.

It is those market needs that are most often misjudged, assumed or even taken for granted. Uncertainty about what the market wants, both now and in the future, is one of the most difficult problems with which businesses must cope. More than ever, decisions in business require robust information. If information on markets is a key to business success, it follows that the people who can supply it hold considerable power.

It is the role of market researchers to provide sound information to guide business decisions, set strategies and monitor the implementations to give feedback on whether it has been successful or unsuccessful. The techniques available to researchers have been developed and polished, especially over the last three decades. There is no area where market research techniques cannot be used. They are as useful in social marketing to probe why people drink and drive as they are to manufacturers selling alcoholic drinks, as useful to the government trying to obtain recruits for the armed forces as for theatre managers trying to measure their audiences. The skill of the market researcher is not just being able to apply a special technique but also knowing which to apply and when.

'Companies now are concentrating on 'knowledge management'. There is a wealth of internal data that needs to be analysed and interpreted – but there have to be procedures to discuss it. Once reviewed a company can decide on what data to collect and use the best technique to do the research needed.

This book reviews all the techniques in market research and is a key reference for knowledge management to be successful.

SECTION 1

PREPARATION

Introduction

Market research is a means of providing management with market and marketing information. Its main purpose is to reduce uncertainty when marketing strategy is being planned, and to monitor performance after the strategy has been put into operation. It has a key role in aiding decision-making, either with a continuous flow of data or dipstick information.

The quality of the information gained from marketing research and its contribution to decision-making depend largely on the definition of the problem. Without this, research becomes an isolated piece of information. This information might be interesting, but it will not necessarily provide management with the means of refining their decisions. The research may also fail to provide the 'lead' towards the sales and marketing actions required. Any approach to designing a research project must therefore start with problem definition. After this, careful discussion – on the type of research that is required and what should be gained from it – is vital if a company is to make an investment in effective and cost-effective market research.

Management needs to ask the following questions to help decide what research to carry out to solve a marketing or sales problem.

- What information will help make decision-making?
- What are we going to do with this information?
- How should we collect this information?
- What are we going to measure?
- How should we analyse the results?
- How much should we spend on collecting the information?

It is also very important to consider the cost and value of information that may be obtained. This in itself is meaningless unless management clearly identifies the benefits of using the research. To do this, it needs to weigh up the likely outcome of not using research against the likely results of using it. It therefore needs to ask:

- What decision are we faced with?
- What is the potential cost of taking the wrong decision?
- What is the probability or risk of taking a wrong decision on the basis of information already available?
- How justified are we in taking this decision without collecting data?
- How will additional information help me?
- How quickly is any additional information required?
- What level of accuracy is required?

The following process will help management think through a problem, define it, assess what alternative courses of action or decisions will follow from the range of information that could be acquired and, finally, decide what must be acquired to be 'safe'.

1. Define the problem carefully, to address the decision that needs to be taken and the information that will help.
2. Review how existing data can address the problem.
3. List what additional data is needed.
4. Select the data collection methods.
5. Select the measurement techniques required.
6. Select the sample.
7. Select the analytical method.
8. Specify the time and the cost.
9. Prepare a research proposal.

All this implies that effective research depends on management adopting a structured approach to decision-making. This means deciding in advance what is required from the research. The preparation in itself helps to define the problem and the extent to which information needs to be collected. It also influences the way in which a research project is designed. It not only identifies who needs to be interviewed, but also helps to shape the nature of wording for the questionnaire.

This section of the book will show how important it is to prepare a research project carefully. Planning is the first step as it is essential to ensure a research project is executed in a definitive way. The quality of the brief will correlate directly with the quality of the finished job, since the objectives of the research should arise naturally from the brief.

Statistics concern the actual numbers in market research. It is in fact the science of numbers and the analysis and interpretation of market research information using statistical theory. Management using research inform-ation should not be concerned with learning statistics. There are, in fact, three key elements research users need to summarize data collected from surveys and to ensure that maximum interpretation of the data can be carried out. First, reassurance has to be gained on the accuracy of the information, as development or investment decisions might rest on what the data have found about the subject being researched. Secondly, in this context the research planner should also be aware of the effect of sample size on the accuracy of the data. And, finally, it is important to be able to identify between real changes measured by surveys, as opposed to random fluctuations caused by sampling variability.

An important development in sampling has been the techniques of geodemographics. These techniques improve sample accuracy and contribute to reducing fieldwork costs. The main implications for market research are that geodemographics provide a link between sample survey results and the population. They can either be used for initial sampling, or for extrapolating from survey data to form a benchmark for the population.

Questionnaires, together with sampling and fieldwork, form the critical part of the data collection process. The content of the questionnaire depends on the survey brief in the context of what information is to be collected and how it should be analysed. Designing a questionnaire is an art, which can be learnt with the benefit of experience. The most important aspect of any research project is to be able to develop a questionnaire that explores all the issues, but also provides the means of collecting the key information.

Desk research, or previously published or commissioned data from both internal and external sources is frequently under-utilized and under-estimated as a source of information. Most companies, whatever their size, have access to a wealth of information. From internal sources there are sales statistics, reports of previous research projects undertaken, internal company documentation and even the accumulated knowledge of colleagues. Published data such as government publications, trade association information, trade journals, etc are important sources of information provided the data are available, relevant and accurate. In the context of preparing a project, desk research forms an important role in helping management to develop its understanding of the market and its ability to develop survey research. Both the design of a survey and the type of questions put in the questionnaire can be greatly enhanced by having done desk research. Knowledge of the market gained from published research ensures that actionable information is incorporated into the survey.

Standards have an increasing impact on the practice of research. They are intended to be implemented at an organizational level, rather than being a matter for individual practitioners – but they need to be followed by practitioners in an organization.

The essential first step in the research design process is to define the marketing problem, which, it is hoped, the research will identify or solve. Preparation for research therefore has a great influence on the quality of the answers gained from research and their contribution to decision-making.

1

Planning Market Research Surveys

James R Adams

This chapter follows the steps that need to be taken in planning a research project, and is illustrated with a case history.

THE BRIEF

In simple terms the better the brief, the better the finished job. However brilliant the researchers may be, if they have not uncovered a clear picture of what the marketer needs to know, they may provide excellent information that is none the less useless for the marketer's purposes.

We put the onus for this discovery on the researchers, partly because discovering is part of their calling, but mainly because it is they who will be in the most trouble if it is not made. Researchers should not be ashamed of admitting ignorance at the briefing session, even if they are in a competitive position.

Clients are experts in their market; if the researcher neglects the opportunity to ask them, he or she may not find anyone else who knows. The best approach to briefing is to get a written outline first, and to consider it before the (essential) meeting. Not only does this give an opportunity to think about techniques, but also to set time and cost parameters. These may put the project beyond the client's schedule or budget. It is better to know this as early as possible, when remedial action may be taken.

The matter of confidentiality is always important to the client company. It is particularly critical in the case of new products (which is why the study in this chapter is some years old). Since it is always important, it 'comes naturally' to most research companies. If the client has any reasonable doubts about the company being briefed, he should go elsewhere.

The quality of the brief will also depend on the quality of the briefer(s). Given the opportunity to study a written outline, the researchers may be able to improve the brief, as well as to clarify the intention, thus making for greater satisfaction all round. We have cheated a little in selecting the following study, because there was no room for improvement on the very clear brief. Life is not always hard!

THE CASE STUDY

A US food manufacturer had a unique pastry base for frozen pizzas. He wished to know whether it could be sold profitably in Europe.

The objectives

Given a clear brief, the research objectives flow logically. In this case, it was necessary to discover:

1. what kind of markets for frozen pizzas existed in Europe;
2. whether this pizza base would be seen as superior to existing products;
3. if so, what kinds of toppings the European markets would prefer;
4. what packaging, pricing and marketing requirements there would be; and
5. what financial projections could be made for the best entry.

These objectives are based on the 4-P approach to marketing, which suggests that success is dependent on product, packaging, price and promotion. Getting these right should guarantee market share. The first objective related to ascertaining what value a given share might have in dollar terms.

Research methods

The choice of research methods is usually determined by a series of constraints. Frequently there is only one method that will satisfy them all, and sometimes none, so that a compromise has to be sought. The primary constraints are usually budget and time. The nature of the information required will also affect methodology (mainly the choice between desk research, qualitative or quantitative techniques), and so should the level of accuracy required. 'Should' is the operative word because managers more often temper their needs to the available budget than vice versa.

Accuracy is largely determined by sample size but a sample four times greater is only twice as accurate, whereas it will cost nearly four times as much. Often sample sizes are determined by the smallest subsample that is required. Most people prefer this subsample to number not less than 100, and, statistically speaking, less than 30 cannot really be called quantitative data.

However, other factors are also important, including the number of sampling points. Again, a national sample should have at least 30 sampling points. If hall tests are involved, divide the sample into as many different halls as is practicable. A perfectly designed random sample that does not allow for evening and weekend interviewing will fail, because it will become a sample of people who are at home during working hours.

Time is well invested in planning, especially the questionnaire. If this involves scales, they will only give true results if they are evenly balanced, for example not ranging from 'excellent' to 'fair'! A pilot (which may not be more than 10 interviews) will help here.

Preliminary decisions

In the present case, a preliminary decision concerned the countries to be surveyed. The 'big four' in most terms were Germany, France, Italy and the UK. It was agreed that if these were not sufficiently promising, the project would be abandoned. If they were promising, others could be added later. However, a subjective decision was that Italy, original home of the pizza, was unlikely to provide a substantial market for frozen pizza, however good it might be. We concentrated our efforts, therefore, on Germany, France and the UK.

The first step that should be taken with any project is to search for published information. There are situations in which most if not all that is needed has already been covered by some published source. Libraries are good sources for such information, and there are also, today, a number of online services that provide (relatively) easy access to sources.

We looked for published data sources, but at the time we could find nothing useful. Data were available on the frozen food markets, but not on such a (relatively) small sector as pizzas. We had, therefore, to collect our own information.

It was very important that the market estimates did not mislead the company about the viability of the project. There would not be any point in spending even further research money if the market were not large enough. For this reason, it was decided to use sample sizes of around 1,000 in each country. To make this affordable, face-to-face omnibus studies were employed.

The cost/benefit ratios of omnibus surveys are a function of the number of questions to be answered and the sensitivity of the data to other questions. We actually wanted to ask about 25 questions, which is quite a large number. However, we were prepared to take the risk that respondents' answers regarding their consumption of frozen pizza were unlikely to be adversely affected by questions about readership, political affiliations, or anything else we could think that others might wish to include. (Omnibus surveys do not carry directly competitive products.)

The number of questions was high because it was felt that, while in contact with the respondent, we should seek as much information as could reasonably be extracted in this type of interview. We therefore asked about awareness of pizza in the context of pasta; consumption of pizza and pasta products; and the opportunity to eat pizzas.

Of those who had eaten pizza, we enquired in detail about the type and place of consumption. Of those who had had frozen pizza at home, we asked (for the last occasion) the brand, how much of the product was bought and how much it had cost. We also asked a series of questions about the serving occasion, with specific reference to ingredients on the top and the quality of the pastry. These were compared to the respondents' ideal for pizza.

Having established that the size of market was of definite interest, the next stage was to explore reactions to the product offer in depth. Six group discussions were held in each country, three with current users (defined as having served frozen pizza at home in the last three months) and three with current non-users (but who had served pizzas other than frozen ones at home in the last three months).

When recruiting groups, it is an enormous help to have quantitative research on which to base quotas (as we now had). On the other hand, there are only a limited number of parameters that can be given to recruiters before it becomes impossible to find respondents, or respondents who can attend at the time of the discussions.

In each country the target for each group was 50 per cent under 35, and 50 per cent over; 50 per cent AB, and 50 per cent C1. It was further specified that there should be an even division between households with and without children. The groups were divided into three pairs (users and non-users), each of these being held in a different part of the country.

Managing the project

With international projects it is necessary to get the highest possible quality in the data while ensuring uniformity across the countries chosen. In this case it also included ensuring that US management was involved and in agreement at each stage, and guaranteeing that the quality of product offered to respondents was at least comparable with that of the eventual product cooked in the home.

It is sometimes possible to find an organization that can mount a multinational project like this entirely within its own resources. If this can be done satisfactorily, it must be the preferred method. We saw problems with all of those purporting to offer such a service, and in the end used five fieldwork companies to cover the six needs (qualitative and quantitative for the three countries). We used one company to conduct the UK quantitative work and also to recruit the groups.

It is good practice to ask for quotations from three companies, since costs can vary considerably for a variety of reasons. We would not recommend asking for a quotation from a company for which a first-class reference is not available. It is always possible to cut research costs by cutting quality. We used group moderators resident in the UK for both cost and communication reasons.

The specification should be as explicit as possible: how is the briefing to be done? How large is the pilot? What is the precise sampling method? What subcontractors will be used?

Having selected the quantitative fieldwork companies, we sent those in France and Germany the English questionnaire for translation. When these were returned we had them translated back into English by a local firm. We strongly recommend this procedure to any company without mother-tongue speakers in the language concerned, since it is the only sure way of producing an acceptable result.

The qualitative stage was more complex since it was decided to videotape the groups, and also to carry out unusual procedures to ensure product quality. To take the latter first, we were fortunate in that the client took the special steps necessary. We repeat them here, since most food products, and some in other fields, will call for special attention of some sort. As the only source of product was the USA, arrangements had to be made for special iceboxes, packed with product, to be air-freighted to each country, met at the airport and quickly taken to local refrigerated storage. In order to ensure that the product was in perfect condition when presented to respondents, it had to be cooked at the right temperature for the right period of time and then served immediately. To facilitate this process, the client provided an industrial oven, together with a technical manager who was able to fit it, and to do the cooking.

Everyone involved was very aware that the product the housewife produced for her family might not get this quality of treatment; in-house placements were to be introduced at a later stage. It was correctly argued that if the product did not succeed with this amount of care, it would never get off the ground.

Our German associates were not confident of producing technicians who were competent on short briefing to do all we required for videotaping the groups. We therefore decided to take a crew from the UK, with complete equipment, spares and technicians. Although they had difficulty in finding one rather rural location, and had tough times with the customs authorities, they performed splendidly otherwise.

Our French associates assured us that videotaping groups was very routine, and required nothing that could not be found in any medium-sized French town. In Lyon things went smoothly. In Lille our operator was prepared to just go home when the apparatus *marche pas* (with the appropriate shrug). It took a lot of improvised swearing in several languages to persuade him that this was not an adequate response! In Paris, we managed to find the only *arrondissement* in the city that was still on 110 volts. There was nothing that could reconcile the video recorder to that power input, and we failed to get pictures.

A potential problem with the German groups is making considerable inroads in the UK at present. This is the habit of providing lavish entertainment for respondents, particularly alcohol. We suspect that some ads are so bad that it takes a degree of inebriation on the part of respondents before they will say a kind word about them. With more serious research, however, it is important that the respondents are clear-headed, and not unduly favourably disposed towards the 'sponsor'. Ideally they should feel quite neutral about the proceedings. Moreover, when testing food products, it is vital that their palates should not be influenced by what has gone before.

A more general problem was that of location. We are very keen on having consumer groups in interviewers' homes. This way the respondents feel more relaxed and less required to give a 'performance'. Finding interviewers with rooms large enough to accommodate respondents, moderator and TV gear is not easy; adding the need for a kitchen big enough for an industrial oven makes it more difficult still.

We had to compromise, and some of the groups were held in hotel rooms. On the same principle, we use the simplest hotels we can find; they are often really pubs. In Germany, however, the practice has been to use the 'studio', something that has gained ground in the UK.

Reporting

Reports had to be made on each stage individually, before the next was authorized. The main difficulty was in assembling data from the three nations in comparable formats. We hit the problem of incompatible hardware and software, and found that we had to re-enter large amounts of information.

We had then, and still get now, beautiful, bound reports on the individual markets, in the appropriate language. There may well be an English summary, but those who want to get into the tables still have to know the difference between *collante* and *étouffante*, between *locker* and *weich*. Our solution to this problem was to produce a report that, while a summary, contained all the information that was necessary to arrive at a decision on the next stage. However, that was our judgement and might not satisfy all clients.

Because of these problems we made verbal presentations from written reports, with simple paper charts. Although the client personnel were not linguists, they were highly intelligent, and this form of reporting was quite acceptable. For larger, more formal organizations we find PowerPoint slides unbeatable, since they give the best visual quality. Overheads may fall between the two stools, and are very subject to projection conditions. Although ideal for lectures, they may not be adequate for the commercial environment because of the use of software packages.

When we arrived at the qualitative stage, we had, of course, the videotapes to help us, except that all the French housewives were speaking in French, and the Germans, funnily enough, in German. To our nil-language clients, this was of limited assistance. However, the tapes justified the cost of procurement when the concepts were shown, and the products tasted. Indeed, even where there are no language barriers, the added value of the reaction shot, over the moderator's interpretation of it, is usually worth the cost. We used the tapes in this way, therefore summarizing the bulk of the discussions, and letting the tapes speak (and act) for themselves at the critical points.

Again, in larger meetings it is possible to use projection video equipment, although we would strongly recommend never using such gear without a technician (from the supplying company) present, and only then after considerable practice.

Timetable

The timetable for the complete project, from brief to final results, was four months. There are, of course, timings that cannot be shortened. Once data have been loaded on to a particular computer, for example, they will take a finite and predictable time to emerge in the form of tables, that is, provided that the machine has been given the correct specification, that there is no power or other mechanical failure and that the operator has remembered to load paper for the printer! It would be possible to plan to shorten this time by giving the job to a bureau with a faster machine or faster software, but the learning curve of those involved would almost certainly lose any advantage gained.

Far more difficult to timetable are the difficulties of getting key personnel to decision-making meetings. Although critical path analysis is an outmoded tool, it had its merits, and illustrating that most delays were in the mind was one of them. In planning a programme of the kind under discussion it behoves the planner to set down the dates at which meetings will be needed, the decisions that will have to be made and the consequences of failing to make them. In our experience, if those concerned understand the reason for such a timetable, it will be met.

In this particular case, the stages covered were as follows. Similar programmes would need similar, if not identical, schedules:

1. briefing research supplier;
2. working out plan;
3. contacting fieldwork companies for timings and costs;
4. providing detailed proposal;
5. getting client approval;
6. translating questionnaires (two ways) (there could also be sampling, but in this case we used omnibus surveys with pre-set samples);
7. briefing field forces;
8. quantitative interviewing;
9. coding, editing and data processing;
10. analysis and report writing;
11. presentation, and approval of next stage;
12. preparation of stimuli and arrangements for product shipment;
13. briefing field forces, moderators and video suppliers;
14. qualitative fieldwork;
15. translation, analysis and report writing:
16. presentation.

From the supplier's point of view, one might have added billing and payment into this timetable. Certainly, with a number of organizations involved and considerable sums being committed over considerable periods, this aspect must be carefully watched. From the client point of view, budgets must be meticulously observed and assurance obtained that the correct personnel are in place to authorize payments, sign cheques and so forth; otherwise, the whole thing may grind to a halt.

Costs

These varied very widely between countries at the time (less so today). To minimize both costs and timing, UK suppliers were used where possible, that is, as group leaders and suppliers of video recording. Competitive quotations were obtained from reputable fieldwork companies (working on a field and tab basis). Translation and transport costs were a significant element.

Currently, a ballpark figure for the whole scheme would be in the region of £100,000–£120,000. The actual total for the scheme looked very reasonable to paymasters accustomed to Stateside figures.

2

Desk Research

Peter Jackson and Robin Birn[1]

INTRODUCTION

In most standard market research texts, desk research is given either cursory mention or none at all. Perhaps the problem is that it is a rather messy subject and offers little potential for professional reputation building. What usually happens is that novice practitioners are left to get on with it as best they can. It is assumed that it is practice that counts and more formal instruction is at best a secondary aid. There is a lot of truth in the view that good desk researchers have some flare, but there is no substitute for experience.

Desk research is messy and untidy. For one thing the outcome of a particular exercise is uncertain, in a way that field market research is not. If we plan and organize interviews with a sample of 500 consumer durable buyers we can be reasonably certain, barring some catastrophe, that we will obtain the required data. In carrying out desk research, days can be spent in libraries with little or nothing found, and inexperience increases the likelihood of this occurring.

On the other hand, desk research, other than online database searching, needs few resources and for this reason everyone can attempt it. The lack of expenditure on outside resources may, however, hide the high staff costs entailed, especially where, through inexperience, time is wasted.

WHAT DOES DESK RESEARCH COVER?

Desk research includes all the following activities:

- **Internet searches** Searching Web sites, library and information sources, and any referrals gained from the cyberspace links.
- **Library searches** This is what is usually thought of as the core of desk research: time spent in libraries finding, reading, copying, searching digital databases or précising available material in the public domain. Some of the sources consulted are written with marketing personnel as the primary readership, but often the material comes from quite diverse fields. The skill of desk research is in finding sources and recognizing their relevance.
- **Information direct from source** Most library access and the material found there is free. Material such as published market research reports usually involves payment direct to the provider and in some cases charges can be substantial. However, this is by no means always the case and some standard sources such as accounts from Companies House involve only nominal or modest costs. The task for the researcher is to identify useful sources and evaluate them, before purchasing anything.
- **In-house sources** Most organizations of any size collect information from a range of sources for a variety of purposes. A researcher should know what is under his or her nose before going anywhere else. Not only does public-domain information flow into the organization, but there may also be spasmodic or regular private intelligence available, such as sales force reports. This may meet *ad hoc* or routine information needs and in large operations may be part of an integrated information system.
- **Online database searches** At least in principle, the types of desk research already mentioned go back a century – they certainly predate market research as a recognized activity. Online data searching is the post-electronic-revolution alternative. Going online gives instant access to the data banks of large computer systems set up commercially, to provide a data provision service. This type of desk research is now open to all owners of PCs with a modem link – commonplace in most organizations. This type of desk research is discussed in more detail below.
- **Near desk research** Pure desk research is an ideal activity for the shy and introverted. There is strictly no need to speak to anybody, although it is useful to seek the help of librarians. Discussions and interviews often, however, have a close and logical link with the written reference and this is what is meant by near desk research. There is more about this topic below.

This, then, is what desk research encompasses. What are its uses? If we think of a market research study in terms of aims and objectives, then desk research often provides a means of gathering some or all of the required data. Here are a few examples of the type of information desk research can provide:

■ **Product details** Desk sources on product details include directories, press reviews, advertising and product or sales brochures. Near desk research sources may include retail visits and other types of observation.
■ **Background economic data** Products and markets exist in a wider economy and even where little is available from published sources of direct relevance, an understanding of the economic backcloth can be an essential part of an overall assessment.
■ **Market size and structure** Usually some estimates of market size can be made from available statistics. Possibly statistics on the specific area of interest cannot be found, but at least an initial estimate can be made from the data on a wider market, perhaps by combining two or more sources. Trade press articles and reviews in specialized directories and published extracts provide data on other aspects of market structure.
■ **Information on companies** Company accounts, press mentions, product literature and directories can all be used in building up profiles of the leading players in a market.

There are clearly some research aims where desk research cannot make a contribution. Consumer reactions (whether individual or corporate) to specific products, companies or marketing activities cannot be obtained unless a piece of original research is reported in the press. Obviously, journalists' opinions of what consumers think are not a substitute for the real thing. For this reason desk research is usually assumed not to be relevant to research allied to new product development, although a general overview of the product field or an analysis of past launches – information that can be obtained from desk research - may form a useful part of the total project.

As well as being a source of substantive information, desk research may be required in planning other types of market research. There may be published sources from where the interview sample is selected and, in business-to-business research, significant desk work may be needed to combine the potential contacts found from various sources. Even in consumer research, compiling probability samples from published lists (eg the electoral register) is a type of desk research. Desk research also has an important role in commercial market research companies at the proposal and quotation stage. Some quickly acquired knowledge may be needed to impress the potential client or for estimating fieldwork strike rates and, therefore, costs.

In market research agencies, desk research is more usually employed in business-to-business than consumer research. Probably most commissioned research of the former type has a desk research element and this will be formally acknowledged at the proposal stage if not put forward as a major reason for choosing the agency ('Using our extensive data banks we shall . . .'). Many consumer research agencies, on the other hand, would probably not think of desk research as a service to charge out. However, the sources available covering consumer markets are extensive and often worth searching for.

A note of caution should be sounded here. *Data from desk research are not infallible.* The temptation to believe whatever is published in hard print is very natural. Having spent days in libraries searching for a few scraps of information, the last thing the researcher wants to consider is its reliability. However, any published data may be misleading or based on unreliable sources. Making judgements about data validity is very much a part of the researcher's job and skill.

GOING ONLINE

Probably any market researcher involved in desk research will now initiate the process by going online. However, a word of warning is necessary. Unless the need is such that frequency of use will enable skill in using databases to be built up and maintained, it may be better to buy in the searches from organizations providing this sort of service (eg the British Library).

The prerequisites for going online are as follows:

1. The right equipment – a PC and modem link.
2. Subscription to a number of database suppliers to provide the means of logging on (and so you can be billed). Many databases charge very little upfront: you pay as you go.
3. Skill in using these databases. Some skill is required and needs to be rapidly built up if access is going to be cost-efficient. Charging is usually time-based and wasted time costs heavily. There are some general skills to learn, more or less applicable to any database, and some techniques specific to individual databases. Both kinds are best learnt through hands-on courses offered by the database providers.

The benefits of electronic searches using key words are enormous. For example, every mention over the last year in the quality daily press of say 'mineral water' can be identified and abstracted within minutes. No commercial researcher could afford the time manually to look through every issue for the year of even one newspaper alone, and the various published indexes are neither wholly reliable nor are they quick to use.

Databases have, therefore, changed the resources available to the researcher, and continuing improvements in terms of coverage (the breadth of data on the database) and user assistance (eg smarter databases that will themselves think beyond narrow definitions) are certain to come. There are limitations, however, which must be recognized.

Even when used with skill, costs can mount up in a search and perhaps with only limited useful information actually produced. However, the staff time that would have been spent in conventional desk research should be balanced against the database billings. An allied danger is rushing to carry out a database search without considering whether data are really needed or useful.

No database is comprehensive, and sometimes the problem is knowing which database to use or start with: there is a lot of choice. In any subject area there is almost certainly important published information that is not on any database. Leading on from this point is that *databases should not be relied on as the sole means of desk research*. The syndrome of 'it is not on the computer and therefore it does not exist' is becoming a real problem. Databases are best used as well as conventional library and Internet searches. Often online searching provides references to follow up by conventional means.

The need to check the validity of data applies with even greater force to online sources. There is a real danger that data in the form of a computer output acquire a spurious and undeserved authority. The origination of the data is the key confirmation of its relevance.

The scope of commercially available online databases is illustrated by the selective list in Table 2.1, that has been traditionally the key source to which researchers have referred.

NEAR DESK RESEARCH

The term 'near desk research' is used to cover discussions and interviews arising from consulting published sources. Usually any interviews will be by telephone and unstructured. Some examples include the following:

■ contacting a trade association (identified through desk research) to find out whether any publications, membership lists, etc are available and perhaps to discuss other areas of interest in the research (many place information on their Web sites);
■ telephoning a government statistics source to establish whether more detailed breakdowns of the data can be ordered (again, information on their Web sites can be helpful);

Table 2.1 *The scope of commercially available online databases*

Supplier of Database	Name of Database	Information within the Database
ONUNE Data Services	Profile	Full text retrieval of media articles, eg *Financial Times, Daily Telegraph, Guardian* and *The Economist*. Also full text retrieval of Euromonitor, Mintel, McCarthy, Jordans and MSI
Reuters	Financial, Media and Professional	Full text retrieval of leading media sources in different geographical regions of the world, eg Africa and Latin America. Also full text retrieval of specialist industrial sources, eg banking and finance, property and construction, computing and electronics
Dun & Bradstreet International	Profiles	Interactive access to information about companies
ICC Online	Training Zone	Financial accounts and information on UK and Irish companies. Also allows comparison of target company with the average performance of companies operating in that sector
Reed Business Information	Kompass Online	Online version of *Kompass Directories*. Covers the UK, Western Europe, Eastern Europe, Asia Pacific, the Middle East and Africa. Allows the compiling of sample frames and mailing lists using complex search criteria

- establishing, through discussions with the publishers, whether a market research report offered for general sale meets specific needs or represents value for money;
- contacting the author of a trade journal article (or the editorial) to discuss the subject in more detail.

Such follow-ups form a cycle, as represented in Figure 2.1.

DESK RESEARCH SOURCES

There are so many sources of desk research that it is clearly impossible even to start to provide a comprehensive guide in the scope of this chapter. All that can be attempted is to give some indication of the range available. The sources mentioned are primarily for the UK, and the omission of a particular source should not be regarded as significant – there are many that could have been mentioned instead or as well.

Guides to sources

There are a number of guides that can be used to find sources relevant to particular subjects. These include:

- *The Index of Reports* (Key Note Publications Ltd);
- *Compendium of Marketing Information Sources* (Euromonitor);
- *MarketSearch* (Arlington Management Publications).

There is also the government's own *Guide to Official Statistics* (HMSO).

As well as such source books, there are various indexes to locate specific information in market reports and the press, eg *Reports Index* – available in most larger libraries – covers a range of sources including newspaper and journal special reports. Such indexes are arranged by subject, and some lateral thinking may be needed to find out how the subject you are interested in is classified; it may be necessary to look under a heading for a more general classification, eg four-wheel-drive cars may be indexed under the general heading of 'cars'.

General marketing compendiums

There are a number of general compendiums giving all sorts of useful marketing data. Often these are the best starting-point in any desk research

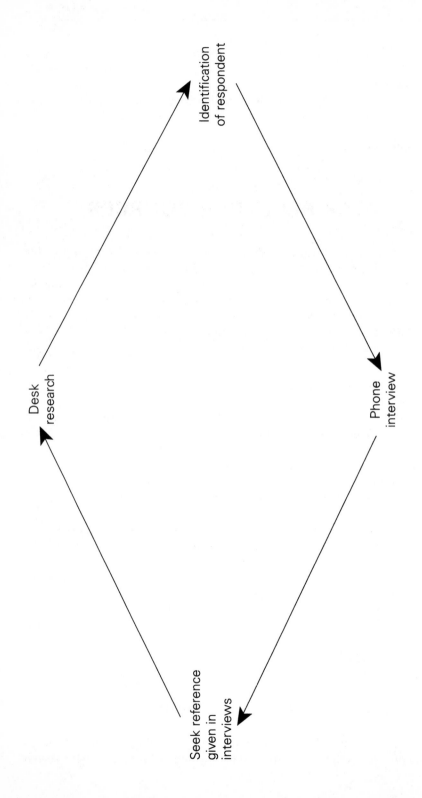

Figure 2.1 *The desk research cycle*

programme. All research staff would do well to have their own copy of the *Marketing Pocket Book* (The Advertising Association, reprinted annually). This is an invaluable quick guide to consumer markets and also gives sources to follow up. Another volume to have on your desk is the summary of key government statistics – *Annual Abstract of Statistics*. NTS now publishes a series of different and very useful data sources.

UK government sources

The two major government offices that collect statistical data are National Statistics, which is concerned with data on companies and business generally, and the Population Censuses and Surveys, whose focus is the population. All government departments also produce statistics related to their own activities. The following regular government publications are commonly used in consumer or business-to-business market research:

Themes	general economic background to markets
Latest figures	these are produced by standard industrial classification and provide data for establishing the market size of product groupings
StatBase	these sources all provide data relevant to consumer markets
DataBank	
Census	

Another important source is the statistics collected on imports and exports by Customs and Excise. For detailed product classifications, value and volume data are available by month and year with analysis of the country of import origin or export destination. This type of data was formerly obtained directly from Customs and Excise, but is now available through a number of private agencies that have taken over the data analysis function.

Company accounts

Every UK limited company and plc is obliged by law to make an annual return and provide accounts to a government agency – Companies House (the Registrar of Companies). There are now strictly enforced deadlines by which returns should be made. Information in a company's accounts and directors' report can be an important source in analysing the structure of a market sector. Turnover data from all the major players may guide estimates of market size.

Changes in regulations have, however, tended to diminish the value of company accounts in market research. Smaller companies now need provide only very scant financial data, and turnover need not be disclosed. In this context 'small' companies can include businesses with turnovers of over £5 million and, in niche markets, these may include the leaders in the field.

Microfiches of company accounts can be obtained direct from Companies House, either in person by visiting City Road, London EC1 (tel: 020 7253 9393) or by post – which will take some days – from Crown Way, Cardiff CF4 3UZ (tel: 029 2038 0107). There are special arrangements for companies registered in Scotland. Although the procedures involved in dealing with Companies House are quite straightforward, it is often easier to use an agent to supply the accounts (the fees are modest). Some will also offer a useful abstraction service to reduce the time you need to spend looking at the raw data. An example is Circare (tel: 020 7739 8424).

Adequate company financial data can often be obtained from secondary sources without the effort and trouble of looking at the accounts themselves. All UK quoted and some other company accounts are summarized on Extel. These are available in larger libraries or can be ordered direct (tel: 020 7253 3400).

Another useful source is ICC publications, which provide financial analysis of particular sectors (eg there is one available on the market research 'industry'). Some general business directories also provide financial data on individual companies.

Market research reports

There is an enormous range of market research reports published speculatively. The charges range from the price of a normal book up to five-figure sums. Cost is not necessarily a guide to either depth of coverage or the reliability of the data. The best guide to what is available is *MarketSearch* – an annual publication of Arlington Publications. Its coverage is international and has a detailed product classification. The prices of the available reports and contact details of the publishing organization are provided.

Another source for locating published reports is Findex. This is also international in scope but with a US bias. Before buying any report, it is obviously wise to find out as much as possible about the contents. Most publishers will provide, on request, descriptive brochures and you can follow these up with telephone calls.

There are a number of publishers producing regular reports with a particular focus or otherwise offering a wide range of titles. Often these are at relatively low cost and in some cases are available in larger libraries. Examples include:

Key Note	industry reports
Jordans	also industry reports, with an emphasis on financial performance of the companies making up the sector, but also including useful overviews
Retail Business	a monthly journal (single copies can be brought) published by the *Economist* Intelligence Unit, containing short analyses of industries and consumer markets (the EIU also publishes other regular and modestly priced reports)
Mintel	similar in scope to *Retail Business* but including data from primary research

Directories

Directories are essential tools in business-to-business market research. Their main role is either to provide data for profiling specific companies (eg as part of a market structure analysis or to build up lists of relevant companies for a sample frame or interview contact list. A major division of directories is between *general* and *specialist* publications.

General directories aim to cover all businesses (more or less) and may be arranged alphabetically (to look up specific companies), geographically (for a sample of companies in a particular area) and by product classification (for a sample drawn from a specific market) – some provide all three classifications. Any researcher regularly carrying out desk research is likely to have one of these volumes to hand. Examples include *Kompass* (there are *Kompass* directories available for many countries, each volume having a similar layout) and *Key British Enterprises* (published by Dun & Bradstreet). Both directories can also be accessed online, and additional services from the publishers include preparing listings of companies to meet individual requirements.

For virtually every trade and business, specialized directories are available and generally the coverage is more thorough than in general volumes. Some also include useful statistical summaries and industry reviews. Directories of available directories can be consulted in larger libraries.

Telephone books also have a role to play in market research. *Yellow Pages* offer a comprehensive listing of businesses within an area and A–Z books provide a sample frame for consumer research by telephone.

The press

The general press is a valuable source for both consumer and business-to-business markets. Often the reports mention source publications that can be followed up for detailed data. To search even a month's copies of the 'heavy' press – *Financial Times, The Times, Guardian, Independent, Wall Street Journal* etc – an index or cuttings system is essential and probably the online search is now the best approach.

Information on specific markets may not be of sufficient general interest to the national press and more will often be found in magazines and journals covering a particular industry or trade. No matter how obscure, every recognized activity has some publication devoted to it – and there are often several. Directories can be used to locate the trade publications relevant to the field of interest. In some journals, indexing is rudimentary or non-existent and it may be necessary to scan past issues laboriously. One limitation of online databases is that only some trade journals are covered.

As well as the press covering a particular activity, general business and marketing publications can be useful sources. The *Investors' Chronicle*, for example, profiles both individual companies and market sectors.

Trade associations

As well as directories and magazines for each type of business there is nearly always a trade association. These vary enormously in organizational complexity, size and usefulness to a researcher. The largest are substantial publishers of information, including industry statistics (eg Society of Motor Manufacturers and Traders), and membership lists may be freely available or on restricted circulation. Some have their own libraries providing the best collections of publications in their field. Other associations publish virtually nothing and have only part-time staff.

Whatever the subject of desk research, the relevant trade associations are well worth contacting. Even if no publications are available, a useful discussion may be held with the staff. Again, larger libraries can be used to locate the relevant trade associations.

DESK RESEARCH FOR OVERSEAS MARKETS

Desk research is also a valuable tool in overseas research. It can provide an overview at low cost, reduce the time and cost spent on fieldwork abroad and may be an essential part in the planning stage of overseas visits. For every developed economy there is a range of desk research sources comparable with what is available in the UK. While some of these data are only accessible in the individual countries, much can be obtained in the UK. Larger general libraries have international as well as domestic sources on their shelves, but the most comprehensive international business library in the UK is run by the government – the Department of Trade Statistics and Market Intelligence Library, based at Victoria Street, London SW1. Any serious overseas desk research programme should also include contact with the Department of Trade and British Overseas Trade Board, which offer information and assistance for exporters.

Another avenue to information for particular countries is to contact the relevant embassy or consulate. The co-operation forthcoming, however, is variable. There are also international organizations producing world-wide or regional reports and statistics. These include the various agencies of the United Nations, the EEC and the OECD.

Some language skills may be needed in carrying out international desk research. This obviously does not apply when researching the USA. In terms of both volume and quality of data this is the best-researched market in the world. The major US published sources are also easily accessible in major libraries as well as at the Department of Trade and the US Embassy. The US government department most concerned with business statistics is the Department of Commerce. Some directories include:

■ *Standard Fund Poors Register of Corporations, Directors and Executives*;
■ *MacRae's Blue Book*;
■ *US Industrial Directories* (Cahners Publications).

STRATEGIES AND TACTICS

Although there is only a limited theoretical framework to desk research, and skill and experience go hand in hand, some general comments on desk research strategies and tactics should be made.

As with any type of research, the starting-point is to know what you are looking for – define the *aims and objectives*, not only of the whole project but also specifically of the part you expect to cover through desk (rather than field) research. A couple of days spent in a library, vaguely seeking information on the 'water industry', for example, will not be fruitful. Instead, before you set foot in a library, pick up the telephone or go online, decide what you need to know about the water industry – organizational structure, waste treatment systems, type of plant used, current capital expenditure – and identify which sources are likely to be worth consulting initially. Obviously additional sources will be identified, and in desk research there is often the chance of stumbling across a key piece of data – you may just see it on the open shelves.

Part of desk research planning is *subject definition* and this is particularly important in online searching. What you wish to cover in terms of products or markets may be obvious, but often the trouble is that the field of interest is classified in a different way in published data. There may be little or no data on the subject you are directly interested in. In this case, the approach may be to narrow your search to *subcategories*, to look to the wider fields of which your interest is a part, or to seek data on *associated* or *analogous areas*.

You may wish to research the field of office communications systems, for example. Possibly little is classified in published sources under this heading. You could instead either seek data on specific examples of office communication – fax, PCs, telephone systems, telex, etc, or look to the wider fields of communication systems or perhaps information technology. You could also look at associated or analogous areas such as office building, employment trends, etc.

Sometimes data from associated or analogous markets is the only route open. If, for example, your objective is to estimate the size of the potential market for a certain type of plastic used in bottling drinks, you may find little or no direct data. However, simple retail checks should identify the sort of bottled drinks where the material is or might be used. You can then seek, and probably with more success, data on the consumption of various drinks. Estimates of the potential market for the material can then be derived.

As well as planning what you will be seeking from desk research, it is desirable to have at least an initial plan of how long you will spend covering the various areas of interest and where you will work. Either because the information is needed to meet a deadline or because limits must be put on the resources devoted to the work, a timetable is needed. You should not spend a disproportionate amount of time on a particular aspect of the study – it is far better to spend two days in covering three-quarters of the subject than to devote all your time to an exhaustive review of one aspect that, in itself, may be of secondary concern. It is worth bearing in mind that in desk research, as in other activities, the law of diminishing returns operates beyond a point; the yield from additional time is often very small (see Figure 2.2).

As a general rule, it is best to move from the general to the particular. At the start of the exercise seek the broad-brush information – who the major players in the market are before starting to profile each one, the overall market size before focusing on specific segments, etc. However, there are exceptions to this principle. You can possibly only obtain data on some individual segments of the market and the overall estimates may have to be made from this base upwards.

Linked to the rule of moving from the general to the particular is the argument that it is often better to refer to secondary sources before going to the primary data. Press coverage of a Monopolies Commission report

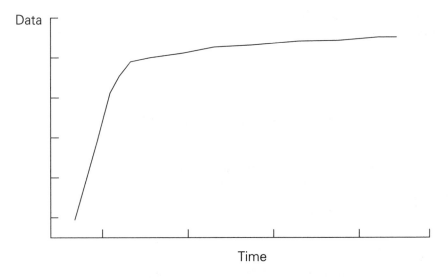

Figure 2.2 *Data yield over time*

should, for example, be read before the full document. This is quicker and easier since the analysis has already been done for you. Also it may be apparent from the press that the coverage of the report is only of marginal relevance to your own objectives. However, this is not an inviolate rule: you would, for example, normally go straight to *Business Monitor* data. There are also dangers in relying on the secondary source even if the coverage seems thorough. Possibly some key details may be missed out and, if the data are an important part of the study, their validity should be established from the primary source.

Note-taking is a vital part of desk research and, for an exercise of any size, it is best to be reasonably methodical. With experience you will develop your own system. But, however it is done, you should be able to backtrack and check which sources (including dates and issue number) you have used, and your final report should include precise source references. It is useful to keep a list of all the sources you look at and note whether or not they were useful. Devise some sort of 'usefulness' code. In the long run you will find it of benefit to have recorded even the dead ends. Keep a separate list of the references you see mentioned which you feel ought to be followed up – references to a source document or other articles and people or organizations worth contacting.

Obviously the data you do find must be recorded – photocopies, your own precise notes, printouts of Web site information or perhaps the full document if it is available. A useful technique is to keep notes of separate topics on individual pieces of paper. You can then put them into a useful order.

Where desk research spans several days, you should periodically take stock of what you have learnt and which data you lack. You can then think about how to find the important missing information and concentrate your remaining time most usefully.

SUGGESTED TACTICS

Finally, to give the reader a better feel for how desk research has been carried out, two checklists are provided below, which are taken, with kind permission of the author, from *The Industrial Market Research Handbook* by Paul Hague (published by Kogan Page). These checklists suggest approaches to establishing market size and providing product information.

Table 2.2 *Action checklist to determine market size by desk research*

Step	Action	If unsuccessful
1	Examine *Business Monitor*.	Phone *Business Monitor* at Cardiff. To step 2.
2	From *Guide to Official Statistics*, search for other government sources of statistics.	To step 3.
3	Identify and contact relevant trade associations from *Directory of Associations*.	Obtain leads from trade association. To step 4, 5, 6 or 7.
4	Search articles in trade magazines and press.	Phone relevant journal for leads. To step 5, 6 or 7.
5	Build up lists of UK turnovers of companies from Companies House, Dun & Bradstreet, Extel. Make estimates of proportion of turnover derived from product of interest.	To step 6 or 7.
6	Determine if any correlation exists with other products or employment. Seek data on that product or employment base as per step 2.	To step 7.
7	Check in directories of published market research for availability of multi-client report.	Consider fieldwork survey to discover market size.

Table 2.3 *Action checklist to obtain product information by desk research*

Step	Action	If unsuccessful
1	Write to company asking for brochures, data sheets, prices.	Contact distributors for same information.
2	Search trade journals and appropriate media for adverts, editorial mentions, articles, product reviews.	Contact journals as a check. Try abstracting service. To step 3.
3	Search buyers' guides and directories for product specifications and background.	To step 4 or 5.
4	Buy or rent sample product for testing (obviously impractical for large or expensive items) or take photographs of product at dealers' or end users'.	To step 5.
5	Search for exhibitions to visit where product may be displayed.	Consider commissioning study to find users of product.

Neither can be followed mechanically to obtain the data you need in your own research, but they illustrate how sources can be used in a logical progression.

ENDNOTE

1. This chapter was originally written by Peter Jackson and has been updated by Robin Birn.

3

Standards and Methods

Peter Jackson

INTRODUCTION

Since the last edition of the *Handbook*, standards of various types have had an increasing impact on the practice of market research in the UK and elsewhere. The purpose of this chapter is to explore the link between these standards and the choice of appropriate methods for market research. It can be stated at the outset, however, that this link is, at least for the present, tenuous and, although the standards influence the process by which methods are selected, they do not as yet determine their selection. In other words, the standards in place now do not define good methods. As will be discussed, this is not implicit in the nature of standards but as yet (and probably for the foreseeable future) the setters of standards have not attempted to move into this potentially contentious area.

The nature of standards will be considered shortly but for the moment it is useful to distinguish between codes and standards in market research. Codes are by far older than standards. They are addressed to individual practitioners (the MRS Code being binding on its members) and are largely a set of prohibitions against what the professional body deems to be unethical conduct amongst its members, in relation to respondents and to clients of commercial research services. These prohibitions do of course impact on methods. The requirements to not mislead respondents and maintain confidentiality, for example, may well rule out some methods that might otherwise be appropriate to meeting the research objectives, and in this context the use of consumer databases as a research tool is relevant. Because of restrictions on breaching respondent confidentiality, market research companies have largely left database trawling to organizations outside the industry. (This and other types of situation lead to some tension between the ethical and commercial aspects of market research and the more cynical may believe that in the long run ethics will adjust to commercial realities.) Data protection legislation, of course, also impacts in this area.

Whilst, therefore, it will be contended that standards in market research, at least as they have developed so far, do not affect choice of methods directly, codes do so if only to rule out some types of data collection. It should be noted that the codes are enforced only in the breach in that flagrant breaking of the prohibitions may set in train quasi-legal action by the professional body, providing, that is, the matter comes to light.

Standards take a different approach with an emphasis on defining what is good practice rather than simply prohibiting the unethical. In this sense, standards address and encourage quality – whatever this means. Standards are also intended to be implemented at an organizational level rather than being a matter for individual practitioners. There are no mechanisms as such to punish breaches of standards but instead there is the more positive approach of assessment – organizations can choose to be assessed to demonstrate that the standards are effectively implemented. However, standards and codes should not be seen as alternatives or competitors. Both have their own place and MRQSA standards (see below) require the MRS Code to be followed by practitioners within the organization.

A BRIEF HISTORY OF STANDARDS

Before going further, some historical context is needed as to how standards in market research evolved and what has come out of the process. The context discussed is mainly the UK.

Although codes are distinguished from standards, it is worth noting that the MRS Code preceded the more recent standards by several decades – the MRS was founded in 1946. But the first true UK standards appeared in 1986 and were those of IQCS (Interviewer Quality Control Scheme). They were developed to set minimum standards for data collection or, more accurately, the management of interviewers. The problems addressed by IQCS were in no sense theoretical, methodological problems but concerned practical issues arising out of how data collection had come to be organized and carried out. If there is any methodological issue addressed it is the need to minimize interviewer variability, although in practice this is more a matter of limiting gross abuses such as made-up interviews. Although first, IQCS standards are still very much live and also form part of the newer and wider standards developed by MRQSA (discussed shortly).

In historical sequence, the next set of standards came into market research from outside the industry. In 1992, the first market research company was assessed to BS 5750 (since replaced by ISO 9000), a standard that concerns how processes should be managed to deliver quality, whatever quality is defined to be. BS 5750/ISO 9000 does not attempt to define appropriate quality levels for any specific activity, and the debate within the UK market research industry over this perceived gap resulted in common agreement that appropriate quality levels should be agreed and developed. To this end, therefore, in 1995 a new body representing all existing organizations in market research – MRQSA (Market Research Quality Standards Association) – was created with the additional role of putting in place effective assessment arrangements so that companies could demonstrate their compliance with the standards to be developed. A first version of these standards was published in 1996 and revised the following year. In 1998, with the support of the BSI and DTI, the standards were again revised and published as a full British Standard – BS 7911. BS 7911 has the full support of the British Market Research Association (the trade body of UK market research companies) to the extent of requiring all but its smallest member companies to be assessed to these standards.

The above history has been exclusively about the UK. However, there has also been a move to market research standards throughout Europe, the US and in other parts of the world, and this has been stimulated by what has been achieved in the UK. The outcome includes national standards in draft or final form in many countries and a European market research quality standard developed through EFEMRA (European Federation of Market Research Associations).

THE NATURE OF THE STANDARDS

For the purposes of this discussion, MRQSA/BS 7911 is taken as the model of market research standards. The scope of the standard covers the research process from proposal/quotation up to reporting. It is broken down into three process areas: those typically handled by professional research staff (proposals including research design, questionnaires, reporting and generally interfacing with the client), data collection (in this case the standard is identical to IQCS) and data processing. There is also a section on 'quality assurance', which is very closely modelled on ISO 9000, and the point of this will be mentioned shortly. Readers looking for more detail must read the standard itself. Of more interest here are its general themes and these can be put under three headings: defining client requirements, ensuring the requirements are met and overall management of the research process.

The emphasis on defining client requirements is very much derived from ISO 9000 and from quality management generally, with a pragmatic view of quality as the process of meeting requirements and particularly those of the customer or client. Ways that the standard requires this are mainly via effective communication including making the research methodology explicit at both the proposal and the reporting stage, confirming the commission in writing along with details of the research plan that the client needs to know, approval of questionnaire drafts and internal communication to ensure the whole organization knows what is required to meet the contract. In all this there is nothing to limit or constrain the choice of methods, only a requirement for transparency so that the client knows what is being provided.

The means specified in the standard to ensure that the defined requirements are met involve review and verification of various types. There is, for example, the need for research proposals to be reviewed by someone other than the drafter as a means of ensuring that the proposed methods are adequate, given the research objectives. Similar reviews are required at the questionnaire drafting and reporting stages. Reviews of this sort should help to ensure methods are adequate but the standard imposes no constraint (or guidance) on what is deemed to be adequate in general or particular. For a given objective, for example, valid arguments might be made for either a broadly quantitative or a broadly qualitative approach and the standard in no way limits the choice at even this level of methodology. The choice depends on professional judgement although this can be (and arguably ought to be) supported by more formal design validation (eg from the results of using the techniques in other projects, standardization of proven questionnaire wording, piloting, etc). In other words effective design review should involve seeking evidence that the chosen method will be capable of meeting the research objectives.

Verification is a more prescriptive area in the standard and covers matters such as interviewer 'back-checking' and the checking of coding and data entry, with levels and methods in these areas specified. However, verification addresses whether some steps in the process have been followed as specified in the research design rather than imposing constraints on the choice of method. Rather than determine the research design as such, verification concerns how the work is organized for effective application of the selected methods.

The final theme of the standard is about the overall management of the research process. This is the quality assurance aspect and is where the historical linkage with ISO 9000 is most apparent. Requirements of the standard of this sort include the need for the organization to work to established procedures (these should set out little more than what is accepted working practice), some level of records (eg what was done in a project), controlling purchases and ensuring staff, including interviewers, are trained for the jobs they undertake. Most of this is recognizably good commercial practice and has no real impact on the selection of appropriate methods.

Overall, therefore, the standard concerns the process by which appropriate methods of research come to be selected and implemented but does not define which methods ought to be used. In other words, the freedom of the researcher is not constrained except in areas where ethical requirements impact (the standard requires organizations to ensure the MRS Code is followed throughout the research process).

COULD STANDARDS DEFINE APPROPRIATE RESEARCH METHODS?

Whilst MRQSA/BS 7911 (and other national standards or the European draft) does not define, therefore, in any real sense, appropriate research methods, could or even should this be attempted?

There is no doubt that prescriptive standards specifying when, where and how specific methods should be used can be defined in standards for at least some professional and knowledge-based activities. The proof is that these types of standard already exist and the best example is account-ancy.

Up to 20 years ago, accountants were more or less free to select appr-opriate methods in preparing accounts subject only to a general principle of presenting a 'true and fair view'. However, what is true and fair can be a matter for legitimate debate and arguably varies somewhat from case to case. But this freedom to exercise professional judgement caused problems when it came to comparing businesses and with some notable disputes arising out of take-overs and acquisitions – the acquirers and acquired had different interpretations of the true and the fair. Despite some hostility within the profession (and with a prospect of legal regulation if matters were not resolved) the profession agreed to develop defined methods in all key aspects of financial reporting and these are now set out as Accounting Standards, which must be followed (not to do so can lead to a breach of the Companies Acts). To give an example of the result of this process, the methods by which goodwill is to be accounted for (ie measured in a business) are defined. In market research the equivalent might be that standards would set out how advert recall should be measured and only this method would be regarded as giving true and fair data.

On this evidence, therefore, it appears that, in principle, standards could define research methods but is this, in market research, realistic in practice and should standards attempt to do so? Is it sensible to apply the approach that is now accepted in another profession to our own? To answer this we need to consider what, in market research, makes for 'good' methods.

In some sense or other, market research is concerned with uncovering the truth, not for the pure pursuit of knowledge but to guide marketing decisions. The most basic assumption is that we need to know what is before we or our clients can consider what ought to be; true findings precede recommendations and action, and our businesses exist because this is accepted. Good methods, therefore, are practices that can be demonstrated theoretically and/or practically to be effective in uncovering the truth of marketing situations. But when we start thinking about the nature of truth – which we must if we are to find right methods – we find less than a consensus. In accountancy, what is true is normative; profit is profit because it is what we define it to be, and the Accounting Standards are very largely definitional. In research, however, we try to look for truth that is in some sense 'real' rather than normative. However, there are widely divergent views on the nature of truth or truths and reality or realities. Take for example what underlies the choice between qualitative and quantitative techniques. Whilst often the practitioners concerned may not realize it, the two approaches aim at rather different types of truth. On the one hand quantitative methods measure, describe and, some would argue, explain a situation (and may be used to predict the effects of making changes in a situation) whilst the qualitative methods aim at a deeper understanding such as how it feels to be a consumer in a market. Different sorts of truths are, therefore, pursued by different researchers, and each group argues for its own approach and associated methods. This difference of approach, it should be noted, is at the highest level of methodological choice and within each of these very broad approaches there are other wide divergences (eg different schools of qualitative research).

The truth in market research and how to get is, therefore, problematical and, whilst there is probably a common understanding that some methods are poor or unacceptable, there is a lack of consensus on some of the basic fundamentals. Perhaps this is hardly surprising given that market research is rooted in social science – a branch of knowledge racked by methodological and epistemological debate. This would be all right if market research was just an academic discipline but it is also meant to be useful to those who pay for it, to the clients of the various research services. In practice these problems have little public airing and most researchers scarcely consider them. However, with these underlying differences about fundamentals it is very difficult to envisage consensual, prescriptive methods of the kind that now exist in accountancy. And it should be understood that market research standards have been developed on the basis of consensus. This is reflected both at the institutional level (eg the composition of MRQSA) and in the process followed. At each step, proposals of what the standards should be have been widely debated and only finalized on a basis of consensus. There is no question at present of outside regulation of market research and, therefore, standards can only be effective if they are based on wide consensus. Whether or not, therefore, the specification of methods in the standards is ultimately desirable, it seems unlikely to be practically feasible within the foreseeable future. (However, EU draft legislation on data protection could have a significant impact, although the implementation of industry-wide standards may be deemed to be adequate self-regulation and so stave off legislation.)

IMPLICATIONS

As things stand now, therefore, it is no use turning to standards such as BS 7911 for direction on appropriate methods. However, these standards will hopefully encourage a more conscious process in the selection of methods so that they best meet research user needs and objectives. Between drafting the proposal and sending it to the client, or developing the questionnaire and putting it into field, the standards require a formal review stage. Such review can be taken more or less seriously; anything from a senior member of staff glancing at the document upwards. What is truly needed though is review that includes rather more formal validation methods and this may well be addressed as the standards develop (future development and revision can be expected). Validation can take various forms but almost anything is better than nothing, and it is nothing that is too often the case now. Many wheels, including faulty ones, are reinvented every research day without any real attempt to determine whether or not they are up to the job. Questionnaire design is a case in point; too often a blank sheet approach is used rather than using wording and structure that have been demonstrated to be valid in other work.

Inevitably, it is the suppliers of research who have to carry out validation but users and buyers of research need to demand it. At least the methodological transparency required by the standards provides the information on which judgements can be made about the effectiveness and validity of the proposed or applied methods.

Standards will also affect methods through improving their application. The work that goes into the wording of questionnaires, for example, is wasted if interviewers do not read it out as written. Standards covering interviewer training, appraisal and verification of work can substantially reduce such problems.

REFERENCES AND FURTHER READING

Alt, M and Brighton, M (1981) Analysing data or telling stories, *Journal of the Market Research Society*, **23** (4)

British Standards Institution (1994) *BS EN ISO 9001*, BSI, London

British Standards Institution (1998) *BS 7911*, BSI, London

Collins, M (1989) Concepts of accuracy in market research, Seminar proceedings, Market Research Society, London

Jackson, P T (1997) *Quality in Market Research*, Kogan Page, London

Sykes, W (1990) Validity and reliability in market research, *Journal of the Market Research Society*, **32** (3)

4

Sampling and Statistics

Paul Harris

SAMPLING

Introduction

The topic of sampling is an essential one for market researchers since almost all market research is conducted using samples. It is therefore important that researchers understand the main concepts of sampling and are familiar with the sampling methods available to them. The aim of this chapter is to acquaint researchers with the main principles of sampling and with the sorts of sample designs that they will be using in practice. Interested sampling specialists and those wanting to know about the underlying statistical and mathematical theory are referred to in Cochran (1977) and Kish (1965).

The first question to be asked is 'Why do we wish to draw samples from a defined population instead of carrying out our research among all members of that population?' In other words, the question being posed is whether we should be using a sample or a census. Clearly in our research we are trying to find out certain things about the whole population and it therefore makes sense to do so with as complete accuracy as possible. This is one point in favour of a census. However, that method of obtaining survey results has a number of obvious drawbacks. Usually the populations from which we select our samples are very large, consisting of many thousands or even millions of members. Thus, to carry out a survey on all of them would clearly take a very long time and this is one thing that market researchers do not have, being required usually to produce results very speedily. A second drawback to the census method is that of cost. It would require an enormous amount of money to carry out surveys on most large-market research populations. It therefore seems that recourse must be made to using samples to carry out market research studies. In practice, this is what always happens and the properly selected sample has a great part to play in research.

A sample is selected from a population to give representative and unbiased data about that population. All the methods of sampling described below aim to have this property, namely that the survey results obtained from the sample are broadly the same as those that would have been obtained had the whole population been surveyed. The use of the word 'broadly' needs explaining. It would not be expected that a sample, no matter how carefully selected, would estimate a population value (eg the percentage who smoke) exactly, but what is required from any sample design is that if it were repeated a large number of times, the true population result being estimated by the sample would result on average. Sometimes the sample survey result might overestimate the true population value and sometimes it might underestimate it, but in the long run the samples should average out to the true population value, giving estimates without bias. This is what is meant by the term 'representative sample'. The second fundamental property that a sample must have is to reflect the population values accurately most of the time. It is not much use to get the right result on average, if repeating the sample design gives very widely scattered results around that average. A good sample design will give the client the true result most of the time with only small margins of error. These margins are known as sampling errors and for the sample designs used in market research it is possible to calculate them. Their magnitude depends first on the size of the sample used, and second on the sample design.

In market research the aim of drawing samples is to make inferences about survey populations and to do so with acceptable margins of error. Fortunately for us this is easily possible and over the years many thousands of sample surveys have been carried out in the fields of commercial and social research, where the sample designs have produced acceptable results.

Population definition

The fundamental question when selecting any sample is 'What is the definition of the population from which the sample is to be selected?' For the sample survey, results will refer to that defined population and to none other. The use of the word 'population' in the sampling context is different from its everyday use as 'the people in the country'. In sampling, the population (sometimes called the universe) is the aggregate of items (eg people, smokers, addresses) from which the sample is to be drawn.

It is essential that the population is rigorously defined before the sample design is contemplated and that it is agreed by the researcher and the client. For example, it may be decided to carry out a survey among 'motorists in this country'. This is far too vague a description of the population and it needs further definition. What does the phrase 'in this country' mean? Does it refer to England, Great Britain or the UK? It can be very embarrassing for the researcher to be asked to analyse the Northern Ireland part of the survey separately, when he has only carried out the survey in Great Britain. Secondly, the particular survey being carried out may lead one to decide what is a 'motorist'. In a survey on the buying of petrol the definition of a motorist may be anyone who drives a car at any time, whereas for a survey concerned with car repairs and servicing it could be defined as a car owner.

How sampling works

In this section an attempt will be made to demonstrate how samples can give accurate information about a population most of the time and how increasing the size of the sample can yield more precise estimates of the population. The approach used here was originally given by Stuart in *Basic Ideas of Scientific Sampling* (1978).

Consider a population of N = 6 students who have been given marks out of 20 for an English examination. The six marks for students labelled A to F are shown below:

A	B	C	D	E	F
1	5	7	9	9	11

The population average (arithmetic mean) mark is $\bar{X} = 7$ and it is this population result that is to be estimated by means of sampling. Of course, in practice the population average is unknown and this is precisely why a sample survey is carried out to estimate it. In this case, as it is known, it is possible to see how well an unbiased and biased sampling plan can perform and what the effect of increasing the sample size will be.

Consider drawing a sample of n = 2 students from the population of N = 6 and forming their average mark as an estimate of the population average $\bar{X} = 7$. It would be possible to do this a number of times with such a small population and with such a small sample size. In fact it does not take long actually to draw all possible 15 samples of size n = 2 (there are $\frac{t(t-1)}{2}$ pairs from t objects). This has been done in Table 4.1 below and the

Table 4.1 *All possible 15 samples of size n = 2*

Sample of Students		Marks		Sample Average
A	B	1	5	3
A	C	1	7	4
A	D	1	9	5
A	E	1	9	5
A	F	1	11	6
B	C	5	7	6
B	D	5	9	7
B	E	5	9	7
B	F	5	11	8
C	D	7	9	8
C	E	7	9	8
C	F	7	11	9
D	E	9	9	9
D	F	9	11	10
E	F	9	11	10

population average has been estimated from each sample average.

It can be seen that the sampling plan only gives an exact estimate of the population average for just 2 of the 15. It should also be noted that for some of the samples the estimate produced is very far from the population average (eg 3 and 10). However, there is a broad tendency for the sample average to be clustered around the value of 7, with sometimes an overestimate and sometimes an underestimate. The remarkable fact about the 15 samples as a group is that if the average is taken of all the 15 population estimates from the samples, then this will be found to equal 7, the population average. Thus, the sampling design that takes all possible samples of n = 2 from this population is what is known as an unbiased sampling plan, that is, if it is repeated a number of times, it will in the long run give estimates that will on average correctly estimate the population value. Clearly some of the time when using this sampling plan an estimate will be produced that is considerably different from the population average, as was the case for the first sample of students A and B. This is the penalty one must pay when using a sample instead of a census. This problem of less accurate samples can be solved by increasing the sample size, as will be shown below.

The distribution of samples is shown in Table 4.2 and diagrammatically in Figure 4.1.

At this point it is convenient to introduce some technical terms connected with the sampling process. If the above 15 sample averages are formed into a *frequency distribution*, then this distribution is known as the *sampling distribution of the arithmetic mean*.

Table 4.2 *Frequency distribution of the sample averages*

3	1
4	1
5	2
6	2
7	2
8	3
9	2
10	2
	15

Just as it is possible to calculate the average of this distribution, so it is possible to calculate its standard deviation. For those not familiar with it, the definition of standard deviation is given later in this chapter. When dealing with a sampling distribution, the standard deviation is given a special name and is known as the *standard error of the mean*. This is to distinguish it from the usual calculation of the standard deviation from the data values of a *single* sample of respondents. The standard error is an important concept and reference will be made to it below, when explaining about sample accuracy and the calculation of sampling errors. Here it is seen to be a measure of spread or concentration of the sample averages around the population average, arising from applying the sampling plan a number of times.

Now what is the effect on the sampling distribution and the standard error of increasing the sample size? Consider all possible samples of $n = 4$ from the same population of $N = 6$ students; there are again 15 of them as can be confirmed by writing them down systematically as with the samples of two previously.

The distribution of their arithmetic means may be shown pictorially in Figure 4.2.

It is visually apparent, and can be checked by calculation, that the average of this sampling distribution is equal to 7, the known population average. The sampling plan is therefore unbiased. More important is that whereas with samples of $n = 2$ the sample averages ranged from 3 to 10, they now, with $n = 4$, only range from 5.5 to 9. In other words the sampling plan with a larger sample size produces estimates that are more closely grouped around the population average. Thus, the standard error is lower and the sampling plan more accurate.

This is a general result and is of wide applicability. It means that the larger the samples taken, the more accurately can the population values

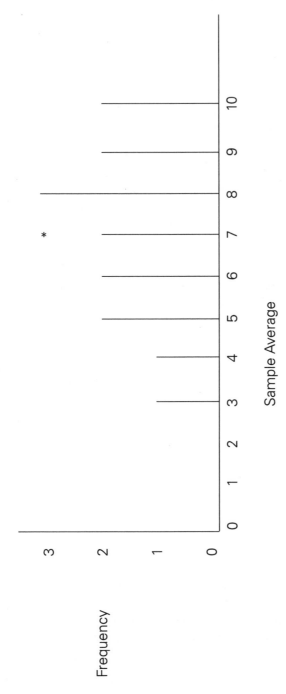

Figure 4.1 *Frequency distribution of the sample averages*

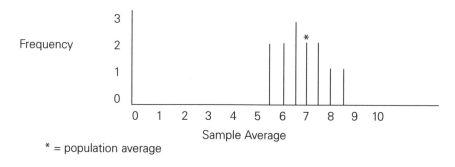

* = population average

Figure 4.2 *Distribution of means where n = 4*

be estimated by the sample. As shown in Figure 4.2, the shape of the sampling distribution is becoming smoother and more regular about the population average. Eventually, as the sample size gets very large (say, greater than 100), the sampling distribution takes on a special shape and becomes a well-known statistical distribution, the normal distribution, with helpful properties. A discussion of these properties and their use in sampling error calculations will be given later in this chapter.

A further point to demonstrate at this stage is that of a biased sampling method. Suppose that in our population of N = 6 students that student F was for some reason a non-respondent. Thus, the samples of n = 2 will not be able to include that student. There are therefore only 10 possible samples of n = 2 that can now be selected and these are shown in Table 4.3.

The average of these 10 sample averages is equal to 6.2, which does not equal the population mean value of 7. The sampling plan is therefore *biased*, as it does not in the long run produce the correct population result on average.

Table 4.3 *The 10 possible samples where F is a non-respondent*

Sample of Students		Marks		Sample Statistics
A	B	1	5	3
A	C	1	7	4
A	D	1	9	5
A	E	1	9	5
B	C	5	7	6
B	D	5	9	7
B	E	5	9	7
C	D	7	9	8
C	E	7	9	8
D	E	9	9	9

METHODS OF SAMPLING USED IN MARKET RESEARCH

Random sampling

With random sampling every member of the population has a known (but not necessarily equal) probability or chance of selection. For this reason it is sometimes known as probability sampling. The sample is drawn by some chance process such that the person drawing the sample has no say as to which members of the population appear in the sample and just accepts the sample members generated by this sampling process. It is to be distinguished from other methods of sampling used in market research and described below, where the sample selector (normally the interviewer) decides which members of the population appear in the sample.

Methods of random sampling

Simple random sampling

This is sometimes known as unrestricted random sampling and is a method of selecting n items from a population of N items such that every item in the population has an equal chance of selection in contrast to more complex random designs, where groups of units are selected at a first stage and then subsampled at a second stage.

With small populations the sampling method may be achieved by numbering the population members from 1 to N and then drawing n random numbers between 1 and N from published sets of tables of random numbers. An excerpt from such a set is shown in Table 4.4. Suppose a sample of n = 10 is required from a population of N = 100. First number the population members from 00 to 99. Then pairs of random digits are selected from a random start-point in Table 4.4 and these form the numbers or the 10 selected population members. Thus, from Table 4.4 the numbers selected could show that population members 95, 73, 10 . . . etc form the sample of n = 10.

In practice this sampling method is not very often used by itself, but is used in conjunction with other more efficient methods of sampling. Readers may wish to use Table 4.4 to carry out their own sampling distribution simulations of random samples of say n = 5 and n = 10 from the population N = 100, as outlined above.

Systematic random sampling

When the population size is larger it becomes very tiresome to use tables of random numbers to select the sample. Therefore a simple alternative is

Table 4.4 *Random numbers*

22	35	85	15	13	60	11	14	10	95	45	07	31	66	49
09	98	42	99	64	24	51	79	89	73	53	94	13	38	47
54	87	66	47	54	88	97	54	14	10	35	80	39	94	88
58	37	78	80	70	88	26	49	81	76	16	04	61	67	87
87	59	36	22	41	23	83	01	30	30	90	89	00	76	33
68	34	30	13	70	84	26	34	91	64	70	29	17	12	13
74	57	25	65	76	83	92	12	06	76	56	62	18	37	35
27	42	27	86	53	44	39	52	38	79	99	49	57	22	77
00	39	68	29	61	99	66	02	79	54	16	08	15	04	72
29	94	98	94	24	08	02	73	43	28	31	16	93	32	43
67	19	01	71	74	60	76	21	29	68	12	41	94	96	36
02	94	37	34	02	47	70	90	30	86	96	93	02	18	29
79	78	45	04	91	16	92	53	56	16	10	47	48	45	88
87	75	66	81	41	40	01	74	34	86	35	81	33	03	76
34	86	82	53	91	00	52	43	48	85	45	37	59	03	09

required and this is supplied by the method of systematic random sampling. It is not necessary to number all the population members from 1 to N, but only to know the value of N, the population size, and have available a list (or card file, for example) of the population members.

To select a systematic sample of n items, first calculate the sampling interval defined as:

$$k = \frac{\text{Size of population}}{\text{Size of sample required}} = \frac{N}{n}$$

Then take a random number between 1 and k, which determines the first selected member for the sample. Counting through the subsequent members of the population and selecting every k'th member after the random start and doing this n – 1 times determines the remaining n – 1 members of the sample. Suppose a sample of n = 10 is to be selected from a population of N = 1,000. The sampling interval is calculated as

$$k = \frac{1,000}{10} = 100$$

and the random number between 1 and k is, say, 41. Therefore, counting down the list of 1,000 population members and selecting every 100th person after person 41 identifies the remaining nine sample members as:

141   241   341   441   541   641   741   841   941

The resulting sample will be seen to cover all parts of the population list and this is a point where the systematic sample scores over the simple random sample, especially if the population list is in a special order (see below). There is no reason why a simple random sample in theory should not give sample members from just the first 100 population members. It is unlikely in practice, but possible. When the population members are in random order this should not matter and then the two sampling methods will give the same results in the long run.

Systematic sampling is especially useful in market research when sampling from directories, professional body list members, etc. The only serious drawback to the method is when the list is in order of values of some key variable (eg a list of building society members in order of amount invested). A systematic sample in such cases with a random start at the lower end of the sampling interval will result in a sample with a much lower average amount invested than a sample based on a random start near the top of the sampling interval.

Stratified random sampling

When drawing samples from certain populations it is often the case that the sampler knows something about the population that may be used to improve the sample design. In the previously cited population of N = 100 used for demonstrating a simple random sample, the following population members were selected for the sample, using Table 4.4.

95   73   10   76   30   64   76   79   54   28

Now suppose that the first 50 members (00–49) listed in the population were men and the last 50 members (50–99) were known to be women. The principle of stratification says that this information, if known, should be used. Consider the simple random sample selected, which ends up with three men and seven women. There is nothing wrong with this as, in the long run, samples of 10 will on average give the correct balance of five men and five women. What is done in stratified random sampling is to divide the population up into known groups, called *strata*, and select a simple random sample from each *stratum*. Thus, in the present example, a simple random sample of five men would be selected from the men's stratum (members 00–49) and a separate simple random sample of five women from the women's stratum. Protection is thus given from any imbalance that may arise from a single simple random sample.

Stratification gives much better random samples than does simple random sampling when the variable or characteristic in which the strata are formed is correlated with the variable being measured by the sample. For example, if the variable being estimated by the sample is the percentage of people who smoke, then if 60 per cent of men smoke and 40 per cent of women smoke (50 per cent overall), the above simple random sample of three men and seven women would give a very distorted estimate of the overall smoking level. If, on the other hand, the level is 50 per cent for both men and women, that particular simple random sample will be no worse than a stratified sample. When the variable being measured by the survey sample varies with the strata, a stratified sample will produce population estimates with far fewer sampling errors than will the simple random sample.

In the above example of stratified sampling an identical sampling fraction was taken in each stratum, ie a sample of 1 to 10 was selected from the men's stratum and the same fraction from the women's stratum. This is known as *stratified sampling with proportional allocation* and is the most popular variant of the technique.

Sometimes it is desired to use different sampling fractions in the various strata. This is known as *disproportional allocation* and is usually done in market research to obtain a minimum subsample size in each stratum. An example here would be a sample in England and Wales, where every one of the nine standard regions had to have at least a subsample size of 300 in a total sample size of 2,700. Because of their very different sizes, a proportionate sample would give some regions only a subsample size of about 100, which could be thought of as being too small for accurate separate regional analysis.

A further occasion when disproportionate sampling is used in survey work is when sampling population with members that vary greatly in size (eg businesses). If the aim of the survey is to estimate the annual turnover in millions of pounds, then 'number of employees' may be used as a basis for forming strata. Then it is argued that it is more important for the sample to contain a much larger proportion of large firms than medium or small firms. The sampling fractions are chosen using a statistical theory known as *optimum allocation*, which gives the lowest sampling errors for a fixed survey cost. Typical sampling fractions in such an example might be as follows:

Small firms	1 in 20
Medium firms	1 in 10
Large firms	1 in 2

Multi-stage sampling

Quite often the members of the population fall into natural groupings. In the population of electors in Great Britain, for instance, the electors live in polling districts, a number of these polling districts will form a ward and a number of wards will in turn group together into a constituency or a local authority area. If a sample of n = 600 electors is required it is possible to select a stratified random sample of them using, say, regional and urban or rural stratification. This would give a widely scattered sample of n = 600 respondents, one each from 600 separate constituencies. This may be judged to be an expensive and time-consuming way of getting 600 interviews since each of the 600 interviewers would have to travel widely to get their assignment of 1 interview.

Multi-stage sampling is a way of getting over this problem and helps to reduce survey costs. What happens is that a first-stage random sample of constituencies (known as primary sampling units, PSUs) is selected. At a second stage, a random sample of one or more wards is selected from each of the *selected* constituencies. Other stages may be added as required until suitable economic interviewing areas are obtained. In the example quoted a suitable design would be to have 60 polling districts, situated in 60 wards of 60 selected constituencies, with each interviewer carrying out 10 interviews.

The advantage, apart from economy, of multi-stage sampling is that stratification may be used at each stage of sample selection. The main drawback is that such samples have increased sampling errors over single-stage stratified samples and measure population variables less precisely. The increased error comes from the sampling errors incurred by each stage of sampling.

Sampling with probability proportional to size (PPS)

Quite often the first-stage or primary sampling units vary considerably in size. For instance, if we take constituencies as PSUs, it is known that they will contain different numbers of electors. When the sampling units vary in size it is not good practice to use simple random sampling to select a sample of them. To do so would mean that a constituency with 80,000 electors would have the same chance of appearing in the sample as a constituency with only 40,000 electors. Now, this imbalance can be corrected by taking a fixed sampling fraction from each constituency and ending up with a variable number of interviews in each area. This gives problems for fieldworkers and can be overcome by sampling PPS. In this method each constituency would be given a chance of selection proportional to its number of electors. An illustration of the mechanics of the method is given below. Suppose it is required to select a sample of four constituencies from a population of 10 constituencies with probability proportioned to number of electors. Table 4.5 gives details of the number of electors in the constituencies.

The procedure is as follows:

1. Cumulate a running total of number of electors (third column).
2. Determine the sampling interval required, which is

$$\frac{\text{Total number of electors overall}}{\text{No of constituencies in sample}} = \frac{400,000}{4} = 100,000$$

Table 4.5 *Number of electors in the constituencies*

Constituency	Number of Electors	Cumulative Number of Electors
1	20,000	20,000
2	40,000	60,000
3	10,000	70,000
4	60,000	130,000
5	60,000	190,000
6	20,000	210,000
7	20,000	230,000
8	10,000	240,000
9	80,000	320,000
10	80,000	400,000

3. Choose a random number between 1 and 100,000, say 50,000, which will be used as a starting-point.
4. Look in the cumulative total electors column and see where this 50,000th elector lies. He or she lies in constituency number 2 and this constituency is included in the sample.
5. Add on the sampling interval successively to the random start three times to identify the other three selected constituencies in the sample. They will be:

50,000 + 100,000 = 150,000	Constituency 5
150,000 + 100,000 = 250,000	Constituency 9
250,000 + 100,000 = 350,000	Constituency 10

The main advantage of sampling PPS at the first stage is that having done so, if an *equal number* of interviews is carried out in each selected primary sampling unit, then the overall chance of selection for each population member will automatically be equal.

Sampling frames

A sampling frame is a list of all the N members of a population, from which the sample may be conveniently selected. One of the first questions to be asked when a random sample is being considered is 'Is there a suitable sampling frame for the population being sampled?' It makes the sampling process so much simpler if there is a good list of population members. Such a list should have the following properties:

■ It should contain a list of members of the defined population or at least those members who are in the defined population should be identifiable.

An example would be a list of the members of an accountancy professional institute with the names of retired members indicated, which could therefore be used as a sampling frame of working accountants.

■ The frame should be a complete, up-to-date list of the population.
■ No population member should be listed more than once. This could occur in the accountant example if a sample of all registered accountants of all accountancy professional bodies was required.
■ The list should contain information about each individual that could be used for stratifying the sample.

It is fair to say that most lists used in practice do not fully meet all these requirements. Researchers in the UK have access to three main sampling frames when drawing samples of the general population of domestic establishments and private individuals. The most used frame is the electoral register, with the postcode listing becoming more popular for sampling addresses.

The electoral register

The register is published on 16 February every year, using data supplied by individual householders in the UK relating to the previous 10 October. It gives the names and addresses of all persons aged 18 and over and also those who are due to become 18 during the life of the current register. It remains in force until 15 February of the next year. Each constituency produces a register and it is available in a number of booklets, one for each polling district. These can be grouped into wards, local authority areas, etc for use in multi-stage sampling. In urban areas the register is arranged alphabetically by street name and within street name by house number. At each house the electors are usually listed alphabetically by surname and then by first name within surname. In very rural areas, however, the names of electors are arranged alphabetically.

Clearly the register is out-of-date by four months when it is published and gets progressively more out of date during its life. It is out of date because some people will have died and others will have moved home (12 per cent of people in any one year) and new houses will have been built. It is obviously a better sampling frame for addresses than for individuals, as people who move are often moving to and from existing addresses.

Some interesting statistics about the register were published by the Government Social Survey in 1967. They reported that 2.9 per cent of eligible persons who qualified were not on the register and that 0.6 per cent of those who were eligible were listed twice.

From what has been said above, it is apparent that the register is an adequate but not perfect sampling frame. It is often used to select samples of addresses or individuals. One essential point in its favour is that it is available in a number of ways. It can be inspected locally at town halls and libraries, and it can be used for sampling at the British Museum or the Government Social Survey, where a full national set is kept. Finally, one may buy copies of the individual constituency registers from electoral registration offices at town halls.

Sampling individuals from the electoral register

The convenient way in which the register is arranged makes it easy to draw samples of electors. Usually systematic random samples of electors are taken from wards or polling districts with varying degrees of clustering. Thus, a random number is chosen that identifies an elector and every nth elector is selected. However, most surveys require more than just a sample of electors and often a sample of adults aged 15 and over is needed. To supplement the sample of electors the following procedure (due to Kish) is often used to obtain the non-electors and those who have moved house. The interviewer, at each selected elector's household, makes a list of all persons aged 15 and over who are not on the electoral register and numbers them from 1 to n. The listing is done alphabetically by surname and initials. The interviewer then selects one of these listed people for interviewing using a Kish selection grid, an example of which is shown in Table 4.6.

If the interviewer was at the fourth elector's household and there were three listed persons not on the register, then the selection grid shows that, in this case, the first listed person would be interviewed. It will be seen that wherever there are three persons listed, one-third of the time it is the second and one-third of the time it is the third person.

Table 4.6 *Kish selection grid*

Address Serial Number	Number of Listed Persons					
	1	2	3	4	5	6 or more
1	1	2	1	4	3	5
2	1	1	2	1	4	6
3	1	2	3	2	5	1
4	1	1	1	3	1	2
5	1	2	2	4	2	3
6	1	1	3	1	3	4
7	1	2	1	2	4	5
8	1	1	2	3	5	6
9	1	2	3	4	1	1
and so on						

Most sample designs ensure that overall electors are selected with equal probability, but this is not true for these additional 'non-electors'. They are selected with varying probabilities that depend on the number of names on the electoral register at their household and the number of 'non-electors' from whom they are selected. They each therefore have to be given the following weight in the analysis of the survey results:

$$\frac{\text{number of 'non-electors' in household}}{\text{number of names on register for that household}}$$

The above sampling scheme for individuals will sometimes result in two interviews in one household. This is objectionable for some studies where the client has good reason for insisting on only one interview per household for, say, a population of people aged 14 and over. An efficient procedure here is to select a sample of electors from the register in the usual way, but not necessarily to carry out an interview with that selected person. The interviewer goes to the *household* of the selected elector and forms a list of people aged 14 and over as for non-electors above and uses the Kish grid to select one of them. Each selected person is given a weight to correct for unequal selection probabilities. The weight is defined as:

$$\frac{\text{number of persons aged 14 and over in household}}{\text{number of names on register for that household}}$$

This gives not too great a range of weights for the selected respondents. If households had been selected with equal probability and then a single person selected, the range of weights would be the numbers of qualifying people in each household, ranging from one to five mostly. Such extreme weighting increases sampling errors and an inefficient sample design will result.

In addition to drawing samples of people it is often necessary to draw a random sample of men or of women from the register. This is done by examining every nth name on say the polling district register and only including it in the sample if it is a name with the required sex. Alternatively, one may select every nth man's (or woman's) name, but this takes slightly longer for the sampling clerks to carry out. Whichever method is used there is still the problem of telling the difference between men's and women's names.

Sampling addresses and households from the electoral register

Because of the way the register is laid out it is possible to draw random samples of addresses (households), usually for samples of housewives or heads of households. This can be done in two ways. One way is to take every nth address from the register using the street address as a guide. The addresses are listed conveniently in street order. The other method is that of 'firsting', where a sample of electors is drawn but the selected elector's address is only included in the sample if he or she is the first-*named* elector at that address. This gives a self-weighting sample removing the imbalance of selection probability caused by addresses having different numbers of electors. Both methods give problems in rural areas where electors are listed alphabetically. The sampling clerk has to inspect the whole polling district register to see whether any selected elector is the first-named at his or her address.

As most addresses contain only one household, the resulting sample of addresses is almost a sample of households. To convert it to a household sample one just includes in the sample *all* households at each address. In practice, however, it is normal to have an upper limit of three households per address.

The Post Office postcode file

All addresses now have a postcode and a premises code and therefore each address can be uniquely defined in this Post Office sampling frame. It can therefore be used to draw random samples of addresses and is becoming increasingly popular for this purpose. Because of the layout of the postcodes, going from a postcode district down through to sector codes and then to postcodes, it is convenient for drawing multi-stage samples. Another plus point is that it is available in various forms including a computer file, from which it is easy to draw systematic random samples.

A typical market research random sample design

When designing a national sample design for a study it is necessary to take into account most of the techniques and ideas put forward above. In this section a typical and well-known market research sample design is briefly described. This survey is used to estimate readership levels for newspapers and magazines. The universe is defined as adults aged 15 and over in Great Britain. A two-stage stratified random sample is used and is selected in the following way. Wards are taken as first-stage sampling units and are stratified in three ways. First, they are formed into 40 main strata by interlacing non-overlapping portions of ITV areas, metropolitan/non-metropolitan counties and Registrar General's planning regions. Secondly, within each main stratum wards are grouped into areas with more or less than 10 per cent of evening newspaper coverage. Finally, within each resulting substratum wards are ordered by the percentage Labour vote at the most recent local government election.

A total of 1,512 wards is then selected with probability proportional to the most up-to-date electorate figures. Within each ward, one polling district is then chosen with probability proportional to the most up-to-date electorate. The electoral register is used as a sampling frame and within each polling district a systematic random sample of electors is drawn. To supplement this sample of electors a sample of non-electors is taken, not using a Kish grid, but a recently developed method (the Marchant-Blyth method) for obtaining a self-weighting sample. The price to pay for a self-weighting sample is that on rare occasions two non-electors as well as one elector are sampled at an address. A full description of the method is given in the *Journal of the Market Research Society*, 1973, **15**, pp 157–62.

Interviewers call and recall on *the* selected respondent and, as in all random surveys, are not allowed to accept substitutes. Obtaining a high response rate is essential for the randomness of the sample to be preserved and in this survey a response rate of about 75 per cent is usually obtained.

Semi-random sampling

The random sampling schemes described above are ones in which the interviewer has no say in the selection procedure. He must interview the people generated by the sampling scheme and no others. There is also another form of sampling used in market research that attempts to 'mimic' a random sample. It goes under the name 'random walk' sampling most of the time, but is also known as 'random route' or 'point and route' sampling. The principle is that the interviewer is given a random address at which to conduct the first interview and thereafter a set of rules to follow to obtain the other addresses. Basically the interviewer continues to interview at every nth address in the street, alternatively turning left and right into other streets when he meets them. Special instructions are given on how to deal with non-private dwellings, cul-de-sac, blocks of flats and open spaces. The method is not purely random as much depends on the detail of the instructions given to the interviewer and his or her bias in carrying them out.

When the starting addresses are selected they are usually part of a normal multi-stage stratified random sample and therefore the resulting sample of addresses can be very similar to a pure random sample as described above. The method is best suited to sampling in urban areas, for example for samples of housewives. It can be used in rural areas where interviewers are given more than one random starting address in case they run out of subsequent addresses on their walk.

It is a method that should be used with call-backs for those addresses where no one is at home when the interviewer first calls. Thus, it does not save much on costs compared with random sampling when it is fully applied. It is useful when there is no time to draw a full random sample from the electoral register. Some researchers do not use call-backs but set overriding quota controls (see next section) for working / non-working to balance what would be a biased sample of households obtained during the day. The prime advantage it has over non-random sampling techniques is that it requires interviewers to interview in defined areas, where they might not necessarily choose to go if allowed any latitude. It can therefore give a much better sample than a quota sample.

Quota sampling

As with random samples, when quota samples are used, one is trying to estimate certain facts about some defined population. This is done by selecting a representative sample that gives results accurately reflecting that population. In the case of quota sampling this is done by building up a sample that looks exactly like the population in some respects and is, it is hoped, similar in other respects.

Method of selection

It is selected in the following way. The researcher chooses certain characteristics by which to set quotas, has or finds some relevant data about the population for those characteristics and then instructs interviewers to select set numbers (or quotas) of respondents with those characteristics. The simplest form is to use independent quota controls, as shown in Table 4.7.

Table 4.7 *Quota sampling using independent quota controls*

Male	19	Age under 35	20	ABC1 class	17
Female	21	Age 35 and over	20	C2DE class	23
	40		40		40

If each interviewer is given these numbers of interviews to carry out, then the total sample will consist of 50 per cent in each age grouping. The quota numbers are set such that a known population age split is obtained. Also, balance is obtained in this example for sex and social class. As long as the interviewer fills the separate cells of the quota, he is at liberty to interview anyone he wishes. Thus, he may end up above with all 19 males under the age of 35, which would clearly not be a balanced sample. To overcome this problem it is possible to set what are known as interlocked quota controls, as shown in Table 4.8.

Table 4.8 *Quota sampling using interlocked quota controls*

		Male	Female	Total	
Under 35	{ABC1	4	3	7}	20
	{C2DE	7	6	13}	
35 and over	{ABC1	4	6	10}	20
	{C2DE	4	6	10}	
		19	21	40	

Now the 19 males are spread into age and class categories according to known population data. Thus, a more representative sample is obtained. In practice, usually one uses mixed quota controls, interlocking some characteristics and leaving others independent, as shown in Table 4.9.

Table 4.9 *Quota sampling using mixed quota controls*

	Male	Female	Total		
Under 35	11	9	20	ABC1	17
35 and over	8	12	20	C2DE	23
	19	21	40		40

It is important to realize that the sample design for national quota samples often follows that for random samples right up until the final respondent selection stage, where of course it differs. Primary sampling units are usually selected using a stratified, multi-stage, PPS sample. The final geographical area defined for carrying out the quota selection may vary from a whole town down to just a single polling district or a few streets. The choice will be dictated by such things as speed and availability of local quota setting information.

Choice of quota variables

The question of choosing the quota variables is governed by such things as:

■ up-to-date available data being at hand;
■ the data being applicable for setting quotas for a wide range of different geographic areas;
■ interviewers being able to classify people correctly on the quota variable, eg social class.

The quota controls should be correlated with the response variables being measured by the survey. For example, a study among housewives for 'convenience foods' should always have a working/non-working quota control, as usage of such products could easily be different for working housewives.

Traditionally, quota samples of adults in the UK use age, sex, social class and working status as controls. In addition, some overriding general instructions are usually given about carrying out some of the interviewing in the evening and at weekends. A point to note here is that interviewers rarely interview in the street, as is popularly assumed, but usually interview people at home. Usually some special pertinent quota control is set for a survey, an example being a heavy/medium/light users quota for a product field.

Advantages and disadvantages of quota sampling

The one overall real asset of the quota sample is its cost, where it can be up to half the cost of a random sample of the same size. Second, it has the advantage of speed, giving survey results much more quickly than random samples, as these require selection processes from sampling frames and time-consuming call-backs on the not-at-homes.

The main drawbacks are those associated with bias and sampling errors. As selection of respondents is virtually controlled by the interviewers, the quota sample always runs the risk of obtaining a biased sample of the population. It can clearly give a sample of people who are more available for interview and this can be important when measuring things that are related to not being at home very often. The second important drawback is that as no probability mechanism is involved in quota sampling, it is not possible, except in special ways, to calculate sampling errors for quota samples. The little conflicting evidence that has been collected in this area suggests that quota samples have the same levels of sampling errors as random samples or have twice their sampling error!

Quota samples are often used where results of the survey are not required to fine degrees of accuracy, eg product tests for preference, and where little or no bias is expected. They are also very useful for minority sampling.

Some of the bias in a particular quota sample may be removed by weighting. For example, suppose we have set an age, sex and social class quota of adults and we find the resulting sample is biased in terms of working/not working. If we know the correct distribution for working status, then we can weight the sample to it.

Where to get quota setting data

In the UK, the Office of Population Censuses and Surveys regularly publishes data on a national and regional basis for such variables as sex, age and marital status. In the years following the decennial census they supply data for more variables and give it down to very small areas. These data soon become out of date.

Most large market research firms carry out large-scale random surveys on a regular basis and some publish volumes of statistics for the setting of quotas. Also, some of them run omnibus surveys on which one single question may be asked (along with others from similar clients). If the question, for example, relates to the ownership of a motor cycle, then analysis by sex, age, class, etc of those responding 'yes' will give quota setting information for the population of motor cyclists.

If time is not available for collecting the quota setting data in this way, then as a last resort one may wish to use the method of contact quota sampling. Here, one sets a national quota sample of adults using say age, sex, class and working status controls. Interviewers fill this quota control and whenever they come across someone who fits the quota control and owns a motor cycle, they complete an additional questionnaire on motor cycling. Other respondents in the quota only complete a short demographic questionnaire.

Random location sampling

In this method, for each sampling point, a few streets are chosen PPS to the number of electors, and interviewers have to quota sample in these streets only using a simple age, sex and working status quota. No social class quota is given, nor would it be feasible in such a small area, but a large number of sampling points ensures a good social class spread. Even so, if a bias on class results, the sample can be weighted.

Use of quota samples

It has been roughly estimated that 60 to 70 per cent of market research is conducted using quota samples. Clearly, if the method was consistently giving badly biased samples and misleading conclusions, it would soon be discredited. It is a fact that general election forecasts using surveys based on quota samples are no less accurate than their random counterparts. Also, for a wide range of consumer goods, brand share data agree well for surveys collected using both sampling methodologies.

STATISTICS IN MARKET RESEARCH

Introduction

A lot of market research data consist of numbers, and statistics is the science of numbers. It is not, therefore, surprising that the analysis and interpretation of market research data involves using statistical theory. This does not mean that all market researchers necessarily have to be trained statisticians – in fact very few are – but it does mean that market researchers should be aware of basic statistical concepts. The main areas that they should understand are related to the variability of data collected from sample surveys. They should know how to summarize the numerical data collected from surveys and assess its accuracy, be aware of the effect of sample size on accuracy and be able to distinguish between real changes measured by surveys as opposed to random fluctuations caused by sampling variability.

Types of data

Market research data come in a variety of forms, the numbers arising from different ways of collecting the data. The basic types of data are described below.

Nominal or classified data

In this case respondents in surveys are asked various questions that produce answers as categories. The simplest example would be demographic information, which would categorize them into classifications such as those shown in Table 4.10.

Table 4.10 *Simple classification of respondents*

Sex	Region of Residence	Working Status
Male	Scotland	Working – full-time
Female	Northern England	– part-time
	Midlands	Not working
	Wales and the West	Retired
	Southern England	Student
		Still at school

A further type of nominal data would arise from the main survey questions, where respondents would reply to areas such as those shown in the example in Table 4.11.

In such cases the statistical numbers arise from a frequency count of the numbers of respondents falling into each cell of the classification. Thus, for a survey of 1,000 adults, we might end up with the data shown in Table 4.12.

Two points should be noted about these data. First, the sum of the frequencies in the classifications equals the sample size, ie each respondent

Table 4.11 *Further nominal data*

Voting Intention	Favourite Daily Newspaper
Conservative	The Times
Labour	Daily Telegraph
Liberal and Social Democrat	Sun
Democrat	Mirror
Other party	Daily Mail
Will not vote	Daily Express
	Today
	Independent
	Guardian
	Financial Times
	Star
	Other

Table 4.12 *Frequency count*

Region of Residence		%
Scotland	112	11.2
Northern England	300	30.0
Midlands	210	21.0
Wales and the West	70	7.0
Southern England	308	30.8
	1,000	100.0

appears once and once only in a classification. The second point is that each frequency has been expressed as a percentage of the total sample size. The percentages therefore add up to 100 per cent. It is percentages such as these that form the raw data of much survey analysis.

Underlying these data is a simple measuring system, which scores the respondent as follows:

■ 1 = Respondent falls into stated classification;
■ 0 = Respondent does not fall into stated classification.

Data of this type are known as binomial distribution data, and we shall return to them in a later section.

It is not mandatory for the frequencies in each category to add up to the total sample size. Consider the example of motorists being asked to state which monthly car magazines they read. The typical data shown in Table 4.13 may arise.

Table 4.13 *Magazines read by motorists*

		% Reading
Car Mechanics	332	16.6
Popular Motoring	991	49.6
The Motor	570	28.5
Autosport	112	5.6
Cars Illustrated	545	27.2
Which Car?	310	15.5
Other	572	28.6
Total sample size	2,000	171.6%

It will be noted that respondents are permitted to state more than one answer and that the calculated percentages far exceed 100 per cent.

Ordinal or ranked data

In the previous section the categories of the classifications could not be put in any particular order. With some classifications there is a natural order of categories. Examples of these would be:

Respondent rating of effect of medicine
– severe drowsiness
– moderate drowsiness
– little drowsiness
– no drowsiness

Product 'A' ranking compared with five other products tested. 'A' ranked
– first
– second
– third
– fourth
– fifth
– sixth

As before, the numerical data arise from frequency counts and percentages for each category.

It must be realized that the numbers sometimes used on ordinal scales are not real numbers but are only used to indicate more or less of a preference for items being ranked. For example, if a respondent rates two products A and B on a scoring system of 'marks out of 10', then a score of 6 for product A and 3 for product B does not mean that A is liked twice as much as B. It only means that A is preferred to B. If A had been scored as 8 and B as 5 (ie the same difference of 3 in scores as above), it does not necessarily mean that A is liked more or less than it was with relative scores of 6 and 3.

When we think that the distances between ordinal scale points are equal, or we make that assumption, then the numbers such as 'marks out of 10' form interval scales and we may wish to calculate average scores, etc.

Measured data

In this case respondents use real numbers in giving their answers to survey questions. For example, men may be asked to state exactly how much (to the nearest pound) they spent on clothes last week. At this stage there are no categories and each man will give a single stated amount. Sometimes it is considered unlikely that respondents will be able to remember exactly how much they spent and they are asked to code themselves into pre-arranged groupings of amounts:

£ spent last week for those buying
1–10
11–20
21–30
31–40
41–50
51–60
61–70
71–80
81–90
91–100
101 or more

This grouping and its associated frequency counts is known as a frequency distribution, and we shall return to it later.

The numbers used here are real ratio numbers. If I spent £40 on clothes last week and my friend spent £20, then I spent twice as much as he did. We can perform all manner of statistical calculations validly on such real numbers.

There is one form of numbering scheme popular with market researchers who use rating scales, which is to attach an arbitrary set of numbers to the words of the rating scale. An example is shown in Table 4.14.

It must be understood that the numbers of such scoring systems are not ratio scale numbers, and it is difficult to assume necessarily that they form even an interval scale. However, it must be said that the practice of assuming interval measurement is widespread in market research and researchers often calculate descriptive measures such as averages on them.

Table 4.14 *Rating scale*

	Score	*or*	*Score*
Very good	5		+2
Good	4		+1
Neither	3		0
Bad	2		−1
Very bad	1		−2

Measures of location

We now turn to descriptive measures that we may calculate from our survey data numbers. Much can be gleaned from our survey data *observations* by tabulation and forming frequency distributions. For example, if we have asked 1,000 women how many fashion magazines they read last week, we would obtain 1,000 numbers such as:

$$2, 0, 4, 0, 1, 6 \ldots\ldots\ldots 0, 1$$

It is difficult to inspect and interpret 1,000 numbers, so we form them into a frequency distribution, as shown in Table 4.15.

Table 4.15 *Frequency distribution of magazines read*

Number Read	Frequency
0	237
1	588
2	97
3	30
4	15
5	12
6	9
7	7
8 or more	5
	1,000

It is now more apparent how the distribution of values lies, and we can deduce the likely range of values. But what we really require is a single number that is typical of the data values. Such single values are known as measures of location or measures of central tendency. (Popularly they are known as averages.)

The first of these measures considered is the arithmetic mean. Suppose we have data consisting of a series of measured numbers and that we have n of them, where n can be any value. The measurements can be denoted symbolically by the labels $x_1, x_2, x_3, x_4, \ldots, x_n$ where x_1 is the value (number) for the first respondent and x_n is the value for the last (nth) respondent.

The arithmetic mean is denoted by the symbol $\bar{x}$ (called x-bar) and is defined by:

$$\bar{x} = \frac{\Sigma x}{n}$$

Now $\Sigma x = x_1 + x_2 + x_3 + \ldots + x_n$ just means 'add up' or sum and therefore Σx means add up the n measurements $x_1, x_2,$ etc (n = the number of measurements being used). In other words, the arithmetic mean is obtained by adding up all the measurements and dividing by the total number of measurements.

As an illustration, let us take a simple example of n = 6 measurements.

$$x_1 = 11;\ x_2 = 9;\ x_3 = 14;\ x_4 = 7;\ x_5 = 12;\ x_6 = 10$$

$$\bar{x} = \frac{11 + 9 + 14 + 7 + 12 + 10}{6} = \frac{63}{6} = 10.5$$

It will be noted that the arithmetic mean lies somewhere in the middle of the six values.

When the measurements contain values that often occur, as with discrete measurements (ie 0, 1, 2, 3, etc), then a different formula has to be used to calculate the arithmetic mean from the frequency distribution.

$$\bar{x} = \frac{\Sigma fx}{\Sigma f}$$

where x = the value for each measurement (0, 1, 2, etc) and f = the frequency of occurrence of that value. In words this formula says: take each value of x, multiply it by its associated frequency (f), sum these products and finally divide by the sum of the frequencies. It will be apparent that the sum of the frequencies (Σf) is equal to n, the total number of values.

As an example, let us return to the frequency distribution of women's fashion magazine reading, as shown in Table 4.16.

Table 4.16 *Frequency distribution of magazine reading*

Number Read (x)	Frequency (f)	fx
0	237	0
1	588	588
2	97	194
3	30	90
4	15	60
5	12	60
6	9	54
7	7	49
8 or more	5	40
	1,000	1,135

$$\bar{x} = \frac{\Sigma fx}{\Sigma f} = \frac{1,135}{1,000} = 1.135$$

A further modification is when we have what is known as a grouped frequency distribution. For example, we might have the one shown in Table 4.17.

Table 4.17 *Grouped frequency distribution*

Amount Spent on Car Service (£)	Mid-point (x)	Frequency (f)
up to 20	10	25
21–40	30	111
41–60	50	244
61–80	70	573
etc	etc	etc

The formula $\frac{\Sigma fx}{\Sigma f}$ is once again used but now x denotes the mid-point of the range values. In some cases the actual data values may be unavailable to us and we have to work with a given set of grouped data.

The arithmetic means that have been calculated are single numerical figures that lie somewhere in the middle of the measurements being considered. They are said to be typical or representative of the measurements from which they have been calculated. They give one a quick understanding of the data under review.

Another use for arithmetic means is for grossing up, eg if one knows the average wage of employees in a company and the number of employees, then a simple multiplication will give the total wage bill. A drawback of the arithmetic mean is that it is greatly affected by one or more very untypical values. A different kind of average will be introduced in a moment, which attempts to get over this problem of extreme values.

Before leaving the arithmetic mean it is worth mentioning a common example that occurs in market research work. This is the rating scale to which numerical scores have been attached, as shown in Table 4.18.

Table 4.18 *Rating scale with numerical scores*

Scale	Score	f
Very important	5	20
Important	4	40
Neither	3	60
Unimportant	2	10
Very unimportant	1	10
		140

The arithmetic mean can be calculated by the usual formula and is often referred to as the mean score in market research reports.

The median

This is an alternative form of average that overcomes a criticism of the arithmetic mean. The median may be defined as the middle measurement when all the measurements have been arranged in order of magnitude.

Formally, if we have n measurements arranged in order, the median is the value of the $\frac{n+1}{2}$ th measurement. If n is an even number, then there is no middle measurement as in the simple example below where n = 6.

$$21 \quad 21 \quad 22 \quad 23 \quad 25 \quad 26$$

The formula says take the $\frac{n+1}{2}$ th = (3.5)th. Thus, we take the mid-point between the third and fourth measurements, and the median value is 22.5.

The mode

A further way of obtaining an average, which is not affected by extreme or untypical values, is to use an average called the mode. It is defined as the measurement or value that occurs most often. For example, we may have the ages of 30 children arranged in a frequency distribution, as in Table 4.19.

Table 4.19 *Frequency distribution of children's ages*

Age	f
7	6
8	15
9	4
10	3
11	2
	30

The age that occurs most often, and is therefore the mode, is eight years. More children are that age than any other age in the distribution. The mode is useful for discrete frequency distributions. An example often quoted of using the mode is where a frequency distribution of shoe sizes can tell a shoe manufacturer which are the most popular sizes of shoes to make.

In our fashion magazine example, the three measures of central location are:

Arithmetic mean = 1.135
Median   = 1
Mode   = 1

Measures of variability (dispersion)

The measures of central location or central tendency we have been considering are valuable pieces of information that summarize the data under review, but they do not tell the full facts about our data. Whereas an average shows where most of the measurements are clustered, it does not tell us how clustered or how dispersed the individual measurements are around the average. If we are told that the average height of Welshmen is the same as the average height for Scotsmen, we might be tempted to think that height frequency distributions are the same. However, by drawing histograms of the two height distributions it might be apparent that Scotsmen's heights tend all to be very close to their average height, while Welshmen are much more spread about the average.

Single numerical values can be calculated from the data to show how dispersed the data measurements are around their average. These values are known as measures of variability or measures of dispersion. The simplest of these measures of variability is called the range, which is defined as the largest measurement in the data minus the smallest measurement. It therefore requires very little calculation.

It is not a very satisfactory measure as it is based only on two of the original measurements, and therefore can be considerably different if the highest and lowest measurements are untypical or extreme values.

The most important measures of variability are the variance and the square root of the variance, which is called the standard deviation. They do not have the merit of simplicity of calculation as does the range, but they are widely used in a statistical analysis, as they have a number of advantages.

For a set of measurements the formulae for calculating the variance and the standard deviation are:

$$\text{Variance} = v = \frac{\Sigma(x - \bar{x})^2}{n}$$

$$\text{Standard deviation} = \sqrt{v} = s = \sqrt{\frac{\Sigma(x - \bar{x})^2}{n}}$$

Using a previous data set with $n = 6$ values, we have an arithmetic mean of $x = 10.5$. The calculation of the standard deviation is shown in Table 4.20.

Table 4.20 *Calculation of standard deviation*

x	$x - \bar{x}$	$(x - \bar{x})^2$
11	0.5	0.25
9	−1.5	2.25
14	3.5	12.25
7	−3.5	12.25
12	1.5	2.25
10	−0.5	0.25
$\Sigma x = 63$	0.0	29.50

$$\text{Variance} = v = \frac{29.50}{6} = 4.916$$

$$\text{Standard deviation} = \sqrt{v} = \sqrt{4.916} = 2.217$$

The standard deviation (or the variance) measures how closely the measurements are grouped around their mean measurement. The more concentrated the measurements are around the mean, the smaller the standard deviation is. The more the spread of the measurements about their mean, the larger the standard deviation.

The standard deviation, which is probably more often used than the variance, is not so affected by extreme or untypical measurements as is the range. It is a very useful quantity, when one starts to learn about drawing random samples of data and wishes to find out the accuracy or sampling error of, say, an arithmetic mean.

When data have been grouped into a frequency distribution a modified formula has to be used to calculate first the variance, and eventually the standard deviation.

$$v = \frac{\Sigma f (x - \bar{x})^2}{\Sigma f}$$

$$SD = s = \sqrt{\frac{\Sigma f (x - \bar{x})^2}{\Sigma f}}$$

When two frequency distributions have the same arithmetic mean, the variability of these two distributions may be compared by calculating their respective standard deviations. The one with the higher standard deviation will be more variable. When the two arithmetic means of the frequency distributions are different, a measure of relative dispersion is needed. This is called the coefficient of variation and is defined as:

$$CV = \frac{\text{standard deviation} \times 100}{\text{arithmetic mean}}$$

Such a coefficient is needed, as a standard deviation of 5 inches indicates relatively greater variability if the mean height is 60 inches than if it is 72 inches.

$$CV = \frac{5 \times 100}{60} = 8.33\%$$

$$CV = \frac{5 \times 100}{72} = 6.94\%$$

The first group with a mean height of 60 inches is relatively more variable in height than the second group.

One vexed question has to be posed at this stage. What is the correct divisor to be used in the formula for the variance (standard deviation)? Is it n (as has been presented here) or is it n − 1 as given in some statistical textbooks? With small sample sizes, say less than n = 50, when estimating a population variance from the sample data, then it is appropriate to use n − 1 as the estimate using n tends to underestimate the population variance. With large samples it makes little difference which is used.

The binomial distribution

When respondents fit a single category or not, then the data follow the binomial distribution. An example would be a buyer/non-buyer of a product; another would be social class ABC1/C2DE.

If we score, for example, buyer = 1 and non-buyer = 0 then, if we have n_1 buyers and n_2 non-buyers ($n_1 + n_2 = n$) (the total sample size), the arithmetic mean is given by:

x	f	fx	
1	n_1	n_1	
0	n_2	0	
	n	n_1	= Σfx

$$\bar{x} = \frac{\Sigma fx}{\Sigma f} = \frac{n_1}{n} = \text{proportion of buyers} = p$$

Similarly, it can be shown that the variance is given by $p(1 - p)$ and the standard deviation by $\sqrt{p(1 - p)}$.

Equivalent terms of expressing the proportion as a percentage p% are $p\%(100 - p\%)$ and $\sqrt{p\%(100 - p\%)}$.

Many market research data are expressed as percentages and therefore these are important formulae that we shall be using later.

Sampling distributions, standard errors and the normal distribution

The fundamental distribution needed to help us with making inferences from sample surveys is called the normal distribution. We arrived at this distribution by explaining how it occurs when sampling from particular populations. We used a very small population of N = 6 members and drew samples from it, forming what are known as sampling distributions, leading to a concept called the standard error of the arithmetic mean.

If the sample size drawn from the population increases and is equal to n = 100 or above, then the sampling distribution is shaped like a bell and results in the most important distribution in statistics, the normal distribution. It is illustrated in Figure 4.3.

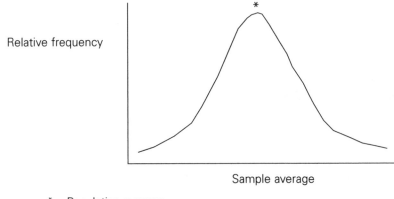

Relative frequency

Sample average

* = Population average

Figure 4.3 *Normal distribution*

The normal distribution has the following property – a known proportion of values lie beyond certain multiples of the standard error. Some typical examples are: 95 per cent of values are within the range of population average ± 1.96 standard errors, and only 5 per cent of values are outside this range; 99 per cent of values are within the range of population average ± 2.58 standard errors, and only 1 per cent of values are outside this range.

This property of the normal distribution is useful when we come to learn how to make inferences about the population average when we have only drawn one sample from that population.

At this point it is instructive to introduce the idea of probability. When it is stated above that only 5 per cent of values are outside this range, we are saying that there is a chance or probability of 1 in 20 (ie 5 per cent) that samples will fall outside the stated range. We will return to probability ideas when discussing confidence intervals.

So far we have introduced the above concepts in terms of drawing many samples from a given population. In practice we only draw one sample from the population. How then do we know the value of the standard error, which has been derived from repeated sampling of the population? Luckily, there is no need to draw a large number of different samples to estimate it: it can be estimated from the single sample we normally select.

If we select a sample n (greater than 100) and obtain a numerical measurement from each person, say personal weekly income in pounds, we can calculate the standard deviation (s) of the actual sample values, as detailed above. The standard error of the arithmetic mean of the sample is then given by:

$$\text{Standard error } (\bar{x}) = \frac{s}{\sqrt{n}}$$

In other words, the standard error is obtained by dividing the sample standard deviation by the square root of the sample size (n).

Example

A sample of n = 200 men in the UK report their weekly beer consumption, and the following results are obtained:

Mean $= \bar{x} =$ 5.6 pints
Standard deviation = 2.1 pints
Sample size = 200
Standard error $(\bar{x}) = \dfrac{2.1}{\sqrt{200}}$ = 0.148 pints

What is the practical use of the standard error? As we shall see later, it is a key statistic for assessing the precision of an arithmetic mean calculated from a sample.

When the sample survey data are in the form of binomial data, such as buyer/non-buyer, then the arithmetic mean of the sample is the proportion (percentage) of the sample who are buyers. The standard error of this percentage is given by:

$$\text{Standard error (p\%)} = \sqrt{\frac{p\%(100-p\%)}{n}}$$

Example

A random sample of n = 400 in an opinion poll yields the result that p = 40% are pleased with the government's performance.

n = 400
p% = 40%
100 − p% = 60%
Standard error $(p\%) = \sqrt{\dfrac{40 \times 60}{400}} = \sqrt{6} = 2.45\%$

We will use this result later to assess the precision of the sample survey percentage (p% = 40%).

Confidence intervals

How can we make use of these calculated standard errors and the normal distribution theory? They can be used to calculate confidence intervals or confidence limits (as they are sometimes called) to determine the precision of the arithmetic mean (or percentage) from the single sample we have selected.

For large samples (n greater than 100) the sampling distribution of the means will follow the normal distribution and we can use certain properties of that distribution. In drawing random samples from a population with a mean of $\bar{X}$ then, as we have said previously:

1. 95 per cent of the samples will have means falling in the range $\bar{X} \pm 1.96$ standard errors of the mean.
2. 99 per cent of the samples will have means falling in the range $\bar{X} \pm 2.58$ standard errors of the mean.

Now we can turn this argument round, and say that the true mean $\bar{X}$ of the population will have a 95 per cent chance or probability of falling in the range:

Sample mean $\pm$ 1.96 (standard errors of the mean)

$$\text{ie } \bar{x} \pm 1.96 \left[\frac{s}{\sqrt{n}} \right]$$

This range is known as a 95 per cent confidence interval. A 99 per cent confidence interval will be given by:

$$\bar{x} \pm 2.58 \left[\frac{s}{\sqrt{n}} \right]$$

Example

The previous data on men's beer consumption were as follows:

Mean $= \bar{x} =$ 5.6 pints
Standard deviation $= s =$ 2.1 pints
Sample size $= n =$ 200
Standard error $(\bar{x}) = \dfrac{s}{\sqrt{n}} =$ 0.148 pints

A 95% confidence interval for the mean $\bar{x} = 5.6$ is given by:
5.6 $\pm$ (1.96)(0.148)
5.6 $\pm$ 0.29
ie from 5.31 pints to 5.89 pints

What is the interpretation of this 95 per cent confidence interval? We have conducted a sample survey to estimate $\bar{X}$, the average beer consumption for the whole population of men in the UK. Because we have only taken a relatively small sample, the average produced by the sample ($\bar{x} = 5.6$) is not fixed quantity. It is subject to sampling variability. What we are telling our client is that we do not know what the population value $\bar{X}$ is but we are 95 per cent confident that it lies within the stated limits for every 19 out of 20 sample surveys we carry out.

There is obviously a 1 in 20 chance that we are making an incorrect statement, when we derive the 95 per cent confidence limits. This is the risk we are prepared to take when we carry out sample surveys. The level of risk can be reduced by setting the wider 99 per cent confidence limits and only having a 1 per cent chance of being wrong. As explained earlier, setting a higher sample size can also improve the precision of the confidence interval.

Example on percentage data

Using the opinion poll data cited above, we have:

n = 400 sample size
p% = 40%
Standard error (p%) = 2.45%
95% confidence interval for p% = 40% is given by:
40% ± 1.96 (2.45%)
40% ± 4.8%
ie from 35.2% to 44.8%

Note how wide the confidence limits are for such a small sample size.

Effect of sample size on statistical precision

It will be apparent that the sample size (n) plays an important role in determining the precision of sample survey results. It is an integral part of the standard error formulae and therefore it determines the width of the confidence intervals. It will have been noted that, in fact, it is not the sample size itself which is important, but rather the square root of the sample size.

This implies that if we wish to double the precision of our sample survey estimates (ie make the confidence interval width one half of what it currently is), we do not have to double the sample size, we have to make it four times as big! Think about the cost implications of this. If an interview costs £20 per head and the chosen sample size is n = 2,000, then the total survey cost is very high. Assume that the survey result obtained is that 50 per cent of people smoke cigarettes. Then the 95 per cent confidence interval is calculated in the normal way and we have the following summary:

Survey statistic 95%	95% confidence interval	Total survey cost
50%	± 2.2%	£40,000

Now, increasing the sample size from 2,000 to 8,000 has a predictable effect on precision and cost.

| 50% | ± 1.1% | £160,000 |

The survey has probably become prohibitively expensive for what is a non-practical reduction in precision. The confidence limits of ± 2.2 per cent are probably good enough for practical purposes. It is probably better to carry out three further surveys on different topics for one's money than spend it on improving one survey from ± 2 to ± 1 per cent.

A further important point is that it is not the overall sample size that is always the criterion. It is quite often the size of subsamples that have to be fixed at a certain size. For example, in a UK tourism survey, we may wish to analyse separately those respondents who took a holiday abroad. Assuming that 25 per cent is the penetration of that group and we wish to sample 2,000 of them to get confidence limits of ± 2 per cent approximately, then we will require that subsample base to be of size 2,000. As they are 25 per cent of the population this means that the total sample size must be 8,000.

Determining sample size for a given precision

Before a sample survey is carried out, the client often states that he requires survey data to be of a stated precision. For example, he may wish a sample survey arithmetic mean, which may be the $\bar{x}$ = 5.6 pints in the previous beer example to be accurate to ± ½ pint and have 95 per cent confidence in this prediction. What size of sample does he need to ensure such precision, and what formula is used to calculate the correct sample size?

Let ± d = the required confidence interval
z = the normal distribution constant to give a specific percentage confidence level
s = standard deviation
n = required sample size
In the beer example:
± d = ± ½ pint
z = 1.96 for 95 per cent confidence
s = 2.1 pints
The formula for n is:
$$n = \frac{z^2 s^2}{d^2}$$

$$\therefore n = \frac{(1.96)^2 (2.1)^2}{(0.5)^2}$$

n = 68

For binomial percentage data:

Let ± d% = the required confidence interval
z = the normal distribution constant to give a specific percentage confidence level
p% = estimate of % being measured
n = required sample size

For the opinion poll data, let us set the desired 95 per cent confidence interval to be ± 1 per cent on the survey p% = 40%
$\therefore \pm d\% = \pm 1\%$
z = 1.96
p% = 40%
The formula for n is:

$$n = \frac{z^2 p\% (100 - p\%)}{d^2}$$

n = 9,220

Significance testing

Often we wish to compare two statistics from one survey or two statistics from separate surveys. An example of the former case would be to compare the statistic 'percentage of men who smoke' with the statistic 'percentage of women who smoke'. The second case would be comparing the 'percentage of men who smoke' from this year's survey with the 'percentage of men who smoke' from last year's survey.

Obviously both statistics, being based on sample surveys, are subject to sampling variability. Imagine two annual surveys of 2,000 adults, which gave the following results:

	% men who smoke
1987	34.3%
1988	35.7%

Has smoking among men increased? We know from our confidence intervals that both results have sampling errors of about ± 2 per cent. The difference 35.7% – 34.3% = 1.4% is less than the sampling error and therefore may not indicate a real change. Could not the truth in both years be that the level of smoking among men is constant at 35 per cent? It is not unreasonable with a sample of 2,000 in 1987 to get a sample survey result that is 34.3 per cent when the truth is 35 per cent. Similarly we may argue that the 1988 result of 35.7 is also not unreasonable.

What we need is a method for determining how large differences in survey results have to be before we can confidently report them as real differences. Significance testing is the statistical method for objectively deciding whether a difference is real or can be explained by sampling variation. When the observed difference between the two percentages is greater than a certain margin, then we say that the difference is statistically significant and we can conclude that a real change in the level of smoking has taken place.

It is not possible in this short exposition of statistics in market research to give a full description of the theory of significance testing. What will be given now is an example of one of the most popular significance tests used in market research.

Test of two independent percentages

This is the case cited above where we wish to assess whether two percentages obtained from two different subsamples (eg age 16–24/age 25 and over) are really different. Alternatively we may be comparing results from two different sample surveys.

Just as single survey percentages have a measure of sampling variability (the standard error) so does the difference between two percentages. The standard error of the difference between two percentages p_1 and p_2 is given by:

$$\text{Standard error } (p_1 - p_2) = \sqrt{pq\left[\frac{1}{n_1} + \frac{1}{n_2}\right]}$$

where n_1 and n_2 are the respective sample sizes

$$p = \frac{n_1 p_1 + n_2 p_2}{n_1 + n_2}$$

$$q = 100 - p$$

A significance test is carried out by comparing the actual difference (ie $p_1 - p_2$) with its standard error. We calculate the criterion

$$z = \frac{p_1 - p_2}{\text{Standard error } (p_1 - p_2)}$$

and if z is equal to or greater than 1.96, we say that the difference is significant at the 5 per cent level. We conclude that the observed difference is greater than would be expected if the two samples were drawn from populations where the two percentages were actually equal. This is the hypothesis being tested – is there really a difference between the two percentages or could their difference be explained by sampling variation? The interpretation of the 5 per cent significance level is that there is a 5 per cent (1 in 20) chance that we make an incorrect decision when we conclude that the two sample percentages are exhibiting a real difference.

The following example shows the use of this significance test in a practical example. Samples of $n_1 = 900$ motorists in Scotland and $n_2 = 1,600$ motorists in England yield $p_1 = 43$ per cent and $p_2 = 40$ per cent respectively who drove more than 15,000 miles in the last 12 months.

The significance test is used to ascertain whether this sample difference of $p_1 - p_2 = 3$ per cent is a real difference among all motorists in these two countries.

$$p = \frac{(900 \times 43\%) + (1,600 \times 40\%)}{900 + 1,600} = 41.1\%$$

$$q = 100 - p = 58.9\%$$

$$\text{Standard error } (p_1 - p_2) = \sqrt{(41.1\%)\,(58.9\%) \left[\frac{1}{900} + \frac{1}{1,600}\right]} = 2.05\%$$

$$z = \frac{p_1 - p_2}{\text{Standard error } (p_1 - p_2)} = \frac{43 - 40}{2.05} = 1.46$$

The value of the z criterion is less than the critical value of 1.96 needed for the 5 per cent significance level and the conclusion is that we cannot state that the proportion of heavy travellers is different for the two countries.

In this example, a significance level of 5 per cent was used as we wished to take a 1 in 20 chance of making an incorrect decision. If we wished to be more cautious and only accept a 1 per cent error level, then the critical value of z would be 2.58. The 5 per cent and 1 per cent levels of significance are those most commonly used in market research. The critical values 1.96 and 2.58 are those values mentioned earlier and are related to the normal distribution.

REFERENCES AND FURTHER READING

Cochran, W G (1977) *Sampling Techniques*, 3rd edn, John Wiley, London
Kish, L (1965) *Survey Sampling*, John Wiley, London

Moser, M and Kalton, C G W (1971) *Survey Methods in Social Investigation*, Heinemann, Oxford

Owen, R and Jones, P (1982) *Statistics*, Polytech

Stuart, A (1978) *Basic Ideas of Scientific Sampling*, 2nd edn, Charles Griffin

Wonnacott, T H and Wonnacott, R J (1977) *Introductory Statistics for Business and Economics*, 3rd edn, John Wiley, London

Worcester, R M and Downham, J, eds (1978) *Consumer Market Research Handbook*, 2nd edn, Van Nostrand Reinhold, USA

5

Questionnaire Design

Alan Wolfe

THE ROLE OF THE QUESTIONNAIRE

Some market researchers refer loosely to all documents from the field as 'questionnaires', although the results of observation studies and retail audits are recorded on documents of a different type. The term questionnaire is here defined in a more restricted sense as a document used in sample surveys to stimulate and record information from individual informants by means of specific questions. Questionnaires, with sampling and fieldwork, form the crucial data collection process. Errors perpetrated on good data at the processing stage of a survey can be rectified later (for example by recoding or reanalysis) with only the loss of some time and money. Researchers should never forget that nothing can be done after the event about bad or uncollected data: no computerized alchemy can turn statistical dross into meaningful gold. It is therefore vital that a questionnaire should:

- be workable to administer and record by all the interviewers involved;
- collect the information specified in the survey brief, with the appropriate degree of accuracy, and as parsimoniously as possible;
- be cheap and simple to handle in the office.

Whenever there seems to be a conflict of interest between the needs of coding and analysis, and the best solution for the interviewer, field must always prevail. The content of the questionnaire of course depends on the survey brief: what information has to be collected and how it is to be analysed. In this chapter we start from the point where the 'information need' has been clearly specified. Designing a successful questionnaire is an art, which cannot be learnt without practice. To help in starting this process, this chapter will classify and describe the basic types of questionnaires and questions, give some general principles of good questionnaire design, and finally apply these principles to some specific types of data and survey.

CLASSIFYING QUESTIONNAIRES AND QUESTIONS

Interviews (and hence questionnaires) can be classified as follows:

- face-to-face;
  - fully-structured;
  - semi-structured (or mixed);
  - unstructured;
- telephone;
- self-completion;
  - mailed;
  - personally-placed;
  - machine-input.

Unstructured interviews ('qualitative', 'intensive' or 'depths') require specially qualified and trained interviewers using checklists or interview guides. These differ greatly from the questionnaires administered by field forces trained in quantitative techniques and are beyond the scope of this chapter.

Structured questions

Structured questions to provide quantitative data can be open-ended, fixed-choice/pre-coded or scales. They can collect three types of information: behavioural, attitudinal and classification.

Open-ended questions

These questions are worded to elicit a wide range of answers, eg 'Why did you buy Brand X lemon curd yesterday?' Possible answers include the following:

- 'Because it has more lemon flavour.'
- 'The store was out of stock of my usual brand.'
- 'I wanted to bake a lemon meringue pie for the family.'
- 'I always do my shopping on Thursdays.'

Such answers legitimately cover a range of aspects, which may not be mutually exclusive. These four alone cover product characteristics, brand loyalty, end use, family-group influence and shopping habits! Informants may have views on all these aspects, which will not be elicited without probing.

A probe is a standardized supplementary question such as 'Anything else?' or 'Can you explain a little more?' An open-ended question without probes can only mislead the researcher, and probed open-ended questions in a structured questionnaire demand special training of the interviewers, who also have the skilled task of writing down lengthy answers verbatim (or of summarizing them, thereby risking eliminating words of great interest to the researcher). Such material is then difficult and costly to code and analyse.

Open-ended questions are therefore rarely used nowadays in quantitative surveys, except for 'housekeeping' purposes. A lengthy and fully structured interview may become very boring for both interviewers and informants.

The latter often wish to express views of their own (not necessarily germane to the research), and there will be no opportunity to offer or place to record such material. Wise researchers therefore offer a few 'open-enders' at intervals through a lengthy questionnaire. If put near the beginning of each new topic they may have the benefit of helping to focus informants' attention on the subject, and at the end of a topic they may act as a 'safety net' to stimulate relevant material that ought to have emerged already but has not been included in the pre-codings.

Other than this, open-ended questions are largely the province of qualitative researchers, who are trained to administer and are allocated the resources to analyse them. Indeed, one of the key outputs of open-ended pilot research is to elicit the topics and range of alternative responses that need to be included in later quantification by structured surveys.

Fixed-choice/pre-coded questions

Open-ended questions can be 'closed' by wording them to make clear to both interviewers and informants the type and range of answers needed.

These can be pre-coded (printed on the questionnaire) and, where appropriate, read out as part of the question itself. If long or complex, they can be shown to informants on a hand-out card.

If, for example, plastic tubes for toothpaste are much cheaper if coloured green, a manufacturer might commission a survey to find out if green is a popular or unpopular colour. An open question such as 'What colours do you like?' would cause problems of interpretation. It would elicit a very wide range of responses, and even the mentions of green would probably be qualified: 'sage green', 'dark green' and so on, with borderline answers such as 'turquoise' or 'ultramarine'.

A researcher might close the question by asking 'Is green your favourite colour?' This logically has only the two answers 'yes' and 'no', but there are always a few informants who cannot or will not answer. These must be pre-coded as 'don't know/not stated' (or DK/NS for short).

A better approach might be to short-list possible colours and show them to informants on a hand-out card (perhaps RED BLUE GREEN YELLOW WHITE with the possible addition of NONE OF THESE), and ask 'Which of these colours do you like best?' This is called a multiple-choice or cafeteria question.

Since people's imaginations differ, it would be even better to provide a visual aid in the form of samples of the actual plastics, or (if practicable) mock-ups of the packs themselves, and approach the problem with more than one question, for instance, 'When you buy toothpaste, which one of these packs would you choose most often? Is there any one you would never buy?' Two or three questions of this type would enable analysis to determine which colours were most popular and unpopular, and which were neutral (perhaps the best choice in a marketing context!).

Alternatively, the colours could be rank-ordered: 'Which colour do you like best? Which second best? Which least?' This is a boring process, and with long lists of items informants often give up after the first few. It rarely gives meaningfully different results from asking about just 'first, second and last' preferences.

Scales

Where the answers to a question will be a matter of degree rather than of kind, it is possible to use scales. The question 'Do you prefer tea or coffee?' can have the responses TEA, COFFEE, BOTH EQUALLY, NEITHER, DK. These in effect form a 'three-point verbal scale'.

It could be made more sensitive to tastes by asking a probe question to those expressing a preference: 'Do you prefer that a whole lot or just a little bit?' This is now a five-point scale, which can be printed on the questionnaire and used in analysis:

PREFER TEA A LOT
PREFER TEA A LITTLE
NO PREFERENCE EXPRESSED
PREFER COFFEE A LITTLE
PREFER COFFEE A LOT

Scales are used most frequently to help quantify opinions, attitudes and brand images. They can be expressed in a number of ways, verbally, numerically and pictorially.

Individual 'opinion scales' can be read out by the interviewer within the sequence of a questionnaire. A hand-out card with the scale points will help informants when several similar scales are administered.

Attitudes and images are more complex concepts, which usually need lengthy 'batteries' of scales. These are printed on separate sheets, which informants fill in after a full explanation of the task by the interviewer. Attitude measurement was first developed by clinical psychologists, who often use scales with 9, 11 or even more points. In a standard market research interview it is almost impossible to achieve this degree of discrimination. Indeed, examination of the results of surveys using such extended scales shows that few informants make use of all the points available. Most concentrate their responses near the centre or the ends, thereby turning long scales effectively into just five points, or even three!

Some researchers believe that scales with even numbers of points elicit more discrimination than odd numbers, which permit 'no preferences' votes at the centre. While this forces the issue for informants with borderline views, some will 'write in' their own 'DKs' if not provided for, and others may resent being forced to express an opinion where they have none.

In practice, five-point scales of the Osgood or Likert type are in most common use. Scaling is a difficult topic, over which inexperienced users should take particular care and seek expert advice.

PRINCIPLES OF QUESTIONNAIRE DESIGN

Many people believe that designing a questionnaire must be easy because asking questions is one of the commonest forms of interaction between people (isn't it?). Yet in ordinary conversation, the reply to the first question affects the content and wording of the next. So two such exchanges that start from the same first question are highly likely to go different ways.

The essence of a market research interview is that each interviewer asks the same questions in the same order to each member of the sample, deviating only where the interviewers' instructions specifically permit.

If interviewers yield to the temptation to modify question wording or order to make their work easier, then a fully structured survey of 1,000 interviews at 50 sampling points degenerates into 50 parallel semi-structured surveys of 20 interviews, the results of which cannot be guaranteed to be compatible with one other. Indeed, this is one of the problems that field supervision systems are designed to prevent.

The fundamental principle of questionnaire design is therefore to make the interview possible for all the interviewers with all the respondents. To be practical, informants sometimes turn up whose circumstances, behaviour or attitudes are so unusual and bizarre that no questionnaire can cope. These have to be treated as 'non-contacts' for analysis purposes, but should form only a tiny fraction of any contacted sample. The researcher should design for 99 per cent success!

The keys to successful questionnaires are: sequence, wording, layout and length. Each is considered below in the context of face-to-face interviews. Variations from this basic approach for telephone or self-completion surveys are discussed later.

Sequence

Interviewers are trained how to 'make contact' and should be briefed on how to introduce each survey. Once the informant has agreed to participate, the interviewer should begin the questionnaire, and from that point on must stick to what is on the paper and record the answers exactly as given. They have standing instructions about what to do where this does not work, but these cases usually have to be treated as 'non-response' at the analysis stage.

If the questions flow pleasantly and logically, the interviewer will maintain rapport and collect the data required without interruptions caused by incomprehension or refusals through boredom or resentment.

Questions that may appear irrelevant or intrusive should be kept to a minimum and not asked early on. Lengthy 'classification data' should not be inserted at the beginning, or at least only enough of them to establish that the respondent qualifies for the survey. The interview should get as quickly as possible into its most interesting part.

Good questionnaires are funnel-shaped, that is they move from the general to the particular. If, for example, you wish to know if the informant is a recent buyer of Brand A baked beans (so as to ask about its brand image perhaps), an opening question such as 'Did you buy Brand A baked beans in the last seven days or not?' is likely to produce a no more meaningful response than an uncomprehending 'Eh?'

A series of questions has to be asked, for instance:

'I want to ask you some questions about food. Do you buy the food for your household?'
(If yes) 'Do you ever buy baked beans?'
(If yes) 'When did you last buy baked beans?'
(If within the last seven days) 'Last time you bought baked beans what brand did you buy?'

Such a sequence will be answerable, will establish that the informant qualifies for the rest of the interview and, best of all, will focus the inform- ant's mind on the topic, facilitating the brand image battery to follow.

It is advisable to proceed from non-controversial questions of fact about recent behaviour to difficult questions about attitude or intention rather than the other way round. Whenever the topic switches (say from one product to another, or from shopping behaviour to usage habits), give the interviewer a 'cushion statement': a sentence to flag the change and get the informant's mind back into gear. ('Thank you for that. Now I am going to ask some questions about the way you use Brand A.') Special types of question (such as using visual aids or performing tasks like filling in scale sheets) also need careful explanation before going ahead.

Embarrassing or intrusive questions (say about incomes or personal habits) are more likely to be answered if put in late in the questionnaire after rapport has been built up. If then refused, most of the required inform- ation will have been already collected. A personal question may be put obliquely: instead of asking about how often the informant takes a bath, ask about how the domestic hot water is heated, and how much is used in a day for various purposes! Some topics are perhaps so difficult that a structured questionnaire should be abandoned in favour of a totally qualit- ative approach.

Wording

Surveys of special populations, for example doctors, the blind or young children, pose problems of wording beyond the scope of this chapter.

Questionnaires aimed at general population samples have to work with people of varied age, sex, education, intelligence, occupation and region. Demotic speech should be used, concentrating on communication rather than grammar and style. Avoid words that are long, technical, Latin-based or the jargon of the business community: 'shops' not 'retail outlets', 'things you buy to save you time' not 'convenience products'. Lists of words found not to be in common use in Britain have been published. For example: normal, average people do not normally use the words 'normal' or 'aver- age' – try 'usual'!

Successful questions are short, specific, clear, unambiguous and about a single issue. Break down complex ideas and avoid double negatives: 'Would you not drink a non-alcoholic wine?' Avoid abstract concepts: 'Would you be interested in buying products that help the environment?' It is better to specify the type of products concerned, even to the point of showing dummy packs or 'concept boards' (illustrations with a detailed description).

Bias is a constant problem in all aspects of survey research. Make it as easy as possible for informants to give true answers. For example, beware the yea-saying syndrome. Co-operative informants like to be helpful, and try to answer what they believe you want to hear. Most surveys get more 'yes' than 'no' answers! Make sure there is no clue to 'the right answer'. Give choices: not 'Do you like X?' but 'Do you prefer X or Y?' This provides a standard of comparison, and informants who have praised one feel free to criticize the other.

When checking on awareness and use of a rare brand or behaviour pattern, include it in a list of familiar and less-familiar names so that most informants can give both 'yes' and 'no' answers. Informants feel inadequate if they have to say 'no' to a complete list, and may invent 'yesses' to keep themselves involved.

In the final choice of words, try to maintain comparability. Unless there are good reasons to the contrary, use the same wording as earlier research or available syndicated surveys. First, this reduces the risk of the question not working. Secondly, it aids validation of results by facilitating comparisons with known data. Thirdly, changes from earlier surveys will indicate trends, thereby greatly increasing the value of the research.

Layout

Every element of a questionnaire is either a question, a pre-coded answer, an interviewer's instruction or an administration/analysis/office aid. It is vital that the interviewer is in no doubt in the heat of the moment which is which, and especially the elements that must and must not be read out.

A frequently used convention is to put all questions and anything to be read out to the informant in upper and lower case, pre-coded answers IN CAPITALS, and interviewer's instructions IN CAPITALS AND UNDERLINED. 'Office use only' will be in italic or a smaller type size.

Print should be uncluttered and large enough to read in poor light. Complex multi-part forms can use several (light) colours of paper. With desktop publishing software now offering wide choices of typefaces and sizes and on-screen editing, there is no excuse for the badly laid-out forms full of last-minute corrections that were traditionally suffered by field forces.

Hand-out cards and visual aids should be large enough to be read by informants with poor sight (and remember there is a significant proportion of effective illiterates in most populations: 'Please read it out, I haven't got my glasses, dear!'), and upper and lower case letters are easier to read than capitals.

Help the interviewers too: SHOW YELLOW CARD is an easier instruction to follow than SHOW CARD D. A large number of cards should be bound in order of use, like a book. Where several successive questions have the same answers (say a choice of a list of brands, or a verbal scale), it is easier to fill in, and saves space if a grid is used. Where the next question to be put depends on the answer to the current question, clear routeing or 'skip' instructions must be given, preferably alongside the relevant answers. Open-ended questions must have large blank spaces to encourage probing and full verbatim recording.

The needs of the analysis department must be discussed both before starting questionnaire design and at final proof stage. Much time and money can be saved by this, although (as has been emphasized earlier) this should not be to the detriment of the interview situation. Most quantitative surveys are analysed by computer, and need numerical codes to be ringed for each answer. If document-reading machines are used, these demand accurate printing of these pre-codes. Each analysis department has its own conventions, which they will explain to questionnaire designers.

Length

How much can be asked in a questionnaire is a trade-off between budgeted cost and the requirements of the brief, within the limits of what is possible in the field. A street or doorstep interview cannot be stretched to more than about 10 minutes; yet a personal interview at home or place of work may last over an hour without the respondent becoming restive. Such long interviews demand a prearranged time convenient to the informant, a topic of high intrinsic interest, a skilled interviewer and a professionally designed questionnaire.

A satisfactory 'interview experience' for the informant depends a great deal on good questionnaire design. All researchers have an obligation to be 'parsimonious' so as to waste neither informants' goodwill nor survey resources by collecting more information than is absolutely necessary for the survey objectives. Despite the high costs of skilled fieldwork, the temptation to push the questionnaire to the limit must be resisted in the interests of data quality in the short term and informant co-operation in the long term.

DESIGNING BEHAVIOURAL QUESTIONS

The rest of this chapter is concerned with applying the principles of good design. Most of the information collected by market research concerns behaviour and attitude patterns with classification data about individual informants to help in analysis and interpretation.

The essence of behaviour is that it is factual: what people actually bought or did in the past. The research problem is therefore one of obtaining complete and accurate recall. Experience recommends asking a sequence of specific questions about the most recent event: 'When did you last buy X? Thinking about this last occasion, what size, price, where . . .?'

A very strong stimulus to accurate memory is the so-called 'pantry check' whereby the informant is shown the actual item under investigation, to act as a visual aid for purchase and usage questions.

Bias is a constant problem. Beware questions about frequency or loyalty that test long-term memory and self-awareness, the answers to which should be treated as 'attitudinal'. For example, an informant may classify himself a 'light drinker' of beer. Finding out his actual consumption will require more elaborate techniques such as a diary. High-interest products are easier. An informant may well recall accurate details of his last car but one, even if bought several years ago. Yet someone who buys chocolate every day may have trouble in correctly specifying the last purchase but one, even if it was only yesterday.

Define your terms precisely without using jargon – 'in the last month' rather than 'recently', 'things you put on your hair like shampoos' rather than 'haircare products'. Watch out for underclaiming because informants are unsure or embarrassed. Try: 'Many people nowadays . . . Have you ever?'

Some topics may be unsuitable for direct questions. The first time a leading jeweller commissioned a 'usage and attitude' survey, the researcher adapted questions tried and tested from branded goods. Interviewers went round knocking on doors asking 'Do you or anyone in your household own jewellery with gold, silver or precious stones?' Several had to be bailed from their local police station!

DESIGNING ATTITUDINAL QUESTIONS

Behaviour is factual and surveys can be checked against other sources such as sales or observation. Attitudes, opinions and images, however defined, are 'all in the mind', multi-dimensional, and their quantitative measurement fraught.

The usual approach is scaling, as described above. The problem is what to scale. The essential start is unstructured research to derive concepts, constructs and statements expressed in informant language. Draft questionnaires need careful piloting, as will be explained below.

Most informants understand verbal scales better than numerical ones, or 'scoring out of 10'. They get bored with long lists, or repetitive tasks like reporting on every brand (try a random allocation of three, or client brand, leading brand and informant's usual brand). Informants can be persuaded to carry out complex tasks (such as sorting packs of cards), but only in a suitably relaxed interview situation and after a full explanation.

Beware scales that do not scale. If 90 per cent 'strongly agree' with a statement, discard it in favour of a wording on which opinions differ.

Minimize bias by offering choices, and randomizing order of presentation. 'Do you prefer plain or milk chocolate?' actually gets a significantly higher proportion of claims to like plain than 'Do you prefer milk or plain chocolate?'

Beware asking about the future or hypothetical questions: 'What do you intend . . .?' 'How likely would you say you are to . . .?' 'If you could not get X, what would you do?' Such statements of intent are frequently not borne out in reality. To identify (say) potential buyers of a video recorder it may be necessary to ask a battery of attitude questions about the product.

DESIGNING CLASSIFICATION QUESTIONS

Classification data are needed for three reasons: to select samples; to validate sample and results against known data; and to act as independent variables for analysis. It is undesirable to collect other classification data because it wastes field and analysis time and is tedious for both interviewer and informant.

Most field forces have standardized methods of asking and recording standard classifications such as age group, size of household and occupation. For these, notes should be given so that the interviewer knows exactly what is required, for example 'number of adults in household including informant, and number of children under 16'.

Otherwise, put the exact question that has to be asked with its pre-coded answers as if part of the 'behavioural data'. Beware asking informants about other people. They frequently do not know (but may guess wrongly) quite elementary facts about other members of the household, such as age, income or favourite brands.

SPECIAL TYPES OF QUESTIONNAIRES

Telephone interviews

The basic characteristics of a telephone interview are that it has to be short (unless by appointment with business executives who make extensive use of the telephone), has no visual aids (unless posted ahead of time and which even then may not be available) and cannot use open-ended questions (the silences while long answers are written down encourage informants to think of something else or even put the telephone down).

However, computer-assisted telephone interview systems (CATI) are now available to supply the questions, record the answers and operate the routeing systems instantly. Using these demands training in the particular software to be used. Similar considerations apply to computer-assisted personal interviews (CAPI).

Self-completion

The limitation of mail surveys and self-completion techniques generally are that informants will see the whole questionnaire before starting, and will refuse to complete it if they find the task daunting in any way.

Unless an interviewer will be present to explain and encourage, they should be kept short, simple and pre-coded for the simple ticking of boxes. Space should be offered for free comment; even though few will use it, the opinionated will otherwise scribble all over the whole document!

Explain how the informant was selected and what the survey will be used for, because personalized mail-shots disturb some people ('How did they know I was here?').

A tried and tested format is a four-page leaflet with an explanatory letter on the cover, two pages of pre-coded questions on the inside, and on the back page: 'Please write here your detailed comments, and anything else you would like to tell us.'

Properly printed forms look important and will be treated more seriously. A stamped or Freepost return envelope is essential. To be worth analysis, response rates should be above 50 per cent, so include and explain a code number to permit a reminder system to non-respondents.

Placement tests

Research such as product tests may include both an interviewer and informant questionnaire. In such cases, unprompted information must be collected first, because the responses to questions later in the interview will be affected by the topics that have been raised early. If you need to know how many spontaneously notice a difference in perfume between two samples, ask about general preferences and reasons before asking 'Which did you prefer for smell?'

Be sure to minimize order-of-presentation effects by carefully explaining the randomization system in the interviewers' instructions. Separate versions of the questionnaire minimize errors.

Unfamiliar situations

Questionnaire design is the area that most clearly distinguishes the professional researcher from the amateur. Experience is the best teacher, but the learning curve can be speeded by reading the texts (a starter reference list is appended) and other people's successful questionnaires. Interviewing is a good idea, but even better is to accompany interviewers to see at first hand what does and does not work well and why.

Even the most experienced researcher sometimes comes across new problems to solve. Whenever an unfamiliar problem arises, the researcher's best approach is to ask around and above all to pilot.

PILOT TESTING QUESTIONNAIRES

There are three types of pilot study:

1. a small-scale survey to obtain approximate results to help design samples, and to enable work depending on them to begin early;
2. qualitative research (usually group discussions among the target population to determine informant language and their range of behaviour and opinions, as input to the questionnaire, especially pre-codes and scale batteries;
3. pre-testing the questionnaire in draft to see if it works.

Type 1 is a luxury except for large projects that break new ground or where time is of the essence in applying the results.

Type 2 is unnecessary when the survey covers ground already well researched, but is otherwise highly recommended as a valuable insurance policy that the questionnaire is designed with the informant in mind and that essential topics are not missed out.

Type 3 piloting is essential to a successful survey. An unpiloted questionnaire may have fundamental flaws (incorrect routeings, misunderstood words, unreadable questions) that will not be detected until substantial time and field costs have been wasted.

While it is a good idea for the designer to try early drafts on a handy colleague or relative, this is not 'piloting', as the parties have too much in common and a good idea of what is wanted, and so may overlook some types of problem. A pilot must be done by an interviewer from the field force that will carry out the survey on genuine target respondents. The pilot interviews should ideally be tape-recorded (or videoed) and be debriefed by the interviewer and designer together.

It is a fact that however expert and experienced the designer, almost all draft questionnaires have to be modified after a pilot at least in detail, and sometimes have to be restarted from scratch. For time planning and budgeting, the minimum pilot is one interviewer's day's work, and a second round may be needed after redrafting.

It can be suggested that more disasters in market research happen through bad questionnaires than anything else, and most of these failures can be traced to inadequate piloting.

REFERENCES AND FURTHER READING

Belson, W (1983) The accuracy of interviewer reporting of respondent replies to open ended and to fully structured questions, Market Research Society Conference, UK

Collins, M and Courtenay, G (1983) The effect of question form on survey data, Market Research Society Conference, UK

Crimp, M (1985) *The Marketing Research Process*, 2nd edn, Prentice Hall, Harlow

Crouch, S (1984) *Marketing Research for Managers*, Heinemann, Oxford

Jobber, D (1985) Questionnaire factors and mail survey response rates, *European Research*, **13** (3)

Macfarlane-Smith, J (1972) *Interviewing in Market and Social Research*, Routledge & Kegan Paul, London

Morton-Williams, J (1986) How much do you care whether your survey results are accurate?, *Admap*, June

Sykes, W (1984) The use of interaction coding and follow-up interviews to investigate comprehension of survey questions, *Journal of the Market Research Society*, **26** (2)

O'Brien, J (1984) How do market researchers ask questions?, *Journal of the Market Research Society*, **26** (2)

Oppenheim, A N (1970) *Questionnaire Design and Attitude Measurement*, Heinemann, Oxford

Shephard, P (1984) Literacy and numeracy and their implications for survey research, *Journal of the Market Research Society*, **26** (2)

Spagna, G J (1984) Questionnaires: which approach do you use?, *Journal of Advertising Research*, **24** (1)

Wolfe, A R (1994) *Standardised Questions*, 2nd edn, Market Research Society, London

Worcester, R M and Downham, J (1978) *Consumer Market Research Handbook*, 2nd edn, Van Nostrand Reinhold, USA

$\boxed{6}$

Geodemographics

Barry Leventhal

INTRODUCTION

Successful market research requires a balance to be struck between the costs of data collection and the value of accurate, actionable information. Geodemographics can be a powerful ally, by helping to improve sample accuracy, reduce fieldwork costs or gain additional value from the results. In this chapter, we look at geodemographic techniques and their potential applications.

We start with the underlying principles and origins of geodemographics, leading to the main classifications currently available and their methods of use. Alternative sources of small-area information are reviewed on the way, including the census and lifestyle data. Primary areas of application are described next, in terms of survey design, target marketing and retailing. Finally, we consider geographic information systems and future prospects following the 2001 Census.

UNDERLYING PRINCIPLES

Geodemographics can loosely be defined as the classification of small areas according to the characteristics of their residents. It is based on two principles:

1. Two people living in the same neighbourhood are more likely to have similar characteristics than two people chosen at random.
2. Neighbourhoods can be categorized on the characteristics of their residents; two neighbourhoods belonging to the same category are likely to contain similar types of people, even though they may be geographically far apart.

These principles mean that geodemographic information on an area can be used to infer the likely characteristics and behaviour patterns of its residents.

The main implication for market research is that geodemographics can provide a connection between sample survey results and the population as a whole, which can be employed in either direction. This may be used either to apply knowledge of the population for managing the sample, or to extrapolate from survey results to make inferences about the population.

ORIGINS

The origins of modern geodemographics, in the UK, go back to the mid-1970s and were triggered by the release of census small-area statistics in machine-readable form. Richard Webber, while at the Centre for Environmental Studies, developed area typologies for research into inner-city deprivation. Using 1971 Census data, he subsequently produced a national classification of wards and parishes. Ken Baker showed the value of this system for analysing the Target Group Index (TGI), and the results were presented at the Market Research Society Conference (1979). CACI took up the classification, which became known as ACORN.

In 1983, ACORN was rebuilt using the 1981 Census, and the remainder of the decade saw developments of different competing classification systems.

The late 1980s also saw the arrival in the UK of lifestyle databases – information compiled from self-completion lifestyle surveys and product registration forms. Although initially built for direct marketing purposes, lifestyle data have come to be used for market analysis, geodemographic systems and some research purposes.

After the 1991 Census, a host of geodemographic systems was launched for the 1990s, with lifestyle data increasingly used in building or describing the categories. The move towards 'one-to-one' marketing has fuelled a shift towards individual-level discriminators and 'fusions' between research and lifestyle sources. However, there is still a valuable role for neighbourhood classifications within the survey process.

INFORMATION SOURCES

As we have implied, the primary information source for geodemographics is the Census of Population, which provides a unique set of demographic data for all neighbourhoods in the UK. Some classifications include additional sources, either to supplement or even replace the census.

Census data

The UK Census is conducted on a decennial basis, the last having been undertaken in 1991 and the next planned for 2001. The sheer size of the data-processing task means that a further two years will elapse before census results are issued; therefore the current range of geodemographic discriminators is likely to be with us, largely unchanged, until some time in 2003.

In the 1991 Census, the smallest geographical unit for output of results was the enumeration district (ED), the territory covered by each census enumerator. Each ED typically contained 160 to 200 households, and was a predefined area on a map. A large number of demographic counts was released for EDs in a dataset known as the small area statistics (SAS), which formed the starting-point for building most geodemographic classifications. In Scotland, the Census Office took a different approach and created output areas that were around one-third the size of EDs, by combining together unit postcodes into blocks.

The release of results from the 2001 Census will mark the starting-point for a new range of geodemographic classifications; the developments planned for 2001 will be considered in the last part of this chapter.

Non-census data

Additional data sources are often employed in geodemographic systems, in order to reflect characteristics of consumer purchasing behaviour and classify at the level of the unit postcode, for more precise targeting.

The most significant such source is lifestyle data – a generic term for information on known, identified individuals gathered from lifestyle questionnaires by various direct marketing companies. Typically, the questionnaires capture demographics, including income, hobbies and interests, and product ownership or usage.

Although lifestyle data falls outside the MRS Code of Conduct, it provides an illuminating and cost-effective information source, which should not be ignored. In geodemographic applications, lifestyle surveys may be summarized at postcode level and used instead of census data. Alternatively, census-based clusters may be profiled and described in terms of lifestyles.

Other non-census sources for geodemographic classifications are listed in Table 6.1.

GEODEMOGRAPHIC CLASSIFICATIONS

Currently, there are seven general-purpose classifications of Great Britain and two financial classifications, all of which are summarized in Table 6.1. As the table shows, the current systems differ from one another in several respects. The number of variables employed in the classification process ranges from less than 50 to 200, depending on the data sources used. However, a large number of variables does not necessarily imply a better product – too many inputs may 'overcook' the clustering and result in a weak discriminator. It is more important that the input variables are relevant to the intended application, and therefore the potential user should obtain details of the actual data that was clustered and how this was undertaken.

Each classification is hierarchical, typically with around 10 high-level groups and 40–60 constituent types. This provides a useful flexibility; for example, sample surveys may be analysed by the summary groups while the more detailed types may be applied in database profiling. Classifications with hundreds of types are rarely of direct benefit, but can provide the building bricks to cluster the user's own data and create a bespoke discriminator.

Table 6.1 also shows that two classifications are based solely on census data, one makes no use of census (employing lifestyle information instead), while the remainder utilize a combination of census and other sources.

Ultimately, the most important issue is whether a geodemographic classification discriminates in a helpful way for the user. It is often possible to 'try before you buy', by running a comparative profiling analysis on a relevant set of test data. Leventhal (1995) discusses factors to consider when assessing discriminators and suggests an evaluation approach.

MECHANICS OF USING GEODEMOGRAPHICS

Geodemographic classifications can be employed in two alternative ways: 1) to describe the population residing in a given area; and 2) to characterize the users of a product or service.

Table 6.1 *Current geodemographic classifications*

Organization	Classification System	Number of Clusters		Number of Input Variables	Data Sources
CACI	ACORN	(a)	6	79	Census
		(b)	17		
		(c)	54		
CACI	Financial ACORN	(a)	4	80 (+20 FRS)	Census; FRS
		(b)	12		
		(c)	51		
Experian (formerly CCN)	MOSAIC	(a)	11	87	Census; credit data; CCJs; ER; PAF; company directors; retail access
		(b)	52		
Experian	Financial MOSAIC	(a)	10	64	Census; credit data; ER; CCJs; company directors; share ownership; unemployment statistics
		(b)	36		
CDMS	SuperProfiles	(a)	10	120 (+30)	Census; credit data; CCJs; TGI; ER
		(b)	40		
		(c)	160		
Equifax	DEFINE	(a)	10	146	Census; credit data; ER; unemployment statistics; CCJs; insurance rating
		(b)	56		
		(c)	1,17		
Equifax	MicroVision	(a)	11	185	Census; lifestyle data; company directors; share ownership; ER; CCJs; risk indices; unemployment statistics
		(b)	52		
		(c)	200		
EuroDirect	Neighbours and PROSPECTS	(a)	9	48	Census
		(b)	44		
Claritas	PRIZM	(a)	4	59 (+188)	Lifestyle data; share ownership; company directors; unemployment statistics; PAF; births and deaths
		(b)	19		
		(c)	72		

Key to sources: FRS = OP Financial Research Survey; CCJs = County Court Judgments; ER = Electoral Register; PAF = Postcode Address File; TGI = BMRB Target Group Index

These two methods may be applied in combination, for example to locate the areas with greatest expected demand for a product. We term these methods 'area profiling' and 'customer profiling' respectively, and will examine the mechanics of each below.

Customer profiling

The starting point here is a sample of postcodes for customers of the required product, service or company. The source for such a sample may be market research, a customer survey or data collection exercise, or the company's database. Geodemographic codes are attached, via postcode look-up, and are again summarized in a profile table, with a comparison against a suitable base. For example, Table 6.2 shows a MOSAIC customer profile of CHORUS lifestyle survey respondents whose next car is likely to be a '4 × 4' four-wheel-drive vehicle. Target types have been highlighted in black and are MOSAIC lifestyle types with an index over 150.

Since geodemographics frequently yields numerous different neighbourhood types, it is helpful to have some means of assessing the significance of results based on small samples. Standard statistical theory can provide a straightforward solution via, for example, Chi square tests, z-scores, or binomial confidence limits.

Table 6.2 *MOSAIC profile at group level*

Target: Respondents whose next car is likely to be a 4 x 4
Base: All respondents

	MOSAIC lifestyle groups					
Classification *Description*	*Record* *Count*	*%*	*Base* *Count*	*%*	*Penetration* *(%)*	*Index*
1 High Income Families	226	13.29	5,308	10.62	4.26	125
2 Suburban Semis	214	12.59	5,534	11.07	3.87	114
3 Blue Collar Owners	235	13.82	7,025	14.05	3.35	98
4 Low-rise Council	127	7.47	7,404	14.81	1.72	50
5 Council Flats	49	2.88	2,616	5.23	1.87	55
6 Victorian Low Status	101	5.94	3,846	7.69	2.63	77
7 Town Houses & Flats	143	8.41	4,924	9.85	2.90	85
8 Stylish Singles	46	2.71	1,607	3.21	2.86	84
9 Independent Elders	76	4.47	3,241	6.48	2.34	69
10 Mortgaged Families	138	8.12	3,445	6.89	4.01	118
11 Country Dwellers	**281**	**16.53**	**3,560**	**7.12**	**7.89**	**232**
12 Institutional areas	64	3.76	1,490	2.98	4.30	126
Total	1,700	100.00	50,000	100.00	3.40	100

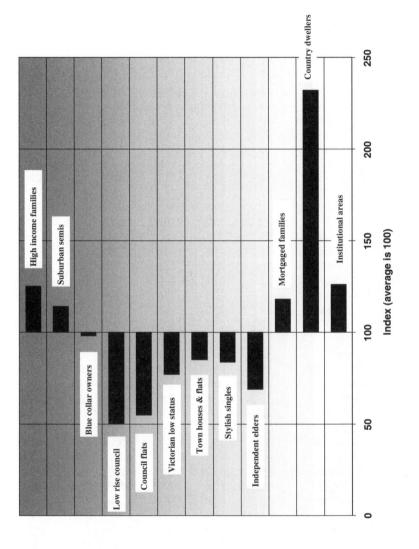

Figure 6.1 *MOSAIC profile at group level (Great Britain)*

Table 6.3 *MOSAIC lifestyle types at type level*

Target: Respondents whose next car is likely to be a 4 x 4
Base: All respondents

Classification Description	Record Count	%	Base Count	%	Penetration (%)	Index
1 Clever Capitalists	20	1.18	466	0.93	4.29	126
2 Rising Materialists	62	3.65	1,478	2.96	4.19	123
3 Corporate Careerists	62	3.65	1,292	2.58	4 80	141
4 Ageing Professionals	32	1.88	628	1.26	5 10	150
5 Small-time Business	50	2.94	1,444	2.89	3 46	102
6 Green Belt Expansion	101	5.94	2,006	4.01	5 03	148
7 Suburban Mock Tudor	43	2.53	1,426	2.85	3.02	89
8 Pebble-dash Subtopia	70	4.12	2,102	4.20	3.33	98
9 Affluent Blue Collar	68	4.00	1,777	3.55	3 83	113
10 30s Industrial Spec	62	3.65	2,018	4.04	3.07	90
11 Low-rise Right to Buy	63	3.71	1,717	3.43	3 67	108
12 Smokestack Shift Work	42	2.47	1,513	3.03	2.78	82
13 Co-op Club & Colliery	42	2.47	1,878	3.76	2 24	66
14 Better-off Council	25	1.47	1,162	2.32	2 15	63
15 Low-rise Pensioners	29	1.71	1,597	3.19	1 82	53
16 Low-rise Subsistence	21	1.24	1,646	3.29	1 28	38
17 Problem Families	10	0.59	1,121	2.24	0.89	26
18 Families in the Sky	7	0.41	490	0.98	1 43	42
19 Graffitied Ghettos	3	0.18	124	0.25	2.42	71
20 Small Town Industry	14	0.82	685	1.37	2.04	60
21 Mid-rise Overspill	2	0.12	172	0.34	1 16	34
22 Flats for the Aged	8	0.47	566	1.13	1 41	42
23 Inner-city Towers	15	0.88	579	1.16	2 59	76
24 Bohemian Melting Pot	16	0.94	724	1.45	2.21	65
25 Victorian Tenements	1	0.06	41	0.08	2.44	72
26 Rootless Renters	15	0.88	590	1.18	2.54	75
27 Sweatshop Sharers	12	0.71	303	0.61	3 96	116
28 Depopulated Terraces	14	0.82	415	0.83	3 37	99
29 Rejuvenated Terraces	43	2.53	1,773	3.55	2.43	71
30 Bijou Homemakers	63	3.71	1,757	3.51	3.59	105
31 Market Town Mixture	59	3.47	2,197	4.39	2.69	79
32 Town Centre Singles	21	1.24	970	1.94	2.16	64
33 Bedsits & Shop Flats	5	0.29	364	0.73	1.37	40
34 Studio Singles	10	0.59	501	1.00	2 00	59
35 College & Communal	2	0.12	162	0.32	1 23	36
36 Chattering Classes	29	1.71	580	1.16	5 00	147
37 Solo Pensioners	14	0.82	777	1.55	1 80	53
38 High-spending Greys	20	1.18	541	1.08	3.70	109
39 Aged Owner Occupiers	34	2.00	1,463	2.93	2.32	68
40 Elderly in Own Flats	8	0.47	460	0.92	1 74	51
41 Brand-new Areas	8	0.47	171	0.34	468	138

Table 6.3 *MOSAIC lifestyle types at type level (continued)*

Classification Description	Record Count	%	Base Count	%	Penetration (%)	Index
42 Pre-nuptial Owners	32	1.88	843	1.69	3 80	112
43 Nest-making Families	33	1.94	874	1.75	3 78	111
44 Maturing Mortgagers	65	3.82	1,557	3.11	4.17	123
45 Gentrified Villages	**45**	**2.65**	**580**	**1.16**	**7.76**	**228**
46 Rural Retirement Mix	14	0.82	312	0.62	4.49	132
47 Lowland Agribusiness	**67**	**3.94**	**927**	**1.85**	**7.23**	**213**
48 Rural Disadvantage	**39**	**2.29**	**646**	**1.29**	**6.04**	**178**
49 Tied/Tenant Farmers	**45**	**2.65**	**309**	**0.62**	**14.56**	**428**
50 Upland & Small Farms	**71**	**4.18**	**786**	**1.57**	**9.03**	**266**
51 Military Bases	**62**	**3.65**	**553**	**1.11**	**11.21**	**330**
52 Non-private Housing	2	0.12	937	1.87	0.21	6
Total	1,700	100.00	50,000	100.00	3.40	100

Most of the large syndicated consumer surveys have been coded by at least one geodemographic, and so a profile of product users can be obtained relatively easily. Profiling is the best way to explore the usefulness of geodemographics for a given market, service or company. It will show the extent of discrimination and enables competing classifications to be compared.

Area profiling

Since geodemographic systems are based on small geographical units – typically EDs or postcodes – area profiling entails the extraction of all units within the required area, followed by analysis of their geodemographic types.

The result is typically an 'area profile', which compares the geodemographic composition of the target area with the corresponding picture for Great Britain as a whole. For example, Tables 6.4 and 6.5 show part of the MOSAIC profile for Hereford, the town with the highest occurrence of the chosen target types for 4 × 4 vehicles. Similarly, target types may also be mapped – Figures 6.1 and 6.2 are maps of the locations of the target types of Great Britain and Hereford respectively.

Table 6.4 *Area profile report for Hereford's major shopping centre (group level)*

MOSAIC Lifestyle groups by adults 15+

		Hereford	Hereford %	Great Britain	Great Britain %	Penetration %	Index
L1	High Income Families	7,952	5.55	5,539,316	11.98	0.14	46
L2	Suburban Semis	9,267	6.47	5,209,299	11.27	0.18	57
L3	Blue Collar Owners	13,896	9.70	6,243,503	13.50	0.22	72
L4	Low-rise Council	10,945	7.64	6,349,976	13.73	0.17	56
L5	Council Flats	1,715	1.20	2,572,311	5.56	0.07	22
L6	Victorian Low Status	8,009	5.59	4,014,054	8.68	0.20	64
L7	Town Houses & Flats	12,711	8.88	4,410,328	9.54	0.29	93
L8	Stylish Singles	1,200	0.84	2,256,011	4.88	0.05	17
L9	Independent Elders	9,033	6.31	2,926,359	6.33	0.31	100
L10	Mortgaged Families	8,991	6.28	3,009,502	6.51	0.30	96
L11	**Country Dwellers**	**58,278**	**40.70**	**3,375,200**	**7.30**	**1.73**	**558**
L12	Institutional Areas	1,198	0.84	335,285	0.73	0.36	115
	Total adults 15+	143,195	100	46,241,144	100.00	0.31	100

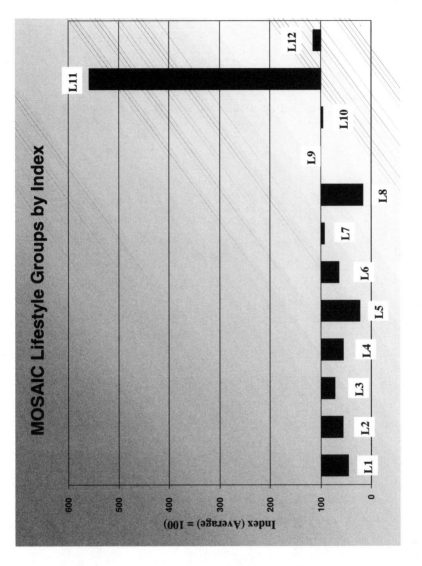

Figure 6.2 *MOSAIC profile at group level (Hereford)*

Table 6.5 *Area profile report for Hereford's major shopping centre (type level)*

	Hereford	Hereford %	Great Britain	Great Britain %	Penetration %	Index
L1 High Income Families by adults 15+						
M1 Clever Capitalists	217	0.15	761,196	1.65	0.03	9
M2 Rising Materialists	1,577	1.10	1,139,319	2.46	0.14	45
M3 Corporate Careerists	995	0.69	1,378,948	2.98	0.07	23
M4 Ageing Professionals	265	0.19	851,045	1.84	0.03	10
M5 Small-time Business	4,898	3.42	1,408,808	3.05	0.35	112
Total adults 15+	143,195	100.00	46,241,144	100.00	0.31	100
L2 Suburban Semis by adults 15+						
M6 Green Belt Expansion	5,458	3.81	1,803,949	3.90	0.30	98
M7 Suburban Mock Tudor	1,408	0.98	1,276,396	2.76	0.11	36
M8 Pebble-dash Subtopia	2,401	1.68	2,128,954	4.60	0.11	36
Total adults 15+	143,195	100.00	46,241,144	100.00	0.31	10
L3 Blue Collar Owners by adults 15+						
M9 Affluent Blue Collar	1,465	1.02	1,619,599	3.50	0.09	29
M10 30s Industrial Spec	3,066	2.14	1,880,430	4.07	0.16	53
M11 Low-rise Right to Buy	6,591	4.60	1,391,301	3.01	0.47	153
M12 Smokestack Shift Work	2,774	1.94	1,352,173	2.92	0.21	66
Total adults 15+	143,195	100.00	46,241,144	100.00	0.31	100

Table 6.5 *Area profile report for Hereford's major shopping centre (type level) (continued)*

	Hereford	Hereford %	Great Britain	Great Britain %	Penetration %	Index
L4 Low Rise Council by adults 15+						
M13 Co-op Club & Colliery	2,995	2.09	1,618,832	3.50	0.19	60
M14 Better-off Council	2,265	1.58	1,038,137	2.25	0.22	70
M15 Low-rise Pensioners	1,206	0.84	1,349,879	2.92	0.09	29
M16 Low-rise Subsistence	1,511	1.06	1,457,158	3.15	0.10	33
M17 Problem Families	2,968	2.07	885,970	1.92	0.34	108
Total adults 15+	143,195	100.00	46,241,144	100.00	0.31	100
L5 Council Flats by adults 15+						
M18 Families In The Sky	0	0.00	446,678	0.97	0.00	0
M19 Graffitied Ghettos	0	0.00	120,732	0.26	0.00	0
M20 Small Town Industry	587	0.41	573,773	1.24	0.10	33
M21 Mid-rise Overspill	30	0.02	306,736	0.66	0.01	3
M22 Flats for the Aged	1,098	0.77	486,047	1.05	0.23	73
M23 Inner-city Towers	0	0.00	638,345	1.38	0.00	0
Total adults 15+	143,195	100.00	46,241,144	100.00	0.31	100

Table 6.5 *Area profile report for Hereford's major shopping centre (type level) (continued)*

	Hereford	Hereford %	Great Britain	Great Britain %	Penetration %	Index
L6 Victorian Low Status by adults 15+						
M24 Bohemian Melting Pot	0	0.00	1,018,282	2.20	0.00	0
M25 Victorian Tenements	37	0.03	66,608	0.14	0.06	18
M26 Rootless Renters	1,590	1.11	545,955	1.18	0.29	94
M27 Sweatshop Sharers	0	0.00	622,052	1.35	0.00	0
M28 Depopulated Terraces	2,044	1.43	350,554	0.76	0.58	188
M29 Rejuvenated Terraces	4,338	3.03	1,410,603	3.05	0.31	99
Total adults 15+	143,195	100.00	46,241,144	100.00	0.31	100
L7 Town Houses & Flats by adults 15+						
M30 Bijou Homemakers	1,239	0.87	1,685,212	3.64	0.07	24
M31 Market Town Mixture	6,208	4.34	1,754,726	3.79	0.35	114
M32 Town Centre Singles	5,264	3.68	970,390	2.10	0.54	175
Total adults 15+	143,195	100.00	46,241,144	100.00	0.31	100
L8 Stylish Singles by adults 15+						
M33 Bedsits & Shop Flats	772	0.54	443,224	0.96	0.17	56
M34 Studio Singles	428	0.30	699,787	1.51	0.06	20
M35 College & Communal	0	0.00	317,485	0.69	0.00	0
M36 Chattering Classes	0	0.00	795,515	1.72	0.00	0
Total adults 15+	143,195	100.00	46,241,144	100.00	0.31	100

Table 6.5 Area profile report for Hereford's major shopping centre (type level) (continued)

	Hereford	Hereford %	Great Britain	Great Britain %	Penetration %	Index
L9 Independent Elders by adults 15+						
M37 Solo Pensioners	2,467	1.72	657,706	1.42	0.38	121
M38 High-spending Greys	1,261	0.88	537,275	1.16	0.23	76
M39 Aged Owner Occupiers	4,364	3.05	1,229,880	2.66	0.35	115
M40 Elderly in Own Flats	941	0.66	501,498	1.08	0.19	61
Total adults 15+	143,195	100.00	46,241,144	100.00	0.31	100
L10 Mortgaged Families by adults 15+						
M41 Brand-new Areas	1,627	1.14	516,768	1.12	0.31	102
M42 Pre-nuptial Owners	3,396	2.37	731,938	1.58	0.46	150
M43 Nest-making Families	2,056	1.44	620,261	1.34	0.33	107
M44 Maturing Mortgagers	1,912	1.34	1,140,535	2.47	0.17	54
Total adults 15+	143195	100.00	46,241,144	100.00	0.31	100
L11 Country Dwellers by adults 15+						
M45 Gentrified Villages	**3,648**	**2.55**	**730,013**	**1.58**	**0.50**	**161**
M46 Rural Retirement Mix	4,004	2.80	276,911	0.60	1.45	467
M47 Lowland Agribusiness	**8,458**	**5.91**	**903,556**	**1.95**	**0.94**	**302**
M48 Rural Disadvantage	**6,508**	**4.54**	**523,116**	**1.13**	**1.24**	**402**
M49 Tied/Tenant Farmers	**7,506**	**5.24**	**296,557**	**0.64**	**2.53**	**817**
M50 Upland & Small Farms	**28,154**	**19.66**	**645,047**	**1.39**	**4.36**	**1409**
Total adults 15+	143,195	100.00	46,241,144	100.00	0.31	100

Table 6.5 *Area profile report for Hereford's major shopping centre (type level) (continued)*

	Hereford	Hereford %	Great Britain	Great Britain %	Penetration %	Index
L12 Institutional Areas by adults 15+						
M51 Military Bases	**607**	**0.42**	**110,039**	**0.24**	**0.55**	**178**
M52 Non-private Housing	591	0.41	225,246	0.49	0.26	85
Total adults 15+	143,195	100.00	46,241,144	100.00	0.31	100

APPLICATIONS TO SURVEY DESIGN

Geodemographic systems are highly recommended in certain situations commonly encountered by the survey designer, as described in the following sections.

Stratification

Sample accuracy will be improved if relevant variables are employed as stratifiers at the sampling stage. As we have seen, geodemographic systems summarize large numbers of census variables and are area-based, so are ideal for survey stratification. Furthermore, geodemographic information may be obtained at various geographical levels, such as constituencies, wards and EDs, and so may be used with complex multi-stage survey designs.

Disproportionate sampling

As an extension of the stratification technique, the survey designer can choose to vary the sampling fractions within different geodemographic types, so as to overrepresent groups of greatest interest. This approach might be adopted either to optimize sample accuracy or to oversample areas of greatest product potential.

For sample optimization, an established principle is to oversample strata with greater variability in the topic of interest and, conversely, to undersample those strata where responses will vary less. This is often achievable using geodemographic types as strata, by first quantifying the variation within each type from previous survey results. Having conducted the survey on a disproportionate basis, the sample results will be weighted back to population proportions at the processing stage, using the corresponding area profile as the 'target'.

Matched samples

Repeat measurement surveys that require matching over time are likely to be improved by the use of geodemographics as a stratification control. The selection of geodemographically matched sampling points will help to reduce sampling errors or 'noise' when monitoring changes in the research results.

Minority sampling

The ultimate extreme in disproportionate sampling is to employ geo-demographic techniques in order to reach minority groups. Dependent on the definition or profile of the minority population, geodemographic targeting can be a highly effective tool for locating its members. This can greatly reduce the number of screening interviews that would otherwise be needed in order to reach the required subset.

Geodemographics can be deployed in this way either for quantitative surveys, eg to find product users, or for qualitative research, in order to locate the most suitable areas for depth interviews, group discussions or hall tests.

Sample control

Having conducted a survey or set up a sampling frame for repeat measure-ment, geodemographics can be used to control or monitor sample balance. Neighbourhood classifications tend to identify the areas where fieldwork may be more difficult or costly, for example inner cities or rural areas. Some surveys are weighted by geodemographic strata in order to improve representation or to compensate for disproportionate sampling, as dis-cussed above.

Analysis

As mentioned earlier, market research has an important role in geodem-ographic profiling – this link is achieved through survey analysis.

The TGI, so important in demonstrating the early potential of ACORN, has continued to be a key market research linkage for geodemographics. Most of the leading classifications are available on TGI, and therefore users may obtain a 'geodem cross-tab' for any desired product or service, and apply the results within their geodemographic systems.

Other syndicated surveys are also geodemographically coded and may be employed to derive equivalent cross-tabs. These sources cover the main sectors of consumer activity, for example:

- financial services – NOP's Financial Research Survey (FRS) and MORI Financial Services (MFS);
- media research – National Readership Survey (NRS);
- packaged groceries – TNS Superpanel and Nielsen's Homescan panel;
- household durables – GfK Home Audit.

Market research cross-tabs are frequently employed to drive the retail, marketing and media applications outlined below.

RETAIL APPLICATIONS

Geodemographic systems have a wide range of applications to retailers – virtually irrespective of size or market. The principal areas of application are summarized below.

Catchment area definition

The tools available in geodemographic systems are ideal for defining the catchment area of a retail outlet, that is the local region supplying most of its customers.

The most accurate methods require a sample of customer postcodes, which can come from either the company's records or a customer survey. One approach is to map the locations of the outlet and its customers and define an area containing the nearest 70 per cent to 80 per cent (say) of customers to the store. Another technique is to use postal sectors as 'building bricks' and define a catchment area of sectors with a required penetration of customers.

In the absence of customer data, a catchment may be constructed by assuming that it covers a given distance or drive time from the store.

Demand estimation

Potential demand can be estimated for any geographical area, by applying research-based purchasing rates to the area population profile. 'Off-the-shelf' retail potential reports are available from the major geodemographic agencies. A primary application would be to obtain the total market value for the catchment area of a retail outlet, and hence derive an estimate of market share by comparison with the retailer's known sales.

Store location analysis

Various approaches are available for evaluating existing stores or predicting the performance of new sites – see Davies and Rogers (1984) or Wrigley (1988) for details of such methods. A model-based approach is often employed, using techniques such as multiple regression or gravity modelling.

Multiple regression entails the analysis of data on performance and characteristics of existing stores in the retailer's portfolio, the outcome being a model that expresses store turnover as a function of site and area characteristics.

Gravity analysis simulates the trading in a region and analyses the flows of purchasing from consumer 'origins' to retail 'destinations'. These flows are modelled in terms of outlet features, which attract consumers to a store, and travel costs, which act as a deterrent.

Store ranging and merchandising

The estimates of consumer demand, for different markets in a store catchment area, can be employed to help optimize that store's merchandise range. Johnson (1989) describes how geodemographics can be applied as part of retailer research into store planning.

Local store marketing

Retailers are heavy users of local advertising media such as press, radio, posters, direct mail and door-to-door distribution. The use of these channels may be planned and targeted with the aid of geodemographics, as we will describe in the following sections.

DIRECT MARKETING APPLICATIONS

'Cold' vs 'warm' targeting

In the 1980s, one of the primary applications of geodemographics was for direct marketing. Having profiled existing customers and identified their neighbourhood types, the next step was to target recruitment of new customers in similar neighbourhoods. Such targeting was invariably conducted using the electoral roll, held on computer and tagged with geodemographic classifiers.

The arrival of lifestyle databases has significantly reduced this use of geodemographics. Lifestyle names may be targeted on specific pieces of information, such as age and income, held for those individuals. Further, due to its method of compilation, lifestyle sources are more likely to contain people who will be responsive to direct mail.

However, geodemographics is often still used in 'warm' direct marketing to a company's existing customers. Within the financial sector alone, most customer databases hold geodemographic codes and employ them as part of activities such as valuing customers and cross-selling them further products.

Door-to-door distribution

'Door-to-door' offers an alternative to direct mail, whereby the same communication is delivered to every household within an area, using teams of 'door-droppers'. This significantly reduces both the unit cost of reaching each individual and the targeting power that can be achieved. Almost by definition, the targeting of door-to-door can be improved dramatically through using geodemographics to help select the areas.

Door-to-door operators generally employ postal sectors as unit areas, although several companies have developed smaller areas for finer targeting. An analysis known as postal sector ranking (PSR) is commonly used to select the best areas for a product distribution. This works by estimating the sales potential for each available sector using geodemographic profiles, and then ranking sectors for selection. The PSR report will show the cumulative number of households that will be reached and the expected efficiency of targeting. The most sophisticated users of this medium, in the fast-moving consumer goods (fmcg) sector, employ precisely targeted door-to-door techniques to gather information for building marketing databases at the same time as distributing product coupons or free samples.

MAPPING AND GEOGRAPHICAL INFORMATION SYSTEMS

With the advent of more powerful and cheaper desktop computers, software packages have become available that enable the user to display data in map form. Such tools range from off-the-shelf mapping packages to customized geographical information systems (GIS), which will store, manipulate and display any forms of locational data.

Sleight (1997) segments the GIS market into three main product types – 'big systems', PC analysis/mapping systems and low-priced GIS/mapping systems.

'Big systems' are typically used by large retailers for storing customer and purchase data, and performing site location analysis. The applications may be customized to client requirements, and a number of users may access the system simultaneously, possibly from different departments within the organization. Suppliers of big systems include ARC/INFO, LaserScan and Smallworld.

PC analysis/mapping systems are designed to provide geodemographic analysis and geographical mapping. All of the classification vendors, listed in Table 6.1, offer such systems and they almost universally run in a Windows environment.

Low-priced GIS/mapping systems provide a reduced range of geodemographic functions, and the necessary input datasets often cost more than the software. Two popular systems in this category are MapInfo and Tactician.

A variety of datasets are required to run a GIS. A typical installation will contain:

- natural geography, eg rivers and coastline;
- human-made geography, eg towns and cities, roads and railways;
- imposed geography, eg administrative districts, postal areas and media regions;
- demographic data, eg census, lifestyle and geodemographic classification;
- geocoding data – grid references for locating and mapping postcodes, eg of customers and stores.

The power of a GIS lies in its ability to interrelate different types and levels of information geographically. For example, a system containing the above data can calculate:

- proximities of customers to stores;
- stores present in a postal area;
- customers living close to certain roads.

The datasets for GIS have been created at a range of geographical scales, according to the level of detail and accuracy required. The potential user has to consider the maps and analyses that will be produced, the geographical features required and the functions needed, when planning to set up one of these systems.

FUTURE PROSPECTS – 2001 CENSUS AND BEYOND

The availability of 2001 Census output will give a new impetus to the geodemographic industry; a new generation of classification systems can be expected to appear from 2003 onwards.

At the time of writing, the details of '2001' have yet to be finalized. However, the Government White Paper published in 1999 indicates that some major refinements of approach are planned. These include:

- a new computerized system for planning enumeration districts and defining them to enumerators, as computer-generated maps and address lists;
- an extended list of question topics, including new questions on religion and, possibly, income – subject primarily to public acceptance;
- a redesigned census form that is easier for respondents to complete;
- post-back of forms by respondents combined with targeted follow-ups by enumerators;
- use of more advanced technology to automate data capture from census forms;
- 100 per cent processing of all census questions (certain questions were previously processed on a 10 per cent sample);
- concurrent release of all national and local census outputs, with some data published in electronic form and greater flexibility to obtain customized outputs;
- a separate geography for census outputs, based on groupings of unit postcodes;
- production of a consistent set of census outputs that have been adjusted for population undercounting, based on estimates from a census coverage survey.

These developments are designed to deliver a package of census results that meets user requirements, while satisfying confidentiality and acceptability criteria, and that is demonstrably value for money. They will help to ensure that the census continues to be the primary driver for geodemographics in the 2000s and that its user base will continue to widen.

REFERENCES AND FURTHER READING

Bermingham, J, Baker, K, and McDonald, C (1979) ACORN – a classification of residential neighbourhoods, Market Research Society Conference

Davies, R L and Rogers, D S (1984) *Store Location and Store Assessment Research*, John Wiley, London

Johnson, M (1989) The application of geodemographics in retailing – meeting the needs of the catchment, *Journal of the Market Research Society*, **31**

Leventhal, B (1995) Evaluation of geodemographic classifications, *Journal of Targeting, Measurement and Analysis for Marketing*, **4**

Office for National Statistics (1999) *The 2001 Census of Population*, Cm 4253, HMSO, London

Sleight, P (1997) *Targeting Customers – How to use geodemographics and lifestyle data in your business*, NTC Publications

Wrigley, N (1988) *Store Choice, Store Location and Market Analysis*, Routledge, London

7

Quantitative Research Over the Internet

David Walker

INTRODUCTION

Although the initial development of the Internet can be traced back to the late 1960s, it has only been in the last six or seven years that it has truly become a globally accessible medium. The Internet has, in effect, become a collection of virtual communities, all focused upon the pursuit or sharing of information.

Business organizations have woken up to the potential of this medium as the technology and its usage has broadened. E-commerce has become the buzzword of the boardroom as companies realize how the Internet can offer a global platform for conducting business at a very low infrastructure cost. The tremendous hype and publicity surrounding the Internet would suggest that no organization can ignore its potential. For many this is not true; the Internet may be no more than a marketing or promotional tool. Organizations that will truly benefit will be those that can operate or distribute their services over the new medium. Market research certainly falls into this category, with the Internet representing an exciting new method of collecting and distributing information.

For many, the online questionnaire holds the most potential for research companies. In effect, the Internet is an electronic data collection tool, which will allow researchers to collect information in a format that can be directly read and analysed without the relatively slow and costly data entry processes that can hinder paper-based quantitative methodologies.

However, before examining the key quantitative methodologies, it is important to understand the unique issues that affect the ability to conduct research over the Internet.

BENEFITS AND DRAWBACKS OF THE ONLINE APPROACH

Like all research techniques, online research has its benefits and drawbacks. Unlike others, however, these are changing constantly as the usage and application of the Internet changes. It is important, however, before deciding on an online approach, to be aware of the context in which it operates.

Benefits

There is a wide range of benefits to be gained from taking an online quantitative research approach, encompassing speed, cost and quality issues:

- **Inexpensive research** In comparison to face-to-face or telephone research, online costs are significantly lower, as the there are no interviewers and minimal telephone charges to pay. It can even be cheaper then postal research, given huge reductions in printing and postage costs.
- **Objective responses** As respondents are typing in their own responses, feedback can be considered totally objective; there is no interviewer influence.
- **Unintrusive** Respondents complete surveys at their own pace, when they want, and this has potentially beneficial effects on response rates and the quality of answers.
- **Speed of response** Experience shows that responses can be received far more quickly than for postal research. This may be because most individuals check their e-mail on a daily basis and normally do so when they have time to respond.
- **Quality of response** Compared to telephone or even postal research, respondents give more articulate responses to open-ended questions. This may be due to the fact that when individuals type, they are more accustomed to producing structured and formatted output (rather than handwritten notes or one-word responses).

- **International research** There are no international boundaries and so questionnaires can be completed as easily on the opposite side of the world as at a more local address.
- **Technical possibilities** Given the methodology is using the latest technology, there is the possibility of using its capabilities in the research questionnaire (potentially using sound, graphics and video).
- **Automation** Data is collected in a predefined electronic format and so there is no need to re-enter responses manually, making considerable cost savings.

Drawbacks

The drawbacks of the online approach relate largely to sampling and sample control issues. However, as usage of the Internet continues to grow rapidly, some of these issues may be overcome in time. At present, key concerns are as follows:

- **A narrow target audience** The types of individuals that are using the Internet have an obvious effect on the scope of research that can be conducted at present. The vast majority of users (up to 85 per cent according to some estimates) are based in the US. The system is also clearly biased towards males aged 25–35, largely the more affluent individuals in this group, although this balance is changing and there is an increasing number of female users (over 30 per cent according to some estimates).
- **Identifying Internet users** Generally the penetration of Internet users, particularly in Europe, is low and identifying who they might be, outside of placing messages on the Internet itself, is difficult. Lists of e-mail addresses are limited and not always reliable.
- **Understanding the sample** Knowing who exactly is participating in research can be difficult. E-mail addresses alone also give little indication as to the type of person using e-mail. Identifying and controlling samples of Internet users is therefore a difficult process and needs to be addressed on a project-by-project basis.
- **Technical restrictions** The ways of accessing the Internet are many and varied. Some Internet users may be using high-speed modems over a digital telephone network whilst others may have something far more basic. With different degrees of access the 'performance' of Internet services will vary between different users. One Internet page may also look different to respondents, dependent upon the browser software that is being used.

Taking these issues into consideration, there is still much opportunity in conducting quantitative research over the Internet. There are two key methods that should be examined. They are: 1) Web questionnaires – self-completion questionnaires undertaken online via Internet Web pages; and 2) e-mail questionnaires – questionnaires transmitted directly to individuals for self-completion and e-mail return. Although these methods have similar approaches, the applications and management of them vary. Each of the methods is examined in turn below.

WEB QUESTIONNAIRES

Broadly defined, a Web questionnaire is a self-completion document placed on a Web site. The data collected can be read directly into the researcher's analysis package at any given point in time and results generated.

Questionnaire types

There are two basic types of Web questionnaire: 1) a form – a number of questions are presented on a page and the respondent completes each question and scrolls down to the bottom of the page; and 2) an interactive questionnaire – questions are shown one at a time to respondents, who submit their answer and are then presented with a new question (which downloads separately dependent upon the answer to the previous questions). An example of each is shown as Figures 7.1 and 7.2. Both questionnaire types are valid and have their pros and cons, as shown in Table 7.1.

The basic rule would appear to be that forms are most effective for the simpler research project, with interactive questionnaires more effective for the complex survey. Certainly forms are a simpler and cheaper alternative, although research objectives may require that a more complex interactive approach is required.

Running a survey

As with traditional research, the bulk of research executive activity is concentrated in the setup and design of the questionnaire. Once in place and active, there is little monitoring or control required, as respondents self-complete the survey.

The design process for a questionnaire remains similar to that of a traditional postal survey, the exception being that the document is programmed into hypertext mark up language (html) to enable it to be placed on the Web.

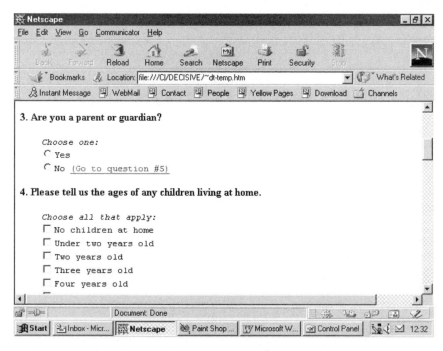

Figure 7.1 *A form-based Web survey* (copyright: RI and Decisive Software)

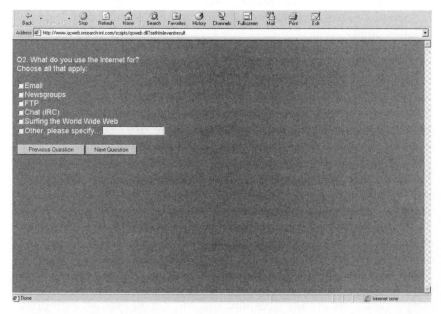

Figure 7.2 *An interactive Web-based survey* (copyright: RI and QCWeb)

Table 7.1 *Pros and cons of forms and interactive questionnaires*

Forms	Interactive Questionnaires
Good for simple, straightforward questions with basic routeing	Good for questionnaires with complex routeing patterns
On one Web page, so will download quickly	Questions download one at a time (may be time-consuming for users with slow modems)
Respondents are aware of the total length of the questionnaire	Respondents are not immediately aware of the questionnaire length
Respondents are not forced to complete all questions before submitting answers	Respondents have to complete all questions correctly before answers are submitted
Relatively easy to set up	More complex programming and routeing required

Programming is relatively straightforward, and three options are available:

1. The survey can be designed and built 'from scratch' using basic Web design tools (such as Microsoft FrontPage).
2. Specialist Web questionnaire design software can be purchased and used fairly simply.
3. Some data analysis agencies will offer a 'bureau' service for a questionnaire, building the Web pages from a specification, and hosting and collecting the data.

Once designed the questionnaire should be allocated a specific Web address (or url). This address could be linked to an existing Web site or a completely stand-alone page dependent upon the requirements of the survey.

Once in place, respondents are invited to complete the questionnaire, which can be achieved in two key ways. The first way is to place an invitation on another Web page, for example by putting a banner advertisement or a link to the survey on a related Web site, or by intercepting visitors to a site with a 'pop up' window link to a questionnaire. This is a very simple method of generating response, but there is little control over the research sample or types of individuals completing the survey. The other way is to e-mail respondents directly with the address (url) of the survey and invite them to participate. This is a more effective method of controlling the sample and access to the questionnaire, but e-mail lists of appropriate respondents are not always readily available.

Respondents self-complete the questionnaire and, when complete, they register their answers (normally by pressing a submit button at the end of the questionnaire). Responses are then automatically saved and can be accessed by the research manager at any point.

Once the fieldwork period is complete, the electronic responses can be fed into traditional analysis packages and data generated. This can be a very quick process, given that the responses (to pre-coded questions) are already in a structured electronic format.

Issues to consider

Although the Web questionnaire is a simple and effective research method, there are a number of considerations that should be taken into account when running a survey, as detailed in the following sections.

Sampling

The true representativeness of the sample should be taken into account. The fact that respondents are all Internet users means that they are not typical of the overall consumer universe (although this may be desirable if the research is aimed at a more technically literate audience).

Inviting response

The location and method of inviting response will have an effect on sampling. E-mailing invitations will mean a more controlled sampling approach, although may not always be possible. Inviting response through links on other Web pages may skew response to individuals with an interest in the pages where the invitation appears.

Response rates

As with any self-completion research, it is difficult to predict the level of response. A wide range of factors will influence this including any incentives offered for participation, the prominence of the invitation to participate, the degree of interest in the topic area and the length of the fieldwork period.

Applications

The applications for this approach are still at their early stages. It provides a highly cost-effective data collection methodology and, if the target audience is relatively small and technically literate, can be useful as a stand-alone research methodology. It represents a highly cost-effective alternative to postal questionnaires or even some telephone research studies but whereas postal research can be used amongst a wide variety of target groups, online questionnaires, at present, have a much smaller potential audience.

Examples

Research International (RI) has been involved in a number of surveys where Web questionnaires have been generated. Examples of these, which give an indication of the capability of the methodology, are as follows:

■ Twenty-two thousand individuals who had registered an interest in a new UK-based Internet access service (by leaving e-mail contact details) were e-mailed and asked to participate in a survey about their perceptions of the product. A prize draw for two electronic organizers was offered as an incentive for participation. The questionnaire took around 10–15 minutes to complete. Six thousand responses were received, 80 per cent of them within three days of the initial invitation e-mails.
■ In March 1999, a forum of 9,000 IT/telecom managers in 11 countries were e-mailed and asked to participate in a Web survey. Web questionnaires were set up in seven languages. Participants were e-mailed an invitation in their own native language and English, and were sent to a central Web page. On this page respondents were presented with the language options for the questionnaire and were able to choose the most appropriate option for themselves. A 20 per cent response rate was achieved.
■ In order to help monitor the effectiveness of their Web site, a leading airline placed a feedback questionnaire on the Web site itself and invited visitors to place their comments. Responses were collected on an ongoing basis and reviewed in relation to promotional activity and developments on the Web site to ensure that online customer satisfaction was kept high.
■ The IT department of a leading telecom company assessed satisfaction with its performance by conducting research over the company intranet. Around 7,000 e-mail invitations were sent and around 2,500 questionnaires were completed.

E-MAIL QUESTIONNAIRES

The majority of Internet users have their own personal e-mail address, which allows them to have private communications with other Internet users. One potential application for researchers is to use this e-mail system

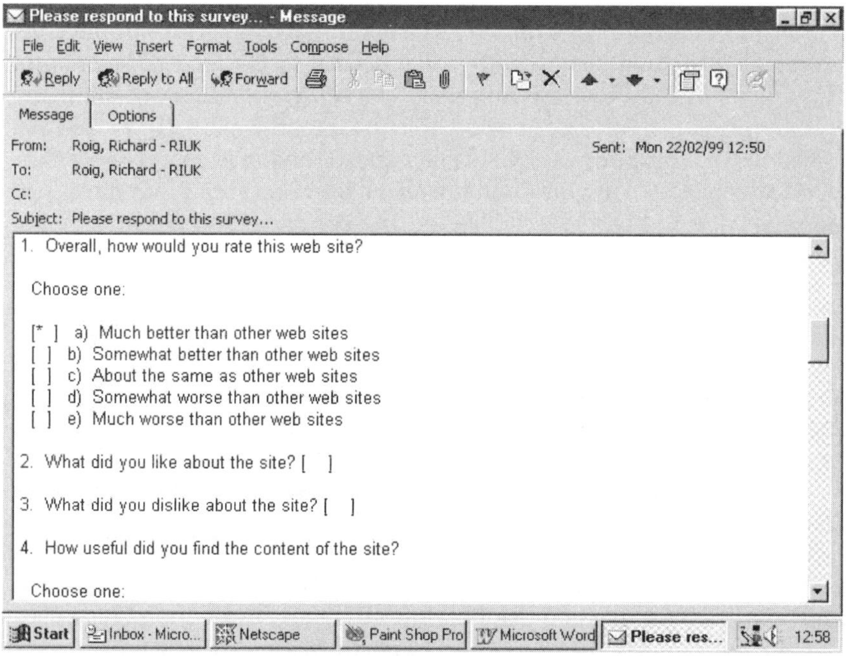

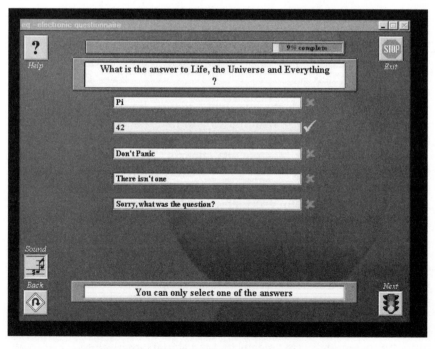

Figure 7.3 *Text-based e-mail survey* (copyright: RI)

Figure 7.4 *Executable e-mail survey* (copyright: RI)

to transmit questionnaires directly to respondents, who can complete the survey at their own leisure and e-mail it back to the research company. This approach combines the simplicity of a self-completion questionnaire with the added advantage of being able to target the research sample.

Unlike Web questionnaires, where a questionnaire is completed online on a Web page, e-mail questionnaires have questions built into the e-mail message itself and can be downloaded and completed offline.

Questionnaire types

There are two key types of e-mail questionnaire: 1) questionnaires that appear as text in an e-mail (with tick boxes and spaces for response as in a paper self-completion exercise); and 2) executable questionnaire programs that are sent as an attachment within an e-mail (and are completed similarly to a CAPI-based exercise).

Text-based e-mail questionnaires contain questions that appear almost as they would appear on paper in a self-completion exercise. These can be generated using an easy-to-use Windows-based software tool. This questionnaire is generated in an e-mail, sent directly to a respondent and appears in the e-mail window as a text questionnaire. The respondent will then scroll down through the questionnaire and enter text or check boxes at the appropriate points. Respondents e-mail the questionnaire back to a central point by using the 'reply' button. The system then collates the responses in an automated manner and allows for the production of automated data and graphics. An example is shown in Figure 7.3.

Executable e-mail questionnaires are mini-questionnaire programs sent as a file attachment in an e-mail. Once received, the respondent clicks on the attachment and starts the questionnaire (which runs as an automated self-completion interview, with routeing built in – similar to a CAPI self-completion exercise). The programs can be written using standard tools such as Visual Basic or Macromedia Director. This form of questioning allows for the production of more complex questionnaires, perhaps incorporating sound, graphics or even video. Figure 7.4 illustrates this.

As this method uses an executable questionnaire program, essentially sending a piece of software, it produces a file that is much larger than a standard e-mail and this can place restrictions upon its usage, particularly when sending files over the Internet. However, this issue is overcome when executable questionnaire programs are used over an internal company e-mail network. In this instance, the executable program sits on the central computer server used to drive the e-mail network and respondents are sent an e-mail with an attachment. This attachment, although looking the same as in the figure, is actually only a 'trigger' to start the executable programme remotely. This means that the actual e-mail sent is very small and that there are no restrictions on the size or content of the questionnaire.

Running a survey

To an extent, the design of an e-mail questionnaire is similar to Web questionnaires, in terms of the thought process employed. The only major difference is in the conversion of the questionnaire into its electronic format. The key stages in the process, however, are described in the following sections.

Questionnaire design

Some companies offer simple menu-driven software tools for questionnaire design, which allow an individual to create a final e-mailable questionnaire. This is particularly effective for questionnaires that appear as text in an e-mail.

For the more complex executable questionnaires, the original questionnaire is more likely to be created on paper and then later programmed into a more interactive electronic format. The only drawback to this approach is that the questionnaire may not have been designed with the full potential of multimedia in mind and so there may be a further stage of creative development involved.

Testing the questionnaire

As individuals use a variety of e-mail systems, before sending a large mailing to all respondents, it is essential that the questionnaire is tested fully, preferably with a small pilot sample. In our experience with RI, we test our questionnaires thoroughly internally with our clients and with a small sample of pre-recruited respondents who have a range of e-mail systems or technical capabilities. This stage is critical in the research process. If an e-mail questionnaire fails to work with a majority of respondents first time, it is unlikely that the same sample will try to complete the survey again. A badly constructed e-mail questionnaire could even cause a respondent's PC to 'freeze' or 'crash' and this could create a very negative impression, so rigorous testing is essential.

Mailing out questionnaires

Having input all relevant e-mail addresses, a custom-written program creates each e-mail individually and sends it on its way. To check that all e-mails have been sent and received effectively, delivery receipts and read receipts can be requested. However the accuracy of this cannot be guaranteed as some organizations will turn off this facility at their server (primarily as they do not want to pay for the cost of sending a receipt back). The time allocated for response may vary from project to project but it has been shown that the bulk of responses will be received within a few days (at RI, fieldwork tends to be no longer than two weeks).

Reminder e-mails

After a given point of time, a reminder e-mail could be sent out to those who have not yet responded. Unlike postal surveys, where this could be a very time-consuming and costly process, it is a very quick automated process and the original questionnaire could be resent. (In some RI surveys, we have sent more than one reminder e-mail, as the cost implications are minimal but response greatly enhanced).

Collecting responses

When a respondent presses the reply button on an e-mail, data can be sent to any address that is specified. Based on RI's experience, our favoured approach has been to set up a dedicated central e-mail address for a given survey. This address can only be accessed and used by the project management team, and all questionnaires are sent and received via this route. This ensures a high degree of control over the process and also ensures a level of data security.

Analysis

Responses are collected in a central point and can be accessed at any time. It is possible, therefore, to monitor the number of responses as they arrive and to analyse findings on an ongoing basis. All e-mail questionnaires produce data in an electronic format that can be translated into most statistical analysis packages.

Issues to consider

Sampling

Identifying the initial sample base can be difficult. The proportion of the population with an e-mail address is still relatively small, and lists of users are difficult to find and can be unreliable. Although this situation is improving (lists of users and online access panels are becoming widely available in the US), this remains the major difficulty in designing an e-mail survey.

Technical restrictions

All e-mail systems are not alike and hence it is difficult to ensure that an e-mail questionnaire will function correctly and in the same way for all respondents.

E-mail failure

It is inevitable that some e-mails will fail to be received or function once opened. In our experience there has yet to be a truly 100 per cent effective hit rate with respondents. Most common reasons for failure include:

- incorrect e-mail addresses (often a very small mistake – an incorrect case, spelling or punctuation);
- an unusual technical setup (normally a personalization or modification of the standard e-mail setup);
- the security restrictions on incoming e-mails that some systems may have (for example, size limitations or restrictions on file attachments), which may limit the design potential of an e-mail questionnaire.

Junk mail

Respondents are beginning to receive e-mails from external organizations on a more regular basis and there are beginning to be some complaints about unsolicited messages (particularly in the US market). E-mail research may be mistaken for sales activity or ignored altogether (although this is a challenge faced by a variety of research methodologies).

Pre-recruited vs 'cold' e-mail

Should respondents be pre-warned that they are to receive a questionnaire before it appears in their inbox? An online survey conducted by US company World Research Inc found that 88 per cent of e-mail users have received junk mail in their account with 66 per cent having a negative attitude towards it. E-mail researchers should think carefully about this issue. E-mail is much more of a 'personal space' than the normal mail and respondents may act negatively to an invasion of their privacy. ESOMAR guidelines on this issue recommend that the unsolicited e-mail approach should be avoided wherever possible.

Confidentiality issues

When an e-mail is received, the address details of the respondent are automatically attached, so it is very easy to identify responses at an individual level. In a way, this is no different from collecting classification and address details in a telephone or postal survey and is useful for quality control (also to identify who has responded if a reminder e-mail is to be sent). If this data is collected by a market research organization, it can then be collated and presented to the sponsoring client in an anonymized manner.

Applications

As a general rule, e-mail questionnaires can be used:

■ where there is a defined sample of e-mail contacts;
■ where users have an e-mail address but no Web access (particularly true for business e-mail users) and so cannot complete a Web questionnaire;
■ on internal company e-mail systems (where the majority of users may have access to e-mail).

The use of e-mail questionnaires amongst respondents who have Web access may reduce over time, as using a Web questionnaire instead will solve many of the technical problems that can be associated with sending e-mail over the Internet. Perhaps the area of growth for this methodology will be amongst users without Internet access and, in particular, business users of e-mail.

One example of this is in conducting research over internal company e-mail systems. This perhaps offers most opportunity for the medium. Internal systems offer the most simple means for conducting research – respondents are easily identifiable and manageable, they are normally using the same e-mail packages and the process can be monitored and managed effectively. There are few technical restrictions to conducting research over an internal e-mail system and hence there are great opportunities at present for using this medium (and indeed e-mail is already proving to be a fast-growing research medium in employee research).

Examples

Although e-mail research would appear to be a fairly structured form of research, aimed at the technically literate respondent, the possibilities for the methodology are fairly wide. Three recent examples of e-mail research are highlighted below, to illustrate the potential applications and success of this tool.

■ Research International UK conducted its own 1997 staff survey using an executable e-mail questionnaire. The questionnaire was fairly lengthy (taking over 30 minutes to complete) and contained a complex ratio scaling exercise and some complex routeing. The questionnaire was sent to over 400 staff around the country with a response rate of over 70 per cent within a three-week period. All staff (regardless of technical ability) undertook the survey (with a small proportion without e-mail access completing the survey on stand-alone laptop computers). A full analysis of the results was available within three days of completion of fieldwork.

Compared to previous years' studies (conducted by post), the e-mail route offered significant savings in administration costs, a higher response rate, more detailed responses to open-ended questions and the ability to design a more complex set of questions (taking advantage of the ability to route respondents effectively).

■ A staff survey for a leading management consultancy was conducted in September 1997. Conducted internationally over their internal company e-mail system (although in English), this was a small executable e-mail questionnaire, which contained a full computerized conjoint research exercise. The key benefit of this approach was a dramatic cost saving on a traditional conjoint research approach, which would have entailed a face-to-face CAPI interview.

■ A customer survey was carried out for a leading international oil company. This was a 'cold' executable e-mail questionnaire sent to 300 international customers of the company. A response rate of just under 50 per cent was achieved, although, because this was a 'cold' e-mail approach, it is not possible to ascertain how many respondents did not reply because of technical e-mail difficulties as against those who were simply not interested in participation in the survey. (Excluding technical failures, we would expect the response rate to be over 50 per cent.) The key benefits of this survey were seen to be the ability to conduct widespread international research at a fraction of the cost of a telephone or postal survey and in a very fast time-scale.

THE WAY AHEAD?

Despite some of the restrictions of Web and e-mail questionnaires, there can be no doubt that these research methods are here to stay and that they are becoming increasingly effective as the user base of the Internet increases and as the speed and infrastructure of the system improve. As more users may move to digital networks or fibre optic cables for their access, many of the technical problems currently restricting these methods will be improved. Improvements in software development will also lead to the 'new age' of electronic questionnaires that will be even simpler to design and transmit if required.

The potential for research companies is substantial, particularly if one compares this method to postal research. There will be substantial cost savings, faster and improved response and the ability to widen the type of questions asked to incorporate stimulus material such as sound or video clips. One must remain realistic, however, and realize that these opportunities are perhaps two to three years away and will largely be in the business environment in the more developed countries. Nevertheless, it is a potential that cannot be ignored.

IMPLICATIONS FOR THE MARKET RESEARCH INDUSTRY

If online research does develop rapidly over the coming years, there will be implications for market research organizations currently relying upon traditional methods.

The resources needed to conduct online research are very small and very basic. The large field force and resources of a major research organization count for little when conducting research over the Internet. There may well be considerable growth in the small specialized agency with online expertise. Indeed some of the larger research organizations may be slow to respond to online developments and there is a good chance that they will be left behind. When reviewing the list of organizations listed on the Internet as currently providing online research services, one can see that the list is becoming increasingly dominated by new, smaller, specialized companies largely based in the US.

As Internet usage grows, it will be increasingly important for executive research staff in all organizations to become aware of the online research alternatives and techniques. Market research organizations will need to consider improving their own Internet infrastructure and access for staff. This will have considerable cost implications, especially for the larger organizations where providing access and training may be a costly process.

Online research does not appear to offer a threat to traditional consumer research in the medium term, but for how long will that be the case? As penetration of the system increases, will market research companies be able to justify field interviewers or will they revert to online or electronic data collection methods? Will the shape and size of these field interviewing divisions change dramatically as online research grows?

SUMMARY

It could be argued that as a research medium the Internet will never be comprehensive and will be ineffective for certain types of research. This is true, but the same argument was levelled at telephone research not too many years ago. In fact the uptake of Internet access can be compared to the uptake of telephone or fax technology, except, according to some commentators, the speed of uptake is much faster and seems to be driven by a very high media profile. As long as one can accept the Internet's strengths and weaknesses, however, Web and e-mail questionnaires can be useful tools in the researcher's bag and ones that are likely to be here to stay.

SECTION 2

DATA COLLECTION

Introduction

Market research is an eclectic discipline. It draws its techniques from other areas – from statistics, economics, business management, marketing, psychology, anthropology and sociology. No single approach is suitable for all products and a technique used to examine a product or service at one point in time might not be thought so appropriate at a later date. Market research is essentially pragmatic, matching its methodology to a specific problem area.

This section is divided into parts on data collection into quantitative, qualitative and new product development. This is for convenience of segmentation. Both modes of research can be used, separately or in tandem, as the research problem dictates. Qualitative research should be used before quantitative to probe attitudes or set hypotheses or even just to understand buying habits and trends. Qualitative research can also be used after quantitative to probe more deeply into the data. Some companies undertake both modes, some specialize in one or the other. One approach is not necessarily 'better', but each approach is different and requires understanding of its advantages and limitations. Other chapters make readers aware of these differences.

Data collection methods are subject to several social and technical influences. Taking the social factors first, the growth of the proportion of women in paid work has affected data collection in two ways. First, it has reduced the number of women who are available for part-time, non-guaranteed and not-very-well-paid work as interviewers. Secondly, it has reduced the availability of key target groups for daytime interviewing – so evening and weekend interviews are a feature in the industry. Another social factor affecting data collection is the number of 'no-go' areas, particularly in the evenings, and the increasing numbers of blocks of flats, especially in large cities, where entry is restricted for security.

Data privacy legislation can also affect data collection and can make follow-up interviews on a sample difficult to achieve.

Face-to-face interviews still account for a high proportion of UK research turnover although there has been a gradual shift away from face-to-face to telephone research in the last 20 years. None the less, although telephone interviewing grew in popularity, it has not done so at the rate predicted. It has been suggested that one of the reasons for this is the difficulty of providing visual aids and stimuli, although techniques for doing this do exist. Telephone research appears to have grown fastest in the areas of opinion research and daytime business-to-business research, but has been much slower in fmcg areas. Postal research has never had a large share of research turnover in the UK, but there is some interest in the potential of self-completion surveys. This technique is particularly appropriate when the subject matter of the survey can be matched to the respondents' interests as a cost-effective way of collecting customer satisfaction information.

On the technical side, the increased use of computers has impacted on data collection approaches. Data collection methods that make direct use of electronic terminals include peoplemeters, scanner data from EPOS (electronic point of sale), CATI (computer-assisted telephone interviewing) and CAPI (computer-assisted personal interviewing). These techniques are described fully in the relevant chapters. Direct face-to-face interviewing with laptops was adopted in the industry in the 1990s, but there are still limitations: the costs involved in equipping a field force with computers, and the remaining heavy concentration of computer literacy among younger people.

The computer is likely to make the largest impact on quantitative data collection in the future although it is being found increasingly useful in analysing qualitative data. Growth in the use of computers does of course depend on heavy investment.

In qualitative research, theories from semiotics, anthropology and even literary criticism are being used to gain richer understanding of people's attitudes, responses and behaviour. Market research works best as an open model – highly flexible and pragmatic, moulding techniques to the project in hand.

It should be mentioned that any techniques carried out in the UK can be adapted for international research. The UK has become the world's foremost centre for the efficient co-ordination of research, and quantitative, qualitative, face-to-face or telephone research can effectively be organized in almost any country, in any language, from the UK. Panels, retail audits and EPOS systems based on market research in the UK are now used in all parts of the world.

Part 1

QUANTITATIVE TECHNIQUES

8

Quantitative Research

Erhard Meier

INTRODUCTION

At the planning stage of a project, a choice has to be made as to whether the study should be based on qualitative or quantitative research methods. The decision may be straightforward, and in favour of one or the other because the objectives guiding the project themselves often imply the most suitable method. If the objective is to obtain exploratory views on a new product or concept, then a qualitative study, based probably on a few group discussions, is in order. If, however, the study is required to quantify the number of people in a population, or a subset of the population that has particular characteristics or views, then a quantitative study is appropriate. This study will have a representative sample drawn by statistical methods.

Quantitative studies are often preceded by qualitative research, which explores the issues to be studied or tests the questions to be asked. Equally, quantitative studies are sometimes backed by a qualitative follow-up to explore the subject in more depth.

Unfortunately, however, the qualitative/quantitative choice is not always so straightforward. There can be conflicting interests and demands, which need to be resolved at the planning stage. For example, the publisher of a consumer magazine might wish to attract new readers by changing some editorial features of the magazine. At the same time he does not want to lose too many existing readers. The research objectives in such a case might be: 1) to find out how both existing and potential new readers will react to the redesigned product; and 2) to give a quantifiable measure of how many new readers are likely to be attracted and how many old readers, if any, will be lost.

The first objective alone can be dealt with in a qualitative study. The second objective demands a quantitative study. However, both objectives can also be addressed in a quantitative study.

The conflict is most likely to be one between the research budget and/ or time available on the one hand and the costs and/or time needed for the quantitative study on the other. Because quantitative studies involve large numbers of interviews, they tend to be more expensive and can take longer to implement than qualitative research. This leads to a temptation to carry out qualitative research alone without the benefit of a quantitative stage. And, worse, decisions may be made without full insights into the subject.

At this point it is appropriate to mention a possible misunderstanding that may derive from the words 'qualitative' and 'quantitative'. As is apparent from the above example, quantitative surveys deal with the quantification of behavioural and other informant characteristics. They can include attitudes and opinions, and these are sometimes referred to as 'qualitative data'. People's attitudes and opinions can of course be measured in quantitative surveys. For example, this could well be the case for the magazine publisher wanting to research reactions to editorial changes. He might want insights into what people think of the editorial and any proposed changes. Qualitative views may be sufficient. Or he may want a measure of the incidence of these views, in which case a quantitative study is called for.

Once a quantitative survey has been chosen as the vehicle of investigation, we are then dealing with a survey employing highly structured procedures. These concern the sampling approach, the data collection method, the questionnaire structure, the fieldworkers' training and competence, the data preparation, data analysis and reporting. These aspects of survey research are all covered elsewhere in this book. The following paragraphs, therefore, only touch very briefly on each.

SAMPLE SIZE

Quantitative research does not necessarily mean very large samples. While it is true that some quantitative studies are based on large samples of 20,000 informants or more, most commercial market research uses samples of (typically) 200, 250, 500, 800, 1,000 or 2,000 informants.

The choice of sample size depends on factors such as the desired accuracy of the estimates to be derived from the sample, the expected incidence of what is measured, the sampling method, the interview method, whether subgroups of the sampled population are to be studied separately, and considerations of costs. A quantitative study may in some cases be based on just one or two hundred informants. The decisions to be taken are then based on the findings of a survey with relatively large confidence limits, statistically speaking. It is a matter of judgement as to whether this is justified in the light of the decisions to be made.

Surveys with large samples tend to be those where subgroups of the sampled population need to be studied separately. In the UK, examples include the National Readership Survey with an annual sample of 38,000 informants (NRS, 1997), the government's Family Resources Survey with a sample of 40,000 households (ONS, 1996) and the Target Group Index (TGI) with an annual sample size of 25,000 respondents (British Market Research Bureau, 1997).

An example of a survey with a very large contact sample is the British Business Survey in the UK. This survey reports a sample of 3,000 business-people. However, these businesspeople are a subgroup of over 60,000 respondents selected by probability sampling (RSL, 1997).

Outside the UK, large sample sizes include readership studies. The National Readership Survey of India has a sample of 132,000, the Spanish EGM survey has a sample of 40,000 and the Dutch Summoscanner has 24,000 informants (Meier, 1997).

SAMPLING METHOD

Most large studies employ probability sampling so that the researchers can qualify each result by quoting its accuracy. Studies in the public domain tend to be based on probability samples because they are generally accepted as less prone to bias (due to non-response) than those using quota samples. While with probability samples non-response can be calculated and its likely effect estimated, this is not the case with quota samples – and quota samples are by far the most common samples used in studies to guide business decisions. Quota samples are accepted in commercial research for most quantitative studies, provided they employ quota control variables that are selected appropriately.

Reverting back to probability samples, the well-documented sampling approach used for the UK's National Readership Survey (NRS) is a continuous survey of the adult population aged 15 or over in the UK. Its purpose is the measurement of reading behaviour covering over 250 newspapers and magazines, and to describe potential readers and target groups in demographic terms. A sample requirement is that each monthly sample is a replica of the annual sample. The NRS uses a two-stage probability sample constructed for one year's fieldwork. In 1997, the design involved the selection of 2,520 enumeration districts as primary sampling units, the selection of addresses from PAF (postcode address file) and the selection of persons for personal interview within these addresses. There are highly sophisticated stratification and selection procedures, including the balancing of the sample over time by month and within month by day of week. Informants are interviewed personally in-home. In 1997, there were 38,000 respondents, representing a response rate of 61 per cent (NRS, 1997).

DATA COLLECTION

Quantitative studies can be carried out face to face, over the telephone, by mail or observation. The common characteristic is that structured question-naires are used, which collect responses to standard questions. Most use pre-coded responses. Where so-called 'open-ended' questions are used, the verbatim answers are subsequently coded in the office using a coding frame, which is a grouping of the responses into a small and manageable number of categories enabling patterns to be observed. It is developed either from a qualitative research stage or more typically from looking over a small sample of responses selected from the study.

FIELDWORK COMPETENCE

All standardized interviewing needs specially trained interviewers. Apart from a basic training in interviewing, a field force must also be briefed and trained for the particular study in hand. The procedures used for the UK NRS may again serve as an example. The sampling and interviewing techniques used for this survey are particularly complex, so interviewers first have their basic training in market research interviewing, followed by a lengthy period of relatively standard interviewing practice. The special training for the NRS then involves a day's briefing session, repeated annually and accompaniment by a supervisor on the new interviewer's very first NRS assignment. To control the quality of work, periodic checks are made on all interviewers' work by a mixture of personal supervision, telephone checks to informants, tape-recording of selected interviews, and inspection and computer analysis of all the data returned by individual interviewers.

DATA PREPARATION, ANALYSIS AND REPORTING

Data preparation comprises the tasks of editing, coding and computer-processing of the completed questionnaires. It is a particularly important aspect of quantitative survey work. (With CAPI (computer-assisted personal interviewing) and CATI (computer-assisted telephone interviewing), some editing tasks are transferred by software to the interviewing stage itself.) These tasks are undertaken in order to produce a database that is internally logical, complete and accessible for users of the survey. Prior to producing tabulations, the survey data may be weighted (by computer) to correct for any imbalance of the achieved sample compared with known characteristics of the survey universe.

However, a most important feature of quantitative surveys is the presentation of data both in the form of tabulations and electronically. For many surveys in the public domain, access to the data is given to any number of individual data users via online systems or other data dissemination methods.

As to tabulations, those produced by the survey organization should always include the bases (sample sizes) from which the percentages have been calculated. And, where these are weighted bases, it should also show the unweighted sample sizes. At the very least, the presence of the stated sample size serves as a reminder that the survey, though quantitative, is still only based on a limited number of respondents and therefore has statistical limitations that increase with decreasing sample sizes. However, when data are made available to users directly electronically, often viewed on screen, sample sizes may be excluded from the display, due to limitations of space and programming. In such cases the user loses sight of sample size and survey limitations. Problems occur when the user is untrained in market research and may not even be aware that these sample limitations exist. This could lead to possible misuse of the data and wrong decisions could result.

In conclusion, it follows that the interpretation of quantitative surveys needs care. Because the ultimate data user of quantitative research is most probably not involved in the planning or execution of the survey, the report tabulations may be all he or she sees. In cases where there is a report with written commentary, or a presentation of the results, it cannot be assumed that all subsequent users of the survey will be privy to the sample sizes on which the results are based. Any statistical or interpretative reservations about the findings, which may be expressed in the commentaries or the presentations, are unfortunately not to be found in the tables and data tapes.

Quantitative research offers the possibility of producing piles of computer printouts from cross-analyses of every question, one with another.

Couple this with the temptation of including interesting but not so relevant questions in the survey and you have a recipe for tabular diarrhoea. The researcher who produces quantitative survey data must be aware of this and endeavour to be selective about what data are presented. At the same time, as much information should be given about the figures produced on the tables as is necessary and practical so that the end user is able to make a proper evaluation.

REFERENCES AND FURTHER READING

British Market Research Bureau (1997) *Target Group Index*, London
Meier, E (1997) *Summary of Current Readership Research, Survey Practices in 44 Countries*, Research Services Limited, London
NRS (1997) *National Readership Survey*, London
ONS (1996) *Family Resources Survey*
RSL (1997) *The 1997 British Business Survey*, London

9

Face-to-Face Interviewing

Ellen Robertson and Steffen Conway[1]

INTRODUCTION

Until a few years ago, if you said at a party that you were a market researcher, the other person's image of you would probably be of an interviewer with clipboard in hand, standing on a doorstep talking to the lady of the house. Other pictures would include stopping someone in the street to ask them various questions. For such interviewing today, it is becoming increasingly likely that interviewers will be using hand-held computers instead of a clipboard. An acronym, CAPI (computer-assisted personal interviewing), is commonly used to describe this newer means of data collection. It is a term that is part of a string of similar acronyms, which in market research include CATI (computer-assisted telephone interviewing) and PAPI (pen-and-paper interviewing). CAPI has been in use for over 10 years now, but has become a key data collection method in the last few years as the cost of hand-held computers has made it a more viable option even for smaller companies.

But whether it is the clipboard (PAPI) or CAPI, the public picture of interviewers reflects the fact that much survey work is conducted via the personal face-to-face interview. In revenue terms, face-to-face interviewing (based on the 1997 AMSO Annual Report as an example) accounted for 61 per cent of all quantitative questionnaire-based research (ie excluding panel, observational and audit research), as shown in Table 9.1.

Table 9.1 *Quantitative questionnaire-based research*

Method	£m	%
Face-to-face	162.3	46
Hall Tests	43.4	12
Street Interviews	11.6	3
Total Face-to-face	217.3	61
Telephone	99.6	28
Postal	38.3	11
Total	355.2	100

The strength of the personal interview lies in its flexibility and diversity. It is a research technique that encompasses a wide range of options, which can be adapted to meet the objectives of any project.

In this chapter we review the choices available in personal interviewing and how to ensure a high standard of data collection. Throughout the chapter a project on canned wine carried out by Metal Box plc (now CMB Packaging) in 1980–82 will be used for illustration. This project is particularly interesting as it involves several stages, employing a range of methodologies, all using the personal interview.

Note 1 The concept of packaging wine in a can grew out of previous research when Metal Box designed the tall, slim 25-centilitre aluminium can for soft drinks. Consumer research on the can design revealed its strong potential for adult-based markets. At the same time the wine market in the UK was expanding rapidly. The British were beginning to enjoy wine outside the dinner party occasion and other packaging innovations such as 'bag-in-box' were being adopted for wine. A logical step was the packaging of wine in cans. Canned wine successfully established a niche market and the packaging format spread across Europe. Subsequently, Metal Box won an award from the French wine manufacturers for its 25-centilitre canned wine pack.

Note 2 To ensure clarity throughout the chapter the pronouns 'she' and 'her' refer to the interviewer and 'he' and 'him' to the respondent.

BENEFITS AND DRAWBACKS OF THE FACE-TO-FACE ENCOUNTER

Quality data

A prime concern in any survey is that the data collected should be as accurate and complete as possible. A relatively high degree of control over the survey can be achieved using personal interviewing, ensuring both reliability and validity of survey results. The face-to-face encounter achieves quality data in a number of ways, although it has to be recognized nowadays that so much research has been and continues to be carried out that respondents are becoming less co-operative than they were 20 or so years ago. Selling under the guise of research ('sugging') or more recently fundraising under the guise of research ('frugging'), as well as telesales still giving the impression of 'being a survey', has made life increasingly difficult. Consequently, previously helpful people have become suspicious and annoyed by any approach to take part in a survey. The data protection legislation has attempted to control abuses in the use of the word 'surveys' or 'research' but this has not been completely successful. Even if it was, damage has been done.

The kind of control that personal interviewing can achieve is in the following areas:

- **Respondent selection** The interviewer can check and ensure respondent eligibility before the interview is conducted.
- **Response** The interview-administered survey can ensure that the target number of interviews is achieved in the end. With the right interpersonal skills, personal contact is a better means of encouraging people to take part in a study.
- **Data collection** A personally administered questionnaire ensures that questions are asked in the right order, all applicable questions are answered, the questions are answered as fully as possible and the respondent understands the question in the first place.
- **Administration** Control over how the interview is administered and use of show material is essential for reliable data. The interviewer ensures that materials are seen in the correct order, properly presented.
- **Innovations in research** The skills of the professional interviewer have allowed methodologies to become more complex and sophisticated, achieving a greater degree of accuracy and finesse from the data.

CAPI has enhanced the degree of control, especially that over respondent selection, data collection, administration and innovations in research. As far as response is concerned, CAPI has had marginal effect, although the novelty (initially) may have marginally improved matters.

Practical considerations

Certain requirements of a survey, such as displaying show materials, preparing and presenting products or showing videos, automatically call for the use of personal interviews. Top-of-the-range multimedia laptop computers do allow for such materials to be included on the computer, although the video playback and sound quality might sometimes be debatable.

Other considerations may limit the use of the technique. The face-to-face interview can become both costly and time-consuming where geographically dispersed sampling is required (one or two respondents to any one locale), or when quota requirements mean that respondents are hard to find.

An extremely tight time schedule and/or research budget may restrict the type of personal interview possible (see below). In such cases it may be beneficial to combine the personal interview with other data collection methods, for example:

- Pre-recruiting by telephone can alleviate a lot of legwork when working in wide geographic areas or on target groups that are hard to find.
- After an initial personal interview, a self-completion questionnaire can be effective for collecting additional information, perhaps from other members of the household.
- If the survey requires an initial interview and a follow-up, the call-back may be conducted by telephone.

Using a combination of techniques in conjunction with the personal interview increases flexibility of research design.

Interviewer and respondent interaction

All personal interviews involve interaction between interviewer and respondent. One benefit of this interaction is the depth and reliability of information the interviewer can achieve, due to her ability to probe and clarify ambiguities in either the question or the answer.

Non-verbal communication also aids understanding. Gestures and facial expressions, as well as tone of voice, can give guidance to the meaning of statements such as 'It's all right.' In-depth interviewing especially benefits from such unstated signals. Equally, however, interviewers need to be careful in how they use such means of communicating since they should not be seen to agree or disagree with what respondents are telling them – a disapproving frown may not be appropriate.

The interviewer can also tell when a respondent is uncomfortable or bored and, therefore, she can try to avoid an abandoned interview or tired answers. The situation may be defused by a simple reassurance ('We will only be a few more minutes . . .'). The interviewer may use her own non-verbal skills to relax the respondent. The professional interviewer will also learn effective non-verbal skills in recruiting the respondent (see below).

Interviewer bias

Interviewer bias can present a problem in personal interviewing and can occur in several ways. It can be introduced at the recruitment stage when the interviewer selects whom to approach as a potential respondent. The way she handles the initial approach can affect whether that person will agree to participate. Bias can occur in the way an interviewer asks a question, how she responds to the answer, how she probes or prompts the answer or in the way she 'translates' the answer (even if instructed to 'record verbatim') for recording. Bias is especially possible when the interviewer probes or prompts for a complete answer or when she attempts any interpretation of the non-verbal communications.

Interviewer bias is limited or at least defused by structuring the fieldwork so that as many interviewers are used as is practicable. It is also important for each interviewer to work across the entire sample so that any bias is equally distributed. In this way any foibles one particular interviewer may have only minimally affect the data as a whole. Such precautions are generally considered good fieldwork practice. However, the key answer to the problem of interviewer bias is the use of professional field forces, thorough training and retraining programmes and maintenance of quality controls. (These issues are further discussed later in this chapter.)

Sensitivity

When the survey involves particularly sensitive issues (eg sexual behaviour, alcoholism or bed-wetting) the personal interview becomes a two-sided coin. A respondent may be reluctant to talk about a particular issue on a face-to-face basis. However, the skilled interviewer can draw respondents out and get them talking.

Respondent response

Not all respondents have the verbal or literary skills necessary to provide a good interview. The personal encounter is beneficial in eliciting viable responses from respondents who may not participate in any other type of survey. This reduces sample bias, ensuring that not only the highly articulate or literate voice is heard.

Ambassadors for the industry

The personal interview plays an important role in maintaining the public goodwill without which market research could not function. Respondents usually enjoy the interview experience as they are made to feel that their opinion is important. Interviewers can assure the respondent as to the legitimacy of the survey and the anonymity of his replies.

VERSATILITY OF THE PERSONAL INTERVIEW

The personal interview is used in all sectors of market research for both qualitative and quantitative data collection. The canned wine project involved a range of surveys demonstrating the versatility of the personal interview.

In order to explore consumer opinion of various packaging formats for wine, qualitative research was carried out using group discussions. Focus groups were recruited by personal interview and the discussions themselves involved face-to-face contact. The survey went on to quantify details of drinking habits and initial reactions to the concept of canned wine. Again personal interviewing was employed. Interviewers were able to maintain an accurate, objective presentation of the concept. The final stage focused on the effect the image of the can may have on consumer opinion of the product. Here the methodology required a high degree of administrative control, and no other data collection method would have been feasible.

A team of industrial interviewers conducted in-depth interviews with key personnel in the wine industry to assess trade opinion of the viability of a canned wine market. These took the form of individual face-to-face encounters. Again, this assured that the concept was properly presented. Also, respondents were able to see and handle the can while evaluating the idea. Furthermore, the interviewer was able to establish a rapport with the businessperson and conduct an in-depth discussion eliciting valuable data, despite the respondent's other pressing business commitments.

Optional techniques in personal interviewing

There are a number of options as to how and where the personal interview is carried out. Each technique has its own benefits and drawbacks and must be chosen carefully in line with the research objectives. When several options can satisfy the objectives, considerations such as timing, costing or the practical considerations of administration may determine which technique is used. This section reviews the options available when using personal interviewing for data collection.

In-street surveys

Normally in-street interviewing is conducted in busy town centres. This positioning ensures a good flow of people representing a good cross-section of the local population.

Recruitment in-street

A good traffic flow means that the interviewer stays in one location and the respondents come to her so that travel time between interviews is eliminated and recruitment is quicker. Another plus is that sampling can be geographically specific since any high street can be used, and towns lacking research venues can be included in the survey.

There are, however, limitations to in-street recruitment. Since it relies on the traffic flow through town, recruitment of particular groups can be difficult. Working people need to be interviewed in their lunch hour or on Saturdays. Groups representing a very low percentage in the population will be difficult to find. However, some minority groups may be easy to find if the locale is well chosen. For example, if you need to interview people who go to wine bars, you might interview in a town with a wine bar on a day it is open.

Interviewing in-street

In-street interviewing severely limits the length of the interview. Respondents are unlikely to stop for more than 10 minutes for even the best of interviewers. It is physically easy for the respondent to walk away.

Use of show materials is also restricted. The interviewer is already holding her clipboard with one hand and writing with the other. She is able to hand over small show cards for respondents to read, but certainly cannot handle any unwieldy show material. She may be able to show the respondent one item, like a can, but this must be light and easy to handle. Something like a full bottle of wine would grow too heavy over the day, and there is a risk of breakage.

CAPI can overcome some of these problems, especially a multimedia machine. However such computers are, by and large, still quite heavy and interviewers tire more quickly in having to hold such machines for a long time. Laptop computers with keyboards are not really appropriate. 'Pen-pads' are easier to operate (these are touch-screen computers where an 'electronic pen' is used to point at boxes or codes that apply to a given response and include the ability to 'write' directly on the screen to enter an open-ended response).

Another disadvantage of street interviewing is the uncertainty of the weather conditions. A warm sunny day in June is a delight for both inter-viewer and respondent. If it is raining, or a cold wintry day, however, respondents will not stop, and even the stalwart interviewer may well wonder 'What am I doing here?' Computers will be inoperable. The devel-opment of enclosed shopping malls has helped alleviate this problem, but this has caused other ones.

Shopping malls in the UK are considered private property and permission of the manager is required to carry out any interviewing. Some places have a 'no market research' policy, while others may charge a fee and must be booked in advance like any research venue. If permission cannot be obtained, recruitment away from the site is more difficult as these malls attract a good selection of respondents off the street.

In-hall surveys

Research venues exist in most towns where interviewers can recruit from the street and then carry out the interview indoors. Any venue that hires out rooms can be used, including town halls, church halls and hotels. Several venues especially designed for carrying out market research surveys have been established in recent years and most major towns will now have such facilities. These are more commonly used for qualitative research, notably focus groups, where one-way mirror viewing rooms and video recording allow for observation of groups. These research venues have all the facilities a survey may require – fully fitted kitchen, video equipment, a number of different-sized rooms, etc. Other less specialized locations may supply only an odd assortment of tables and chairs. It is essential to make sure that the hall test venue adequately meets the needs of the survey for both location and facilities. Venues with good facilities and in a good location can be hard to find and may be fully booked months ahead. Guaranteeing a good hall in the required location on a specific day can be difficult. There is always a further danger that such good halls become overused and the local population becomes overresearched.

Recruitment to in-hall

Since recruitment of respondents into a hall is carried out in-street, it is subject to similar benefits and restrictions as the in-street survey. An added benefit is strict maintenance of quota controls monitored by the hall supervisor.

Interviewing in-hall

The respondent's agreement to enter the hall is a commitment in itself and once in the hall it becomes awkward for him to walk out. Therefore, an interview may run for up to half an hour, even 45 minutes at a stretch. The interviewer should tell the respondent how long he is likely to be kept.

The respondent can be made comfortable and even served a coffee if appropriate. The interviewer can make herself comfortable and set up her own area. All materials for the interview are close at hand and can be freshly arranged for each interview.

The hall venue is particularly effective for showing a multitude of items. Large concept boards can be shown. Elaborate displays can be set up. Videos can be used. Products can be prepared and served in standard ways and, in all cases where food is served, full compliance with current hygiene laws is an absolute requirement.

Benefits of using a central location

Hall testing is centralized with a team of five to eight interviewers working under an area supervisor. The supervisor can monitor and motivate the team throughout the day. Any ambiguous aspects of the survey can be discussed and clarified. All aspects of administering the survey (setting up displays, product rotations, etc) can be tightly controlled. Surveys requiring a higher degree of confidentiality (eg new product development) can be better secured in such a controlled environment.

Strict deadlines can be met as all finished work is gathered in one place and can be returned to the office the next day. Dispatch of products and show materials is easier and more cost-effective, since all items can be sent in one trip to one location. Costs can also be saved in the production of show material. Ideally, each interviewer should have her own set of materials, but when items are very expensive to produce, or difficult to obtain, interviewers working in a hall can share materials.

Drawbacks to using a central location

Centrality means that the sample cannot be geographically spread. However, as most surveys will need several days to achieve the required sample size (see below), a geographic balance can be achieved by using a different location each day.

Another drawback to carrying out a block of interviews in one place is that if anything goes wrong with that day's testing, a high proportion of the data can be affected. Typical problems would be adverse weather (rain or snow), a security alert closing the area, interviewers being delayed on their journey to the hall, or questionnaires or products not being delivered on time. In most cases mishaps will only affect the number of interviews completed and not the data themselves (see below). Any shortfall in the number of interviews can be made up in future halls, or an extra day's hall organized.

Replication in-hall

In-hall interviewing limits a survey's ability to replicate the real-life situation, although it is better in this respect for some projects than others. Store displays can be effectively replicated in-hall, but any product testing can only provide a quick assessment. Not all surveys require true-to-life replication. Some will benefit from the control situation achievable in hall. The objectives of the research must be carefully considered.

The canned wine survey took place in-hall as it proved to be the ideal environment for controlling the taste testing of the canned versus the bottled wine. However, the objectives of this survey focused on establishing any effect the image of the can may have had on the perception of the wine and not on evaluating the wine product itself. The survey did adequately assess whether consumers could detect any strong differences between the canned and the bottled product by eliciting reactions to both glasses of wine (blind) before introducing the concept of the packaging. However, if the survey had required a comprehensive evaluation of the product, in-hall interviewing would not have been used.

In-home surveys

The in-home quantitative survey uses the home (or occasionally doorstep) of the respondent with the interviewer recruiting door-to-door. Qualitative surveys may use the home of an interviewer (or hostess) to conduct groups or depth interviews. The principles of in-home interviewing apply to both formats.

Recruitment in-home

This method is popular when a spread of geographic areas is required. Each interviewer conducts a small number of interviews in her location.

The sample can also be specifically located, down to one particular street. In-home recruitment is particularly suited to sampling from residential listings.

Door-to-door recruitment can be time-consuming and relies on people being at home. When specific listings are used for sampling, several call-backs may be needed. Many surveys will require interviewers to work in the evening and/or at weekends, which all adds to the cost of the fieldwork.

Interviewing in-home

The interview itself can benefit from the in-home venue, as the respondent may be more relaxed in his familiar environment. Longer interviews can often be achieved, especially if an appointment is made in advance. Psychologically, it is difficult for a respondent to throw the interviewer out if the interview is running longer than expected. However, interruptions are always possible (telephone, family, pets).

Use of show material is also restricted during the in-home interview. The amount and size of the show material must be manageable. At best the interviewer can leave items in her car during recruitment and fetch them for the main interview, but all this takes time. Also, the interviewer must rely on the facilities available in the respondent's home. It cannot be assumed that all households have videos, microwaves or computers, or that the respondent will be happy for the interviewer to use such items. Nor can one assume for CAPI interviews that respondents will freely permit an interviewer with a computer to plug the machine into their electricity supply.

It is also difficult to control the environment so as to assure that requirements for concept or product presentation are being met consistently. The physical space itself may not suit the needs of the interviewer. Use of space can be especially important for group discussions.

Replication in-home

Product testing in-home can replicate the real-life situation taking into account how the product is actually used and the influence of the opinion of other members of the household. Thus, if the canned wine had been tested in-home, the respondent would have been able to evaluate it in the context in which it would normally be tried, perhaps with a meal or in the evening as a nightcap, or even on an outing. Such usage information would have been interesting in itself.

The respondent has the opportunity to drink the entire contents of the can, not just taste a few sips. Other family members may have tried the product and their opinion may have influenced the respondent's opinion. Simply discussing the product with others, and considering it over time may affect respondent's reactions. However, the time gap between product trial and the recall interview does mean that the respondent must rely on memory to evaluate the product. Therefore, the evaluation may not be as stringent as if the questions were asked immediately after trial.

Surveys other than product tests can also benefit by being able to obtain precise information in-home. For example, if we need to know the type, make and model of electrical appliances the respondent has in the kitchen it is more accurate to be able to go into the kitchen and record the data from observation than to rely on the respondent's memory of such details. Similarly, if we wanted to know the types of wine the respondent drinks it would be beneficial to check his wine stock.

The respondent can also provide more accurate information for any surveys, which may require reference to maintenance records or receipts or just direct observation by the interviewer.

Practical considerations

Production of show materials can be expensive. Since the interviewer works alone each one requires her own set. Dispatch can be costly for heavy items, breakable items or refrigerated products. Time-scales can also be affected if recall appointments need to be rearranged. In some cases road delivery by a specialist company becomes necessary, for example using a refrigerated lorry to ensure food products are transported according to correct hygiene and storage parameters to guarantee delivery to respondents of safe products.

In-store surveys

Many surveys take place in a shop, or just outside the shop. Personal interviewing in-store will meet the requirements of a limited number of surveys but should be considered in line with research objectives.

Recruiting in-store

Recruitment in-store is similar to street recruitment and carries with it similar pros and cons. Also, the survey company must obtain permission from the store and in many cases co-operation of the store personnel. However, it is a good way to recruit specific types of shoppers.

Interviewing in-store

Interviewing at a store may bias responses, as the survey is likely to concern some aspect of shopping related to that store. However, it is a good way to immediately assess shoppers' opinions about aspects of their shopping experience, rather than relying on their memory of the experience.

Shop displays

The interviewer can handle show materials in-store if she is given an interviewing area. There is no better way to evaluate a shop display than in the shop, although setting up a display, which does not already exist, can be costly and no items requiring confidentiality should be used in such a display.

Business surveys

The respondent's office is a popular venue for carrying out face-to-face business or industrial interviews. Usually the interview will be pre-arranged. Interviewing on respondent's territory for business research is akin to in-home interviewing with similar benefits and drawbacks (see above). The businessperson will have any records or information required at hand. Interruptions may be kept to a minimum if the respondent considers he is 'in conference', but the interview is usually peripheral to the businessperson's workday. Pressing matters may interrupt or in extreme cases shorten the interview. The office environment may inhibit responses in certain cases, especially if colleagues can overhear the respondent.

Specialist research venues

The use of specialist venues for face-to-face interviewing is becoming more popular. Centres designed for carrying out group discussions are serious alternatives to the traditional front room. Hall test venues are being designed to cater for research surveys. Hotels are providing conference-style venues to cater for business interviews.

Such venues can enhance the personal interview. Purpose-built facilities ensure that the interviewer is provided with adequate equipment and never has to 'make do' by readapting available items to meet her requirements. These facilities are always more comfortable for both interviewer and respondent, and ensure the smooth running of the interview. Interested third parties can also observe the interview through one-way mirrors or via video links, without interrupting or influencing the interviewing procedure. A formal venue provides a neutral environment. This may mean it takes longer for the respondent to settle in than he would at home, but it eliminates any problem of interruptions or restrained responses.

The main drawbacks to using specialist venues are cost and availability. Professional research venues can be expensive to hire and do limit the survey to locations where they are available. An additional cost may include the transporting of pre-recruited respondents to and from the venue.

GAUGING THE FIELDWORK

The researcher must accurately judge how many interviewer days are required on a survey. Typically one interviewer working six hours plus one hour's travel time equals one interviewer day. Two key factors will determine the number of interviewer days. One is how long it takes to recruit a respondent and the other is how long it takes to conduct the interview.

Recruitment time

If the survey is using a quota sample the researcher must determine the 'strike rate' for recruitment, that is, how many people the interviewer will have to approach before finding an eligible respondent. This is determined by the penetration of the required criteria in the general population and the venue for such work. For example, if we want to recruit wine drinkers we must know the proportion of the general population that drinks wine. If 30 per cent of the population qualify we would expect that three out of every ten people we stop would be eligible on that criterion. However, penetration figures do not take into account how many eligible respondents are willing to be interviewed. A rule of thumb fieldwork research executives use is that an interviewer recruiting on a general quota (eg all housewives) will need to stop five eligible housewives before achieving an interview.

What an interviewer can achieve in a day of contacting people needs, furthermore, to take into account all the sample criteria involved. Thus if we are looking for female wine drinkers aged 24–34, the strike rate would be reduced substantially and we would expect the recruitment procedure to take longer.

When penetration figures are unavailable, some 'guestimates' must be made based on available data and past experiences. On pre-selected names and/or addresses, recruitment time must take into account how many call-backs are required to make a contact and the travel time required to get from one address to the next.

Interviewing time

The length of a structured interview is easily determined by testing out the questionnaire. The time to administer a more open-ended interview will vary somewhat depending on the verbosity of the respondent.

Calculating the time it takes to administer a questionnaire must allow for the practicalities of the real-life situation. Time must be included for recording answers, probing, showing materials, waiting for considered replies and repeating a question. If videos are being used the machine must be switched on, the video viewed (some reels may run over five minutes), and the reel rewound. If products are being tested they need to be prepared and presented. The respondent must then be given adequate time to try the product.

The fieldwork doesn't always go according to the best office calculations. Some practical considerations of fieldwork need to be included in the formula.

There is always a gap of time between recruitment and the main interview. In-home the interviewer is usually invited in and must settle. In-hall the respondent must be brought into the venue. General interaction between interviewer and respondent eats into interviewing time and must be accommodated into the schedule.

The unforeseen

Unforeseen events are always lurking in the background to destroy the best-planned scheduling. These cannot be calculated in, but it is important to be aware of the pitfalls.

The weather is always an unpredictable variable, which can hinder the interviewer's best efforts. Illness is another gremlin, which can hinder recruitment. Holiday periods reduce the number of available respondents (although this should be considered when scheduling the job). Even major events such as the World Cup or the final at Wimbledon can limit traffic flow.

Technical mishaps can also cause problems. Any equipment required for the survey (computers, videos, cookers, tape recorders, etc) may malfunction. Vital materials may arrive late, or not at all. 'Lost in the post' or 'broken in transit' aren't just excuses, they can be realities that cause havoc to a fieldwork schedule.

It is always wise to overbook a survey, that is, schedule the survey to achieve at least 5 per cent over the required sample size and, allowing for mishaps, preferably 10 per cent more; in some cases, such as CAPI, maybe 15 per cent is desirable because of computer and data transmission problems.

A GOOD INTERVIEW

Surveys must be *reliable* (ie they would achieve similar results if administered to another sample based on the same sampling technique and population) and *valid* (they measure what they claim to measure). If we cannot achieve these requirements the entire accuracy of the survey and the value of the results come into question. In order to achieve reliability and validity the interview must be free from ambiguities that may result in a misunderstanding of what is being asked and from any bias that may influence a respondent's answer in any way.

Questionnaire design

Questionnaire design from the methodological point of view is covered elsewhere in this book. However, the issue of questionnaire preparation is also essential for quality data collection.

Quantitative surveys use a highly structured questionnaire, which the interviewer must follow precisely. Qualitative surveys are by nature more free-flowing, and the interviewer or moderator will follow a flexible discussion outline. A half-way house between these two formats is the semi-structured questionnaire, which can be adapted for both quantitative and qualitative surveys. The semi-structured questionnaire is usually a series of open-ended questions, which the interviewer will follow as written, but which require skilled in-depth probing. Whichever format is used the data collected by the interviewer can only be as good as the questionnaire itself.

A well-laid-out questionnaire with clear instructions is instrumental in reducing the kinds of ambiguities that can reduce the quality of the data collected. The interviewer should never have to ask herself 'What do I do now?' or 'What does that mean?' Although an interviewer is professionally trained (see below), she is not necessarily versed in all the skills a researcher acquires. Nor will the interviewer be as familiar with the whys and wherefores of the survey as is its creator.

Comprehensive routeing and coding instructions are essential, yet they must be easily understood and clearly visible on the written form. Technical terms should be avoided, or at least fully explained. Clear instructions about the use of show materials are also vital.

Piloting

In order to ensure that a questionnaire works well it ought to be tried out in advance. The more complex the questionnaire, the more important it is to pilot the survey.

Ideally the questionnaire is piloted in the field where an interviewer recruits and interviews legitimate respondents. The interviewer then reports on any problems she or the respondent may have had. The researcher can then review these comments, examine the data collected and readjust the questionnaire as required. This procedure goes a long way to ensure that the survey is reliable and valid, but formal piloting is costly and time-consuming.

Since many market research surveys tend to follow set patterns that the professional is trained to handle, in such cases those surveys would not in fact benefit greatly from such an exercise.

In most cases a thorough piloting of the questionnaire in the office will adequately reveal any problems. The interviewer should preferably be someone not involved in the survey, and someone who is not a researcher should be the respondent. Even the most straightforward questionnaire ought to be tested in some way.

Briefing

It is important on all surveys that the interviewing team is briefed as thoroughly as possible. The briefing session is the last stage before interviewer meets respondent, and potential problems should be adjusted now. Briefings can be done in a number of ways.

- **Formal personal briefings** At a formal briefing session all field staff and office staff are gathered together. The researcher explains all aspects of the survey and makes sure that all interviewers achieve a common understanding. This procedure is costly and time-consuming and is worthwhile only for the more complex surveys.
- **Sequential personal briefings** A cost-effective form of personal briefing can be achieved using a chain of command. Personal briefing sessions are conducted for supervisors of interviewing teams, and the supervisors then personally brief their interviewers.
- **Self-briefing** The interviewer briefs herself using a detailed set of written instructions. She actually pilots the questionnaire with a friend. If she has any queries she telephones her supervisor or the office for clarification. It is imperative that the researcher provides a comprehensive set of written instructions. Self-briefing is the most common format used. Annotating a final questionnaire with comments is a useful

way of giving interviewers something to take with them when they are out working, to which they can easily refer.

- **Telephone briefing** The researcher telephones the interviewer once she has received her paperwork and goes through the questionnaire with her. If the number of interviewers working on the survey makes this option impractical the researcher can brief each area supervisor who will in turn telephone each of her interviewers. The advent of conference call networks makes this option more accessible.
- **Central location briefing** Whenever a group of interviewers is working together (in-hall or in-store), a face-to-face briefing session can be conducted before interviewing begins. The most senior member of the team will lead the session. It is also possible for an executive to be present and conduct the briefing.

Briefing techniques can be combined. For example, a supervisor can be personally briefed and she can then brief each interviewer by telephone. Conversely, supervisors can be briefed by telephone and they can personally brief interviewers. Whatever method is used, interviewers working on any survey must be fully briefed.

THE PROFESSIONAL APPROACH

The onus of ensuring quality interviewing lies with the companies employing interviewers. These companies achieve high standards of data collection by:

- maintaining a professional field management team;
- having well-planned training programmes;
- following a formal schedule of quality controls;
- complying with industry quality guidelines.

Field management

A typical structure in field management is a head-office team led by a senior manager or director with a number of regional supervisors working from home, controlling local teams of interviewers.

Good quality interviewing is dependent on a strong team of supervisors. They may be salaried or free-lance depending on the quantity and nature of the company's business. They are always senior members of the field force who have been thoroughly trained and are versed in both research and people management skills. Interviewers usually work on an *ad hoc* basis and are attached to a company through their supervisor. The interviewer looks to her supervisor for guidance and motivation. In larger field forces supervisors may be called area managers or regional managers, but the role is the same.

Training programmes

All interviewers will be put through a training programme, the extent of which depends on company policy, although guidelines for such training do exist within the industry (see below). Training should be two-fold: teaching the interviewer the skills she needs to carry out a good interview; and integrating her into the industry.

The interviewing skills she must acquire include mastering how to approach respondents, successfully persuading them to take part and then maintaining their interest throughout the interview. She must also learn how to classify respondents accurately in market research terms (who falls into the C1 social group and how you define head of household, for example). She must be made aware of the pitfalls of administering a questionnaire and how to avoid interviewer bias. She will also be introduced to the various types of surveys she may be asked to work on.

Her integration as a market researcher is important since most of the time she will be working alone and will experience a sense of isolation. Such isolation can result in a blinkered attitude of 'get the numbers' and may lead to the use of short cuts to achieve that goal more easily. It is important for the interviewer to understand the reasons for the rules she is asked to follow, and to see how her role fits into the greater research picture.

Training programmes usually involve an in-house session (between one and three days) where a prospective interviewer will attend lectures and participate in exercises. She will be given a comprehensive interviewer manual to study and for future reference. The next step should be a session of in-field training, when she will work from a training questionnaire administered to the public, under the supervision of an instructor. Finally, she will be assigned to a survey and carry out legitimate interviews while accompanied by a senior interviewer or supervisor on her first assignments with each type of survey. Once her supervisor is satisfied with her standard of work, the interviewer will then be allowed to conduct interviews on her own, although she will continue to be accompanied on each new type of work to which she is assigned, as each requires different skills.

Quality controls

There are a number of checks that can be carried out on the quality of the data being collected. These should be used in a regular programme of quality control.

Feedback

Most questionnaires go through a process of editing, coding and computing. Comments from the data processing team on the quality of the data (how open-ended questions are being probed and recorded, and how filters and instructions are being followed) should be fed back to field management. They in turn should advise supervisors on the standard of work of their interviewers. Interviewers who need improvement must be informed and their work monitored. Those who are performing well should receive recognition. With effective control checks and proper motivation, the interviewer will reach and maintain quality standards.

Validation or back-checking

Accuracy of data and legitimacy of recruitment are checked by re-calling on respondents and readministering part of the interview. In a regular programme of such validating (also called back-checking), the industry standard is for a minimum of 10 per cent of respondents on each survey to be recontacted. This may be done by telephone, by post or by a personal visit. Interviewers are aware of these re-calls and realize the importance of the validation.

Appraisal or accompaniment

Together with feedback and validation, interviewers in the field are accompanied by their supervisors on a regular basis. This directly checks the quality of their interviewing and provides an ongoing training programme. Any bad habits an interviewer may pick up can be checked and rectified. The industry standard is that at least one full appraisal should take place each year with one other shorter appraisal being carried out over the phone or on some other occasion.

Record keeping

In order to maintain a successful programme of quality control, good record keeping is essential. Office personnel should be involved in maintaining and updating records on training programmes, appraisals/accompaniments and validations/back-checks for each interviewer. These records are used to ensure that the field force is continually monitored.

Industry guidelines

The industry, through the Market Research Society (MRS), provides a Code of Conduct for research, parts of which apply directly to interviewers. An interviewer's basic training should include a discussion of these rules and guidelines.

The Interviewer Quality Control Scheme (IQCS) is a voluntary programme set up for monitoring data collection procedures. Members are made up of agencies employing interviewers and clients who use these agencies. The scheme, endorsed by the MRS and British Market Research Association (BMRA), ensures that all member companies operate the same minimum standards of fieldwork by carrying out annual inspections of record keeping. The standards checked apply to interviewer recruitment, training, supervision and validation of interviewers' work.

The MRS has introduced a uniform interviewer identity card. All bona fide interviewers should carry such a card, assuring the public of the legitimacy of the interview. A category of membership to the MRS has been introduced for interviewers in order to help integrate them into the industry.

IQCS procedures have been adopted as valid parts of quality assurance systems (ISO 9000) as far as fieldwork is concerned. The Market Research Quality Standards Association (MRQSA) has been set up to provide a formal standard for the industry, which includes the IQCS fieldwork standards. Increasingly research agencies are seeking accreditation for MRQSA, ISO 9000 and now the BS 5911. BS 5911 is the first standard of its kind to have been agreed within an industry as diverse as market research and approved by the British Standards Institute. Increasingly the concept of this standard is being adopted in overseas countries.

IN THE FIELD

The interviewer has the final responsibility for making sure that her job is carried out in accordance with survey requirements and rules of good practice and that the data she collects are as accurate and complete as possible.

Office checks

Completed work is returned to the office for processing. Further checks are carried out on the quality of the work and the accurate completion of assignments by the sampling instructions given at the outset. Checking-in systems are increasingly computer-driven, and these include scanning questionnaires for speedy processing. In this respect CAPI interviews are checked in as the survey progresses.

Preparation

The interviewer's job begins when her package of work arrives (or her computer receives the working files). She will probably be working alone and expect to be self-briefed. She must go through her pack (or the computer files) carefully to make sure that all the materials and information she needs have been provided. The interviewer is the last person to look over the survey and should catch any errors or omissions that have fallen through the office safety nets. If there are any problems, she must contact her supervisor or the office and have the queries sorted out before she goes into the field.

She must also prepare her strategy for recruitment. There is usually some leeway as to exactly when she carries out the interviews and where within her locale she works. Interviewers quickly learn the art of matching time schedules and locations to survey requirements. She must choose the best time of day or evening to contact the type of respondent she is seeking, and know her area well enough to pinpoint the best concentration of particular groups.

When she is thoroughly familiar with the questionnaire, and has organized her game plan, she is then ready to face the public.

Winning the interview

Employing the most appropriate interviewers for the job is the first step in making sure that potential respondents agree to participate. Wine drinkers, traditionally profiled as up-market consumers, will react most favourably to interviewers who are well dressed and well spoken. Interviewers learn to adopt the most appropriate demeanour to suit the circumstance of the survey. Non-verbal communication plays an important role in the initial approach. Her body language must reveal a positive attitude, but not be too aggressive. She must be saying, 'I am going to ask you to do something that you will want to do.'

Once the potential respondent stops, the interviewer must conduct the screening interview quickly and efficiently. If the respondent is eligible to continue the interview, the interviewer must quickly gain his interest and point out the positive aspects of taking part. Interviewers rely to some extent on natural human curiosity and willingness to help. If the respondent is not eligible for the survey, the interviewer must remain tactful in rejecting his potential offer of assistance. She again should adopt a positive approach. ('I am looking for people who drink wine, in the age group . . . perhaps on another occasion.') Trained interviewers know how important it is to maintain the public's goodwill for future market research projects.

They are also aware of the need for strict confidentiality of the survey subject and will not reveal its nature beyond a general description – 'We are talking to people about wine drinking', *not* 'We are testing wine in a can.'

Conducting the interview

Establishing a rapport with the respondent at the recruitment stage is essential. The relationship must then develop in the early stages of the main interview. It is always best to ask the more personal questions at the end of an interview, when the relationship is well developed. The interviewer shows that she is interested in everything the respondent has to say, while at the same time controlling irrelevant deviations. Body language is used throughout the interview as a way of encouraging the respondent to continue. She may incline towards her respondent period- ically, smile and nod encouragement, although these gestures must not indicate agreement with the answers, but merely show interest.

Pacing an interview correctly is critical. The aim is to get the interview completed as quickly as possible while not rushing through it. The respondent must be given enough time to consider his answer. Moving on to the next question before he is ready may affect how he answers the next question. It may also make him feel that *his* opinion is not important.

All aspects of the interview must run smoothly so that it flows as naturally as possible. The interviewer must be thoroughly familiar with the questionnaire and show materials so that she is never working out what to do next while the respondent is left waiting. However, if the interviewer is unsure of anything, it is essential that she gets it right before continuing.

Concluding the interview graciously is important too. Interviewers are taught to show appreciation to those who give their time, to maintain a positive image of market research. Apart from thanking the respondent for his participation, it is usual to hand him an explanatory leaflet about market research and the industry. This is a useful device for answering any questions he may have later on. On occasion a small gift may be used to thank a respondent. The use of incentives must be carefully considered in relation to the survey and the amount of time and effort required by the respondent.

CONCLUSIONS

Personal interviewing is a well-established, practicable and reliable method of data collection. It provides the researcher with a wide range of techniques from which to choose, effectively meeting the needs of almost any project. The use of professional fieldwork teams ensures high standards of interviewing, maintains a good public image for the industry and is the mainstay of reliable and valid surveying.

ACKNOWLEDGEMENT

In the first edition of this handbook, this chapter was written by Ellen Robertson (then of Research & Auditing Services Ltd and now of Analytica). For that, Ellen expressed her appreciation of the help given by Val McGregor on the sections 'Professional approach' and 'In the field'. The main changes since the original was written have been in the matter of computers and specifically CAPI. The case history example is the same as that used in the original: although dated it does not alter the lessons to be gained from it.

EDITOR'S NOTE

Steffen Conway passed away after illness in the same week in which Kogan Page delivered the proofs of the book to me.

As an industry colleague for 15 years and an MRS co-activist for 10 years, I always appreciated his teamwork and support.

This chapter is now dedicated to recognizing the contribution he made to the industry.

ENDNOTE

1. This chapter was originally written by Ellen Robertson and has been updated by Steffen Conway.

10

Telephone Interviewing

Janet Weitz

SUMMARY

Only 20 years ago in the UK, telephone interviewing was an innovation that was in some senses ahead of its time. Today it has become a mainstream and widely used survey method. Its rapid growth was fuelled by changes in technology and survey management, and driven by client needs. But its rate of expansion was also limited by the speed of social changes that determined its usefulness and its reliability.

As we enter a new century, use of the telephone for research interviewing is facing new threats that come from non-research use of the telephone and from the rapid growth in ex-directory numbers.

THE FORMATIVE YEARS

By the mid-1970s telephone interviewing was well established as a technique for business surveys among managers and professional people. These people were bound to be accessible by phone. Indeed, appointments for face-to-face interviews had in any case to be made on the telephone.

As travel and time costs grew it was a logical progression to carry out the actual interview by telephone.

But telephone surveys with the general public were limited by the skewed penetration of home telephones. This generally restricted their use to up-market people, or to lists of purchasers that clients might have compiled. At that time, telephone interviewers usually worked from their homes, with a proportion of interviews being checked by a supervisor who also worked from home.

Domestic penetration of telephones grew rapidly through the 1970s, but remained biased toward the affluent and those in London and the South-East. For research into many consumer products this was not a problem, as the biases that resulted from sampling by telephone could be reduced by weighting. In any case, the most important market for many consumer products was among households with telephones.

The proportion of households with access to a telephone has risen rapidly since the early 1970s, when it stood at under 50 per cent. By the early 1990s this proportion had reached 90 per cent and currently stands at over 96 per cent (see Figure 10.1). Consequently, now that nearly all households are connected, telephone samples have become suitable for a wide variety of research applications.

However, the problem posed by lack of universal telephone ownership has now been superseded by another development: the increasing proportion of households in the UK that are ex-directory.

The drivers of growth

While the domestic telephone was becoming more widespread, there was also a growth in the number of research organizations offering telephone-based services. This expansion was partly the result of greater use of telephone surveys among executives and businesses. But telephone surveys among *consumers* contributed most of the growth.

While domestic telephone penetration grew, interviewers' pay rates also rose, so that face-to-face interviewing became more expensive. This shifted the cost per interview in favour of telephone interviewing. Moreover, clients needed the results of surveys more quickly, placing a premium on speed of turn-round. Telephone surveys became increasingly competitive, and supplanted work that might previously have required face-to-face interviews. The most dramatic influence on the relative cost and speed of telephone surveys was the development of central location interviewing.

At the same time, the whole social and cultural environment has changed. Through the 1980s the telephone acquired a new status as the normal medium for many new areas of communication. The real cost of using the telephone fell, as telecom monopolies were broken up and suppliers faced increasingly sharp competition. As a result, businesses and

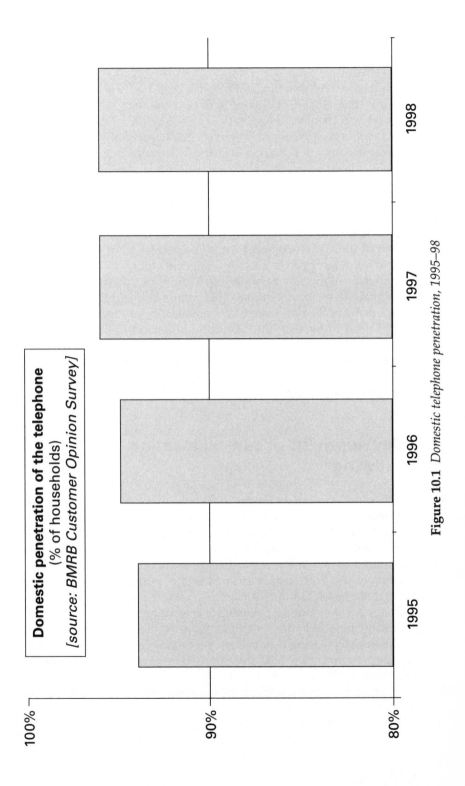

Figure 10.1 *Domestic telephone penetration, 1995–98*

private individuals in the 90s were far less reluctant to use the telephone, and developed the telephone habit to an extent that was unknown just a generation before.

BT reported in 1998 that nine out of ten Britons had used the telephone for banking, ordering products or services, checking bills or making complaints to companies. The growth in the daily use of credit cards has made the telephone a viable commercial channel in almost every household. Several consumer market sectors (insurance and banking, for example) have been transformed by the creation of wholly telephone-based businesses. Enterprises of all sorts now routinely offer ordering facilities, customer helplines and information over the telephone, and a whole new industry has grown up around the management of telecentre resources to supply these functions. BT forecast that in 2000 some 200,000 people (1 per cent of the UK work-force) would be employed in call centres. In the United States the figure is already 3 per cent and rising.

The general public has become much more receptive to telephone interviewing over the past 20 years. This greater co-operation has in turn eliminated some of the old procedures (pre-alert letters, for example, that sometimes used to be sent out before the initial call). But the research industry is not alone in making cold calls to people's homes. The telephone is increasingly used as a selling tool by a variety of suppliers of goods and services. Growth in telemarketing has presented new problems, which we return to later in this chapter.

The development of central location interviewing

Until 1980, most telephone surveys in Britain involved interviewers and supervisors working from home. But with continuing expansion it was no longer practical to employ fieldworkers that way. The early 1980s saw the establishment of central location telephone interviewing, in which the work is concentrated in closely supervised centres. This change eliminated the administrative and time costs associated with sending out and returning fieldwork documents. Central location interviewing rapidly displaced the previous approach by offering benefits of cost, quality and speed.

At the same time software companies were developing technology that meant interviewers using a paper questionnaire could enter responses directly into a computer. This too required interviewing from central locations.

Today a typical central telephone facility (telecentre) uses dedicated outgoing lines, with interviewers working in individual booths each equipped with a computer terminal, in an area set aside specifically for the unit.

The shift to central location interviewing was originally driven by the need to control an expanding telephone interview work-force, and to finish surveys faster. But it soon became apparent there were other broader benefits, which included:

■ immediate supervision and management of the interviews;
■ more effective sample administration;
■ greater efficiency in finding and interviewing the right people;
■ improved quality of data;
■ logging call costs (precisely);
■ faster access to survey results, thanks to direct computer entry of the data.

The result was an increase in the quality and cost-effectiveness of surveys, from which in turn came greater client demand.

The development of CATI

Increasing demand for telephone surveys, and the development of central location interviewing created the environment for the next major stage of development – computer-assisted telephone interviewing (CATI). Many telecentres already used computer terminals for direct data entry. The logical extension was to incorporate both the questionnaire and the resulting data capture into a single computer program. This major innovation added significant new advantages of productivity, quality and speed to central location interviewing. In consequence it was an important new contributor to the growth of telephone research. In the simplest form of CATI, the questionnaire appears on a monitor, the interviewer enters replies directly by keyboard and the program automatically routes the interview to the next question.

Various CATI systems are now able to offer a variety of benefits, but every standard package offers these features:

■ presenting and routeing through the questionnaire;
■ accepting the data;
■ managing the sample;
■ managing appointments and repeat calling;
■ helping develop and pilot the questionnaire;
■ real-time monitoring of progress and quota control;
■ help in processing and presentation of the results.

CATI systems continue to evolve, as software companies build in ever greater sophistication and functionality. Later in this chapter we review some of the latest developments and look forward to future innovations.

Market demand for telephone interviewing

Central location telephone interviewing is now well established, using both paper-based and computer-assisted questionnaires. The Association of Market Survey Organizations (AMSO) includes all the UK's largest research companies, and in 1997 it reported that telephone surveys accounted for 20 per cent of total research turnover among member companies. In that year, AMSO member companies carried out 5.7 million telephone interviews, amounting to 32 per cent of their total interviewing (see Table 10.1).

Table 10.1 *Growth in telephone interviewing*

	Percentage of Turnover %	Percentage of Interviews %
1987*	10	26
1997**	20	32

Source: Technical and Development Committee of the Market Research Society
**Source: AMSO*

TELEPHONE INTERVIEWING AS A MODE OF DATA COLLECTION

The advantages of telephone interviewing

Our review of the development of telephone interviewing has shown that its advantages over other survey methods have increased with successive innovations. These advantages can be summarized as:

- speed of collecting and processing information;
- control of the interviews;
- management of the sample;
- access to respondents (especially in geographically dispersed samples);
- cost-effectiveness.

Speed

Central location telephone interviewing eliminates the time-consuming preparation and dispatch of documents. All interviewers on a project can be briefed simultaneously, and start work straight away. Using CATI and direct data entry speeds the analysis and presentation of results. Short lead times and fast response make it possible for surveys to take place immediately after topical events. This is particularly important in, say, advertising tracking and opinion polling.

Control of interviews

Centralized interviewing affords maximum control of a survey at all stages. Interviewers are uniformly briefed, supervised and monitored. Help is at hand for the interviewers if they face difficulties, as the executives in charge can be consulted for their decisions. It is easy to validate and amend the questionnaire in the early stages. *Ad hoc* coding and tabulation specifications can be developed effectively. Comprehensive quality control is combined with a degree of flexibility when adjustments become necessary.

Management of sample

The sample is centrally controlled as the survey unfolds. This makes it easy to check progress, for example in meeting quota requirements, compared with controlling a set of individual assignments dispersed across a field force. Handling the sample source list and the questionnaire data within an integrated system means that informants' characteristics can be transferred direct from database to survey analysis. If the same people might be approached for interview from time to time it is easy to remove duplication from successive sample lists, avoiding over-interviewing the same people.

Access

Telephone samples can overcome geographical barriers that would impede other methods of interview; samples need not be clustered. The remoteness of a potential respondent is not a consideration in survey planning. If informants are busy when first called, the interviewer can key in a call-back appointment and the CATI system will place the call automatically at the appointed time. If there is no reply or the respondent is unavailable when first called, the system can call again at pre-programmed intervals until answered.

Cost-effectiveness

Centralized organization provides a combination of reduced field costs, high productivity and quick turn-round of quality-controlled data. This makes for highly cost-effective use of research budgets.

Sampling in telephone research

As in all research, the key sampling considerations are the end use of the data, the degree of accuracy required and the perceived direction of any bias. The following sections detail issues that are of particular relevance to telephone research.

Sampling the public

In earlier years the relatively low level of telephone ownership was the chief obstacle to using telephone research methods. In most situations, this problem was surmountable. When research was designed to consider the opinions, attitudes and habits of certain defined groups, then samples of respondents with access to the telephone were satisfactory. For measuring trends, whether market, social or political, etc, telephone samples were also acceptable, as demographic weighting could be used to diminish bias.

However, some general cautions had to be borne in mind where the research wanted to measure accurately the occurrence of a particular factor in the population as a whole. This might be ownership, readership, voting intentions or opinions on social issues. Under those conditions, telephone interviewing could produce different estimates from face-to-face interviewing among a national sample of the population.

Not having a telephone tended to be associated with a different set of personal values and opinions. This presented difficulties in precise measurement of readership, voting intentions and views on social issues, etc within the population as a whole. Those who did own a telephone were also more likely to own other durables and thus give an overestimate of ownership if taken as representative of the national population.

Furthermore, non-owners were more frequent among older people, the less well off or those living in the North. It was not possible to compensate for their exclusion simply by applying demographic weights to bring the sample profile into line with the population. But more satisfactory weighting procedures helped overcome this problem.

More important, though, was the expansion in telephone ownership. In the UK, domestic access to a telephone is now over 96 per cent. Although differences persist with the remainder of the population, these are far easier to overcome by reweighting in surveys. Only when looking at exceptional areas, particularly those targeting young less well-off people, are these sorts of sampling problem likely still to be an issue.

However, the sources from which samples of telephone owners can be drawn (particularly directories) also have deficiencies. These can affect the viability of telephone samples for accurately measuring the incidence of a particular feature in the population as a whole. In particular, the problem of telephone penetration has now been superseded by the increasing proportion of UK households that are ex-directory. This currently stands at around 38 per cent, and is as high as 60 per cent among those moving home in the last year. By contrast, only 25 per cent of people who have lived in the same home for over 10 years are ex-directory.

Although ex-directory people show fewer biases than before in social class, age and income, they are markedly more common in London and among certain minority groups (in particular, younger people are far more likely to have unlisted numbers). This matters more for representative studies of the general population than for surveys among customers of a particular company. Most studies suggest, age profile apart, that people with unlisted numbers are not measurably different from those appearing in directories.

Business and industrial sampling

Potential respondents are invariably on the telephone, so problems of coverage in business-to-business surveys are minimal. The main consideration is the relevance, accuracy and adequacy of the proposed sampling frame.

Sampling methods

There are essentially three methods of sampling for telephone interview:

1. using ready-made lists and databases;
2. directory-based methods;
3. random digit dialling.

Using ready-made lists and databases

Providing the researcher is satisfied that the lists are as representative as possible of the universe to be sampled, then sampling can be carried out using any systematic method.

Lists and databases can be used for business and industrial sampling. There are many third-party sources that provide lists, and in many cases they can also provide a custom-made database or sample of potential respondents with required characteristics. Organizations such as trade directories, business information services and publishing houses are listed in the *Guide to Sources of Samples for Telephone Research* (Market Research Society telephone research working party). In some cases the client will be able to provide a list of potential respondents from their own records.

Lists and databases can also be used for members of the public. Again, when sampling members of the public, it is possible to use unclustered lists of potential respondents with defined characteristics. There are many sources. In some cases the client may provide a list of subscribers to their publication, or users of their services. A manufacturer, for example, may hold a list of customers who bought a washing machine in the past six months and are willing to be interviewed. The members of organizations or societies may also constitute suitable sources.

Directory-based methods

Direct sampling can be carried out from the telephone directory. Theoretically, with a set of up-to-date telephone directories, and knowing the number of entries in each directory, the researcher can draw a random fixed interval sample by taking the 'nth' number from each selected directory. The sample can be stratified or unstratified, clustered or unclustered, as deemed necessary. In most cases an unstratified, unclustered sample should be viable, since telephone research can access all areas, and the remoteness of a potential respondent presents no problems. This means sample size can be held to a minimum – and so, therefore, can costs.

In practice there are two major drawbacks to sampling from directories. First, residential and non-residential numbers are often mixed together (although in the UK this problem is now reduced, since in many areas the two sets of numbers are published in separate volumes). In addition, numbers can be missing from directories, or out of date. Only the newest directories include the numbers of new subscribers and take account of those who have moved and changed numbers; and missing are all those subscribers who have chosen to be ex-directory. Despite these drawbacks, most UK interviewing firms use directories as part of their resources.

In the USA the direct use of directories is not considered viable, because of the high mobility of the population and the large number of subscribers who pay to be ex-directory. The preferred method of sampling is random digit dialling. Plus 'n' dialling is also sometimes used.

Plus 'n' dialling is a modified version of a randomly drawn sample, and is used to give missing numbers a chance of being selected. This involves adding a constant (usually one or five) to the number selected. The probability of the missing numbers being selected is unknown, so a sample generated this way can no longer be described as random. (A random sample is one where the probability of being interviewed is known for all members of the universe.) It should more properly be described as a 'plus one', 'plus five', etc sample. The method works well in practice, although the interviewer has to overcome the difficulties of not having a name associated with the number, and possibly meeting a greater reluctance to be interviewed.

This procedure can also be used to produce matched samples for tracking research. The original plus 'n' sample is used, and the match generated by adding two to the original number. Two is chosen to avoid duplication of households with two lines and adjacent numbers. Few households have more than two numbers.

Random digit dialling (RDD)

Where qualified lists are not available, this is the preferred method in the USA. It is used less often in the UK, because directory-based approaches offer greater viability and ease of use. With the growth in ex-directory numbers, though, this is likely to change; because unlisted numbers are not randomly distributed, it is not possible to draw an unbiased sample of the population using listings. RDD offers a potential solution to this problem.

Within a specified exchange code or area code, random number tables or computer random number generators are used to pick telephone numbers. In a list generated this way, many of the numbers do not exist; and residential numbers are mixed with businesses. In this simple form the method is not very cost-effective.

For residential research in the USA pure random digit dialling is modified by two-stage sampling to increase the proportion of household numbers. Computer-based variants are also available to increase effective household incidence.

The implementation of such methods in the UK is now conceivable given the standardization of the numbering system. However, the reluctance of British Telecom to release information about number structures actually in use remains a barrier.

Interviewing procedures

Selecting the individuals to be interviewed

In common with face-to-face interviews, at any particular address or telephone number the interviewer must find and interview the right person, whether the one who 'is responsible for telecommunications', 'buys the breakfast cereal' or 'celebrates a birthday next', etc.

We have already noted that call-backs and appointments are relatively simple and cost-effective to manage by telephone, especially when this is handled by the CATI system. So the specified respondents can be found with the minimum administration.

In more demanding methods of selection, where all members of a household have to be listed and the individual respondent randomly selected, then telephone interviewing again has an advantage over face-to-face interviewing. The CATI program can handle the random selection of a respondent, rather than the interviewer having to choose manually using a system such as a Kish grid. But this type of selection requires details of all the adults in the household, and so extends the opening of the interview. This initial period is crucial in telephone interviewing. Without visual signals to help establish rapport, the interviewer must take particular care to hold the first contact's attention, perhaps using a script describing the purpose and value of the study.

Making contact with the respondent

In face-to-face interviewing, when a specified person must be interviewed, it is usual to make up to three call-backs. Using the telephone it is easy to make more calls. The CATI system handles this automatically, and can be programmed to vary the time of day and the day of the week until a successful interview is achieved. Company policy or an individual decision per survey should specify the pattern of call-backs. Similarly, the events that constitute 'no reply' should be consistent.

Introducing the interview

In telephone research very few respondents withdraw once the interview is under way. The crucial period is the initial contact.

As in face-to-face research, interviewers introduce themselves and their company by name. Using a prepared script they explain the subject of the research in a way that seems relevant to the respondent without causing suspicion or offence. This is particularly important since, unlike the face-to-face counterpart, the telephone interviewer cannot show an official interviewer identity card. The growth of telemarketing has made it imperative to make clear that the call will be an interview and not a sales approach.

When respondents understand why they have been selected for interview they become more willing to co-operate. Where possible, using a well-known client company name (with prior permission) in the introductory script will often reinforce the probity of the proposed interview and encourage the respondent to take part.

Length and timing of the interview

A notional interview length of 15–20 minutes is acceptable to most people. If necessary, a longer interview can often be obtained using a preliminary letter that names the research company and the (well-known) client, and explains the purpose of the survey. In business surveys, respondents are willing to participate longer if the interview seeks their professional opinions and judgements, rather than merely recording facts.

It is vital to be honest about the length of the interview. The interviewer must not be tempted to understate the time in order to get an interview. If the call runs over the stipulated length (which will already seem long enough to the respondent), the co-operation already gained is put at risk.

Residential interviews should take place between 9 am and 9 pm during weekdays, and 10 am and 6 pm at weekends, unless by appointment. However, individual companies have different views on the advisability of interviewing in the morning, as late as 9 pm at weekends and on Sundays. Business calls must take place during working hours; between 1 and 2 pm is not usually very productive.

Telephone manner

Obviously the only means of communication for a telephone interviewer is the voice, and it must be readily understood. As long as the speaking voice is clear then, in general, age, appearance and sex make no difference. However, when interviewing elderly people at home or when working on sensitive subjects, it is important to take care to select appropriate interviewers.

Regional accents are not an impediment, providing they can be understood. Indeed, some UK research studies have shown people actually *favour* interviewers with particular accents – particularly those from Scotland and North-East England. Interviewers need to speak slightly faster and higher than their face-to-face counterparts, and to avoid pauses (which can seem endless on the telephone). This has a bearing on the speed required for interviewers to take notes or enter data on the computer.

The interviewer must also be well prepared to deal with respondents who refuse to be interviewed, are suspicious or demand more explanation. Refusals usually occur right at the beginning of the interview, and people can be more abrupt and rude on the telephone when there is no face-to-face contact. Interviewers must be well trained, and prepared with specimen scripts and set phrases to deal with questions such as 'What's all this about?' 'Where did you get my name from?' or 'I'm not interested.' Individual companies provide their own versions of suitable phrases and scripts.

In the face-to-face situation, the respondent can see the answers being written down or pre-coded, and be encouraged to go on to the end of the questionnaire. Telephone interviewers can also indicate their continuing interest in the respondents' comments and replies, even if they seem trivial or boring. Suitably anodyne remarks such as 'Ah', 'I see', 'I understand' and 'Mm' can be used to establish the necessary rapport and prevent the interview sounding more like an interrogation. The interviewer must sound efficient, relaxed and in command.

Closing the interview

At the end of the interview, when thanking the respondent, the interviewer must offer the name of the company and telephone number of the executive in charge (even if not asked). An alternative is to offer the name and number (sometimes a freephone number) of an executive of the client company.

If, having been offered this, the informant wants any further assurance, an interviewer can suggest the respondent checks the bona fides of the company by ringing the operator and asking for Freephone Market Research Society. This free (and international) service, run and manned by the MRS, operates from 9 am to 9 pm on weekdays, and 10 am to 6 pm at weekends. All companies with an entry in the UK's *MRS Buyer's Guide* will automatically be verified. Any specific queries relating to the interview or content of the research are referred back to the company concerned.

These numbers may indeed be offered at the beginning of the interview. On occasion they may help establish the difference between genuine market research and telephone selling, and so help secure an interview.

International studies

Central location telephone interviewing makes light work of multi-country studies, or remote surveys of one country from another. International telephone connections are now of such a standard in quality and reliability that interviews are normally as easy to execute over thousands of intervening miles as they are within a city.

For such studies it is highly desirable to interview in the respondent's own language (except in a few highly globalized markets, where English may be acceptable). Best practice requires the research company to recruit bilingual (native-speaking) interviewers and give them the appropriate training.

Question wordings also require special attention, and it is important to have any translation checked for sense in the remote country whenever possible. It should also be 'back-translated' into its original language to identify any idiosyncrasies that arise in translation.

Despite the variety of languages used in multi-country studies, data can still be compiled using the same coding, to produce unified tables of findings.

Qualitative interviewing by telephone

While the bulk of telephone interviewing is concerned with broad-scale numerical studies, it is becoming increasingly common to use the telephone for qualitative interviewing studies too. Depth and semi-structured interviews, using a topic guide or outline questionnaire, can both be carried out successfully by telephone.

This application requires a higher level of interviewer training, and usually a greater involvement with the project's background and aims than the more conventional telephone survey. The cost per interview is correspondingly higher. But the approach also benefits from the generic advantages of the telephone – especially the ability to interview across large distances, completing interviews more productively and consistently. In appropriate cases, qualitative research by telephone adds an important new element in the research toolkit.

Interviewing management and control

Continuous supervision raises the standard of central location interviewing, through high levels of control over interviewing procedure and survey administration. Grouping the interviewers together in one place ensures constant supervision and allows consistent quality control. It also provides a high level of support and encouragement for the interviewer resulting in greater confidence and efficiency.

The role of the supervisor

The supervisor is vital for effective and efficient telephone interviewing. This is equally true in the simplest and most sophisticated interviewing centres.

By watching and listening to the interviewer (usually with a remote headset), supervisors can offer immediate support and advice. They can deal with any difficulties with the questionnaire or sample, counteract any bad practices, and act as backup if respondents have queries or want a higher authority. Above all, supervisors should be making sure that the quality of the interviews is maintained to a uniform high standard and that the interviewers are coping with their work efficiently and confidently.

The supervisor will be responsible for back-checking. Using a listening device, supervision and back-checking are accomplished simultaneously, and there is no need to trouble the respondent further with a call-back. Moreover, the supervisor can deal with issuing paper questionnaires and allocating the sample, when these are not being handled by CATI.

Industry standards and quality control

Bona fide market researchers in the UK belong to the MRS, and must follow the Society's Code of Conduct about responsibility to informants. The Code of Conduct guarantees the anonymity of respondents, and requires that all information will be presented in statistical form only. It covers telephone and other types of interviewing.

Individual companies adopt their own quality control procedures to cover the recruitment, training, supervision and back-checking of interviewers. Some UK companies belong to a quality control scheme known as the IQCS (Interviewer Quality Control Scheme), and all these companies conform to or exceed defined standards of quality control. This scheme and its standards are defined, reviewed and regularly updated.

In addition, growing numbers of companies now adhere to ISO or BSI quality accreditation schemes that regulate their approach to administration, training and management of projects.

Executive participation

With central location, it is easier to consult the executive in charge of the survey if any problems arise. Any difficulties that interviewers experience can be dealt with more rapidly during a survey. Decisions can be relayed straight back to the interviewer. As with the supervisor, the executive is available for advice and support when needed.

A properly supervised and sympathetically administered telephone centre generates an enthusiastic atmosphere of mutual support and corporate endeavour. This is reflected in a high proportion of successful interviews being administered precisely as intended with the correct respondents.

THE QUESTIONNAIRE IN TELEPHONE INTERVIEWING

General considerations

Of course, the principles and criteria of good questionnaire design that are important in face-to-face interviews also apply in the case of telephone interviewing. But there are some aspects of the latter that demand particular attention.

We have already noted that the introduction to the interview is important in gaining co-operation, but the actual wording of the questionnaire is also especially important. There is no visual backup to indicate when the respondent does not understand or is bored. The script must 'flow' and maintain interest, yet there must be enough time allowed for the respondent to absorb the question without creating an awkward pause. If necessary, the interviewer may repeat a whole question. The questionnaire should be succinct, clear, concise and leave no room for confusion or worry. It is vital to use reassuring, simple language. It is also important to guard against assumptions that reflect the writer's vocabulary and education. For example, technical words like 'statistical' and 'trends' are best left out of questionnaire wordings among non-technical samples.

Differences between telephone and face-to-face response

In general what can be asked face to face can also be asked by telephone, providing the question is suitably modified. The replies from the two formats are remarkably consistent. Nevertheless, experimental studies comparing the two modes do indicate some differences in responses obtained. It is invidious to consider the replies from either mode to be 'wrong', but researchers must bear these disparities in mind when considering telephone research, particularly if comparisons will be made between similar surveys using different modes.

Academic studies continue to reveal degrees of variation in response between the two modes, although the results are not always consistent. The following differences occur with sufficient regularity to warrant consideration:

- **Sensitive and personal questions** There is evidence in both the UK and USA that questions of a sensitive nature dealing with personal or private matters are answered more 'honestly' when asked by telephone. The absence of visual signals to establish the rapport noted above can also have a positive value. It seems that with the relative anonymity and confidentiality of a telephone interview, respondents are more willing to admit to attitudes and behaviour that are not so socially acceptable. There is less need to conform. Thus, in telephone surveys a higher proportion of people will admit to having had dealings with the police, will agree that they have no religious beliefs, etc. For one item of a personal nature – income – the levels quoted by telephone are consistently lower than face-to-face responses. Social grades also differ somewhat between the two modes; assessing the occupation of the head of household is less easy by telephone without visual clues. The main problems seem to be in distinguishing between grade B and C households, and deciding whether pensioners are grade E or not.
- **Scaled questions** Where scaled questions such as 'agree/disagree' are used in telephone interviews there is more inclination to opt for the extremes of the scale, ie a higher proportion say they agree/disagree strongly. But some studies suggest that this may be partly due to the 'unfolding' techniques described in the next section.
- **Other variations** Again there are signs that unprompted awareness (for example, of brands) is lower by telephone and that prompted awareness is higher. Answers to open-ended questions also tend to be less expansive so that research design must pay particular attention to the wording of questions and to prompting and probing.

Specific telephone questionnaire techniques

Simple pre-coded questions can be read out, and present no problems, and open-ended questions are also straightforward to ask. The techniques are discussed in the following sections.

Reading out

Even for lengthy or more complicated pre-coded questions, reading out can be as effective as showing a card in the face-to-face situation. CATI systems help ensure that the order in which the items are read out is rotated or randomized.

Writing down lists

As an alternative to reading out items, respondents can be asked to find paper and pencil and write a list down. The interviewer must ask the respondent to read back the list to ensure it is correct. This takes longer, but makes it possible to ask about all the members of the list at once, rather than working individually through the list. Subsequent questions are quicker, such as:

> 'Which of the makes of baked beans on your list have you heard of?'
> 'Which of the manufacturers in your list make fax machines?'
> – rather than:
> 'Have you heard of X brand of baked beans?' 'Yes' / 'No'
> 'Y brand?' 'Yes' / 'No'
> 'Z brand?' 'Yes' / 'No'; etc.

Respondent-written lists are particularly useful where the respondent is asked to consider, say, concept or attitude statements, which are more easily understood when written down, and may require a moment's thought before replying. They can also be used so that respondents can pick out, say, the company with 'the best', 'the next best' and 'the worst' reputation. Simple scales (liked / disliked; very satisfied / moderately satisfied / dissatisfied) can also be used to address a substantial number of items on a written list. In general, the paper-and-pencil method should be used sparingly, when a pilot study indicates that other methods are not working well.

Unfolding

Four- or five-point scales can be obtained by 'unfolding' the question in two parts.

> 'Would you say you are satisfied or dissatisfied with the service you get from your bank?'
> 'Is that very . . . or quite . . .?'
> 'I am going to read out some statements made recently by members of parliament. Would you tell me whether you agree or disagree, or have no opinion on the subject?'
> If agree / disagree, 'Would you say you . . . strongly or slightly?'

The technique can also be used to obtain numerical data within specified ranges rather than asking for outright figures. This is most commonly used for assessing gross income or take-home pay.

'Thinking about your take-home pay, that is your earnings after tax and National Insurance have been deducted, do you receive it weekly or monthly?'
If weekly, 'Is it more or less than £150 a week?'
If more, 'Is it more or less than £175 per week?' and so on.
If less, 'Is it more or less than £125 per week?' and so on.

Marks out of 10

Most respondents appreciate the idea of 'marks out of 10' from their schooldays. It is worth remembering this type of question for telephone research for, although it does not give in any way an absolute measure of the different items in terms of the criteria under consideration, it does enable performance comparisons to be made between various items. 'Now, thinking about the quality of the goods you have bought from each of the mail order companies, please give each company a mark out of 10.'

Stimulus material

Where a visual stimulus is necessary (such as copies of advertisements, maps, concept cards, photographs or equipment), it can be sent by post, either when the respondent has agreed to participate or with a preliminary letter. A variant of this, designed to increase the response rate and also elicit instantaneous reactions, is to send the information by post, with instructions not to be opened until called by telephone.

The advent of the fax has considerably improved the situation for business and industrial interviews. Stimulus material can be faxed ahead rather than posted, an appointment for an interview being made at the same time. Alternatively, after the initial introduction and agreement to be interviewed, the interviewer faxes the information and calls back, say 10 minutes later, to carry out the actual interview. It is also possible to foresee a domestic version of fax being used in the future.

Aural signals can also be transmitted to the respondent. For example the interviewer can play out the background music of a particular advertisement to aid recall, or read out a short narrative describing it.

The Internet provides new opportunities to present stimulus material to respondents equipped to see it, using either the World Wide Web or a company's own intranet. Digital television also promises new channels for showing stimulus, using either an unused TV channel or the new digital teletext services. In both cases (as with faxed material) the sample is restricted by the need for special equipment at the respondent's end of the communication.

Open-ended questions

Open-ended questions are easy to ask by telephone, but companies have had to develop new techniques to capture the responses.

At its simplest the interviewer writes down the reply to a particular question, and this is then coded by the usual pen-and-paper method, the codes being entered later into the answer file of the relevant respondent. The interviewer can also type the reply directly into the computer for later retrieval and coding as above. Alternatively, 'keywords' can be typed in and then used as a kind of shorthand, with the interviewer amplifying the answers after the interview is completed. In addition, techniques have been and are being developed in which the computer carries out the coding, by searching for 'keywords' and coding accordingly.

Using the latest refinements in CATI systems, it is also possible to capture verbatim responses by digital recording of sound directly into the computer. These can then be played back as required, as part of the presentation of results. So, for example, all the opinions about a local supermarket given by women aged 25–30 with one or more pre-school children can be heard immediately. The verbatims can also be coded either manually or by computer as above.

In general, open-ended questions should not be a dominant part of the structure of a telephone interview study, because of the extra work and cost they incur in analysis.

THE USE OF CATI IN TELEPHONE INTERVIEWING

Our outline of the history and development of telephone research noted the major role played by CATI in driving growth of the technique as a whole. This will now be considered in more detail. This subject does not stand still. The explosive growth in processor speed and power continues to impact on CATI as on any other computer application. What was unthinkable 10 years ago is now commonplace, and the future promises continuing advances.

Managing the sample

Administering a sample by pen-and-paper methods involves:

■ a large number of contact sheets;
■ logging every attempt to contact the prospective respondent at different times of the day and different days;

- recording (and keeping) appointments to call back;
- noting the final outcome of each contact/non-contact.

This is in order to make maximum use of the sample, to ensure the right geographical distribution and to spread the interviews over the interviewing period. The CATI system can manage the interview scheduling and call-back scheme much more effectively than a paper-based approach. It can also be integrated with broader database management software, for example to regulate the frequency of the interviewing of people from a tightly defined small group.

Managing the questionnaire

CATI removes from the interviewer the responsibility for following the correct routeing and making the appropriate jumps in the questionnaire. This means that interviews flow smoothly and faster, without interruptions for routeing. It also means a survey can use a more complicated questionnaire without loss of accuracy. The CATI system edits the input for incorrect and incompatible replies; instructions and questions are then given to the interviewer to reduce any inconsistencies.

CATI systems can automatically rotate or randomize the starting-point within questions that include lists of items or statements, to reduce order effects and biases. They can also handle alternative versions of a question, or put the questions in a different sequence. Respondents' answers to earlier questions can be recalled later in an interview for further probing.

Monitoring progress

Visual display of the questionnaire, together with remote listening devices, enables both supervisors and executives to monitor interviews in progress. Up-to-the-minute online hole counts, simple cross-tabs and analysis of the sample are also available.

Latest features

The newest CATI systems also allow third parties (such as the client) to dial in and listen to live interviews while they are happening, even from remote locations. Such facilities include password and other controls to ensure security. Recent CATI systems can incorporate the random selection of individuals within a household, and surveys involving complicated (factorial) designs.

Current state-of-the-art systems benefit from high-speed computer networking and digital telephone lines, and integrate the telephone dialling process with the software that manages the sample and the response data. Taking full advantage of ISDN technologies, they detect busy signals and no answers, immediately dialling other respondents to minimize interviewer waiting time. Compared to analogue technology, ISDN provides extremely fast dialling and call result detection. The tedium of manual dialling and recording the call result is eliminated, freeing interviewers to concentrate on interviewing. The result is faster completion of projects, lower staff costs and increased control. This automated dialling ('power dialling') delivers big gains in productivity.

Further integration

The improved efficiency and quality that CATI offers will continue to increase with further integration. At the moment, samples that are in the form of paper lists have to be entered into the computer manually, or by scanner and optical character reading software. Even if they are supplied as computer output from a database, further processing is often required for entry into the CATI computer. It increases efficiency to use compatible sample databases that can be fed directly into the CATI system. In both these systems there will be a saving in the time and personnel required for typing and programming.

Because most CATI systems lack a user-friendly interface for questionnaire design, most companies still design their questionnaires and routeing on paper, which is then entered into the computer by a programming specialist. Piloting and amending the survey means repeating the hard-copy-to-computer process. Direct entry via a word processor would permit *ad hoc* piloting. Researchers could try out alternative wordings and check their routeings, with the executive actively participating. Ideally the executive should be able to input the questionnaire. Further integration with compatible systems already enables companies to transmit tabulated data both nationally and internationally.

Future development

As technology becomes cheaper and demand more sophisticated, we can expect the development of interactive systems (especially in the field of business and industrial research) in which respondents reply to a set of questions posed by the computer, videophone, fax and possibly electronic mail services or Web pages.

Increasing domestic use of e-mail and the World Wide Web is likely to offer new possibilities in telephone interviewing, particularly in more prosperous homes, and may be followed by other new media. Web pages can be used as an interviewing medium in their own right, or as a medium for showing stimulus materials (pictures, sound and video clips) remotely in the course of a telephone interview. The new digital TV channels also have the potential to carry research materials for the respondent to view in real time, either in unused channels or using the high resolution of digital teletext. The use of 'written' replies received by e-mail, fax, etc will increase as part of mixed-mode interviewing that also involves CATI.

The continued (if not explosive) expansion of telephone research can be expected in all fields where structured interviewing is required (in particular for residential surveys), as access to the telephone becomes even more universal.

Telemarketing

Telemarketing is the use of the telephone to generate sales, either directly or by arranging for a representative to visit prospective purchasers. As telephone has become more widespread and commonplace, so companies have recognized its role as a sales channel that gives them direct access to potential purchasers. Home improvement companies, financial services and catalogue marketers have pioneered telemarketing, and many further companies join in every year.

Sales canvassing activities pose a threat to telephone interviewing that has not yet been resolved. As in the case of 'sugging' (selling under the guise of research), the initial telemarketing contact with consumers is often disguised as market research.

Telemarketing uses similar mechanics to telephone interviewing: telephones and computers grouped together in central facilities under close supervision. Indeed, many of the systems and facilities, and even some of the people manning the telephones, overlap with those used in research.

While the aims of telemarketing are totally different from those of research, this is not necessarily obvious to the majority of consumers, who are not familiar with such activities. These consumers will not appreciate that genuine market research will always maintain confidentiality and will only provide clients with aggregated data.

A substantial drop in response rate (whatever the mode of interview) in the USA has been attributed to the effect of telemarketing, where the initial approach is often disguised as research. The distinction has become more blurred as telemarketing companies increasingly include market research as part of their package. Research and telemarketing will merge not only in the minds of the general public, but also of legislators. Already in Germany and parts of the USA, cold calling for telemarketing is legally restricted. Only constant vigilance has so far ensured that telephone interviewing is not inadvertently subsumed into legislation, or that interviewing is not considered or assumed to be covered by the current law.

Apart from educating the public to help them distinguish between 'selling' and 'research', researchers must emphasize their role as consultants, and their ability to interpret data and help plan a marketing programme, giving added value to the data obtained by telephone.

REFERENCES AND FURTHER READING

Birn, R (1988) Chapter 1, in *The Effective Use of Market Research: A guide for management*, Kogan Page, London

Bowles, T (1989) Data collection in the United Kingdom, *Journal of the Market Research Society*, **31**

Brennan, M, Esslemont, D and Hini, D (1995) Obtaining purchase predictions via telephone interviews, *Journal of the Market Research Society*, **37**

Brighton, M (1980) Data capture in the 80s, Market Research Society Conference

Clemens, J and Watson, P (1980) Telephone panels, Market Research Society Conference

Collins, M *et al* (1988) Chapter 14, in *Telephone Survey Methodology*, ed R M Groves *et al*, John Wiley, New York

Consterdine, G (1989) Telephone research: directory and social grading biases, *Market Research Society Newsletter*, November, **18**

De Leeuw, E D, Hox, J J and Snijkers, G (1995) The effect of computer-assisted interviewing on data quality, *Journal of the Market Research Society*, **37**

England, L and Arnold, P (1986) Chapter 10, in *Consumer Market Research Handbook*, 3rd edn, ed R M Worcester and J Downham, Elsevier, Holland

Frankel, M R (1989) Current research practices: general population sampling including geodemographics, *Journal of the Market Research Society*, **31**

Goodyear, J (1989) The structure of the British market research industry, *Journal of the Market Research Society*, **31**

Hague, P N (1987) Chapter 22, in *The Industrial Market Research Handbook*, Kogan Page, London

Hoinville, G (1985) Telephone interviewing on a survey of social attitudes: a comparison with face-to-face procedures, SCPR Survey Research Centre

Honomichl, J (1989) US research industry structure, *Journal of the Market Research Society*, **31**

Hyett, G B and Allan, G M (1976) Collection of data by telephone (CDT): its viability in consumer research, Market Research Society Conference

Kiecker, P and Nelson, J E (1996) Do interviewers follow telephone survey instructions? *Journal of the Market Research Society*, **38**

Lysaker, R L (1989) Data collection methods in the US, *Journal of the Market Research Society*, **31**

Market Research Development Fund (1986) Comparing telephone and face-to-face surveys, **1** Seminar proceedings, **2** Marplan technical report and (1988) Telephone or face-to-face polls

Marplan Ltd (1985) Comparing data collected by telephone and face-to-face, A report on a methodological research survey

Miln, D and Stewart-Hunter, D (1976) The case for telephone research, 19th annual conference of the Market Research Society

Nicholls II, William L (1988) Chapter 23, in *Telephone Survey Methodology*, ed R M Groves *et al*, John Wiley, New York

Noble, I, Moon, N and McVey, D (1998) Bringing it all back home – using RDD telephone methods for large-scale social policy and opinion research in the UK, *Journal of the Market Research Society*, **40**

Rothman, J and Mitchell, D (1989) Statisticians can be creative too, *Journal of the Market Research Society*, **31**

Sykes, W and Collins, M (1988) Chapter 19, in *Telephone Survey Methodology*, ed R M Groves *et al*, John Wiley, New York

11

Postal Research

Peter Mouncey

WHY USE POSTAL RESEARCH?

The annual statistics covering 1997, compiled by the Association of Market Survey Organisations (AMSO) from returns submitted by its members, show that postal and self-completion accounted for 4.6 million interviews, an increase of 9 per cent on the previous year. These accounted for 26 per cent of the total number of interviews conducted by AMSO members – third behind face-to-face (off-street) at 4.66 million and telephone (5.73 million). However, by value postal accounted for only 7.6 per cent of revenue (£38.34 million), compared to 32 per cent for face-to-face (£162.34 million) and 19.8 per cent for telephone (£99.66 million). These figures will underestimate the totals for the whole UK market research industry, but the only recent attempt at a census was in 1987, conducted by the Technical Development Committee of the Market Research Society, which estimated that postal/self-completion methods accounted for 4.86 million interviews with a value of £11.3 million.

The extent to which these figures provide a complete picture may be open to debate, but they do indicate two factors: firstly, that despite the growth in telephone research, mail/self-completion surveys remain a very important interview method in the UK; and secondly, the revenue figures underline the cost-effectiveness of this as a research tool, as the average costs per interview for the three main methods show:

	£ per interview
Postal/self-completion	8
Telephone	17
Face-to-face (off-street)	35

(Source: AMSO, 1998)

Of course these figures do not tell the full story. One of the advantages of postal research is its flexibility. It can be conducted cost-effectively by the research user without the need for significant investment in either interviewers or telephone systems. In all probability the numbers of postal/self-completion interviews is an understatement compared with telephone and field interviewing methods. It is also likely that, over time, the cost of postal research will continue to increase by inflation levels only. Two immediate advantages of postal research are therefore cost-effectiveness and flexibility.

Research undertaken by the Henley Centre on behalf of the Direct Marketing Association indicates that a postal questionnaire is also the method preferred by the public for supplying information, closely followed by face-to-face at-home methods, as shown in Table 11.1.

Table 11.1 *Preferred methods for supplying a company with information*

	%
Postal questionnaire	46
Face-to-face interview on the doorstep	44
Application form	34
Personal call to the company on a freephone number in response to an advertisement	28
Questionnaire completed on premises	20
Personal call to the company	19
Face-to-face interview in the street	20
Telephone call from the company	19

Source: Dataculture, Henley Centre/DMA

So popularity with the public is another factor in favour of this interview method.

The low cost of postal research has attracted much academic interest, especially from the USA. However, there is a dearth of published case studies relating to actual applications in a commercial environment – especially in Britain.

With careful planning, and when used in the appropriate circumstances, postal research can provide a very cost-effective way of producing high-quality data with the flexibility on the one hand and centralized control on the other.

Two key impetuses to postal surveys have been firstly the continuing rapid growth in direct or database marketing and secondly the rise in monitoring levels of customer service. These are often linked – financial service institutions are an important example.

Postal research is most effective and appropriate where there is an established and positive relationship between the researcher and the recipients of the questionnaire, such as between a company and its customers. Postal research is unlike telephone or field interview methods in that the recipient of a postal questionnaire cannot be persuaded into responding except through the covering letter, the questionnaire and, at the margins, any incentive that might be provided. Examples are 'clubs' and subscription-based organizations such as book or record clubs, motoring organizations and others where customers' names and addresses are held on record, for example car dealers, privatized utilities, financial institutions and mail order companies. Postal surveys also enable the researcher directly to replicate the method that will be used for promoting and distributing the product or service itself. It is therefore an ideal research method for those with access to a customer database, providing a reliable and low-cost method for undertaking surveys, for example to forecast demand for a proposed new product or undertaking post facto research amongst samples of those who might be or have been mailed an offer.

Thus, in many respects, the postal survey must deal with the same problem as that faced by a direct mailing agency – how to elicit the highest possible level of response from the customer base – and this will affect the survey's design.

Many of the communication issues are also similar – the same care and attention need to be taken in the design and testing of all the elements within the pack. For example, the covering letter must 'sell' the benefits of the survey to the recipient and encourage the person to respond. The questionnaire topics need to be of some interest to the respondent and written in a language and format that recipients can clearly understand. A suitable reply-paid envelope should be provided and an appropriate low-cost 'thank you' gift may be considered necessary to increase the response. The response tends to be higher if the letterhead used and the response address are those of a company with which the respondent has a relationship – even if an agency is being used to conduct the survey.

Increasingly, retailers and fast-moving consumer goods (fmcg) companies are realizing the advantages of collecting customers' names and addresses to help stimulate brand loyalty. For these companies the opportunity to use databases as a sampling frame for market research is expanding all the time. Using a database as the sampling frame provides additional data that can be used for analysing the responses to the survey and for compiling comparable profiles for responders and non-responders. This helps assess any bias in the response.

Postal surveys can work well if there is a need to re-interview people who have taken part in an earlier survey. It may be necessary to return to them, for example, to collect more detailed information from a minority group in the original sample. Increasingly, respondents in omnibus and other field surveys are asked if they would mind being re-interviewed. Most respond positively to these requests. For example, the IPSOS-NFO panel of 30,000 households is drawn from respondents in *ad hoc* surveys who have agreed to then participate in this ongoing activity. Panel members are usually contacted by post, sometimes by telephone or occasionally face to face. The large overall sample enables minority groups to be identified, and allows surveys to be conducted simultaneously without overloading respondents. Typically, about 70 per cent of those agreeing to join the panel will subsequently return questionnaires. The success of this panel is due to creating an initial relationship with respondents to the *ad hoc* survey and then maintaining it over time.

By comparison, it is much more difficult to achieve an effective response rate for postal surveys from a general sample of the population, unless much higher value incentives are used (such as a major prize draw), or the research is undertaken by an official body.

Set our below are the basic advantages and disadvantages of using postal surveys. The advantages are:

- **Low cost** Postal surveys are likely to be up to a third of the cost of telephone and an eighth of the cost of field interviews for comparable unclustered fieldwork.
- **High response** Correctly designed and executed postal surveys exceed the effective response rates from telephone surveys and in many cases approach those achieved from field surveys.
- **Central control** There is no reliance on external factors in the field.
- **Unclustered sampling** There are no cost advantages in clustering as might be the case for field interviewing.
- **Questionnaire length** More time is available for completion, as it can be left to a convenient moment.
- **Timing of interview** The recipients can complete the questionnaire when it is convenient for them to do so.
- **Conferring** There is the opportunity to confer with other members of the household, or give more considered thought to the answers.
- **Demand forecasting** This is especially useful to those in direct marketing.
- **No interviewer bias** The interviewer cannot lead by tone or inclination since the question is not read out.

- **Response level** Very accurate records can be kept of the true response levels, including undelivered items returned by the Royal Mail as 'gone-aways'.
- **Deliverability** Imprecise address details can be successfully used, whereas this would not produce a match for telephone interviewing. For example, it would be difficult to obtain a telephone number if the name differs from that in a directory.

The disadvantages of postal research are:

- **(Perceived) low response** This is a traditional perception but is often related to either the inappropriate use of the technique or poor questionnaire design.
- **No control of respondent** There is no interviewer to assist or control the respondent, or ensure that the named individual answers the questions.
- **Questionnaire content** There are constraints on attitude-related questions and the effect of pre-reading the complete questionnaire in advance; there is limited success with certain types of open-ended questions.
- **Questionnaire design** Any errors in routeing instructions, etc cannot be rectified once the survey is in the field.
- **Data quality** Incomplete responses can be a problem.
- **Time** Response usually takes longer than other main methods.

Inevitably some topics are of less interest to recipients than others, and this acts to lower the response. One way of overcoming this problem is to insert a short set of questions at the beginning of the questionnaire that are known to have wide appeal. For example, the Automobile Association (AA) sometimes includes questions related to the performance of the breakdown service to aid response.

As there is no interviewer to provide feedback, questionnaire piloting is very important. It is also possible to test at low cost any of the other variables that might increase response, for example:

- response to an agency compared to response to your organization;
- incentive versus no incentive, or different types of incentive;
- anonymous versus personalized or identity-coded questionnaires;
- personalized versus non-personalized or identity-coded questionnaires;
- pre-contact versus no pre-contact (or postal pre-contact compared to a telephone call);
- effectiveness of follow-up letters (or telephone calls);
- pre-paid versus stamped address return envelopes;
- pre-notification (postal or telephone call).

Table 11.2 shows the extent to which various factors can lift response above the base line.

Table 11.2 *Factors increasing response*

	Increase in Response %
Established relationships (eg up-to-date customer file or database)	+ 150
1st reminder (letter)	+ 26
2nd reminder (telephone)	+ 25
High-interest questions section	+ 19
Appropriate incentive	+ 18
2nd reminder (letter, questionnaire and envelope)	+ 12
2nd-class return post	+ 8
1st-class return post	+ 5

Source: Market Research Development Fund (1985, November) Increasing response

One leading market research agency undertook an analysis of 89 postal surveys conducted between 1991 and 1993. This unpublished 'survey' showed a mean response rate of 44 per cent, varying from 11 per cent to 80 per cent. The main positive conditions that led to increases in response (excluding the source of the sample) were the use of a pen as an incentive and/or a follow-up letter. Other factors varied from survey to survey.

The example in Table 11.3 shows that, used in the right way, a postal research survey can achieve response levels as good as the best that can be achieved with fieldwork. The results for the two postal surveys are from projects conducted by the Royal Mail and the AA, whereas the face-to-face example is based on survey work undertaken by British Gas.

Table 11.3 *Response levels*

No of Call-backs/Follow-ups	0 %	1 %	2 %	3 %	4 %
Postal (Royal Mail)	41	64	77*		
Postal (AA)	43	66	79		
Face-to-face	45	66	81	85	87

Source: MRDF (1985, November) Increasing response
* 92 per cent where telephone follow-up used instead

These results should also be seen in the context of the marginal improvements in data quality achieved at high cost through three or more follow-ups in field surveys.

MECHANICS OF POSTAL SURVEYS

Advanced planning is essential to ensure success. Procedures for recording completed questionnaires to track response rates, and sending out reminder letters should also be decided before the mailing.

To estimate the number of stamps, envelopes and questionnaires that will be required, a decision must be made about the number of reminder letters to be sent and whether or not duplicate questionnaires and return envelopes will be sent. For example, if two reminder letters are to be sent on an original mailing of 1,000 with a duplicate questionnaire and return envelope with the second reminder, it is necessary to have 3,500 envelopes and stamps and 1,450 questionnaires as shown in Table 11.4.

Table 11.4 *Calculation of envelopes, stamps and questionnaires*

	Envelopes	Stamps	Questionnaires
Initial mailing (1,000)	2,000	2,000	1,000
1st reminder (assuming 40% response)	600	600	–
2nd reminder (assuming 55% response)	900	900	450
Total	3,500	3,500	1,450

Franking of the mail-out envelopes will obviously reduce the number of stamps required and is easier.

As discussed earlier, if there is sufficient time, it is always worth while to conduct a pilot survey. Not only will this provide the opportunity to pilot the questionnaire but it will also provide indications on speed of response, response rates and the quality of the sample (from the number of undelivered returns).

RESPONSE RATES

The response levels to postal surveys are variable and depend on many things, but the key influences are the level of interest in the questionnaire, whether or not there is an established relationship between the respondent and researching company, and the extent to which there is an up-to-date mailing file. In 1988 an unpublished survey among members of the postal research special interest group (MRS) showed that while a number of postal studies achieved response rates of 70 per cent plus, 40–69 per cent is probably more typical. Worst cases show response levels of well under 20 per cent. It is the appropriate use of the technique that is the key factor. However, there is evidence from some organizations that the average response rate is falling, so attention to the factors described above and in other sections of this chapter is of even greater importance.

One advantage with postal research is that response rates are easily measurable in comparison with telephone and face-to-face surveys, especially when quota sampling methods are used, where the number of attempts made to achieve the interviews have to be taken into account.

The following sections offer guidance on how to conduct a postal survey and how to maximize response rates.

Sampling frame

The sampling frame is one of the key elements of postal research. Obviously one of the most important considerations is the quality of the name and address. These should be as complete as possible and in Royal Mail preferred format, including postcodes. Apart from that, the usual considerations apply in terms of lack of duplications, how up-to-date the list is and how accessible it is. For example, can representative samples be drawn, and can the list be pre-profiled in any way?

Sources for sampling frames that might be considered are customer databases and lists, club/organization membership lists, directories (eg Kelly's), and so on. The new generation of commercial marketing databases offered by bureaux may also be considered.

Increasingly, details from the database are being combined with the research results to produce a more detailed profile of respondents. This should be undertaken by the agency to ensure that the requirements of the MRS Code of Conduct are adhered to in respect of maintaining the anonymity of those in the sample. In addition, the MRS have produced a set of guidelines for researchers working with databases.

Pre-contact

There is some evidence to suggest that pre-contact or pre-notification by telephone, face-to-face or card/letter accelerates the rate of return, but against that the improvement may be marginal and will add to the cost of the survey. If the sample is drawn from previous respondents in face-to-face surveys who have agreed to be recontacted, a higher response rate is likely to be achieved.

Send-out envelopes

An official-looking envelope has been shown to work well. It is best to avoid anything that looks like a direct mail approach, as this is least likely to be successful. A return address for undelivered questionnaires on the reverse of the envelope will help in monitoring 'gone-aways' and undelivered questionnaires.

Covering letter

This takes the place of the interviewer and is a very important element in a postal survey. Its role is to encourage the recipient to respond. Therefore, the recipient needs to have a very clear understanding of the benefits of responding. Excellent advice on the contents of covering letters can be found in Dillman (1978) and Hoinville *et al* (1978). The letter should cover the following:

- why the survey is being undertaken;
- why it is important for people to participate, eg only a small number of people contacted and a high response needed;
- who should complete the questionnaire;
- an assurance of confidentiality;
- how the survey will help people in the future;
- how people were selected for the survey;
- how to return the questionnaire;
- the need for quick response;
- a thank-you for co-operation.

If it is possible for the results to be communicated back to respondents (eg through a customer magazine), then reference to this might also increase response. A Research Development Foundation study on public co-operation in market research clearly underlined the importance of all these points in reassuring potential respondents that the survey is both genuine and of value.

Where the questionnaires are numbered to identify those requiring reminder letters, this should be explained in the letter, together with an assurance that this number will be removed from completed questionnaires, thus preserving anonymity. There is some debate about whether or not the covering letter should be personalized. Dillman believes that personalization increases response, but only if a date of posting, a blue ink signature and individually typed addresses on the envelope are also used. However, personalization, particularly where the covering letter is part of the questionnaire rather than a separate page, may also lead to fears of loss of anonymity on the part of the respondent.

To help reassure recipients of postal surveys that the information provided will be used responsibly, the MRS has an MRS Mark symbol, which can be included by their members on postal surveys to identify them as genuine market research projects that conform with the MRS Code of Conduct.

Incentives

The use of an incentive adds to the cost of the survey but can be useful in increasing or accelerating response. Enclosing an incentive with the mail-out questionnaire may create a sense of obligation for the recipient and seems to be more effective than withholding rewards until the questionnaire is returned. A pen or pencil is often used but these may cause problems in handling through the postal system. Entry into a prize draw is another alternative and can be used to speed up response if a closing date is given. Experience shows that second-class mailings are as effective as those sent first class.

Return envelope

Again there are conflicting views about the use of stamps as opposed to franking or postage-paid imprints on return envelopes. In the Automobile Association's experience, a stamp produces a higher response rate, possibly due to the perceived monetary value. Within the AA a second-class stamp is used as first-class postage is viewed as wasting members' funds.

Follow-ups

The use of reminder letters is a successful way of increasing response rates. The first letter can double as a thank-you letter if sent to the full sample. The second follow-up letter should be specifically targeted at non-respondents and may include another copy of the questionnaire and return envelope. The covering letter should seek to reinforce the need to respond.

The timing of the first reminder letter can be decided by plotting returns on a graph and sending it out when returns begin to plateau. A similar procedure can be adopted for the second reminder. As a rule the first reminder should be mailed 10 days after send-out and the second letter 10 days to two weeks after that. Telephone or face-to-face can be used for the second or final follow-up. Obviously this increases response rates, but the additional costs are high.

Questionnaire design

An important difference between self-completion questionnaires and those administered by interviewers is that the respondent can answer questions in any order, read through the questionnaire before completion and consult others for their views. Also, there is no control over who actually completes the questionnaire or the conditions under which it is completed.

The absence of an interviewer imposes certain limitations on question-naire design. Question ordering such as spontaneous and then prompted awareness cannot be controlled in postal surveys, as there is every chance that the respondent will read through the whole questionnaire before starting to tick the boxes. Self-completion questionnaires are unsuitable for asking open-ended questions of the type used in attitude research. Probing or seeking an explanation for a particular answer is clearly impossible. There is, however, the advantage that the respondent can work through the questionnaire at his own pace and at a convenient time and this may be particularly useful where the survey requires personal or household details that are not readily to hand. Any potential interviewer bias is obviously overcome.

It is always advisable to pilot the questionnaire, as there is no interviewer to advise of errors or problem questions. Factors to consider when design-ing the questionnaire include those set out in the following sections.

Length of questionnaire

Scott (1961) concluded that the length of the questionnaire makes no significant difference to response rates. The issue is the relationship between the organization, the recipient and the recipient's interest in the topic.

Open-ended questions

In the experience of the AA, open-ended questions can be used effectively. The responses will sometimes lack depth but are useful for obtaining strongly held or top-of-mind responses. A single open-ended question at the end of the questionnaire can be used to give respondents the opport-unity to mention topics important to them not covered elsewhere and this in itself can raise overall response rates.

Length of questions

Long or complex questions should be avoided.

Routeing

Routeing should be clear and concise, eg 'Please go to Q number . . .'

Content

All recipients should be required to answer a reasonable proportion of the questionnaire to ensure a good response. Above all it should include some questions that are likely to be of interest even if this means including questions that are not directly relevant to the aims of the survey.

Layout

The questionnaire should look easy to complete and should not be compressed to make it look shorter. There is some debate about whether the questionnaire should be printed to look like a booklet or be printed single-sided. While the questionnaire should look attractive, a glossy, typeset presentation may be counterproductive if mailed to groups of people who would view this either as a waste of money, adding to subscription rates/costs, etc or as a direct mail approach. Optional mark reading (OMR) technology can be used in the design and automation of processing self-completion questionnaires.

Coding

This can be included on the questionnaire, but is best put in the right-hand margin to ensure that it does not interfere with the clarity of the questionnaire from the recipient's point of view.

Non-response

There are two aspects to consider here: non-response to the survey overall, and partially completed questionnaires.

If the response rate is low this may raise questions about how representative the final sample is. The postcode may be used to help with geodemographic analysis. For example, by ACORN-coding each questionnaire before mailing and comparing this with the completed questionnaires, weighting factors may be generated. If the questionnaires have been individually identified, any information available from a database such as demographic data, product purchasing, etc can also be utilized.

Where the purpose of the survey is to forecast demand for products or services it may be appropriate to base the analysis on the total mail-out volume (net of Royal Mail returns), thus treating non-responders as rejectors of the product or service, provided the sampling frame is known to be reasonably up to date. Where the questionnaire is partially completed, these responses can be totally omitted from analysis or treated as 'no answers' with analysis based on total numbers of questionnaires returned.

POSTAL RESEARCH IN ACTION

This final section includes examples of postal research surveys to illustrate the points made in this chapter.

Using postal research to collect data on people's perceptions of grocery brands (City University Business School)

As part of a research project to evaluate people's perceptions of grocery brands, a large sample of respondents was required. Householders were asked to look at a colour photograph showing eight competing brands in a frequently bought product field and complete an attribute-brand battery (eight brands to be evaluated across 10 attributes). A further 11 pre-coded questions were concerned with grocery shopping behaviour and classifying respondents. The only criterion for recruitment was that the respondent had to be the person responsible for household grocery shopping. With all the questions pre-coded, no complicated routeing procedures and the need for respondents to complete the questionnaire at their own pace (on average 20 minutes), a postal survey appeared ideal.

A covering letter was designed explaining the purpose of the survey, assuring confidentiality in reporting and explaining why householders should reply. Each respondent was addressed personally (on the letter and envelope), along with a blue ink signature at the end of the letter. Second-class stamps were used on the mailing and a second-class business reply-paid envelope was included with the questionnaire. Due to budget constraints, there was no incentive included with the questionnaire. One follow-up letter was sent. By allocating and recording serial numbers, non-respondents were sent the reminder. The decision about when to send out reminders was based on plotting daily cumulative responses; when a plateau was apparent, reminders were sent out.

A questionnaire was prepared and presented in such a way as to appear interesting and easy to complete (ie no column punching codes included). To enhance respondents' confidence, easier questions were placed early on. The questionnaire and letter were tested by observing the way 12 householders completed the survey. The pilot showed that respondents preferred the questionnaire produced as two double-sided pages stapled together, rather than photo-reduced to all fit on two sides of A4.

The daily replies slowed to a plateau 12 days after the original mail-out and the reminder letters were sent. By this time, a 29 per cent response had been achieved (636 replies). A further 429 replies were received after the reminder was sent, giving a total of 1,065 returns (49 per cent response).

Of the replies, 78 per cent had correctly completed the entire questionnaire, ie an effective sample of 829 respondents. Thus, in terms of the original objectives, postal research was considered to have sufficiently satisfied the data collection needs.

The European Businessman Readership Survey 1989 (Research Services Ltd)

The 1989 European Businessman Readership Survey (EBRS) is the 12th in a series of surveys conducted by IPSOS-RSL. First conducted in 1973, the surveys investigate the readership and business responsibilities of heads of functions in medium and large business establishments in 17 European countries. The universe of such individuals was estimated at 406,955 in 1998. The survey is used to plan national and international advertising campaigns aimed at senior business individuals.

In each country, business establishments are sampled from published directories. A telephone call is made to establish the name of up to two randomly selected eligible heads of functions. The survey uses a mailed questionnaire and up to four mailings in some countries, sample individuals being sent a covering letter and four-page typeset questionnaire in the local language together with a reply-paid envelope. All packs are mailed from Great Britain. Incentives such as dollar bills are used where appropriate.

The results were as follows:

Mail-out	21,538
Replies analysed	9,180
Response rate	43 per cent

Response was lowest in the Netherlands (35 per cent) and highest in Sweden (54 per cent).

The postal method was selected as the most appropriate and cost-effective method of gaining sufficient response from busy executives. The high response rate amongst the audience was achieved by experimentation with various techniques over the series of surveys (such as offering a summary of results to respondents), detailed attention to the letter and questionnaire design, and various monetary incentives.

Direct Marketing Collection Club (Sample Surveys Ltd)

The objective of the survey was to profile customers, including behavioural and attitudinal differences. Postal self-completion surveys were conducted between 1992 and 1996, and achieved a consistent response rate of around 35 per cent. The sample size was 16,000. The mail pack included a questionnaire (with integral covering letter) and a reply-paid envelope. In 1997, the client decided (in the interests of cost) to use a 'tuck and fold' questionnaire and integral envelope. All other design features remained constant ie sample selection, questionnaire coverage and time of year. The response rate, however, fell to 25 per cent. The survey was conducted again in 1998 reverting to a separate reply-paid envelope, and the response rate increased again to 35 per cent.

The process of completion and return needs to be made as easy as possible for the respondent. The process of tucking and folding the questionnaire appears to have been a real irritant and ultimately suppressed response.

Vehicle Warranty Breakdown Assistance (Automobile Association)

The AA provides breakdown cover as part of the new car warranty scheme for a number of car manufacturers. As part of the AA's programme to monitor satisfaction with the core roadside service, those who call out the AA under the warranty schemes are sent a single-page two-sided questionnaire. Whilst the covering letter is manufacturer-branded, the questions are common to all schemes and match those included in the more detailed survey conducted amongst personal members of the AA. Each questionnaire also includes a label containing details of that particular call-out, to match for analysis with the opinion data. The covering letter refers to this label, and also includes the MRS Mark, to reassure recipients that the survey complies with the MRS Code of Conduct. Questionnaires are dispatched within 72 hours of the breakdown service experience with a reply-paid envelope. There is no follow-up letter. Response rates average 55 per cent, but do vary by brand. Two of the surveys are personalized but this does not appear to have an effect on response rates.

REFERENCES AND FURTHER READING

Blythe, I and Essex, P (1981) Variations on a postal theme, Market Research Society Conference, UK

Chilvers, D and Langford, R (1982) Research techniques to isolate and separate segments of the PO letter market, Market Research Society Conference, UK

Dillman, D A (1978) *Mail and Telephone Surveys, the Total Design Method*, John Wiley, New York

Erdos, P L (1970) *Professional Mail Surveys*, McGraw-Hill, New York

ESRC Newsletter (1987, Summer) Survey Methods Seminar Services: First class postal surveys, Social and Community Planning Research (SCPR), London

Evans, N (1995) *Using Questionnaires and Surveys to Boost Your Businesses*, Pitman Publishing

Guidelines for Handling Databases, Market Research Society, London

Henley Centre / Direct Marketing Assocation (1995) *Dataculture*

Hoinville, G *et al* (1978) *Survey Research Practice*, Heinemann, Oxford

Johnson, F (1983) Price and relevance of accuracy of market research data, Market Research Society Conference, UK

Market Research Development Fund (1985, November) Increasing response, Seminar papers, Market Research Society, London

Scott, C (1961) Research on mail surveys, *Journal of the Royal Statistical Society*, Series A, **124** (2)

Whitley, E W (1980) The case for postal research, Market Research Society Conference, UK

Windle, R (1996) *Public Co-operation in Market Research*, The Research Development Foundation

12

Omnibus Research

Tony Lees

INTRODUCTION

Omnibus (meaning 'for all' in Latin) research is a term used to describe a vehicle that runs at regular intervals and where the costs are shared by a number of participating clients.

To the layperson, the term means either 'a volume containing a number of books or stories previously published separately' or, more commonly, 'a large (red) vehicle for transporting a number of fare-paying passengers from one place to another'. The analogy between the market research omnibus and the 'large (red) vehicle' fits better, in that a client can get on at any stop (any tranche of fieldwork), can travel as far as he or she wants (buys into one or more stages of fieldwork) and pays for the number of seats taken up (is charged according to the number of questions asked).

Historically, many companies started by setting up high-quality regular studies for a specific client and then, mainly due to cost constraints, offered part of the available space/time to other clients. With omnibus surveys a part of the 'everyday life of a researcher' for some three decades, niche-market services are more apparent than they once were.

The advantage of omnibus as a data collection vehicle is that costs for setup, sampling, respondent contact and collection of demographic information (ie the overheads) are shared by all participating clients. This, allied to the fact that surveys are available regularly, allows clients to ask quest-ions when required at costs far less than one might pay for an *ad hoc* study.

This chapter explains how omnibus surveys work, the advantages and disadvantages compared with other data collection techniques and how best to select an omnibus company. Over the past 10 years omnibus research has become more popular, varied and competitive, giving clients the opportunity to buy cost-effective research as and when required.

One can find omnibus surveys covering consumers, new businesses and company directors. Within the consumer category, omnibus surveys cover:

- the adult population;
- children and adolescents;
- motorists.

Omnibus surveys operate domestically in Britain and internationally, both within the EU and beyond its frontiers. European ownership has in some cases given British omnibus operators such as RSL (IPSOS Group) ready access to the omnibus surveys operated by their counterparts based in other European cities. Other companies, NOP for example, have formed close working relationships with their opposite numbers to ensure harmon-ization of data collection. Pan-European relationships and/or ownership have long since rendered the ability to make cross-frontier comparisons a far simpler task than it once was. The British-based operator will ensure consistency throughout the countries being researched, whilst ensuring that local cultural conditions are not overlooked.

Given that the majority of omnibuses are conducted among consumers – either face to face or by telephone – most comment in this chapter is related to studies among this group.

METHODOLOGY – HOW OMNIBUS SURVEYS WORK

Sampling procedures

The basic method of sample selection offered by face-to-face consumer omnibus companies is random probability or random location. In both cases respondents (or potential respondents) are grouped or clustered so that interviewers work across a manageable geographical area. While this somewhat reduces the statistical reliability of the data it increases the interviewers' 'strike rate', thereby offering cost advantages.

Companies offering a telephone omnibus service generally use a random selection methodology for selecting the telephone number and then impose overall age, sex and class quotas. In order to reach ex-directory consumers (estimated at perhaps 25 per cent) a 'digit plus one' technique is employed, where numbers are selected at random and then one is added to the last digit, eg 020 7207 1234 becomes 020 7207 1235. (This obviously results in selection of non-consumer numbers that are excluded.)

Frequency and sample size

The frequency of any omnibus is naturally dependent on market demands and the company's success in marketing its offer. The more specialized omnibus surveys (eg business-to-business, GPs, etc) tend to run quarterly, or perhaps monthly. In contrast, most of the successful consumer face-to-face and telephone omnibuses in Britain run weekly. It is worth noting that Britain leads the world in the sheer range and frequency of its omnibus services. For example, on the European mainland fortnightly or monthly frequency is the norm, although both France and Germany offer weekly availability. It should also be said that the further south in Europe one goes, the longer everything takes.

Sample sizes per wave tend to vary. Consumer telephone omnibus surveys are likely to offer samples of 1,000 adults per wave, whereas companies offering consumer face-to-face surveys have sample sizes of either 1,000 or 2,000 adults per check. All of the major omnibus surveys offer the following subsamples as part of their standard package:

■ all adults (either 15+ or 16+);
■ men;
■ women;
■ housewives;
■ heads of households.

Additionally, special discounted rates are normally available if the required sample is a specific age group, socioeconomic class group or geographical region (ITV/Registrar General's standard region, etc).

INTERVIEWING

Whether conducted via the telephone or face to face in-home, omnibus companies train their interviewers to the same standards as they would if the work were *ad hoc*. Indeed, most agencies claim to conduct specific training sessions related to the differences in *ad hoc* and omnibus interviewing techniques. The majority of telephone omnibuses are conducted at central location interviewing centres with listening-in facilities where supervisors constantly check the quality of each interviewer's work.

For face-to-face studies, agencies have a degree of supervisor accompaniment, but all agencies employ back-checking procedures to ensure the quality of their interviewing, mostly to Interviewer Quality Control Scheme (IQCS) standards.

QUESTIONNAIRE DESIGN

Everyone wants to be first on the questionnaire! This is a natural request, as omnibus research buyers have two basic fears: 1) that other questions will bias the answers to their own questions; and 2) that the questionnaire will be long so, if they are near the end, the quality of their data might suffer. To be first also guarantees consistency of data when research is conducted across a number of waves.

The ordering of question sets has to be left to the agency and it is its responsibility to ensure that conflicting sets of questions are not carried on the same wave. Some agencies have continuous contracted clients who are always placed first, while others offer the spot on a first come, first served basis. Within the main body of the questionnaire, agency researchers will place question sets as most appropriate, eg fmcg questions together, financial questions together and more personal questions generally at the end. In terms of the overall length of questionnaire, this varies company by company and indeed, to a certain extent, week by week. At certain times of the year (eg pre/post-Christmas) demand equals or sometimes exceeds capacity, and the 'better' agencies try to restrict their questionnaires to a reasonable length.

All agencies carry a standard classification section, which is completed at the end of the interview (for quota-controlled studies some variables, eg age, class, etc are asked upfront). This section normally covers demography, regionality and other important classifications, eg telephone ownership, car ownership, tenure, etc. Some omnibuses collect other classificatory information that can be used for analysis (NOP – trade union membership, cable/satellite TV households, etc).

It is common to use visual aids as stimuli on face-to-face surveys. These may be storyboards of commercials, pack shots, copies of newspaper ads, etc. Given that the size of the visual can be handled easily, they create no problems, since most companies will stipulate A4 size. If, however, the visual aid is a large pack, box, tin or similar, most omnibuses will not accept them as the logistics of getting them to interviewers would be problematic, not to mention that the poor interviewers would have to carry them round.

All agencies will offer a questionnaire design service and the better ones will be gentle but firm over what may or may not be acceptable to the average respondent. These days, there are few taboo subjects as such, but sensitively worded questions are vital and the omnibus company's advice should always be accepted. It is, after all, their job to know what will work and what will merely serve to offend.

DATA COLLECTION

Just as the mid-80s saw the advent of CATI (computer-assisted telephone interviewing) and the subsequent benefits it brought to telephone omnibus surveys, the early 1990s saw CAPI (computer-assisted personal interviewing) adopted as the norm for face-to-face omnibus surveys. All British consumer omnibus studies operate this technique and have done so for some years. However, it has still to gain widespread acceptance on the European mainland –with the notable exception of the IPSOS European Capibus.

ANALYSIS OF DATA

Client and agency will agree a reporting format. The discussion will cover details of the demographic splits required, whether the data shall be grossed up to population estimates and what cross-analysis shall be included. At this stage, possible limitations due to subsample base sizes should also be an important consideration.

Most agencies offer a flexible but restricted package of variables that can be used for cross-analysis. In the main, clients are offered the facility to analyse all of their paid-for questions by one or sometimes two outlines or banners containing up to about 16 variables. Internal cross-analysis, that is question by question, is often 'thrown in' at the quoted price. Should a client require further analysis after receipt of the report, a fee is usually levied.

Omnibus companies vary in terms of tabular presentation but the example table shown (Table 12.1) represents most of the detail that is normally presented, namely unweighted base (number of actual respondents), weighted base (grossed up to population estimates), absolute figures (weighted and grossed-up numbers) and column percentages. It is generally the case that special analysis (cluster/trend/ACORN) and statistical testing are at an extra cost.

The time between end of fieldwork and provision of a tabular report varies between two or three days for CATI studies to eight or ten days for a face-to-face omnibus. A client should, however, be given an exact report

Table 12.1 *Tabular presentation by omnibus company*

GENETICALLY MODIFIED CROPS

Q3. NOW THINKING ABOUT ORGANIC FOOD – I MEAN FOOD GROWN WITHOUT USING ARTIFICIAL FERTILIZERS, PESTICIDES, ETC – HERE ARE SOME THINGS THAT OTHER PEOPLE HAVE SAID ABOUT IT. WHICH ONE OF THE FOLLOWING BEST DESCRIBES YOU?

BASE: ALL

	TOTAL	SEX		AGE			SOCIAL CLASS		TV REGION		
		MALE	FEMALE	15–34	35–54	55+	ABC1	C2DE	NORTH	MIDLANDS	SOUTH
UNWEIGHTED TOTAL	997	483	514	340	341	316	474	523	349	321	327
		48%	52%	34%	34%	32%	48%	52%	35%	32%	33%
WEIGHTED TOTAL	999	480	519	356	322	322	453	546	348	318	332
		48%	52%	36%	32%	32%	45%	55%	35%	32%	33%
I EAT OR BUY AT LEAST SOME ORGANICALLY GROWN FOOD	356	169	186	119	119	119	194	161	127	178	171
	36%	35%	36%	34%	34%	36%	43%	30%	30%	37%	33%
I HAVE TRIED ORGANICALLY GROWN FOOD, BUT COULDN'T TASTE THE DIFFERENCE AND STOPPED	180	123	56	76	76	53	84	96	84	49	47
	18%	26%	11%	21%	21%	16%	18%	18%	24%	15%	14%
I'D LIKE TO BUY ORGANICALLY GROWN FOOD, BUT IT'S TOO EXPENSIVE SO I DON'T	464	187	276	160	160	154	175	288	138	152	174
	46%	39%	53%	45%	45%	48%	39%	53%	40%	48%	53%

timing as soon as the work is accepted and, if necessary, an extended timing if extensive or complex analysis is required.

REPORTING

The provision of printed copies of tabular data and/or data on disk is always included in the price quoted. Some companies will offer either a full interpretative commentary or a management summary report at extra cost.

AFTER-SALES SERVICE

Omnibus clients vary in terms of their experience of research, information needs, budgets and availability of time and people to interpret data tables. Some clients present the agency with a finalized questionnaire and analysis specification at the outset and others are no further along the line than having an outline topic guide. As such, omnibus researchers have to be able to design and present research programmes and/or simply provide a tabular report. The standard quoted cost will certainly include question-naire and analysis design (if required), but, as mentioned, will not include debriefs, interpretative reports and charted presentations.

PRICING

In general, the cost of including questions on an omnibus will be significantly less expensive than conducting an *ad hoc* study to ask the same questions (plus classification questions) of the same sample. There are, however, significant differences between omnibus agencies in both the methods used to price an omnibus question set and the end cost.

First, we will look at the comparison between telephone omnibuses and face-to-face omnibuses. Perhaps surprisingly, there is very little difference between the cost of studies conducted by telephone and those conducted via face-to-face quota omnibuses. There are, however, significant differences between the face-to-face omnibuses, not least because in a competitive commodity market such as omnibus the buyer may be able to negotiate a significantly discounted price.

A comparison of some of the major face-to-face rate cards has been indexed to show some of the differences in pricing as at 1998 (all prices are based on the equivalent of a 2,000-adult sample). This is shown in Table 12.2.

Table 12.2 *Comparisons of prices for omnibus surveys*

	A	B	C	D	E
Cost per question	85	80	84	100	86
Entry fee	NIL	NIL	NIL	NIL	100
Show cards	NIL	57	100	NIL	86

Notes: 1) Letters A to E represent five different omnibus surveys.
2) Prices are expressed as an index where 100 is the highest of the 5 surveys.

Though entry fee and show cards are an important cost consideration, the price of a question is generally the most important determinant of final cost. As can be seen above, the cost per question of 2,000 adults can indeed vary. The view taken on entry fees and show cards varies even more dramatically, and for a very short questionnaire they can be a significant part of the overall cost. Additionally, companies take differing stances as to what constitutes a question (particularly for semantic scales), how much extra an open-ended question will cost and volume discounts for commissioning multi-stage / wave projects.

APPLICATIONS

Strange requests have been made, such as the following:

- measuring the height of beds;
- checking brand names on electric blankets (necessitating unmaking the bed);
- verifying 'vital statistics' during the actual interview.

But more common uses include:

- **Tracking** This is done for new product launches, advertising monitoring and brand share measurement. Omnibus surveys are regular and thereby able to accommodate the required timetable. They offer consistent quality, providing well-matched samples over time.

  Geographical or target group sample sizes can be a problem but can be built up over a number of waves of fieldwork.
- **Usage and attitude** They are an efficient way of undertaking small-scale (in terms of questionnaire length) usage and attitude studies.
- **Image research** They are ideal for measuring the image of brands or manufacturers (brand association techniques are particularly cost-effective) and tracking across time.

- **Concept testing/name research** They are excellent for screening and short-listing a range of concept stimuli in the form of either visuals or verbal descriptions.
- **Product testing** Face-to-face omnibuses can be used to 'drop off' products to relevant respondents for subsequent in-home testing. Recalls can be in the form of self-completion questionnaires or telephone follow-up. Remember that the product must be small, light and available in sufficient quantities to allow spares – the number of qualifying respondents is likely to vary between interviewers. (NB: some companies may well refuse to place products via their omnibus.)
- **Media research** They are particularly useful for obtaining interim readership levels between standard NRS reporting periods (eg following editorial changes) and for building up sample sizes of minority titles.
- **Editorial** They are a simple and efficient method of obtaining data for editorial usage for press, TV and radio.
- **Minority samples** They can provide the location of qualifying minority samples for subsequent follow-up interview. (Note that omnibus suppliers will often not release respondents' names and addresses to third parties and will therefore expect to be commissioned to conduct the follow-up research.)
- **Retail research** Large multiples can obtain reliable data on who shops where and why. Omnibus research can be used to collect 'spend' data on a recall basis, but one must ensure representation of all days of the week within the fieldwork period (buying 'yesterday' is also a problem if the omnibus is biased by day of interview). Often relatively large sample sizes are required to provide reliable data for individual chains or regionally based outlets.

Some other uses of omnibus research include the following:

- It can be used as a 'toe-in-the-water' measure, ie as an extra to desk research or where desk research cannot yield basic measures. It is often used by ad agencies in 'account pitches'. For some non-research-oriented companies, it may be their first real experience of 'hands-on' market research.
- Respondents can be interviewed at home about their working environment, ie as employee or self-employed person. This is particularly useful when respondents work in an industry or profession that is generally accepted as being 'overresearched', or where the development of a working environment sampling frame or a screening process would be difficult.
- It can be used as a means of establishing profiles for setting quota controls for *ad hoc* research or to post-weight or gross up existing *ad hoc* data.

■ It can be used as a basis for recruiting panels – large sample sizes tend to make it easy to establish panels of suitable size and to top up or balance panels as they age.

SETTING UP A STUDY

There are a number of variables that will affect the choice of which omnibus agency or type of omnibus to select. Listed below are some of the more important considerations:

■ sample size;
■ frequency of fieldwork;
■ speed of reporting;
■ pricing;
■ reputation of supplier.

Additionally, there are a number of fundamental questions that need to be asked:

■ average length of survey in total;
■ positioning of questionnaire;
■ classification data available for analysis;
■ timetable – commissioning to reporting;
■ client service.

In order for the agency to be able to provide an accurate quotation and to ensure that the question set can be accommodated, there are a number of questions a client might (in fact, *ought to*) be asked (and should be aware of) before a price is given, namely:

■ subject matter;
■ number of actual questions (1a–d is not one question!);
■ proportion (or guestimate of proportion) answering each question;
■ structure of questions (open-ended/scales, etc);
■ necessity for show cards/special visual aids, etc;
■ overall sample (adults, housewives, etc);
■ analysis requirements (level of cross-tabulation);
■ timing and frequency of study.

In many respects, an omnibus is a series of *ad hoc* studies. Therefore, when using such a service, exactly the same level of care has to be taken in formatting questions, designing analysis specifications, interpreting data, etc, as one might for a 'custom-designed' study. If this is adhered to, a client using an omnibus facility should be able to take advantage of a quality service, obtained at a less expensive cost than that of comparable *ad hoc* research. It should never be considered, however, as research 'on the cheap'.

13

Panels and Diaries

W G Blyth

WHAT IS PANEL RESEARCH?

The essential distinguishing characteristic of panel research is that the same data are collected repeatedly from a representative sample of the defined survey population. Typically, these data are behavioural, rather than attitudinal, but not exclusively so. The frequency of the data collection and the data collection media vary depending on the subject matter, the application of the data, the desired level of accuracy, the budget available for the research and the required speed of reporting. As with all research, the final design represents a trade-off between these factors.

From the purely statistical perspective, replicated measurements on the same respondents provide a much more accurate measurement of changes over time than measurements from matched independent samples.

With regard to marketing applications, panels provide the opportunity to combine accurate absolute measurements of such parameters as expenditure and volume with the ability to analyse individual micro-behaviour and its change over time. These analyses can be used to provide guidance in areas such as pricing, advertising effectiveness, new product sales projections, stock range, etc. The advent of more powerful and cheaper computing coupled with more flexible software tools has greatly expanded the range and facility of such analysis.

TYPES OF PANEL RESEARCH

In the last decade market research world-wide has doubled in real value. This has been caused by both strong growth in mature industrial economies and the penetration of large-scale research into new countries particularly in Asia-Pacific and South America.

One of the results of this growth has been an expansion in the use of panel research, both in the products that are measured and the countries these are measured in. Alongside of the impact of real growth and globalization have been the impact of new technology and the integration of computing and telecommunications; the effects of this latter are still only really starting to be understood.

Thus in the 10 years that have passed since the first edition of this handbook the panel research area has been substantially transformed. This transformation has not, however, been a step change, but rather has been evolutionary. As techniques employing technology and high-investment labour reduction have been introduced into mature markets such as the UK and Germany, existing techniques such as interviewer-administered data collection have been extended to developing markets.

Within Western Europe the best-known examples of panel research are the continuous consumer purchasing panels either of households or individuals covering grocery, food and drink, and toiletries. The provision of these panels is dominated by a small number of large multinational research agencies. These now consist of Taylor Nelson Sofres, GfK and ACNielsen, which has moved increasingly into consumer panels in recent years. The other major use of panel research has historically been for television audience research (which is covered in Chapter 21).

The first commercial continuous consumer panel in the UK was the Attwood panel, launched in 1948, which was developed out of work carried out during the Second World War for the government. Since then the number of panel services available internationally has steadily increased. The 1960s saw the development by AGB of the Television Consumer Audit (TCA) and the conjunction of this services launch with major changes in the retail environment led to panels being increasingly used for market measurement as well as diagnostics. The 1970s also saw the growth of panels in Europe and their extension to individual products, and in the USA. The application of more sophisticated marketing techniques to mass industrial markets such as agrochemicals, ethical pharmaceuticals and office equipment also led to the development of a number of panel-type services in these product areas.

Finally, there are instances of panels being used to collect opinion and attitude data. The best known of these are the Nuffield electoral studies initially reported by Butler and Stokes, which still continue under different control and, more recently, the British Public Attitude Survey, funded by the ESRC and carried out by Roger Jowell of SCPR. While these are strictly speaking panel research, the methodological issues involved in asking such questions from the sample over time are distinct from the more general application of panel research. They are not covered in this chapter.

WHEN PANELS ARE APPROPRIATE

Panel research, as defined above, is not about answering 'Why?' It is about asking 'What?'-type questions that are capable of validation. As a simple model, one can divide research into two data types:

1. What?
   - Who are you?
   - What do you buy?
   - Where do you buy?
   - How much?
   - Price?
   - When?
   - What else could you have bought?
   - Where else could you have bought it?
2. Inferential
   - Why?
   - What will you do next?
   - How do I influence/change this?

The 'What?'-type questions fit into a model of every market, be it a good or service, and these are what panels are about. The art is the trade-off that exists between breadth and depth.

Typically in a commercial research context, panels are used to provide quantified grossed-up measurements drawn from samples of individuals or households. To provide accurate market measurements down to individual brands or brand sizes requires very large sample sizes.

Two other primary aspects of panels that make them particularly suitable for fmcg markets are the ability to provide frequent measurement, and the ability to provide consistent trend data. These points are discussed in more detail below.

In summary the key characteristics of panel research are:

■ grossed-up quantification of 'What?' questions;
■ large sample sizes;
■ frequent data collection;
■ repetition of the same data over time;
■ larger user base.

DESIGN AND CONTROL ISSUES

Superficially, panel research design is similar to that of one-off quantitative survey design – a defined sample universe, sampling frames, sample design, a data collection methodology, data encoding and processing, data weighting and analysis. Generally what is good practice *ad hoc* is also so in panel design with regard to response rates, quality control, document design and, where appropriate, interviewer training. However, by virtue of being a continuous measurement over time of the same data from essentially the same sample, panel design and conduct vary from *ad hoc* in a number of significant ways.

Panel research can only meet its objectives if it provides consistent trend data over very long time periods. The purchase of any continuous data series is a large investment, which is undermined if there is any uncontrolled variation in trends or where some exogenous factor forces a change in methodology. It follows that once a panel methodology has been specified and put in place, it is rarely changed. The initial design must therefore be as accurate as possible, and also be capable of maintenance at the same level of quality over time. The latter forms the greater part of the science or art of panel research. It should be borne in mind that in today's marketing environment most users of panel research have either continuous production or sales data relating to their own products or services. These data series will be used to monitor the consistency of the panel measurement and thus provide the confidence to use the measurement as part of marketing planning and evaluation.

In methodological terms one can summarize panel control as having the objective of keeping all biases constant, and panel design as minimizing the initial bias. In the next sections we will discuss design and control in detail.

SAMPLING, RECRUITMENT AND PANEL MEMBER CONTROL

The statistical theory of sampling applies in the same way to panels as to any sample survey and is not addressed here. Reference has already been made to the statistical theory underlying the fact that replicated measures from a panel provide more accurate measurements of change over time. This section is concerned with the practical aspects of panel management:

■ recruiting a representative sample of the required population to a panel;
■ keeping the maximum proportion of that recruited sample reporting over time;

■ replacing panel members who leave with similar entities so as to maintain consistency of trend measurement.

The launching of a new panel service is not a frequent event. In consequence there is not an established methodology. In addition, different services will have different cost constraints depending on their area of application, and their designers will have access to different facilities. Note that the approach outlined below is the author's personal preference.

Recruitment

One can identify the following stages:

1. Sample design;
2. Sample selection;
3. Sample contact, classification and task description;
4. Sample recruitment (ie agreement to task).

Stage 4 is the additional step for the panel researcher. Stage 3 is much the same as interviewing in *ad hoc* research and, if a random sample is used, will get similar response rates.

Recruitment rates to panels are not as high as response rates to random samples. Generalizations are difficult to make, as the recruitment rate will vary depending on the perceived scale of the task in terms of time, the complexity of the task, the perceived personal and social relevance or value of the task and the value of the incentive offered. Generally speaking, between 30 and 60 per cent of the contact sample will agree to join a panel, once its purpose has been explained. It is undesirable to minimize the task that is involved in panel membership when briefing potential panel members. This will only result in high levels of panel dropout in the early periods of operation. This is costly, inefficient and causes great problems in maintaining representativeness.

Recruitment rates to panels will vary by demographic subgroup. The nature of the variation will depend on the subject and the data collection methodology. If the process of recruitment is completely integrated into the contact sample screening, it will be realized that the size of the contract sample will be driven by the lowest subgroup recruitment rate. If proportionally representative screening samples are being employed, this differential recruitment rate results in large numbers of wasted contacts in the easier subgroups, again costing time and money. For this reason the accepted approach has become to separate contact sample screening, classification and recruitment.

Given the low levels of recruitment rates, and their differential aspect by demographics and other key variables, the preferred method of sample design and recruitment is via some form of quota sampling. Quotas act as explicit stratifiers, so as with all sample design the issue is which variables to stratify by. Again, this will depend on the subject matter. However, in addition to basic demographics it may be desirable to have some behavioural controls, if possible. Thus, for example, a panel designed to measure cigarette brand purchasing should be controlled by weight of consumption. For household-based samples the classic controls would be region, household size, age of housewife and some social grade measure. Housewives' working status, presence of children, car ownership, etc may also be desirable. One approach is to group variables as in life cycle, another to control by geodemographics. There is no one or simple answer. There is a limit to the number of variables by which the sample can be controlled, as there is a limit to the number of variables by which it can be weighted. Clearly, in the absence of prior experience, piloting and modelling have a role to play.

The most efficient way to recruit a panel is to have a large-scale screening or establishment survey on which the relevant classification questions may be asked. Respondents can be asked about their willingness to take part in further research and the responses stored on a database. From a cost point of view it is preferable that such screening be undertaken as part of another survey, eg an omnibus, *so long* as the host survey's basic design, in terms of numbers and size of sampling points, will permit the attainment of the basic panel sample design. Such an establishment survey provides the contact sample for recruitment. Researchers should also make sure when following such procedures that they are complying fully with both the ESOMAR Code of Conduct and whatever data protection legislation is operating in the country in which they are working. Indeed, as a general point of caution, panel research by its very nature requires details of respondents to be maintained over time. It follows that panel researchers in their operations cannot make their data completely anonymous, but rather at best can only hold it in an unidentifiable manner, which will require especial care in the design and security of their databases.

The panel researcher should pilot alternative methods of recruitment, and on such a scale as to enable quantification by demographic subgroup of the likely response rates. This will permit differential issuing of contacts to the field to maximize the speed and efficiency of the recruitment operation. Depending on resources, recruitment can be by telephone, post, in person or a mixture of the three.

Some panel operators are now experimenting with the use of the Internet both to recruit panel members and to collect data, and we are likely to see an expansion of the use of this new medium in the next few years, particularly in those countries or amongst those population subgroups where penetration is highest. I would stress that the same principles will apply to the use of the Internet as to any other media of communication or data collection. Some panel tasks are best explained in person and require on-the-spot training. Others, which are simpler, may only require post, or post and telephone.

Recruitment invariably involves panel member training, ie showing what one wants people to do. Given that the eventual success of the research depends on the goodwill of panel members and the skill with which they perform the task, the greater the resource put in at this stage, then the greater the benefit. Opportunity should be taken at the recruitment stage to check the classification details are already obtained, and to extend them where relevant.

Continuous sample maintenance

At this stage one should have achieved the target sample size, balanced by its controls. The next task, both to protect that investment and to ensure the fullest utility of continuous panel analysis, is to keep as many panel members reporting consistently for as long as is desired. Note that in the absence of any evidence of either conditioning or reporting fatigue (see the section on quality control below), the preferred policy is not to discard panel members except in the case of poor compliance.

There is an implicit contract between the researcher and the panel member, which must be honoured on both sides. The task must be as described and not suddenly increased, although occasional variety is to be desired. People should not be made to feel inadequate. It's not an exam! For members of the public, levels of incentive do not have to represent a rate per hour similar to paid employment, but neither should payments be so small as to be derisory. Panel operators are naturally secretive about the exact levels and methods of incentives that they use, representing, as they do, the result of much experimentation over time. Typically they will follow some kind of points scheme, building up over time to encourage longer panel membership, although examples exist in some panels in the USA of a percentage of the value of shopping measured. Incentives may be varied to include prize draws and mystery gifts, and there may not be a flat rate for all panel members.

Communication is just as important as incentivization. The use of a newsletter with information about other panel members will increase the sense of being members of a team. Such a newsletter can also be used to give examples of how the answers are used to support the sense of the utility of the task, and to provide reminders of specific aspects of the panel member task. The implicit contract that exists also provides the opportunity to communicate when mistakes are made. Panel members will not respect an organization that ignores blatant and repeated non-compliance. Quality control procedures need to be put in place to deal with this.

Finally, there should, where feasible, be more than simple written communication. A personal visit or a telephone call once or twice a year enables classification to be checked, any problems to be dealt with (eg incentive receipt) and comments taken. Today's computer systems enable simple little touches such as the correct despatch of birthday and Christmas cards, or other personal gestures.

A panel should have as its objective a continuity in excess of 80 per cent. By that it is meant that 80 per cent of those who are panel members on 1 January are still panel members the following 31 December. Achievement of such a level of continuity will ensure that there is a reasonable probability of a close correspondence between the data from the continuous panel and the 'live' panel. This makes the dual use of the data for market measurement and diagnostics easier in terms of analysis and reconciliation needs.

Panel replacement

There is always a constant, though hopefully small, turnover of panel members. Some people stop because they no longer find it rewarding, others die or become sick, others move and others are discards. In the same way that recruitment is differential by demographic subgroup, dropout will be differential within that. Care also has to be taken to check that dropouts are not behaviourally different in a manner that affects results, eg heavy buyers, multiple-grocer-only users or price-conscious. Detailed analysis of dropouts, both by demographics and earlier reporting, enables such characteristics to be identified. Care must then be taken, as far as possible, to replace them with similar people, again via an ongoing screening sample.

DATA COLLECTION

The detail of the data collection method is critical both to the quality of the data and to the complexity and scale of the task (and hence to the length of panel life). Excluding television research, the choice until only a few years ago was simply between some form of self-completion diary returned by post and an interviewer-administered check. Today the options are substantially greater and increasing rapidly, to include CATI-operated data collection, personal computers in all their manifestations, smart cards, touch-tone phones, videotext, bar code readers, the Internet and, further down the road, such developing technologies as speech recognition. There follows a brief outline of the primary systems.

Diaries

Internationally, self-completion diaries have been the most common form of data collection media. Depending on the product field, diaries are designed for either the individual or the household. In the latter case they are normally completed by the housewife. A diary will cover a finite time period, typically a week, and will consist of a number of product field 'questionnaires'. These will follow much the same format. Depending on the size of the product field, the level of detail required and the volume of purchasing, the diary format may be either structured, ie all answers pre-coded, or semi-structured, ie respondents writing in brand, variant, shop, price, offer type, etc. Pre-coded diaries are easier from the data entry side, but for today's markets may require either very long code lists or very small print to keep the diary to a reasonable size.

Semi-structured diaries require less space and can rely on the 'training' aspect of panel research to obtain good quality response. However, they need to be supported by sophisticated screen-based data entry systems to eliminate the vagaries of manual coding, and unacceptably slow report delivery times.

The most complex part of diary design of either type is the ability to update or amend the diary as needs change over time, eg measurement of new product fields, or the need to identify new types of brand variant, eg additive-free.

Levels of response can be affected by among other factors:

- change of diary length;
- change of paper size;
- change of paper colours;
- change of product field order;
- change of space allocation to a specific field.

For all but minor changes, it is judicious to test the impact of planned diary changes. By their very nature panels are very suitable for testing design impacts by taking a test sample and matched control group.

It is not intended to go into great detail about the actual layout of diaries. The same rules apply as with any self-completion questionnaire: clarity, succinctness, simplicity, adequate signalization and the use of all design techniques available. Any researcher who is experienced in such matters, but who has to design such research, may be well advised to call in the services of a design consultant at an early stage.

In-home interviewer checks

For many years the UK panel research market was dominated by an interviewer-administered service called the TCA. Conceived and operated by AGB and highly important in their success, it was known as 'the dustbin audit' because the interviewers originally used to check the details of the products that had been bought and used in the home. Its introduction in 1964 was in a society whose everyday characteristics have long disappeared. These characteristics included a society with little divorce, stable family units, non-working housewives who were invariably female, retail price maintenance (ie no price cutting), no supermarkets or superstores, and no private label. Shopping was frequent, food was fresh, and low car ownership and little use of refrigeration in-home meant small and consistent pack sizes.

Low labour costs enabled the use of a field force to visit personally the 6,000 homes in the sample each week to collect purchasing data. This approach ensured a high level of data accuracy, fast reporting and good panel continuity. These virtues, combined with proprietary software and data entry systems, enabled this method to last successfully until the beginning of the 1990s. By then the combined effects of rising labour costs, product proliferation and retail competition had made this a formula whose time had passed in the UK and indeed the rest of Europe. The TCA was replaced by a system using in-home bar code scanning (see below). However, the same principle of interviewer data collection is now being successfully introduced into markets such as China where the growing need for panel data is still within a labour market where this approach is affordable and where the level of literacy and comprehension amongst consumers gives this approach certain merits compared with pure self-completion.

Thus we have an example of the transfer of methodology from one market to another, and this is going to be an increasing phenomenon. The challenge this offers researchers is that there is a need to ensure that data collected using different methodologies is sufficiently understood, so that clients combining data across countries are able to use it in a consistent manner if the methodology used in one country results in different degrees of accuracy from those of the data provided in another.

Bar code reading

One innovation more than any other is changing the face of panel research. This is the introduction of EAN coding (electrical article numbering or bar codes on products) and the increasing utilization of scanning technology at the point of sale (EPOS or scanning). EAN coding gives unique identification of products down to brand, size, flavour and offer. The information embedded in a bar code is the same as required to be given by panel members, but is much more succinct if the meaning of the bar code is known. Simultaneously, retailers have been using EAN codes to increase the efficiency of their check-out operations through faster entry of purchases, and by the information such computerized scanning check-out systems provide. Such systems are revolutionizing not just panel research but also retail-based measurement.

The advent of this technology first occurred in the USA. It was recognized in the early 1980s by a company called Information Resource Incorporated (IRI) that such retailer systems could be used passively to provide consumer-based information. The panel smart card approach involved issuing panel members with a smart card – similar to a credit card – which was presented at the check-out. Details of household demographics were linked via the card ID number, and details of the purchases in the 'shopping basket' downloaded from the retailer's own computer.

To achieve accurate data required not only the co-operation of the panel member, but also that of all retailers in the sampling points forming the master sample, who unsurprisingly charged for the data and/or needed to have the relevant scanning equipment installed on their premises. The load on the panel member was relatively transparent and, *if* retailer co-operation was achieved, offered substantial benefits against paper-based systems. It did, however, require a very high level of existing scanning usage by retailers, and the presence of defined shopping catchment areas. Such conditions were more easily met in the USA than as yet in Europe. Indeed, given the high concentration of the UK population in conurbations, such conditions will never be met on a widespread geographical basis.

Subject to these caveats, this approach offered many permutations in terms of datasets and applications. Data could be linked with in-store activity regarding prices, range and facings to examine the efficiency of below-the-line activity. Panel members' homes could be linked to TV meters to provide single-source data integrating advertising exposure, below-the-line and purchasing. A representative sample of areas could be grossed up to provide national sales estimates integrated with total retailer sales estimates.

This approach has now been superseded by the use of in-home bar code readers, which are issued to panel members, linked to a small personal data terminal or PC. Building a panel in this fashion removes the need for retailer co-operation and the use of a small number of areas. The investment involved is substantial. One is essentially replacing a paper self-completion diary with an electronic device that is one of several thousand linked telephonically to a central computer. This alone requires a high level of investment in IT and telecom infrastructure and support resource. Additionally the research company needs to be able to interpret the meaning of many hundreds of thousands if not millions of bar codes, as it requires to know not only the bar codes and their meaning for the products it is interested in, but also the bar codes it is not interested in, so that they can be discarded at analysis stage. This is because it is not accurate to ask panel members to read only certain bar codes. Rather, panel members essentially record the bar codes of everything they bring into the house.

The scale and complexity of these systems mean that there will only be a market opportunity for a small number of suppliers in total and rarely more than two in any one country. In the UK, AGB replaced the TCA with a service known as Superpanel, which with a panel size of 10,000 households is now the leader in the market. Competition comes from ACNielsen's Homescan service. AGB, which is now part of Taylor Nelson Sofres, operates similar panels in France, Spain and Ireland. GfK operates them in Germany, the Netherlands, Italy and Switzerland. The service ACN competes in most of these markets with panels as well as retailer measurements.

The data collected from these panels are the same as in self-completion, but with the panel member recording purchases as they are brought into the home using the terminal. Details of the product are collected via the bar code with purchaser price details (if required) entered via the keyboard or a master codebook of bar codes. The panels are recruited and managed as previously described. The details of the data are then transmitted via the telephone line to a host computer in a way similar to TV audience researchers' 'peoplemeters'.

It should be borne in mind that the data provided by such services are essentially the same as from previous services. EDC presents the opportunity for more accurate data capture techniques, but the use of technology typically designed for industrial purposes requires researchers to absorb new skills – for example, ergonomics – to position these methods properly for the ordinary household member.

CATI panels

Some product fields by their very nature do not lend themselves to data collection by bar code readers, for example products bought and consumed outside the home. Other types of behaviour may be so frequent or complex or diverse as to be unsuitable for purely self-completion recording, either because the data is not recorded accurately enough or because it is under-recorded. To redress these difficulties some panels have been designed and implemented using a hybrid technique combining some minimal level of data recording by the panel member, which is then supplemented by data collection and amplification by a CATI interviewer supported by state-of-the-art software for call scheduling and data entry. In these panels one could liken the data collection to semi-structured interviewing, as the task of the interviewer is to collect the fullest possible dataset by probing or prompting supported by past behavioural information. Because the panels involved are concerned to collect hard behavioural data the use of the interviewer in this manner is a positive contribution rather than a biasing or conditioning role as it would be, for example, in attitude research. Taylor Nelson run a number of panels employing this approach on such markets as confectionery and soft drinks.

The technique does require a well-equipped CATI unit, but can clearly provide international application, consistency and economies of scale. This is an area that is likely to grow as manufacturers and service providers increasingly research personal and leisure markets. The technique provides the benefits of personal interviewer contact at a lower price and at a time tailored to meet the busy lifestyle of people in today's society. It is particularly good for the younger consumer and those who find detailed self-completion onerous or too intrusive. As the costs of telephone collection fall and international call centre co-ordination grows this technique will prove cheaper in real terms over the next 10–15 years. CATI interviewing is increasingly seen as providing better-quality, better-motivated and better-managed interviewers. The lower cost barriers to entry of this approach make it a growth candidate for the future.

One possible extension of this area as technology evolves will be the integration into it of speech-recognition and text-to-speech technology. The combination of the two could provide most of the same benefits without the need for interviewers. It is the most cybernetic of all the panel methods on the current horizon. It will be feasible within the next five years!

The Internet as data collection medium

When this chapter was written 11 years ago the PC was still a new phenomenon whose impact on the world IBM had not yet grasped. The Internet has arrived and, like it or not, is here for the immediate future. It will provide an alternative to the PC in that it can be used for interactive self-completion rather than passive EDC. From the panel research perspective the design of self-completion questionnaires with an electronic display is not a new problem. The Internet presents some special problems in some areas outside the panel members' control. For example, the setup of the screen is in the hands of the user including the colour of the back screen. This may be important for some types of research where emotions are involved, but is unlikely to be important for panel researchers. Problems of representativeness of the Internet-using population are not particular to panel research and require no special comment.

It will become important and in the short term in Europe this will be for specialized user populations, eg veterinarians. Its longer-term future for research, and panels in particular, will depend, I believe, much more on how we see the technology of the Internet converging with that of digital television and the services provided by cable owners and especially in the features of the equipment with which such services are delivered in the home. Since companies like Microsoft and BT don't seem as yet to know the answer to this question, it is too early to provide a prognosis of the implications of all this for panel research!

Quality control

Irrespective of whether one is using high-tech data capture or pencil and paper, a panel will stand or fall by the quality of its measurement, particularly, as already stated, that of data trend.

Attention has already been drawn to sources of uncontrolled bias in both recruitment and diary design. In addition there is the question of compliance. Are panel members doing the allotted task? Are they doing it consistently? Improved computer software allows an ever greater range of quality control procedures. Some examples are as follows:

■ In the period immediately after recruitment, panel members may overrecord their purchasing, as it is a high-profile task. Typically, early panel recording is not to be used.
■ Norms can be established for certain types of behaviour, either at recruitment, eg cigarette consumption, or against the panel as a whole, eg volume and value of purchasing increases with household size. Variations around the average can be checked, and queries followed up with further questioning.
■ Purchasing of staple products can be checked as indicative of the overall completion quality.
■ Homes that give rise to relatively high numbers of editing corrections can be identified.
■ For individuals, variations in recording from period to period can be checked.
■ Abnormally large purchasing volumes can be identified and queried.
■ Reporting over time can be normalized to check for evidence of decay or conditioning. (No systematic evidence of the latter has ever been identified.)

Such checks, together with validation (see below), serve to ensure the consistency of the measurements.

WEIGHTING, PROJECTION AND ESTIMATION

Weighting is widely practised by market researchers but rarely discussed in detail, either theoretically or practically. Most panels employ some form of demographic weighting to take out the effects of variations in panel balance. This is typically matrix-type weighting similar to that used on other major industry surveys such as the National Readership Survey, although rim weighting is increasingly popular. Data is normally projected to national totals. Again this presents little problem since the issue here is one of the sourcing of updates for universe estimates, and the frequency with which they are applied. For example, external control data, eg government statistics, are only updated annually, but where there is rapid universe change this may result in discontinuities in the data source. The alternative is to use some moving average based on a forecast, which can be adjusted once the new control data becomes available. In the UK the speed of demographic and population change is insufficient to warrant this.

Estimation is a term to cover a more complex set of issues. In recent years many more sources of data, particularly retail data and manu-facturers' delivery data, have reached a high level of accuracy, sufficient in some instances to be used as separate control data. With modern weighting, imputation and fusion systems it is becoming increasingly feasible to produce 'best estimates' based on a variety of sources, but fed into a single adjusted raw dataset. Readers are referred to the paper by Bowles and Blyth (1985) for a discussion of this issue.

VALIDATION

Panels measure sales to domestic consumers, primarily purchases brought into the home. In consequence there will always be a gap between sales as measured by a manufacturer or retailer and sales measured by a panel. This will be due to damaged stock, returns, purchases by the catering trade, office purchasing, export leakage, double retailer buying and pilfering. The level of this will vary from product field to product field. For washing powders nearly 100 per cent of produce is sold into homes, for beverages such as tea or coffee it will be substantially lower. For validation, allowance has to be made for this and for how change may occur over time, eg due to a greater percentage of eating occasions being out of the home. Ex-factory figures will also vary from purchasing due to changes in stock levels in the retail trade. However, once account is taken of such facts, experience over many years in many countries shows an extremely high correlation between panel measurements and sales. Otherwise panels would not have reached the scale they are at today.

PANEL ANALYSIS

The primary outputs of panels are four-weekly or monthly reports on market value, volumes and consumer penetration. Data are also provided on a regional basis and by retailers. In the UK and a number of other countries, panels are unique in being able to provide brand shares within named retailers, a facility unavailable to retail audits owing to the contractual arrangements that exist with the data providers.

In addition to providing such regular aggregated data, panels are also used for the analysis of individual/household purchasing over time to give an understanding of market dynamics. In addition to demographics of both purchasers and purchasing, panel operators have, over time, developed a range of analyses that capitalize on the special unique characteristics of panel data.

Repeat purchasing over time is unique in that it has been shown that brand and product field purchasing is subject to law-like relationships, which have been empirically derived and unified within a single theory by Goodhardt, Ehrenberg and Chatfield (1980).

For such analyses it is feasible to predict long-term brand share from early trial, cannibalization of existing brands by new brand launches, duplication of purchasing between brands, the importance of heavy buyers in a field and where sales are being lost or won, to name a few. It is possible to install television audience measurement meters into panel member homes so that the effect of advertising on sales can be modelled. It is possible to isolate homes that have received promotional material through their letter boxes and examine the effect of special offers on brand loyalty.

Panel operators have become increasingly sophisticated in the analyses they carry out. A good description of these is given in the chapter on panel research in the new edition of the *Consumer Market Research Handbook* (Parfitt, 1986).

The future

Writing 11 years ago, I made the following predictions:

Data collection

- In-home electronic EDC will replace self-completion for nationally representative panels.
- Costs will drive international convergence and standardization of techniques.
- True single source will fail under the combined pressure of costs, analysis difficulties, incongruities with established currency measures and the encroachment of fusion techniques.
- Smart card technology will provide test market/in-store testing, but will otherwise develop slowly.
- Experimentation will continue with other media, eg videotext and data broadcasting.

Commercially

- Panels will expand into the economies of South America and the Asia-Pacific Basin, including Japan.
- Investment will require further international amalgamation.
- There will be increasing integration of retail and consumer data.

Analytically

- The data explosion that is occurring will increase the investment in output and expert systems.
- Attention will be focused on looking to generalize the existing theories of buyer behaviour.
- There will be a growth in specialist information systems and analysis consultancies. Initially this will be outside the existing accountancy-based management consultancies.

Human resources

- There will be a significant shortage of personnel with the skills needed to design and use the panel data.

Of these, the data analysis area has yet to come true. The human resource shortage has been avoided in part by standardization and sharing of resources through rationalization. The rest has largely come to pass although, as with all of life, not necessarily in the manner one might have expected. The next 10 years will be more of the same with, I believe, the data analysis aspect coming true.

What will be new is the use of panels in totally new areas, in particular behaviour. Manufacturers, and more urgently service providers and governments, will want to understand the answers to the big questions.

HOW DO PEOPLE PASS THEIR TIME? CAN I HAVE MORE OF IT?

Western economies are locked in a battle to provide consumers with new ways of saving time or new ways of wasting it. Panels will be the answer. There will be a profitable future for the agency that measures this!

Readers wanting to find out more about the panels that are currently available around the world should visit the Web sites of the major providers, where much detail is available. These are Taylor Nelson Sofres, GfK, NPD, and ACNielsen.

REFERENCES AND FURTHER READING

Advertising Research Foundation (1989) The ARF scanner-based services fact sheet, ARF, New York

Bowles, T and Blyth, B (1985) How do you like your data: raw, al dente or stewed?, *Journal of the Market Research Society*, **27**

Buck, S F (1982) Consumer panels in the UK: past, present and future, Market Research Society Conference, UK

Ehrenberg, A S C (1988) *Repeat Buying*, Griffin, London

Goodhardt, G J, Ehrenberg, A S C and Chatfield, C (1980) The Dirichlet model, *JRSS* (A), **147**

Kent, R A (1989) *Continuous Consumer Market Measurement*, Edward Arnold, London

Lievesley, D and Waterton, J (1985) in *British Social Attitudes*, ed R Jowell, SCPR, London

Moser, C A and Kalton, G (1979) *Survey Methods in Social Investigation*, pp 137–43, Gower, London

Parfitt, J (1986) Panel research in *Consumer Market Research Handbook*, ed R M Worcester and J Downham, McGraw-Hill, London

Parfitt, J and Collins, B J K (1968) Use of consumer panels, *Journal of Marketing Research*, **5**

Wellan, D M and Ehrenberg, A S C (1987) A successful new brand: Shield in the UK, London Business School, C Mac working paper

14

Retail Audits

Terry McCarthy

Retail audits measure volume and availability of products at the point of sale, being based on data collected or at least identified at individual retail outlet level. There is no reliance on consumer response, merely a measure taken as to what has been purchased from the outlet – thus there is no knowledge of who did the purchasing or why a purchase was made.

An audit requires considerable commitment from both the client and agency. The client must not only take account of the cost – often a significant part of the research budget – but also realize that the value of the data is limited, unless he or she is buying into an existing syndicated service, while history is being built up. Similarly, the agency needs to set up a large field and/or data processing capacity to handle the enormous collection and inflow of data for any national survey. Thus, as mutual protection, contracts are normally signed on the basis of several years' commitment, with a minimum cancellation period even after this. The stability of the service is often further guaranteed by syndication, whereby either the agency has agreements with several companies that wish to research the same trade sectors or several companies agree among themselves on the need for a service into a trade sector and approach agencies who might be interested in setting up a survey. Despite the relatively high spend needed for retail audit research, the documentation of techniques and uses can at best be described as sparse, as illustrated by the absence of reference to other works in this chapter.

The syndicated nature of such surveys has meant that traditionally they have been carried out in specific trade types, and this has left the client with an incomplete picture of the total market-place. Such a compromise has been justified on the grounds of cost-effectiveness. Recently, there has been a greater demand by manufacturers for a complete picture of their retail market-place. This has manifested itself in either a joint approach to an agency – as for example the tobacco companies – or occasionally an approach from a larger company that considers the high investment in a non-syndicated service geared to its own specific needs to be worth while in terms of the competitive edge gained. Generally, non-syndicated projects are more likely to be limited in scope. They may be special area test market measurements or limited time period monitors (with or without a controlled environment) rather than an attempt to measure the ongoing national performance of the total market.

TECHNIQUE

The traditional method of data collection in audit surveys was for a fieldworker to call on a sample of retail premises at a designated point in time, and record the stock levels of all products that were of interest. Often, in a successfully run syndicated service, this meant counting stocks for a large proportion of the goods handled by that particular outlet. The fieldworker (and in the interests of fostering an ongoing relationship, it was often the same person) returned, normally one or two months later, and repeated the stock counts. At the same time he or she ascertained via delivery notes, invoices, cash-and-carry records, etc the deliveries of each product that the outlet had had since the previous visit. While in the store, there may have been a requirement to collect other information such as the selling price of items, or the amount of stock actually on the shelf as opposed to in the stock room.

The measurements actually made allowed many other details to be calculated:

- **Consumer sales** These can be derived by adjusting retailer purchases (deliveries) by the difference between consecutive stock counts.
- **Incidence distribution** This is the presence or otherwise of a product in the outlet.
- **Sterling distribution** This is the presence or otherwise of a product, but taking account of the total sales of the outlet for all products.
- **Product class weighted distribution** This is the presence or otherwise of a product, but this time taking account of the total sales of the outlet for only products in the same defined product field, eg any lagers, any beer or any alcoholic drinks. These sales can be calculated on a volume or value basis.

- **Averages** After combining with other stores, average figures can be derived for any of the measures. These can further be related to any of the distribution characteristics, eg average consumer sales per outlet stocking.
- **Stock cover** If sales are maintained at the same rate as over the last period measured, how long would the present stock last?

The above is merely an indication of the depth of detail that can be derived. Not all audits are set up to collect all details. Indeed, in some cases practical limitations exist. Thus, ACNielsen (previously as Stats MR), which has been running a regular monitor of licensed on-premise beer volumes for 30 years, has limited this service to a purchase audit, never expecting their field-workers to acquire the necessary skill to be able to enter a publican's cellar and estimate stocks of draught beer in kegs, casks, tanks, etc merely by sounding the container! Obviously this limitation is acceptable where a product has a short life, but could not be applied to the measurement of slow-moving products.

In many areas, traditional audit collection methods have now been refined with modern technology. Stock counting still goes on, even in large superstores and hypermarkets. However, for many multiple organizations, actual store deliveries are much more likely to be available accurately and quickly on computer tapes. (Later in this chapter is a consideration of scanning, where sales can be collected directly without the need to count stocks or record deliveries.)

UNIVERSE

In order to set up any retail audit, it is essential that details are available on the trade types that are to be sampled. In its simplest form, this detail (universe) must accurately define the total number of stores trading by sector and provide a guide as to how to select sample stores to represent every sector. Ideally, every outlet is listed by name and address, and appropriate detail, such as value of total sales, is available.

Until 1974, audit companies in the UK relied heavily on a five-yearly government retail census to set the base. However, for economic reasons the census was dropped. Moreover, the UK retail scene changed rapidly and this, together with the four or five years it took to publish results, meant that the actual scene was so different as to make the data unusable. In 1971, Asda was classified in the Government census as a dairy company. By the time the results were published, it had become a leader in superstore development. Other universe data sources were clearly needed.

Even in the context of this expensive form of research, the cost of wide-scale unsyndicated census work can still be prohibitive. In the past, companies such as ACNielsen, MGS, and ICI set up their own surveys, and attempted to defray some of the costs by selling on information to smaller users. Published sources were eagerly sought, especially to provide lists by individual outlet. These varied in accuracy from lists where a register was essential to run a business (pharmaceutical register, liquor licence registers), through trade affiliations where it was seen by the consumer to be beneficial (Association of British Travel Agents), to trade associations of less obvious consumer benefit with a much lower percentage membership (for example, the Horticultural Trades Association). Desk researchers spent many an hour with trade directories, *Yellow Pages*, etc.

Currently, in most of the trade sectors that are monitored, a few retail organizations dominate the universe in respect of their contribution to sales value. Nearly 60 per cent of UK outbound packaged holiday bookings are concentrated in five organizations; therefore it has become relatively easier to acquire a considerable part of the required universe knowledge by direct negotiation with these few retailers. However, there is still the need to make reasonable estimates for other sectors. Moreover, there are other trade types such as on-licences, where the multiple penetration is still much lower and agencies have to fall back on published sources.

The key to accurate retail audit research is not just the need to invest in a one-off exercise to derive detailed universes; rather it has been recognized that regular and frequent surveys are necessary if accurate trends are to be maintained.

SAMPLE DESIGN

Overall sample sizes of audits are determined by client budgets. Statistical departments merely function in this respect to advise when this is insufficient to yield any meaningful results at the level of detail required. Once this obstacle is overcome, techniques can be applied to maximize the accuracy of the data projections from a given total sample size.

Ideally a disproportionate technique is used, whereby the larger outlets and those with a greater variance are oversampled. This can only be applied where detailed universe data exists, both for design purposes and later to allow this disproportionality to be removed through 'weighting' (see below). In a well-designed retail audit sample, the proportion of sample outlets by sector matches throughput much more closely than the number of outlets in the sector. Where there are large numbers in one sector compared to another, this rule may be somewhat constrained. Furthermore, there may be requirements to show in detail particular analysis breaks that are a relatively small part of the universe. Where this is the case these may need to be boosted for this particular purpose. Typically in a national analysis, the smaller commercial television areas are disproportionately oversampled for just this purpose. Care must be taken to ensure a sample outlet does not represent too many other outlets, whatever the statistical design may suggest. It is always important to be aware of practical limitations, such as enforced sample outlet changes through closure.

SAMPLE SELECTION

Often additional controls on the sample are necessary. The detail available on the universe determines the depth to which this can be applied. If selecting a sample of independent grocers in Scotland, the only data that might be available are census estimates of total number of stores. This means that little can be done except possibly control the sample on the basis of population spread, eg 20 per cent of the population lies in Glasgow and so 20 per cent of the sample should be in Glasgow. However, if selecting a sample of multiple grocers in London, the actual name and address of every branch with its all-commodity turnover may be available. In this case a three-dimensional matrix of geographic location to ownership to size is possible, and controls can be superimposed by all these variables.

Seldom is the researcher able to select every store that would ideally be included in a sample. At store level, the permission of the owner or group must be obtained. An agency therefore approaches all the major national retailers in a trade type to be surveyed prior to agreeing to set up a service for the client. Unless agreement for access is gained from most of these, there is no point in continuing with the proposal. Usually there are one or two groups that do not wish to participate, and once again the experience of the agency then comes to the fore. Compromises may be necessary whereby only store purchases are available because of the unwillingness of a group to allow stock counts, and sales may have to be estimated from these.

In return for participation in an audit, retailers normally are compensated by money payments and/or information from the survey. Information is more likely to be made available to multiple groups where a large enough sample of their own stores has been selected to provide comparisons between themselves and their competitors. The provision of data identifying a group was historically only made available to that group itself. Competitor data was aggregated in order that no single organization could be identified. This rule applied throughout retail audit research. The confidentiality of data was similar to that of an individual in any consumer survey and clients were not able to identify individual outlets or groups. Recently, there has been a move to much wider disclosure of information. In many audits, access is now allowed to at least some of the multiple group specific information – commonly notated as KAD (Key Account Data). Obviously this access depends on the individual retailers agreeing to disclosure. The development of such additional services has led to a 'sub-industry' where this data might be made available either directly to the client or to its retail audit agency via 'data brokers' contracted by the retailer. The advantage of using the agency as an intermediary is that the client continues to receive all its outputs in a similar (and hopefully user-friendly) format.

WEIGHTING

The successful design and selection of retail audit samples depend on the availability of accurate universe data. Putting those sample outlets into context with all stores in the trade type being measured is achieved through 'weighting'. A ratio between sample and universe is calculated, and applied to every measure collected or derived in the sample stores. In its simplest form, a sample store might represent 'x' stores. If a sale of 'y' units is made in the sample, then this is equivalent to 'yx' after weighting (y units sold multiplied by x stores represented). Disproportionate sample designs can therefore be used, as different sample outlets can have different weighting factors applied to them. The value of continuous up-to-date universes is again obvious, as the ratio calculation is based on universe levels.

Seldom is the calculation of this grossing-up factor as simplistic as in the above example. Consider the following example:

Store A, with a turnover of £5 million on all goods, sells 5 of product 'y' in a period of time.
Store B, with a turnover of £15 million on all goods, sells 15 of product 'y' in the same period of time.

SIMPLISTIC WEIGHTING

Option 1

Select A to represent A + B
 ie 1 store represents 2, so weighting factor is 2
Thus total market is A sales of 5 × 2 = 10
BUT we know the answer is 20

Option 2

Select B to represent A + B
 ie 1 store represents 2, so weighting factor is 2
Thus total market is B sales of 15 × 2 = 30
BUT we know the answer is 20

STERLING VALUE WEIGHTING

Option 1

Select A to represent A + B
ie £5 m represents £5 m + £15 m (£20 m), so weighting factor is 4
Thus total market is A sales of 5 × 4 = 20

Option 2

Select B to represent A + B
ie £15 m represents £5 m + £15 m (£20 m), so weighting factor is 1.33
Thus total market is B sales of 15 × 1.33 = 20

Using the sales value weighting factor gives the known answer, whichever outlet is selected. However, this example assumes certain statistical relationships between the sales of product 'y' and the turnover of the store. It is in this area that once again the skills of the statistician are employed to minimize the variability of this relationship. In an ideal world the estimated product sales would always be weighted to the known universe of that product. In the real world, if this were possible, the retail audits would not be necessary! We look at the compromises in the next section.

ACCURACY

The greatest benefit of a retail audit panel is that it remains relatively stable through time. For this reason more reliance can be placed on trends or movements in brand share than on absolute levels.

The accuracy of volume levels projected from a retail audit sample, at design stage, can only be realistically considered against the variable that is to be used for weighting. Thus, if a sample is designed to minimize the error for estimates of total annual turnover of outlets, then the accuracy can only be specified as a ± percentage, at a given level of confidence, of the generated total annual turnover of the universe. Similar calculations can be made for any analysis breaks to be shown based on subsamples, and these subsamples may need to be increased to improve accuracy to acceptable levels.

Once again, the greater the detail available on the universe to be sampled, the more chance the experienced researcher has to make subjective decisions to improve the accuracy of the final product. With total co-operation from a retail multiple group, many of the vagaries of sampling can be removed. The 'answer' in respect of total group sales may already be known, and it may just be a case of building this into the overall design by weighting the group individually. We will look at the ultimate of removing sampling error at brand level from parts of the universe in a later section on future developments.

Initially, in this chapter, the cost benefits of syndication were considered. However, the penalties of this are often apparent when one measures accuracy. A panel designed to measure sales of all liquor products for the take-home market will oversample the larger and more variable outlets. Such a design may well give a good measure of the majority of products where sales are closely correlated to the control variable of total liquor turnover. In the UK, supermarkets are unhappy with the handling problems of returnable bottles, so such items are more likely to be (or even exclusively) sold in the smaller, less variable outlets.

A design based on total liquor sales thus gives an inferior estimate of sales for that product and it is up to the client to decide on the value of such data, with guidance from the agency. Other problems may occur when products are in very low distribution, as this immediately reduces the 'effective' sample for measurement. Equally problems occur where the distribution of sales within stockists is considered skewed, as this greatly increases the chances of not selecting the correct blend of stockists for a product. Sophisticated statistical techniques are available to measure these variables, but can only be applied retrospectively once data have been collected.

USES

Traditionally, retail audit findings from a syndicated database have been used to plan long-term strategy by monitoring changes in the strengths and weaknesses of the various channels of distribution through rate of sale, product availability, etc. An audit can be the only monitor in sectors that are not supplied directly by the manufacturer such as where the product is purchased via wholesalers or cash-and-carries. Moreover, even where a product is supplied directly to multiple retailers, an audit enhances knowledge by allowing estimates to be made of warehouse pipeline or excess stock-holding at branch level. There is a thin dividing line between using ex-factory sales in conjunction with an audit to 'prove/disprove' audit accuracy and monitoring real distribution problems such as stock build-up or shortage – indeed discrepancies should be of more use to a client if acted upon.

In the past, considerable expenditure has been made for these strategic purposes – even to the extent of the results being more a comforter that the correct decision has been made. Audits would not have retained their share of research budgets, unless more tactile uses were made of the data. The short-term uses have also meant that audits have proved actionable data before a long history has been built up. Disaggregation (outlet-by-outlet detail) has allowed the value of audit data to be almost infinitely increased. Outlets behaving within certain constraints can be grouped together and the impact on sales observed, for example where certain brands have price advantages or disadvantages, and where certain brands have higher or lower stock cover factors. To make the most of data interrogation, direct interaction with the database is highly desirable. This has been helped by the widespread availability of online facilities. Limitations still have to be imposed, whereby the confidentiality of individual stores and groups (where still required by them) is protected.

General uses of retail audits are often complemented by requests for special add-on surveys, to test specific ideas. Thus, an audit sample database makes an ideal test-bed, whereby in-store observational data at individual outlet level can be collected and merged with these volumes to investigate further the relationship of volume movement with other variables such as:

■ position in the traffic flow of the product group;
■ shelf layout of the product group;
■ space allocation to your product within the group;
■ special displays or promotions.

These surveys can be an end in themselves, or can be a means to provide an 'ideal' shelf layout, etc, to present to retailers, in support of a product or product group.

As well as collecting additional information from a syndicated panel, special non-syndicated surveys can be set up to test advertising campaigns or promotional events. A good example of such a project was a study carried out by ACNielsen on behalf of International Distillers and Vintners (IDV) before Christmas 1988. The hypothesis tested was whether a promotion to encourage earlier consumer purchase of IDV major brands before the normal pre-Christmas sales peak from mid-December would boost product sales against major competitors. (The normal problem encountered by all suppliers is a high out-of-stock for successful products during this period.) In order to test this, panels of off-licence stores (high sampling fractions of about one in four) were set up in four matched test towns, and weekly audits carried out during October. The special promotional bottles were introduced into three of the towns (two variants were used – to monitor further different campaigns), while the fourth town did not receive any special bottles, but was merely retained as a control. Weekly audits were continued through November and early December to monitor any increase in sales in the test towns compared with the control town. The survey was then extended for the next month to see if any of the additional volume that might be engendered was offset by falling sales in the normal peak period, and whether the overall impact during the full period was to increase volume sales over the level that would otherwise have occurred. The results could then be considered in the light of estimated national impact as against the cost of national campaigns, and a decision made as to whether such a promotion would be cost-effective.

This case study illustrates the key components of such a test:

- pre-test audits – in control and test towns;
- regular audit periods – differing period lengths can lead to differing purchase pick-up rates;
- maintaining a control panel;
- post-test audits – to monitor any compensatory movements.

The recruitment of such panels requires a high level of retailer collaboration, and can only be carried out by an agency that is already well known in a particular trade type and has ongoing agreement with the major retailers.

THE FUTURE

There are developments over the last few years that have lead to a reassessment of audit techniques and the uses of audit data. Examples of these are:

- Key Account Data (KAD) – already discussed earlier in this chapter;
- Scanning/EPOS input;
- Live universe controls for weighting;
- Saturation sampling of independent sectors;
- Total group input – forecasting/modelling opportunities;
- 'Single source' – linking with consumer monitors.

Scanning/EPOS

In-store scanning systems provide a wealth of detailed data down to individual shopping basket level. The uses of this in a microanalysis situation (eg specific store tests) are obvious. However, care has to be taken when considering this input as an alternative for inclusion in traditional retail audits. The degree of disaggregation is so high that processing time and costs escalate, even given the rapid advances in computer technology, before the data can be reduced to manageable levels.

Live universes

Universes change every day, so theoretically every audit period should be weighted to a different level. Realistic trends can only be preserved if the information is accurate. Tinkering with universes in an imperfect world can often lead to additional unquantifiable errors. However, where such data are available, as is increasingly becoming so in the multiple retail sectors, then positive cognizance can be taken.

Saturation sampling

Detailed universe data in the independent sectors can only be obtained by regular large-scale census operations. As many trade sectors have become more dominated by a few major organizations, the interest in expanding to such techniques has reduced.

Total group input

Electronic data supply from retail groups for live universes is in itself a small advance when compared with the possibility of obtaining detailed data on all outlets for those groups taking part in a retail audit. As the volume of trade concentrates in fewer groups, this possibility becomes more worth while, as a considerable proportion of any audit can be removed from the 'vagaries of sampling'. Once such a database is established, the extended use of forecasting and modelling techniques can greatly enhance the value of retail audit data – especially for the retailers themselves, where interest is generally in small catchment areas.

Single source

The ability to be able to link consumer profiles – portfolios of shopping and/or lifestyles – with quantitative audit measures has seen a major breakthrough in expanding the use of formerly potentially rather static historical data.

Traditionally, retail audits were large, cumbersome and limited to tightly defined trade sectors. Researchers must now remember the dinosaur, increase both the speed and the flexibility of data manipulation, and consider the wider context of the total marketing environment in order to survive!

Part 2

QUALITATIVE TECHNIQUES

15

Qualitative Research

Mary J Goodyear

INTRODUCTION

Qualitative research is an important sector of the total research industry: one that has frequently been underrepresented, both in value terms and in terms of the space it has been allocated in research handbooks.

Historically, qualitative research seems to have received less than its fair share of appreciation and review for two reasons. First, it was dismissed as 'not serious': it lacked scientific rigour; it tended to be based on very small samples; its interview form made it non-replicable and it was labelled 'subjective' since it quite evidently benefited from the past experience, insight and creative or intuitive skills of the researcher.

Secondly, it wasn't properly understood: its practitioners and protagonists failed to provide any comprehensive categorization or description of the many different qualitative approaches and techniques, leading its detractors to perceive it as a large, undifferentiated and imprecise area of research.

Even today, too many researchers and research buyers or users tend to see the qualitative sector of the industry as supplying a more or less homogeneous product based on a particular style of data collection in either group discussions or individual 'depth' interviews. In reality, there are almost as many different styles of qualitative research as there are practitioners.

In this chapter, I will describe and comment on some of the differences between qualitative and quantitative research, and also indicate some of the very wide variety of styles, approaches and techniques that can be found within qualitative research.

A DEFINITION

Qualitative market research provides a disciplined approach to gathering and analysing information using a repertoire of open-ended interviewing techniques and formal and informal analysis methods.

The qualitative research consultant normally plays an active role in gathering the data, as well as in their analysis and interpretation – and one of the strengths of qualitative research is the extent to which its experienced and skilled practitioners can provide an interactive and creative consultancy role as an input to marketing decision-making.

At its most simple level, qualitative research is all about observing and listening to people as they respond in a carefully constructed environment of enquiry, and gaining the understanding and appreciation of their attitudes and behaviour that will in turn lead to the creation of successful strategies for reinforcing or modifying their attitudes and behaviour. This style of research is equally appropriate for the commercial world and for the formulation of strategy in social policy.

Its main strength is that it enables the decision-maker to see the world through consumers' eyes, and understand the bases for their attitudes and behaviour. Qualitative research provides insight.

HOW DOES QUALITATIVE DIFFER FROM QUANTITATIVE RESEARCH?

In general, it can be said that where quantitative research is concerned with describing and measuring, qualitative research is all about explaining and understanding. The two types of research differ in a number of ways:

- the type of problem each can solve;
- the method of sampling;
- the methods and style of collecting information;
- the approach to and techniques of analysis.

One key point of difference is that with quantitative research the conceptual approaches to problem solving are explicit and fixed, an agreed conventional tool for measuring. Statistical tests, for example, will indicate if a particular measurement is significant, and probabilistic sampling will help the buyer to know if the findings from the interviews with respondents can be held true for the whole of his target market.

The conclusions reached in qualitative research, however, are the product of individuals using their own, usually implicit, models of assessment and evaluation. Their way of thinking and their previous experience and predisposition run through every aspect of the project. The end result is a series of hypotheses, which the research buyer either submits to some form of quantification or may accept as self-evident.

WHAT TYPE OF PROBLEMS CAN QUALITATIVE RESEARCH SOLVE?

There are four major 'modes' of qualitative research, and each tends to be employed to address a different type of problem:

1. **Exploratory research** Qualitative research is used when there is a need to explore a particular country, a market, an idea or even the emotional or psychological state of the consumer. The open-ended, flexible, interactive qualitative approach means that it is used in uncharted marketing territory in order to hypothesize about the parameters and the basic structure and dynamics of the market or the problem area. Here, qualitative research is usually employed prior to quantitative research.
2. **Explanatory/diagnostic research** In this approach the client has a specific problem, perhaps a downturn in sales, or a loss of share in a particular sector, which needs investigation. Qualitative research can be the search for an explanation of a phenomenon, an explanation that can help corrective decision-making. In this context, qualitative research is often used as a follow-up to quantitative research.
3. **Evaluative research** Here, qualitative research is used to assess whether or not a particular marketing proposition (say, new advertising or perhaps a new pack design) will satisfy its strategic objectives. Group discussions are commonly used 'to test' advertising concepts and roughs. This can be a useful procedure but only if the criterion for evaluation, the benchmark of success or failure, has been clearly identified and agreed by the client and, where relevant, agency. All too often researchers are asked to evaluate consumers' response to, say, advertising concepts, with no clear statement of advertising and creative strategy and certainly no agreed benchmark against which to set the findings.

4. **Creative development research** Qualitative research, in the form of individual interviews, group discussions or brainstorming sessions can be used with the deliberate objective of getting consumers to help create either new product ideas or new advertising directions.

It is important to recognize which type of problem the client company has so that an appropriate choice of research mode can be selected. The type of problem will determine the approach to sampling, interviewing, analysis and reporting.

Sometimes, of course, the brief from the client may encompass several different research problems, which require the researcher to combine, say, both an exploratory and a creative approach, eg the research problem may be to explore the attitudes of elderly people towards fire prevention and encourage them to help to refine and modify the fire brigade's current communication strategy. A project like this involves both exploration and creative development.

Once the mode of enquiry has been determined, then decisions about sampling, the procedure of the interview, the way to ask questions and how to approach the analysis will all fall into place.

SAMPLING

Qualitative research uses non-probabilistic sampling methods. Recruiters (ie interviewers, normally part-time or free-lance, whose task is to carry out short 'screening' interviews to identify consumers who 'fit' the quota sample requirements, and then to invite qualifying consumers to attend an interview at a subsequent date) are asked to work to very specific quota samples with, typically, sex, age, socioeconomic status and product or brand usage characteristics being specified by the client. Increasingly, as markets become more competitive, so other criteria are employed to ensure that the key target consumers or most useful people are recruited. This has resulted in recruitment based on life stage, lifestyle and attitudinal affinities. For creative development research, there is sometimes the requirement to recruit people who are particularly creative or good lateral thinkers.

Consumers meeting the quota are found by various ways and means (for example, a sample of 'young mums' may well be recruited at the school gates at the end of the school day). Care is taken to avoid recruiting people who are relatives or friends and likely to come into the same sphere of influence) and to avoid people who have been frequently or recently interviewed in market research. Thus, in recruiting 'young mums', the sample would need to be drawn from several different schools to avoid the respondents knowing each other.

For business-to-business qualitative studies, business directories are invaluable and so too, increasingly, are specialized mailing lists.

Some extremely hard-to-get respondents, for example the 'very rich', may need to be approached through the reassurance of a social network by the process of 'snowballing' – using various contacts to suggest the names of others who might be within the quota constraints, and using second-generation contacts to suggest others, and so on.

The sample sizes in qualitative research are generally much smaller than those used in quantitative research, which is yet another reason why qualitative information can rarely be the basis for extrapolation about the total target market. Project size must depend on budgetary constraints, the nature of the problem and, in particular, how many 'cells' exist within the target group that need to be interviewed as discrete subgroups. In considering typical project sizes for strategic projects, it may be reckoned that exploratory research could be anything from 8 to 30 group discussions, sometimes more. As most 'groups' consist of about eight people this would mean a total sample size of between 60 and 240 respondents. Small tactical projects, most commonly used for advertising creative development and evaluation, tend to involve anything from about two to eight groups.

THE METHODS AND TYPES OF DATA COLLECTION

Methods – group discussions or individual interviews?

The choice between 'groups' and individual interviews can depend on a variety of factors:

- **Problems of recruitment** Sometimes with hard-to-recruit or widely dispersed consumers the only practical solution is to interview individually rather than try to get them together as groups, eg the very rich, wheelchair users and key opinion-leaders.
- **Homogeneity/heterogeneity of sample** If a sample for research is very heterogeneous, it may prove too costly to bring people together into group discussions, and individual interviews may be the only cost-effective approach.
- **The nature of the product under survey** Some subjects are considered too sensitive for people to want to reveal their attitudes to a group of strangers. Topics in Western Europe that might be considered sensitive could include sexual practices, some bodily ailments and remedies,

'personal' finance and political issues. And surveys on religion, too, would probably be difficult to cover in detail in groups.

■ **The sort of information required** The processes involved in making a decision to purchase, the history of brand or product ownership, products that are privately used or consumed and advertising that will be experienced in private rather than public media (eg magazines compared with television or cinema) are more appropriate for the one-to-one rather than the group environment. Where the product culture belongs in the social arena (for example beer, or fashion clothes), or will be advertised in the public media, then groups are usually a much more appropriate method.

■ **The constraints of budget and time** Group discussions offer better value for money in terms of cost per respondent and this factor sometimes influences the decision about which to use. Moreover, a project consisting of groups can usually be carried out in a shorter period of time than one with a similar-sized sample consisting of individual interviews – and the need for information quickly can be a determining factor.

COLLECTING DATA – INTERVIEWING

Most of the interviewing in quantitative research takes the form of pre-coded questions on a structured questionnaire. The respondent's replies are fitted into a predetermined response frame, and the question wording and question order are fixed. Although there is an interview guide in qualitative research, to a great extent the consumer's responses dictate the path taken through that guide.

The interview is interactive and resembles a conversation, with interviewer and respondent reacting to each other and pursuing topics as they arise. The qualitative interviewer's role is many-sided; he or she must create a conducive atmosphere for the discussion, guide respondents through all the topics that need to be covered, pursue deviations from the guide if they seem relevant, probe into areas where some things seem left unsaid and, through all this, allow the respondents to speak freely, using their own words and their own parameters.

In quantitative work, the questionnaire is king; in qualitative, the respondent rules. Despite the differences, there is much similarity between qualitative and quantitative research in the rules that govern how questions are phrased. The same basic principles apply:

■ asking questions that are not ambiguous;
■ asking questions that have the minimum amount of 'information' within them;

■ asking questions in such a way as to avoid leading the respondent to believe there are right and wrong ways to answer.

THE APPROACH TO ANALYSIS

The analytical method in quantitative research is an integral and explicit part of the overall research design, and it is usually based on statistics. The analytical approach in qualitative research should also be an integral part of the research design, but statistics are not part of the many theoretical or methodological constructs employed.

Exploratory research

Exploratory research tends to use the aggregation of data as one of its key analytical tools. The researcher's objective is to look for patterns of attitudes and behaviour and thereby create a conceptual framework as to how a particular universe (or market sector) operates. This framework may then be related to secondary constructs of sociology, or anthropology, according to the qualifications and inclinations of the individual researcher, and the client's objectives. From the analysis emerges a set of hypotheses, which might subsequently be subject to quantification.

Diagnostic research

Diagnostic research is problem solving and, therefore, calls for lateral thinking, logical analysis and intuitive insights, rather than a mechanistic sorting of data. Diagnostic researchers very often use psychology or other social sciences to help understand the processes that are going on. Researchers with academic experience of clinical psychology are appropriate for this type of approach and they base their analysis on the interpretation of consumer information, be that linguistic or schematic (as the result of using projective techniques). The resulting report is likely to include models of behaviour that explain, and can be used to predict, how consumers and markets behave.

Evaluative research analysis

Evaluative research analysis is relatively straightforward and, crudely speaking, is based on the null hypothesis. The researcher's job is to compare the response from consumers with the intended or desired response required by the client or advertising agency. If there is a match of input and output, the evaluation is positive. If there is a mismatch, then the proposition is deemed not to have worked. Where the researcher's skill and experience are demanded is in knowing how to recommend the modification and development of propositions, communication strategies and executions.

Creative development

Here, too, the analytic process is relatively simple, with the end result being created by respondents themselves. The particular skill required by the researchers is that of being able to identify and empathize with the respondents, or to 'speak their language'. The analysis very often consists of the researcher absorbing the attitudes of the target group and then reproducing those attitudes in the presentation to the client. By feeling and thinking like their consumers, they are able to help develop the creative process.

The obvious limitations of this approach are the limitations of an individual's ability to empathize with consumers. Researchers in this category tend to work with consumers of their own age, socioeconomic status and cultural background. Thus, for example, products or communications intended for the 'youth' market may well demand researchers of a similar age and, ideally, a similar background.

THE QUALITATIVE RESEARCH PROCESS

It is perhaps useful to look in detail at the process of a 'typical' qualitative project, a process that holds good no matter what the subject or what kind of conceptual framework the researcher prefers.

Let us imagine a manufacturing company is planning a market entry with an established brand into a new territory. This new territory may be a region of their own country or it could be an altogether 'foreign' country. Either way, they feel they need to learn about their consumer and how that consumer will respond to their brand before they make marketing plans and contact distributors, etc. How will their brand fit into the new territory? What sort of competitive context will it be in and how will it be seen to shape up? How will it be perceived by consumers? What will be its perceived shortcomings? What will be its benefits? What impact will all aspects of the marketing mix have on the consumer, especially the key target group?

Briefing

The company decide to commission a qualitative research study to explore consumers in the new territory. They ask a research company to come in and be briefed on the situation. The briefing, ideally, should be extensive and, if this is the first time that client and research supplier have worked together, this is a good time for some familiarization with the history of the company, the history of the brand and what the client feels about prospects for the market entry. The researcher should be encouraged to ask questions and in general be given as much information as possible concerning:

- the background to the proposed project;
- the repercussions and implications of success or failure;
- any hypotheses that the marketing team subscribe to concerning how best to make the project successful.

Some clients may feel that by giving the researcher a lot of information they are likely to bias the approach to the research. With really experienced researchers this doesn't happen: they are trained to be concerned only with what they learn from their respondents, and to disregard both their own prejudices and assumptions, and those of others. By withholding information, all that happens is that the researcher's learning curve is lengthened and the early interviews will, therefore, be less useful. It is important, however, that the researcher questions the information given by clients, and challenges the assumptions that have been brought to the research. The real problem for research is not always the problem as perceived by the client.

The proposal

The researcher replies to the client's brief with a formal written proposal for research. This, typically, will include the information detailed in the following sections.

Background and reasons for research

In this section of the proposal the researcher attempts to summarize the information he or she has been given at the briefing: 1) in order to demonstrate understanding of the task; and 2) so that it can act as a reference throughout the research and, in the (usually unlikely) event of there being any disagreement as to whether the research has met the objectives, clearly indicate the jointly accepted basis for the research proposed.

The research objectives

These should be listed separately and in some detail. This detail acts as a reassurance to the client and also helps the researcher to think in detail about the problem and select an appropriate methodology and interviewing approach. The qualitative researcher should have lots of hypotheses about the project as well as having an open mind about whether these hypotheses will stand the reality testing of fieldwork.

Methodology

Here the researcher identifies what form the data collection will take: observation or, more frequently, some type of face-to-face interview, either individual or group. It is also important to indicate here what kind of procedure will be adopted and why (will respondents, for example, be shown the proposed packs for the new variant before they discuss the existing brand or afterwards? Should the competitive advertising be shown before or after the client's advertising?).

There are few cut-and-dried rules about procedure, but it is often a useful generalization to see the interview as developing in two ways: from specific information to the more general to, finally, the more specific (so respondents might start off by talking about their purchasing habits, move on to discuss general market dynamics and then end up focusing on new product modifications); and from the tangible to the more abstract (respondents are 'warmed up' on topics such as purchasing behaviour, which they will find easy to discuss, before being asked to get involved in brand imagery and their emotional response to advertising, subjects that are more abstract and demand greater rapport between interviewer and respondent).

Procedure is obviously important when it's necessary to understand respondents' attitudes before giving them some new information that may modify those attitudes. It is no good giving them the new information and then trying to find out retrospectively if this has influenced them at all. They will want to respond (as always) in the way that presents them at their most knowledgeable and intelligent. They may in those circumstances deny that the information was even new. Therefore, the logical process of an interview can be crucially important and can resemble a gradual layer-by-layer exploration of the respondent's attitudes and feelings, a bit like peeling an onion.

Again, there are few rules about procedure that can hold good for all projects. Each interview guide must be developed according to the specific objectives of that job, and may need to be modified by the particular reality of the interview. If a certain procedure just isn't working with a particular respondent or group of respondents, then the moderator may have to change the planned procedure to generate the right level of energy and involvement, and to ensure obtaining data that are most true to the consumer's way of thinking and belief structure.

This flexibility and sensitivity to the needs of the moment, as well as the intellectual understanding of the longer-term requirements of the research overall, is what makes the task of moderation difficult and demanding. Not everyone is good at it. It's certainly not a part of the process that can be delegated. In qualitative research, unlike quantitative, interviewer and analyst are one and the same person.

The methodology section will also describe any special techniques to be used or tasks that respondents will be asked to do. These may involve the respondent in:

- creating material such as word pictures, or real pictures;
- completing material, or responding to half-finished material;
- sorting material such as pictures or words;
- role-playing, or acting out various scenarios.

There are many different special techniques that are in common use and have been so since the 1960s. Equally, however, there is no reason why the researcher shouldn't create his or her own tasks or techniques. Qualitative research is itself a creative process and is not something that can be entirely learnt by diligence and following the rules.

Topic guides and interview guides

There's an important difference between mapping out what procedure, methodologies and general topics are going to be covered in an interview (a topic guide) and producing a full interview guide. The interview guide explains how respondents are going to be asked to take part in all stages of the interview and, obviously, their response can vary according to the way they are questioned.

One prime example of this is in the case of creative development research. Here the respondent is being asked to work with the moderator in helping to improve, not evaluate, ideas for new advertising and new products. If the questions incorrectly imply that an evaluative function is required of the respondent, then the interview may never get going in the right way. Questions that encourage a positive, constructive response, such as 'How could this new product idea be modified to suit your needs?' would be more appropriate than 'Do you feel this idea is good?'

Inexperienced researchers (those who have handled fewer than, say, 20 projects on their own or who have worked in very limited research areas) need to write out interview guides in as much detail as possible in order that they can work out how much they are going to phrase their questions, including the all-important introduction, which should serve the dual function of: 1) putting people at their ease and helping to create a rapport; and 2) informing respondents exactly what is required of them so they can feel confident about responding and are aware of their own and the moderator's role.

Sample

The details of how many people will be interviewed, of how they will be defined as eligible and where they will be interviewed, must all be set down in writing beforehand and agreed before the recruitment starts. Typically, a proposal will specify: the sex, age, marital status and socioeconomic group (SEG) of respondents, and their product and brand usage. And increasingly in highly sophisticated consumer societies, it may be important to identify and select respondents according to values and attitudes. If a manufacturer is considering the introduction of a breakfast cereal product with extra healthy ingredients, then it makes sense to specify that respondents should be to some extent 'health-conscious' as well as being cereal eaters. Questions asking about their attitudes and behaviour concerning healthy eating might be a useful filter in the recruitment questionnaire.

As well as specifying who is going to be interviewed, the sample section will also outline how those people will be grouped together. The researcher will have to decide if it is appropriate to recruit narrow-cast or wide-cast on age, whether men and women should be mixed or interviewed separately, whether loyal users should be grouped with occasional or non-users, etc.

Again, there are few hard and fast rules; each job must be assessed in terms of its own objectives and needs. But for the easy dynamics of the group – at least in the UK – it is wise to keep usually to single-sex groups and to people of similar socioeconomic status.

Personnel

A good proposal will also specify which researchers are going to work on the project and which aspects of the project will be shared (if any) and with whom. Thus, this section might read:

> The project would be the direct responsibility of Sheila Smith, Senior Associate Director, who will:
>
> ■ undertake all the planning and the development of the interview guide;
> ■ personally conduct four of the eight group discussions;
> ■ personally transcribe at least two of the tapes from those discussions;
> ■ share the analysis process;
> ■ share the oral presentation;
> ■ personally write the conclusions section of the report having monitored the writing of the content analysis.
>
> She will be working with Alan Richards, Research Executive, who will be responsible for:

- conducting four of the groups;
- transcribing the rest of the tapes;
- sharing the analysis and presentation, and writing the content analysis.

He will work closely under Sheila's supervision and direction.

If these details are not specified the client might well find that, with some less scrupulous companies, while the researcher of his or her choice appears to have headed up the project and shows all the signs of having been involved in the back-room work, in fact much of the process has been fielded out to nameless people (sometimes not even part of the company), who have little contact with the research objectives and the integrity of the data.

The resulting research may look and sound perfectly feasible but it will necessarily be less intelligent and sensitive than a project where one or two experienced minds have worked on the project right through from briefing to producing the final report.

Cost

Costing for qualitative research is traditionally based on the number of interviews rather than executive time. This appears to have been an approach borrowed from quantitative research and has encouraged the erroneous belief that 'a group is a group is a group' among some buyers of research. This is not appropriate, as will be explained below.

Group discussions and individual interviews are only a description of how the information will be collected. They do not indicate how much time and what level of seniority will need to be spent on the job. And time and experience are all that the qualitative researcher has to sell.

There are many variables that affect the cost and profitability of a project and these should be identified when a job costing is submitted to the client. The variables include:

- how full and formal a written proposal is required;
- the number of briefing meetings required;
- any familiarization time required because of the nature of the product or the problem;
- whether there is a need to create a new technique or interviewing approach;
- how difficult it will be to recruit the sample;
- how many people will be recruited for each group;
- how long the interviews are likely to last;
- whether the interviews will require video as well as audio recording;
- whether the interviews can be conducted in a private home or require a purpose-built studio or hotel room;

- what kind of analysis is required;
- how formal the presentation will be;
- what sort of report is required and how long it is likely to take to prepare;
- whether further debriefs will be required and, if so, where.

Two projects of, say, four group discussions may superficially appear to be similar, but one may involve as little as 20 executive hours – telephone briefing, no written proposal, one-and-a-half-hour groups, listening to the tape recordings but no transcription of the tapes, rapid 'intuitive' analysis and a five-page summary of findings – while the other may take 120 hours or more – formal proposal, out-of-town briefing, two-and-a-half-hour groups, full transcriptions made by executives, full coding and analysis, a 60-page detailed report and formal debriefing to senior client members. Yet many buyers still assume that there should be a sort of 'market average' cost for an interview unit.

The proposal, then, should clearly identify what sort of executive time is likely to be involved and the costing should be clearly based on that estimate. Additional costs over and above executive time costs (such as travel, hire of video equipment, etc) are usually quoted separately.

Timing

If the executive time involvement has been clearly scheduled, then it will be easier to know what sort of timing is possible and whether the client's needs can be met. Timing usually includes:

- a lead-in time;
- however many days it will take to complete fieldwork;
- however many days in addition it will take to complete transcription and analysis;
- how long it will take to put together a formal debrief;
- how long after that debrief the written report will take to be produced.

Terms of business

Finally, the proposal should set out the terms of business that the client agrees to in accepting the proposal and commissioning the research. This section will include payment terms, proposal copyright terms and any special conditions that might be relevant.

This, then, is what is involved in a proposal: a document that identifies and articulates all the issues that are likely to arise during the course of the project and which therefore acts as a form of contract and reference in the event of any subsequent problems or disagreements between buyer and research supplier.

Fieldwork

Once the proposal has been accepted it is then time to set up the fieldwork according to the sample requirements agreed. Many qualitative researchers have their own internal field and team of part-time recruiters based around the UK, usually in major towns.

Setting up fieldwork and the niceties of good recruitment cannot be dealt with in detail here, but suffice it to say that it is a task requiring obsessional and intelligent attention to detail, and very good social skills and understanding. The actual process of recruitment is often a thankless task demanding courage and confidence as well as interviewer skills, and the company field manager's job is to offer a sympathetic ear to recruiters as well as to ensure that standards are met.

Although the job of setting up fieldwork and recruiting respondents is nearly always delegated, it is still important for the research executive to be closely involved to ensure that the sample requirements are realized, in the form of respondents who are as useful and appropriate as possible.

The fieldwork itself usually takes place in the evenings, or whenever people are home from work and able to spend an hour or two in a relaxed frame of mind. The researcher and respondents convene at a set hour, in a private home (often the house of the recruiter), a purpose-built research facility or a private meeting room in a hotel, pub or village hall. The researcher usually arrives some time in advance of respondents to ensure that the room is set out properly and that they themselves are prepared and ready.

The general approach of the interview, as we have seen, will vary according to the requirements of the project, and so too will the researcher's interviewing style and form of questioning. In the hypothetical 'exploratory project' we have suggested, that of the client making an entry into a new market, the interviewing style is likely to be very open-ended. This means that the researcher will be alert at all times to absorb the details of surroundings, of how the respondents are dressed, how they behave and how they interact, as well as what they actually say. In a foreign territory, even the location and surroundings of the interview will be subject to scrutiny, as all and any information will help the researcher 'get a feel for' the consumer and his or her environment.

The questioning style in exploratory research starts off with very open-ended invitations to speak such as 'Tell me about this part of the world . . .', 'What sort of work do you do?' or 'Tell me how you use this product', all questions which invite respondents to disclose themselves, and none of which can be summarily answered by 'yes' or 'no'.

Later on in the interview, the researcher will find that, having got the respondents to describe certain aspects of their lives, he or she now needs to understand why things are as they are. At this point the questioning becomes more investigatory, looking for the reasons why people do what they do. Respondents may not know why they behave in a particular way, in which case it is useful to look at the phenomenon by standing outside it, for example by asking 'What do you feel about someone who doesn't use this product? What do you think their reasons might be?'

The understanding of consumer values and attitudes is also helped by encouraging respondents to carry out an informal benefit analysis by asking them to explain and continue explaining what benefits they get from a certain piece of behaviour, say choosing a particular brand, for example:

> *Interviewer* You've mentioned you use this brand only during the Easter celebrations, why is this?
>
> *Respondent* Because I can't afford it all year round.
>
> *Interviewer* What advantage is there in affording it at Easter?
>
> *Respondent* It makes a better meal.
>
> *Interviewer* And what do you feel about that?
>
> *Respondent* It helps to make the family realize that it's a special occasion.
>
> *Interviewer* And what do you feel about that?
>
> *Respondent* They understand that I know how to do things properly, that I can help to make an event special.
>
> *Interviewer* And how does that make you feel?
>
> *Respondent* I suppose a bit more in charge.
>
> *Interviewer* And why is that important to you?
>
> *Respondent* Well, much of my time I am cooking with no comments or praise from the family at all. They seem to think I am there to serve them.

This sort of line of questioning helps relate descriptive behavioural information back to primary benefits and motivations and is an important technique for charting consumer dynamics in an exploratory study.

Other interviewing techniques that would be relevant in an exploratory study would include market and brand mapping (to understand how consumers view the structure of the market) and information about the decision-making process in order to learn who or what are the major influences affecting the choice of brand in this product sector. For the latter the researcher might select one or two respondents in the group and ask them to tell the story of exactly what happened the last time they bought a new brand in this particular product sector. More effectively, the decision-making process can be explored through individual interviews rather than groups.

The overall character of exploratory interviewing is initially to get the respondents talking, during which time they define their own terms of reference, and then to explore their constructs to elicit basic values, rewards and patterns of influence. The interviewer's role is to put his own prejudices aside, to cast the conversational net very wide and then to listen with an open mind. This is more difficult than it might sound. At the end of exploratory fieldwork the researcher(s) will have tapes, notes and lots of personal impressions, which form the raw material for the process of analysis that follows.

Analysis

The qualitative research process is like an iceberg. Most of it exists unseen. There has been little written (in the UK at least) about the analysis of qualitative information. This, I believe, is because for many researchers it is an intuitive and often fairly superficial process, one that hasn't been sufficiently formalized for it to be communicable. Recognizing that there are different types of research problems and different categories of problem-solving approaches is a first step to understanding why the process must vary from job to job.

Analysis of the exploratory study described above is time-intensive and the process will consist of three major stages:

1. transcribing tapes and organizing, in writing, notes and mental observations;
2. coding the information on a framework or matrix consisting of the sample characteristics as the vertical axis and the individual topics as the horizontal axis;
3. analysing the coded information with possible reference to one or two different intellectual or conceptual frameworks, and against the researcher's own hypotheses.

In the exploratory study, the researcher will be looking for aggregates of like information, which will help to develop an understanding of the structure of the market, and of user types and attitudinal trends. He or she will also be looking for the dynamic links, which involves evaluating words and phrases that will help in understanding the nature of the relationship between consumer and brand. Informal benefit analysis (identifying the key motivators and how they are linked to brand and product) also helps to explain what role the product plays in the consumer's life.

In the broader sense of the word the 'analysis' process is ongoing throughout the research. The client's problem and the research objectives are tucked away in a corner of the researcher's mind, demanding both conscious and unconscious attention. The researcher 'lives with' the project and a part of the analysis is carried out at odd moments during the day.

Other approaches to qualitative research may involve other analytic methods. In the diagnostic type of research the key to solving the problem may lie in paying attention to one particular aspect of the information. In creative development research, the thinking work is largely accomplished during the course of the interview with the analysis thereafter involving, for the most part, continued development of the main ideas that have evolved.

Similarly, with evaluative work, where the structure of the research problem has already been determined, and the benchmark for a successful evaluation identified, the research objectives are met largely as the field-work progresses, and the analysis 'proper' is more a matter of detailed confirmation of impressions that have been formed throughout the process.

Once again, however, one must stress that the processes of analysis are many and various, and one chapter cannot provide room for full description. The ideal qualitative researcher would have a good working knowledge of all the social sciences, and familiarity with marketing and communication theories, but what happens in real life is that most buyers of research have a repertoire of different researchers, each of whom may only have knowledge or skills in one or two disciplines.

In this situation the research buyer needs to have a good idea of the nature of the research problem and what is likely to be the most appropriate discipline (individual psychology, anthropology, sociology, economic theory or semiotics) and the most relevant conceptual framework (for example, whether, in individual psychology, Freud, Adler or Jung would offer the best solution, or whether transactional analysis or Gestalt psychology should be used). There are currently specialists in most of these areas in the UK.

The debrief

When the analysis has been completed, and before the report has been written, the researcher will present and discuss the findings with the client. It takes time to convert findings into a well-structured oral presentation.

First of all, the researcher must check that the findings really address the problems presented by the brief. Looking at the client's language in that briefing document, as well as at the nature of the research objectives themselves, will help to remind the researcher what is expected of the research. Secondly, consideration must be given to the language used in presenting the findings. Market research has plenty of its own jargon. The best presentations avoid too many words and untranslated concepts from other disciplines. As a general maxim the inexperienced researcher might well be advised to 'think clever but talk simple'. That same principle is also worth remembering when it comes to writing the report. Thirdly, the researcher should be mindful, in planning what format the presentation should take, to learn from the client:

- who will be at the presentation;
- what their particular concerns are;
- what time is available;
- whether the presentation should be on overhead transparencies, on flip charts or by informal interaction;
- what order they would like the information in (eg conclusions first or at the end);
- what special sensitivities there might be.

Regarding sensitivities, it is not suggested that the research findings should be modified in any way because of any sensitivities. The researcher's allegiance is to the brand that pays the salary of client and researcher alike. However, there are ways of conveying information that can have a short-term negative impact. Tact and diplomacy, without compromising on what appears to be the true character of the data, must be part of the researcher's stock in trade. Lastly, the debrief should be a positive and, as far as possible, an enjoyable occasion. It can be an opportunity for a creative interaction of ideas, for seeing the brand in a new light and for being re-enthused about a planned project. With this in mind the qualitative researcher should attempt to make the presentation entertaining and involving for all those attending.

Presentation skills are rarely a natural talent of the more intellectually minded of researchers, but they are very necessary in qualitative research, where the debrief plays a very important part in the communication of the results, and they can be learnt.

With an increasing volume of research being commissioned by overseas clients, there appears to be a growing need to make video recordings of the presentations of findings, which can be couriered to the client and watched at a time convenient to all. Questions and answers can take place by telephone at a later date. This tends to demand lengthier preparation, but it can save dramatically on executive time and travel costs.

The written report

Not all projects require a detailed written report. Much of the more simplistic creative development work for advertising needs only a written summary to act as 'evidence' of the findings, since the decisions based on the research will be taken at the debriefing.

In our hypothetical market entry exploratory project the written report will probably be very important. There is likely to be too much information to be communicated at one single debriefing meeting and, besides, the information may well be required as a planning 'bible', a reference book for decision-making. This kind of report (likely to be around 60 pages on a project of four to eight group discussions) takes time to write.

The structure of the report is likely to follow the debrief quite closely, and the debrief format, in turn, will probably be related to the procedure of the interviews. It may, however, be modified at the client's request, or by the researcher. In exploratory projects there is often the need to add an extra scene-setting section to the report – usually right at the beginning – which would include much of the information that came from general observation, or from other background reading, rather than directly from the interviews. Reports are usually structured in such a way that the data, and the researcher's interpretation of those data, are clearly distinguished. A typical report structure might follow this format:

1. **Introduction, objectives, method and sample** This section of the report describes the background to the research and details the objectives, the methodology employed and the criteria by which the sample of respondents was chosen. It should indicate if and where the final sample or method employed deviated from the proposed plan. Very often this can be a finding in itself, rather than a failure on the part of the research company. For example, in one recent project MBL conducted, the researchers were asked to run two groups with current users and two groups with lapsed users who did not intend to buy the brand again. There was a shortfall on the second category because most of the lapsed users contacted (in this case the readers of a Sunday newspaper) proved unexpectedly to be willing to try the product again at some time in the future. This, in itself, was a finding of some value, and worthy of reporting.
2. **The conclusions and recommendations** This section of the project summarizes the findings from the research, the researcher's interpretation of those findings, their implications and any appropriate recommendations for future action. This section is the most important part of the report and, ideally, should be able to stand alone as a summary of the entire project, so that readers with time constraints can be well informed without reading further.
3. **The content analysis** This consists of a detailed and impartial description of what took place and what was said during fieldwork. It should be clearly structured; very often it will follow the order of topics on the interview guide. It often includes verbatim comments from the respondents to add substantiation and interest, as well as providing 'consumer language'. In a well-written report a clear distinction is made between reported activity and the researcher's own interpretation of what happened or was said, and of what it means in the context of the research objectives. This distinction is valid even though it has to be acknowledged that qualitative research is always a personal and therefore partly subjective interpretation of events.
4. **Appendices** The last part of the report, the appendix, should contain copies of the interview guide, the recruitment questionnaire and any

stimulus materials (copy propositions, new pack designs, etc) used in the research. Collecting everything into the one document often proves to be invaluable later on, if concept boards and interview guides get lost and forgotten.

REFERENCES AND FURTHER READING

There is a limited selection of literature available about qualitative research, but a better way to get acquainted with it is to get access to qualitative research reports and read them. Although reading may help the beginner to acquire some skills there is no doubt that learning on the job is the best way to become involved and skilled in one of the most interesting of research activities. The titles that follow will help to provide an understanding of the elements of the problems and issues commonly encountered in qualitative research.

Adler, A (1955) *The Practice and Theory of Individual Psychology*, Routledge & Kegan Paul, London

Brand Positioning Services Ltd (1987) *Positioning brands profitably*

Cowley, D, ed (1987) *How to Plan Advertising*, Cassell Educational Limited

Douglas, M (1980) *The World of Goods*, Penguin Books, London

Harris, M L (1980) *Culture Materialism: The struggle for a science of culture*, Vintage Books, Random House, New York

Jung, C G *The Collected Works of CG Jung*, Routledge & Kegan Paul, London

King, S (1973) *Developing New Brands*, The Garden City Press Limited

Munn, N L (1961) *Psychology: The fundamentals of human adjustment*, George G Harrap & Co Ltd

Williams, K C (1981) *Behavioural Aspects of Marketing*, Heinemann, London

Williamson, J (1978) *Decoding Advertisements: Ideology and meaning in advertising*, Marion Boyars Publishers Ltd, London

Worcester, R M and Downham, J, eds (1986) *Consumer Market Research Handbook*, 3rd edn, Elsevier, Holland and ESOMAR

16

In-depth Interviews

Kate Willis

INTRODUCTION

The in-depth interview is a qualitative research technique that is as important and useful as the discussion or group interview. As the name implies, the objective of in-depth interviews (as with group discussions) is to understand the nature and make-up of the area being researched, rather than to measure the size and shape of it:

- It has an open-ended, dynamic, flexible nature.
- It can achieve a greater depth of understanding.
- It taps consumers' creativity.
- It 'gets beneath' rationalized or superficial responses.
- It provides a richer source of material for the end users of research (often marketing and creative teams).

The key to all effective qualitative research lies in a flexible approach. The qualitative research project is inherently evolutionary in nature, and needs to be as flexible as possible to incorporate new learning and, where necessary, to modify the interviewing approach as the research progresses. There is therefore no such thing as the 'standard' in-depth interview. Although most practitioners and users of qualitative research have a clear idea of the basic structure of a typical depth interview, its exact nature will change considerably according to the following circumstances:

- the objectives of the study (if the objective of the research is to carry out a communication check on a piece of finished television advertising, the structure of the depth interview will clearly be very different from an interview designed to look at shoppers' in-store behaviour for a large supermarket chain);
- the type of questioning used (a semi-structured interview using set questions in a predetermined format as against an open-ended, unstructured interview);
- the type and number of people being interviewed (individuals, pairs of people, a family unit and so on);
- the length of the interview;
- the skill and level of input of the interviewer;
- the location of the interview (in-home, in a central location, within the actual retail or purchase environment).

Despite the enormous number of potential variations within the depth interview, there are generally agreed rules about the application of the depth interview and when this is the most appropriate research tool to use. In this chapter, we will therefore begin by looking at when to use the in-depth interview in qualitative research, and will then examine the logistics of conducting and analysing in-depth interviews.

WHEN TO USE IN-DEPTH INTERVIEWS – THEIR STRENGTHS AND WEAKNESSES

In-depth interviews can be applied across a very wide range of areas and types of study including:

- exploratory, broad market studies;
- diagnostic studies;
- creative development (advertising, packaging);
- tactical research studies.

As already discussed, the broad focus and aim of the in-depth interview is similar to that of the group discussion in that it aims to achieve a depth of understanding. However, the in-depth interview is clearly able to achieve very different things from the group discussion, and is therefore a more appropriate choice on certain occasions, particularly those that fall into one of the following two groups.

First are the occasions when detailed behavioural or attitudinal information is required, or a particular decision process needs to be understood in detail. For example, how does an individual go about choosing a particular building society in which to house his or her savings? What exactly is he or she looking for? What other influences are brought to bear upon the final decision?

Second are the occasions when sensitive issues such as highly intimate, personal matters need to be explored. These can be more sensitively examined within a one-to-one environment, for example, consumers' reactions to an advertising campaign for contraceptives. Using in-depth interviews offers the dual benefit here of being able to explore precisely what the advertising is communicating to individuals and providing a 'safe' environment for the discussion of sensitive feelings and emotions.

In-depth interviews also avoid undesirable 'hothousing' and peer group pressures that sometimes affect responses in larger group discussions. Less 'acceptable' views can be expressed more openly in the interview, including those that reflect the majority and the minority view.

Because of its one-to-one nature, the in-depth interview can also provide a valuable sense of perspective upon qualitative research findings, often lost in the group context, where the opinions of individuals can be lost or swamped in the peer environment. (Interestingly, using the in-depth interview to avoid the danger of conformity of group responses in Japan may not be completely successful. Japanese respondents, adhering to the polite rules of their society by agreeing with one other in groups may be equally prepared to conform to what they believe is the interviewer's view in a depth interview!)

Individual interviews are also often useful where the sample is difficult. It is considerably easier to recruit one respondent at a time for depth interviews than to try to ensure that a group of difficult-to-find individuals will meet at a specific time or place agreeable to all. This is particularly true of countries where populations are spread out, in South America, Sweden and the Far East, for example, and is also a major consideration when interviewing businessmen and women.

In-depth interviews also have disadvantages:

■ They are time-consuming. The interviewer often has to move from location to location to conduct the interviews: a maximum of three or four per day can be conducted, and travelling time and costs between interviews can be high.
■ They provide far less opportunity for creativity and interaction between respondents and interviewer; responses can be very rational and considered in the one-to-one context, not mirroring the range of emotions that may affect the true purchase decision.

■ They can lead to misplaced numerical interpretation. The one-to-one interview is perceptionally closer to the quantitative interview, and can result in the sample and data being viewed 'quantitatively'.

CONSIDERATIONS BEFORE USING THE IN-DEPTH INTERVIEW

The approach to in-depth interviewing must be a considered one in which there has been deliberation of all possible variables. The success of any research project depends upon the standard of initial planning and thought undertaken, to ensure not only that the choice of research technique is appropriate and will best answer the research objectives, but also that the structure of the interview itself is relevant and effective.

KEY ISSUES IN DESIGNING THE IN-DEPTH INTERVIEW

The research objectives clearly have a major role to play in determining the exact nature and structure of the in-depth interview within any one research project. For example, to fulfil a brief in which broad exploration of a market sector is required, the interview will need to incorporate research stimuli and projective techniques that tap each aspect of that market and explore less rational, top-of-mind responses.

If the subject matter is of a personal or intimate nature, this will dictate that the interview should probably take place in the respondent's own home, and will need to be conducted by a more skilled qualitative interviewer. If, on the other hand, the major objective of the study is to identify how a finished piece of television advertising is communicating, a shorter interview will be the order of the day, looking at immediate and spontaneous reactions.

The issues detailed in the following sections need to be considered when designing the structure of the in-depth interview.

Who to talk to

The nature of the unit selected for interview should reflect the key requirements of the research objectives. The in-depth interview can incorporate pairs, triads or even family units and is by no means restricted to solus interviewing. More than one individual may be required either to mirror the context in which the product is consumed or purchased (buying a house or a car is usually a decision in which both husband and wife participate) or to encourage dialogue, debate and sometimes even conflict within the interview.

Length of interview

The time over which a respondent is interviewed should be dictated primarily by the research objectives rather than cost, time deadlines or the availability of the researcher. Shorter interviews are usually conducted to evaluate a specific piece of communication, for example a new pack design, where immediate reactions and initial impressions need to be identified and interpreted. A longer interview in this type of project might serve to overfocus the respondent on the issue, and the original objective of the research would be lost.

A longer in-depth interview may be necessary when exploring attitudes and behaviour in a particularly sensitive and personal area, such as sanitary protection for women. Here, sufficient time is needed to create a rapport between interviewer and respondent, and to allow the interview to be conducted at the interviewee's own pace. Wide and free-ranging responses can emerge in studies of this nature, and projective techniques can be satisfactorily used within the longer time-scale of the interview.

Location of the interview

The in-depth interview is almost always pre-recruited (an exception to this rule may be in-store interviewing where respondents are approached 'cold') and may take place in the respondent's own home or office, or in the recruiter's home (UK only), in a central location (such as a hotel) or, occasionally, in a viewing room. The location will be determined by a number of practical factors: the nature of the topic to be discussed (does it demand a very 'secure' atmosphere or, if the subject is to do with work or business, would the interview be better held in a work-like atmosphere?), the status, availability and location of the interviewees themselves, the nature and amount of research material to be exposed, the need for the interview to be observed by others and so on.

On this last point, the one-to-one nature of the in-depth interview makes it less suitable for observation than the group discussion, and there is a danger that the respondent becomes very inhibited by being transported into an alien environment. For this reason, clients should generally also be discouraged from attending in-depths in-home.

Level of interviewer skill and involvement

The in-depth interview should usually be conducted by an experienced qualitative executive interviewer who also has experience of moderating group discussions. This is vital, since the skills necessary to all qualitative research – sensitive interpretation of data obtained via open-ended and projective questioning – are vital for the successful outcome of in-depth interviews and group discussions alike. Understanding and interpretative skills cannot be supplied by a novice to qualitative research, and the mistake of thinking that in-depth interviews are easier for beginners (to learn the skills of the profession) should not be made.

A skilled qualitative researcher interviewing a respondent in depth will establish a rapport with the individual that grows throughout the session. The researcher will be sensitive to a host of influences upon the interviewee in establishing a rapport, for instance how the respondent dresses and the lifestyle he or she leads. It is important that the interviewer should project the feeling that, although the views of the respondent are paramount, the interviewer is reciprocating or sharing the experience, to encourage the sort of atmosphere where the respondent can talk openly and honestly, and in which any enabling or projective techniques can be properly intro-duced and managed.

On occasion, a less skilled interviewer may conduct the in-depth inter-view, in instances where the emphasis is more upon the collection of fairly straightforward data, by means of standard, pre-set questions in a semi-structured questionnaire. Here, the interviewer (often a recruiter or quantit-ative interviewer) will have been fully briefed upon the project beforehand, and will have been instructed about which areas to probe in detail.

SETTING UP AND RECRUITMENT

As mentioned above, in-depth interviews are pre-recruited, either by a qualitative recruiter from a standard field force, or by the qualitative interviewer him or herself. At recruitment, essential behavioural, attitudinal and sociodemographic details are elicited to ensure that a respondent conforms to the quota demanded for that interview. The respondent's overall willingness and availability to participate in the study will be sought, and an incentive will be promised on recruitment, such as money, a gift voucher, a donation to charity or, as is often the case with industrial research or research among professionals, a summary from the completed study may be offered.

In the unstructured in-depth interview, a discussion guide (an outline of agreed topics and the order of the interview) will be drawn up prior to the interview via discussions between researcher and client, and the types of stimulus material and projective techniques will also be agreed. The discussion guide is merely an outline and the order of the interview itself may well differ dramatically across different interviews. This is because the open-ended nature of the in-depth interview and the type of questioning employed are designed to allow the respondent to express his or her views, and the respondent often dictates the course of the interview through the responses given.

It is vital that the interviewee is sufficiently relaxed to participate fully in the study. This is best achieved where the qualitative interviewer clearly sets out the parameters of the interview, makes it clear why the respondent is there and what is expected of him or her, and establishes sufficient rapport to ensure that the interview is an enjoyable experience for both.

THE USE OF STIMULUS MATERIAL AND PROJECTIVE TECHNIQUES

The nature of the stimulus material and projective techniques used in any in-depth interview depends upon the objectives of the study and the developmental stage of the project.

Stimulus material

As with any research project the less finished the form of stimulus material, the less danger there is of the consumer evaluating concepts or ideas as finished pieces of advertising or promotional material.

The choice and design of research stimuli for in-depth interviews need to differ from those used in group discussions, in that they must be appropriate to the one-to-one nature of the interview. In this context, more detailed information can be obtained, and it is a waste of resources available not to take advantage of the level of attention and concentration in the single respondent, who is not distracted by the interaction of the group environment. Hence, the in-depth interview is an ideal environment in which to show respondents complex pieces of stimulus material (perhaps a press advertisement) and ask for detailed comments. Similarly, large pieces of stimulus material, designed to convey an idea to a larger group of people, can sometimes be rather overwhelming for the single respondent in the in-depth interview. Where possible, it is generally a good idea to try to 'normalize' the stimulus for depths as much as possible.

Projective techniques

Projective techniques provide an invaluable tool to reach below superficial and rationalized responses to a more emotional level. They are as useful in the in-depth interview as in the group discussion: respondents are just as likely to 'posture' and hide their true feelings, despite the one-to-one nature of the interview. There are a number of types of projective techniques that lend themselves equally to depth interviewing and to group discussions, but a few rules do need to be followed.

First, in an individual in-depth interview, it is a wise precaution to introduce a dummy projective technique at first, since respondents often need to practise and will feel much more comfortable once they have completed their first projective task.

Secondly, when using projective techniques in any context, the respondent him or herself must describe and interpret the response he or she has given.

Thirdly, and perhaps most importantly, projective techniques must be applied in a flexible way. If a particular exercise is unsuccessful or unproductive with any one interviewee, another may prove more appropriate, and it is important for the researcher to be armed with a battery of projective techniques designed to approach the same problem in different ways. (It is also important that the interviewer is completely comfortable with the techniques to be used, otherwise there is little chance that the respondent will 'perform' with ease.)

VARIATIONS ON A THEME

The 'standard' in-depth interview commonly lasts 45 minutes to an hour, and is conducted with one respondent in-home in the UK. However, there are a number of other types of interview, broadly referred to as in-depth interviews, which fulfil the objectives of the standard in-depth interview. These include:

- mini depth interviews;
- extended depth interviews;
- paired depth interviews;
- triangular depth interviews;
- family interviews;
- accompanied depth interviews;
- observational depth interviews;
- interviewer-administered interviews (semi-structured).

Mini depth interviews

Mini depth interviews are conducted over a 15–30 minute period, and may be used to test a specific piece of communication (such as pack design, pack copy or advertising copy), or to explore specific, clear-cut research objectives in more detail, such as improved or adjusted pack copy. It is possible to use mini depths alone for a complete study, but they are more frequently employed as an adjunct to more comprehensive quantitative research.

Pre-recruited mini depths are convened in a recruiter's home (UK only) or a viewing room, and respondents are paid a small incentive for their participation. A topic guideline is used, and data are usually tape-recorded and analysed subsequently by the qualitative researcher conducting the depth interview.

The advantages of these interviews are that they offer ready access to consumers and data, so that marketing decisions may be made quickly regarding adjustments to marketing or product strategy. Clearly they are not appropriate when a deep level of sensitivity and understanding is required, since interviews of this length are not sufficiently long to build up high levels of trust and rapport between interviewer and interviewee.

Extended depth interviews

Extended depth interviews lasting one and a half to two and a half hours are generally used for diagnostic or broad market studies, or creative development, and are a valuable qualitative tool. A longer in-depth interview may prove useful when discovering attitudes and behaviour in particularly sensitive and personal areas, as discussed earlier, where sufficient time is needed to encourage rapport between interviewer and interviewee.

These interviews are pre-recruited and convened in a recruiter's home, respondent's home or, more rarely, a viewing room facility or central location. The interview must be conducted by a qualitative researcher. Incentives are given, and the interview is generally tape-recorded. Such interviews are time-consuming and are heavy on qualitative research resources, but used as an adjunct to group discussions they can add enormously to other qualitative insights gained from the group situation.

Paired, triangular and family depth interviews

Paired depth, triangular depth and family depth interviews share a similar format to the standard in-depth interview, although in each case the unit interviewed consists of more than one individual to mirror the purchase decision, encourage dialogue in a sensitive area or with a sensitive audience, or set up an interview between individuals where conflicting usage and behaviour emerge in order to understand a market-place more quickly and easily.

All such interviews are pre-recruited, conducted by a qualitative researcher or researchers, and convened as for other depths. Family interviews more often take place in-home so that the family is interviewed in context. Young and very young children can often be more successfully interviewed within a family interview than in a peer group environment. Paired depth interviews may be used to reflect the purchase or decision-making process, such as investigating first time buyers' approaches to the housing market. A couple considering such a purchase can be interviewed in the privacy of their own home, where they are encouraged to share and discuss without inhibitions their feelings and apprehensions approaching this important life stage.

Triangular interviews, often consisting of three participants who know one other, are very useful among teenage audiences, particularly in sensitive product areas such as sanitary protection, contraceptives or skin treatments. They encourage interaction in a relatively 'safe' atmosphere, and can be set up to encourage debate by, for example, deliberately recruiting together a user, non-user and lapsed user.

Family interviews are essential for understanding the influences individual family members bring to bear on the purchase of shared products such as cereals, biscuits or soft drinks. Here, two qualitative researchers may be required to interview different members separately and simultaneously, prior to interviewing the whole family together as a group. Interesting insights are obtained, such as the mother's perceived and actual influence in purchasing a healthier brand, the children's desire to satisfy or reject this need and meet peer group approval, and the father's role in the matter.

Accompanied depth interviews

An accompanied depth interview is one where the participant is accompanied by a qualitative researcher, usually throughout the purchasing process at the chosen purchase outlet. It is frequently used in exploratory and diagnostic studies as well as in retail outlet redesign programmes, to understand the process of deliberation and purchase at first hand.

The interview usually takes place over a period of one and a half to three hours, and starts at the respondent's house. It will be pre-recruited and the respondent will receive an incentive. A topic guideline will be used pre- and post-visit. Permission to conduct such research in-store should be sought from the store manager beforehand.

The first part of such an interview consists of a discussion about the respondent's current state of mind towards the purchase he is about to make, and the influences that may affect his decision. The interviewee and interviewer will then proceed to the store, bank or shop, where the respondent will be encouraged to ignore the interviewer and carry on looking, choosing and buying as normal. The interviewer will watch and annotate the respondent's progress through the store in order to discuss recalled, forgotten and inaccurately recalled behaviour later.

The last part of the interview will involve a full discussion of what has taken place, how this matched expectations, and how in practice this differed from respondent recall of the expedition. In this way a deeper level of understanding will be achieved as to what really affects the purchasing decision and process.

The home decorating market is one of many that has benefited from such an approach. Research has demonstrated how much purchase is influenced by the store range and display of alternative materials and products. Another more unusual area where accompanied interviews are appropriate is within the audio-visual market. Research has shown an unconscious need for consumers to touch and feel such equipment in-store, carrying important implications for store layout and accessibility to products.

Such research is very time-consuming but has tremendous value in assessing consumer perceptions (as may be gleaned from off-site qualitative research) against reality.

Semi-structured depth interviews/observational interviews

Both semi-structured and observational interviews have their place in a battery of research techniques, but do not fulfil the objectives achieved by in-depth qualitative interviews. As such, both will be dealt with briefly within the qualitative context in which this chapter is set.

When used wisely, such interviews can be conducted quite economically by less experienced personnel in large numbers and can be used effectively if a mere description rather than an interpretation of current behaviour is required. The data can then be analysed by a more experienced researcher who has been closely involved in the nuts and bolts of the research project, and has been fully briefed on background, research objectives and points of issue.

However, all too often such interviews are used to economize on more expensive qualitative researcher resources to boost a client's sample to an acceptable size. Given the title 'depth interviews', such interviews are a long way removed from genuine qualitative in-depth interviews.

Semi-structured depth interviews

Semi-structured depth interviews (sometimes referred to as non-executive depth interviews) are conducted usually by a trained interviewer from a basically quantitative field force or by a trained 'depth' interviewer.

Such interviews are conducted over a period of anything from 15 minutes to one hour, during which a semi-structured questionnaire or a very detailed discussion guide is used. The interviewer is carefully briefed by the qualitative researcher responsible for the project, and is instructed to conduct the interview in precisely the way and order detailed.

The responses may be annotated either on a provided questionnaire or in note form, although ideally all interviews should be tape-recorded so that the qualitative researcher may refer to the taped interview later and use his or her own interpretative skills, experience in the market-place and understanding of the desired objectives to aid and elaborate the research results.

In international market research, semi-structured depth interviews are used quite frequently, particularly where populations are widely distributed, and comparability of results across cultures is important. Such an approach facilitates the collection of specific comparable data across countries, while also allowing the views of respondents to be probed and recorded in greater detail. When well briefed and experienced, such interviewers can use projective techniques to facilitate the expression of less rational, more emotional views and feelings.

Such an approach has proved useful in international research when, for example, a detailed understanding of the attitudes of company decision-makers regarding the issue of credit cards was concerned. This study required some scale of coverage, but also in-depth probing of the issues. Some 60 interviews were conducted, with the written questionnaires and tape recordings subsequently analysed by qualitative researchers.

Another approach would be to combine discussion groups with semi-structured depths, thus attaining the level of qualitative understanding required along with an increased degree of coverage.

Observational depth interviews

This system of interview takes place on-site – at the point where information is collated to effect a purchase decision. Realistically, observational interviews cannot be construed as true depth interviews, since recruitment takes place immediately prior to the main interview so that the respondent is not ready or willing to provide in-depth answers. Additionally, a number of other consumers will be present who will unconsciously or consciously interrupt the social interaction between interviewer and interviewee.

An outline to be discussed may be drawn up, but clearly its progress may be seriously affected by more practical considerations. Projective techniques and stimulus material cannot be introduced for the very practical reason that the interviewer is 'on the move'. Arguably too, a very experienced qualitative researcher is not entirely necessary here because the interview itself can do little more than discover how consumers really behave in such a context, rather than how they recall and believe they behave at some point in the future.

Such interviews are useful when needing to interview literally mobile consumers and identify the way in which a number react in context. For instance, within motorway service areas, short observational interviews were an essential part of a larger model of research, in which more conceptual issues were discussed within group discussions away from the service areas. On-site, a whole range of respondents was interviewed, including private drivers, business drivers, drivers of HGV vehicles, families and so on. Ready access to such an audience is also invaluable when a particular tactical problem requires some prompt evaluation and some degree of sensitivity in the data.

ANALYSIS OF IN-DEPTH INTERVIEWS

Analysis of data from in-depth interviews is dealt with in detail elsewhere in this book. However, there are some important principles that need to be stressed here.

Analysis is another part of the evolutionary process of the qualitative research project, and should not be conducted in a vacuum. It is a process that begins at the initial briefing for the project, and continues through the interviewing stage up until the final debrief.

There are no 'right' ways to analyse qualitative in-depth data. Methods of analysis will depend upon the skill, experience and preferences of the researcher, the objectives of the study, clients' requirements and many other factors. For example, international research, which requires cross-country comparisons to be made, demands a more formal, structured content analysis, where the outline structure of the analysis conforms across all countries, in order to achieve comparable data. On the other hand, advertising development research requires a far more flexible approach, to follow the train of thought and the emotional responses of the interviewee.

Analysis can be conducted either from the raw data (a tape recording of the interview) or a transcription of the interview. Neither method is better, although there is an argument that the tape recording reflects the original interview more accurately. Either way, the researcher must choose the preferred method, but must be prepared to be flexible and change, should circumstances demand a different approach.

17

Group Discussions

Sue Robson

INTRODUCTION

In this chapter we will examine the following themes:

- the historical context, which has strongly influenced the way group discussions have developed as a methodology in the UK;
- the setting up and general administration of a group discussion study;
- the importance of learning about the dynamics of small groups as a basis for developing the skills of a qualitative researcher and as a basis for assessing when this is a relevant methodology to choose;
- interviewing techniques;
- the analysis and interpretation of group discussion data.

So we will hopefully begin at the beginning and end at an end; after all the analysis and interpretation of the data is an end point of sorts, although many, including clients, could regard it as another beginning.

The aim of this chapter is to demonstrate the complexity and fascination group discussions can offer. Most practitioners who stay in qualitative research do so because they enjoy the process of doing group discussions. People are fascinating and perhaps especially so when they mix with others in small groups. On a more practical note, people in small groups can provide researchers (and hence clients) with real insight and understanding about their relationship with the world of marketing, advertising, PR and so on. Hence, groups are of value to us all.

THE HISTORICAL CONTEXT

The roots and origins of group discussions mostly lie in two related psychological disciplines: psychoanalysis and group psychotherapy. The themes and practices of these disciplines have been borrowed by qualitative researchers and adapted to the commercial framework of market research (Schlackman, 1989a). That process of borrowing and adapting still goes on today as new approaches to understanding human behaviour are developed by psychologists, sociologists, anthropologists, psychoanalysts and the like (de Groot, 1986; Sampson and Bhaduri, 1986).

It is often said that the 'founding father' of group discussions was Ernest Dichter. Indeed, it was Dichter who brought what was then termed motivational research from the USA to the UK (Schlackman, 1989a). This occurred in the mid-1950s and many of the market research units operative in the field of qualitative research in the 1960s were therefore still influenced to some extent by Dichter, although they had developed a more empirical approach, sticking more closely to the data than Dichter was alleged to have done. The success of group discussions as a research tool in the UK today owes much to the empiricism and integrity of these UK pioneers of the 1960s.

Prior to Dichter, practitioners of qualitative research could be found, but their approach was more anthropological and sociological. An example is the work of the 'Mass Observation Project' (Calder and Sheridan, 1984), founded before the Second World War to provide 'an anthropology' of the British people going about their everyday lives. (The address of the Mass Observation Archive is given at the end of this chapter.) The Mass Observation work, however, was not done by means of group discussions. They used a mix of individual, unstructured interviews and 'observers' who went about everyday places and situations and recorded what they saw and heard. A 'National Panel' of volunteers, who kept a detailed account of everything they did from waking until sleeping on one day of each month, was also used during the war.

Observation of consumers going about their everyday lives is still part of the armoury of qualitative research methodologies, although more usually used in conjunction with some form of interviewing. Self-accounting is rarely used nowadays, although qualitative researchers do often look inside themselves to seek their own attitudes, values and prejudices before conducting a project to explore other people's views on a topic. This can be an important early stage in planning the research project.

Use of the group discussion methodology has increased in the UK since the 1950s and 1960s. By the mid-1970s, the use of group discussions had grown significantly in the UK. The development of different types of group discussion occurred (eg extended groups, reconvened groups and sensitivity panels) as did the development of many varied techniques for use within the discussion itself (Wells and Lunn, 1986).

This has led today to moves being made to categorize and assess the different approaches that are in use (MRDF seminar, 1988; Sykes and Brandon, 1990). This development is a welcome one as it is as misleading to categorize all group discussion approaches under the one heading as it would be to categorize all *ad hoc* quantitative research under the one heading.

THE REASONS FOR GROUPS

The arguments in favour of using group discussions often go hand in hand with arguments in favour of using qualitative research generally, as much qualitative research nowadays is conducted by means of group discussions.

Group discussions have been used more and more as a result of the perceived limitations of quantitative surveys, due to the problems of the responses given by people to structured and public questioning. Group discussions cannot provide 'hard' data, with precise percentages indicating behaviour patterns or beliefs, but they can provide a deeper level of understanding about people's behaviour and beliefs. They can also uncover 'private truths' that people would not be willing to divulge in the public arena of a quantitative doorstep or telephone-type interview (Schlackman, 1989b; Tarrant, 1978).

In the early days, qualitative research was often used as a precursor or pilot stage to a quantitative survey, defining the parameters, helping in questionnaire design and so on. Currently, qualitative research, and group discussions in particular, are more often used separately from quantitative research, to provide strategic guidance or creative insights. This is perhaps particularly true for advertising creative development research, when group discussions would often be the only research carried out at the early stages of idea development. Also, group discussions are more often used to explain quantitative data than to set the parameters for a quantitative follow-up.

SO WHAT IS A GROUP DISCUSSION?

A group discussion is a gathering together of a small number of people for a set period of time, to discuss a series of topics under the leadership and direction of a qualitative researcher – often called a moderator.

Some people seem to regard group discussions as being little more than a convenient way to gather the views of more than one person at a time. But that is only half the truth. Group behaviour differs from individual behaviour and also differs according to the size and dynamics of the group. Groups take on a life of their own and the group has an influence back on the individual. Thus, what is said in the group relates to people's experiences in the group. It is for these reasons that group discussions are such an excellent means of revealing respondents' way of thinking. They provide an opportunity to observe the exchange of ideas in a dynamic way and to construct hypothetical models of the way people think.

The group environment has been shown to influence what and how much is said. Seating arrangements, lighting, room temperature, etc will all influence respondents' degree of participation in the discussion. So, too, will the number of people in the group, the presence of an observer or outsider, the length of time or number of times a group convenes and, not least, the subject matter.

A number of studies have explored the optimum number of people in a group. Some of these studies are conflicting, but generally it has been found that a small group size, of around five people, allows greater and more equal participation of all members, leads to a higher level of consensus after discussion and provides more satisfaction for group members. Members of larger groups, particularly those of over seven people, contribute less equally and participants can feel that the group has been disorderly and a waste of time.

A wide variety of types of groups are conducted today in the UK (Sykes and Brandon, 1990), but a UK norm can still be defined. A 'standard group' will consist of eight respondents, with 'mini groups' of five or six respondents being used, for instance, when interviewing children or teenagers, when interviewing on sensitive or complex subjects, or when there is a need to explore individual behaviour at a more detailed level, but still in the context of a group discussion.

There are also UK industry norms for the length of time a group lasts. The majority of groups in the UK last a maximum of one and a half hours and this is usually sufficient. But experimental work done in the UK (Schlackman, 1984; Fuller, 1984) shows that it takes time to build up a trusting, cohesive atmosphere in any group discussion. The standard one-and-a-half-hour group discussion does not always allow for personal conflicts and game playing to be resolved. Unless this resolution occurs, the responses are 'true' to that group but difficult to interpret in the context of what the same people may have said in a different set of circumstances. For these reasons, there is a growing tendency to utilize longer (extended) groups when using more complex interviewing tools, such as projective techniques. These are described later in the chapter.

The choice of type of group will usually be made on the basis of the problem given. Equally, the choice of group versus individual (depth) interviews will also be made on the basis of what information or answer is required. Chapter 16 deals with depth interviews in more detail, so a comparison of the strengths of the two methodologies will be given only briefly here.

THE ADVANTAGES OF GROUPS

When considering the advantages of using group discussions, it is usual to compare and contrast them with the other main methodological approach of individual (depth) interviews. Most advantages centre around the interaction that occurs when people discuss topics together in a small group. (Equally the disadvantages can be related back to this fundamental feature of groups.)

Groups provide a social context that is a hothoused reflection of the real world. There was a lot of debate, in the image-sensitive 1980s, of the value of brands and it is now well recognized that a 'brand' is the sum total of the product or service plus all the other elements of the marketing mix (Lannon, 1986). All these add up to form a 'brand image' to which consumers can strongly relate. Group discussions are usually considered to allow respondents to explore the images they have of brands in a more dynamic and insightful way than they would in an individual interview (Hedges, 1985).

Another strength of group discussions is the stimulation they provide. There is more variety of opinion represented and therefore expressed in a group than in an individual interview. This can also stimulate the moderator to address new questions and explore new, fruitful avenues of thought.

Group discussions are often said to be more creative than individual interviews and thus to be more useful for idea generation. There is contradictory evidence, however, that individuals are more creative and produce more and better quality ideas than groups (Sykes and Brandon, 1990). It is probably true to say that the outcome is at least in part a result of the moderator's approach and the techniques utilized. A final reason for using group discussions instead of depth interviews is their relative cheapness and speed. This is not a good reason perhaps, since the methodology may not be appropriate, but it is nevertheless true that cost and time are often considerations in the marketing world, where deadlines can be critical. Quick qualitative research may be better than no research at all.

The main disadvantage of groups, which practitioners and buyers alike should be concerned with, is that a group takes on a life of its own and what is said in the group may only have real validity in that context. For example, people are not immune to showing off or trying to impress others in the group – perhaps about the frequency with which they clean the toilet, or take a bath, or perhaps about the whisky they prefer, or the type of holiday they like. Another example is the area of dominance versus passivity. Some respondents play a very quiet, passive role in a group discussion and, while they may be quietly assenting to the views of others, they could equally well be quietly disagreeing, but not wishing to take on a more assertive role.

This is why it is so important that qualitative research practitioners make the effort to learn about the behaviour of small groups. This can provide a valuable framework for interpreting group responses, ensuring that misleading conclusions, eg about preferred whisky brands or consensus views, are not drawn.

PLANNING AND ORGANIZING GROUP DISCUSSIONS

We will assume for the purposes of this section that the decision has already been made that the problem is researchable and that qualitative research will provide the relevant type of data and answers to the brief. There is a trap that both buyers and research practitioners can then fall into – that this means the project should be done by means of group discussions. It is always worth reflecting whether depth interviews or a combination of the two basic methodologies would not be a better solution. There is a welcome trend towards combining the two methods or, indeed, combining qualitative with quantitative.

But let us assume that groups are the most appropriate method. This could mean, for example, that the problem is one of creative development research, or new product development, or a strategic marketing problem for an established brand. So, what size should the project be? Jokes are often made about the ubiquity of the four-group discussion project, but in practice this is often a sensible size to choose. One or two groups run the risk of responses being atypical with no comparisons against them. Three groups may be feasible, but often one wishes to contrast different segments, for instance different ages, social grades or user types, so an even number of groups then becomes the sensible choice.

Hence, much qualitative work is done by means of four-, six- or eight-group discussions. It is, at times, necessary or desirable to do larger projects than these, but there does come a point of diminishing returns with extra numbers interviewed. Unless one is working in a highly segmented market (eg financial services), it becomes unwieldy and expensive to conduct a large number of group discussions (Gordon and Langmaid, 1988).

Times have changed with regard to preferred sample structures for group discussions, and this has also led to smaller sample sizes being the preferred option. A quantitative view used to be taken of the group sample structures to cover sex, social class, age and region, so that the simplest matrix could lead to a minimum of 16 groups. Now it is recognized that this could be overkill and that an emphasis on usership and life stage could be most important, with the end result that filling ever one of those 16 cells is wasteful and tedious (Robson and Burns, 1989).

There is also the point that the human brain is programmed for pattern recognition – to recognize the similar – and this can prevent the researcher analysing the material from a large series of groups from seeing small, but important, differences. This is the reason why qualitative researchers often prefer to work in teams of two or three on larger projects. Some also prefer to work in teams, believing that this reduces the risk of subjectivity and brings extra insight to the problem-solving process.

RECRUITMENT

Recruitment is the identification of relevant people ('respondents') and inviting them to attend a group discussion. The process is normally handled by the researcher or field manager in the office putting out the job to free-lance field supervisors or direct to field recruiters. Recruiters normally work from written job instructions, recruitment questionnaires (designed specifically to identify the right respondents) and a telephone briefing.

The accepted recruitment approach is door-to-door interviewing and screening, but nowadays many group quotas are highly demanding. If the sample required is complex or a minority one, then the recruiter does need to supplement the standard approach with creative initiatives, such as recruiting mums of 0–2 year olds outside health clinics or recruiting businesspeople on their return to the local station in the evening. If the group is extremely difficult to recruit then the client would be well advised to change the approach to one of individual interviews.

Standards of recruitment need to be high, as interviewing the 'wrong' people can lead to misinterpretations (Robson and Burns, 1989). Clearly it is important that moderators get the respondents they asked for – such as within the right age or life-stage group, or within the right social grade classification. It is even important that they are correct in usership terms. Usership can include such definitions as loyal or heavy users of a brand, lapsed users who do not reject the brand, those who are aware of the brand but have never tried it and so on. The moderator will use the differently segmented groups to make judgements on which user types have certain images and attitudes towards the brand, and will be misled in these judgements if recruitment is not correct.

There is always much debate about issues such as overresearched areas and experienced respondents (Hayward and Rose, 1990). Research into this debate, such as Hayward and Rose's, does much to put this into persp-ective. In brief, they found that the levels of concern expressed about the problem of repeat attendance at group discussions, particularly by client buyers of qualitative research, were needlessly high. Control levels do need to be set but, reassuringly, some experience at previous groups is of little or no consequence to the content or process of consequent groups.

GROUP INTERVIEWING

The interview experience can be explored at three levels – structure, content and process (Foster, 1989) – each of which interacts with the others.

Structure

Structure is all predefined and under the control of the moderator. It includes the time, the place and the membership. Thus, it involves decisions at the planning stage about sample structure, recruitment criteria, venue used and the presence or not of observers. Recruitment, venues and observers are all dealt with in this chapter.

Content

Content is partly decided in advance as it relates to the research brief. The moderator should prepare an interview or discussion guide on the basis of the client's brief and use this to guide respondents through the topic headings.

An important point to make here is that the interview guide cannot anticipate all the questions in advance. A good interview guide is a rehearsal for the group and should be an automatic part of every moderator's prep-aration on a project. But the good moderator is always alert to other relevant things said – or perhaps unsaid – in the group, that were not anticipated at the preparation stage.

This is because the interviewing process is flexible and dynamic, with the moderator working on an inductive level, both interviewing and interpreting at the same time (Blyth and Robson, 1981). Each question the moderator asks is dependent on the content of the previous answers; it is also dependent on the moderator's perceived meaning of those answers. Thus, a part of the content is determined by the type of respondents recruited to the group and what they choose to say.

This results in a common pattern of no two group discussions on any one project being the same in content, or topic order. The moderator learns from each group and explores new hypotheses at every consequent group. Others have dubbed this inductive process 'rolling hypotheses' (Wells and Lunn, 1986).

Another aspect of the content of the group is stimulus material. This is discussed below.

Process

The process is the way all these elements react together to determine the way the group functions. This is the emotional dimension. It is this part of the group that the moderator has no control over. It is this part that the moderator needs to work with to enable respondents to perform the tasks required of them effectively. This element of small groups has been the subject of much study and discussion. It will only be dealt with briefly here. For a fuller discussion, the interested reader should refer to Angela Foster (1989), plus all the references given in that chapter.

People bring with them to groups an emotional dimension that is a function of their learnt behaviour in previous groups. Human beings are, essentially, group animals. Our personalities are formed in groups. We are born into and most of us grow up in a natural group, the family, and this probably has the most influence on us. We learn to contribute to the family group in certain ways, performing certain roles, both spoken and unspoken, and we take these with us into the other groups we experience throughout childhood and into adulthood – school groups, peer groups, work groups and so on.

Market research groups are no exception. Although the groups that qualitative researchers work with are unnatural – in that they are not the normal groups that we experience in our daily lives, they mostly only occur for one short session and they are highly task-orientated – they are nevertheless groups. Respondents invited to market research groups bring their common behaviours and also all sorts of anxieties to these groups.

Part of the moderator's skill is to enable a group that has been brought together for a short length of time, with all its individual and collective anxieties and defences, to gel quickly, so that the respondents can perform the task efficiently in the time available. An understanding of the stages all groups go through is essential to effective moderator performance. These stages have been described as: forming, storming, norming, performing (Tuckman, 1986) and mourning (Brown, 1986). The moderator needs to help the group through each of the early stages and apportion tasks appropriate to that stage in order for the group successfully to achieve the performing stage.

The forming stage is characterized by superficial chat. The moderator should therefore give respondents easy tasks to do, like discussing straightforward behavioural issues. He or she should also be encouraging the group to form as a group and not remain a bunch of individuals. This can be done by addressing the group, rather than any one individual, and encouraging debate across the group.

Gradually, respondents begin to size one other up and competitiveness will creep in. This is the storming stage. The anxious moderator may try to suppress the rivalry and struggles for power and control, but this is counterproductive. Unless the group is helped through the storming stage, participants cannot move on to work effectively together. The moderator has to learn to 'sit on' her anxiety and let respondents get on with working out their own relationships. As the group passes through this stage, people gradually settle down. The feature of this, the norming stage, is the establishment of a group culture, an accepted way of doing things. By this time the group is ready to perform and the moderator is now free to give the group demanding tasks, such as non-rational areas for discussion, image work, creative work, projective techniques and so on.

The importance of ending the group well, the mourning stage, is often neglected. A group that has been functioning well together, even for just one and a half hours, needs time to dismantle, to adjust again to being individuals. The moderator needs to be alert to the appointed finishing time of the group, and signal to group members that the discussion is nearly over – thus allowing them to finish off all they want to say and allowing them to disentangle themselves emotionally.

In all, the group process is one of the most significant aspects of the group experience, for moderator and participants alike. Untrained moderators will experience more difficulty working with the process than they will with the structure or content.

THE ROLE OF THE MODERATOR

Implicit in the above description of the group process is the belief that the moderator is an integral part of the group with a specific role to play.

It is now accepted by leading qualitative practitioners that the moderator has an effect on the group, simply by being there, as well as by the way he or she conducts the group. The 'fly on the wall' model (Worcester and Downham, 1978) of a passive, invisible role is no longer accepted (Robson, 1989).

Common sense should tell us that, just as the moderator will react towards group members, so they will surely react towards him or her. The moderator will have a presence, a personality and prejudices, all of which may be brought to the group. This has implications for training, particularly self-awareness training.

Common sense can be supported by some research. Gordon and Robson (1982) have shown that respondents are very sensitive to the moderator and his or her projected personality and role, particularly during the introductory phase of the group discussion. This is partly because they are seeking clues about the 'real' reason behind the interview, as well as how to behave and what answers to give. It is also partly because they are curious to know about the moderator's opinions of the subject under discussion and even the moderator's personal circumstances, ie the 'human element'.

INTERVIEWING TECHNIQUES

There are many varied techniques that skilled moderators use and adapt to their own personal style of interviewing. Most importantly, there is the basic approach of non-directive interviewing. This means asking little, asking only open-ended and non-value-loaded questions, and using body language (eg eye contact and nodding), short probes (eg 'ah ha' and 'um') and silence to explore the respondents' worlds. Silence is a powerful tool and, of course, when used positively and not threateningly, is the most non-directive of all.

The next point to stress is that there is no one right way to interview (Robson, 1989). As every individual researcher is different, so is every group of people interviewed. The good moderator is someone who has developed skills that match his or her own personality and ways of socially interacting, skills that overcome weaknesses, skills that allow every group of strangers to form a cohesive group and perform well.

The main task of the moderator is to gain an understanding of the group: how they live, think, talk, feel, believe and experience things, and how much they say freely and how much they withhold. The moderator can only do this by listening, and being response-oriented rather than question-oriented. A common experience of the novice is to be so anxious about covering the brief and asking all the right questions that, at the end of the group, or, worse, while it is occurring, he or she cannot remember anything anyone said. Basically this means that he or she did not listen. Only in the novice is this understandable.

The corollary of listening well is that the moderator must not impose his or her social values and beliefs on to the group. Even if communicated only at the non-verbal level (eg facial expressions), they will affect how much is said in the group. The moderator should therefore be using non-verbal communication, ie body language, to keep the social interaction proceeding smoothly – using posture, tone of voice, eye contact and facial expressions. For instance, no 'cold-shouldering', regularly making eye contact all round the group yet addressing the group and not one individual, are important, as is using body language to quieten down the dominant members and bring in the quiet ones.

STIMULUS MATERIAL

Stimulus material can form a helpful part of many group discussion projects. It is useful to separate it into three very different types of material:

1. 'Real' material
   - products
   - advertising
   - promotional material;
2. 'Rough' material
   - concept boards
   - prompt/word boards
   - animatics
   - photomatics
   - narrative tapes (plus key frames)
   - storyboards
   - flip-over boards
   - mock-up packs
   - mock promotions (eg direct mail)
   - mock editorial;
3. 'Open-ended/ambiguous' material
   - words and picture sorts
   - collage boards
   - thought tapes
   - mock interviews.

The category of 'open-ended/ambiguous' material almost overlaps with projective techniques requiring stimulus material, such as sentence completion or bubble cartoons (see later in the chapter).

Most researchers and users have little problem with using 'real' material, either to understand its relevance and appeal or as a means of understanding consumer perceptions, imagery and values. Thus, for instance, showing a range of competitive products can be a way of exploring the consumers' perceptions of the dynamics operating in the market (qualitative market mapping).

Most researchers and users also have little problem working with 'open-ended/ambiguous' material. This area is a relatively new one and has been developed, in part, out of dissatisfaction with researching 'rough' material (of which more later). 'Open-ended' material allows the consumers to project their own meaning on the material, thus allowing the researcher to understand the dynamics of attitudes, beliefs and imagery that exist and the symbolic triggers of these. Semiotics and the theory of projective techniques have played a strong part in assisting the development of useful 'tools' to use as stimulus material (Silverman, 1983; Williamson, 1978).

'Open-ended/ambiguous' material can be used to explore and develop, but cannot be used to evaluate concepts, packs, advertising, etc. This is where 'rough' material comes into its own. This is also the area fraught with the most problems. The two key issues are: 1) it may be 'rough' to us, but to the consumer it is 'real'; and 2) there is no coherent body of knowledge that gives professionals an easy framework for deciding what type of material best suits which type of problem or idea. Both of these issues are discussed by Rose and Heath (1984). To quote their conclusions:

> Consumers do not see advertising ideas when they are shown research stimuli, they see advertisements . . . If reactions to a close approximation of the finished advertisement constitute the basic objectives of the research . . . then existing forms of stimulus material may well suffice. But if . . . it is reactions to the advertising idea that are required, then they do not appear to be adequate.

The problem still remains unresolved. The more recent developments of 'open-ended/ambiguous' material only go part way, as there is still often the need to translate that creative expression of the 'idea' into something more structured for a later piece of research, eg creative development research for alternative advertising executions.

PROJECTIVE TECHNIQUES

Projective techniques have been developed in response to theories of human psychological development that have their roots in psychoanalysis. These theories, at their simplest, argue that as babies develop from an undifferentiated sensory state to cognitively aware children and adults, they learn to deal with those aspects of their behaviour and personality that are unwanted by projecting them out on to the environment or repressing them, that is denying their existence (Schlackman, 1989a; Branthwaite and Lunn, 1985). As adults, therefore, there are parts of our personality, feelings and emotions that we are not aware of at a cognitive level – and therefore that the market researcher cannot tap through straight-forward, non-directive interviewing. Projective techniques utilize this propensity to project by allowing individuals to share thoughts and feelings that they are either anxious or embarrassed about, or unaware of at the level of normal social interchange.

Not all qualitative researchers would subscribe wholeheartedly to this theory of projection but most would nevertheless agree that projective tests are a way of getting in touch with people's imaginations and are thus a way of getting beyond the rational, objective expressions that people often limit themselves to in straightforward interviews.

Projective techniques can be used in individual interviews or group discussions, but the group dynamics can often be harnessed to great effect with some shared projective games, such as the obituary, role play or guided fantasy. Many practitioners will have their own list of preferred projective techniques, but some of the most commonly used are the following:

■ association procedures – such as word association, collage building (from a wide collection of scrap art or magazine cuttings) or psycho-drawing (asking respondents to express their feelings about a brand by drawing these using coloured pens and paper on boards);
■ completion procedures – such as sentence completion, story completion or bubble cartoons (asking respondents to fill in 'thought bubbles' of people drawn in simple cartoon style – see Figure 17.1);
■ transformation procedures – such as personification ('if this brand came to life as a person, what would he/she be like?'), turning brands into animals, or personal analogies (when the respondents imagine themselves as the object/brand);
■ construction procedures, such as role playing (asking people to act out a situation, dialogue or event) or obituaries (asking people to give the last sayings of a brand and the thoughts and feelings of the family, best friends, enemies and so on).

In essence, projective techniques are an extremely useful way of exploring areas of feelings and belief that would otherwise be untapped. However, they are not to be used casually. It requires skill and sensitivity to judge when is an appropriate moment in the discussion to introduce a projective task. The type of response given will be very different (more rational, guarded and superficial) at the early forming to norming stages than at the performing stage.

Equally, it requires skill and experience to interpret the responses (Sampson and Bhaduri, 1986). Most established practitioners will use the group discussion both to explore the deeper levels of experience and emotions through projective techniques and to help in the interpretation of the responses. Getting people to explain and discuss what they have done is a very valuable learning process.

THE OBSERVER EFFECT AND VENUES

There is a growing tendency in the UK for clients to wish to attend group discussions, and in the USA and continental Europe this is a widespread practice. While a one-way mirror or video facilities are the common method of allowing observation in the USA and continental Europe, they are less frequently used in the UK. Their use has grown significantly over the past few years, but most UK consumer groups are still conducted in recruiters' or hosts' homes, and thus in a location close to respondents' own homes. It is important to reflect on the advantages and disadvantages of having observers at a group, in the same room (the host's living room) or in a separate room with a large, obvious one-way mirror or camera connection.

The experience of having an observer sitting in the same room is a different one (for moderator and respondents) from having observers behind a camera or one-way mirror. Some research has been done on the observer effect (Robson and Wardle, 1988) that demonstrates both situations are stressful and affect the group in detrimental ways, but that the one-way mirror viewing facility has a more severe effect.

Nevertheless, the one-way mirror facility does allow many clients to be present at the one group, which can mean that the rest of the groups on the project are left unobserved. The value of this approach is that it can provide some control groups to compare and contrast with the bias introduced by the viewing facility imposed on the one group. Although there is no doubt that the observer and viewing facility affect the nature of the discussion, the problem is in knowing what effect this has in any particular set of circumstances and then how to interpret the responses.

Finally on the subject of observers, there is the thorny question of 'How do I introduce the observer(s)?' Clients do not like being identified as 'the man from the ad agency' and moderators are anxious that if respondents are told this, they may withhold some views, such as appraising comments about advertising. The problem can be even more daunting in a viewing facility when the moderator has to give a reassuring explanation as to why a number of people want to listen to them and why these people will sit invisibly in another room.

Thus, commonly, researchers evade their ethical and professional responsibilities to respondents and introduce the client as 'a colleague'. This may be the truth, but not the whole truth. How often do respondents pick up the rest of the truth from the non-verbal cues that will always be there? And if they do 'see through' the evasive information they have been given, what result does this have on the group process and on respondents' conclusions about the integrity of the market research profession? These are questions that qualitative researchers should address more frequently. The issue is currently being ignored by many and yet it will not go away.

Figure 17.1 *Bubble cartoons*

ANALYSIS AND INTERPRETATION

Both of these terms are used to describe the non-numerical process of deliberating on all that was said during the groups, structuring it in a meaningful and relevant way, and identifying the key areas of usefulness for the client. It involves much more than relaying back to the client what was said in the groups. What was said may not be as important as how it was said or what was left unsaid. The meaning of what was said will relate to the context, who said it and at what point during the process.

Overlaid on all of this needs to be the qualitative researcher's conclusions on what the client should do as a result of what was said. 'Do' can refer to such actions as: carrying out further, perhaps quantitative, research; redefining the brand strategy; developing more finished advertising treatments; and so on.

None of this is possible if the group discussion is not carefully recorded. It is normal practice nowadays to use high-quality tape recorders and then make use of the tape recording at the analysis and interpretation stage. Practice about accessing the data from tapes can vary considerably: from preparing a short impressionistic report of each tape to producing complete transcripts of the tapes and then proceeding with the analysis and inter- pretation. A case can be made for utilizing different procedures, dependent on time, budgetary considerations and the objectives of the research. But, in every instance, those using the research should be aware of how thorough this stage has been and therefore the soundness of what they have been given. Whether or not moderators transcribe their own tapes, they should certainly listen to them if they possibly can. Listening to the tapes allows the researcher to relive the interviewing experience, explore the hypotheses generated at that stage and consider whether, on reflection, alternative ways of looking at the data are more valid.

The next step, from transcripts, is to structure or restructure the data in meaningful ways and make judgements about the implications of this restructuring. This is an important part of the interpretation process. The best practitioners in the UK may vary (across projects even) in the concept- ual frameworks they use to judge the relevance and meaning of the data, but they will always use some framework (perspective) when approaching the data (Robson and Foster, 1989). They need to, because group discussions rarely deal only with the rational and descriptive; more usually they explore the intangible, the emotive, even the subconscious motivations and value systems of respondents (Hedges, 1985).

The restructuring process of transforming the data from transcripts into collated, interpreted and reframed insights about respondents can take many forms: annotating transcripts, listing responses and codifying ideas under headings, mapping the information showing causal links or even using computers to sift and sort (see Robson and Foster, 1989; Hedges,

1985; Gordon and Langmaid, 1988). However, the underlying process will be the same: thinking about what it all means, assessing the levels of importance of different topics, and deciding what to recommend to the client as a result. Thus, throughout the analysis and interpretation process, just as throughout the interviewing stage, the qualitative researcher is response-oriented, with the ultimate goal being one of answering the questions in the client's brief.

THE END POINT?

Of course, completion of the analysis and interpretation is not really the end point. The researcher then has to prepare a verbal (aural) presentation for the client and, after that, a full report. Various people have written interestingly about the importance of the verbal presentation to researcher and clients alike (Wigzell, 1989; Gordon and Langmaid, 1988). It is beyond the scope of this chapter to go into this in more detail here.

CONCLUSION

In this chapter we have provided a brief exploration of group discussions from setting them up, through moderating them, to analysing and interpreting what was said during the discussion. The interested reader is encouraged to follow up at least some of the references that follow, as a lot of worthwhile material debates the issues in more depth than is possible in this chapter. The books and the Market Research Society (MRS) Conference papers make for particularly useful further reading for would-be practitioners.

REFERENCES AND FURTHER READING

Blyth, W and Robson, S (1981) Resolving the hard / soft dilemma, Market Research Society Conference, UK

Branthwaite, A and Lunn, T (1985) Projective techniques in social and market research, in *Applied Qualitative Research*, ed R Walker, Gower, London

Brown, A (1986) *Group Work*, 2nd edn, Gower, London

Calder, A and Sheridan, D, eds (1984) *Speak for Yourself: A mass-observation anthology 1937–49*, Jonathan Cape, London de Groot, G (1986) Deep, dangerous or just plain dotty? ESOMAR seminar on qualitative methods of research

Foster, A (1989) The dynamics of small groups, in *Qualitative Research in Action*, ed S Robson and A Foster, Edward Arnold, London

Fuller, L (1984) Use of panels for qualitative research, Market Research Society Conference, UK

Gordon, W and Langmaid, R (1988) *Qualitative Market Research: A practitioner's and buyer's Guide*, Gower, London

Gordon, W and Robson, S (1982) Respondent through the looking glass: towards a better understanding of the qualitative interviewing process, Market Research Society Conference, UK

Hayward, W and Rose, J (1990) We'll meet again: repeat attendance at group discussions – does it matter? Market Research Society Conference, UK

Hedges, A (1985) Group interviewing, in *Applied Qualitative Research*, ed R Walker, Gower, London

Lannon, J (1986) The contribution of qualitative methodology to creative advertising, ESOMAR seminar on qualitative methods of research

MRDF (1988) Reliability and validity in qualitative research, Proceedings of an MRDF seminar

Robson, S (1989) Group discussions, in *Qualitative Research in Action*, ed S Robson and A Foster, Edward Arnold, London

Robson, S and Burns, C (1989) The life history of a qualitative research project, in *Qualitative Research in Action*, ed S Robson and A Foster, Edward Arnold, London

Robson, S and Foster, A (1989) The analysis and interpretation process, in *Qualitative Research in Action*, ed S Robson and A Foster, Edward Arnold, London

Robson, S and Wardle, J (1988) Who's watching whom: the effect of observers on group discussions, Market Research Society Conference, UK

Rose, J and Heath, S (1984) Stimulus material: a dual viewpoint, Market Research Society Conference, UK

Sampson, P and Bhaduri, M (1986) Getting the basics right: qualitative data – interpretation or misinterpretation, ESOMAR seminar on qualitative methods of research

Schlackman, B (1984) Discussion of the use of sensitivity panels in market research, Market Research Society Conference, UK

Schlackman, B (1989a) An historical perspective, in *Qualitative Research in Action*, ed S Robson and A Foster, Edward Arnold, London

Schlackman, B (1989b) Projective tests and enabling techniques for use in market research, in *Qualitative Research and Action*, ed S Robson and A Foster, Edward Arnold, London

Silverman, K (1983) *The Subject of Semiotics*, Oxford University Press, Oxford

Sykes, W and Brandon, K (1990) Quantitative research models – towards a typology, Market Research Society Conference

Tarrant, M (1978) *Interpreting Public Attitudes*, JWT, London

Tuckman, W B (1965) in (1986) *Group Work*, 2nd edn, A Brown, Gower, London

Wells, S and Lunn, T (1986) The paradox of the new qualitative research - from Dichter to self-destruction? ESOMAR seminar on qualitative methods of research

Wigzell (1989) It's not just what you say, it's also the way you present it, in *Qualitative Research in Action*, ed S Robson and A Foster, Edward Arnold, London

Williamson, J (1978) *Decoding Advertisements, Ideology and Meaning in Advertising*, Marion Boyars Publishers Ltd, London

Worcester, R M and Downham, J (1978) *Consumer Market Research Handbook*, 2nd edn, Van Nostrand Reinhold, USA

The source for the Mass Observation Project is the *Tom Harrison Mass Observation Archive, The Library, The University of Sussex, Falmer, Brighton, East Sussex BN1 9QL.*

Part 3

NEW PRODUCT DEVELOPMENT

18

Hall Tests

Bill Dunning

WHAT IS A HALL TEST?

Hall tests (sometimes referred to as central location tests or studio tests) are used when it is necessary to test the reactions of people to a product or concept that it is impractical to take to homes or into the street. For example, many food and drink products need to be carefully prepared and presented at the right temperature if a fair reaction is to be obtained.

Hall tests are so called because they involve hiring a suitable hall, which could be anything from a room over a pub, a hotel room or any other venue close to a shopping area. Respondents are recruited to the hall by interviewers who work outside in the main pedestrian thoroughfares, screening people to determine their eligibility for interview. If eligibility is based upon difficult recruitment criteria, then respondents are often pre-recruited some time earlier and appointments made to visit the hall.

The technique sometimes has an advantage over street or home placements in that tests can be set up quickly and central supervision is at hand to see that all goes smoothly. Clients can attend the hall to observe their survey being carried out and a quick count of key responses provides an immediate feel for the results.

PRODUCT TESTING IN HALLS

Not all products are appropriate for testing in halls. Personal hygiene products, soaps and shampoos, for example, are better tested in the home environment. Products that have to be tested over a period of time (eg a plant fertilizer) or in a complex way (eg an adhesive that needs to be mixed and allowed to set) must similarly be tested at home.

There are many products that are not sensitive to where they are tested, and a hall is a perfectly suitable location. Many food products and alcoholic and non-alcoholic beverages fit this description. However, food and drinks are by no means the only products tested in halls. Other typical examples are:

- fragrances and perfumes;
- design and colour appraisals of furniture;
- kitchen displays;
- tableware;
- household durables or electricals, etc;
- new packaging evaluations that may involve the use of electronic exposure and timing equipment (eg for recognition and stand-out measures);
- ad testing, particularly where controlled exposures and rotations are important.

Every product must be presented in as realistic an environment as possible and this is not always easy. Researching certain foods and drinks is not without its difficulties. For example, the time of day can influence attitudes to what we eat and drink. Many people may not be in the mood for tasting an alcoholic drink before the sun is over the yard-arm. Eating hot quiche straight after a large breakfast may be equally distasteful.

The location of a hall near to a particular supermarket or specialist food shop could cause bias if certain foods are being tested. People passing close to the hall can be expected to shop in the vicinity and, as such, may have preferences that distinguish them from other consumers. For example, if the hall is close to a baker's, this could influence a test of bread.

In the hall the respondent is asked to view, touch, smell or taste the products. This is always in a controlled fashion and the brands that are under test are often presented 'blind', being identified by numbers or letters rather than their names. However, it can be appropriate in certain circumstances to reveal the brands and see how this affects attitudes to the products. The order in which the respondents are asked to evaluate the products is rotated so that bias effect caused by consistently presenting them in the same way is minimized.

Since the objective of a product test is often to measure the attitudes to taste, it is usual to proffer only a small sample of the product. However, if appearance is also to be judged there may be full-size versions of the product to hand. When foodstuffs or drink are tested, the respondent may be asked to nibble a dry biscuit or sip water to clean the palate between tastes.

Occasionally, products are tested on their own (a monadic test) or, more commonly, two or three products are rated against each other (a multiple test). Testing more than three products can be tricky as the senses and judgements may become blurred in being bombarded by the many sensations. However, such constraints do not apply to hall tests that involve measurements of reactions to visual stimuli. For example, in the case of packaging or design and colour evaluations, successful tests have been carried out on 25 pack designs and on 300 different designs and colours of ceramic wall tiles.

Most hall tests aim to measure the acceptability of the products on a number of different attributes including taste, smell, touch and appearance. Each of these attributes can be further subdivided to take account of views on degrees of sweetness, texture, etc. The researcher is working towards determining the preferences for the various products and obtaining insights into the reasons for preference. Typically, new products are compared with a client's existing products and others that are often brand leaders. The rating against existing and brand leader products, together with an understanding of the new product's strengths and weaknesses, may lead to a reformulation or a redesign prior to launch.

SAMPLE SIZES AT HALL TESTS

Hall tests are essentially a quantitative technique. It is usual to carry out hall tests in more than one location in order to overcome the possibility of regional bias. A total of at least 100 interviews (more usually 200 to 300 if the budget will allow) is the aim in order to achieve statistical reliability. This total may be made up of the number of interviews carried out at more than one hall.

Quota sampling is nearly always used to select the sample for hall tests. The quota will reflect the target market for the product and is likely to be expressed in terms of demographics such as sex, socioeconomic class, age and purchase or usage behaviour.

VENUES FOR HALL TESTS

A major problem in the UK and on the continent is that currently the number of suitable sites for hall tests is limited. The better halls are often overbooked and the streets surrounding them are overresearched. It is not unknown for people actively to avoid the area close to well-used halls for fear of being accosted by interviewers. Certain local town councils may also restrict hall test interviewing through local by-law legislation.

Furthermore, the number of good halls with two or three separate rooms for the various stages of an interview can also be difficult to find at short notice. The hall may be required to have kitchen facilities to prepare the product or, at the very least, provide a retreat for the interviewing staff to recuperate and have a cup of coffee. Depending on the products under test, fridges and freezers may be necessary to keep them in top condition.

The first requirement of the hall is that it is located close to where respondents can be recruited. Individual halls should be selected very carefully because their particular location often reflects pedestrian traffic flows that can be very 'up-market' (ABC1 social grades) or very 'down-market' (C2DEs). Similarly, some hall locations are excellent if one is recruiting women but poor if men are the target respondents.

In the UK such halls are often in pubs, hotels, community centres or church halls. This contrasts with hall tests in the USA ('mall intercepts') where special facilities in shopping malls are owned by research companies and are hired out to other research agencies together with interviewers. Such special facilities are becoming increasingly available in the UK and are also available for hire in the larger cities in Germany.

Halls should be easily accessible from the street and ideally will not involve the negotiation of stairs and lifts, which are difficult and off-putting to older respondents or harassed mothers laden with carrier bags and children.

If the products to be tested are heavy or bulky, then loading and unloading facilities need checking. The use of any electrical equipment, special lighting, etc means that power points must be adequate and tested beforehand. Security is also often important. If a hall test is booked to run in one location for two or more days, then overnight security for product displays is critical. Otherwise you may find you have to take down a display and remove all the products overnight so that the hall can be used for a dinner dance or a local bridge tournament. Then of course there is the setting up of the display again the next morning!

The fittings and décor in halls are usually quite plain. However, sufficient tables and chairs will be needed to seat respondents and interviewers and to display the products. Screens may be necessary to separate the respondents and to prevent people overhearing the answers given by others.

It is essential that the appropriate furniture is available in the hall and arranged in advance of the test. This demands that the venue is checked out by a supervisor or researcher prior to the day of the test.

If there are lots of stimulus products to be displayed then it is a good idea to draw up a floor plan and prepare a design for displaying the products. In all tests involving visual material, attention must be given to lighting conditions (both artificial and natural), as often one finds a mixture of bulbs and tubes, which can undermine the research. If in doubt hire extra lighting!

RECRUITING FOR A HALL TEST

The recruiters work in the close vicinity of the hall. They are armed with a recruitment screener questionnaire, which is completed for likely-looking candidates. This both provides a record of who attends the test and guides the interviewer as to whether the respondent meets the recruitment criteria. The recruiter's job is twofold: first to locate respondents who meet the recruitment criteria and secondly to persuade them to take part in the test.

When the interviewers approach the respondent, they run through the recruitment questionnaire without mentioning the test specifically, since the effort of persuasion is only required once the respondent has been judged as relevant to the quota. On learning that the person fulfils the requirements, the interviewer describes the task (ie 'take part in a product test') and then 'sells' the benefits of attendance. The respondent may be told for example that:

- it will be an interesting experience tasting new products;
- it will be helping companies produce better products;
- it will be an opportunity to sit down and have a cup of tea or coffee;
- there will be a small gift as an appreciation for helping.

On the latter point, it should be noted that in the UK a gift for participation is not always given and much depends on the length of time the respondent has to forgo and the extent to which recruitment will be aided by a material incentive. In Europe payment in cash seems to be a common practice, although the amounts are invariably small.

Almost certainly the respondents will ask how long they will be involved in the test and it is unethical to suggest anything other than the truth. The average person in the street can be assumed to have little time to spare and it must be assumed that people cannot be held up for more than 25 minutes and ideally it should be less. If longer interviews are required then it is usual to pre-recruit respondents one or two days before the hall test and arrange a suitable time for the interview. Payment for this longer interview is invariably required to achieve the requisite number of interviews.

The throughput that can be achieved at a hall test depends on the staffing levels and the availability of potential respondents. This latter factor is in turn affected by the weather, the time of day and the day of the week. As a good working average, five recruiters, with the same number of interviewers backing them up in the hall (plus a couple of support staff), can cope with around 100 respondents in a day if the interview is short. Of course, much depends on the constraints of the quota. Often a target interview rate of 50 per day is more realistic. In some instances 35 per day without pre-recruitment may be the maximum possible.

In the UK, Scantel interviewers prefer to recruit and interview the respondents, rather than doing only the recruiting or only the interview inside the hall. The benefits of this are: 1) that the personal contact is maintained throughout; and 2) the flow of interviews is maintained without creating bottlenecks or delays.

QUESTIONNAIRES AND DATA ANALYSIS AT HALL TESTS

The questionnaires that are used at hall tests are usually structured or semi-structured, since this is a quantitative technique. Questions enquire about preferences, usually with scalar responses. Open-ended questions may be included; these are to probe reasons for likes and dislikes, reasons for non-purchase, etc. The sequence of the questions is important since it is necessary for the interview to be 'unfolded' in a logical manner. Precise interviewer instructions must be printed on the questionnaire, as it will undoubtedly be necessary to manage each interview differently, perhaps by rotating the order of products tested or skipping questions according to responses. It is good practice to give a personal briefing to the interviewers at the start of each hall test and also to provide a written interviewer guide, especially where a lot of stimulus material has to be evaluated in a tightly controlled sequence.

Data analysis packages are now available to run on PCs so that, on a job with critical timing, a PC at the venue can be used to enter responses as each questionnaire is completed. Even if computers are not used at the hall, simple counts of key questions can provide an indication of the final result, although reaching conclusions on the basis of first results may be dangerous. Increasingly, CAPI interviews are conducted using laptops or hand-held computers. There are many benefits from the use of the new hardware/software developments particularly in respect of conjoint and trade-off interviews for new product development and pricing studies.

Many clients nowadays may ask for a qualitative dimension to be added to hall tests. Executive interviewers may attend the tests and take the opportunity to hold depth or mini depth interviews with a subsample of respondents who complete the main hall interview.

THE FUTURE OF HALL TESTS

Hall tests are a well-proven means of testing products from foodstuffs to furniture, from perfumes to packaging. City and town centres will for a long time remain the place where most shopping is carried out and hall tests will take place in the surrounding streets as long as halls are available. However, the value of city-centre property could persuade the owners of some halls to sell out to developers, and the old church hall off the high street could eventually disappear. At the same time the trend to out-of-town shopping may encourage the establishment of purpose-built rooms in the shopping precincts following the example of the USA.

The costs of setting up the halls will put pressure on research buyers to get as much as possible out of them. The trend of 'qual/quant' halls will continue in which research executives run through a depth interview with a small sample of respondents after they have sampled the product. As more and more people are approached and/or interviewed, particularly in the locations used frequently for hall tests, there may be an increasing need to provide some form of 'incentive' to achieve sample targets. The costs of hall hire have increased (in some cases dramatically) in the past, and could do so again as competing pressures build up for the use of the space. New developments in data entry systems (eg hand-held computer devices) may facilitate faster production of results, either in the hall itself using PCs, or through electronic transfer.

One problem area where uncertainty will remain high, especially in the UK, is the weather. It is to be hoped that we don't have to rescue our hall test interviewers by boat again, following unexpected downpours and subsequent flooding, as once happened in a suburban shopping centre!

Hall tests are here to stay; we expect them to continue to remain cost-effective whenever logistics and practical considerations preclude all other methods.

19

Sensory Evaluation

Derek Martin

INTRODUCTION

In its practical applications, sensory evaluation has traditionally been more the province of research and development, close to technical research and manufacturing, than part of marketing and market research. Market research has principally been involved with researching the consumer and the consumer's response to the marketed product, and the aspects of marketing and promoting it.

When testing products, market research often concerns itself with relatively simple tasks: measuring overall liking plus some measurement or evaluation of limited aspects of the product. A competitive product is frequently used as a benchmark, and the number of product variations assessed is usually small in number. Sometimes the consumer tests out formulation changes, usually for cost reduction purposes.

Sensory evaluation is used more in the technical development of a product, in quality control, and in exploring and developing raw materials and manufacturing processes. Typically, this work is carried out by trained panels, often in-house, who have concentrated exclusively upon measuring products against agreed criteria of specific or generalized product quality.

The 1980s saw the beginnings of an interchange of information and techniques between these two areas, but there has tended to be an emphasis upon one or the other approach, depending on whether the issue is seen as a marketing or technical one.

As will be seen from this chapter, there is a considerable case for integrating the techniques of sensory analysis with those of market research, to develop a programme of product assessment that clarifies the tasks of both marketing and R & D in developing and maintaining successful products. In particular, greater understanding of the preferences and requirements of the consumer can be achieved in terms that can be related directly to the physical attributes of the product, which R & D can manipulate.

THE HISTORY OF SENSORY EVALUATION

While marketing concentrates upon aspects of a product that principally act upon consumer psychology, and R & D concentrates upon the physical features (its ingredients, formulation and manufacturing), sensory evaluation addresses itself to both aspects.

Human perception may be regarded as the psychology of the interaction of the physical object, or the physical energy coming from it, and the perceiving organism. While concern with what we perceive and the process by which this is organized into an experience was for a long time principally a question for philosophers, it became a discipline of scientific interest with the advent of psychology in the 19th century. What was the process by which the sensations of seeing, hearing, tasting and smelling were translated into experiences that we all recognized, even if we could not always describe them?

Not only could they not always be described, which we shall see remains an important issue in sensory evaluation, but they could not be directly observed. Perceptions are 'covert events' (Dember and Warm, 1979), and we rely upon either accurate reporting by the person experiencing the perception or controlled measures that enable us to interpret accurately what is being perceived. This has considerable relevance to how sensory evaluation can be carried out, and how much the results can be relied upon.

The range of measures involved in collecting and analysing data on perception are grouped under the general term of psychophysics, which has been defined by Dember and Warm as the 'quantitative relations between change in physical stimulus, and concomitant changes in the reported aspects of sensory experience'. This, of course, is exactly the main issue on which a product developer needs information – what the effect is on the consumer of changing the product, and how it is reported – so that changes can be made in the physical product in the consumer's desired direction.

The father of psychophysics is generally considered to be Gustave Fechner (1801–87), who first formulated rules about the relationship between the stimulus – the physical object – and perception, and how to measure it. He was aware of Weber's Law, devised by E H Weber, who had concluded that an increase in the level of output was perceived as a proportional increase to the previous state, from whatever level that was. Weber produced a series of fractions to demonstrate this relationship for different types of stimulus – taste, sound and vision. Fechner took from this a scaling procedure to demonstrate that there was a log function between the increase in the stimulus and the perceived magnitude of the increase. Thus, progressively larger increases in the stimulus are needed to give an equal increase in perception. The principal value of this for our purposes is that it demonstrated there was a measurable consistency in recorded perception that could be related directly to changes in the object being perceived.

Fechner's theory held good until Stevens developed his concept of a power function being the relationship between the object and the perception of it, and he managed to demonstrate this relationship with a series of experiments over some 40 years. In particular, Stevens developed ratio-scaling by which he demonstrated that subjects could record directly their perception of magnitude, whereas Fechner's work relied on the indirect recording of this by measuring a series of jnds (just noticeable differences).

There is still considerable debate among psychophysicists about the validity of the power law, and further complexity has been added by the more recent concepts of signal detection theory, and information theory.

Nevertheless, the basic concept of psychophysics, that there are measurable relationships of a consistent nature between increases in a stimulus and the recorded perception of them, holds good. That this is so is highly relevant to the techniques and design of studies for sensory evaluation. In complex products such as food, fragrances and drink, there is a multitude of elements competing for attention and combining with one other to deliver a sensation. Distinguishing these effects and recording as accurately as possible how they are perceived is the first major task of sensory evaluation. The second is to relate these perceptions to consumer requirements and preferences, to help deliver the most appealing and satisfying product. Sensory evaluation is therefore a valuable tool for the technical developer. What has been less well developed is applications of sensory evaluation and analysis techniques to areas more traditionally the province of market research.

WHAT TO MEASURE AND HOW TO MEASURE IT

It is clear that we need to measure perception if we are to understand the ways in which the formulation of a product can be altered to suit consumer needs. This is of course the first task of the technical developer – what ingredients or elements should be used and in what quantity and proportion.

It is also clear that what the consumer wants, and what will satisfy needs, is not just going to be a 'pure' sensory experience. More or less of a certain element in a product may be detectable but may not be important, because the major expectations of the product are being met. The perception of the product as a whole, and the perception of individual characteristics, will also be affected by the context in which it is used or consumed in its widest sense. There may be social, political and cultural factors that impinge on what is acceptable and, further, on what is the most desirable taste, odour and texture of what we consume. If Australians think rabbit is like rat, people from the USA cannot stomach steak-and-kidney pie, Poles think lamb is for the dog and Koreans think dogs are delicacies for humans, then it is hard to contemplate a sensory experience that is uncontaminated by a mass of factors affecting the psychology of the consumer. Marketing and promotion add their own influences to the scene, and any research into the sensory experience of consumers and their requirements has to take these issues into account. Figure 19.1 demonstrates product perception.

This is particularly relevant when considering how perception should be measured. It is well established that individuals may differ quite markedly in their perceptions of the same product. Experimental work has shown considerable differences between men and women in their ability to detect certain odours or flavours, and other work has demonstrated clear differences with obese people. Individuals may also vary in their ability to detect certain types or classes of odour (Koster, 1989).

This problem has usually been addressed in sensory research by developing a trained panel. The descriptors may or may not be developed by them. From a given list, they are trained to identify certain characteristics in the product and describe them with agreed terminology. Obviously this can take some time. Panels can spend several months in training and the panel is therefore quite small, usually between 8 and 20 in number. A further disadvantage is that training in one product is not necessarily relevant to any other, although it can be argued that the individuals are more knowledgeable and sensitized to sensory experience, having been trained once.

Sensory trained panels, because of these issues of specialization, have been mostly used by manufacturers in-house. However, now they are also available from research companies and laboratories specializing in this type of work.

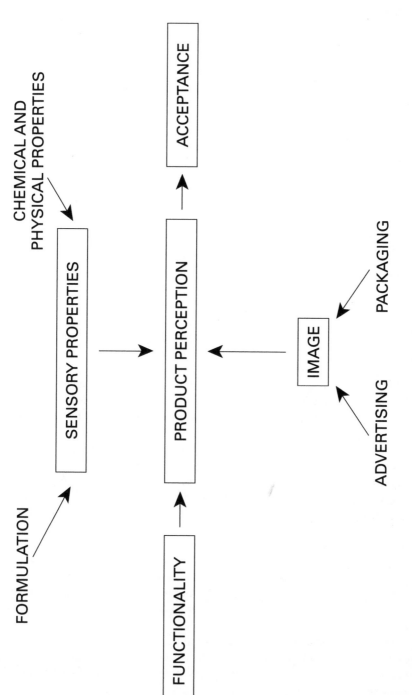

Figure 19.1 *Product perception*

The greater accuracy of a trained panel in its ability to 'profile' a product on its key attributes means that the panel is a more specialized instrument of measurement than a sample of consumers. Panel members cannot be expected to be typical of consumers in their preferences for the formulations they profile because of their training. They are 'noses' and 'palates', 'ears' and 'eyes'. However, for a product that is to be marketed to the consumer, it is obviously vital to know what the consumer likes and prefers in the formulation of a particular product. Thus, at the very least, information must be collected about consumer likes and dislikes.

The problem of developing sufficiently accurate and consistent consumer descriptors of products, and the greater reliability of the trained panel in this regard, have led some sensory scientists to pursue the two issues entirely separately. The trained panel is used to profile the product and to analyse the magnitude of the effect of various changes to the formulation, thus giving detailed 'instrumental' information on its sensory characteristics, while consumers simply provide hedonic data on a range of samples. Combining the two data sources should provide clear indications of how to optimize the product (Koster, 1989).

Other solutions to this central problem have been proposed. One that has received a good deal of attention is the use of 'free-choice' profiling. Using this method, individuals are allowed to use a range of descriptors that suit them. All the individuals in the sample evaluating the product may use a different range of terms. The list of terms is most satisfactorily developed in initial sessions using elicitation techniques such as free discussion, product comparison, repertory grids and any other techniques suitable for developing descriptors. Respondents then choose from the list those terms they think most suitable for the product they are testing.

Subsequent multivariate analysis can then combine the individual data into descriptive maps of the main product features and show the similarity of various terms that refer to the same physical quality of the product. This has the benefit of using the consumer directly in describing the product and, of course, at the same time the consumer can indicate levels of liking and preference (Williams and Langron, 1984).

A further problem that can arise from the rigid separation of product description and profiling from consumer liking and preference is touched upon earlier in this chapter. That is the extent to which 'psychological' factors may impinge upon the perception of product characteristics. Market researchers are used to exploring image, and a large part of product research is devoted to positioning, and promotional and communication development. The virtue of sensory analysis is that it provides reliable and detailed information about the product itself. However, while some aspects of the product may be considered to be merely physical, many have an image content, even when they are rooted in the physical features of the product. This being so, the perceptions of consumers are likely to be considerably affected by image, and an understanding of what elements of the product image impinges upon is necessary in order to optimize it. A trained panel is unlikely to be able to give reliable data on these aspects.

Exploring the influence upon sensory perception of image, branding, name, packaging and other elements in the marketing mix is important in order to establish what is demanded of the physical product. There is no point in attempting to increase, say, strength of taste, the amount of chocolate or some other product feature, if it has reached the acceptable sensory level, but needs to be enhanced on this aspect by image. This can happen if consumers want more of this feature to satisfy their 'idea' of what it should ideally be. The respective roles of R & D and marketing in developing the product can be more clearly defined by research that addresses itself to these issues (Martin, 1989).

SENSORY PROCEDURES

While it is necessary to be aware of the complexities that surround measuring perception, and liking or acceptance of a product, frequently it is necessary to examine some aspects in detail, particularly if a technical issue of formulation is to be resolved.

Sensory procedures are particularly good at providing accurate information, usually from relatively small samples of respondents. Conscious of the problems of accurate measurement and the influence of external factors on perception, sensory researchers prefer to test products in a controlled environment. This can help ensure that extraneous noises and odours are excluded and proper ventilation avoids the build-up of odour, which might affect perception. Lighting is also controlled to provide a consistent visual environment for the product, unaffected by the time of day or the weather. Frequently studies are carried out in specially constructed booths, which permit the respondent to concentrate solely on the product, free of distractions from other respondents and indeed interviewers. The task is usually self-completion and it is important to allow the respondent as much time as is needed to complete the assessment of the product. Such a laboratory environment also makes for more accurate controlled experiments (Wilton and Greenhoff, 1988).

Sensory work is well suited to problems of product difference or matching, and is particularly useful when changing a formulation, possibly because of changes in raw materials, suppliers or the manufacturing process or for cost-reduction purposes. Alternatively, it may be to check on how well a product replicates a competitor's.

Typically, the procedure would be to conduct a triangle test, in which respondents are told that two products are the same and one different. Picking out the odd one is measured against chance, to see if it is different.

A more rigorous form of this test is the duo-trio test, where two and three of the products are the same. Paired comparison tests can also be used, but the order effect is considerable and, where two very similar products are being tested, reliable measurement may be difficult.

CHARACTERISTIC INTENSITY

It is often necessary to compare formulations or rival products for a particular characteristic. Here the task is to measure the magnitude of the perceived characteristic across a range of product samples. The relationship of the perceived magnitude or intensity of the characteristic with the formulation variables that underlie it can then be plotted.

A further development in this area is the measurement of time-intensity – how a particular characteristic changes in the process of eating, drinking or smelling. While this has always been an important measure for fragrance, where the character develops and changes on the skin over hours, measures of the magnitude of a taste characteristic on smelling the product, at the front of the mouth and as it is swallowed can now be undertaken. Thus, the patterns of taste intensity and fade-away for different formulations or ingredients can be plotted.

PROFILING

Profiling has been referred to earlier in this chapter. It provides a picture of the major characteristics of the product and the perceived level of each. Products or different formulations can be compared. The most common application of this approach is quantitative descriptive analysis (QDA), which produces line or 'star' diagrams of the major product dimensions and the perception of each product on these dimensions. What the dimensions should be depends upon what is already known about the product or product field.

Figure 19.2 is an example of taste differences in tap water from different locations in Britain and Europe. The terms were developed by a trained panel.

Dimensions can be developed by discussion or other elicitation techniques, as mentioned earlier, or the researcher can rely on already-developed flavour or odour lexicons, which may be generally applicable to the product field. These have been developed for whisky, for instance – the 'whisky wheel' – and extensive work has been done on fragrance, eg Harper, Bate-Smith and Land (1968).

STAR DIAGRAM

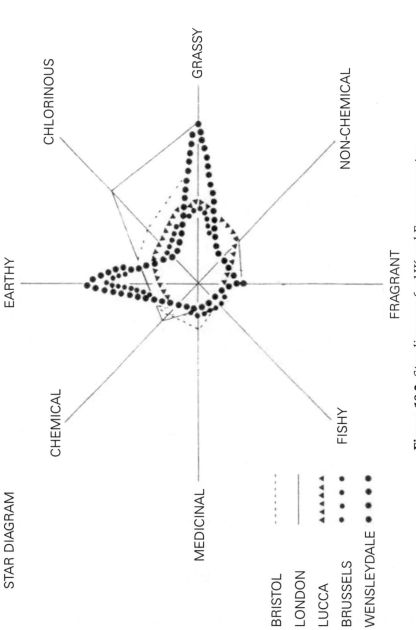

Figure 19.2 *Star diagrams for UK and European waters*

MEASUREMENT

Measurement of sensory response is a matter of some importance, since the scaling of magnitude and the sensitivity of response that the scale permits can have a major effect on the reliability of the apparent relationship between the magnitude of what is perceived and the formulation elements affecting it. There are considerable sources of potential bias in most scales, and it is important to be aware of these and the ways of designing out such bias or of allowing for it in subsequent analysis (Poulton, 1989).

As already noted when considering the development of psychophysics, Stevens and Galanter (1957) developed the magnitude estimation scale as a reliable method of obtaining direct recording of magnitude by respondents. There have been various criticisms of the scale, but it does have good practical value, giving improved sensitivity among untrained respondents. It also enables them to record more accurately their responses simply by avoiding 'end-effect' problems where tasters run out of places to score what they are perceiving, even though they do clearly differentiate a product from those tested previously. It does require a degree of numeracy since respondents are required to develop their own scale of numbers, but not to an arduous extent. Children under the age of 12 can also use the scale by means of 'cross-modality' methods. These can also be used by adults of course. Cross-modality simply means using one form of scale (say an increasing light intensity or sound, using a hand control) to match the increase or decrease in the magnitude of the sensory experience. For product tests, flexible rulers can be used, pulled out to one length to represent a magnitude of, say, sweetness, and adjusted to represent the next level of sweetness experienced. This also has the benefit of not requiring any special equipment, and having scale numbers that can be read directly off the ruler.

The simple open-line scale is also frequently used on which the respondent marks the level of magnitude. Category scales can be used if the respondent is allowed the facility to go back and amend previous judgements on products tasted; otherwise the 'end-effect' problem raises its head. The 100-point scale has also been used to good effect, since this gives sufficient points for relatively fine judgements, without the requirement for explanation and training that applies to magnitude estimation.

SAMPLE SIZE

It is commonly accepted that perception is more stable and uniform than liking. Thus, although care must be taken to look for respondents who may perceive different aspects of the product, or be particularly sensitive to features that others do not notice at all, measurement of product characteristics can normally be undertaken with relatively small panels. Specially trained panels of 10–20 are common, and work with untrained panels, undertaking simple tasks of difference, or free-choice profiling, needs samples of around 30.

If, however, there seems a good chance that image factors may play an important role in influencing aspects of perception, then it will be necessary to undertake larger samples, of the type more commonly found in market research. This is because imagery is prone to a wider spread of response than sensory evaluations, in the same way as hedonic response. In these circumstances, it may be opportune to complete limited profiling with hedonic measures in one test among samples of around 200 or more if demographic or usership subgroups need to be explored separately.

ACCEPTABILITY

As has been discussed already, the detailed sensory evaluation of products can provide reliable information on what is perceived. Since there can be a very wide range of product features it is particularly relevant to examine which are the most important sensory characteristics relative to product liking or 'acceptance' (as it is commonly referred to by sensory scientists).

The issue of context is also significant here. The extent to which the product should or can be tested within a context will depend on the stage of development or the nature of the existing market. The social, cultural and market elements need to be identified and considered, as has been commented on before, and the product presented consciously in the relevant context. This is especially important when the environment may be changing rapidly. A good example of this is the low-alcohol beer market where legal and social pressures rapidly increased product acceptability, and affected taste perceptions as well (Martin, 1989).

While there may be such an experience as a 'pure' sensory one, this is more a matter of academic research than practical applied research for marketable products. If product concepts, brand identity, packaging or advertising are available to provide this context they should be used as soon as possible in testing. Isolating their influence on perception or liking should be part of the overall research design.

DESIGN

Experimental design is a key element in any research project where the influence of individual variables needs to be isolated. Since this is the particular task of sensory research – identifying product variables, showing how they are described, measuring them and providing indications of what the consumer wants – it is obvious that careful experimental design is critical to enable such variables to be isolated, and to identify which of them are of key importance to the acceptance of the product.

Given the complexity of many products, it is unlikely that the formulation can be reduced to, say, two major ingredients. Even with three, four or five major variables in the formulation, a design that examined each of these variables at, say, three levels, very rapidly produces an extremely large number of product variants for testing. There are statistical designs that reduce the total number such as the central composite designs of Cochrane and Cox (1957) but, even with these, five variables at three levels yield a minimum of 43 variants to test. This can obviously be time-consuming and very expensive by traditional consumer testing methods, and the required quantities may be difficult to prepare in the laboratory or factory.

Sensory testing methods permit relatively large numbers of products to be tested within one session. Up to 12 usually present no problem, if suitable breaks are given to respondents between products, or blocks of products. Higher numbers than this can be achieved with reliable results providing sufficient time is taken and the product itself is not highly demanding on the sensory apparatus – very spicy food, for example, or many subtle taste elements. Repeated sessions with respondents over a few days can cover a large number of variants with ease. This makes a panel the easiest operationally, but work can be conducted with samples of consumers specially recruited for the study as well. The relatively small sample sizes required also make production of many variants more feasible.

Fatigue should be looked for routinely in such tests, but respondents often prove to be more resilient than is commonly believed. Order effect analysis and analysis of variance will indicate whether there have been too many demands placed on them. The other issues of a controlled environment – lighting and lack of distraction – have already been commented upon.

ANALYSIS

Because sensory research largely concerns itself with product issues in which there are a number of independent variables – the elements of the formulation, the marketing and design factors, and the purchase and usage pattern – it greatly benefits from multivariate analysis. Perceptual space mapping is widely used to indicate what the key product dimensions are, where the products in the test appear on those dimensions in relationship to one other, and what the directions of consumer preference are. Such mapping can also be applied to the respondents, to look for segmentation of requirements, and to isolate any individuals or groups who have different perceptions of the products tested. Principal component analysis, canonical analysis and other multivariate methods can be used.

The chocolate example shown in Figure 19.3 is based on data from participants in a seminar, and is not representative of the market, merely illustrative.

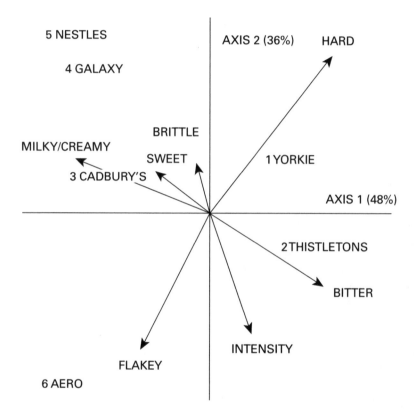

Figure 19.3 *Principal component analysis of milk chocolates*

The question of individual differences also points to the value of some form of individualized data analysis, avoiding the potential errors arising from averaged data on quite complex responses. Free-choice profiling, which allows the individual to use different terms from a broad lexicon, obviously requires individualized analysis, and generalized statistical Procrustes analysis has proved particularly useful in matching individual responses using different terminology. The example of coffee in Figure 19.4 is from Dr A A Williams (1989).

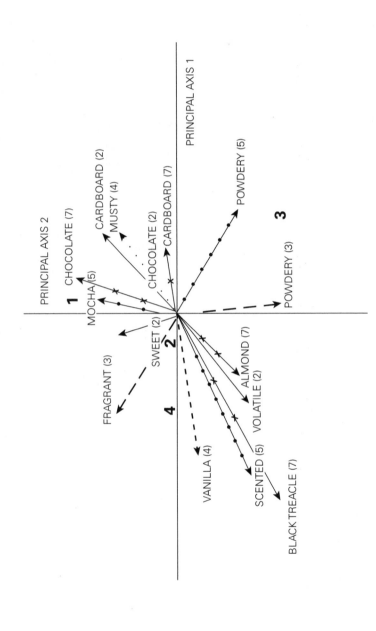

Key: 1 = Angolan Robusta; 2 = Brazilian Robusta; 3 = Instant Coffee; 4 = Costa Rican Arabica (numbers in brackets = assessors)

Figure 19.4 *The perception of coffees using free-choice profiling*

Optimization analysis can be carried out when sufficient data points are collected on formula variables, in a controlled design. Multiple linear regression and surface response modelling (see Figure 19.5) have proven effectiveness in:

■ isolating the perception of the main product characteristics;
■ relating them to formulations;
■ modelling the picture of consumer response to demonstrate the projected ideal product in formulation;
■ showing whether there is an overall consensus or taste segmentation in the market.

Perceptual maps can also be combined with liking or preference data, either from the same data source, or from different ones. Vectors can then be

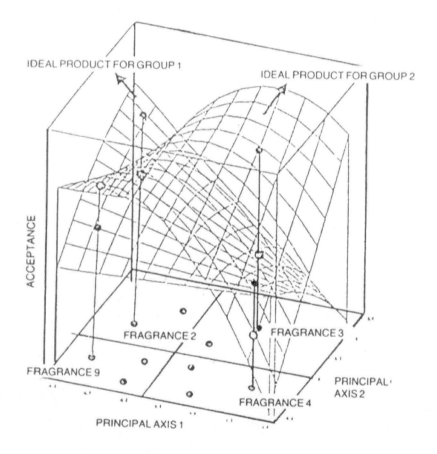

Figure 19.5 *Surface response modelling of the acceptance of the fragrance of a typical proprietary product for two subgroups with differing requirements*

produced to show the direction of maximum consumer appeal, the products closest to it and the characteristics of the products most likely to provide that appeal. Figure 19.6 shows an example of a perceptual map.

Care should be taken to analyse for sensory segmentation where different taste, odour or appearance requirements are held by groups in the population. Experience has shown that these are most likely to be independent of demographic differences. Preference mapping gives further insight into how the individuals in the sample have responded and what

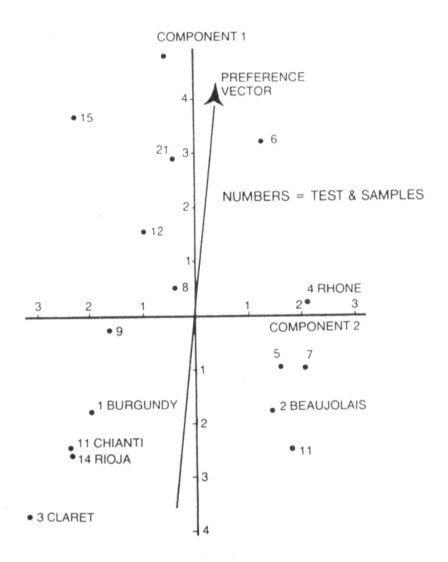

Figure 19.6 *Perceptual map*

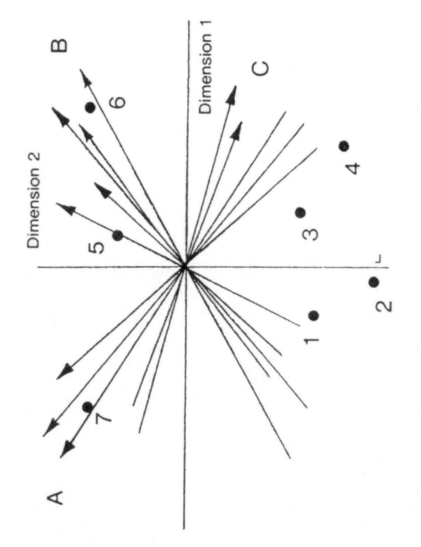

Figure 19.7 *Preference map – overall acceptance*

tastes or brands they prefer. This is particularly useful for developing strategic positioning of new products. Figure 19.7 shows an example of a preference map.

CONCLUSION

Sensory analysis provides a more detailed, sensitive and reliable insight into the ways consumers perceive products, how they describe their perceptions and what they want from them. While the techniques have been used principally for detailed examination of the product's physical characteristics, they are equally relevant to examination of consumer psychology – the image, brand and other factors affecting consumers. These techniques should be taken up more thoroughly in market research exercises to aid product development and promote a clearer understanding of what the respective roles of marketing and technical development should be.

REFERENCES AND FURTHER READING

Cochrane, W G and Cox, G M (1957) *Experimental Designs*, 2nd edn, John Wiley, New York

Dember, William N and Warm, Joel S (1979) *Psychology of Perception*, 2nd edn, Saunders International Edition, Holt, Rhinehart & Winston

Harper, R, Bate-Smith, E C and Land, D G (1968) *Odour Description and Odour Classification*, I & A Churchill, London

Koster, E P (1989) Research for flavours and fragrances, ESOMAR seminar, Lyon, France

Martin, D C (1989) Research for flavours and fragrances, ESOMAR seminar, Lyon, France

Poulton, E C (1989) *Bias in Quantifying Judgements*, Lawrence Erlbaum Associates, Hove and London

Stevens, S S and Galanter, E H (1957) Ratio scales and category scales for a dozen perceptual continua, *Journal of Experimental Psychology*, **54**

Williams, A A (1989) Research for flavours and fragrances, ESOMAR seminar, Lyon, France

Williams, A A and Langron, S P (1984) The use of free-choice profiling for the evaluation of commercial ports, *Journal of Sci Food Agric*, **35**

Wilton, V and Greenhoff, K (1988) Integration of sensory techniques into market research, *Food Quality and Preference 1*, Longman Scientific and Technical, London

SECTION 3

COMMUNICATIONS, ADVERTISING AND MEDIA

Introduction

The amount of money spent on advertising of all kinds now accounts for a small proportion of the gross national product in many countries. Communications is big business by any standards. And yet many people claim they are not affected by advertising. They assure us that they can't be persuaded to do something they don't want to do. Many claim they are not aware of advertising. If this is the case it is a lot of money wasted!

The problem is that a lot of money is wasted. Good market research can help keep advertising waste to a minimum by ensuring four things:

1. the messages that are communicated are relevant and have impact;
2. the media that are selected are appropriate to reach the target audience;
3. the audience appreciates the features and benefits of a product or a service;
4. there is impact being achieved by the advertising.

In this context the word 'advertising' is used in its broadest sense. It includes all types of promotions and PR, but not selling. Market research plays a vital role in making this advertising pound work harder. Qualitative research throws up ideas about motivations, which the creative people can develop into campaigns. Thereafter, research tests and modifies the campaigns to ensure that they are meaningful. Quantitative research has, perhaps, a larger part to play, measuring readership and viewing. It can track the degree to which awareness, interest and action are stimulated. It can also measure image and its impact on continued readership or viewing.

Advertising agencies and companies with a large advertising purse would not dream of launching a campaign without carrying out market research in one or other of these areas. In this section of the book the authors provide the latest thinking on communications research. They give clear examples of how researchers have developed, tried and tested techniques.

The chapter on advertising research is a good starting-point, as it covers planning research, creative development research, pre-testing research and campaign evaluation studies. These four stages of research can be used to show the effect of any form of advertising including TV, radio, press, poster, direct response, classified and the Internet.

Researching TV and radio is a major area of research. Advertisers and their agencies need to know who reads, listens to or watches what and in what numbers. This is easier said than done when people quickly forget, become confused and even try to impress when answering market research questions. Techniques have been developed for arriving at measurements that can be trusted.

Ask any confectionery shopkeeper about the influence of television advertising and he will confirm that it works. He is used to watching his sales of a product jump following an advert on television the previous night. There is plenty of empirical proof that television advertising moves consumer products. However, measuring the viewing audience has become harder, not easier, as many programmes are now watched on video and via the Internet and opportunities exist to fast-forward over the commercials. Multiple television sets in the home are now commonplace and they introduce another complication. Fortunately, the electronic chip is again there to help researchers, this time providing devices that record who watches what and when. These are 'peoplemeters'.

The section rounds off with a chapter that covers packaging research, another vital topic given the fact that for every pound spent on advertising, the same amount is spent on packaging. Packaging not only protects goods, it is also a medium for informing consumers about the contents of the goods they buy. Packaging researchers are in great demand as they help create packs that are more environmentally friendly, but no less stimulating, informative or functional.

With these techniques the researcher can help the advertiser communicate more effectively. However, communications is a complex subject. It would be nice if researchers could consider communications in a laboratory – away from the confusions of the big wide world. Unfortunately, the media 'noise' is phenomenal and we are attacked by messages from every direction. Consumers become punch-drunk by communications so that it is not easy to separate out what has had an effect. It is hardly surprising that consumers claim they are not influenced by advertising.

Certainly, researchers must learn to apply specific techniques to help improve the efficiency of specific lines of communication. However, they must also bear in mind that advertisers need help deciding what to put into their communications mix and in what proportions.

$\boxed{20}$

Advertising Research

Tim Broadbent

INTRODUCTION

The subject of this chapter is advertising research, that is market research that is carried out in order to check the effect that advertising might have on the people who receive it. In one sense almost any piece of market research that is carried out on a product or service that is going to be advertised could be defined as advertising research, but the main studies involved are usually classified under four broad headings.

1. Strategic or planning research – to help define the objectives of the advertising within the context of the overall marketing strategy and marketing plan.
2. Creative development research – to provide guidance on the development of a creative execution or treatment.
3. Evaluative or pre-testing research – to check a finished or fairly finished advertisement against the objectives set before it is aired.
4. Campaign evaluation research – to check how far the advertising has achieved its objectives after it has appeared in paid-for media. The same research is often used to help set objectives for the following year.

These four broad stages of research would be relevant to any form of advertising including direct mail, direct response and classified advertising, as well as the television, press, poster, radio and cinema campaigns that come most readily to mind. In the same way, the questions raised in the research would be relevant whatever the subject of the advertising, whether it was trying to increase the sales of a breakfast cereal, decrease the use of heroin or explain the benefits of the pension scheme to replace SERPS. However, for simplicity and clarity we will focus mainly on above-the-line media advertising for branded products and services, since these are the areas where research is more likely to be conducted, though the principles and the techniques described apply equally well to other advertising for other subjects.

STRATEGIC OR PLANNING RESEARCH

If a national advertiser is proposing to spend several million pounds advertising a brand, the marketing department will have certain objectives in mind. At the broad level, the objective will be to sustain or increase sales and share, but there may also be certain sub-objectives such as to increase profitability, secure distribution or successfully introduce a new variant. Strictly speaking these are marketing objectives and the advertising is part of the marketing strategy, but within the overall marketing plan the advertising itself will have objectives and a strategy.

It might well be, for example, that in order to play its part in increasing sales, share or profitability, the advertising will set out to increase frequency of usage among current users, to increase trial among young consumers, to generate awareness of the existence and benefits of a new variant or even to sustain current levels of usage when the brand is under pressure from a competitor.

These examples all relate to objectives that the advertising might be asked to achieve in relation to the brand, but it is also common for further objectives to be set in relation to the advertising itself. An increase in the overall level of awareness that advertising for the brand has taken place or the achievement of a certain level of awareness of a specific message in the advertising are typical examples of objectives relating to the advertising.

In order to define these advertising objectives within the overall marketing plan, the marketing department and the advertising agency must first agree an advertising strategy. Most marketing companies and advertising agencies will have their own preferred format for the advertising strategy but the key elements will usually be:

- a definition of the role advertising should play within the overall marketing plan;
- the primary target audience for the advertising;

- key messages it should try to impart about the product or the brand;
- attitudes, beliefs or images of the brand it should try to address;
- behaviour that it will try to modify or reinforce.

Research techniques

The research techniques that are most widely used to help define the advertising strategy are large-scale quantitative studies designed to monitor the overall performance of the brand and to identify areas of competitive strength and weakness.

Market studies or usage and attitude studies

These are substantial quantified studies, usually with samples of at least 1,000 representative consumers and a detailed questionnaire, which may take 30 or 40 minutes to administer. They are expensive studies and it is not normally necessary to conduct them more often than every two years unless the brand or its market is going through a period of major development and change.

The method is as follows. Usage and attitude studies are normally conducted by face-to-face interview using a largely pre-coded questionnaire. However, some companies use postal self-completion techniques and others collect somewhat simpler data more cheaply by using omnibus or telephone surveys. A consumer diary may also be included to provide further purchasing or usage information. Many basic awareness and usage questions cover a long list of competing brands but, for the attitude and advertising questions, shorter lists are advisable. This may be achieved by restricting the list to key competitors only or by rotating the complete brand list so that each informant deals with only a small number of brands.

Sections of the questionnaire are tailored to issues of specific interest to the company commissioning the research, but the following question areas are likely to be covered on all such studies:

- brand awareness;
- purchasing patterns;
- usage patterns;
- attitude or image scales relating to the brands, brand users and product performance;
- awareness and sometimes recall of advertising;
- respondent demographics.

As with all major quantified studies, the precise design of the questionnaire, the wording of questions, the structure of the rating scales used and, indeed, the briefing and supervision of the interviewers, coders and data processors play a vital part in determining the value and the validity of the information collected. Guidance on these points can be found within Sections 1 and 2 of this book.

Interpretation of results

The initial analysis will be a straight run of all questions against standard cross-breaks – typically age, class, region, category usage groups, brand usage groups and those who are aware of the advertising. There will also be other questions that will be known to discriminate between brand or product field user groups. These will vary according to the market being studied so, for example, for a food brand, size of family or age of children might be relevant, and for a financial product, having a bank account or credit cards might reveal useful differences of attitude or behaviour and so on.

A good deal of useful information about the commissioning brand and its key competitors can be gleaned from these basic tables, but the full value of these major and expensive studies can only be obtained through extensive and intelligent cross-analysis. Increasingly, such cross-analyses are done directly using desktop computers by those analysing the data.

A cautionary note is appropriate here. With all major market studies it is very easy to fall into the 'too much or too little' data traps. Either you just skim the surface and waste much of the data, risking drawing misleading conclusions as a result, or you drown in computer printout and lose the key findings in a bewildering sea of numbers. Contrary to popular belief, subjective misinterpretation is just as prevalent in relation to quantified data as it is in qualitative studies. The conclusions may have the appearance of validity because hard numbers are attached to them but without diligence, creativity and the nose of a detective for tracking down elusive clues, they may nevertheless be misleading. Most quantified research companies now offer sophisticated computer analysis packages that are extremely useful in both the manipulation and the presentation of data.

Information that helps to shape the advertising strategy by highlighting areas of strength or weakness for the brand in relation to its competitors can also be gleaned from other studies. These include continuous diary panels such as those offered by AGB or Taylor Nelson Sofres, syndicated multi-product studies such as the TGI, the Financial Services Monitor or the Alcoholic Drinks Survey, and *ad hoc* 'before and after' or advertising tracking studies. Qualitative studies of behaviour or belief patterns in relation to a product field or market may also be used in this way either on their own or in conjunction with quantified data. Information on how to conduct such studies is contained in Part 2 of Section 2.

CREATIVE DEVELOPMENT RESEARCH

The advertising agency is always likely to be very closely involved at this stage of research and, indeed, the research is often commissioned and even conducted by the research or account planning department within the agency. The purpose of this research is to help the creative team develop a piece of advertising that not only incorporates the message that best meets the strategy but also conveys that message in an interesting, stimulating and persuasive manner that is both appealing to the target group and in keeping with the values of the brand.

If we were writing a 'For Sale' notice to go into a newsagent's window, the communication task would be relatively simple. We would only need to describe the object in brief detail and indicate the price we hoped to get. Even at that simple level, the precise words we used would materially affect the number of enquiries we received. However, an advertisement is a much more complex piece of communication. Advertising frequently uses visual images, music to help convey a mood, a storyline to help illustrate the point, a variety of visual or verbal metaphors to enrich the message, or humour to make it more sympathetic and involving. Even a comparatively simple poster will usually be a multi-layered piece of communication.

Creative development research can be used to help focus and refine the development of advertisements at any one of a number of stages, but preferably not at all of them for any particular advertisement, otherwise you can get dangerously close to getting consumers to take the decisions rather than informing those decisions.

To refine the strategy

In a perfect world the creative strategy would be very tightly defined at the end of the first stage, but in practice strategic planning research will probably have been very helpful in isolating areas where effort might usefully be directed, although less helpful in suggesting how the desired result might be achieved. For example, the strategic research may have revealed a weakness in the brand among young consumers. Analysis of the rating scales for the brands they buy more frequently may also provide some indications of the sort of qualities they value, but these data will stop short of isolating the single compelling message that should be the basis of the advertising.

To continue the simple example, advertising concepts built around say convenience, flexibility, modernity or, more subjectively, style could be put into research that would throw more light on which of these qualities was more relevant and appealing to young people in relation to your brand.

The strategy might then become 'to make the brand more appealing to young consumers by emphasizing its flexibility within a young lifestyle context'.

To choose between alternative advertising routes

Most creative departments can devise more than one way of fulfilling an advertising strategy and it is not always easy to choose between them. So, for example, if we imagine that the same agency had come up with both 'It's for you-ou' and Maureen Lipman as embryonic campaign ideas to promote further use of the telephone, creative development research might have been used to help client and agency decide which campaign to progress.

To refine executional details

Even when the strategic focus is tight and the creative route is agreed there will often be different candidate scripts (many advertisers only make one a year) or press or poster executions.

In many instances advertising executions will be selected, rejected or modified on the basis of experience and judgement, but research can also be immensely useful. Often research at this stage delivers a reminder of the old adage that communication is more about the message received than the message transmitted. A presenter thought to be authoritative can be seen as patronizing, a humorous pastiche may be taken literally, a detail in the set could move what was intended to be a mildly aspirational lifestyle out of reach and even the core message may be distorted by its context. Many of these points are difficult to research when the material is in rough form, but consumer reactions to the rough advertisements can, nevertheless, suggest modifications that enhance the clarity or the appeal of the finished advertisements.

Research techniques

By far the most common technique used for creative development research is the group discussion, but individual depth interviews or even small-scale quantified studies may sometimes be used. Qualitative research is appropriate here for several reasons:

■ The creative work is invariably at a rough, unfinished stage and commenting on such material is an unfamiliar task. This means that the interviewing situation must be designed to make informants feel relaxed and at ease (apart from expense, this is the main reason groups are usually preferred to depths).

■ By the same token, informants usually need an experienced convener rather than an interviewer to encourage them to use their imaginations and to respond at an emotional as well as at a rational level to the stimulus material.

■ A large part of the value of creative development research lies in its diagnostic information.

It is not enough simply to know that version F was preferred; the creative team need to know what it was conveying, where those ideas, thoughts or feelings came from, what elements in the advertising treatment sent informants off on the wrong path, and what elements were strong and meaningful and could be built on. This kind of information simply cannot be obtained from a pre-prepared questionnaire: the convener has to follow up and probe the spontaneous comments.

Last but not least, there is no requirement at this stage that the information collected should be quantified. Creative development research is essentially part of a learning process; testing or evaluating will be carried out when the advertising ideas are in much more finished form.

Group discussion techniques are discussed fully in Chapter 17. It is usual to convene groups of eight informants in a sitting-room environment. Often they are conducted in interviewers' homes, but increasingly viewing-room facilities are used. Several of these are available across the UK for general hire, and some qualitative research companies and advertising agencies have their own.

Essentially these facilities provide the opportunity for several people (creative teams, or other agency or client personnel) to watch the group discussion without disturbing the informants by being in the same room. Some have a small viewing room behind a two-way mirror, while others videotape the group and relay the video to another room with a television monitor.

Interpretation of results

At a simple level group reactions to outline advertisements are often unequivocal. If everybody hates an idea or totally misinterprets it, subtlety of interpretations seems hardly necessary. However, even a strong adverse reaction should not be dismissed out of hand in that the very strength of the reaction may indicate that there is a germ of a very powerful idea in the advertisement that might be worth revisiting with an alternative treatment.

Over and above this, however, there is a very real skill involved in working with rough creative material and providing positive and constructive feedback for the creative team. The convener needs not only to be skilled in running a group and drawing out responses from the informants, but also to understand the creative process and appreciate the difference between those elements in the rough advertisement that can easily be changed and those that are fundamental to the creative idea.

Everybody involved with creative development research understands that some ideas will be rejected, so a negative conclusion in itself need not cause problems. The real skill lies in being able to draw constructive guidance from the research, enabling the researcher to suggest a way forward rather than simply saying everything bombed for these 14 reasons.

Quantitative studies

Quantified techniques using a structured questionnaire are not suitable for checking rough advertisements. They may, however, be useful in narrowing product concept options when this is an extension to the strategic planning stage. If, to take a rather simplistic example, a new food product could claim new foil technology, convenience or authenticity of recipe, you might want to prioritize those claims before briefing a creative team. This could be done using simple verbal descriptions of the product characteristic and its benefits in a small-scale quantitative concept test in the following way.

Matched samples of consumers are each shown one of the concept alternatives and asked to rate it. The key question is usually likely interest in trial or purchase on a rating scale, but diagnostic information like reasons for interest or lack of interest, believability and uniqueness of the concept would also be collected. Basic demographics and information on current product and brand usage habits would also be covered. Samples of 100–150 are usually considered adequate for these tests.

A straight comparison of the interest scores across the legs of the test is usually the key result because at this stage the primary objective is to remove weak options rather than to select just one. An analysis of the relative scores within broad demographic or user groups may sometimes be useful as a tie-breaker, but the target group should have been defined in an earlier, much larger study. The concept test sample should consist only of members of the target group, and the primary analysis should be between total samples. A precaution against progressing the 'best of a bad bunch' is the use of norms or average scores from previous tests.

Note that product concepts are sometimes conducted comparatively, where the informant is shown all the options and asked to choose or put them in order of preference. In the main, however, this kind of check is better done qualitatively. The simple preference ratings tend to conceal more than they reveal.

A cautionary note should be added here: concept tests of this nature are not precision measuring instruments, and they are enormously dependent on the exact wording of the concepts tested. Used with common sense they can, however, be a quick and fairly cheap way of weeding out low-interest product promises and improving the copy focus.

EVALUATIVE OR PRE-TESTING RESEARCH

This stage of advertising research is normally carried out on finished or near-finished material since the core objective is to test the performance of the actual advertisement not the strategic thought or the creative idea behind the advertisement.

It is, however, quite common for television advertisements to be tested in the form of an 'animatic' or 'photomatic'. These rough versions of the proposed finished script are sometimes very sophisticated with the visuals rendered by either drawings or photographs and a professional voice-over and music track. The advantage of testing at this stage is, of course, that you get feedback before you go to the considerable expense of making the commercial for real. When £100,000 is often regarded as a cheap production cost, this precaution is understandable. The disadvantage is equally obvious in that the animatic or photomatic is not the actual commercial and may perform slightly differently on the test measures, therefore giving rather misleading results.

Some companies actually 'pre-test' with both versions in order to overcome this difficulty, but then the animatic research is properly part of the creative development or learning phase even if pre-testing measures are used.

Objectives of the research

There are two distinct, if slightly overlapping, schools of thought about pre-testing research.

The first holds that the only thing that can be measured with any validity is whether the advertisement said what it set out to say – where 'said' is extended beyond the transmission of rational, verbal messages to include successfully conveying a mood, emotion or association. In many cases these tests will include a persuasion measure or two, but their primary orientation is towards the measurement of communication.

The second holds that the only thing really worth measuring is whether the advertisement will influence sales. It is usual for these persuasion or effectiveness tests to include several measures of communication, but the sales effectiveness measures are the focus.

Over and above this basic difference of opinion about primary objectives, there is a great deal of contention over the measures that are considered relevant and the questioning techniques that are considered to be most fruitful. Pre-testing is a major source of business for the market research industry and, since it is also an area fraught with difficulties, there has been no shortage over the past 30 years or so of fresh ideas and new techniques designed to narrow the area of risk and increase the feeling of confidence in the results.

Many research companies market their own proprietary techniques with fervour, and many advertisers select one technique that they use consistently in order to develop company or category norms to increase their level of confidence in the decisions taken on the basis of the results. It is, however, the author's belief that while all of the techniques available generate useful information that reduces the level of uncertainty about whether the effect of running the advertisement will be beneficial to the brand, accurate predictions of market-place effectiveness are, and are likely to remain, unattainable.

The basis for choice as between the techniques available (apart from simple technical competence) must be the advertiser's personal or corporate model of how advertising itself works.

If, for example, you believe that advertising influences people to the extent that it conveys rational, and primarily verbal, information about the performance benefits of a brand, then your primary interest will be in measures that tell you whether the messages you believe to be powerful have, in fact, been conveyed. Most communication and recall measures will tell you that, within the limitations imposed by the forced viewing context.

If, on the other hand, you believe that overall 'liking' of an advertisement is important, there are measures that will tell you that. Persuasion measures are rather more contentious except in the cases of new brands or genuinely new information, but several companies can claim validation of their measures against in-market brand performance.

Research techniques

The three basic research techniques used in pre-testing are:

1. group discussions;
2. quantified hall tests;
3. quantified theatre tests.

Group discussions are organized in the usual way with groups of eight target consumers invited to an interviewer's home or a research viewing facility. The groups normally last for 90 minutes, though two hours is not uncommon, and the moderator probes for general and specific reactions to the test advertisement after one and then repeated showings.

Hall tests are held in research centres or hired public halls. The total sample is usually between 100 and 150 but this will be split across two or three hall day sessions using different locations. Normally, target respondents are recruited off the street and invited to go to the research session there and then.

Theatre tests are rather different in that respondents are pre-recruited for a designated session and are often told they will be asked to rate a television programme. This is an expensive procedure and more than one commercial is usually tested in a single session. The test commercials are shown first in a reel of commercials inserted in the test programme and then, later, given a repeat showing. Respondents sit as an audience and fill out self-completion questionnaires. Sample sizes are 100–200 per test.

Measures used

Many research companies offer a standard, proprietary pre-test service that uses their own selection of measures and their own preferred question wording. However, many of these measures are common across many services.

Impact, stand-out and brand registration

It is difficult, if not impossible, to get a realistic measure of impact in an enforced viewing situation, and group discussions do not even try. However, most hall and theatre tests put the test advertisement in a reel of five, six, seven, nine or ten and ask informants to name spontaneously any advertisements they remember seeing. Unnamed advertisements are then prompted with a list of brand names.

This procedure usually produces high recall scores, but there is variation in the levels achieved and, when compared against the other advertisements in the test and against norms, it is certainly possible to see when you have a low-impact advertisement (or a poorly branded one – see below).

A more severe measure of impact is provided by the DAR or day-after-recall test. For this the test commercial must be screened on air, usually in one television region in the middle of a high-rating programme. A sample of target consumers is then contacted by telephone the next evening and, after a series of questions to establish whether the informant was watching the relevant part of the programme, spontaneous and prompted advertisement recall questions are asked.

Millward Brown set great store by the extent to which commercials are branded, not in the simple sense that the brand name can be recalled after forced exposure in a reel, but in the sense that the brand mentions are fully integrated with the creative highlights and the main message. They have developed a series of questions that measure branding in this way and claim that their Link pre-test technique is a good predictor of their tracking study results.

Communication

All pre-tests set out to measure communication in the sense that, in one way or another, they ask informants what the commercial was saying about the brand and this is checked against what the advertiser and agency set out to say. Depending on the point of view of the testing agency, these questions may be asked immediately after viewing, after two or three minutes or 20 minutes or, indeed, 24 hours. With groups and hall tests, the questions are then asked a second time immediately following repeat exposure of the advertisement.

A good deal of controversy surrounds the question of the relevance of recall of message points to the eventual effectiveness of the advertising and the built-in bias of these measures towards rational and verbally encapsulated messages, but many advertisers use message recall as their primary measure. Some attempts are often made in subsequent questions to pick up messages that were heard and recalled but disbelieved, or heard and recalled but judged commonplace and boring, but in the main those who value recall of messages take this at face value.

Comprehension

Comprehension questions ask informants to describe what was going on in the advertisement, what was seen, what was heard and what happened. Many tests include such questions. The answers may be used to supplement the communication questions if a message is mentioned at this question but not at the main recall question. The answers are also used diagnostically in that they may reveal confusion or lack of understanding or, indeed, simple failure to 'see' part of the commercial at all.

Liking and involvement

These subjective response measures obviously interrelate in terms of the respondents' overall reactions to the advertisement, but they are usually measured in different ways. Some tests ask about things in the commercial, particularly whether it was liked or disliked. Some collect general impressions of the advertisement, while some ask 'What was going through your mind when you watched?' Some administer a prompt list of adjectives or phrases describing the advertisement rather than the brand, and ask informants to choose. Still others give informants a dial or lever to move or buttons to press as they watch. The question is usually phrased in terms of interest in what is on the screen or of feelings about the advertisement, and informants are encouraged to register their reactions to each sequence.

The lever or buttons then produce a computer-generated line, which is plotted on to a copy of the commercial so that high or low points of interest, involvement or attention can be analysed and interpreted. These frame-by-frame reactions are a feature of both the PEAC testing system from Pegram Walters and Link from Millward Brown.

Attitude or brand image questions

Many pre-tests include questions on brand image. Six or seven attitude or image statements are rated on a five- or seven-point scale, and the statements are likely to include one or more that relate specifically to a message point in the test advertisement. One should not normally expect shifts in attitudes or beliefs about a brand as the result of two exposures to an advertisement, but they do sometimes happen. This question can also be used as a supplementary communication question, and the ratings can be useful in making comparisons between advertisements if the advertiser habitually uses the same testing system.

Diagnostic questions

All of the above questions can be used diagnostically in that they can reveal elements of strength or weakness in the commercial that can be used to explain the overall results and perhaps suggest changes that might be made. Over and above this, however, most tests allow the opportunity to probe particular elements in the commercial. Commonly this is the music, the presenter or main characters or the end line, but any element can be the subject of a specific question if extra information is required.

Persuasion measures

This is a controversial issue and practitioners and advertisers differ widely in the degree of importance they attach to measures of persuasion. Many so-called communication tests include a direct or projective persuasion scale, typically 'Having seen the commercial do you feel more or less interested in buying the brand?' or 'This commercial has been shown in another part of the country. Do you think sales of the brand went up or down?' However, in the main these questions are presented as just part of the overall evaluation, supplementing communication or involvement or attitude scores, rather than as a critically important measure.

There are tests, however, and these are usually theatre tests, where this measure is used as the critical measure. Typically, informants are asked to choose from a list of brands, and told they will get a free supply of their selected brand if they win a raffle. The question is asked before the advertisement is seen and then again afterwards, with the difference being the persuasion score. It is usual to get quite small differences between scores for well-established, heavily advertised brands, but, nevertheless, taken together with other key measures the research suppliers claim good correlations with subsequent in-market performance.

These techniques fell out of favour in the UK after the demise of the Schwerin and ASL testing systems, but the two companies CRL and RSL have recently introduced new systems based on techniques that are widely used in the USA and elsewhere.

Pre-testing press executions

In the UK, television commercials are much more likely to be subjected to quantified pre-testing than press or poster advertisements. This is largely a function of the cost of the test itself against the cost of producing and running the advertisement rather than any deficiency in techniques.

All major companies who offer a television communication check also test print ads. The test advertisement is inserted in a folder or even a copy of a newspaper or magazine in order to simulate a real reading situation and it is then exposed on its own later. The questionnaire follows broadly the same pattern as the television questionnaire and there is usually a mechanism that enables the test to discriminate between information gleaned from a brief look and information communicated after a read.

Reading and noting checks take this one stage further. The tests are usually carried out on advertisements printed into special editions of a newspaper or magazine, and additional questions establish which particular elements of the advertisement have been read or noted.

Interpretation of results

Interpretation of results depends fundamentally on the objectives of advertisers and their agencies in setting it up. Objectives broadly fall into four groups:

1. to check whether the advertisement communicated what it was intended to communicate;
2. to check whether the test commercial reaches an acceptable standard on key measures compared with other commercials tested for that brand;
3. to predict, in general terms, market-place success in building (or holding) business for the brand;
4. more simply, to provide general reassurance that the advertisement contains no serious negatives.

All advertising pre-tests are designed to meet the first of these objectives and, in theory at least, the results are easy to interpret against this objective. In practice, however, it is not uncommon for difficulties to arise. These usually stem from a lack of absolute clarity at the outset about the desired performance level on the key measures. Many commercials score somewhere in the middle rather than being obviously poor or excellent. Many also perform differently on the different measures and that lends a certain ambiguity to the overall results.

All these problems are, of course, simplified if the advertiser and agency have clear views about the most important measures and if the same test is used routinely so that category or brand norms form a benchmark. It is, therefore, much easier to reach a conclusion in relation to the second objective than the first.

Where companies have the third objective in mind, evaluating the results can, paradoxically, be easier. Prediction of likely market-place effects is obviously a much bigger theoretical issue than evaluating communication effectiveness, but those who are interpreting the results usually have a much clearer picture of what they are looking for.

To a greater or lesser degree of rigour, the results for a given advertisement will be evaluated against data showing in-market effects of previous advertising. In the main, such data will also focus primarily on one or two measures only.

Some advertising theorists would argue that advertising effectiveness is far too complex to be reduced to one or two pre-test scores, but it is undeniable that companies that systematically build a model of how advertising works in their market can have more confidence in their judgements. At the very least, the whole process of preparing advertising strategies, developing advertisements and evaluating them will be more focused if it is working against a defined model represented by a proven recall score, a persuasion index or measures of the extent to which the brand is fully integrated into an involving commercial.

Decisions that can be taken

A large number of pre-tests seem to be carried out in order to confirm the decision already taken, ie to run the advertisement. However, it is also the case that a commercial may be rejected, re-edited, substantially re-shot or aired for a very brief time while a new version is being prepared.

Opinions differ about the extent to which tinkering with a finished commercial can substantially improve it, but there are certainly many instances where problems can be traced to a particular element in the advertisement and this element can often be changed. In the nature of things, the revamped commercial is rarely retested, but learning has been accrued and confidence is boosted.

CAMPAIGN EVALUATION RESEARCH

In 1970 the systematic evaluation of advertising campaigns was relatively rare. Advertisers would, of course, evaluate the performance of their brands but links between market performance and the concurrent advertising was, in many cases, made on judgement or on the basis of measures taken at infrequent intervals on usage and attitude surveys.

All that has changed. With the increasing sophistication of marketing departments, research techniques and econometric models, major advertisers now commonly conduct research in order to give them some feedback on the way their advertising is working. Here again, however, there are significant differences of opinion about what constitutes effective advertising and, therefore, in the type of research carried out.

For some advertisers the only relevant measure is sales and, while one cannot deny that the end objective of all marketing activity is sales, this tends to lead to a focus on short-term sales gains. Sometimes this is a highly appropriate measure, but there are many instances, especially with mature brands, where holding sales is a considerable achievement. Obviously, this is an issue of interpretation not of measurement, but the question of the specific longer-term effect of advertising is much more difficult to address through research. A good deal of work has been done on advertising decay rates, but in the end the advertiser either would have to stay with a campaign despite disappointing early results in order to be able to measure any longer-term effects or, more drastically, would need to stop advertising for a while (at least in an area) to see whether an apparently disappointing advertising performance was, in fact, contributing to sales, share and profits.

At the other end of the theoretical spectrum, some advertisers make no attempt to relate advertising performance directly to sales or share. Objectives for the advertising are set in terms of so-called 'intermediate' variables. Such an objective might be to increase spontaneous brand awareness if the product is new or if the brand has only recently benefited from a significant advertising appropriation. The objective might also be to modify the image of the brand along certain dimensions, to sustain a strong image in a competitive context, to achieve awareness that a product improvement has been introduced or simply to relay the information that it is now available at a lower price.

In each case the advertising and marketing strategy will have estimated that satisfactory achievement of these advertising objectives will result either in short-term incremental sales or in increased brand stature, which will lead to longer-term sales benefits. However, in this approach, no attempt is made directly to attribute sales results to the advertising. Advertising and sales will be measured separately and a relationship may be inferred, but no attempt will be made to calibrate the increased sales volume directly against the cost of the advertising.

Techniques

The technique chosen for the evaluation study will obviously depend upon the objectives that have been set. Some of the main ones are outlined below.

Sales measures

At the very simple level, advertising can be related to sales with ex-factory shipments in one hand and a media plan in the other, so a separate advertising evaluation study is not required. Sometimes this is literally what happens, but the analysis would more usually be supplemented by knowledge of competitive activity and of any other changes to the marketing mix of the competing brands during the period in question.

In those instances where the advertising is designed to achieve very fast sales results (eg direct selling off the page, or sales or special offer announcements especially in the retail sector), a good evaluation of the advertising will be achieved without survey information: the advertising runs on Thursday and by Saturday you know how well it has worked.

For manufacturers of fast-moving consumer goods (fmcg) without direct access to till receipts, research data (of the kind produced by Nielsen or AGB) will be required to check consumer off-take. Again, advertising effectiveness can be inferred simply by looking at the purchasing or share data against the media plan. The problem with this very straightforward approach is that it makes no direct allowance for anything else that was going on in the market apart from the client's advertising. Obviously this can be done informally in that client and agency usually know about, and can make some allowance for, competitive advertising or promotional activity, changes to product, pack, distribution and so on. There are, however, more formal ways of taking account of these other factors so that the relationship between sales and advertising is more clearly exposed.

Area tests

Area tests are usually used to isolate advertising effects in one of two ways: 1) to compare the achievement of different advertising executions; and 2) to compare the achievement of the same advertising at different spend levels. Care must obviously be taken to match the test areas as closely as possible (which is not easy) but, nevertheless, area tests often provide a very clear basis on which to evaluate the sales performance of advertising. Even when sales or share results are the primary criteria of advertising effectiveness, the basic data are often supplemented by survey information that throws light on how the advertising was working.

Information on the 'intermediate' measures such as brand awareness, advertising awareness, advertising recall, brand image or user profile is collected but, in this case, the results are used diagnostically to inform the development of the next advertising (or to help decide its level) or to explain the sales differences, rather than as the primary evaluation measure. This information might be collected on an *ad hoc* one-shot study, or a 'before and after' study, or on a regular or continuous basis.

Econometric modelling

Econometric modelling takes the process of isolating the influence of advertising on sales a stage further. Those who want a more detailed explanation of econometrics in this context are referred to the relevant chapter by Jeremy Elliot in *How to Plan Advertising* (1989) produced by The Account Planning Group and to the five editions of *Advertising Works* produced by the IPA (Broadbent, 1981, 1983; Channon, 1985, 1987; Fieldwick, 1989).

Reduced to its bare essentials, econometric modelling uses a mathematical formula by which a value is put on each of the marketing variables where the formula best explains variations in the key dependent variable, that of sales. The development of such a model requires not only a rigorous process of statistical testing, but also a reliable series of prior data on all the key variables before the formula can be derived. It follows, then, that the technique is only available to those companies that routinely and consistently collect all the necessary input data.

Intermediate measures

The tracking study focuses on intermediate measures, and its great advantage is that the measures are taken continuously so that it is possible to relate responses to specific bursts of advertising activity. In the same way, of course, continuous measurement also enables the analyst to pinpoint competitive advertising activity, significant promotions, or changes in the product, price, pack, distribution or any other element in the marketing mix of the major brands.

Typically, tracking studies use samples of 100 a week from the main target group (all housewives, all adults, all motorists, etc), but present data in rolling four-weekly periods to smooth small sample variations. Results are usually presented in graphic as well as tabular form in order to highlight variations in the trend lines on the different measures during or between bursts of advertising activity. Advertising bursts (indicating weight and duration) are usually plotted on the graphs for the test brand to facilitate interpretation. Core questions will be asked about up to a dozen brands and will normally cover the following areas:

- spontaneous and prompted brand awareness;
- spontaneous and prompted advertising awareness;
- detailed recall and communication from advertising;

- attitudes to advertising – from a checklist;
- recognition of key campaigns from stills;
- brand image batteries;
- brand usage questions (primarily for analysis).

If the survey is tailor-made for one client, the questionnaire may be extended to include questions on:

- promotions;
- new brand launches;
- brand personality batteries;
- more detailed usage questions.

Several companies offer tailor-made tracking studies but, in addition, tracking questions can be included on weekly omnibus studies. Tracking studies are frequently used as the primary advertising evaluation measure where advertising is judged to be successful or not according to the scores it achieves on the advertising related measures. Self-evidently, tracking study results can also be used in conjunction with sales or share data though relationships between the two sets of results will usually be inferential.

Strictly speaking, the term 'tracking studies' should only be used when interviewing is continuous. However, some companies 'track' four times a year or in bursts around their own advertising activity. Ad tracking questions are also routinely included in usage and attitude studies and in some syndicated surveys within broad product categories.

CONCLUSION

Advertising research covers a broad range of studies and research techniques, many of which are covered elsewhere in this book, as the same technique frequently has many applications. It is a subject that generates strong opinions and arouses strong emotions, not so much because the techniques themselves are contentious, but because each technique is rooted in and dependent on a particular theory about how advertising works. Since there are almost as many theories on this subject as there are theorists and since, in truth, advertising works differently for different products and different brands in different circumstances, the debate may never be resolved.

In such a situation it is more than usually important that the researcher who is designing and conducting research about advertising should be absolutely clear about the specific objectives of the study in question. With a tight and agreed set of objectives, research can increase the understanding and confidence of the decision-taker substantially. Without this clarity of objective it may simply add to the confusion and dissension.

REFERENCES AND FURTHER READING

Broadbent, S, ed (1981) *Advertising Works*, IPA and Holt, Rhinehart and Winston, London

Broadbent, S, ed (1983) *Advertising Works 2*, IPA and Holt, Rhinehart and Winston, London

Channon, C, ed (1985) *Advertising Works 3*, IPA and Holt, Rhinehart and Winston, London

Channon, C, ed (1987) *Advertising Works 4*, IPA and Cassell, London

Elliot, J (1989) in *How to Plan Advertising*, ed D Cowley, The Account Planning Group, Cassell, London

Fieldwick, P, ed (1989) *Advertising Works 5*, IPA and Cassell, London

21

Researching Television and Radio

Peter Menneer

BROADCASTING, COMPETITION – AND THE AUDIENCE RESEARCHER

Audience research is a source of key information for marketing and editorial management in television and radio companies. For those TV channels and radio stations funded by advertising (the majority), it provides the critical currency for the trading of airtime. ('Channel' is the conventional term for television and 'station' for radio. Constantly to refer to 'TV channels and radio stations' becomes repetitious. In this chapter the two terms are used interchangeably.) The price for a commercial slot will reflect its demand, and demand will be determined by the size of its audience at that time and by the composition of that audience – whether containing a disproportionate number of adults, a high socioeconomic profile and so on. Audience research figures generate a channel's revenue. They are, in this way, the source of its programme budget – and of the dividends payable to its shareholders.

By comparison with most manufacturing or service companies, the audience research function in a broadcasting organization is – or should be – relatively high-profile. The stakes are high. The head of the marketing (or audience) research function needs to be a member of the senior management team, contributing to decision-making both at a strategic level and in the rough and tumble of daily competition – whether advising on promotional activities or on tactical scheduling manoeuvres. The opportunity for the audience researcher to contribute to the development and success of the channel should be personally and professionally rewarding – with luck, in more senses than one.

The literature and papers given at professional conferences tend to be dominated by the arcane subject of audience measurement. This is inevitable. A channel depends on the 'numbers' for its revenue – in most cases. But inside the broadcasting organization the researcher should be operating on a much broader front, adding to the significance of the function – and job satisfaction for the individual.

Broadcasting is nowadays a highly competitive business. Some years ago the number of channels available to the viewer was traditionally limited by spectrum scarcity. Governments, particularly in Western Europe, therefore believed that it was important to ensure that the limited number of possible channels or stations should be deployed to contribute to the welfare of the public as viewers of television and listeners to radio. Out of this political aspiration arose the concept of 'public service broadcasting'. In many countries of Europe what emerged was a highly regulated system, based in part on public funding – often a licence fee was required from all families owning a radio or (later) a television set. The United States went the other way. It was the commercial stations that developed first. Public broadcasting in the US has always been a poor relation.

The transition from analogue to digital transmission is revolutionizing the structure of broadcasting. There is now an engineering capability to deliver hundreds of channels to the home – whether by the rooftop aerial, by satellite dish or by cable. There is similarly a multiplicity in funding mechanisms: from the licence fee, to spot advertising, to subscription, to pay-per-view. Broadcasting has become highly competitive. The early years of the 21st century are likely also to see a degree of convergence between traditional broadcasting and the personal computer, through the interactive possibilities of the new technologies. However, the fundamentals will remain for the managing directors. They will be hungry for audiences – even those in the fortunate position of receiving public funding, who increasingly have to justify their privileged status. Public accountability has been the order of the day for such channels, whether for the BBC in the UK, NOS in the Netherlands, or Danmarks Radio in Denmark.

Competition for audiences has been good for the business of audience researchers. They can and are expected to contribute to the positioning of their channels in a fragmented market with an increasing number of niche channels, for example:

News	CNN, BBC World
Sports	Sky Sports, Eurosport
Children's programming	Cartoon Network, Nickelodeon
Movies	Sky Premier
Natural history and documentaries	Discovery, National Geographic

Each channel's success is dependent on the talent it acquires, whether this be writers, comedians, Hollywood archives or football clubs. Since in the short term the supply of talent available to a station is finite, the cost of talent has risen dramatically. The audience researcher can contribute his or her professional skills in a major way to the identification of the talent appropriate to the station, its deployment and promotion.

A BROAD AGENDA FOR THE RESEARCHER

So researchers need to apply their craft across a broad front of issues, as indicated, for example, in Table 21.1.

Table 21.1 *Research issues*

	Possible Research Approach
Are the long-term trends in the country's demography going to be helpful to us competitively – or not?	Latest governmental population projections.
When is my audience available to view / listen to my station? When do they return home in my part of the country at the end of the working day?	Time budget studies.
If prime time (say the five hours from 6 pm to 11 pm) accounts for over half of the day's total viewing/listening, what is my optimal strategy for maximizing my peak-time audience share? How can I compete aggressively and efficiently with the competition in peak time?	Detailed interrogation of the audience measurement database.
Given an overall fixed programme budget, how much can be devoted to drama? A high cost per hour but, if it	Cross-analysis of programme costs with audience data: to obtain cost-per-viewer-hour comparisons

Table 21.1 *Research approaches (continued)*

	Possible Research Approach
catches the public imagination, very effective in delivering audiences. What impact will that have on the budgets available for the rest of the programme schedule – and its competitiveness?	between different types of programming.
The channel has committed a major investment to a soap opera – to improve its competitiveness in early prime time on specific days of the week, with subsequent programmes to benefit from their audience inheritance. Unfortunately the soap opera is simply not delivering. What is the problem? The stakes are high.	Almost certainly, focus group research in the first instance – and involving the production team directly to 'own' the research. Audience appreciation data (if available) could identify the sectors of the population to which the soap opera is/is not appealing – with diagnostic data to identify the underlying problems.
A decision has been taken to commission a programme series on the bird life of the planet and how this is adapting to or under environmental threat from humans. The natural history researcher has drawn up an initial candidate list of 50 species. Only 10 can in practice be covered. In terms of potential audience appeal, which should be short-listed?	Pre-testing research, qualitative or quantitative – or a combination of both.
The company's pop music radio station is losing market share. In what directions should the station's music policy be developed to reverse this trend – or at a minimum to halt this decline?	Consider auditorium testing – playing short samples of (eg) adult contemporary artists to a sample of the station's listeners and potential listeners.
The broadcaster is coming under attack from a particular political party for alleged bias in its coverage of news. Is this fair criticism? Is this the perception of the public too? Is the correct response to reject the allegation robustly, or to encourage action to be taken to ensure more scrupulous even-handedness in the channel's political journalism?	Detailed content analysis of news and current affairs coverage of particular issues. Corporate image research: to establish public perception of any partisanship.

Table 21.1 *Research approaches (continued)*

	Possible Research Approach
The company is coming under attack in the press for the (alleged) high incidence of excessive violence in its programmes, especially in the early evening when there is a substantial children's audience. Is this true? Is this also the view of significant numbers of the viewing public?	Formal content analysis is an important information source. This needs to be repeated and updated at regular intervals. The key to this debate is usually trend data. Is the violence (and of what kinds) depicted on the TV screen actually growing, stable or falling at these times of day? Also obtain regular measures of public perceptions. The public threshold of tolerance for violence seen on the TV screen may itself be changing.

The broadcasting researcher will need to deploy a wide range of research tools. It is often useful to develop a continuing relationship with a short list of research companies who will come over the years to understand the complex relationships that exist between the broadcaster and their audiences.

AUDIENCE MEASUREMENT

Inevitably, however, a major preoccupation for the researcher will be the audience measurement system to which the channel subscribes. These tend to be expensive, for reasons that will become apparent. It is likely that about 75 per cent or more of the research budget will be devoted to the measurement of audiences.

In countries with highly developed advertising and broadcasting systems, the 'market' sees itself as needing TV audience figures on a daily basis – all 365 days of the year. The market is the interaction of the buying and selling of airtime: advertisers and agencies as the buyers, and broadcasters as the sellers – often through sales houses that are distinct from the programme-making companies themselves. They need what is called a 'common currency' for this purpose. The outcome is usually a single source of audience data for the country or market in question.

In most countries radio is the (relatively) poor relation. It may generate only some 10–20 per cent of the advertising expenditure attracted to television. There is therefore less of a commercial imperative for the detail and frequency of radio audience information that is expected and required for the television medium. Radio audience data tend in most markets to be published on a quarterly or even six-monthly or annual basis.

How a country's audience measurement system is designed, controlled and funded is a critical issue. The key principle is that there needs to be effective consultation with all sectors of the industry to ensure that the system is customer-led in its priorities. Each country needs to determine what precise organizational arrangement best fulfils this objective – a continuum ranging from a joint industry committee (JIC) that awards a fixed-term contract to a supplier and inherently ensures that the interests of all users are represented, to a media owner committee (MOC), to a particular data supplier's own service (OS).

RECALL AND THE DIARY

In terms of technique there are, in theory at least, a number of options for the broadcasting researcher to choose between. The two classic techniques, still widely used today, are recall and the diary.

For radio audience measurement, the world is divided between those who believe in recall and those who put their faith in diary measurement. Disciples of the diary ask sceptically whether people can accurately recollect their radio listening 'yesterday'. They argue that respondents will tend to report their habitual radio listening behaviour, and not what they actually heard the day before. Equally non-peak-time listening is likely to be understated. To the extent that these problems arise (and much depends on the structure and rigour of the recall interview itself) it is the minority stations that are likely to lose out. They will tend to be secondary stations for their listeners – not tuned to every day. The end result for smaller stations is the familiar double jeopardy. Apart from the disadvantages of being small in terms of their share of total radio listening, they are also penalized for being small. What listening they have can be understated by a recall system.

Diary supporters also point to one major limitation of the 24-hour recall system: no longitudinal analysis (beyond 24 hours) is possible. The number of people who tune to a particular daily show at least once across the average week (its 'weekly reach') cannot be measured other than by modelling. With a diary, reach and frequency across days can be established empirically, whether for programmes or for commercial breaks.

The recall camp have their equivalent doubts about the diary. Response rates tend to be lower for diaries. It is more difficult to persuade people to keep a diary over the conventional seven-day period. The system is therefore more exposed to potential bias. Secondly, to what extent are diarists conscientious in their diary keeping? How many actually enter their listening at least once a day? How many forget and have then to attempt to reconstruct their listening over a number of days that have elapsed? On this particular issue, see van Lil and van Meerem (1987) and Joint National Listenership Research Committee (Ireland)/MRBI (1989). About two-thirds of diarists in these experiments were established to be up to date with their diaries or at least to have completed them up to 'yesterday'. However, there remains of course a worry about the other third.

Across Western Europe recall nations outnumber diary nations for radio audience measurement by a ratio of two to one. Amongst the larger countries of Europe, France, Germany, Italy and Spain all deploy recall, but in widely different ways, while the UK belongs to the diary camp together with Denmark, Finland and the Netherlands. In the USA the diary is *de rigueur* for local market radio audience measurement, while national radio is measured by 24-hour recall via a CATI interview, with respondents being telephoned and interviewed about their previous day's radio listening on seven successive days.

Evidence as to whether one technique tends systematically to deliver higher audiences is inconclusive (see Menneer, 1994). There is a suggestion that the seven-day diary appears to pick up more listening than 24-hour recall. But recall proponents may reasonably raise the possibility that diary samples, with usually lower response rates, could underrepresent the light listener less interested in keeping a diary, and hence overstate average hours of listening. So both sides have faith in what they do, and distrust what they don't.

The structure of the classic recall interview, whether about TV viewing or radio listening, is usually along the following lines. The day is divided into about eight day parts appropriate for the country in question and, for each (eg between 6 and 9 am), respondents are asked whether they watched TV (or listened to the radio) yesterday. If they did, they are asked:

- when they switched on (by 15-minute intervals);
- when they switched off (similarly);
- which channels/stations they tuned to over this period and, for each, from when to when.

This process is repeated for the next day part.

Traditionally it was often the practice for the interview to be aided by the detail of the previous day's programme schedule for each station. But this is becoming less and less practicable as the number of stations to be measured has multiplied in recent years.

The use of programme schedules for the diary technique is again rarely practicable nowadays. Most diaries divide the day into 15-minute segments, and print these down the left-hand side of the diary page. For some diary designs the station names are preprinted (the 'rostered' diary) and the diarist simply draws a line under the appropriate station for the quarter-hours of listening to that station. However, in many (if not most) countries nowadays the sheer number of stations available makes any form of channel prelisting procedure particularly difficult, if not impossible. Instead the respondent is required to enter the station name or call sign (and sometimes the programme name as well) into the diary. This is the 'unrostered' diary. As the Global Guidelines for Television Audience Measurement (GGTAM) point out (ARM Group, 1999):

> New problems now arise:
>
> ■ This unaided technique will often register less viewing than a technique involving channel pre-listing. Viewing is relatively understated.
> ■ Secondly, this relative understatement can disproportionately affect channels rarely viewed. Channels with large numbers of viewers are also usually the channels in the regular repertoire of their viewers. 'Minor' channels can have proportionately fewer regular viewers. Paradoxically, the outcome of what appears to be scrupulous even-handedness can be bias.
> ■ Thirdly, there is the problem of precise channel/programme identification. The respondent may not have clearly identified it. It may be necessary to get in touch with diarists again over the coming weeks at the diary editing stage to try to establish which particular channel was being viewed on a particular day.
>
> The totally unprompted approach to channel identification therefore also has its difficulties.

GGTAM concludes:

> In summary, recall of channels viewed is a serious problem, especially in markets with a large number of channels due to widespread cable/ satellite, etc. Some type of prompt (such as diary roster) should be provided wherever possible. Where this is not possible, research should be conducted on diary design and fieldwork techniques to minimize recall bias to the greatest extent possible.

For TV audience measurement, the diary continues to be used widely to supplement peoplemeter systems (see below). In the USA, for example, diaries continue to be used in local markets. Equally, diaries are recommended by the ARM Group (1997b) for measurement of:

■ non-domestic viewing;
■ holiday homes;
■ international TV channels.

However, recall is also a realistic and appropriate technique to use if this is linked to the establishment of a random day for each individual. 'Yesterday' data are deployed if the person was at home on their Random Assigned Day (RAD). If, however, they were away on the RAD, reported viewing on their last 'away day' is used (Menneer, 2000).

OTHER MEASUREMENT TECHNIQUES

Other techniques also have their place to meet particular objectives of TV audience measurement. They are detailed in the following three sections.

Set meters

These remain widely used for local markets in the USA. They measure set usage in the household and are methodologically superior to most TV audience measurement systems in that they require no day-to-day co-operation ('compliance') from the household members. Of course the principal limitation of this technique is that it does not provide any data about the audience and their demography – a key item of information for both broadcasters and advertisers. Audience and demographic information is then derived from supplementary research such as diaries.

The coincidental interview

The coincidental interview sets out to establish the viewing behaviour of a randomly selected individual at a particular moment. This technique is principally deployed nowadays for validation studies of other systems. By its nature it is expensive to employ, each interview being restricted to the moment of the call. It is customarily conducted by telephone. Despite its apparent simplicity, it presents its own technical problems, for example the interpretation of unanswered calls (not a valid private household member, everyone is out, the family is too engrossed with their TV soap opera to answer the phone, etc) and refusals (whether it can be safely assumed that those who refuse to participate have the same viewing behaviour as those who do).

Passive techniques

There are a number of experimental systems under development at the moment that are particularly interesting for the future. These involve miniaturized equipment (about the size of a pager or worn as a watch) that incorporates a microphone that 'hears' the TV channel or radio station. Broadcasters will have undertaken to include their identification code on their signal. Alternatively, audio samples are compared and matched with sound recordings taken by the data supplier for each channel or station. If and when such technologies are proven and available in the market-place at a price competitive as against the diary and peoplemeter, they will offer the exciting potential of a 'single-source' system for measuring both television and radio audiences.

This passive technology has another major technical attraction. It is much less demanding of respondents. They have simply to agree to wear the miniaturized portable meter or watch. The problems of respondent compliance should be less of an issue. For the time being, however, radio audiences will continue to be measured in most markets by either a diary or 24-hour recall, and TV audiences principally by the peoplemeter, which is the subject of Chapter 22 of this handbook.

THE PEOPLEMETER

The peoplemeter was first adopted by a number of Western European countries as their principal TV audience measurement system in the early 1980s. Over the years it has become the preferred system around the world, and by 1997 was being deployed in over 50 countries.

The technique requires the metering of all TV sets in the home and a handset for each by which each member of the household (down to a predetermined age, such as four) registers as a viewer by pressing his or her personal button on the handset. Each night the data supplier's computer rings each panel household (the phone bell having been suppressed) and retrieves the data: for each set, whether it is switched on or switched off and to which channel it is tuned; and, for each individual in relation to each set switched on, whether he or she has registered as a viewer or not.

In principle the data are captured second by second, but for most peoplemeter systems the standard time unit for audience measurement is usually the individual minute, with each minute being derived by an arithmetical averaging procedure from the original second-by-second data. The minute data can be manipulated by PC-based analysis software systems to provide a wide range of conventional audience measures, such as ratings, gross rating points (GRPs), channel reach and share of viewing.

Some principal audience measures are:

■ **rating** – the average percentage of a population (or projected population estimate), as estimated from the sample, viewing across a defined time period;

- **GRPs (gross rating points)** – the sum of the individual spot ratings in an advertising campaign (also known as ratings, rating points, TRPs – target rating points, and TVRs – TV ratings);
- **HUTs/PUTs (households/people using television)** – the average percentage of households/people using television (in total across all channels) across a specified time period;
- **cover/cume/reach** – the cumulative percentage of a population (or projected population estimate) registered as viewers to a sequence of programmes or schedule of advertising spots at least once;
- **frequency** – the average number of times that members of a population, who have been counted at least once as viewers to a schedule of advertising spots or sequence of programmes, have counted as viewers;
- **amount of viewing** – the amount of viewing (per day or per week) per head of population, by channel or in total, and expressed decimally in hours;
- **audience share** – the amount of viewing obtained by a particular channel or programme as a percentage of total viewing by a population across a defined time period;
- **channel reach** – the percentage of a population (or projected population estimate) viewing a television channel across a specified time period for a specified minimum number of minutes.

The operational task of a peoplemeter system is in essence to persuade a sample of households, that is an accurate cross-section of all private households in the market in question, to allow their TV sets (and usually their VCRs as well) to be metered, and for each member in that household (down to a predetermined age) faithfully to remember to 'push the button' to indicate when he or she is in the audience for each set. The two key concerns about peoplemeter data usually arise from relatively low levels of household response at recruitment (and attrition thereafter) and panellist compliance with button pushing.

The art of a well-designed and managed peoplemeter system is the development of proven techniques to minimize exposure to bias. For example, it is likely to be more difficult to persuade families who do little television viewing to join the panel in the first place. Equally, young adults tend to be the least conscientious in registering their viewing.

The outcome of a well-designed and well-managed TV audience measurement system is valid and reliable data. Senior management and schedulers within broadcasting organizations then have accurate information on their own audiences and those of their competitors as an input to programme content and scheduling decisions. For channels funded wholly or partly by advertising, the TV ratings become the 'currency' for the buying and selling of commercial airtime. For channels funded in whole or in part by a public licence fee or the equivalent, audience data provide measures of public accountability.

GGTAM

For international advertisers and advertising-funded channels, GGTAM is an attempt to establish an international 'exchange rate' for TV audience measurement systems throughout the world. These guidelines will be of interest to general readers intrigued by the art and the craft of audience measurement, in addition to those professionally responsible for the setting up or development of peoplemeter systems in their own market.

REFERENCES

ARM Group (1997a) *Towards Harmonization of Radio Audience Measurement Systems*, European Broadcasting Union, Geneva

ARM Group (1997b) *Non-Domestic Viewing, Holiday Homes, International TV Channels*, European Broadcasting Union, Geneva

ARM Group (1999) *Towards Global Guidelines for Television Audience Measurement*, ed P Menneer, European Broadcasting Union, Geneva

Joint National Listenership Research Committee (Ireland)/MRBI (1989) *Radio Listening Pilot Study*, JNLR

Menneer, Peter (1994), *Radio audiences: figures to be taken at face value?*, ESOMAR, Athens

Menneer, Peter (1995) *Radio audience measurement systems across Europe: currencies in common or in conflict?*, ESOMAR, Paris

Menneer, Peter (1997) *The Story of GGTAM*, ARF, New York

Menneer, P, Normesse, D and Nye , J (2000) *The Random Assigned Day: An innovative technique for measurement of broadcast audiences amongst high status populations*, ARF/ESOMAR, Miami

Syfret, Toby, ed (1995) *TV audience measurement in Europe*, ESOMAR

Syfret, Toby, ed (1997) *Radio audience measurement in Europe*, ESOMAR

van Lil, Jan and van Meerem, Leendert (1987) *The validity of radio measurement: differences in quality of listening behaviour*, ESOMAR, Amsterdam

22

Peoplemeters

Stephan Buck

INTRODUCTION

Everyone accepts the need for accurate measurement of TV audiences, in the interest of the programme makers, the TV contractors and the advertisers. The proliferation of channels, the growth in the additional uses for a TV set and the increasing number of sets in an average household have invalidated old measurement techniques and required researchers to find ever more sophisticated means of achieving their objectives. Fortunately, technology is even-handed: at the same time as it raises measurement problems, it provides the basis for a solution.

The original peoplemeter was introduced in the early 1980s in the UK because the old set and diary system was no longer adequate. Its subsequent spread to most developed countries shows that both the problems and the solutions are international. Each generation of peoplemeter is somewhat more sophisticated than the previous one, capable of monitoring more channels and more types of set usage. However, the launch of digital TV, which is expected to become significant early in the new millennium, requires a more fundamental change in measurement technology, and this is discussed below.

WHY MEASURE TELEVISION AUDIENCES?

Over the past 30 years television has established itself as the world's most important mass medium. Taking the UK as an example, 98 per cent of homes now have a television set and some 59 per cent have two or more. The average person spends approximately 25 hours a week watching television. This experience is not unique to the UK, but is repeated in many countries throughout the world. For the populations of these countries, television has become the major form of entertainment and the main source of information and education. It shapes political ideas, creates trends in fashion and establishes personalities. In consequence television has developed into the most powerful medium and has become a force for creating as well as for reflecting change in society.

Given the unique position television holds, the importance of measuring television audiences is easily understood. Broadcasters produce an enormous variety of programmes ranging from those with a mass public appeal to others designed for small, specialized-interest groups. Programme quality and audience appreciation are important criteria, but a programme's success will be judged in the first instance by its ability to attract the size and type of audience for which it was designed. Television advertisers use the medium to communicate a particular message. How effectively that message is communicated depends, in the first place, on how many and what type of people see it. The behaviour of television audiences is a subject of profound interest for government; the public's reactions to government policies frequently depend on how those policies are perceived through television. At the same time, government has the responsibility of ensuring that television itself does not have a harmful effect on society (eg the effect of violence on television). For both government and advertisers an understanding of how many and what type of people watch particular programmes is essential for the effective carrying out of their policies.

These, then, are some of the reasons why the measurement of television audiences is so important and explains the progress made over the years in developing measurement techniques leading to the peoplemeter.

MEASUREMENT SYSTEMS OVER TIME

The techniques used in the past to measure television audiences appear rather simple and unsophisticated today, but must be seen against the relatively simple television environment of the time. For example, in 1954 in the UK there was just one television channel, which transmitted for only six hours a day. Only some 25 per cent of homes had a television set, and there was no television advertising. In those days, television viewing was a memorable event. It was also in the main a family event, and the stereo-typical picture of the mother, father and 2.4 children gathered together in the evening at the fireside watching their small monochrome television set is not very far from the mark. It is true that with such a low penetration of television households, the number of visitors invited to view television was relatively great, but for them too the activity was memorable and easy to recall. In such a simple situation, relatively simple research methods were sufficient and these included aided recall techniques through an interview (covering 24 hours, three days or seven days) and the diary method, which provided information on the patterns of viewing in the short term. Much of this kind of work in the UK was carried out on a regular basis by the BBC in daily surveys of television viewing and radio listening behaviour. Data were aggregated to produce information relating to programmes and / or time bands, and audience appreciation data were also included in the research.

The advent of commercial television in the UK in 1955 caused a fresh view to be taken of the requirements for television audience measurement. The complexity(!) brought about by two channels rather than one and the growing penetration of television households all added to the interest in new techniques. But it was the market-place that brought the additional impetus required that moved the industry towards a meter-based tech-nique. Thus, the commercial medium's value to the advertisers had to be demonstrated and information was therefore needed, not only about the number of homes capable of receiving independent television, but also about the numbers and kinds of viewers it was reaching.

This time of change is covered in some detail in Audley (1986). In short, the industry committee that was inaugurated in 1955 and in various guises has continued ever since decided that there were a number of advantages to a panel approach, particularly the ability to analyse an individual's view-ing over considerable periods of time (see Buck, Sherwood and Twyman, 1973, 1975). The use of a panel of households also allowed the employment of mechanical methods for recording the status of the television set (ie on or off, and the channel being viewed) on a second-by-second basis.

Television meters had been used in the USA since the late 1940s, a technology lead that, interestingly, is not held today. Of course, the early meters were very basic compared with the current electronic instruments, relying in the main on moving mechanical parts. For example, one of the earlier meters (the setmeter) recorded the status of the set on to a moving, heat-sensitive tape, on which 'burners' in the meter recorded the detail in binary form. Large lengths of the paper tape were then fed through special decoding machines in order to obtain the basic information ready for processing.

The setmeter brought a new accuracy to the measurement of household viewing, but for programme producers and in particular for advertisers it became important to monitor the viewing habits of the individuals within the home and not simply the household in total. In the 1960s and 1970s a combination of set meter and diary was found to be the most generally acceptable solution to the problem of audience measurement adequate for commercial purposes. Even within this consensus, different techniques could be used. For instance, in Britain, diaries were kept by individuals within the metered homes (a monitored diary technique), whereas in the USA the set and individual information were provided by different samples.

The UK system had advantages over that of the USA in the sense that the respondents' task was lower (only needing to record *whether* they were viewing, not *what* they were viewing, since the meter gave the latter information) and the two streams of information (TV set and individual) were consistent. A penalty of the US system was that the task was so onerous that the diary panel was only asked to complete their diaries for one week in every three, and so the advantages of data continuity were largely lost. Nevertheless, while the viewing scene remained relatively simple and stable, the accurate information about set usage could be used as a reasonably efficient proxy for the less robust data on individual viewing.

In the 1980s the television environment changed beyond recognition in almost every developed country in the world. The number of television channels increased as more commercial stations were allowed to broadcast in countries where public broadcasting had been the main or only supply. In the UK, for instance, the number of commercial broadcasting hours doubled with the introduction of Channel 4, breakfast television and generally longer broadcasting hours. The rapid growth in penetration of VCRs helped to cut the link between the broadcasting of a programme and its viewing: popular peak hour programmes no longer had to be seen in peak times by the entire family. Perhaps most significant of all, and usually underrated, was the growth of multi-set households and the effect on viewing habits (Taylor, 1986).

At the start of the decade, although the developments described were in most cases only just beginning, it was becoming obvious in the UK that changes had to be made if television audience measurement was to maintain its credibility. The system installed by AGB (now Taylor Nelson Sofres) in 1968 had worked well for more than 10 years – an extremely good record – but the world was changing and the UK system had to change with it. As a minimum, the new system had to deal with three areas that were not then adequately covered: first, the ability to measure multi-set usage more efficiently and in finer detail; secondly, some measure of how the VCR was used, particularly showing whether live programmes were being watched (using the VCR as a tuner) or whether recorded materials were being viewed; and thirdly, and most important of all, some means of adequately measuring individuals' viewing was required, as the fragmentation of viewing and the growth of multi-set households made the old diary technique increasingly incapable of following the more complex viewing habits of different members of the household.

In 1984, following a considerable degree of planning, testing and validation, an entirely new generation of meter (the peoplemeter) was installed throughout the UK, which went a long way towards solving these problems.

It is worth looking at the nature of the meters that were introduced in 1984 in the UK since their strengths and weaknesses determine the extent to which they can be expected to perform adequately as the technical environment of television changes still further. It proved technically simple to deal with the problem of measuring the state of multiple sets in homes. The bulky old meter that used to sit on the top of the old (static) TV set was replaced by a much smaller meter (monitor display unit) capable of being placed on either static or portable television sets. These meters on all sets in the house communicate with a central display storage unit through the existing electrical mains (see Figure 22.1). The storage unit in turn is linked to the domestic telephone line and by this means can pass the whole day's electronic data every night to the research company computers, which can and do have the viewing figures processed by the following morning.

The major revolution compared with previous meter and diary techniques occurred in the measurement of individuals' viewing, and this is where the peoplemeter really justifies its name. The diary is replaced by a remote control handset (similar to the remote control unit for a television set or a VCR). The handset has numbered buttons (with an adjacent name tag) for each person in the family, together with buttons permitting guests to the home to be entered if they view television. The push-button activity is registered on the small screen on the set-top meter, which is capable of displaying messages and prompts to the panellists (see Figure 22.2). The respondent load is small, simply depressing a button on starting to view and depressing it again when viewing ceases; the meter does the rest.

Like that of the TV set itself, the measurement of individuals' viewing is electronically recorded, which means that people data can be collected as quickly and as automatically as information about the status of the television sets. Furthermore, these data can be provided in far greater detail than was possible with the old diary technique. The latter could only break down the day into quarter-hour sections with the instruction that if viewing had taken place over more than half of any individual quarter-hour, the whole period was to be counted as viewing. For an advertiser interested overwhelmingly in a 30-second commercial spot, such broad categories lacked precision, and it was now possible to report individual viewing by finer time periods.

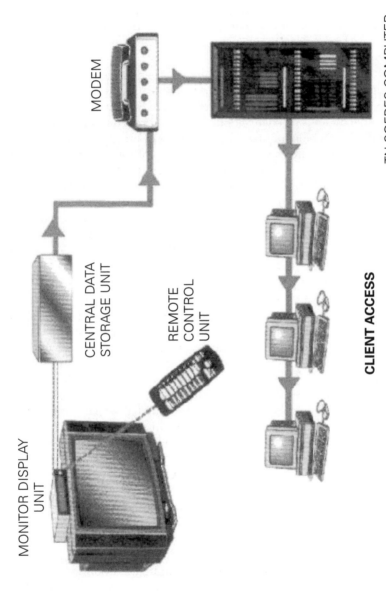

MONITOR DISPLAY UNIT

CENTRAL DATA STORAGE UNIT

REMOTE CONTROL UNIT

MODEM

TN SOFRES COMPUTER

CLIENT ACCESS

Figure 22.1 *The peoplemeter system online*

Shown above are TNS's remote-controlled peoplemeter handset (lower left), and the peoplemeter monitor (upper right), which sits on top of the TV set and at periodic intervals provides a reminder to individuals to use the handset. It also records the channel the set is tuned to and stores the viewing information transmitted by the handset.

Figure 22.2 *Peoplemeter handset and monitor*

FURTHER DEVELOPMENTS OF THE PEOPLEMETER: DEALING WITH DIGITAL TRANSMISSIONS

Since the first peoplemeter was conceived in the 1980s, the television environment throughout the world has continued to evolve with ever increasing sophistication and choice for the consumer. This has manifested itself especially in the explosion of channels available through satellite or cable systems. Table 22.1 provides some idea of how this has affected the UK population.

Table 22.1 *Changes in the TV environment in the UK (percentage of homes penetrated)*

	1978 %	1983 %	1988 %	1993 %	1998 %
2 or More Television Sets	12	34	46	52	59
3 or More Television Sets	–	–	12	16	22
VCR	–	16	50	72	82
More than 1 VCR	–	–	–	8	18
Remote Control	–	22	49	77	91
Teletext	–	5	22	48	70
Multi-Channel Reception through Cable/Satellite	–	–	–	14	29

Source: Taylor Nelson Sofres/BARB

Early peoplemeters dealt with simple terrestrial reception via a single TV set to the home, and collected limited information about viewers. Over time the peoplemeter has evolved, such that the latest versions embrace the following:

■ monitoring of any number of sets and VCRs in a home;
■ detection of cable and satellite channels in addition to terrestrial sources;
■ detection and measurement of the details of VCR time shifting, fast-forwarding, etc;
■ acceptance of demographic information relating to guest viewers;
■ registering the opinion of viewers (audience appreciation) regarding programmes and commercials.

Current developments centre on the ability of the peoplemeter to identify digital television transmissions, be they terrestrial, cable or satellite. Traditional peoplemeters identify the frequency of reception of the TV, satellite receiver, etc and in any one geographic area there is a stable one-to-one correspondence between this frequency and the broadcast being received. The advent of digital broadcasting destroys this relationship, since one frequency now carries a digital multiplex comprising several broadcasts digitally encoded and combined together. Knowing the reception frequency identifies the multiplex but not which broadcast within that multiplex is being decoded and watched.

Solutions to this problem include the use of PictureMatching™. The PictureMatching peoplemeter designed by TNS collects a continuous electronic sample of part of the picture from the television screen and this is stored in the meter. These picture samples are retrieved from the panel homes overnight and compared with corresponding samples for all channels broadcasting at that time. A correlation system then identifies which TV stations were viewed in the panel home across the viewing day. The system can identify channel switches to the nearest second. A similar job is done using 'audio' rather than 'picture' matching techniques. These methods can monitor the ever more complex home television environment more economically than the frequency measurement systems of the past.

In some broadcast environments, broadcasters transmit channel identifier codes within the vertical blanking interval (for example, teletext codes). Where such codes are broadcast by every measured TV station, on a consistent basis, a version of a peoplemeter can detect the codes and hence the channels being viewed.

The best system will depend upon the circumstances in the markets being measured. An advantage of the 'matching' system is that it can operate independently of the broadcasters and avoids any danger that implanted codes are lost or distorted in some way. On the other hand, reliable broadcast codes provide a comprehensive and cost-efficient way of identifying TV channels.

SETTING UP A PEOPLEMETER SYSTEM

It is probably clear from the foregoing that the introduction of a system cannot be taken lightly. For a start, a large investment is necessary in capital and setup costs. Typically, panel sizes for a television region or a small country are of the order of 500 to 1,000 homes, with meter equipment and setup (depending on the complexity of the environment) costing £1 million plus.

More important still, the experience and know-how for running a peoplemeter system successfully needs to cover a wide range of different disciplines:

■ survey design and sampling techniques;
■ panel member recruitment, motivation and incentives;
■ meter design, development, production and maintenance;
■ meter installation and setup;
■ telecommunications;
■ quality control, editing and panel member re-education;
■ systems design and development;
■ computer operations;
■ software support;
■ data interpretation and analysis;

- statistical techniques, modelling, standard errors, etc;
- liaison with third-party processors;
- management and control.

Thus, it is essential with a relatively small sample size to select and maintain a fully representative sample of households, not only in demographic terms, but also related to television reception, video equipment and intensity of viewing. Panel members have to be recruited and educated to respond reliably over long periods of time, but without conditioning them in television viewing terms.

Meters that are suited (and accepted by local regulations) must be customized, installed and maintained. Data must be retrieved (usually by phone lines) on a regular basis for each household. Large databases are involved and, as an example, the UK meter system involves some two million viewing statements each week. If commercial audiences are to be reported upon, there is also a need to deal with calculations on number of commercial spots (over 120,000 per week in the UK).

Increasingly, data dissemination is required not only in printed form, but through electronic means including tapes, online and file transfer. In a competitive television environment each of the literally millions of report figures is important to someone.

PEOPLEMETER SYSTEMS AROUND THE WORLD

There has been a dramatic increase in the number of peoplemeter systems around the world. In 1995 only four countries were equipped, but by 1998 this has risen to 52 and is expected to exceed 60 by the end of 2000. The main driver of this has been deregulation in many countries leading to an increase in TV channels funded by advertising. More recently the launch of commercial television in the new markets of Eastern Europe has fuelled the growth.

In parallel with this, many peoplemeter systems, mainly in Europe, have increased the size of their panels, which in some cases have doubled. This has largely been as a result of the proliferation of channels following deregulation, many of which are thematic with tightly targeted audience groups. Along with the continued growth in multi-set ownership this has led to more audience fragmentation and hence the need for larger panels.

With the growth of peoplemeter systems, and the increase in international advertising as well as international broadcasting, there has been a pressure for harmonization of methodologies for peoplemeter research. Sponsored by the European Broadcasting Union (EBU) and with the co-operation of many European bodies, *Towards Harmonization of Television Audience Measurement Systems* was published in the early 90s.

More recently this has been updated and expanded geographically. Still sponsored by the EBU but with input from the Advertising Research Foundation (ARF) from the USA and by others, the Audience Research Methods (ARM) Group of international experts has produced GGTAM, *Global Guidelines for Television Audience Measurement*.

The operational guidelines are based on 10 overriding principles to ensure that all users of the service have confidence in the system:

1. meeting total market-place needs;
2. effective industry consultation;
3. full disclosure;
4. optimal resource allocation;
5. scientific method;
6. best research practices;
7. quality control;
8. maximizing response;
9. equal access to data;
10. methodological experimentation.

If the tasks of setting up and maintaining a peoplemeter system are complex and expensive, rewards can be great for the television market-place in providing accurate audience estimates and a commercial currency for trading airtime. For the researcher, there are intellectual challenges across the whole spectrum of research techniques and in the international expansion of the business. For research companies, the huge investment in capital, development and expertise is justified by the revenue streams and the growing use of peoplemeter techniques around the world.

REFERENCES

ARM (1998) *GGTAM Global TV Systems*

Audley, G B (1986) in *British Television Advertising – The First 30 Years*, ed Brian Henry, Century Benham

Buck, S F, Sherwood, R and Twyman, W A (1973) Operating effective panels for television audience measurement, Proceedings of ESOMAR Conference

Buck, S F, Sherwood, R and Twyman, W A (1975) Panels and the measurement of changes, Proceedings of ESOMAR Conference

Buck, S F (1982) The future of television audience measurement in Europe, *Admap*, April

Buck, S F (1986) Central's panel beaters, *Media World*
EBU (1990) *Towards Harmonization of TV Audience Measurement Systems*
Ogilvy & Mather Europe (1986) *The Television Guide*
Taylor, L (1986) It's where you watch, not what you watch, *Media World*
Young & Rubicam (1986) *Time and Space*

23

Packaging Research

Tony Schlaeppi

WHY RESEARCH PACKAGING?

Packaging is a major component in the marketing mix of any brand. It is at least as important as the other components that we take care to get right: advertising, pricing and product formulation. If these others benefit from research, so must packaging.

The research that is relevant to packaging arises from the job that packaging has to do for the brand or product. There are two main functions for a pack. The first is the structural function. A pack is a container for the product. It protects the product, and enables it to be transported to the shops, displayed and bought in acceptable units. Properly designed, it makes the product easier to use: it can make using the product a relatively pleasant or unpleasant experience.

The second main function is the visual function. The pack conveys messages about the product: information and also impressions. It carries the product's name and colours, so that it will stand out clearly on the shelf against the competition. It will list ingredients, show sell-by or 'best before' dates, carry bar codes and sometimes instructions for use and warnings against improper use, but these must not detract from the overall impression. The pack has to be attractive as well as visible, and to contribute in a helpful way to the product's image.

A wide range of detailed variations arises from within these two functions, as wide perhaps as the range of things that can be packaged. It is worth noting that we are not necessarily thinking of cartons, tins or jars on shelves, although that is what the term 'pack' brings naturally to mind. The same principles apply more widely, as do the research techniques that follow from them. For example, shop design may be thought of in terms of convenience of layout (the shop being the container for the product, which in this case is customer service), or in terms of the visual impact and message transmitted by the shop-front and interior décor. A car must handle well and convey a good image from its appearance. We will not necessarily think only of packs in the hand in exploring packaging research techniques.

The purpose of packaging research is to check how well current packaging, or potential new or revised packaging designs, fulfil these functions, and to give guidance for their selection or improvement.

Typically the research involves pre-testing before a decision is taken to commission a new design or to launch one already commissioned. Will it do the job intended, without undesirable side-effects on the existing image of the brand? Can it be modified or improved to enhance the effect? As with most product development work, including advertising pre-testing, the task is to ensure that the product is as good as we can make it. Whether in the event a new pack design actually increases sales is not often published and is hard to disentangle for the familiar reason that there are so many uncontrolled variables interacting in the market-place.

STRUCTURAL TESTS

Research into the materials of which a pack is made is a matter for the manufacturers' R & D rather than for market research. It is important that the materials are long lasting, will not react chemically with the contents, will stand up to long storage and rough handling, will not dent or scratch easily, will be lightweight, etc. Where market research comes in is in assessing how the pack structure affects the ability of the consumer to use the product effectively. Is it easy to hold and carry? Is it convenient to store? Can the pack be opened or closed easily? How easy is it to dispense the product from the pack?

Practical observation is the technique to use here: to ask people to handle the pack as required, open and close it, pour from it, etc; to observe them doing it and note any difficulties; to ask them to comment as they are doing it, and answer specific questions afterwards.

This process of physically working a pack can be used qualitatively, in group discussions, or quantitatively, in a hall test. Informants can, for example, be asked to open rip-top cans or screw-top bottles. Sometimes the setting has to be specially designed to be realistic. In pouring tests for motor-oil containers, it is appropriate to interview motorists on the petrol station forecourt. A test can be set up on the forecourt, so that oil can be poured through the normal filler opening into a removable sump. Informants pour from different containers, and observe and comment on the ease or difficulty of doing so: speed of pouring, avoidance of spillage, etc.

A possible method of collecting information in situations like these is to ask informants to comment while they are performing the operation and to video-record their comments and actions on tape for subsequent analysis. This method is recommended where the operation is a complex one, in which informants may have a number of relevant thoughts passing through their minds, which they will forget quickly unless stimulated to reveal them in passing. Examples of situations where this 'stream of consciousness' technique has been used to good effect are shop layout studies, in which informants are asked to re-create the experience of actually walking around a store looking for something (or just browsing), and new car evaluation clinics, in which informants comment as they drive a test vehicle. The informant is accompanied by an interviewer who stimulates him or her to keep saying whatever passes through the mind.

The opening and closure of packs is an important issue in the medical field, where closures are obliged to be child-resistant, and yet accessible to elderly and possibly arthritic people. Considerable effort has been spent by the pharmaceutical industry in testing forms of closure. This has often involved the use of large panels of young children, and of elderly people, opening different packs and being timed and filmed while doing so. The problem is that children on such panels can quickly learn how to open the closures and the test rapidly ceases to reflect the abilities of the average child as opposed to the 'expert'.

THE VISUAL COMPONENT

Research into the visual function of the pack can be considered under two heads: 1) the effect of the surface design or appearance in drawing attention to and identifying the brand or product and commanding attention; and 2) its effect on perceptions of the brand or product image. Often both of these are covered in the same study, as part of the same brief, but it is helpful to keep them apart conceptually. It is rare to see a design brief that does not specify both that the pack design should communicate 'quality' and that it should also have 'impact' or be 'attention-getting'. But, in theory, it is quite possible that one could be achieved at the expense of the other.

A visually arresting and dominating design can easily be produced that gives the wrong impression of the product; conversely, a design may communicate key product values on close inspection, but be too quiet and dull, or too similar to others, to be noticed. Operationally, it is appropriate to distinguish perceptual research techniques, in which visual effectiveness in various forms can be objectively measured, and image association research, which relies on enquiring into attitudes.

PERCEPTUAL RESEARCH TECHNIQUES

The surface design of a pack may include a large number of variables: colours, type sizes, typefaces, illustrations, the mast-head of a magazine cover (since that is also a 'pack' leading consumers to the contents), and so on. These variables, interacting together, may make it more or less difficult for customers to notice the pack in a typical display situation. A European research study carried out in supermarkets revealed that shoppers spend only seconds in front of different product display sectors, eg biscuits 21 seconds, yoghurts 18 seconds, pet foods 25 seconds. Individual packs within these sectors are scanned and have to identify themselves in split seconds. In studies seeking to optimize effective pack design, some of the following questions may arise:

- Will it 'brand' the product well?
- Is the copy legible?
- Should the name be highlighted?
- Should the name be angled?
- Does the pack stand out on the shelf?
- Are the varieties of the range distinguishable?
- Will users recognize the brand in its new pack (or how long will it take them to do so)?

These and similar questions can be answered by the tachistoscope (or T'scope) and specially structured tests. Tachistoscopes have been used since the early days of market research but there are regular calls for them today, especially since the development of sophisticated, discriminating and easily portable models has facilitated their use in comparative international projects.

'Tachistoscope' comes from the Greek 'tachista' (very quickly) and 'skopein' (to look). T'scopes are electronic instruments that provide controlled exposures to a stimulus (a three-dimensional pack or other surface, or a picture of one). The respondent sees exposures, which at first are too rapid for identification; the exposures are progressively lengthened in a precisely controlled way until the respondent is able to identify what is being shown. Test items can thus be compared in terms of the exposure times taken to identify them.

The T'scope measurement is essentially a physiological one, which will vary from person to person according to their visual ability. It is therefore essential to standardize the scores obtained by calibrating them against an independent and objective visual ability measure. The first part of every T'scope interview involves the application of a standard visual acuity test against which each individual is scored for ability; these scores are then applied as weights to convert the same individual's answers. Because of these control procedures, very small samples provide statistically significant results in T'scope tests: cells as low as 30 are common. This advantage makes it much easier to design and finance the experimental comparison between alternatives (of design or sample) that gives T'scope tests their main strength.

Though they have many applications in design research, three standard tests address most of the problem areas:

1. legibility tests;
2. shelf impact tests;
3. recognition tests.

These are used to answer different types of question.

Legibility tests

Legibility tests are the simplest. A pack or design is shown for sequentially increasing periods until identified. It can be used to assess how well the design communicates the brand, the manufacturer, the nature of the product and any other specific piece of copy. The effects of these key communication points of different type styles, layouts, background colours, etc can be assessed; most commonly the test is used in experimental designs in which two or more different treatments are compared for their ability to communicate the brand or other message.

Shelf impact tests

In legibility tests the designs are shown on their own. Shelf impact tests assess the ability of a pack to stand out and be quickly seen and identified from a display of competing products. The test pack – or several facings of it – is exposed in the T'scope. The respondent is required to identify the packs seen in the T'scope from a display of competing products either on shelves alongside the T'scope or from products in computer-generated photoboards simulating a real shelf situation. Among these products is a duplicate set of the test designs shown in the T'scope. Packs with strong features – such as brand names, logos or other visual triggers – are more easily distinguished than recessive designs, which demand longer exposure for their identification among the display. The nature of this shelf impact or 'stand-out' test removes many of the prompting effects of familiarity, and new designs can be assessed against current, established packs. Shelf impact is determined by the physical dominance of the pack and not by recognition of familiar names or devices on its surface.

Results from a recent international research study comparing the shelf impact of two confectionery bar packs in the UK, France and Sweden provided results favouring the same design in all three markets not only amongst the total samples of 50–100 employed but within sub-cells of age, user and non-user groups.

Recognition tests

Recognition tests are, however, useful when new pack designs are proposed for an existing well-known brand. Some elements in the design may be much more closely attuned than others to the collective 'memory' of the brand, and it may be important to establish which these elements are. To assess the possible negative effects on recognition, users of the test product are shown a display of products competing in the product field tachistoscopically, and the exposure time for them to identify the position of the brand being tested is measured. Their performance is compared with the mean recognition times of other matched samples shown the new and unfamiliar designs in the same display. In one study, two new designs for Heinz baked beans were tested against the design then current. The results showed that one of the new designs (new pack A) was just as recognizable to users as the current design, but the alternative new design (new pack B) took longer for users to find in the display. Its mean score of 3.34 is significantly more than the other two at the 99.8 per cent level of confidence. Table 23.1 shows mean recognition score.

Table 23.1 *Mean recognition score*

New Pack A	2.14	}	
		}	Not sig
Current Pack D	2.23	}	
New Pack B	3.34	}	Sig from A and D at 99.8% level

A legibility test on the same designs showed that new pack A also communicated the brand name Heinz significantly more efficiently than the current. Table 23.2 shows mean identification score.

Table 23.2 *Mean identification score*

New Pack A	0.73	}
		} Sig at 99.8% level
Current Pack D	0.93	}
New Pack B	0.96	

An alternative to the T'scope for recognition tests is the eye-camera, which can record accurately in which order the eye travels to different elements in a design and for how long it rests on each one. Eye-cameras have been known in print media research since the 1960s, but were discredited largely because of the clumsiness of the equipment and the constraints that had to be placed on the viewer. Modern eye-cameras are lightweight and strapped to a respondent's head, enabling him to move freely. There remains some suspicion of the technique on grounds of artificiality, but there is increasing support for it.

T'scopes were used in a legal dispute between Laura Ashley and Coloroll, which was alleged to have plagiarized the Laura Ashley logo. The T'scopes were used to compare the identification times of the two logos, and it was noted what proportion at each timing gave the *wrong* identification (said Laura Ashley when it should have been Coloroll, and vice versa). Sample matching and interview conditions were tightly controlled, and the entire procedure was video-recorded. Since market research evidence is seen to be based on 'hearsay', it is not admissible evidence in law. The video recordings of the procedure however were observations of respondents' behaviour when they were exposed to the symbols, providing undeniable evidence of confusion.

T'scopes were also used to compare the recognition effectiveness of a number of different new designs for the BP logo, as part of a major research project in connection with the company's international re-imaging in the late 1980s. The tests and other interviews were carried out in the UK, Germany, Australia, Singapore and the USA.

In this case the T'scopes were used as distance simulators. Photographs were taken, under day and night conditions, of a service station from different distances away (100 yards, 200 yards, etc: five different distances). This was done for each logo design. The same service station was used, the signs being changed for each set of photographs. The results made possible the ranking of each design at each distance, both day and night, in terms of average identification distances.

A test of two pack designs used the same approach. Displays of packs in each design were set up for two different brands after shop hours in a supermarket – a total of four displays. A series of 12 slides was taken, simulating a housewife's approach to the display area covering a distance of 41 to 5 feet.

In the subsequent hall test, after each T'scope exposure to the display, the respondent was asked to describe what she had seen – providing a brand identification level for each distance. Design B prompted more identifications in total than A and at longer distances for both of the brands tested. Table 23.3 sets out the results.

Table 23.3 *Pack design test results*

Pack Design:	BRAND 1		BRAND 2	
	A	B	A	B
	%	%	%	%
Distance (feet)				
41–32	43	56	12	24
29–31	11	16	23	24
17-28	32	28	43	45
5–16	4	–	7	7
Not Identified	10	–	15	–
Average Distance Identified:	26.3	28.9	17.9	20.9

NEW DESIGN RESEARCH: PUZZLE BOARDS

Design recognition (the question of what elements are important in the existing impressions people have of a brand) arises at the very beginning when a designer is being briefed to develop a new design. Too often research is not considered at this stage, but is only brought in as a cross-check to designs that have already been produced without any of the assistance that research at the start of the process might have given. This is a pity. It ought to be helpful to a designer to know at the outset which are the elements in the current design that are important to the brand's identity in the mind of the consumer and therefore should be retained in some form, and which others may be dispensable.

We have a device called a puzzle board, which can be used to provide input to design briefs for pack or label changes before the production of even rough prototypes. Puzzle boards arose from the finding, after much experimentation, that it is not practical to ask consumers to verbalize descriptions of packs. Mental pictures of even very familiar products cannot be put into words. In a puzzle board test, the respondent is given elements of the design and asked to build it up as he sees it.

It is a kind of game. The respondent is given a board with a recess in the shape of the pack and several dozen pieces of the pack or its label mounted on plastic strips. Each 'element' is given in at least four different versions. The respondent builds up the pack as he recalls it. He has to select the correct form of the brand name, remember its position on the pack, remember whether there are pictures and where, select the correct colour backgrounds and typefaces, and so on. The 'finished' pack represents that individual's idea of the current design. Analysis of 50 packs built up in this way provides insights into which elements may be sacrosanct or redundant in any design revision.

An alternative use of the puzzle board method is to ask respondents to build up not the pack as they remember it but the pack as they would like it to be, from the options offered. What colour and design combination would they like? This was useful in helping to decide between three alternative new designs for the signage and facia of high-street branches of a leading bank.

IMAGE ASSOCIATION RESEARCH

Perceptual tests are seldom used on their own, without reference to what the perceptions suggest to people. A new design may be more arresting and may help the product to be identified more quickly, but it may also radically change impressions of the product for the worse.

Image research involves exploring attitudes and therefore uses the same qualitative and quantitative methods of measuring attitudes as are used in other contexts. Fortunately it is easy, and common practice, to combine this type of interviewing with perceptual tests. Relevant samples are invited to a hall test, carry out an appropriate T'scope exercise, and are then subjected to an interview in which the product is rated on various communication objectives and brand images. When this is done the T'scope cells are combined into larger samples, to give minimum bases of 100 for quantification. Sometimes such quantitative interviews are combined with mini depth interviews that explore some aspect of reactions to the pack in a more unstructured way among, say, 10 per cent of the sample. Another possibility, as with advertising research, is an open-ended question, asked early in the interview, in which respondents are asked to describe the product in detail (eg to a friend who has not seen it), simply going by the pack they have just seen, and without any ideas being suggested to them by the interviewer; this can then be subjected to detailed content analysis by some method such as linguistic coding, which enables the emotive nuances of the response to be captured in full.

An example of the effects of a layout change was found at the time of the launch of Cadbury's Caramel bar. Two alternative layouts produced very different product expectations. In its upright form, and before they tasted it, 56 per cent of respondents thought the product would be a bar of chocolate. Sample B, shown a landscape version of the wrapper, thought it would be a 'countline' type of product. After tasting the product, however, it was the people in sample A who changed their minds. Table 23.4 shows the results.

Table 23.4 *Changes in product expectations*

	A %	B %
Before tasting		
Bar	56	35
Countline	44	65
After tasting		
Bar	44	35
Countline	56	65

These expectations of different products, not surprisingly, affected price expectations. In its upright format the bar was priced significantly higher than in its landscape form. Overall impressions of the product (before tasting) were also significantly more positive from the landscape format. This is shown in Table 23.5.

Table 23.5 *Overall impressions – before tasting*

	A %	B %
Excellent	3	4
Very good	28	30
Good	24	30
Fairly good	32	10
Neither good nor poor	10	6
Slightly poor	2	2
Poor	1	–
Mean score	**23.0**	**33.3**

Since the production costs of the countline wrapper were very much less than the alternative this was the clincher and the product was launched in the landscape format.

Where more than one test design is involved, a good approach to assessing the effect of design on product appeal is to set up a comparative situation in which the packs themselves are not compared but only the products, which respondents are told are 'slightly different'. Respondents say which they would prefer to buy and what sort of product each one would be. Differences can only be ascribed to the pack, but we avoid the classic research 'sin' of asking direct questions about packs and therefore asking respondents to be design experts.

It is a powerful research tool. For example, in a test of two different designs, A and B, for salad relishes, each design tested was shown in a range of three varieties. At one part of the interview respondents were shown one variety in design A and another variety in design B and asked which they would buy. All the possible combinations of the two designs were paired in this way. This comparative evaluation provided two results. First, it told us which variety was preferred overall.

	Total choice %
Variety 1	67
Variety 2	28
Variety 3	53

Secondly, by adding all the choices for each design together, it told us design A had an effect on choices of variety.

	Total choices %
Varieties in design A	55
Varieties in design B	45

Ideally the product variables chosen for tests like these would have fairly equal popularity – to allow the design variable maximum effect – but even though in this example of relishes one variety dominated choice, again the design itself influenced that choice. Here the less popular variety 2 polled almost twice as many votes when it was shown in its A design form – 30 to 70 per cent compared with only 19 to 78 per cent.

	Variety 1 %		Variety 2 %
Design A	78	Design B	19
Design B	70	Design A	30

TEST MATERIALS

Wherever possible in image association tests, the use of 'real' 3-D packs is strongly advocated. Though the extremely high costs of providing hand-made mock-ups may exceed the research costs, it is important that at the initial stage of the assessments the respondent should see the 'reality' of the pack and appreciate its surface texture, size and presence. Subsequent stages of the interview might then use high-quality same-size colour photographic reproductions of the new designs. It would never be recommended to employ projected slide presentations of design materials that totally fail to communicate the 'feel' of the pack.

CAD has provided a cheaper way of generating new pack designs that can simulate 'real' packs. Photoboard displays of computer-generated packs can show them amongst relevant competitors, obviating the need for the construction of shop shelving in research centres.

CONCLUSIONS

There is a considerable battery of specialized tests that can be applied in the development of packs for new products or in redesign exercises or 'uplifts' of existing products. Usually more than one is used together, but which ones will depend on the requirements of the marketing and creative briefs, and on the practicalities of timing and budgeting constraints. We have not attempted to produce a catalogue of every packaging test devised or to evaluate the importance of one against another. As in all areas of market research, pack studies can only contribute information in areas relevant to the decisions to be taken. In our experience, however, these are likely to be concerned with effectiveness in the two main areas we have described. The first is in structural terms. As a container, does the pack work efficiently? Could its functions be improved? The other is in visual terms. As the product's clothing, does it signal itself and identify the brand, and what characteristics and imagery does it communicate about the brand?

It is appropriate to finish with two observations. The first is that pack and design research, of the sort described, should not be seen as a device for inhibiting design creativity. As with advertising, it is the function of research to aid the creative designer, not to thwart him or her. Some of the methods described (puzzle boards, and recognition and association tests) properly form part of the design audit, so that the designer can fully understand the situation he or she is either to build upon or change. At the other extreme, again as with advertising, research can provide important reassurance as to whether a new design will achieve its aims and which new design will do so most effectively. It is not the case in our experience, as is so often feared, that research will always favour the safe, conservative, non-creative approach. Yet every brand must weigh up the risk of damage to its existing loyal franchise when seeking to update its image; good design research can greatly help in that judgement.

The second observation concerns the place of packaging and design research in the present world of retailing. Major retailers with electronic point of sale systems can obtain daily read-outs of what is moving off the shelf, and can rapidly decide whether a brand should be delisted from this hard evidence. This means that the whole marketing mix, including the pack, must do its work quickly and effectively.

The rationale for pack testing in this context is that packs are expensive to develop and expensive to change. Pricing, advertising and merchandising can be tested, tried out in an area and changed fairly quickly; that is not true of packaging, which must be either right first time or an expensive mistake. Good-quality research is needed more than ever to give that reassurance.

SECTION 4

ANALYSIS AND MODELLING

Introduction

Data analysis has an important role to play in turning the information that is collected in research into actionable sets of interpretable facts, conclusions and ultimately recommendations. As a discipline, it is a set of techniques that can be used to obtain information and understanding from the data.

This is, in itself, a very important fact for the potential users of research information to understand. Data analysis can lead a user of market research information to aspects of the data and insights that may not otherwise have been acknowledged. It can help to ensure that poor or ill-conceived evaluations and conclusions are avoided. It can also provide a means to assist in interpreting and understanding analyses carried out by others who might want to apply specific techniques to the data, to be added to the basic data analysis. Indeed, getting to know the extent of the parameters of data analysis techniques can, in time, start to influence the overall objectives of research and the research design itself. Good analysis can often provide detail that had not been anticipated in the research design, but has been a result of the research being done.

Data analysis can also 'kill' a well-designed research project. Inappropriately or incorrectly analysed data can provide interpretations and conclusions that could be unclear or even completely wrong. It is therefore important to appreciate the influence and contribution of data analysis.

There is a definite sequence for analysing data. Initially it must be 'edited' and 'coded'. Editing is the process of finding omissions, errors and (where relevant) inconsistencies and ineligibility of the final response. Coding is the means of deciding how the responses are going to be put together in a frame so that they can be entered into the computer.

The most interesting factor to the manager who is less familiar with research techniques (and even in some cases to some market researchers) is that there are a variety of data analysis techniques available. The basic analysis technique is to specify that each question in a questionnaire is analysed by the classification data and by itself. This provides the initial 'picture' of the results of the research and provides the data user with an insight into which aspect of the data is both useful and actionable. This type of analysis can be one-way frequency distribution or the simple tabulation of one variable.

Only sound analysis will provide information from raw data in a way that leads to sound interpretation and decision-making. Apart from the tabulation information that forms the basis of most research reporting, researchers have a large array of statistical methods, which may be more or less appropriate in individual projects. Applied use of these techniques increases the chances of interpreting research findings in a way that adds confidence to decision-making, maximizes the return on the research investment and makes the research worth while and effective for decision-making.

In this section of the book, the chapters illustrate the analysis and modelling techniques available for market research.

When quantitative research data have been collected they need to be aggregated and digested into a form that presents the summary of answers from respondents, so that the data are transformed into information.

Segmentation is concerned with identifying the size and nature of identified subgroups of the population being researched. It helps to establish how they behave and their attitudes towards the manufacturer or service provider of the products or services being bought. In the past research has been used to monitor the similarity between buyers, but now it is being used more and more to assess their differences, as these are of increasing commercial interest in building future markets. It has become even more effective as mass markets fragment into smaller sub-markets or market niches.

Market research can be used effectively, by analysing past experience or data to produce a forecast. Past data can be assessed to highlight a trend, which can then be applied to the future. More complex forecasts can be developed by creating the subject being forecast and a factor that has an influence on that subject. The essential thing is to decide whether a simple or more detailed forecasting system is required. Ease of use, ease of interpretation and the management time required to set up, run and maintain the system are very important when considering the type of technique that should be used.

Stationary data or information that exhibits no trend or seasonality is best assessed by moving averages or exponential smoothing. Trend data are best assessed by trend analysis or Holt's exponential smoothing. Seasonal patterns are best assessed through classical decomposition or Holt-Winter's exponential smoothing. And for data that show no real trend and indeed might have peculiarities, the Harrison and Stevens technique is used. These techniques are important in their application to data to help develop a forecast. It is essential for the user of the techniques to assess the adequacy of the model chosen and the accuracy of the forecast provided. In doing so the user will ensure that the data are both meaningful and actionable as part of the overall marketing information system.

All market research is concerned with developing models of the market under study, as the research seeks to provide a representation of key characteristics of a given market. Attitude and behaviour models include 'trade-off' (conjoint analysis), pricing and simulated test market models.

Conjoint analysis is a method of analysing experimental data. It has become the basis of a wide variety of modelling approaches that re-create the decision process consumers go through when evaluating or selecting products or services.

Price modelling is said to be 'an aid to judgement', providing all the facts required about buyers, and leading to the price makers' understanding of the acceptable price to buyers. Purchase intention modelling is a relatively cheap survey method and is used at the new product concept stage and all stages up to and including the product launch.

Simulated test marketing systems are concerned with estimating the likely potential of a new product or an existing product if relaunched. They provide an estimate of sales volume or brand share for a given marketing mix. As the cost of launching and relaunching products increases and as markets become more and more competitive, the need for estimating sales through such techniques will become more and more important.

Data fusion is a technique that has been tried and tested, and presents opportunities for the future. Data fusion takes place between two sample surveys or even between two or more different sectors of the same broad survey. One survey is described as the 'donor' survey and contains data that can be transferred to the second or 'recipient' survey. So that the data can be transferred there have to be a number of variables that are common to both surveys. These common variables are the basis for deciding which respondents in the donor survey will pass data to which respondents in the recipient survey. The actual fusion process depends on some statistical measure of similarity between donors and recipients to find the most effective pairings. The common variables are used to determine the similarity between the data and, when the best match is found for a recipient respondent, all the missing data from the matching donor are transferred.

24

Analysing Data

Peter Jackling

When quantitative research data have been collected they need to be aggregated and digested into a form that presents the summary of answers from respondents, so that the data are transformed into information. This process is called analysis: the examination and interpretation of survey data to test hypotheses and form conclusions to drive actions.

Questionnaires will have been designed with analysis in mind: what are the hypotheses to be proved (or tested), what are the anticipated key discriminators, what are we trying to predict, what are we trying to find out? Analysis in this context is the link between raw questionnaire data and the research report, looking at relationships between variables and how the target market may be segmented. For the purposes of this chapter we will be looking at the practicalities of getting analysis done rather than the interpretation of the results.

Table 24.1 is a cross-tabulation, the most commonly used form of analysis and presentation in quantitative survey research. The purpose of this chapter is to describe the various methods of data analysis, showing when and how they may be used, and the implications for other aspects of the research process. This will be done under the following headings:

- Types of survey data;
- Fundamentals of tabular analyses;
- Questionnaire design considerations;

Table 24.1 *Example of simple cross-tabulation*

Q1 Have you used the executive lounges at London Heathrow this year?
Base: All who have flown business class in the past 12 months

	Total	Men	Women	North	South
Total	200	105	95	98	102
	100%	100%	100%	100%	100%
Yes	166	80	86	86	80
	83%	76%	91%	88%	78%
No	24	16	8	11	13
	12%	15%	8%	11%	13%
Refused	10	9	1	1	9
	5%	9%	1%	1%	9%

- How to specify tabular analyses;
- In-house or bureau;
- Software packages;
- Beyond tabulations.

TYPES OF SURVEY DATA

Answers to survey questions may be provided in four ways:

1. Single-choice, eg 'What is your favourite airline?' 'Do you agree or disagree with this statement?'
2. Multiple-choice, eg 'Which airlines have you used in the past 12 months?' 'How did you travel to the airport?'
3. Numbers, eg 'How many times have you flown on business this year?' 'What price did you pay for this ticket?'
4. Text (characters), eg 'Why do you prefer that airline?' 'How can the service be improved?'

Grids, usually of rating scales, are effectively a series of single-choice questions. The type of questions will determine the way the responses are encoded for the data record (see the section, 'Questionnaire design considerations', below) and, in some ways, how the analysis will be done. Single- and multiple-choice questions may be analysed as they appear on the questionnaire, although sometimes answers may be grouped, or netted (eg combining 'excellent', 'very good' and 'good' as 'favourable'). Answers given as numbers will usually need to be grouped into sensible ranges for analysis (eg 1–5, 6–10, 11–20, 21 or more).

If responses given as verbatim text are to be analysed, they first need to be coded into responses of the same or similar groups. For example, in response to the question 'Why do you prefer that airline?' respondents will give a wide range of replies, which is why such questions are often known as 'open-enders'. Single- and multiple-choice questions are known as 'closed-choice', since the range of answers is known in advance. Although it is necessary to review a proportion of the actual replies given for open-enders, the responses in this example may turn out to be grouped and coded along the lines:

- positive comments about price or value;
- positive comments about service;
- positive comments about comfort;
- comments about timetable;
- other comments.

Thus the question becomes a multiple-choice one for analysis purposes, although clearly much of the qualitative feel for the response may be lost, which is why some researchers prefer to have verbatim answers typed as well as coded.

Other chapters, even books and learned papers, have been written on the subject of coding and open-ended responses. There is as yet no universally accepted way of using computers to analyse and code verbatim text responses, unless they are short and non-contextual, such as responses about brand or location. Colin McDonald (1985) explained the limitations (and uses) of such software in his paper on linguistic coding, although there is a useful update on the latest software by Joseph Leung and Ching-Long Yeh (1998) in their paper, 'Natural language processing: verbatim coding and data mining'.

FUNDAMENTALS OF TABULAR ANALYSES

For very small surveys it may be possible to analyse the data by hand. Any survey comprising only 10 questions, each of an average of nine possible answers, will require 90 counts. For just 200 respondents this is likely to take some seven or eight hours, depending upon accuracy, and result in a one-dimensional summary of observations, which after manual transposition and percentaging would look something like this:

	Total:	200
Prefer Airline A	36	18%
Prefer Airline B	20	10%
Prefer Airline C	48	24%
Prefer Airline D	42	21%
Prefer Airline E	54	27%

Realistically, only very small surveys would be analysed in such a manner now: time and accuracy problems would usually make the task daunting, if not impossible. Furthermore, there is no profile of respondents, since counts within each cell would take even longer.

However, it can and sometimes should be used to give the researcher an immediate feedback on one key aspect (eg brand preference) prior to the main analyses, since it can be produced as questionnaires are returned from field. Since they represent the fundamental survey responses, a set of these counts is sometimes known as the 'top-line results'. They are sometimes presented in the form of the questionnaire, with numbers instead of codes.

The power and speed of computers have opened up many possibilities for data analysis, especially since special software packages have been written to cope with the multi-response questions typical of market research data. These packages will be discussed later in the chapter. The most basic form of computer analysis is called a 'hole count'. This name originates from the days when data were entered via punch cards, each of 80 columns and 12 rows (or positions), ie 960 possible responses could be recorded on one card. One or more columns would typically represent a question, and the answers were recorded by punching a hole, or holes, in the appropriate row. Nowadays the columns are replaced by 'field' numbers, although some packages still refer to cards and columns. An example of a hole count is shown in Table 24.2.

We can see, for example, that 106 people have given answer number 2 to the question represented by field 03. So a hole count is another form of 'top-line report', without the text labels. Some packages can also present these counts laid out in the form of the questionnaire.

Table 24.2 *Example of a hole count*

Field	Base	1	2	3	4	5	6	Blank	Total
01	400	29	42	123	19	130	57	–	400
02	400	–	59	182	118	–	57	6	416
03	400	73	106	25	–	197	64	–	465
04	400	27	35	42	18	12	–	266	134

Hole counts are used as a first pass at the research findings and to provide the basis for groupings of answers for the main analysis (for example, to decide which age ranges should be reported) and to see what possible errors may exist. Tabulations of the sort demonstrated at the beginning of this chapter give deeper analysis of the research findings.

Tabulations comprise the following basic elements:

- **Table and page number** These are usually generated automatically.
- **Title** This is usually a précis of the question text.
- **Base** Normally this will represent the group of people who were asked the question, but may be used to focus on a subgroup, eg 'all who use airline A'.
- **Rows** Also sometimes called 'stubs', typically these will be the answers to one question, which may be single or multiple response, and answers may be grouped (eg 'all positive opinions'). In most cases responses will be shown in the order in which they appear in the questionnaire, but this may be changed if required – a frequently used option is to show responses to some types of questions, eg open-enders, in descending order of numbers of mentions. A set of rows is also known as the 'row variable'.
- **Columns** These may be known as 'cross-breaks', 'profiles', 'banners', 'columns variable' or simply 'breaks', and represent the subgroups that the researcher wishes to study and compare.
- **Content** The most common form of content for the 'body' of the table is to show numbers for each cell with column percentages underneath, as in Table 24.1. However, options include row percentaging, just numbers or just percentages, percentages next to the numbers and percentages to one or more decimal places. Tables based on responses given in numerical form may be shown as aggregates of the numbers in each cell.
- **Presentation** Specialist software packages will usually show tabulations in non-proportional fonts, unlike, say, in a word processing system. If presentation is important then it is possible to improve the overall appearance in a number of ways:
  - boxing, around the table and sometimes around the profile groups;
  - shading, possibly of the responses pertaining to the client's brand;
  - table titles in a larger or emboldened font;
  - addition of the agency's (or client's) logo;
  - export to a word processing package, or the use of a specialist post-processing package such as YAPS.

Thus cross-tabulations show the survey results in greater depth, indicating where any significant differences arise in various subsamples, be they demographic (eg sex, age, lifestyle), attitudinal (eg inclination to try new products, preference for environment-friendly products) or behavioural (eg brand-switching tendency).

There are also some 'in-table' statistical measures that can provide the researcher with further summaries of the survey findings. These relate particularly to questions where ratings have been requested in the form of rating scales or scoring. The tabulation in Table 24.3 is an example of these statistics. Respondents have been asked to state how much they agree or disagree with a particular statement.

Table 24.3 *Example of tabulation with statistics*

Q42 Agreement with the statement: 'The ozone layer hole is a serious threat to the quality of my life in the next 10 years.'
Base: All respondents

		Total	North	South
Total		400	200	200
Agree strongly	(+2)	150 37%	20 10%	130 65%
Agree	(+1)	40 10%	30 15%	10 5%
Neither	(0)	50 13%	40 20%	10 5%
Disagree	(−1)	100 25%	80 40%	20 10%
Disagree strongly	(−2)	20 5%	20 10%	–
Don't know	(–)	40 10%	10 5%	30 15%
Mean score		0.56	−0.26	1.47
Standard deviation		1.405	1.166	1.039
Standard error		0.074	0.085	0.080

In such tabulations, the software allocates a score to each positive answer – in this case score +2 for 'agree strongly' down to score –2 for 'disagree strongly'. Any 'don't know' responses are excluded from the calculations. Multiplying the number of respondents by each score enables the software to give the following measures:

■ mean score – an arithmetic average within subgroups, and a measure of central location;

- standard deviation – a measure of the average deviation of the sample from the mean;
- standard error of the mean – an estimate of the standard deviation of the population from which the sample is drawn;
- error variance – the square of the standard error, which is usually only required when calculating independent T-tests by hand.

Another table-based statistical measure is the T-test, which is a test to see if two reported means are significantly different from each other. There are two basic types of T-test: 1) independent tests, where the two means come from different samples; and 2) dependent tests, where the reported means are from the same sample. Independent tests can easily be calculated from the summary statistics available in Table 24.3, but dependent T-tests can only be calculated by going back to the original data. The use of this technique is explained more fully in Wyndham and Goosey (1997).

The Chi square test is another common test that can be applied to nearly any table containing frequency data. This test can be used for either 'goodness of fit' (that the observed frequencies of any one particular variable are similar to a set of expected or theoretical frequencies), or for tests of independence, where the frequencies of two variables are compared with each other to see if they are indeed independent. A good reference for further information about these and other tests that can be applied to tabular data is Ferguson (1981).

QUESTIONNAIRE DESIGN CONSIDERATIONS

The fundamental rule is: think about the analyses you will require before designing the questionnaire! Most of this is common sense, but even the most experienced researcher occasionally gets caught out with data he cannot analyse in the way he wants. Chapter 5 has already dealt with general questionnaire design considerations, including interviewer and routeing instructions, so this section will concentrate on considerations that may affect the analysis phase.

Survey data are usually entered in the form of codes to represent each response, in 'fields' or data locations, so that software can locate each data item for analysis. These codes will normally be shown next to each possible response, and the field numbers next to each question. Questionnaires that do not show these field and code numbers can be used, and may be preferred for self-completion surveys, but data entry is likely to be slower and more error-prone. Apart from research that uses a computer to gather data (eg CATI, CAPI or the Web), the researcher needs to be aware of the planned method of data entry.

There are two basic approaches, depending on the package to be used for analysis: 1) simulation of punch cards (necessary for some analysis packages, with data in BCI format); and 2) key-to-disk (used to prepare ASCII data files). Examples of questionnaire pages designed for both methods are given in boxes. The simulated punch card format involves the emulation of physical card punching with the constraint of 80 columns per card and 12 positions per column, although responses may be recorded over several 'cards' per respondent, in which case a card number must be provided and entered, together with the serial number, on the same place on each card image. The benefit of this approach is that 'card' columns may be multi-punched, ie if you have a list of up to 24 'brands heard of' to record, it can be done on two columns. Similarly, up to 12 possible groups of answers to an open-ended question can be coded on one column, 24 on two, etc, so the researcher just has to anticipate roughly how many responses to allow for. There are direct data entry systems available that emulate punch card formats and include some of the benefits of the key-to-disk option, such as having built-in edit checks for data validity.

Outside of the market research industry, where multiple answers are far less common, key-to-disk is the normal form of data entry. This method entails allocating a field to every logical single-choice question. Multi-response questions thus have to be regarded as one 'Yes/No' question for each possible answer. However, fields may be of two sorts: numeric (single choices and quantities) or character (for recording text or answer codes as alpha characters).

Often the researcher will not have any choice as to the data entry methodology. This is not a problem, since accuracy, cost and speed are generally on a par.

The factors that affect data entry cost are clarity, page turns and key depressions. Non-card-format key-to-disk will only be significantly more expensive when the survey has a very large proportion of multi-choice questions, when the record length will be much longer, but even then it may be outweighed by a lack of resources with card format experience.

Whichever method of data entry is chosen, there are a few basic rules in questionnaire codification:

■ Design the questionnaire without data codes first.
■ Put column or field numbers in brackets.
■ Don't spread columns or fields over a page break.
■ Work from left to right, and then top to bottom.
■ Don't leave gaps in column or field numbers.

At this stage it is worth mentioning another method of data entry: page scanning, or OMR (optical mark reading). Systems such as 'eyes and hands' and 'formic' allow questionnaire pages to be read with a scanner, which detects responses and creates a data file. Scanning should be considered for large-volume surveys, perhaps over 1,000, with relatively few pages (or sides). Questionnaires prepared for page scanning do not need to have field and code numbers, and should not require any special page markings. All responses are captured through detecting marks in discrete boxes, be they tick boxes or handwritten numbers. Technology has not yet come up with a sufficiently inexpensive and reliable system for picking up handwritten text, except carefully written characters in individual boxes (reasonable for postcodes), rather than handwriting.

There is one final factor: when asking about several items (eg cars in the household), do take care to ensure that responses about each item can be related back to one another, asking (and coding), for example, specifically about first car, and then second car, etc.

Naturally, once the data are entered, analysis can start. The researcher should first check some top-line counts to see that things appear to be sensible – no punches out of range, single-coded answer lists added to the base, etc. Such brief manual checks are worth doing before proceeding to tabulations, since computers work on the GIGO principle: garbage in, garbage out. The subject of data editing is too broad to cover here, but most data entry systems now produce an edit setup as a matter of routine – valuable time could be saved later on if a computer edit is run on the key variables.

EXAMPLE OF QUESTIONNAIRE DESIGNED FOR PUNCH CARD FORMAT

EXAMPLE SURVEY – BCI Format

Serial number:_____ (1–4)

Q1 Single-choice question:
Age of respondent:
18–29 .... 1 (5)
30–39 2
40–49 3
50–59 4
60–69 5

Q2 Multi-choice question:
Brands heard of:
BMW 1 (6)
Ford 2
Jeep 3
Ferrari 4
Jaguar 5

Q3 Numeric question:
Number of years driving: _____ (7–8)

Q4 Character question:
Dealership where car is serviced? _____ (9–30)

Q5 Open-ended question:
What are the benefits to you of driving a BMW?
_____ (31–32)
(allowing for up to 24 different answers and up to 24 answers for each respondent)

EXAMPLE OF A QUESTION DESIGNED FOR KEY-TO-DISK FORMAT

EXAMPLE SURVEY – ASCII Format

Serial number:_____(1)

Q1	Single-choice question:	Q2	Multi-choice question:
	Age of respondent:		Brands heard of:
	18–29 ....1 (2)		BMW....................1 (3)
	30–39 2		Ford 1 (4)
	40–49 3		Jeep 1 (5)
	50–59 4		Ferrari 1 (6)
	60 or over 5		Jaguar 1 (7)

Q3 Numeric question:
Number of years driving: _____ (8)

Q4 Character question:
Dealership where car is serviced? _____ (9)

Q5 Open-ended question:
What are the benefits to you of driving a BMW? (write in)
_____ (10)
_____ (11)
_____ (12)

(allowing for up to 15 different answers, multi-response, up to three answers per respondent)

Computerized questionnaire design

Recently, computer packages have become available for questionnaire design. These often utilize libraries of previous studies and will allocate question numbers and data definitions automatically – especially useful when there are revisions to the questionnaire. Examples of this software are QSL/Research machine, MerlinPlus, QPS, SNAP and Quanquest. Although all will print a questionnaire, only a few are flexible enough to produce a document close to the one that would have been designed manually. With the other systems, however, there are links into industry-standard word processing and desktop publishing software to enhance the appearance. A benefit of each system is that the question-and-answer text and data definitions can be taken over into the tabulation package supplied by the same company, avoiding the need for error-prone and wasteful duplication of effort. Some suppliers also offer links to other tabulation systems, either through specific export routines, or through an industry standard format called Triple-S (survey specification standard), available through Mercator, Merlinco and PTT.

HOW TO SPECIFY TABULAR ANALYSES

Having already said that the researcher should consider the analyses required before designing the questionnaire, this stage should be easy! The first consideration is layout options, in other words factors affecting the overall appearance. Some packages are more flexible than others, and at least one system has over 250 decision criteria! Researchers, or their companies, will often have a standard preferred layout, so this should be conveyed to the survey analysts. The main factors are:

■ Portrait or landscape printing, landscape being more common.
■ Whether you require an index of tables (table of contents).
■ Print size(s) – laser printers offer a choice of fonts, but the general rule will be the larger the print, the less information you get on a page.
■ Whether you want spaces between breakdown groups or lines – again, the more white space, the less information.
■ Whether you want the full question text – useful as a reminder.
■ Whether you want any forced editing of key variables – some packages allow you to force errors (out-of-range codes or multi-punches in single-choice fields) in a specified category. If you take this option then everything will add up nicely, but do make sure you know how many respondents have had forced editing applied on each variable.
■ For each cell in a table there are at least three figures that may be calculated – the raw number, the vertical-based percentage and the horizontal percentage. One, any two or all three can be shown, side by side or above one another (vertically or offset).
■ Whether percentages should be shown to zero, one or more decimal places, and with or without the percentage sign.

It should be clear from the above abbreviated list that the choices are enormous – probably far more numerous than really matters, but the options are there. A full list can be obtained from your DP bureau or in-house department.

The main elements of a cross-tabulation were described above as being: what is to appear down the side of the page, what across, and on what filter (base). These three things need to be specified for each tabulation in a form that is unambiguous:

■ **Down** Typically this will simply be the full list of answers to the quest-ions as posed in the questionnaire. The researcher may also consider netting groups of answers, for example 'all positive feelings' or 'any Ford'. This technique may be taken further, to generate completely new variables from existing ones. These are called 'derived variables', the most common use of which is to create an 'ever heard of' variable from spontaneous and prompted awareness questions.

■ **Across** Normally the researcher will decide upon a standard set of breakdown groups to be analysed by each question. These will be the perceived key discriminators, based on either experience or similar previous research, rather than simply 'age, sex, region', or they may be profiles designed to test a hypothesis. Beyond that, extra cross-breaks should be requested where the researcher considers that additional detail could be enlightening on a particular question: crossing 'attitude to test product' by 'brand used now', for example. Derived variables, made up from items within the questionnaire, may also be useful for cross-breaks – age within sex, for example, or 'brand awareness' derived from separate spontaneous and prompted awareness questions.

■ **Base** The filter to be applied to the entire table will normally be the one that applies in the questionnaire. However, it may be useful to look at the data in a third dimension, using filters to generate sets of tables where there may be variance in subgroups such as urban versus rural, presence of young children versus none, or combinations of these. The permutations escalate rapidly, and so does the numerical base, so the data must not be overstretched. In a 50-question survey there are 2,450 possible two-dimension combinations of variables before any special filters are added, so the need for selectivity is fairly obvious.

Tables may be based on respondents (eg all people answering the question), or responses (eg on a multi-choice question, it may be sensible to base percentages on the number of answers), or the appropriate strata of a hierarchical database (eg when the data comprise trips within individuals within households).

One way of generating less paper output is to combine tables. An example of this is shown in Table 24.4 where the first question is 'Have you heard or seen any adverts for Yorkshire Bank?' and the second is 'If so, in what media?' with the percentages in the second question being based on those who replied 'Yes' at the first question.

Table 24.3 showed an example of a tabulation with a rating scale and scores. The researcher must decide what scores to apply to this type of scale question. The example shown has five scores, of +2 through to -2, since there is a mid-point of opinion, but scoring five through to one might also have been chosen. A further option, to magnify the differences between mean scores, is to allocate scores of 100, 75, 50, 25 and 0. Rating scales may consist of more points than the five in the example – scores must be given to each point, and respondents who have not answered will be excluded from the calculation of the mean score.

Table 24.4 *Example of 'nested' tabulation*

Awareness of recent advertising for Yorkshire Bank (YB)

	Total	North	South	YB Account
Q24 Yorkshire Bank advertising seen or heard?				
Base:	400	200	200	50
	100%	100%	100%	100%
Yes	240	160	80	48
	60%	80%	40%	96%
No	160	40	120	2
	40%	20%	60%	4%
Q25 If yes, where did you see the advertising?				
Base:	240	160	80	48
	100%	100%	100%	100%
Television	105	85	20	22
	44%	53%	25%	46%
Magazine	30	15	15	18
	13%	9%	19%	38%
Newspaper	110	44	66	29
	46%	28%	83%	60%
Poster	15	2	13	2
	6%	1%	16%	4%
Radio	45	42	3	26
	19%	26%	4%	54%
Don't Know/Not Sure	40	14	26	8
	17%	9%	33%	10%

Frequently, rating-scale-type questions are asked of a 'grid' or 'bank' or set of similar statements; for example, degrees of agreement with 15 statements about a new service. In such cases, the researcher may choose to have one table per statement, showing the full frequency distributions (as in Table 24.3), or alternatively show them two to a page, or even condense the information further by suppressing the detailed lines and showing just one table with the mean scores only as summaries (known as a table of mean scores).

An alternative presentation in summary form shows the attributes down the side and the frequency distribution and mean score across the top. This style also allows researchers to combine all positive responses (eg 'agree' with 'agree strongly'), for comparison with all negative responses (eg 'disagree' with 'disagree strongly'), a form that is frequently used in reports and presentations.

Weighting

Occasionally it is necessary to apply a weighting procedure on the data to correct differences between the sample and the population it is attempting to represent. These differences may occur by accident or design. For example, you may end up with a disproportionate number of employed as against non-employed people, or simply more women than men, or have difficulty getting sufficient interviews in certain areas, or have to oversample for certain small populations (eg cigar smokers). Most tabulation systems can apply weighting factors to balance the sample – usually through the researcher providing targets (raw numbers or percentages) to be achieved. Some analysis packages allow weighting to be done against 'rim' targets (eg 50 per cent men, 50 per cent women, 30 per cent North, 30 per cent Midlands, 40 per cent South) and the best systems can do this while minimizing the size of weights in order to limit the effect of weighting on the sample design factor.

If weighting is used the analysis must show that this is the case, usually by adding a 'weighted base' line on each page below the unweighted total row, indicating the impact of weighting.

A useful reference work summarizing the reasons for using weighting is provided by Martin Frankel in his paper at the 1989 ARF Conference, 'Making up the numbers: why we do it, and why we don't'.

Table selection

It has been mentioned earlier that computers can generate thousands of pages of analysis very easily – the problem comes when a human being then has to digest it all! The researcher should therefore avoid simply requesting 'everything by everything' but, with common sense and a little planning, consider what is most useful. Even so, there are some computer-based 'hunting' techniques to find variables that show significant differences in the data (see the Chi square test described above). Nevertheless such an approach can be time-consuming and expensive. There are some survey analysis tools aimed at helping researchers explore the data after the main batch of tabulations, running extra analyses quickly (in seconds) on their own PC. Examples of two packages aimed at this application are Fastab and Quanvert, which allow considered analysis and experimentation after the first phase of 'number crunching', and can be used without training by researchers or clients. Another package, ESPRI, allows researchers and clients to conduct data mining and use multivariate analysis techniques in conjunction with graphical presentation. John Bound (1983) warns of the dangers of 'data dredging', and provides advice on the use of data exploration techniques in his paper 'Survey analysis for decisions, rather than "just the usual"'.

It is worth making one final common-sense warning: avoid dissecting the data into groups so small that the bases will not stand up to sub-analysis – bases of under 50, for example, should be examined closely.

IN-HOUSE OR BUREAU?

Twenty-five years ago, when computers cost at least £250,000, only three UK research companies had a computer of their own. A review of the latest MRS year-book, which lists all major companies, indicates that at least 30 now have their own DP department (more than one person) for tabulations – these tend to run powerful mini-computer or PC network environments, which often include data capture (eg CATI) facilities. Indeed, of the 30 largest BMRA (British Market Research Association) member companies, only two do not have such departments, and even these do have PC equipment for most other applications. The ubiquitous and increasingly powerful PC, and software to run on it, has resulted in more in-house options. Even so, specialist bureaux have continued to do well. Some of these, such as IDA and Quantime are independent and benefit from association with the developers of the packages they use (Merlinco and SPSS-MR). Others, such as Numbers and Digitab, benefit from affiliations with research companies. All of these offer high-quality services through using the best packages and people.

Factors in favour of the bureau

People are the most important single factor in quality of service and, since their livelihood depends on it, bureaux tend to employ only the best personnel, and they become the most expert across a broad range of projects. Similarly, bureaux tend to be closer to the leading edge of technology and developments: to survive at all they have to provide the best service, and bureaux take the risk in investment in hardware and people. The use of a bureau means you only pay for what you need. Bureaux survive by getting tabulations right and on time, enabling the researcher to provide the best possible service to his client – this should be the buying criterion for any service.

Factors in favour of in-house

An in-house operation is clearly totally under the control of the agency management, so if there is a resource clash they can decide on priorities, and control their own destiny. Once a company has invested in the hardware and staff to establish in-house services then management and shareholders will want to see a return on that investment. The internal charging system will probably reflect the view that the DP department is an overhead where costs are recovered against the work it does – work put out to bureaux is thus making no contribution to recovery of the overhead cost. Consequently, arguments regarding cost comparisons of bureau versus in-house are impossible to resolve at a job level. If the company thinks it could save money by going outside then this would be investigated at the company level. The corollary of this is that the more work an in-house department does then the greater is its contribution to overheads – hence the creation of some bureaux that are owned and run by research agencies (sometimes known as 'field-and-tab' operations) to offset costs.

In smaller agencies some researchers do their own analysis, given that the Windows-based software is now so much easier to use. This means that researchers may get closer to the data, but on the other hand researchers who spend time doing their own cross-tabulations are not spending that time doing market research, their main task.

SOFTWARE PACKAGES

Computer-generated cross-tabulations are created from four components: data, hardware, software and liveware (people). Apart from the data themselves, the most important element is people, as described above. Software is the next priority, although a researcher will often not be aware of the package used when he gets tabulations run.

The UK-based Association of Survey Computing (formerly the Study Group on Computers in Survey Analysis – SGCSA) is a British Computer Society special interest group, affiliated to the Market Research Society. This group publishes a catalogue of software for statistical and survey analysis – a recent edition shows 242 such packages from various parts of the world. As with most software, the more powerful and flexible it is the more expensive and complex it is likely to be. Of the packages with the most commercial sites there are two broad groups.

First, there are 'professional' packages, which will cope with all types of survey, being rather like programming languages. However, they require considerable investment in training, since if you do not use them frequently the 'language' will become unfamiliar. In this group we have Merlin, Quantum, QPS-CL and STAR from the UK, Donovan, Uncle and Mentor from the USA, and Surveycraft from Australia. These all run on mini-computers, of which the most popular is the VAX from DEC, and on PCs of course.

Secondly, there are the 'user-friendly' type packages, which are inevitably PC and Windows-based, and menu-driven. Essentially these are easier to learn but tend to have fewer options. In practice they may take longer to specify a set of tabulations after the user becomes familiar with the system since the menu system imposes steps that are not always relevant. The most common of these systems are SPSS and SNAP, although Pinpoint, and Windows versions of Merlin and QPS also have good penetration in Europe. An additional benefit of this group is their compatibility with other Microsoft Office applications.

As a researcher in the UK, if you are using a DP bureau then your cross-tabulations will be produced by Merlin or Quantum. These two packages are also the ones used by the larger research agencies. It is beyond the scope of this chapter to compare packages in detail – if such comparisons are important because you are considering purchase, then the best source of action is to seek references and independent advice. If a move to in-house DP is being considered then these are the key questions:

■ **Cost** Some software is leased while other packages may be purchased outright, although you always pay for the right to use, never for 'source code'. Be sure you know what is included – training, support and maintenance, for example, are often extras. How much will you have to pay for the hardware and its maintenance and for qualified people to run the system, set against savings on bureau costs?

■ **Capacity** Do you wish to plan for peaks or troughs?

■ **Time-scale** Over what period will you become self-sufficient? What happens in the interim?

■ **Support** What is the quality of support? This may best be ascertained by speaking with existing users. For the main suppliers there is a user group, and a hotline support number. Does the supplier have a reputation for listening to its clients and responding to their needs? Does it fix bugs, and quickly?

■ **Features** Match the features and strengths of the package to your own business.

■ **Growth** How is the choice of system affected by plans for the business to grow? Even without financial growth, it is possible to overstretch the smaller systems and give yourself a handicap in pitching for future business. If in doubt, choose one that you can grow into rather than one you may grow out of. Some software suppliers, such as Merlinco (Merlin) and Quantime (Quantum), now owned by SPSS-MR, offer starter packs so users can start simply and grow into the more complex things later.

■ **Experience** Is there a 'reservoir' of local experience in the package or will you have to train everyone from zero? If you select one of the packages the bureau uses then you have external capacity for overflow work to be done to the same specifications – indeed, the computer files can be brought back in-house after processing so that future processing can be done internally.

■ **Training** What level of training is required and for what levels of skills? If several weeks are required then it is likely that the package is a powerful one, unless it is overly complex.

■ **Integration** Consider associated tasks and modules such as questionnaire design, data entry, CATI, CAPI, Web surveys, editing, postprocessing, statistics, reports, graphics – what degree of integration exists between these phases? Once text and numbers are in the PC, it should be possible to transfer them across applications, and across suppliers, to avoid wasteful and error-prone re-entry.

■ **Architecture** Is the system a 'closed' or 'open' one with regard to file formats? That is, how easy are files transferable into other systems? You may need to use other formats for data capture or delivery to clients.

BEYOND TABULATIONS

In the process of turning data into information, cross-tabulations are often supplemented by other computer-based tools. Occasionally there are computer 'bridges' available for the transfer of text, data and data definition files from one package to another. These export/import facilities are valuable since they eliminate the need to type files in again in a new format, a duplication of effort that can also introduce errors. It is beyond the scope of this chapter to review all the available software, but since the researcher should be aware of the possibilities the main points of the following subjects are described briefly:

■ multivariate analysis;
■ graphics;
■ spreadsheets;
■ databases;
■ better tabulations;
■ report writing.

Various multivariate analysis techniques

This summary of techniques is supplied by Chris Johnson, Statistical Services Director at IDA.

Sometimes interrelationships within the data are too complex to be expressed by tabulations. Statistical techniques are available to examine many variables simultaneously and present findings that are often simplified approximations. These are valuable analysis tools, almost invariably done through computer packages, often available on a PC, but caution is advised: for correct interpretation, the fundamental approach (not necessarily the detailed statistical tests) must be understood. Some bureaux such as IDA, Digitab and Probit specialize in these applications. Software in this area is often specific to one particular aspect (eg correspondence analysis), but the two most common packages, SPSS and SAS, cover a wide range of applications and both are available on PCs or Unix machines.

Multivariate techniques used in survey research fall into four broad categories: those techniques used for market segmentation, preference analysis, forecasting and product positioning.

The two principal types of analysis performed to segment markets are factor analysis and cluster analysis. Factor analysis is a statistical technique that examines the responses to a battery of questions, and groups those questions that have been answered in a similar way with one another. This is normally achieved by performing a 'principal components analysis' and then subjecting the resulting factors to some form of factor rotation such as varimax or promax.

In general, factor analysis comes into its own when applied to batteries of attitude scales that can be reduced to component factors. In many market segmentation exercises these resultant factors can then be analysed by cluster analysis, which is a range of techniques for grouping respondents who answer particular questions (or factors) in the same way. 'K-means' cluster analysis is often used to achieve this clustering.

The essential difference between factor and cluster analysis from the user's point of view is that factor analysis groups variables into factors, while cluster analysis groups individuals into clusters. Most cluster analysis programs allow the researcher to allocate individuals to their nearest cluster and thus these can then be retabulated against other questions in the same survey.

Other tools often used for segmentation include automatic interaction detection (AID or CHAID) and discriminant analysis. These techniques differ from factor and cluster analysis in that the segmentation is not based on a battery of interrelated variables, but upon one or more dependent variables. Essentially, the sample is split to ensure that the resulting subgroups have as different as possible profiles on the dependent variable.

Techniques used for preference analysis also take many forms. Round-robin analyses can be used to indicate if there are significant differences between preference ratings given to a collection of brands, and multidimensional scaling techniques such as prefmap can be used to map out the differences between brands and products in terms of preference.

One other major area of preference analysis techniques is conjoint analysis. In this case the object of the exercise is to develop individual utility values for each category of a descriptive variable. For instance, conjoint analysis can be used to determine whether package style is more important to respondents than pack size, and also which package style or pack size is preferred.

It is then possible to run simulations by adding all the utilities (or multiplying, depending on the technique used) for all the attributes represented in a particular product and seeing if its overall utility is higher than another product made up of different levels of each attribute. Trade-off and full concept conjoint are just two forms of this type of analysis.

Forecasting techniques are all methods of predicting information based upon information already acquired. In survey research, multiple regression and related techniques are probably the main type used in forecasting. Multiple regression allows one to look at the linear relationship between one dependent variable and a collection of predictor variables in such a way that the dependent variable can be expressed as a linear combination of the predictors (each multiplied by a particular weight). Time series analysis is another family of techniques used in forecasting.

Product positioning and brand mapping can be achieved in many ways. Correspondence analysis and multi-dimensional scaling techniques are just a few methods that can be used to position products. Correspondence analysis is a method by which a contingency table (any cross-tabulation of frequencies) is analysed by performing a principal components analysis on the Chi square distances between each row item and between each column item. The resulting analysis produces maps that can help in the understanding of which products are viewed as being similar and why. Product positioning can also be understood by analysing preference data collected using such methods as the assessor model, and it is possible to place preference surfaces over normal perceptual maps.

It must be stated that many of the techniques mentioned above can be used in most of the four categories; multiple correspondence analysis lends itself to segmentation studies, and factor analysis techniques have been used in many preference analysis studies. There is a wealth of learned publications on the subject of multivariate analysis; three the author recommends are Greenacre, Lilien and Kotler (1983) and Green, Carmone and Smith (1989).

Graphics

If a picture paints a thousand words then a graph can save almost that many words in a report. It is difficult to get very much data on a chart without it appearing cluttered or confusing, but a well-drawn chart can make a point most effectively. The main forms of charts are bar charts (may be horizontal or vertical bars), pie charts and line graphs (see Figures 24.1,

24.2 and 24.3 respectively as examples). Computer software, and demands by management, have made their use much more common over the past decade.

Even in black and white, graphs are still quite expensive to produce because of the relatively high proportion of people-time involved, so they are normally produced to summarize the main findings of the research, either in a report or as part of the researcher's presentation. Tracking movements over time (brand awareness during an advertising campaign, for example) is an excellent use of graphical presentation.

Although most computer bureaux offer facilities for producing graphics, most researchers prefer to do this task themselves unless it is on a repetitive project (eg tracking studies). This is because of the convenience and simplicity of producing your own charts on a PC, and the facility for experimentation without building up external costs. The particular chart type used will depend upon the information to be projected and the amount of labelling text required.

Of the many PC software packages available, ranging in price from £300 to £6,000, four can be mentioned here:

1. Harvard Graphics – more advanced facilities but still on a PC;
2. Excel – within the Microsoft Office suite, so easiest to transport files (eg to PowerPoint);
3. Freelance – considered to be the most featureful, but not the easiest to learn;
4. Tel-A-Graph – a professional tool for designers.

Excellent graphics software is also available on the Apple Macintosh.

Spreadsheets

Spreadsheet software is one of the main applications of PCs, being aimed at individuals who want to assess 'what if'-type hypotheses. They work on 'aggregated' data files, ie not raw data that can be cross-analysed at the individual response level, but data in their summarized (tabulated) form.

Either by typing in numbers from tabulations or transfer via an 'export' program, tabulation data may then be manipulated through a series of simple commands to perform arithmetic functions on columns, rows or entire tables (eg adding the first two columns, or multiplying by the third column to give a new fourth column). This software is also most useful for summarizing data from several waves of a continuous study since the numbers do not have to be reprocessed – any spreadsheet-based formulae (for example, moving annual totals) would be applied to data as they are entered. The most popular packages are Excel and Lotus, both of which have the advantage of a considerable user base.

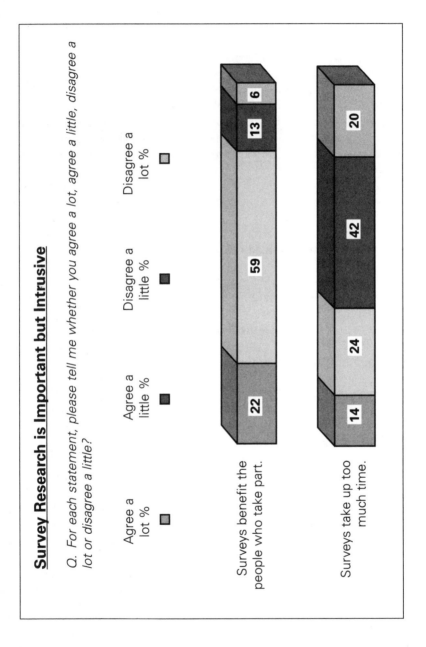

Figure 24.1 *Bar chart*

Captains of Industry

Q *Please tell me how favourable or unfavourable your overall impression of market research is?*

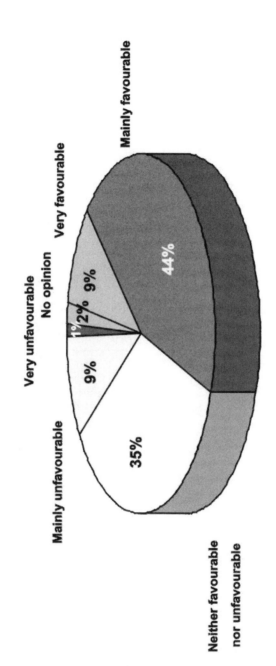

Figure 24.2 *Pie chart*

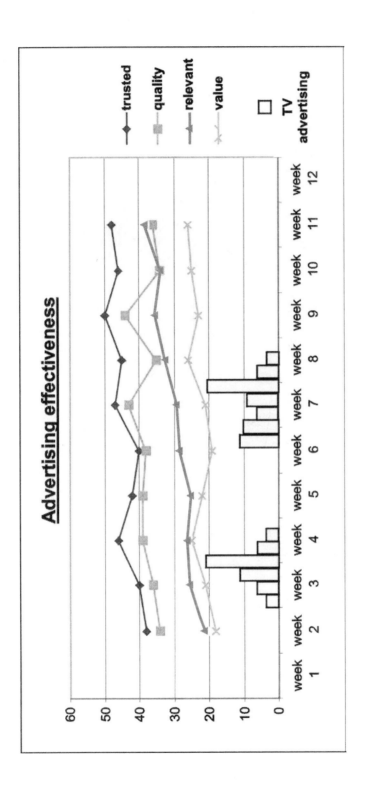

Figure 24.3 *Line Graph*

This later example shows graphically how four key attitudes change over time in the context of bursts of advertising; techniques explained much more fully in Wigzell (1994).

Database management

Database management systems range from simple electronic filing to relational database management control with integral programming tools.

For a researcher their applications therefore vary from client contact records through to panel management systems. The selection of software will depend on the database(s) to be held and the sophistication of reporting required. Holding and manipulating market research data, their main benefit is in being able to pre-program calculations to be performed on each new wave of continuous surveys, but there are restrictions on their ability to handle multi-coded data. Data are held in a predefined, structured way with user-defined 'labels' to facilitate easier access for non-experts. Most management information systems (MIS) are based around database software, most usually Access as part of the Microsoft Office suite. Research data in an MIS can be handled in the same way as (and compared with) other management information such as sales, shipments, advertising and complaints.

Better tabulations

Earlier in this chapter there is a description of how the researcher may prepare a reduced set of summary tabulations supporting the 'story' he wishes to tell from the survey. These may be done by a bureau, or by the researcher using survey exploration tools. This approach is best presented by Andrew Ehrenberg (1975). However, even the most sophisticated survey software still uses a limited range of non-proportional fonts, which make tabulations look rather dated compared with the report produced in Word. There are ways round this: export the tabulations to Word or Excel, or use a specialist survey presentation tool such as YAPS or 'ite'.

Reports

Apart from a presentation, the main outcome of a piece of survey research is the report. Clearly, the better looking a report the more credibility it has for the client. Apart from graphics, two further pieces of software help to improve the appearance of reports: word processing (WP) and desktop publishing (DTP). Both have features for producing well-presented documents, including the use of various type fonts, sizes, underlining and italics. Nearly all research agencies use WP – the selection often depends upon previous experience of the operators.

If an individual is considering using a WP package then there are three important considerations:

1. What does it have to interface with (eg if you are using it at home, what system is used at the office)?
2. Which printer(s) will be used?
3. Will you use it often enough to benefit from the advanced features some of the packages offer? The risk of having more features than you are likely to use is that they can form a confusing trap.

Following many market battles, there are now only two significant PC-based WP packages: Word and WordPerfect. Both now offer many of the features of DTP, taking report writing further into graphics, and allowing the user to call pictures (charts and scanned photographs) in with text. In practice, most agencies use Microsoft Office's PowerPoint for presentations – this is an extension of Word – to produce images of slides.

Qualitative research data

This chapter has been concerned almost entirely with quantitative survey data, apart from aspects of responses to open-ended questions within a quantitative study. This is because nearly all quantitative data are analysed by computer, whilst nearly all qualitative data are digested by people, with very little help from computers at the analysis phase. For completeness, and a review of developments in software for the analysis of qualitative research data, the author suggests two key papers: Guedfond (1989) and Moore, Burbach and Heeler (1995).

SUMMARY

In a way, computers have made analysis more difficult for the user: since there are now more options there are more decisions to make, and it is all too easy to generate hundreds of tabulations irrespective of the sample size. The use of computerized techniques for data capture – CATI, CAPI, Web surveys – means that there is more pressure than ever to deliver results quickly, without proper time for considered analysis of the data. In fact, IT offers researchers and agency managers many opportunities: ignoring those opportunities could turn them into threats since other agencies will seek to use IT to add value to their services. Meanwhile, quality standards have been developed for the research industry in respect of data capture and analysis. The UK has led this development, known as MRQSA (Market Research Quality Standards Association), which has become recognized British Standard charter mark BS 7911, and is increasingly used as the basis for industry standards in other countries.

Skilful use of the techniques, together with common sense, will enable the researcher to turn data into information. Independent and experienced advice should be sought on subjects that are beyond the researcher's usual area of activity, to make the best use of technology.

REFERENCES

Bound, J (1983) Survey analysis for decisions, rather than 'just the usual', Market Research Society Conference

Ehrenberg, A (1975) *Data Reduction*, John Wiley, London

Ferguson, G (1981) *Statistical Analysis in Psychology and Education*, 5th edn, McGraw-Hill, Maidenhead

Frankel, M R (1989) *Making up the numbers: why we do it, and why we don't*, ARF, USA

Green, P E, Carmone Jr, F J and Smith, S M (1989) *Multidimensional Scaling, Concepts and Applications*, Allyn & Bacon, Boston

Greenacre, M *Theory and Applications of Correspondence Analysis*, Academic Press, London

Guedfond, G (1989) *The third generation of qualitative research*, ESOMAR

Leung, J and Yeh C-L (1998) *Natural Language Processing: Verbatim and data mining*, ESOMAR

Leung, J and Yeh, C-L (1998) *The Death of Lady Di – Automatic textual analysis from the Internet*, ESOMAR

Lilien, G and Kotler, P (1983) *Marketing Decision Making*, Harper & Row, Cambridge

McDonald, C (1985) Linguistic coding – how it can be used – computer aided coding, Market Research Society Conference

Moore, K and Burbach, R and Heeler (1995) Using neural nets to analyse qualitative data, *JMRS*

Wigzell, J (1994) A new approach to survey analysis, Market Research Society Conference

Wyndham, J and Goosey, R (1997) *It's Time We Started Using Statistics*, ESOMAR

$$\boxed{25}$$

Modelling: Pricing

Michael Thomas

Pricing can be said to be the most neglected area of marketing decision-making. Even though price is the means for harvesting cash flow into a company, and for creating value perceptions among customers, experience indicates that too often the pricing decision is approached in a mechanistic fashion, overshadowed by the dark cloaks of accountants, rarely strategic and frequently not even tactical. In order to underline the point, everyone involved in price making should consider this list of questions:

- Do you know the economic value of each of your products to your customers?
- Do you know how your customers perceive price in the product field in which you compete?
- What is the relationship between price and market share for each of your products over the past five years?
- Do you use the industry's price–volume curve as a tool of analysis?
- Who is the price leader in each of the product fields in which you compete?
- Do you know how to go about establishing price leadership?
- Do you understand your competitors' pricing strategies?
- Do you have a strategy for dealing with competitors' price changes?
- Do you anticipate competitors' price changes correctly?
- Is your approach to price making cost-, competitor- or customer-orientated?

- How is intra-company (transfer) price managed – is it dictated from the top (accountant-dominated) or by market considerations?
- Do your contribution margins for the same product differ widely from customer to customer?
- Are your prices set to reflect customer-specific costs?
- How are price changes communicated to customers, to salespeople and to distributors?

There are very few managers, even in sophisticated international companies, who could sit down and comfortably answer more than half of those questions, and how they would long for answers to the other half!

Pricing research is clearly the tool to investigate the answer to all these questions, and in this chapter I shall attempt to provide a framework for using the tools, for there are many. Remember that pricing occurs in a dynamic environment, so there are no set rules for determining optional pricing strategy. Pricing is part science, part art, with the balance leaning toward science.

Nault (1983) has produced a convincing list of fallacies about price, which should serve as a warning to those who are overwhelmingly confident that they know how to make a price. The 10 common fallacies about price are:

1. **The consumer buys rationally** There is no homo economicus in the market-place. Buying motives are often emotional, illogical or impulsive.
2. **Quality determines price** This sounds like a truism and many marketers would assess the quality of their product and then set the price accordingly. But the example of wines is a clear illustration that a higher price is often an indicator of quality for the consumer.
3. **Price can be soundly based on margin goal** To apply a rigid margin policy may lead to an overcautious price (or vice versa). The key is to test for upward pricing limits and take all opportunities.
4. **Recession favours low price products** This has not been observed, as value for money is more important than the absolute price level.
5. **Consumers know the market prices** Apart from high frequency purchases or indispensable goods like cars, consumers are rarely aware of the real prices. It may therefore be risky to rely only on their spontaneous price consciousness.
6. **Wise pricing is relative to competition** This is a manufacturer's point of view. What is really important is how the targeted buyers will perceive the product and what value they'll see in it.
7. **New products are to be priced at today's cost of goods** In an economy that is no longer stable the costs are bound to increase!
8. **Only the market leader can control the price** In fact, number two or three often has more flexibility and initiative.

9. **Manufacturers can control the retailer's selling price (RSP)** This is only true of mail-order goods or medicines. In most cases there is a very powerful intermediary, the retailer, who has the last say.
10. **Price low at entry, then increase once share goals are achieved** Introducing a product at a low price creates a defined price–value relationship, which then becomes very difficult to change. To make a higher price acceptable would require much higher advertising investments. The initial price positioning must be the long-term one.

These 10 fallacies yield a number of points that price researchers and price modellers should not forget:

■ Buying motives are complex.
■ Since costs bear no necessary relationship to price, either in manufacturing or in customer attitudes, the key test is for the upward pricing limit.
■ The key to price making is to understand how targeted buyers see price.
■ Inflation erodes customers' price expectations.
■ Where customers shop (consumer goods) and how customers shop (industrial goods) is critical to understanding attitudes towards price.
■ Initial price positioning is critical to long-term pricing strategy.
■ So new product pricing research has to be of the highest quality.

Hendon and Hendon (1994) usefully describe 14 critical factors in making a pricing decision and creating an expert system.

This preamble is intended to underline that price sensitivity measurement, which is what price modelling is all about, is an aid to judgement, not a replacement for it. No model, hence no estimation technique, can reproduce or simulate all of the factors that enter into the purchase decision.

It follows from the questions raised above, the fallacies concerning price and the deductions to be drawn from them that price makers must know all that can be learnt about buyers, both indirectly and directly, and that both qualitative and quantitative data (and impressions!) contribute to price makers' understanding and hence judgement.

Table 25.1 shows the scope of this chapter, Chapter 26 and Chapter 27. Experimentally controlled pricing models are discussed in the chapters that follow, while this chapter is restricted to models deriving from uncontrolled measurement.

Actual purchases are of course recorded in sales data, and price makers must attempt to exploit the information held in internal sales data banks. Chapters 11 and 12 in this volume describe the many sources of sales data that can be purchased from market research companies. If the data are rich enough they can be used to explore the effect of price changes over time. Such data are by definition historical and, given the dynamics of the marketplace, *ceteris paribus* assumptions are likely to be dangerous. Price changes

Table 25.1 *The price modeller's toolkit – conditions of measurement*

	Uncontrolled	Experimentally Controlled
Actual Purchases	Aggregate sales data Store audit data Consumer panel data	In-store experiments Laboratory purchase experiments
Preferences and Intentions	Monadic tests Direct questions Perceived value Sensitivity analysis	Competitive tests Randomized testing of buy Response Simulated purchase surveys Trade-off (conjoint) Analysis

rarely occur without changes in other marketing variables, such as advertising and sales support, and the competitive environment is itself dynamic over time.

All products and brands have a sales history, hence aggregate sales data should be available. Their form and frequency should determine their use to price makers. Desktop technology now makes the possibility of (almost) real-time data being available, on a retail outlet basis. Weekly panel data are obviously richer than out-of-date sales data and, combined with in-store scanning, researchers and price makers now have heightened possibilities of understanding in real time how consumers are behaving as far as household goods purchases are concerned. Store audit data (see Chapter 14) now offers rich possibilities for estimating price sensitivity for a wide range of consumer goods.

Studies of uncontrolled preferences and intentions are potentially the most fruitful source of data for price modelling. Monadic testing only will be covered here, since competitive testing – conjoint analysis – is fully discussed in Chapter 26. Monadic testing attempts to measure a consumer's reaction to the price of an item (a brand or a service, for example) without consideration being given to alternatives or competitive products or services. The consumer's decision is considered to be an absolute one, inducing the response 'I would definitely buy' at one end of the scale to 'I would definitely not buy' at the other. Purchase intention modelling has a long history in price research and, despite its shortcomings, which will be described, it still has an intellectually respectable pedigree. Its attraction stems from its relative cheapness as a survey method – it costs much less than commercially available purchase data. It can be used for a wide variety of goods – most consumer goods and many industrial goods. It can be done at the new product conception stage, and at all subsequent stages up to product launch. Data can be collected reasonably quickly.

Its primitive form is direct questioning, but price researchers are fully aware of the pitfalls of such a simplistic approach. The classic model, which owes much to two British researchers, Andre Gabor and Clive Granger, is the buy-response model. It is an important model because the buy-response curve is in fact a demand curve, a concept fundamental to all price theory.

Customers are asked for each price shown from a set of randomized price cards, whether they would purchase. Purchase intentions are measured by asking respondents to indicate which of the following statements best describes the likelihood of purchase:

- definitely would buy;
- probably would buy;
- might/might not buy;
- probably would not buy;
- definitely would not buy.

From aggregated data, the percentages claiming to buy at each price can be graphed as in Figure 25.1.

Market research firms can ask hundreds of respondents and produce a range of responses: '70 per cent would definitely buy' to '20 per cent would definitely not buy'. This technique can of course be elaborated by introducing a competitive display, asking respondents to answer with reference to more than one product or brand. This has led to conjoint analysis, much more reflective of real purchase situations, a technique more fully described in Chapter 26.

Buy-response modelling is the progenitor of most price modelling in use today. Its limitations are well understood, hence the development of more sophisticated versions of the original model. It is capable of yielding insights into price sensitivity at different points in time or place; it can yield a range of acceptable prices for a new product; it may yield information that will be valuable in predicting probability of purchase before and after trial (see Figure 25.2).

Recent work on pricing emphasizes the need to deliver true value to customers and price must signal such value (Monroe, 1993). The perceived value approach to pricing has been successfully applied to industrial buyer behaviour. It is described by Kortge and Okonkwo (1993). A useful holistic framework appears in Smith (1995). He clearly points out that: managerial pricing orientation is the pattern of policies, activities and behaviours that business units typically engage in with regard to information gathering and processing; objectives, decision rules and beliefs; organizational decision processes; and organizational responsiveness relating to setting or changing price.

Normative pricing models are important and useful, but readers should be reminded that implementation is both critical and a managerial responsibility – models can contribute to making the process more sophisticated,

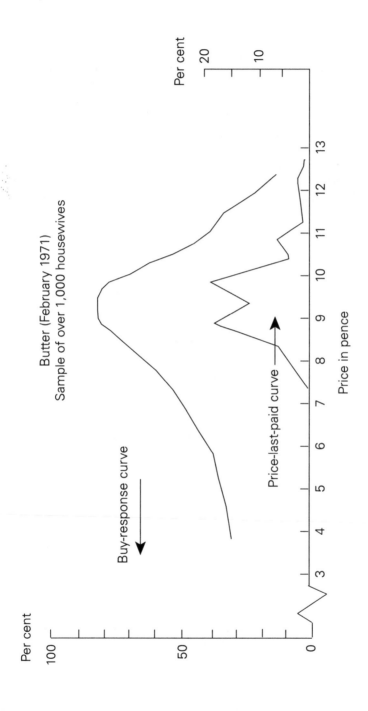

Figure 25.1 *Buy-response model*

Source: Gabor 1988

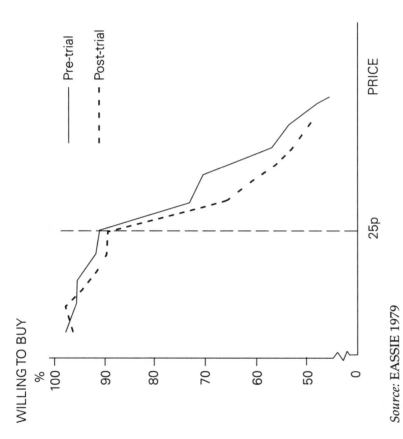

Source: EASSIE 1979

Figure 25.2 *Buy-response before and after trial*

Table 25.2 *Summary evaluation of the pricing models*

			Evaluative Criteria			
	Clearly Specified	Realistic	Variables Clearly Specified	Information Accessible	Relationships Specified	Uses Current Evidence
New Product Models						
Classic microeconomic	+	–	+	–	–	–
Multivariate extension	+	–	+	–	+	–
Market potential	–	–	–	–	–	–
Price discrimination	+	–	+	–	+	–
Perceived value	+	+	–	+	–	+
Product-line Models						
Related products	+	–	+	–	+	–
Product-line changes	+	+	+	+	+	+
Interdependent demand	+	–	+	–	–	+
Price differential	+	+	+	+	–	+

Note: A plus (+) means yes, a minus (–) means no.
Source: Adapted from Monroe and Della Bitta (1978)

Table 25.2 Summary evaluation of the pricing models (continued)

			Evaluative Criteria			
	Clearly Specified	Realistic	Variables Clearly Specified	Information Accessible	Relationships Specified	Uses Current Evidence
Price Change Models						
Cost-orientated	–	–	+	–	+	–
Price–volume	–	–	+	+	–	+
Heuristic simulation	+	+	+	+	–	–
No of discounted units	+	+	–	+	–	+
Optimal discount size	–	+	+	–	–	+
Price sensitivity measurement	+	+	+	+	+	+
Price Structure Models						
Cash/discount/credit policy	–	+	–	+	–	–
Quantity discount	–	+	+	+	+	+

Note: A plus (+) means yes, a minus (–) means no.
Source: Adapted from Monroe and Della Bitta (1978)

hopefully replacing the continuing use of the *ad hoc* approach in what is still the most important element of the marketing mix.

The summary in Table 25.2 describes the evaluative criteria associated with the most frequently used pricing models. Readers should seek more detail in the quoted source.

The author is grateful to Dr Nikolaos Tzokas for help in updating this chapter.

REFERENCES AND FURTHER READING

Coughlan, A and Mantrala, M (1992) Dynamic competitive pricing strategy, *International Journal of Research in Marketing*, **9** (1), pp 91–108

Diamantopolous, A and Matthews, B (1995) *Making Pricing Decisions*, Chapman and Hall, London

Eassie, R W F (1979) Buy-response analysis: a practical tool of market research, *European Journal of Marketing*, **134**

Eliashberg, J and Chatterjee, R (1985) Analytical models of competition with implications for marketing: issues, findings and outlook, *Journal of Marketing Research*, 22 August, pp 237–61

Gabor, A (1988) *Pricing: Concepts and methods for effective marketing*, Gower Press, Aldershot

Gijsbrechts, E (1993) Prices and pricing research in consumer marketing: some recent developments, *International Journal of Research in Marketing*, **10** (2), pp 115–51

Hendon, R A and Hendon, D W (1994) Creating an expert system: design and building considerations, *Pricing Strategy and Practice*, **2** (1), pp 26–40

Kortge, G D and Okonkwo, R A (1993) Perceived value approach to pricing, *Industrial Marketing Management*, **22**, pp 133–40

Lilien, G L, Kotler, P and Moorthy, K S (1992) *Marketing Models*, Englewood Cliffs, New Jersey

Monroe, K B (1993) Pricing practices which endanger profits, *Pricing Strategy and Practice*, **1** (1), pp 4–10

Monroe, K B and Della Bitta, A J (1978) Models for pricing decisions, *Journal of Marketing Research*, **XV**, August, pp 413–28

Moorthy, K S (1993) Competitive marketing strategies – game theoretic models, in *Handbooks of OR and MS*, ed J Eliashberg and G L Lillien, **5**, Elsevier, Amsterdam

Morgan, R (1987) Ad hoc pricing research – some key issues, *Journal of the Market Research Society*, **29**, pp 109–21

Morris, M H and Joyce, M L (1998) How marketers evaluate price sensitivity, *Industrial Marketing Management*, **17**, pp 169–76

Nagle, T and Holden, R K (1994) *The Strategy and Tactics of Pricing: A guide to profitable decision making*, 2nd edn, Englewood Cliffs, New Jersey

Nault, T (1983) Common fallacies in pricing practices and strategies, *Elsevier Business Intelligence Series*, **2**, Conference Board Report No 751, pp 3–6, Elsevier, Amsterdam

Parker, P M (1992) Price elasticity dynamics over the adoption of the product life cycle, *Journal of Marketing Research*, 29 August, pp 358–67

Rao, V R (1993) Pricing models in marketing, in *Handbooks of OR and MS*, ed J Eliashberg and G L Lilien, **5**, pp 517–52, Elsevier, Amsterdam

Smith G E (1995) Managerial pricing orientation: the process of making pricing decisions, *Pricing Strategy and Practice*, **3** (3), pp 28–39

26

Modelling: Conjoint Analysis

Rory Morgan

BACKGROUND AND ORIGINS

Conjoint analysis is a particular method of analysing experimental data in such a way that the contributions of different experimental conditions can be systematically separated and quantified. However, in addition to this, it has become in recent years the basis of a wide variety of modelling approaches that attempt to recreate the decision process that consumers undergo when evaluating competing products or services.

Its origins derive from a classical form of statistical analysis known as 'analysis of variance', which aims to investigate the manner in which particular experimental conditions affect some specific outcome. For example, in a food product the analysis may seek to determine the consumer preference for different levels of sugar, and different levels of colouring. A research project investigating this might handle the problem by testing a variety of combinations of product having different combinations of formulation. The analysis proceeds by separating the effects of the different variables, and estimating the contribution of each, together with the way that these variables 'interact' with one another.

However, a problem exists when more than a small number of variables are tested, since this can easily lead to an impossibly large number of hypothetical products to test – all the combinations being statistically known as a 'full design'.

In order to cope with this problem, it is possible to test a reduced number of combinations taken out of the full design, known as a 'partial balanced design'. This is a subset of the full design, but with combinations chosen in a very careful way so that the representation of each variable level, and its pairing with other variable levels, is balanced so that the analysis is not biased. This end result is known as an 'orthogonally balanced reduced design'. The entire process of examining the effect of more than one variable by testing combinations of them is known as 'factorial testing'.

In the late 1960s and early 1970s, experiments began to be conducted in which the variables being tested in a factorial experiment were less 'hard' than the kind of physical product composition type of variable described above, and did not require actual product testing by respondents. For example, motorists could be asked to examine alternative automobile concepts described in terms of variables such as 'engine size', 'fuel economy', 'seat comfort' and so on.

The assumption here was that, with this sort of variable, rather than test the actual physical expressions, respondents could themselves assess their likely level of liking or preference from a simple description of its composition. Moreover, the variables used did not even need to be so hard as to involve a physical issue (such as engine size) – an example in the airline sector might include variables such as 'quality of food', 'punctuality', 'pleasantness of cabin crew' and so on.

In terms of the analysis of such experiments, a further refinement was possible in circumstances where it was not expected that any of the variables tested were likely to interact with one another – a condition known as 'independence'. In these circumstances, that aim of the analysis is to measure the 'main effect' of each variable and its levels, and the major benefit of this approach is that, with no interactions between variables to measure, the number of product concepts required to measure the main effects can be very much reduced.

Another development dating from the 1970s involved the scope of the analysis itself. In conventional factorial product testing, the aim of the analysis is to identify the main effects (and possibly interactions too) at the aggregate level – that is to say, average values derived across the sample. In contrast, the aim of the reduced design main effects experiments is to identify the main effects values for each individual in the sample. This approach has considerable implications, as will be described below, since it makes possible not just the identification of segments of individuals with similar values, but also the possibility of a wide range of modelling activity.

This adaptation of factorial testing is generically known as conjoint analysis and, in general, these applications commonly have the following characteristics:

- A reduced design is used (except on the simplest experiment).
- Analysis is for main effects only.
- The analysis is conducted for every individual in the sample.
- Modelling and segmentation analysis are commonly applied to the resulting individual values.

THE PROBLEM OF 'IMPORTANCE'

In market research, it can be argued that the main use of conjoint analysis is in measuring the degree of 'importance' that consumers (ie respondents) attach to product characteristics. In fact, the measurement of importance has been a problem that has bedevilled researchers for many years. In contrast to other areas of research requiring measurement – such as behaviour, brand image, core attitudes and so on – it has proved to be a considerably more difficult type of data to collect than other data types.

DIRECT MEASURES

It is sometimes difficult to see why this should be. After all, nothing could be simpler than asking people to consider a range of product characteristics and communicating directly how important each of these is to them. A number of collection systems might be used – importance rating scales, ranking exercises and so on. However, researchers who attempt this approach – sometimes known as the 'direct' approach – find themselves running into a number of problems.

The first of these is discrimination. It is frequently found that importance rating scales exhibit poor discrimination, ie all scores tend to be the same. This is understandable, since there is nothing to stop respondents making the task easier for themselves by declaring all attributes to be 'important' to them. This ignores the fact that, in the real world, obtaining good performance on one attribute frequently has to be at the expense of another attribute.

The second is 'social attributes'. Another problem arises when 'softer' attributes are used in studies that possess a social content – in other words, telling the interviewer how important you rate a topic 'says something' about the sort of person you are.

For example, motorists asked to rate a number of car features for importance to their purchasing decision have been shown to rate safety features far more highly than seems plausible compared to other features such as styling and performance. It is easy to see why – motorists would prefer to regard themselves as prudent, safe citizens. This is responding to what psychologists refer to as 'socio-normative pressure'.

This effect does not arise in all studies, but it can occur where high-image attributes are used that possess a large degree of social or emotional content.

INDIRECT MEASURES

In order to avoid the problems of the 'direct' approaches, researchers have frequently adopted other, more statistical, forms of approaching the problem more indirectly. One way of doing this is to ask respondents to rate a number of products or brands on the attributes concerned (ie obtain brand image ratings), and examine the statistical correlations between these and some overall rating for preference. The argument is that a strong positive correlation – arising when the image scores given to brands for a particular attribute rise and fall in step with overall rating – suggests that the overall rating is strongly associated with the opinion on the attribute, ie caused by it.

The problem with the correlation approach is twofold. First, it makes the assumption of equating simple correlation with causation, which is a notoriously problematic assumption to make (in other words, assuming, because two things appear to rise and fall together, that one causes the other). Secondly, image data derived from market research exercises frequently exhibit high levels of 'autocorrelation' – that is, a tendency for attributes to correlate with one another. This is caused by the 'halo effect', a tendency for respondents who like a product to rate it consistently highly across all attributes. The converse is also true for products they like less.

Conjoint 'importances'

In many senses, therefore, conjoint analysis is a better technique for measuring attribute importances, partly because it is an 'indirect' method (that is, it does not ask the respondent to think about what is important, only what is preferred) that obtains a measure of importance by 'decomposing' stated preferences so that the importance of contributory factors can be inferred.

At the same time, conjoint analysis also scores over other methods of measuring importance by specifically dealing with stated levels of attributes, rather than dealing with them as complete entities. For example, it might be more valuable to know the importance attached to different specific sizes of engine, rather than the importance of engine size as an overall issue.

DATA COLLECTION

Although the principles of the analysis are similar, a variety of different methods exist for collecting information from respondents for conjoint analysis. The principal ones are:

■ full concepts;
■ pair-wise grids (trade-off);
■ computer elicitation.

These will be discussed below, with the aid of a hypothetical set of three attributes, with the following levels:

Size	Colour	Shape
large	red	square
small	green	round
	blue	

Full concepts

The full concepts system has the closest links with the origins of conjoint analysis as a variant of factorial testing. With the example above, a full design would consist of 2 × 3 × 2 = 12 combinations, as shown below.

Concept	Size	Colour	Shape
1	large	red	square
2	large	red	round
3	large	green	square
4	large	green	round
5	large	blue	square
6	large	blue	round
7	small	red	square
8	small	red	round
9	small	green	square
10	small	green	round
11	small	blue	square
12	small	blue	round

Since the number of attributes and levels is small, leading to no more than 12 concepts, it is not necessary to employ a reduced design of concepts, so that all 12 could be evaluated by respondents.

The task would be for the respondent to examine all 12 concepts, and either put them in order of preference (a ranking exercise), or to 'rate' them on some scale. In the case of a large number of concepts (and 20 to 30 are not unusual here), the ranking procedure might be a two-stage process where the respondent first classifies the concept into a number of piles corresponding to 'very interesting', 'quite interesting', 'so-so', 'not particularly interesting' and 'very uninteresting'. Having done this, the respondent would then be asked to rank the concepts in each pile in turn, which would give us an overall ranking for all of them.

The big advantage of the full concepts approach is that the respondent is asked to react to 'realistic' descriptions of concepts in terms of all the attributes used, ie each concept is described as fully as possible. However, a major disadvantage with this approach is that with more than seven or eight attributes used in a study, each concept is liable to exceed respondents' 'span of attention', in other words, their ability to keep track mentally of more than seven or eight simultaneously varying issues. The overall effect of this is to restrict the method to studies where no more than seven or eight attributes are used, or to break the study up into separate sets of attributes.

The pair-wise approach (trade-off)

One way of avoiding the limitations of the full concepts approach is to break up the task for the respondent into smaller and easier-to-perform tasks.

In the pair-wise system, attributes are presented to respondents in pairs. For the three-attribute example above, this would lead to three possible pairings:

- size–colour;
- size–shape;
- colour–shape.

These pairs are presented to the respondent in the form of grids, such as the one shown in Figure 26.1.

SHAPE

		Square	Round
SIZE	Large		
	Small		

Figure 26.1 *Pairs grid*

Taking this grid as an example, this leads to four possible combinations for the respondent to consider, and put in rank order of preference. This is typically done as a self-completion exercise, with the respondent being handed a booklet containing a number of such grids, and asked to work through each grid in turn, entering the ranks. Note that it is usual to train the respondent on some sample grids beforehand.

With small studies, all possible pairs of attributes would be used. However, on larger studies, a subset of pairs would need to be chosen along the same lines as for full concepts – such a reduced design would need to be statistically balanced to avoid bias. As stated above, the principal advantage of the pair-wise system is that, although the respondent is asked to make more explicit judgements than with full concepts, each judgement is conceptually 'easier' since only two attributes are involved. Using this system, considerably more attributes can be used (eg 20 or so) in the same design.

Against this, some researchers feel that the task is less 'natural' to the respondent, and fails to present concepts as an expression of all the attributes considered in the study. The task itself can also appear repetitive and difficult to understand to some respondents. Nevertheless, the approach has been used successfully in many studies where full concepts were not possible, and validation studies (where both approaches were used using the same attributes) have given similar results.

Computer elicitation

The most recent form of elicitation to emerge is one where respondents are asked to make choices between combinations of attributes and their levels, which are chosen and administered by a computer.

It may seem at first sight that this is no more than a sophisticated recording method where the underlying system is still a full concepts or a pair-wise approach. However, this is not the case, since the computer need not administer a fixed list of attribute choices by rota, but can be allowed to compute from previous answers given the next attributes to present to the respondent. This can be done on the basis of the 'information gain' that would arise from obtaining data on some attributes rather than others.

Moreover, the task can be made simpler for the respondent by allowing him to indicate attribute levels that would be totally unacceptable – thus shortening the entire task. At the same time, the computer can continually monitor the degree to which the model of preference that it is building up for a respondent is actually 'explaining' the choices made – when it seems a good enough fit, the computer can terminate the elicitation process.

In effect, the computer-driven process homes in on a respondent's preference structure. The net result is to lead to a typically shorter interview and one that many respondents report as being more interesting.

Although from a fieldwork administration point of view this approach can present some difficulties (not least the ones involved in equipping and training an interviewer force with computers), the accelerating tendency towards powerful and cheap portable micro-computers has meant that this system is becoming increasingly used to administer conjoint tasks in many countries.

ANALYSIS

As stated above, the main aim of conjoint analysis is to obtain estimates of the 'main effects' of the variables being examined, which can be regarded as measures of the contribution or importance of them in determining preference.

The usual terminology for describing such conjoint importance weights is in terms of 'utilities'. The fact that these are fractional numbers (ie they are expressed with decimal places) may seem odd, especially since the elicitation procedures may ask for nothing more than rank orders of preference.

The way in which this is done is illustrated in the grid (Figure 26.2), taking as an example a single pair-wise grid of two of the attributes we have met before: shape (square/round) and size (large/small).

	SHAPE	
	Square	Round
SIZE		
Large	1	2
Small	3	4

Figure 26.2 *Pair-wise grid with ranked preferences*

In the grid above, the respondent has taken the large–square option as the most preferred (ie rank 1) and the small–round option as the least preferred (ie rank 4) one. A conjoint analysis of this single pair-wise grid might assign the following utilities:

Size	Shape
large +100.0	square +50.0
small –100.0	round –50.0

These utility values have a number of very useful properties.

Reproducibility of data

Utility values are derived by 'decomposing' a respondent's stated preferences into estimates of the main effects. A number of statistical methods
can be used to do this – monotonic analysis of variance (MONANOVA),
multiple regression and linear programming, to name but a few.

If the estimates are good, they have an important property – they can
be used to reconstruct the original preferences. Take for example the single
grid above Figure 26.2). Given the utility values calculated, it is possible to
calculate the 'utility sum' for each of the four choices, as follows:

Combination	Rank	Utility Sum
large–square	1	+ 150
large–round	2	+ 50
small–square	3	– 50
small–round	4	– 150

As can be seen, the original rank orders of preference have been preserved
in the ordering of the utility sums. This is a very important feature of
conjoint analysis, since it makes possible the building of computer simulation models, which will be described below.

It might seem that in the above case, the utility values are somewhat
arbitrary, since quite significant changes might be made to them while still
preserving their ability to reconstruct the original ranks. This is true in a
small attribute system. However, the method depends upon the fact that
as the number of attributes grows, the actual values that would satisfy the
constraints of such a system get more and more precise – in fact, turning
rank values into 'real' fractional values. This is exactly the same principle
as used by other techniques, such as non-metric multi-dimensional scaling
(MDS).

Note that in some computer programs, utility values are calculated as
multiplicative rather than additive, although multiplicative values can
clearly be made additive by using logarithms.

Scaling

As can be seen, the values within an attribute span both positive and
negative ranges. This is arbitrary, and indeed utility values are often
expressed purely as positive numbers. The main point is that they can be
expressed in a variety of ways.

Relativity

However, although they can be scaled differently, they have one important
property in common: ratios between levels are preserved. Thus, the utility

values for large and small in the above example could have been expressed as +100 and -100, +1,000 and -1,000, +1.0 and -1.0, or even 2 and 0. All these values preserve the central relationship, which is that the utility or value of large is twice that of small.

Moreover, in our two-attribute system, the value of going from small to large (200 points) has twice the value of going from square to round (100 points). This is an extremely important point, since it means that importance measures derived from conjoint exercises are not absolute, but have meaning only in a relative context alongside other variables collected at the same time.

This type of relative value is known in the mathematical world as a 'ratio scale' – having no absolute start or end point. Another common example of such a scale would be temperature. In the same way that we cannot really say that a temperature of 60 degrees is 'twice as hot' as a temperature of 30 degrees, we cannot say that a utility value of +60 is 'twice as important' as a value of +30. However, in the same way that we can interpret ratios of temperatures, we can interpret ratios of utilities. The best way to interpret utility values, therefore, is in terms of differences between levels, rather than in absolute terms.

Span of utility

Having said this, it is often useful to identify the overall effect of the attribute as a whole, rather than in terms of its constituent levels. This can be done by finding the 'span of utility' for each attribute (ie the distance between the level having the greatest value and the level having the least value) and percentaging these across all the attributes present in the system. This is done in Table 26.1 for our two-attribute case above:

Table 26.1 *Utility span*

Attribute	Largest Value	Smallest Value	Span	%
Size	+100	−100	200	67
Shape	+50	−50	100	33
			300	

In fact, this calculation can be done in two ways, which might not necessarily give the same answer.

The first way is to perform the calculation as shown above, working on the mean utility values. This gives a good overall summary of the net effect for the sample in question, but could potentially disguise a situation where half the sample might prefer one level of an attribute, and the other half prefer another level. The net effect in zero-centred utilities would be to 'average around the mean', with the outcome that the resulting small span of utility for that attribute would not indicate that for a large number of people it was significantly higher. Clearly, if there is a broad consensus concerning the order of preference for attribute levels, this is less likely to happen.

Another way of performing the calculation, therefore, involves computing the span of utility for every individual in the sample, and then taking the average of these. This will provide a better measure in situations where large-scale differences of opinion exist.

The 'span of utility' can be a useful summary measure, but needs to be used with caution, since it is clearly derived from the particular attribute system used. Any change to this (such as a comparison with another study having different attributes, or even different levels of attributes) would result in different values, making such a comparison invalid.

INTERPRETING UTILITY VALUES

Having conducted a conjoint study, and having obtained the utility values described above, the task of the researcher is to interpret these. In general, there are three major ways of using them, as described in the following three sections.

Predefined subgroup means

In the same way that ordinary survey data can be broken down for subgroup analysis (such as a comparison of social class groups, or age bands, etc), so utility values can be grouped together and the mean values examined and compared with other groups. This provides a useful means of checking the relative importance of attributes and their levels among predefined groups of interest – possibly marketing target groups, or behavioural groups.

In the (hypothetical) example shown in Table 26.2, despite similar levels of importance attached to the attributes overall, considerable differences in preference between levels exist between men and women. While both sexes tend to prefer large sizes to small, this is a greater issue to men than women; and in the case of shape, the preference is actually reversed. Finally, in the case of colour, while both sexes prefer red to other colours, men clearly prefer green to blue as their second choice, while for women both green and blue take second place to a similar extent.

Table 26.2 *Mean utility values*

	Men		Women	
	U	*% span*	*U*	*% span*
Size				
Large	+35.6	46	+26.4	47
Small	−35.6		−26.4	
Shape				
Square	−24.8	32	−18.3	33
Round	+24.8		+18.3	
Colour				
Red	+15.4	22	+13.5	20
Green	+3.7		−8.2	
Blue	−19.1		−5.3	

Segmenting utility values

Looking at predefined subgroups of interest is one way to examine the way in which individuals vary in terms of the importance that they attach to issues. However, this depends by definition on identifying criteria beforehand for specifying subgroups that are likely to prove discriminating, in the sense that the different groups have different importance weights. Naturally, if the subgroups are of no intrinsic marketing interest in themselves, but are merely used to expose differences between individuals, the risk is that the prior definitions that are used may not reveal the principal differences between individuals.

Another way is to approach the problem the other way around. Instead of predefining the groups of interest, why not approach the problem with a clear mind, and search for groupings of individuals who are similar in terms of attaching similar levels of importance to the same attributes?

This can be done using a particular multivariate technique known as cluster analysis, which searches through the utilities and identifies groups of individuals having similar patterns of utility values. It can provide a very useful form of segmentation in marketing terms, since it is essentially able to identify and define 'need groups' that exist in a market, which often provide a more actionable basis to market studies than other forms of segmentation based on behavioural characteristics or general attitudes. This forces the research to concentrate on the structure of primary demand in a market, rather than deal with variables that may only have a tenuous (or ill-defined) link with future behaviour.

There is another more practical reason for performing a clustering on conjoint utilities, and this is because the nature of the conjoint exercise forces respondents to 'trade-off' one attribute to obtain another. This frequently leads to a clearer differentiation in the data than is the case with attitude statements (for example), and this can in turn lead to a 'cleaner', more understandable (and ultimately more actionable) segmentation outcome.

It is probably true to say that needs segmentation via conjoint analysis is one of the most useful applications of the method.

Simulation modelling

The third, and some would consider the most appealing, way of analysing conjoint values is through the process of simulation modelling. This is made possible by the property possessed by utility values referred to earlier, that of being able to reconstitute the original order of preferences given by respondents.

For example, in the case of reduced designs (where respondents were not exposed to all possible combinations of attribute levels), it would be possible to estimate the likely preferences that might be shown towards hypothetical combinations that had not actually been tested. Moreover, this can be done at the individual level. As an example, consider the utility values generated by three respondents, A, B and C, shown in Table 26.3.

Table 26.3 *Utility values*

	Respondent		
	A	*B*	*C*
Size			
Large	+55.6	+27.6	−16.9
Small	−55.6	−27.6	+16.9
Shape			
Square	−23.8	+34.5	+48.3
Round	+23.8	− 34.5	−48.3
Colour			
Red	+37.1	+12.8	−0.7
Green	−27.1	+15.9	−36.1
Blue	−10.0	−3.1	+36.8

Now, suppose that we were interested in five possible 'packages', as described below. It is possible to compute the 'utility sum' for each of these. For our three respondents in the example, the utility values for each package are shown in Table 26.4.

Table 26.4 *Utility values for packages*

Package	A	B	C
1 Large/Square/Red	+68.9	+49.3	+31.7
2 Small/Round/Green	+4.6	–57.5	–67.5
3 Large/Round/Blue	+69.4	–10.0	–28.4
4 Large/Square/Green	+4.7	+78.0	–4.7
5 Small/Square/Blue	–89.4	+3.8	+102.0

Taking the view that the item with the highest utility sum will offer a respondent the best combination of desired properties out of the five possible candidates, a simple modelling rule would be to take the item with the highest utility sum as the item 'chosen': ie A chooses item 3, B chooses 4, and C chooses 5.

A conjoint simulation exercise therefore works in this way: a set of hypothesized attribute combinations is 'tested' on a sample of individuals who have completed a conjoint exercise. For each individual, the 'best' option is simulated to be 'chosen', and shares of items chosen can then be accumulated across the sample, as shown in Table 26.5.

Table 26.5 *Sample choice shares*

Sample Size = 300	Simulated Choice Shares %
Item 1	24
Item 2	13
Item 3	35
Item 4	7
Item 5	21

This kind of modelling is an example of 'micro-modelling' – so called because the decision process is modelled at the individual level. This makes the modelling process of particular interest in situations where full account should be taken of individual differences (eg in segmentation exercises). Since no average importance values are calculated, there is much less danger of an average misrepresenting the true diversity of opinion on an issue.

The modelling process allows a large range of simulation possibilities: current market specifications can be created, new products introduced and products optimized (in the sense of finding the exact combination of attributes that maximally satisfies the greatest number of customers).

In reality, the modelling process can be more sophisticated than the simple account given above, and various techniques can be used to mimic the following situations:

- **Joint choice** – such as with respondent A in the example above, where items 1 and 3 have similar utility sums. In these cases, it is unrealistic to assume that a respondent would radically prefer one to the other, given the very small difference that might be within the precision of the method. It is possible to define a resolution factor for a model, which would then take items with utility sums within a certain band as 'joint choices'.
- **Probabilistic choice** – such as that occuring in markets where consumers purchase from a repertoire of products. In these cases, the aim of the modelling is not to predict a certain outcome, but to predict the probability of purchase in a given purchasing situation. These can be estimated from the ratios of the relevant utility sums.
- **Respondent weighting** – for example, situations where it is advantageous to weight people according to some criterion, such as heaviness of consumption in the product field, level of disposable income, and so on.

Much of the computer software now available to conduct conjoint analysis is made particularly user-friendly, so that end users can experiment with the simulation possibilities themselves. For example, Research International's SIMGEN package will operate on a conventional IBM-compatible micro-computer, can be used with minimal training and yet offers all the sophisticated simulation options described above.

EXTENSIONS TO CONJOINT ANALYSIS

There are a number of important extensions to conjoint analysis, which are aimed at specific problems, and which conventional conjoint approaches are in many ways less good at handling. Some of these have become generic techniques in their own right.

Brand/price trade-off

Conventional conjoint analysis 'sees' a product as the sum total of its constituent attributes. For example, a particular car model is a function of engine size, styling option, interior fittings and so on. The more complete the list of constituents, the better the description of the product.

However, for short-term tactical purposes, it is possible to see the product or brand as a total entity, which has a given appeal to consumers and which they can be regarded as 'trading off' against the price they can buy it at. In other words, 'brand' is a summary attribute.

Thus, it is possible to harness the power of conjoint analysis to specific problems of pricing, where the brand or product lists are simply levels of one attribute, and specific prices are regarded as levels of another. In other words, we have a two-attribute conjoint case, which is very appropriate for pricing research in well-defined markets (ie markets with competing products).

In fact, there are a number of problems with using conventional elicitation procedures. For one thing, there is a potentially large number of brands and prices in a typical pricing study. For another, it is common to use an 'evoked set' procedure to allow respondents to nominate only those brands that are relevant to them.

The most widely used elicitation procedure is called the 'buying game', where respondents are shown an array of brands (their evoked set) at specific pricing points. They are asked to specify their most likely purchase, after which the price of that brand increases, and the question is asked again. The process is repeated until all prices have been exhausted.

The net effect of this is to obtain a matrix of ranks similar to a single pair-wise conjoint grid, which can be analysed in the same way. Utility values are calculated for brands and price levels in the study, and these can be analysed by predefined subgroup. Segmentation techniques can also be used to identify groupings with similar importances, for example to identify groups of 'price-sensitive' and 'brand-loyal' consumers.

It is worth mentioning that the utility values calculated for individual brands are very valuable measures of the brand equity possessed by a product, since they are effectively measures of the price premium that the product will sustain. This is frequently regarded as a valuable base measure for evaluating changes in a brand's position in a market over time, and as a dependent measure for evaluating marketing campaigns in advertising, promotions and distribution, etc. In fact, so valuable is this measure that it is frequently the principal reason for conducting the study.

However, probably the most widely used analytic approach in brand/price trade-off is that of simulation, since it is possible to create sensitive pricing models of markets on which hypotheses can be tested. In simulation, specific pricing scenarios can be constructed in which brands are represented at particular prices, and market shares predicted. The modelling also allows the possibility of 'delisting' (ie removing from simulation), and identifying patterns of gains and losses with other brands.

Another common simulation approach is the construction of demand curves for particular products, by conducting a series of simulations in which the prices are sequentially increased against a background of other brands at (usually market) prices. The shares of the target brand can be plotted as a demand curve, allowing an estimate of elasticity of demand to be made.

SMART

Another variant of conjoint analysis was developed by Research International specifically for research into services, or customer research. The SMART technique (salient multi-attribute research technique) takes the view that a better way to measure interest in a service company's change is in terms of improvements.

Thus, an important attribute in the banking area might be 'length of time spent waiting in a queue'. Conventional conjoint might identify say three levels: 'more than ten minutes', 'five to ten minutes' and 'less than five minutes'. The SMART analysis, however, would not attempt to measure the utility associated with the levels themselves but the utility attached to movements between levels. Hence, for an attribute with three levels, there would be two possible movements between them, for which utilities (or relative importance weights) would be calculated on an individual basis.

The system also differs from conventional conjoint analysis, in so far as customers identify the key attributes of interest to themselves from a potentially very long list of possible service attributes. An 'evoked set' system ensures that each respondent examines the set of issues most relevant to him or herself.

Moreover, the analysis also takes into account the perceptions that customers have of the service levels with which they are currently being provided. This allows the analysis to identify areas of maximum leverage for the company – by searching for areas of improvement that are important, and on which current perceptions are poor. Equally, in common with conventional conjoint analysis, need segments can be identified.

The aim of the analysis is therefore somewhat specialized, since it concentrates on identifying areas of highest cost–benefit in service areas.

REFERENCES AND FURTHER READING

Green, P and Srinvasen, V (1978) Conjoint analysis in consumer research: issues and outlook, *Journal of Consumer Research*, **5**

Lunn, J and Morgan, R (1982) Some applications of the trade-off approach, in *Applied Marketing and Social Research*, lst edn, Van Nostrand Reinhold, USA

Morgan, R (1987) Brand/price trade-off – where we stand now, EMAC/ESOMAR Symposium on macro and micro modelling, October, Tutzing

27

Modelling: Simulated Testing

Peter Sampson

BACKGROUND

The idea of a test market, as opposed to a launch across an entire country, may have one or more of the following objectives (Fitzroy, 1976):

- to predict the results of a later national launch;
- to assess the relative effectiveness of different marketing plans in different matched areas;
- to confirm the operational features of the launch are adequate.

With the advent of commercial television in the mid-1950s, test marketing became a common feature of new consumer product development programmes. The efforts of regional television companies in the UK to promote their areas as suitable for test marketing drew a response by local press groups suggesting that particular towns could equally well be used.

In the USA the early advent of cable television and the ability to split television transmissions led to the highly sophisticated use of test marketing. Areas were split by differential expenditure levels, different campaigns, different below-the-line support, etc and the effects of these variations measured, to assess the probable outcome of a particular marketing plan at national level.

The theoretical paradigm of test marketing is consistent with the principles of experimental design. If a small area can be selected, representative, say, of a larger area such as the entire UK, and a marketing activity conducted there without interference or contamination from variables outside that area, the measured test results may be extrapolated to the larger area.

For example, if it was decided that a new product was to be launched in the UK with a Year 1 marketing support budget equivalent to £2 million nationally, this may be equated to £140,000 in Tyne Tees, 7 per cent of the whole country. And, furthermore, the outcome in Tyne Tees, in terms of key measures such as brand awareness, retail distribution, brand trial, brand repurchase and sales volume could be taken as what it would be for the UK as a whole. So, before risking £2 million to see whether or not a new product would succeed or fail if launched nationally, or on the relaunch of an existing product, a company could conduct a test market by spending £140,000 in 7 per cent Tyne Tees to see if its marketing objectives could be met for the plan. And, moreover, it would have the opportunity to discover the strengths and weaknesses of that plan and refine it. This may be something of a simplification, but it serves to illustrate the principle.

In the two and a half decades from the mid-1950s until the end of the 1970s, area test marketing was widely used by many manufacturers. The general idea of an area test market is, theoretically, straightforward. However, in practice, there are enormous problems, which have led, in today's highly competitive market-place, to the virtual demise of traditional area test marketing in favour of simulated test marketing.

The problems of test marketing are well set out by Davis (1986), with references for further reading. In essence, these problems can be summarized as follows:

■ **The choice of area** The selection of a small area that may be assumed to be representative of a larger area, or the whole country, is difficult if not impossible to make. Sociodemographic, geodemographic, purchasing and consumption patterns may differ, and so may the pattern of retail distribution.

■ **The replication of advertising campaigns** Whereas television advertising can be replicated between areas, it is more difficult to do this for mixed media campaigns, especially utilizing the national press.

■ **The difficulty of isolating an area and avoiding effects arising from outside the area that may impinge on it** There are the issues of overlapping television areas, consumers and product crossing geographical boundaries, and retailer and competitive activity, which result in the performance of the brand launched into the test region being artificially affected.

- **Timing** To allow a test market to be 'read', it must run for a suitably lengthy period, at least for six months, possibly longer. During that time, many things can change in both the market-place and competitor activity, which make an extrapolation difficult.
- **Competitive activity** The marketing literature is full of stories of how competitors have 'spoilt' test markets via such tactics as:
  - buying up much of the new product put into the distribution system to give the false impression it has been successful;
  - 'flooding' the area with their own product to make it less easy for the competitor to sell in or sell out;
  - vastly increasing their advertising expenditure in that area, 'out-gunning' the new launch;
  - pre-empting the test market by launching their own equivalent of the product nationally.
- **Cost** As media and other product launch costs began to rise, area test marketing, while a cheaper option, was no longer a cheap option.
- **Security** Increased market competitiveness makes it difficult for a company to spend 6–12 months engaging in a test market. During that time, competitors can prepare their own plans to gain an advantage.
- **Projecting, predicting and forecasting** Conducting a test market is all very well – assessing its outcome and extrapolating to provide a national picture is reliant on a 'complex series of calculations'.

The sum of Davis's observations adds to the conclusions that 'simple projection' is inaccurate, 'prediction' depends on how good the model being used is, while 'forecasting', being time-based, is fraught with problems.

If area test marketing has been beset by such recognized difficulties, why, we may ask, was it so widely used for so many years? The simple answer is that, while being very much less than perfect, it was probably the best way available of obtaining some reasonable estimate of the likely success or failure of a new product or measuring the effectiveness of a particular marketing plan. The fact that most new product launches were failures, and many of these went through an area test market, may be held up to show the failure of traditional test marketing. So what is the alternative?

WHAT ARE SIMULATED TEST MARKETING SYSTEMS AND WHEN ARE THEY USED?

At the beginning of the 1970s, following the publication of several noted texts (including Howard and Sheth, 1969; Engel, Kollat and Blackwell,

1970), there was considerable interest in micro-analytical behavioural models (Sampson, 1974). Here, each person in the database is represented and processed at the individual level, aggregating to the total market. These models were more concerned with aspects of current behaviour than with behavioural outcomes. They were complex, attempted to handle too many variables and had little practical value. As such, they did not prove attractive to marketing management.

At the same time, an alternative modelling 'school' was developing macro-models (Parfitt and Collins, 1968; Massy, 1969; Eskin, 1973; Nakanishi, 1973; Lin, 1979). They were simpler, operated at the aggregate level, provided greater accuracy and set out to estimate brand share or sales volume of a new product if launched. Eminently practicable, they proved to be much more attractive to marketing management. Progressing through different names such as 'sales decomposition–recomposition models', 'pre-test market models', 'marketing mix testing', 'total proposition testing' to, eventually, 'simulated test marketing models' (STM models), they form the subject matter of the remainder of this chapter. (For a detailed history of STM models, see Factor and Sampson, 1983.)

The term 'system' is, in fact, much more appropriate than 'model', since they have developed into strategic tools falling within the mainstream of marketing decision-making. (This term will be used throughout the remainder of this chapter.)

The 1980s saw a continual decline in the traditional area test market. Growing problems relating to cost, speed, security and logistics resulted in a substantial decrease in their use. STM systems that estimate the potential of new products prior to their launch or the likely outcome of a product relaunch developed rapidly. These include ASSESSOR, BASES, COMP, LITMUS, LTM and SENSOR, all macro-systems, and MICROTEST, a micro-system. (Note: It is incorrect to think of STM systems as being only applicable to new product development. They are equally used in the case of relaunching existing products, or in launching line extensions, although these require special consideration. Line extensions will be discussed later.)

WHAT INFORMATION DO SIMULATED TEST MARKETING SYSTEMS PROVIDE?

The usual format is a test in which a product and its concept are evaluated. The precise methods within each system and the actual data provision differ slightly. However, they are all concerned with estimating the likely potential of a new product if marketed, or an existing product if relaunched. They provide an estimate of sales volume or brand share for a given marketing mix. (STM experts prefer to talk about 'estimating' rather than 'forecasting' or 'predicting'. They are fully aware of the limitations of their systems and provide confidence limits that will vary according to product field, price point, country, etc, or any combination of these.)

The different systems may be regarded as building bricks, providing modules to address different problems. The major problem areas dealt with are covered as follows:

1. For a given concept, presented either on board or as a television commercial, concept evaluation (eg BASES I) will estimate trial penetration – the percentage of the target market who will buy the product in Year 1, for a given marketing plan. (Although it is not usually possible to provide a volume estimate from a concept evaluation, sophisticated STM users are often able to 'plug in' a repeat purchase estimate and obtain an 'approximation' of likely sales volume for different marketing scenarios.) The fact that no actual product trial takes place means estimates must be viewed more cautiously, and are provided with wider confidence limits.

2. Concept and product evaluation (eg BASES II) will estimate, for a given concept and product, the following:
   - Trial penetration (as BASES I).
   - Repeat purchase (ie the proportion of trialists who will buy the product again). BASES II, the most sophisticated model, provides two repeat purchase rates – 'true repeat' (the proportion of trialists who will buy the product again within 12 months of their initial purchase) and 'measured repeat' (the proportion of trialists who will buy the product again within 12 months of its launch). (In order to provide a time-based volume estimate, ie to say what the volume will be in Year 1, Year 2, etc, both repeat rates should be derived.)
   - Depth of repeat – the long-term repeat purchase for the brand, leading to a 'stability level' of core, loyal buyers who account for the majority of the brand franchise (van Westendorp, 1989).
   - Brand share or sales volume estimate for Years 1, 2, 3, etc – some systems provide what is termed 'long-term brand share', which can be a problem if the product is creating a new category (share of what?) and the 'long term' is not specified. Much more useful is an estimate of sales volume that is time-related. To know how many units/cases/ tonnes, etc will be sold in Years 1, 2 and 3 is more easily handled as management information, and poses no problems for innovative new products that do not allow a sensible estimate of brand share to be made (Lin, 1979; Pioche and Standen, 1986).

3. Tracking (eg BASES IV) may be used. It could be that the decision has already been taken to launch or relaunch a brand. Or, alternatively, following an STM, many aspects of the marketing plan, or the entire plan, may need to be changed. Under these circumstances, it may be decided to launch the product and track its performance in the market.

By combining tracking with an STM system's ability to estimate volume, conventional tracking data can be used to project forward trial, repeat purchase and sales volume for different marketing plans, via simulation (Sampson, 1987).

Input data

Several sets of input data are required, as follows:

■ They may derive from consumers as conventional survey data (a concept/use test). This is conducted in two stages. Stage 1 is usually at a central location, where respondents are shown the communication for the test product, either in print or rough commercial format, and asked to react to it. (There is often no need to show finished advertising, since one of the advantages of some STM systems is that it is unnecessary to go to this expense before the test product looks like being a success.) The product is given to some or all respondents to try, depending on the system used. Stage 2 is usually a telephone re-call after an appropriate period for product trial has elapsed.
■ Data may derive from management, comprising details of the proposed marketing plan such as distribution, awareness, advertising expenditure, promotional activity and out-of-stock position.
■ They may derive from the market-place, and take account of such factors as seasonality, regionality, market expansion and likely competitive activity.

Most systems provide a simulation capability that enables management to examine different marketing mix scenarios. Indeed, whereas the original prime use of STM systems was to make 'go, no-go' decisions for new products, much greater advantage will be taken of their versatility to perform tasks such as examining the effects of different marketing plans and estimating the effects of launching with different levels of promotional expenditure or launching at different price levels. This trend has been noted in the 1980s and the 1990s.

More recently a whole subset of models has evolved concerned with the complex issues of line extensions, as these continue to be a common feature of companies eager to exploit brand equity. BASES-LX, for example, identifies five different types of line extension, each requiring a very different treatment when estimating.

Nowadays STM systems are being used far more as a strategic marketing tool. The amount of data required for estimating is considerable. The BASES II marketing inputs document runs to 22 pages, for example. What the collection and collation exercise certainly does is make management consider every single aspect of the marketing plan. This is a salutary exercise.

The following paragraphs set out the sort of inputs required in order to provide a sales volume or brand share estimate for Years 1, 2 and 3. These are typical inputs (but not universal, because every system's questionnaire will vary slightly).

First are the inputs from a consumer survey, both before and after product trial:

- intention to purchase on a five-point scale;
- product evaluation on a six-point scale;
- value for money on a five-point scale;
- claimed purchase frequency;
- average number of units purchased at trial and subsequently;
- competitive/substitute product usage.

Apart from standard questions, there is much scope for additional open-ended questions to obtain diagnostic information and questions relating to particular areas of interest.

Second are the inputs from management:

- awareness build on a quarterly basis, ie what level of total awareness for the brand is expected quarterly, in Year 1 and then by the end of Years 2 and 3 (it is appreciated that awareness may be difficult to estimate, especially if there is no prior experience for comparison; for BASES, a sub-model exists that examines the media plan in terms of its ad spend, media mix, timing, etc, converts it to a rating point delivery over time and estimates the likely awareness);
- distribution build, ie what sterling or 'acv' – all commodity volume distribution – is expected in the distribution channel or channels quarterly, in Year 1 and then by the end of Years 2 and 3 (for some products, there may be more than one distribution channel, like grocery plus confectionery, or chemists, in which case input data must reflect distribution in both channels, plus an estimate of the likely relative throughputs for the brand or category between the different channels);
- promotional plans, in the form of below-the-line activities such as couponing, sampling, etc, anticipated across the first three years after launch;
- competitive activity expected, in terms of new launches or general marketing response;
- out-of-stock levels, if expected.

Third are the inputs from the market-place. The environment into which any new product is launched, or existing product relaunched, is a complex, ever-changing one. Consequently, in addition to inputs based on market size, other data must be provided. In general, market-place factors include the following:

- **Market size** This is in terms of number of households or individuals.
- **Seasonality** Do sales of the product vary across the year? If so, this must be taken into account, especially in terms of the timing of launch (sell-in, awareness and distribution build), since, for a given marketing plan, product performance, being seasonal, will result in different sell-out rates according to seasonality.
- **Regionality** Do sales vary by region within a country? If so, this must be taken into account.
- **Category development** Is the category expanding, static or contracting? Consumer markets like health foods, in recent years, have an organic expansion rate that must be accounted for in any STM system.

Output data

Table 27.1 (from Factor and Sampson, 1983) shows typical output data from an STM, in this case, an actual BASES II study for a household cleaning product. Five plans for different levels of distribution and awareness are shown.

Table 27.1 *Typical output data from an STM*

Plan	1	2	3	4	5
Distribution (%) end Year 1	50	60	40	50	50
Awareness (%) end Year 1	60	60	60	50	70
Cumulative trial rate*					
Year 1 (%)	18.5	21.8	15.0	15.8	21.2
Year 2 (%)	24.6	28.9	19.9	21.0	28.2
Year 3 (%)	31.2	36.7	25.3	26.7	35.8

* At the concept stage, the top two boxes on the purchase intention scale were 67 per cent

Consumer volume (x million units)					
Year 1	13.4	15.8	10.9	11.5	15.4
Year 2	16.4	19.6	13.1	13.9	18.9
Year 3	19.6	23.6	15.6	16.5	22.7

Estimates constant for all plans

(i) First repeat rate

True repeat rate (% of trialists who will make at least one repeat purchase within 52 weeks of their initial trial) = 56%

Measured repeat rate (% of trialists who will make at least one repeat purchase within 52 weeks of product launch) = 49%

(ii) Depth of repeat

	%
Penetration	100 (ie all trialists)
1st repeat	49
2nd repeat	33
3rd repeat	27
4th repeat	24
5th repeat	22
6th repeat	21
7th repeat	19

Stabilization point 17 (ie core 'loyalists')

(iii) Average number of units purchased on each occasion

(a) At trial = 1.00

(b) At repeat = 1.02

Sample sizes for simulated test market systems

Again, this will vary according to the system and also, more importantly, according to the actual method of collecting data, which has a major implication for who is actually given the product to test. STM systems divide into two main types: 1) those that collect data by straightforward survey methods; and 2) those that collect data by setting up a simulated shop.

With the former, typified by BASES II, where product is only placed with those respondents showing positive purchase intention (the 'top two boxes' on a five-point purchase intention scale), the objective for a standard test (ie a single monadic cell) is to end up with recall interviews from N = 200 product trialists. If top two box scores are estimated to be 66 per cent then N = 340 of the target market are screened, product placed with N = 224 (66 per cent) to achieve, typically, N = 200 recall interviews (89 per cent of placements, but the usual level of successful recalls is above 90 per cent). Communication material and packs do not have to be finished.

With the latter, eg ASSESSOR, a simulated shop is set up with both test and competitive product 'on-shelf'. Respondents are given 'seed money' to make purchases from the display, but the test product is given to everybody – both those positive and negative to it. Again, somewhere in the region of N = 200+ placements are made to achieve N = 200 recalls with product trialists. The disadvantage of this method is that the product has to be available in finished packs, and both finished and competitors' advertising have to be available too. There is also the problem of defining what the competition is or should be. Which competitive brands? (All of them?) Which varieties or sizes? (All of them?) What about a really innovative product? In passing, it may be noted that for a really 'innovative' product, market share may be meaningless: volume of sales is the key measure.

Organizing a field force to undertake simulated test marketing systems

It must be remembered that an STM is a 'test' and not a 'survey'. Consequently, although sampling is an important issue, no attempt is made to obtain a large, representative or random sample. It is important, however, to have a good regional spread of fieldwork, since reactions to new products or, indeed, old ones relaunched, vary enormously by region. BASES, for example, undertakes fieldwork in four regions, usually using two or more different sampling points per region. The data are weighted at the analysis stage to account for different regional population sizes. However, what is especially critical is quality of fieldwork. To ensure this, an STM field force must be well trained and supervised. It is essential that respondents are allocated correctly between those who react favourably to the communication material shown and those who do not.

Quality is such an issue because the data are being used to provide estimates of likely test product sales. If the input data are not accurate, the estimate cannot possibly be.

Methods of analysis for simulated test marketing systems

Each system has its own analytical approach, comprising a series of complex mathematical formulae into which the data are put. (For details of the mathematics of three typical systems, BASES, LTM and SENSOR, see Factor and Sampson, 1983.)

An essential feature of all STM models is a future purchase intentions measure and the need to recalibrate this for overclaiming, which varies by country, region within a country, product category, price level, social class, etc. If 66 per cent of respondents, after seeing concept communication material, claim they will buy the product, this figure must be revised to provide a more likely one (which will be much less). Not only does over-claiming reduce this, but eventual awareness and distribution levels, as well as perceived value for money, also need to be taken into account. STM systems use vast databases of normative data to make the appropriate, and often fine, adjustments necessary to factor back to realistic levels of likely trial for a given marketing plan.

How reliable is simulated test marketing and what should be looked for in selecting an STM?

Accuracy is determined by comparing the estimates of an STM with what actually happened if and when the product was launched. However, it must be remembered that an STM estimate is provided for a given market-ing plan, so comparing estimate with actual must be based on the original marketing plan, or the resimulation of the estimate for a different plan.

By and large, STM systems are extremely accurate. For example, by the end of 1989 BASES had carried out over 8,000 tests in 34 countries and across dozens of product categories. It is possible to validate and tune the system by comparing estimates with data from several hundred product launches. Typically, its level of accuracy is to achieve a sales volume estimate within ±10 per cent of actual in 70 per cent of cases, and within ±15 per cent in 90 per cent of cases. This is far more accurate than conventional test marketing ever was.

In conducting an STM the things to look for and the questions to ask are the following:

- Is the fieldwork quality of the highest possible standard?
- What experience does the system have, in terms both of the number of tests ever done and of the number of tests done in the product category I am interested in?
- Can the system handle well the kind of product I have? (This includes existing product or line extension and, for line extension, the type. Are sizes, varieties or flavours involved? Do I need to consider innovative versus existing category? Do I require a child influence/gift purchase sub-model?)
- What is the track record of the system in terms of its estimating accuracy? How many validations does it have, and how good were they?
- What diagnostic information will it provide?
- Do the 'modellers' have the experience and ability to make marketing recommendations? (Remember, many people who operate STM systems see far more product launches and relaunches in a year than you may see in a lifetime. Their experience can prove invaluable.)

As the cost of launching and relaunching products escalates and markets become ever more competitive, the need for marketing management to achieve an even sharper cutting edge for their brands will become imperative. In terms of sales estimating, the contribution that STM systems can make is immense.

REFERENCES AND FURTHER READING

Davis, J (1986) Market testing and experimentation, in *Consumer Marketing Research Handbook*, 3rd rev edn, ed R Worcester and J Downham, ESOMAR, Amsterdam

Engel, J F, Kollat, D T and Blackwell, R D (1970) *Consumer Behaviour*, Holt Rhinehart, New York

Eskin, G J (1973) Dynamic forecasts of new product demand using a depth of repeat model, *Journal of Marketing Research*, **10**

Factor, S and Sampson, P (1983) Making decisions about launching new products, *Journal of the Market Research Society*, **25**

Fitzroy, P T (1976) *Analytical Methods for Marketing Management*, McGraw-Hill, London

Howard, J A and Sheth, I N (1969) *The Theory of Buyer Behaviour*, John Wiley, New York

Lin, L Y S (1979) A procedure for estimating non-linear repeat curves using diary panel data, presented to *American Statistical Association Business and Economics Statistics Section*, August

Massy, W F (1969) Forecasting the demand for new convenience products, *Journal of Marketing Research*, **6**

Nakanishi, M (1973) Advertising and promotion efforts on consumer response to new products, *Journal of Marketing Research*, **10**

Parfitt, J H and Collins, B J K (1968) The use of consumer panels for brand share prediction, *Journal of Marketing Research*, **5**

Pioche, A and Standen, P (1986) Estimating sales volume potential for new, innovative products with case histories, ESOMAR Congress proceedings, Monte Carlo

Sampson, P (1974) Consumer behaviour prediction and the modelling approach, ESOMAR Congress proceedings, Hamburg

Sampson, P (1987) The tracking study in market research, in *Applied Marketing and Social Research*, ed V Bradley, John Wiley, Chichester

van Westendorp, P (1989) NSS target monitor – an instrument to assess consumer franchise, ESOMAR Congress proceedings, Stockholm

28

Data Fusion

Ken Baker

TECHNIQUES FOR HANDLING MISSING DATA

Data fusion techniques may be categorized among a range of techniques available to the researcher designed to handle the problems of missing data. Before describing and defining data fusion, it is helpful here briefly to review other commonly used techniques within the research industry.

By far the most commonly used of these methods is weighting. Within most surveys, any key data cell with a significant imbalance compared with a known population may be, and usually is, weighted to that population. Effectively, for those data cells that are upweighted, each non-respondent is assumed to have a value equal to the average value for that cell. The non-responders thus receive a set of information equivalent to the average value of each statistic provided by respondents deemed by the choice of weighting cells to be similar to them.

Weighting frequently deals with respondents whom we ought to have interviewed, but didn't. The next set of techniques deals with respondents whom we have interviewed, but who have missing data items within their responses. These techniques are known as ascription or imputation techniques, and have been widely used to handle missing data, for example on the 1981 Census (Brandt and Chalk, 1985) and major industry surveys such as the National Readership Survey. Perhaps the most commonly used of the ascription techniques is the procedure known as hot decking. This technique requires the survey to be sorted into an order so that respondents with similar answers on a range of key variables are placed together. Brandt and Chalk (1985) describe the work carried out on the 1981 Census in England and Wales, and relate the use of hot decking to more traditional ways of automatic data editing. As an example they quote the method of ascription of 'number of cars in household'. The Census data records were sorted first on a criterion of the number of persons in the household and, within this stratum, in terms of tenure type. Thus tenure and household size were considered key discriminators on the variable 'cars per household'. When a missing data case was found, the data value was ascribed with the equivalent data value for the previous respondent. Hot decking thus sorts data records into similar groups on chosen criteria relevant to the problem in hand and passes missing information to a problem respondent from his or her nearest neighbour.

Both methods of handling missing data use the concept of similarity when ascribing the data. However, when two or more data items are being ascribed, eg readership of the *News of the World* and the *Sun*, how well do these techniques preserve the interrelationships between these data items? Weighting neatly side-steps the problem, since it is imputing average values for each data item in the survey. However, most ascription techniques impute on a one-variable-at-a-time basis, and in order to preserve perfectly say the interrelationships between the *News of the World* and the *Sun*, one of those newspapers would have to become a stratum in the ascription technique.

It is easy to imagine that, in a survey where many variables are being ascribed, the number of strata required to preserve interrelationships may become unwieldy, and other methods of handling missing data may be preferable. Thus over the last 30 years data fusion techniques have been used to handle problems of sets of missing data.

DATA FUSION – A DESCRIPTION OF THE TECHNIQUE

In order to describe data fusion, it is necessary first to establish some terms. A fusion takes place normally between two sample surveys, or sometimes between two or more different sectors of the same broad survey. The terminology used relates to the separate survey situation. One survey is deemed to be the donor survey, and contains data that are to be transferred to the second survey, the recipient survey. We will call the data to be transferred the 'missing' data.

In order for the data to be transferred between donor and recipient survey, there must be a number of questions or other information that is common to both surveys, and these common variables are the basis for deciding which respondents in the donor survey will pass data to which respondents in the recipient survey. The fusion process depends on some statistical measure of similarity between donors and recipients to find the best pairings. The common variables are used to determine similarity and, when the best match is found for a recipient respondent, all the missing data from the matching donor are transferred. Small wonder, therefore, that data fusion is normally known as statistical matching in academic circles.

Data fusion techniques thus go one step further than classical ascription techniques. The key principle for fusion is that once respondents from the donor and recipient files are matched in some way, all the missing data are passed from donor to recipient, thus preserving the interrelationships between variables passed together from donor to recipient files. By such means are the possibilities of using say media data from survey A on to product data on survey B created. Fusion thus frequently attempts to create 'single-source' information from two separate surveys.

DEVELOPMENT OF FUSION TECHNIQUES

In a paper published in the *Journal of Applied Statistics*, JT Barry (1988) gives an overview of the development of these techniques. Barry refers to early attempts at fusion, such as the work carried out in 1968 by the Bureau of Economic Analysis (BEA). The matching process was designed to supplement the March 1965 Current Population Survey (recipient file) with information from the 1964 Internal Tax Model (donor files). The matching variables were marital status, wage and salary income, self-employment income and property income. During the 1970s such techniques were largely conducted by academic or governmental institutions. However, the impetus for the use of fusion techniques in the market research industry in Europe occurred in the early 1980s and involved the fusion of media studies in France and Germany. The readership symposium held in Salzburg in 1985 included two major experimental studies.

Case studies

The first, entitled Media-Market, was conducted in France using an algorithm derived by Gilles Santini. In this experiment, three waves of press and cinema data were collected over time. At the end of each interview of the second and third waves, self-completion questionnaires relating to product and brand consumption were placed with each respondent. Just over 70 per cent of respondents returned the self-completion questionnaire. Fusion techniques were used to deal with non-response on the second and third waves and, in addition, the product or brand data from the second and third waves were fused on to the first wave file. The results of the experiment are described by Jacques Antoine (1985).

The second experiment, entitled Arbeitsgemeinschaft Media-Analyze (AG MA) was conducted in West Germany (as it then was) using a fusion technique derived by Friedrich Wendt. The experiment involved the fusion of broadcast media data into press media data, and vice versa, by means of common variables involving both classificatory variables and readership of daily newspapers. The results were generally favourable, and are reported by Schieler and Wiegand (1985).

In Britain, the first major step was taken in 1987 with the fusion of the National Readership Survey (NRS) with NOP's Financial Research Survey (FRS). This fusion was designed to relate financial data with readership data. Although the technical committee in charge of the fusion did not sanction the release of their fused data to the wider industry, this fusion generated considerable interest within the British market research industry and led to the experiment conducted by the Market Research Development Fund (MRDF), which was reported in the *Journal of the Market Research Society* (Baker, Harris and O'Brian, 1989). Many of the data shown in this chapter relate to this experiment. Since the MRDF experiment, many major fusion projects have been undertaken in Britain. Perhaps the best-known fusions within the public domain are the BARB/TGI fusion and the experiment conducted within segments of the NRS.

METHODS OF DATA FUSION

Data fusion techniques involve the matching of respondents on some distance criterion based on the common variables. Methods differ with regard to both the matching process and the calculation of distance measures. To illustrate, let us assume that two surveys are to be fused. There are seven variables that are common to both surveys. These are as follows:

1. sex;
2. age;
3. class;
4. region;

5. income;
6. presence of children;
7. working status.

For the purposes of matching respondents on some distance criterion, these variables could be treated with equal importance, or some could be deemed more important than others. A further consideration is the level of correlation between the variables. Class and income have a significant level of correlation, as do age and presence of children. Clearly, some form of data reduction methodology such as factor analysis may be useful in accurately determining the distance between individuals.

Common variables

Different methods have been developed to overcome these problems. Many fusion practitioners divide the common variables into two categories.

First, there are the critical variables. These are variables where the match between donor and recipient must be exact. Commonly age, sex and class are chosen as critical variables. In this case, a male ABC1, 15–24-year-old respondent in the donor file may be matched only with a male, ABC1, 15–24-year-old respondent in the recipient file.

Second, there are the matching variables. These are the remaining chosen common variables. These will influence the choice of donor and recipient, but boundaries are not inviolate.

Techniques for handling matching variables differ between practitioners. Some place weights of importance on the variables, the importance weight reflecting their predictive ability on the data contained within the two surveys to be fused. Correlation, regression analysis and analysis of variance are commonly used to determine importance. The problems of intercorrelation between common variables are usually overcome by some form of factor analysis, and multiple correspondence analysis is favoured by many practitioners. The basis for a 'pure' distance measure between donor and recipient respondent has now been formed.

Two popular measures for determining the distance between respondents are squared Euclidean distance (much favoured by writers of cluster analysis algorithms) and a complex form of Mahalonobis distance, a distance measure that takes into account the intercorrelation between variables.

Once distance measures have been formulated between individuals, the marriage or statistical match between donor and recipient may be undertaken. Some techniques use straightforward nearest neighbour or least distance techniques to match donors and recipients. However, even in surveys where the number of respondents in both donor and recipient surveys is very similar, it does not necessarily follow that each donor will marry once. One donor may be the nearest neighbour to several recipients and another donor may not be anyone's nearest neighbour. Some practitioners argue that uneven use of donors may result in the fused sample having a somewhat unrepresentative supply of donor data. Hence, in order to encourage a relatively even use of donor respondents, many fusion algorithms place a 'penalty' distance on a donor who is already married. Effectively that donor's distance from any other recipient is upweighted by a factor imposed by the analyst using the fusion technique.

Other algorithms use more complex procedures than nearest neighbour marriages. The argument goes as follows. In reality, if A is closest to B, it does not necessarily follow that B is closest to A. B might be closest to C. The nearest neighbour technique would automatically marry B with both A and C, unless the penalty distance given to B eliminates this possibility. Thus, multiple marriages are highly likely. In the more complex algorithm, A and B may be married if and only if A is closest to B and B is closest to A. If this is not the case, A and B may be married to other donors or recipients by more complex methods determined by the algorithm. This form of statistical matching may be given attractive labels, such as 'love at first sight' to the most natural marriages and, for marriages not quite so associated with statistical heaven, terms such as 'adultery' or 'shotgun marriages' may apply. Whatever form the algorithm takes, all are designed to match donors and recipients as efficiently as possible to maximize the chances that the fusion will be successful.

DATA FUSION IN ACTION – THE MARKET RESEARCH DEVELOPMENT FUND (MRDF) EXPERIMENT

In October 1988, in order to investigate the strengths and weaknesses of fusion, the MRDF, a body affiliated to the Market Research Society (MRS) in Great Britain, undertook an experiment involving the fusion of two separate subsamples of the Target Group Index (TGI), a large single-source media/product survey conducted annually among about 24,000 respondents. Three separate fusions were undertaken, each involving two separate subsamples of the TGI:

1. Fusion 1 – 6,000 donors into 6,000 recipients;
2. Fusion 2 – 6,000 donors into 6,000 recipients;
3. Fusion 3 – 3,000 donors into 6,000 recipients.

Fusions 1 and 2 differed in the number of common variables used, Fusion 1 using 14 and Fusion 2 using 25 such variables. The fusion algorithm used was the IMS France System, which, at the time the fusion was conducted, was the most readily available.

For each of the fusions, age, sex and class were chosen as critical variables. A variety of demographic, socioeconomic and geographical variables were chosen as common variables on each of the fusions. However, Fusion 2 had as additional common variables certain behavioural variables such as smoking, trying to slim and method of holiday taking, which it was thought might add further information to the 14 variables used throughout the experiment.

Both donor and recipient files contained five levels of data relating to:

1. classificatory variables;
2. readership of national press;
3. readership of magazines;
4. consumption of products;
5. leisure activities.

However, the recipient files given to IMS France contained only the common variables. IMS France were asked to fuse the five levels of data from donor to recipient file. The relationship between the fused file and real 'recipient' behaviour formed the basis of the MRDF analysis. The experiment was designed to check:

■ the accuracy of data fusion;
■ the influence of the common variables on accuracy;
■ the influence of the size of the donor file on accuracy.

The full results of the MRDF experiment are detailed in the article in the *Journal of the Market Research Society* (Baker, Harris and O'Brian, 1989). For the purposes of economy, in this article the case study concentrates on demonstrating the accuracy (or potential inaccuracy) of data fusion in some detail, and the arguments relating to sample size and number of common variables are summarized.

The MRDF experiment is described below in some technical detail. Some readers may prefer to skip to the section summarizing the conclusions from the experiment.

An examination of marginal totals

The first and obvious step, in analysing the results of a fusion, is to check the results of the fused file against that of the donor file. However, if we are in an experimental situation we may also check the results against the recipient file, ie the 'truth'. Table 28.1 shows the results for Fusion 2. Similar patterns were obtained for the other fusions. The results are based on the average percentage differences between a sample of some 300 statistics selected systematically from the fused file.

Table 28.1 *Average percentage differences between files relating to marginal totals*

	Average % Difference
Fused sample versus recipient sample	0.53
Donor sample versus recipient sample	0.51
Donor sample versus fused sample	0.36

The fusion achieved a high level of accuracy. On average, differences were less than 0.4 per cent between donor and fused file, and differences between fused and recipient file were almost identical to the differences between donor and recipient file. At this level of looking at the results of our fusion, the results are commensurate with the accuracy expected from two independent samples of size 6,000. The reason for this level of accuracy is demonstrated in Table 28.2, where the average percentage differences between fused and donor file are broken into strata relating to the size of the statistic in the fused file presented in percentage form.

Table 28.2 *Average percentage difference between fused and donor file*

	Fusion 2
Statistics measured at:	
0.1%–1.9%	0.14
2.0%–3.9%	0.20
4.0%–9.9%	0.27
10.0%–19.9%	0.64
Overall	0.36

It is clear from the table above that the differences are approximating to a sampling distribution; the larger the variance in the donor file, the greater the difference between the fused and donor files.

Conclusion – first 'law' of data fusion

This leads to the first major conclusion of how data fusion works, namely, that when looking at marginal totals of fused data and comparing them with the donor data, the analyst should consider the fused data to be a sample of the donor data, albeit often a complex sample. However, if the sample sizes are large, the fusion would appear to be very accurate indeed. For Fusion 3, where the size of the donor file was only 3,000, the average difference between fused and recipient file was 0.63 per cent, with a difference of 0.61 per cent between donor and recipient files. This is somewhat larger than for Fusion 2. This is exactly as would be expected. Since at marginal total level, fusion is in the sample situation, the larger the size of the donor file, the greater the accuracy of the results.

An examination of simple cross-tabs

One of the great advantages of data fusion over other ascription techniques is that when donors and recipients are matched, all the data are passed from donor to recipient. To demonstrate how accurate this can be, a sample of cross-tabs was selected, in which both the column and the row were fused data (ie data that had been passed across together), and compared to the respective cross-tabs in the donor and recipient files. The results shown in Table 28.3 are based on Fusion 1.

Table 28.3 *Average percentage difference of cross-tabs*

	Average % *Difference*
Fused sample versus recipient sample	3.4
Donor sample versus recipient sample	3.2
Donor sample versus fused sample	1.8

The same patterns are determined as for the examination of marginal totals. The fused results are remarkably close to the donor sample, and are as accurate as the difference between the donor sample and the recipient sample. As with marginal totals, data fusion is in the sampling situation when simple cross-tabs are compared with the donor file. Again, the accuracy of these results will be related to the sample size, both of the donor survey and of the sample size relating to the column in the cross-tab, as the MRDF paper demonstrates.

An examination of complex cross-tabs

In a real fusion situation, the marginal totals and simple cross-tabs are, with few exceptions, the only thing the analyst can compare in order to assess the likely accuracy of the fusion. However, this is not the real test of fusion. Imagine a situation where readership of daily newspapers is fused on to a survey measuring leisure activities. The purpose is to estimate statistics such as 'How many *Observer* readers have travelled abroad on holiday in the last year?' In this situation the cross-tab is fused *Observer* readers (sampled from the donor survey) versus real holiday takers, as measured by the recipient survey. If one knew from some other source the real relationship between these two variables, one could determine the accuracy of the fusion for those variables. It will seldom be the case that these interrelationships are known, but in an experimental situation the results may be compared with the real recipient data.

Data fusion is trying to recreate a 'single-source' survey situation, when, say, products and media are asked of the same respondent. In comparing complex cross-tabs with the real interrelationships, the toughest test we could give data fusion is to treat the real data as a tablet of stone, ie having no sampling error attached. Thus, the only source of sampling error is the fused cross-tabs. This equates to the 'single-source' situation where there is only one source of variance in the data.

The MRDF experiment compared 2,000 complex cross-tabs with their real counterparts. In 75 per cent of cases the real results lay within the 95 per cent confidence intervals of the complex cross-tabs. Clearly viewed at this level, data fusion cannot regenerate the accuracy of single-source data. In order to allow for the effects of a clustered sample design, a design factor of 1.25 was then attached to the standard error calculations, after which 84 per cent of the results fell within the criteria. Although this is an improvement, clearly the fused results are not as good as single-source data.

Dropping the single-source criterion, the fused and real cross-tabs being both allowed to contribute to the variance of the results, some 94 per cent of the complex cross-tabs fell within acceptable limits, allowing for the design element of 1.25 discussed above. Viewed at this level, the MRDF results were almost as accurate as two independent surveys, but the inclusion of a design factor of 1.25 may be considered somewhat arbitrary.

Within the MRDF experiment, however, an examination of major differences highlighted the biggest potential problem with data fusion, namely that of regression to the mean.

Regression to the mean

Before examining cases of big differences on the MRDF caused by the phenomenon of regression to the mean, it is perhaps best to demonstrate this hypothetically with the following extreme example.

Survey A, among other statistics, measures dog ownership. When analysed by age, sex, class, etc, discrimination is poor. Dog ownership is randomly distributed across the groups, with 10 per cent of the sample owning a dog.

Survey B, among other statistics, measures incidence of purchasing dog food. Again this is randomly distributed across the groups and discrimination is poor, with 10 per cent of the sample buying dog food.

The surveys are now fused together, using age, sex, class, etc as common variables. Because there is nothing within the common variables to link a dog owner with a dog-food buyer, allocation will be random. The true relationship between dog-food buying and dog ownership is anything but random – we would expect 100 per cent of dog owners to buy dog food. Those readers who know their probability theory will now know what results would be expected in the fused survey. They are shown in Table 28.4.

Table 28.4 *Expected results in fused survey*

All Respondents	100%
Respondents who:	
own a dog and buy dog food	1%
own a dog and don't buy dog food	9%
don't own a dog but buy dog food	9%
neither own a dog nor buy dog food	81%

Thus of the 10 per cent of the fused sample who own a dog, only one-tenth of them would buy dog food. The expected cross-tabs are shown in Table 28.5.

Table 28.5 *Expected cross-tabs*

	All Respondents	Dog Owners
Base	100%	100%
Buying Dog Food	10%	10%

If we now cross-analyse dog-food buying with dog ownership, we notice that the interrelationship has regressed to the mean for the whole population, ie 10 per cent.

However, supposing we now introduce into both surveys the variable 'own a dog lead', and the fusion is conducted so well that only dog-lead owners marry dog-lead owners. Now, through the common variables we have the perfect link between dog owning and dog-food buying, and the resultant table would now be expected to look like Table 28.6.

Table 28.6 *Link between dog owning and dog-food buying*

	All Respondents	Dog Owners
Base	100%	100%
Buying Dog Food	10%	100%

The true relationship between the two variables has been reconstructed by the fusion.

Given a sample of some 2,000 complex cross-tabs it would be expected that some regression to the mean would occur on 50 per cent of occasions by chance. In the MRDF experiment, on over two-thirds of occasions this phenomenon was observed. The MRDF paper covers in detail the problems caused by a faulty matching of C1s and C2s, owing to a poor choice of critical variables by the authors. However, not all of the more severe cases of regression to the mean were caused by the misapplication of the fusion algorithm. The following statistics show clearly the major pitfall of fusion:

38 per cent of all adults drink at least once a week
58 per cent of adults who bet drink at least once a week

The 'fused' betters crossed with real drinkers showed:

43 per cent of all betters drink at least once a week.

Whether the respondents were male or female, young or old, up-market or down-market, if they were betters they were 'boozers'. There was nothing in the common variables to link these two cells together.

Conclusion – second 'law' of data fusion

This leads to the second major 'law' of data fusion, namely regression to the mean will occur unless all the possible explanation of the relationship between two variables is contained within the common variables. If there is any variance unexplained by these variables, selectivity or discrimination will be reduced.

However, the MRDF experiment showed much that was of considerable merit. In particular, despite the problems of the number of unwanted C1–C2 marriages, the fusion of media and products worked extremely well, as Table 28.7 shows. The data are shown in index form, the national average being 100. Here the products are fused and the newspapers are real.

Table 28.7 *Indices of readership for Fusion 1*

| | Holiday Abroad | | Restaurant in Evening | | Own Stocks and Shares | | TV-am | |
	Fused	*Real*	*Fused*	*Real*	*Fused*	*Real*	*Fused*	*Real*
Dailies
Express	117	133	104	178	114	129	79	85
Mail	113	130	113	127	126	145	79	71
Sun	80	83	82	92	68	63	114	141
Star	84	76	101	102	61	51	132	149
Mirror	91	92	85	81	77	74	117	112
Telegraph	135	158	106	163	162	195	73	42
Sundays
Mail	113	147	131	182	105	140	79	100
News of the World	84	88	102	96	76	72	110	136
Express	125	122	109	129	142	150	75	74
Mirror	89	94	97	85	89	66	113	116
People	94	88	71	74	87	71	112	129
Post	94	82	73	61	113	111	115	135
Observer	140	145	209	206	146	167	67	58
Times	151	167	186	216	150	182	69	64

Although the reader will notice that the variation in the fused indices is less than the variation in the real indices, ie some selectivity has been lost in the fusion, the authors calculated that about 70 per cent of discriminatory power had been retained in the fusion, with media, and, without the problems of the C1–C2 intermarriages, higher levels could have been reached.

Conclusions from the MRDF experiment

The experiment showed clearly that, when looking at the data in terms of marginal totals and simple cross-tabs, the underlying principles of sampling apply. Thus, the larger the donor file, the more accurate are likely to be the results.

In addition, if the algorithm is one that includes 'critical' variables, ie boundaries that must not be crossed in the matching process, the larger the sample size of the donor file, the greater the number of critical cells that can be used.

However, the experiment showed that common variables should not be used without thought. With minor exceptions, Fusion 2 with 25 common variables was no more accurate than Fusion 1 with 16 common variables. A series of regression equations showed that, for most statistics that were fused, most of the explained variance was contained within the 14 common variables, the remaining 11 adding little. This led the authors to conclude that too many common variables may lead to a worse fusion. The use of common variables that do not discriminate will tend to divert the fusion programme from matching on the variables that discriminate strongly. The need for considerable preliminary work into the relationships between the variables to be fused and the common variables, before deciding on the final list of matching variables was clearly demonstrated.

The major pitfall of fusion is regression to the mean, which results in loss of discriminatory power, and it was estimated that on 1 per cent of occasions the problem was severe. However, when the data was put into potentially actionable form, eg the media/product data, the authors were able to conclude that data fusion is potentially a very powerful and acceptable tool for market researchers, although it was not as good as single-source data.

THE VALIDITY OF DATA FUSION

The MRDF experiment clearly indicated the problems of checking the results for validity. Given a large donor file, both marginal totals and simple cross-tabs will be very close to the donor file (assuming some similarity in the sample structure between donor and recipient file). Fusion will thus appear to be highly impressive. However, the real problems with fusion occur in the interrelationships between 'real' recipient data and data fused from the donor file. In most circumstances these cannot be checked. However, if all the data are fused or passed across from the donor file, the matching variables will also be fused. They can be compared with the real recipient matching variables. This will give many clues to the likely quality of the fusion. For example, if a high proportion of 15–24 year olds were fused with respondents aged 65-plus, we would find a high proportion of silly results, eg squash-playing pensioners. In the absence of other control data, a thorough examination of the matches or marriages is recommended. The MRDF working party, for example, to its dismay, found a higher than expected level of marriages between C1s and C2s, and this predictably affected the quality of the fusion.

The acceptability of matches will not necessarily guarantee the success of a fusion, however. Only if the common variables explain most of the link between variables to be fused will fusion work well.

THE FUTURE OF DATA FUSION?

I think it is fair to say that most fusions so far conducted in Britain have been conducted on databases or surveys not necessarily set up for the purpose. As a consequence, the practitioners have conducted the fusion using each common variable as efficiently as they could, but without having choice over the common variables. Fusion works best if we understand which variables have the greatest predictive power on all variables on both the donor and the recipient surveys. Once this homework is done in advance, the variables with maximum predictive power should be included on both prospective donor and recipient surveys, ie 'the surveys are designed in advance with fusion in mind'. If the fusion algorithm then does its job properly and achieves a high level of matching on all common variables, the fusion will be as efficient as it could possibly be. There is increasingly greater demand for more complex datasets for individuals. Market research surveys are increasingly being merged or matched with large databases collected for the purposes of database marketing. Internal marketing databases held by commercial organizations are being fused together. Given that the rules for good fusion practice have now been widely documented, it seems likely that data fusion will be an increasingly important ingredient of the marketing information industry of the 21st century.

REFERENCES AND FURTHER READING

Antoine, J (1985) A case study illustrating the objectives and perspectives of fusion techniques, Proceedings of the Salzburg Readership Symposium

Baker, K, Harris, P and O'Brian, J (1989) Data fusion: an appraisal and experimental evaluation, *Journal of the Market Research Society*, **31**

Barry, J T (1988) An investigation of statistical matching, *Journal of Applied Statistics*, **15**

Brandt, J D and Chalk, S M (1985) The use of automatic editing in the 1981 Census, *Journal of The Royal Statistical Society*, Series A, **148**

Schieler, H E and Wiegand, J (1985) A report on experiments in fusion in the 'official' German media research (AG MA), Proceedings of the Salzburg Readership Symposium

29

Segmentation

Chris Blamires

MAPPING AND SEGMENTATION WITHIN THE BROADER DATA ANALYSIS CONTEXT

At the very broadest level, most quantitative market research is initiated with the intention of answering two fundamental questions, 'Who?' and 'How many?'

Secondary interests in many projects lie in establishing the motivations behind each of these questions, but ultimately the vast majority of quantitative research projects are designed to give quite specific direction to marketing decisions, and hence are less concerned with motivations, and more concerned with numbers.

Segmentation becomes relevant once that first question 'Who?' is asked. In other words, segmentation is concerned with ascertaining the size and nature of subgroups of the population under study, how they behave and what their attitudes are. Of necessity, it is therefore clearly a quantitative-orientated technique, and in many senses it seeks to impose a greater understanding on quantitative data, of a type that in other contexts might be achieved qualitatively.

A useful initial division to bear in mind in the context of segmentation is the one between research that seeks to create static models of a given market-place and research that seeks to generate dynamic causal models.

In the widest sense, all research is concerned with creating 'useful' models of the market under study, in that each study, whether qualitative or quantitative, seeks to provide a representation of key 'useful' characteristics of a given market. 'Useful' must be defined here according to the objectives of the research. The model or representation created of a given market, via a sampling exercise in which a questionnaire is administered, will identify certain characteristics – these are 'useful' to the degree to which results provide actionable information in relation to the objectives set for that study.

Within such an all-embracing definition of model building, quantitative research falls into either the dynamic model-building category, or the static model-building category. Within the latter category would fall a standard set of tabulations, or a graph derived using the data collected from the research – either of which could be deemed 'useful' or otherwise only in the context of the specific application of the results.

Also within this category falls the large area known as 'mapping', which seeks to represent, in a static spatial form, the structure of the market under study, either in terms of the buyers or, more frequently, the brands themselves. In much the same way, for example, the London Underground map shown in tube stations is a static model of the Underground itself, that is, it shows 'useful' characteristics for tube travellers that would be entirely useless for an engineer or train driver, each with differing objectives in relation to any map of the underground.

By contrast, a dynamic (or causal) model is one that seeks to define a causal relationship between variables. Attitude or behaviour models including 'conjoint' models (discussed in Chapter 26) fall within such a category, as do some forms of pricing models (Chapter 25) and all forms of simulated test market models (Chapter 27). Macro-modelling (ie forecasting that is based on total market trend data rather than individual consumer-based information) provides further examples of dynamic models (Chapter 30).

Segmentation, as a bank of techniques for identifying the size and nature of subgroups, cuts across both dynamic and static model categories, but the division is useful in discussing the individual techniques concerned, and will be returned to in the penultimate section of this chapter.

Within the following discussion, use is made primarily of fmcg and retail examples. While these form the majority of segmentation studies, in the author's own experience, the major growth area for segmentation is now in the more specialist markets of pharmaceutical, finance and new technology. The techniques and comments below apply equally to these markets.

THE THEORY

A historical perspective

Historically, prior to the 1960s, marketeers had (knowingly or unknowingly) adopted a passive approach to segmentation – the pattern of distribution of their brand (manufactured or retail) determined the nature of the individuals buying that product or service. Thus, geographic region or catchment area determined the nature of the franchise. With the growth of 'added values' to the basic product or service (ie the growth of the consumer society), the nature of motivations to purchase any particular brand became increasingly varied and complex.

In a market where only the Model T Ford was available (and then only in black), there were clear divisions between those who bought and those who did not – a basic (if important) segmentation. By comparison, the relative positioning of a Rolls-Royce, Porsche, Mercedes and 7-series BMW create significantly more complex positionings, and highlight the need for a more sophisticated segmentation policy on the part of marketeers.

It was at the point at which such 'consumer-driven' options emerged that market research as an industry began to develop the necessary techniques to identify the nature of the segmentation that was evolving within different markets. Marketeers, in seeking to position their brand or product field, were now actively seeking to increase the probability of purchase by certain groups rather than simply 'the market' as a whole, and the definition of these groups is the prime requirement from segmentation research as such.

Objectives of market segmentation

The underlying rationale for marketing segmentation is that there is an opportunity in identifying those with a greater propensity to undertake a given act (eg the purchase of a product or brand) and to direct a message at that group, rather than directing a more broad-based message at a larger group of consumers, with, on average, a lesser probability of purchasing.

For the researcher, therefore, in an effort to build up a total picture in any survey, segmentation is a natural weapon – providing greater understanding and opportunities for targeting, by identifying more clearly the particular nature of the target markets, even where 'segmentation' as such is not explicitly the prime objective of the study.

In general, then, there is a requirement for segmentation procedures to perform one, or both, of two functions: 1) to improve understanding – that is, to generate a clearer picture of the nature of the individuals who are buying within the product field, or are buying particular brands, or who divide in ways that may be exploited in a marketing context; and 2) to target directly – that is, to provide information that would identify the vehicles by which such subgroups should be reached (to assist media scheduling, sale promotion activity, choice of distribution channel type, etc).

It might be done via the use of intermediary measures (eg social grade – an analysis common to most media research), or direct (via measures taken within the subgroups of weight of TV viewing, exposure to tube advertising, readership of identified titles, and so on).

Usually, the ultimate pragmatic reason for segmentation is to identify and segregate consumers into those with higher and lower probabilities of buying into the client's product field, or, more specifically, buying the client's brand. Thus, a segmentation study within the tomato ketchup market might seek to segment consumers into those with a greater and lesser consumption of tomato ketchup, but alternatively might be concerned with segmenting the market into those with a greater and lesser probability of purchasing the brand leader, among many other possible segmentations.

Objectives of research involving segmentation

In one sense, the researcher is constantly searching for ways in which to understand more clearly the nature and motivations of the group that has been sampled, and hence the results that have been obtained, and segmentation is one element within the armoury of techniques available.

However, there is a useful distinction between studies whose primary objective is segmentation and those that utilize some form of segmentation purely as a secondary approach, to meet more effectively entirely different objectives. Thus, there is division within market research studies into implicit and overt segmentation studies.

Implicit segmentation studies

A typical and perfectly valid approach here would consist, very simply, of a study of standard tabulations in which breakdowns are instituted based on age, sex, social grade, weight of purchase or brand orientation, etc (see Chapter 24). By study of this subgroup analysis, the researcher is attempting to identify groups of individuals (younger, older, up-market, down-market, etc) who have a greater propensity to act or think in a certain way, with the intention of increasing the understanding obtained from the study as a whole, and hence increasing its value. Primarily because the central objective of such 'implicit' segmentation studies lies elsewhere, the more complex segmentation techniques are largely (and justifiably) ignored.

Overt segmentation studies

Here, as will be discussed below, there is a range of techniques available to the researcher when considering the possibility of dividing the market up in a meaningful way, each of which allows for more sophisticated segmentation, each with its own strengths and weaknesses.

THE PRACTICE

Requirements of measures used for segmentation

As indicated in the previous section, segmentation can be based on individual measures as simple as age and social grade – identifying whether a particular brand has more potential among a younger or an older audience, for example. Equally, as will be discussed below, there are opportunities for far more complex segmentation.

However, all are based on the ability to collect meaningful information from the identified consumers – either directly by interview, or indirectly from known characteristics of the individuals concerned. Hence, whatever measures are used as input to the segmentation procedures, those measures must have certain characteristics:

■ Most obviously, it must be feasible to obtain a measure on a particular dimension, either directly by interview, or by more indirect means.
■ That measure must be meaningful both to the consumer and to the marketeer, and must be generalizable to the market-place as a whole.
■ The measure used as the basis for segmentation must have some actionable value – there must be the ability to translate the measure, and the subsequent segmentation, into marketing action.
■ The measure must discriminate between both consumers and their commercially related activities (the purchase of products and brands, usage, etc).

Segmentation measures frequently utilized

There are broadly five areas of consumer activity (in a commercial context) within which measures are taken, and which are then used as the basis for subsequent segmentation analyses. Within each area, a division can be made into simple data collection and analysis based on single variables, and more complex data collection and analyses, as detailed in the following sections.

Consumer demographics

The nature of the consumer in terms of the age-old categories of social grade, sex and age are utilized almost without fail in every quantitative study (segmentation or otherwise), in order to pursue the objective of greater understanding of the results, and to identify specific targets. As above, such data can be utilized to segment the market either on an individual single variable basis (eg younger versus older consumers), or on a more complex basis – by interlacing variables on the basis of some model of consumer development. A typical example here would be to analyse by life-cycle stage. Obvious groupings are possible, for example single young adults, through marrieds/no children or with children to 'empty nesters', etc.

More sophisticated cross-referencing of variables, such as disposable income and occupation, in addition to age and household composition, can produce finer groupings within the overall life-cycle stage classification. SAGACITY is probably the best-known proprietary classification here (Cornish, 1981).

Geographic

Once again analysis by region, for example, is commonplace in standard tables and provides a simple means of imposing certain 'segmentation' on any market. However, more complex analyses are similarly possible, with the development of geodemographic classification, of which ACORN (developed by Richard Webber) was the first example (1980).

Subsequently, Webber developed MOSAIC, which incorporates other, more financially orientated variables, while competing systems are increasingly available (eg the PiN types developed by Pinpoint). Most such systems commence with an analysis of census data (usually cluster analysis – discussed below), and subsequently allocate all UK postcodes to individual cluster types.

Example types (from the ACORN 12 cluster solution) are 'affluent suburban housing' (15.9 per cent of the population), 'less well-off council estates' (9.4 per cent) and 'older housing of intermediate status' (17.6 per cent). Given that every individual postcode (typically a single postcode consists of around 15 dwellings) has been allocated an ACORN (or MOSAIC or PiN) code, segmentation by these household types is clearly possible.

Consumer behaviour

At the simplest level, segmentation can most obviously be undertaken on the basis of those who buy within a given market as against those who do not and, more specifically, between those who buy a given brand and those who do not. Equally, more complex segmentations are possible, which are based on use occasion, weight of purchase, degree of loyalty, etc, in combination.

Consumer attitudes

Studies that incorporate measures of consumer attitudes, in terms both of attitude to 'life' in general and in relation to the target market, are frequent. Thus, consumers can be divided into those with a more modern attitude and those with a more traditional attitude, for example, or those who specifically prefer more modern or more traditional brands within a given market.

Once again, it is possible to go beyond the use of individual agree/disagree scales, into the area of psychosociological measures. Here, respondents may be faced with a battery of statements designed to identify their underlying orientation to life (eg on scales such as introversion–extroversion). The use of so-called psychographics is one major development in this area (Thomas, Bunting and Nelson, 1982).

Consumer situation

This is a global category, which depends upon the specifics of any given study. A simple segmentation example would be within the market for perfume where an obvious buyer segmentation would be into purchasers of gifts and purchasers for own use. Any or all of the types of measures discussed above might be collected for each respondent in a segmentation study.

Once these data have been collected and analysed on a total sample basis, they can be used as input to segmentation programs, and subjected to the type of techniques described in the next section.

One point worth noting at this juncture is the increasingly sophisticated use of existing databases in segmentation, that is, segmentation should not be seen solely in the context of analysis of data collected via relatively limited *ad hoc* samples, but as a bank of techniques with wider applications. ACORN and MOSAIC are obvious examples here, but the principles can similarly be applied by any company with a database of information on its customers. Financial institutions and mail-order companies, among others, are coming to realize the importance of targeting subgroups, while the National Shopper Survey (with a database of several million consumers) has as yet unexploited potential in this area.

THE STATISTICAL TECHNIQUES

As noted above, the simplest level of segmentation is the use of the cross-tabulation. To examine, for example, brand purchasing by age of respondent immediately offers the opportunity to segment the market in terms of younger and older individuals, should such a variable prove to discriminate usefully in the market under study.

In every quantitative study, researchers (subject to sample size) undertake such analyses, and 'data-dredge' in order to highlight points of interest. In the researcher's terms, this is 'implicit segmentation', as defined above. The basis of cross-tabulation is discussed elsewhere in this volume (Chapter 24).

However, beyond such a simple segmentation approach, it is possible to utilize the different measures discussed in the previous section in a more sophisticated manner. At the point at which such procedures involve more than cross-analysis of two single variables, they are, quite reasonably, known as multivariate analyses.

With the well-documented growth of increasingly powerful personal computers, use of multivariate techniques in segmentation has been, and should continue to be, a growth area for researchers, and in that sense the techniques are becoming ever more accessible to researchers. Sadly, the expertise necessary to administer such analyses correctly has not kept pace with the computational power to generate them, and the ability to specify appropriate procedures correctly and understand the output remains concentrated in too few hands.

The area of multivariate analysis is a very broad one in its own right, and this chapter can only seek to provide an overview of the subgroup of techniques relevant to segmentation. Kendall, in a discussion of multivariate analysis (1965), divides analyses into those concerned with dependence versus those concerned with interdependence, while Harris (1981) convincingly divides cluster analysis out from other 'interdependence' analyses, as a third category in its own right.

However, while such a classification of the full range of multivariate analysis techniques is certainly valid, in practice those specific techniques relevant to segmentation can instead be usefully classified into those that impose segmentation, and those that allow segmentation to emerge from the data.

Segmentation emerging from market data collected

Models that attempt to divide up a given market (ie segment it in a meaningful way), but where the model does not itself imply or state any form of causal relationship, are classified by Kendall as 'interdependent'. Within our current categorization these are techniques that allow segmentation to emerge (though not entirely unaided).

Within this category as a whole would be included principal components analysis, factor analysis and cluster analysis. Within the subject matter of this present chapter, however, our prime interest lies in cluster analysis, where the result is the creation of distinct homogeneous groupings of respondents.

At the same time, the use of principal component analysis and particularly factor analysis is likely to be a precursor to cluster analysis, and both might feature, quite separately, in 'mapping' procedures (discussed below). Hence, this area will be discussed briefly in total. Principal components analysis and factor analysis both seek to establish the underlying dimensions of data collected in a way that minimizes the degree to which variables emerging are correlated.

It is possible to visualize, geometrically, the first principal component that might be derived from information collected on, for example, the height, breadth and weight of several individuals. Since height and weight are clearly correlated (ie the greater the height, the greater the weight is likely to be), and weight and breadth are correlated (the greater the breadth, the greater the weight is likely to be), and breadth and height are similarly correlated, then readings could be plotted as shown in Figure 29.1.

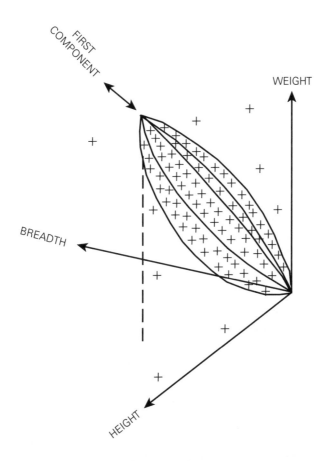

Figure 29.1 *Plot of a series of objects and resulting first component*

Division of the data into their principal components would provide a first clear component as shown in the figure. The use of this component, and measurement of each of the individual objects (in terms of position along this component) would provide a meaningful measure that could be used to group (ie segment) respondents.

Considered visually, factor analysis operates similarly, in identifying dimensions that explain the data in a non-correlated way, and hence allow further, more sophisticated analyses based on these dimensions.

A basic distinction between factor analyses and principal components analyses is that in the earlier principal components example, three components would be generated (in line with the three original variables). By contrast, in factor analysis the prime aim would be data reduction – the number of factors would be less than the initial number of variables (and generally considerably less). An example in which the author was involved was a study of 950 housewives, where grocery-shopping behaviour was under scrutiny (Blamires, Lunn and Seaman, 1986).

A detailed series of questions on attitudes was administered (to find, for example, degree of agreement with 'I take pride in being a well-organized shopper'), and views were sought on specific issues ('I don't often buy the supermarket's own brand'). Thirty-five such statements were administered, with the nature and wording of the statements evolved from earlier qualitative work.

Factor analysis applied to these 35 statements, on the basis of results obtained from the 950 housewives, allowed the derivation of 10 factors that explained a significant part of the variance in the 35 statements. The derived factors included ones subsequently labelled as:

■ 'willingness to shop around';
■ 'pro-own brands';
■ 'shopping confidence';
■ 'need for social contact'.

As for all factor analyses, the labels applied above were purely an interpretation of the degree to which individual statements contributed to each of the 10 factors, within the 10-factor solution adopted. Factor analysis, as noted above, is frequently only one stage in the ultimate use of cluster analysis, and this was the case in this study.

In the present grocery shopping example study, the 10-factor solution generated was used as the basis for clustering consumers. Cluster analysis undertaken on the 10 factors for the 950 housewives produced eight clusters or shopper types. Once again, labels were applied on the basis of the degree to which the individual groupings scored on the 10 factors, and clusters such as 'disorganized Diana' (does not keep stocks, is unable to budget and has certain specific demographic features) emerged. Different, but identifiable, quantifiable and targetable shopper types similarly emerged (eg 'professional Prudence' and 'utilitarian Ursula').

One prime benefit of the development of such typologies is that understanding gained from such a clustering allows for more sophisticated marketing. However, as discussed above, the scores achieved by such clusters on individual media vehicles (weight of TV watching, titles read, etc) also provide the opportunity for the targeting of identified clusters. For example, individual clusters in the above project exhibited significant deviations in terms of shops utilized for main grocery trip, a finding that provides actionable information in targeting high-spending main-trip shoppers at competing stores. The degree of discrimination revealed is highlighted in the following (disguised) chart, Table 29.1.

Table 29.1 *Deviation from average main-trip usage*

Cluster Type (Examples)	Retailer 1 %	Retailer 2 %	Retailer 3 %
Utilitarian Ursula	–11	–1	+16
Extravagant Eleanor	+6	–9	–18
Old-Fashioned Olive	–2	+5	–11
Roving Rosie	+12	0	–3

Lotti and Nurmilaukas (1986) discuss similar retail issues in relation to supermarkets in Finland, but using more basic analysis techniques, while Morgan and Purnell describe a factor/cluster programme based on political allegiance (1969). A further example from the retail trade is given by Lunn and Blamires (1996), where six fundamental shopper types were identified. Illustration of this topology was provided in relation to the baby and young child market, where two very different attitudinal types were discussed: 'Rosie Glow' (prime focus on baby), and 'Designer Diana' (fashion over quality), each with unique behavioural and demographic characteristics.

By contrast, and as an indication of the versatility of the technique, Blamires, Ray and Askew (1997) discuss the results of an international disk-by-mail modelling study conducted on behalf of the Economist Intelligence Unit, which resulted in the identification of four clusters within the EIU market intelligence customer base:

1. the Energetic Professional, with high regard for concise, up-to-the-minute information, placing major credence on the publisher's reputation;
2. the Information Gatekeeper, with an arm's length relationship with suppliers and most concerned about cost;
3. the International Techie, with a firmly global perspective and strong commitment to online services;
4. the Traditional Librarian, conservative, and happiest with the printed word.

Additional examples and more detail on the technical aspects of cluster analysis can be found in Blamires (1995).

Segmentation imposed on the market data collected

Alternative procedures exist that impose a segmentation, rather than allowing the market under study to evolve its own segmentation. The intention here would almost certainly be to segment directly on the basis of the degree of probability of purchasing a given product or a given brand – the market would be examined from the viewpoint of segmenting into brand buyers and non-buyers, for example.

In the earlier context, the simplest such approach would be to provide a standard cross-tab breakdown across the total sample data of those who purchase the brand at all, purchase most often, usually purchase or purchase in greater volume. Beyond this simple, single-variable segmentation, there are a number of techniques (which Kendall classifies as dependence-related) that are relevant in a segmentation context. Among these are the development of linear and multiple regression equations, canonical analyses and multiple discriminant analysis, each of which can be used in a segmentation context, and for each of which references are provided at the end of this chapter.

However, it is in practice unlikely that the reader will be exposed to such techniques in connection with segmentation, given their greater applicability in other areas of research. So, discussion within the present section will be restricted to that set of techniques most appropriate to segmentation – sequential dichotomization techniques, which, because of their simplicity and efficacy, are far more frequently used in market research.

There are two basic techniques within this category – the Belson sort and AID analyses (Sonquist and Morgan, 1965). In each case, the intention is to divide the total sample into groupings that most discriminate between those with a high probability of falling into a given category and those with a low probability of doing so.

In the current context, segmentation of the market into Brand X users and non-users of Brand X (or, more widely, into respondents who do buy within the market and those who do not) might be the basis of the intended division. The application of the two techniques (which differ only in terms of the method used for calculating the basis of the split) is quite straightforward, as follows.

A dependent variable is identified (eg users of Brand X versus non-users), and a series of possible variables that might discriminate between users and non-users (perhaps up to 20) is identified. These might include such elements as age and social grade, but also any other aspects that might be considered remotely relevant and that have been collected during the same study.

AID (automatic interaction detector) analysis on these data then divides the sample sequentially into smaller and smaller groups, on the basis of maximizing the proportion of brand users in one grouping and minimizing the proportion in the other, at each new split. Figure 29.2 indicates a typical (hypothetical) series, with the right-hand side groupings increasingly containing those who are most likely to buy the brand, and the left-hand side groupings, working down the chart, increasingly containing those who are unlikely to buy the brand.

Doeblin (1982) gives an example in a different area: AID analysis of the attitudes of 2,000 Japanese, using their rating of 'Made in Germany' (1 positive, 2 negative) as the basis for the analysis. An excerpt from the full tree is shown in Figure 29.3. Of the variables entered for consideration by the program, the sample split initially by sex (this being the greatest discriminator in attitude), then (within the male subgroup only) by income, and subsequently by other variables that are not shown.

Partly because of its visual appeal, but partly because of the degree to which the analysis immediately clarifies the existing situation and identifies groups of potential in the market-place, AID analysis is frequently used as an element within any segmentation-related programme of research. In practice, it can be used as a 'stand-alone' analysis, or as a practical tool in identifying those key characteristics that are to be subsequently considered in developing clusters, using cluster analysis as described earlier.

CHAID (Chi square AID) is a more recent development of AID, based on the same principle. CHAID allows of more than the simple two-way branching at each division shown in Figures 29.2 and 29.3. Using Chi square calculation, the program determines the optimum number of groups to create from each split, in order to maximize differences on the dependent variable, but will retain the two-way split if this is identified as the most relevant.

MAPPING PROCEDURES

Mapping versus segmentation

Mapping, although frequently considered in the context of segmentation, relates to a quite independent set of analyses. The point of contact between segmentation and mapping is that both are concerned with 'grouping' subjects, and both are subsumed within the range of techniques known as multivariate analysis.

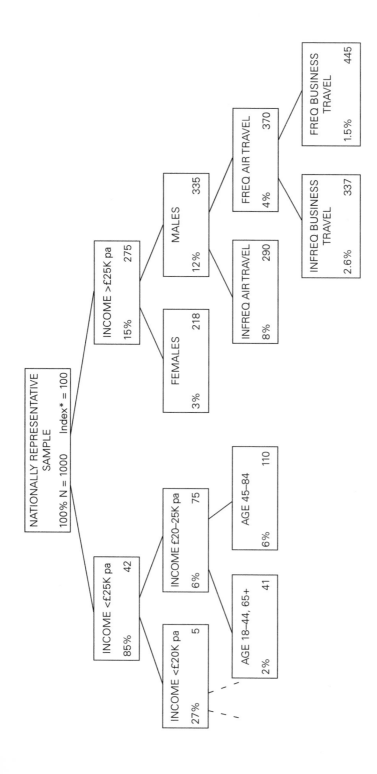

Figure 29.2 *AID analysis*

* INDEX INDICATES CARD PENETRATION LEVEL WITHIN THIS GROUP

While in practical use there is considerable overlap, there is a prime difference between the two in that 'mapping' techniques seek only to identify, and often visually represent, the relationships that exist between subjects (people or, more often, brands) for a given population or sample; there is no a priori intention to 'segment'. Segmentation, by contrast, seeks to identify relationships within subsets of a population, with the accepted intention of creating or identifying those subsets.

Certain mapping techniques are, of course, of direct relevance to segmentation; 'unfolding' is a technique that could be used to cluster respondents by their views on a given subject or market, and generates output that could be 'mapped'. Equally, both factor analysis and principal components analysis generate, respectively, factors and components with scores that could be 'mapped' in two or more dimensions.

Very rarely, however, is mapping as such used as a technique for dividing up a market in the way that is implied by 'segmentation', although it is frequently one stage in a global 'segmentation' study. Instead, mapping is concerned with identifying the relationships between all defined subjects under scrutiny, to clarify and illuminate the structure of a market in a way that may not be possible with standard analysis.

Output, typically though not exclusively, is in the form of points or vectors on a two-dimensional 'map', hence the term 'mapping'. Subsequent comparison of maps derived separately from two or more segments will certainly aid judgements about the segments, but the segments themselves are unlikely to have been derived by mapping.

The techniques

In addition to principal components analysis, which was discussed earlier in its role as a precursor to cluster analysis, there are two other frequently used techniques available for mapping, detailed in the following two sections.

Correspondence analysis

Specifically in a mapping context, principal components analysis generates output similar to that of correspondence analysis, and, purely in this context, can be taken as similar, even though the mathematics differs considerably. Here, the input for correspondence analysis can be simply a brand association matrix, such that shown in Table 29.2, data having been collected for brands A to F on attributes 1 to 10.

Resolution by the computer program of the similarities and differences between the rows, on the one hand, and the columns, on the other, generates a map as shown in Figure 29.4. The relationship of each brand to every other brand, each attribute to every other attribute, and each brand

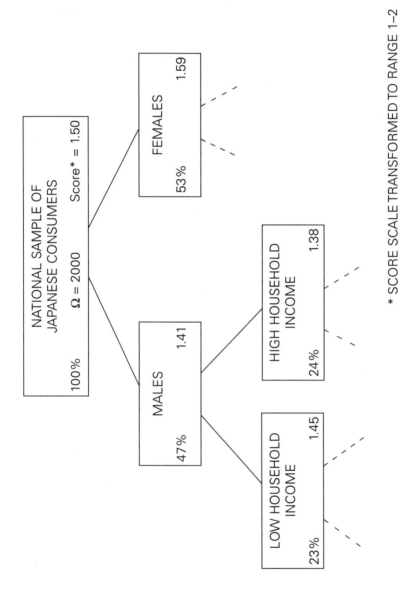

Figure 29.3 *AID analysis of Japanese consumers*

* SCORE SCALE TRANSFORMED TO RANGE 1–2

Table 29.2 *Hypothetical image battery (positive attributes)*

	A SKODA	B MINI	C METRO	D 2 CV	E FIAT UNO	F FORD FIESTA
Attribute:	%	%	%	%	%	%
Economic (1)	24	52	47	60	48	51
Efficient (2)	17	39	58	38	52	47
Modern (3)	5	18	38	11	46	39
Traditional (4)	19	64	31	48	19	42
Sophisticated (5)	2	42	45	36	39	27
Higher-priced (6)	4	12	17	5	28	31
Low cost (7)	52	31	22	59	17	19
Value for money (8)	37	51	57	42	30	45
Exciting (9)	7	51	24	57	45	21
Fashion-conscious (10)	6	41	18	55	32	18

to each attribute is represented by spatial distance on the map (as faithfully as is possible in two dimensions – a 'stress' factor indicates the degree of success).

For simplicity, brands are shown as points, while attributes are shown as vectors, although in practice the analysis makes no distinction between the two. The relationships between, for example, Brand C and each of the attributes can be determined by dropping a perpendicular to the appropriate vector as shown; a similar procedure can be used for the remaining brands (and attributes).

Study of the strengths and weaknesses of each brand on each attribute in Table 29.2 by the reader will confirm that the map in Figure 29.4 is a reasonable representation here. However, there is a range of possible interpretations of such a solution, some extremely misleading, and the interested reader is recommended to follow up the references listed at the end of the chapter before using the technique in earnest (eg Sampson, 1977).

Such a map, correctly interpreted, can be used in a range of circumstances – to compare positions of brands before and after image building campaigns, to assess market gaps, to identify alternative pack design positionings or to compare views held by subgroups identified via segmentation techniques, as well as simply to provide total sample data in a more accessible and often more useful format.

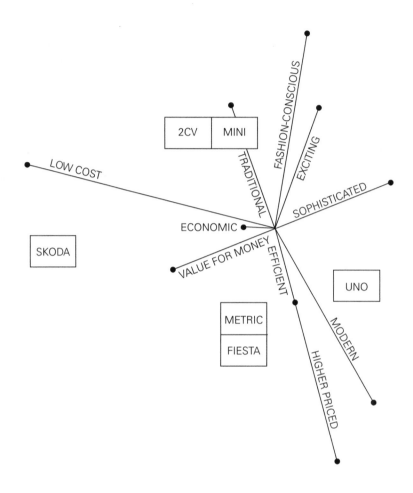

Figure 29.4 *Hypothetical image battery (positive attributes) – brand map*

(Non-metric) multi-dimensional scaling (MDS)

This second range of statistical techniques should be mentioned for completeness, given its growing importance in market research. In the present context, it differs from correspondence analysis in that the only input to the program is the stated relationship between the subjects – nothing else about the subjects is required. Specifically in the case of non-metric MDS, the input is ordinal, ie non-metric.

An illustrative example of multi-dimensional scaling would be to take measures of each distance between nine trees in a park (there would be 36 measurements) and use these data to generate a two-dimensional map. The program used should be able to recover, and map, the spatial positioning of the nine trees, without any further data.

Note, however, that it would require researcher interpretation to impose the underlying dimensionality on the map, ie north/south versus east/west (see Willson, 1974 for a similar, real example). A specific market research equivalent example would be to ask a respondent to identify how similar each of nine brands were (on a 10-point scale, for example) by separately presenting him or her with each possible pair (36 pairs – 36 measurements).

By inputting and solving these data only, the derived map would then reveal the overall positioning of the nine brands, but once again it would be the researcher's interpretation that identified the underlying (and unstated) dimensions on which the brands were being judged. Correspondence analysis, of the type discussed above, demands no such interpretation, with attribute vectors clearly labelled on the map output.

However, the usefulness of a correspondence analysis map clearly depends crucially on the initial inclusion of all relevant dimensions within the image battery administered. Non-metric multi-dimensional scaling, as noted above, does not even require metric data for input – rank order data can be input and, in fact, used extremely effectively (Guttman, Brown and Sigman, 1969 have some relevant points here).

One major example of non-metric MDS is that of conjoint analysis, which is one important step within multi-attribute trade-off modelling. Since this is reviewed elsewhere in this book (see Chapter 26), the application will not be discussed further here.

THE OUTLOOK

Over the period from 1970 to the present day, the market research industry has moved increasingly to smaller, more tactical, surveys, and away from the 'blockbuster' surveys conducted in the 1960s and early 1970s. This is partly a result of the increasing sophistication of marketing management generally. Thus, increasing use of market research is made by smaller and smaller companies, which recognize the potential of research but whose budgets will be such that tactical, rather than all-embracing, market studies will be conducted.

At the same time, an increasing history of research behind each company, large and small, means that there is simply no longer the need for the large-scale usage and attitude (U & A) studies of the past. In one way, this has been bad news for 'segmentation studies'. Where overt segmentation projects are conducted, they are usually of necessity of large sample size, time-consuming and costly.

The good news, however, is that implicit segmentation projects are seeing a distinct upward trend, with the use of cluster analysis, AID analysis and brand mapping particularly becoming an increasingly recognized part of the researcher's armoury. As a result, two points are worth making in conclusion. First, there is always a requirement for a basic understanding by the researcher of the nature of the specific technique utilized in segmentation, within the wide range available, and this requirement will not change. In the face of increased computing power and ever-easier access to suites of programs that offer techniques 'on tap', it becomes ever easier to derive incorrect conclusions, based on a lack of understanding of the limitations of the particular technique.

Secondly, because of the trend towards smaller sample sizes, used more tactically, there is an increasing danger related to limited sample sizes. Accurate segmentation of necessity demands minimum sample sizes of upwards of 400 respondents, and blind application of the more sophisticated techniques discussed in this chapter to sample sizes significantly below this level will result in segmentations that are more apparent than real.

Despite these caveats, segmentation as a suite of techniques has a bright future. Almost certainly the days of large-scale segmentation surveys have disappeared, but their place has been taken by surveys that utilize the theory and practice of segmentation to answer key objectives in specific areas.

Arguably, such a move represents a transition away from the use of segmentation in a strategic and, at times, academic context, and towards its use as an active, carefully directed marketing tool. The author would argue that such a transition is to be welcomed in encouraging the future application of what remains an extremely powerful bank of techniques.

Poised at the beginning of the new millennium, when mass markets are increasingly fragmenting into smaller sub-markets and there is a noticeable move away from standardized production, segmentation techniques should become increasingly important to the research industry.

It is becoming less and less the case that what is important is a monitor of the similarity between buyers, and more and more the case that differences are of increasing commercial interest in building future markets. Segmentation, like mapping, is an important weapon in identifying those differences.

REFERENCES AND FURTHER READING

Blamires, C (1995) Segmentation techniques in market research: exploding the mystique surrounding cluster analysis, *Journal of Targeting, Measurement and Analysis for Marketing*, **3** (4)

Blamires, C, Lunn, A and Seaman, D K (1986) Applying strategic research to the retail area, Proceedings of ESOMAR seminar on retail strategies for profit and growth, Brussels

Blamires, C, Ray, A and Askew, P (1997) Electronic data capture: taking advantage of a new era, Market Research Society Annual Conference

Cornish, P (1981) Life cycle and income segmentation: sagacity, *Admap*, October

Doeblin, J (1982) The image of 'made in . . .' labels in Japan as a criterion for market segmentation, Market Research Society Annual Conference

Eiermingham, J, McDonald, C and Baker, K (1979) The utility to market research of the classification of residential neighbourhoods, Market Research Society Annual Conference

Guttman, L, Brown, M M and Sigman, S (1969) The relevance of the nonmetric breakthrough of marketing research, Market Research Society Annual Conference

Harris, P (1981) Recent developments in the multivariate analysis of market research data, Market Research Society Annual Conference

Holmes, C (1986) Multivariate analysis of market research data, in *Consumer Market Research Handbook*, ed RM Worcester and J Downham, ESOMAR

Journal of the Market Research Society (1989) **31**, 1 January

Kendall, M G (1965) Introduction, in *A Course in Multivariate Analysis*, Chas Griffin

Lotti, L and Nurmilaukas, V (1986) Will clients of different supermarkets be split into segments? Proceedings of ESOMAR seminar on retail strategies for profit and growth, Brussels

Lunn, A and Blamires, C (1996) The new face of retailing, Market Research Society Annual Conference

Morgan, N and Purnell, J M (1969) Isolating openings for new products in a multi-dimensional space, *Journal of the Market Research Society*, **11** (3)

Sampson, P (1977) Some experiences with mapping, Market Research Society Annual Conference

Sonquist, J A and Morgan, J N (1965) The detection of interaction effects, *Monograph No 35*, Survey Research Centre, Institute for Social Research, University of Michigan, USA

Thomas, S, Bunting, C and Nelson, E H (1982) Social change analysis – a new era for the application of research, Market Research Society Annual Conference

Webber, R (1980) Basic principles of ACORN, Seminar on ACORN in action, CACI International, London

Willson, E (1974) Computational segmentation in the context of multivariate statistics and survey analysis, *Journal of the Market Research Society*, **16** (2)

30

Forecasting

Stephen Howard and Roy Norton

GETTING STARTED

What is a forecast and how is it made? A forecast is a subjective view of an uncertain future. The means by which forecasts are made can be based upon anything from pure intuition to the most sophisticated computer models. However, it is far more rational to introduce some logical framework to forecasting in order to provide both understanding and continuity to the forecasting process.

A forecast is made by using past experience or data. The data may be qualitative (opinions or judgements) or quantitative (sales or economic information). Opinion juries or Delphi methods incorporate opinions or views of a large number of key people to generate forecasts of the subject under review and in general are applicable to long-term forecasting (more than two years into the future).

Quantitative information such as sales data, if measured over time, is known as time series. The most popular approaches to forecasting time series data can be classified as univariate and multivariate (sometimes known as causal models). A univariate method will use only the time series back data to forecast the future while a causal model is used when the forecaster assumes there is a relationship between the item being forecast and one or more different explanatory variables. For instance, product sales could be forecast by using their past relationship with price and advertising (their own and competitors').

Generally speaking, quantitative techniques are used to provide forecasts for the short and medium term (up to two years). How then does a forecaster choose a technique to apply to a set of data?

Without question, the technique applied must be understood by the decision-maker so the forecasts derived are made with confidence. In many situations the forecaster has to trade off the pros and cons of a complicated method with a simpler technique from the viewpoint of ease of use, understanding and the time and effort required to develop and maintain the system.

For instance, using a causal model to generate forecasts for product sales also involves forecasting each individual explanatory variable in the relationship. In practical terms the effort involved to provide these additional forecasts may not be worth while, and there is evidence from a number of different forecasting competitions that simple forecasting methods are as accurate as, or even better than, more sophisticated procedures.

Another consideration is the availability of historical data. The use of quantitative methods rests on the assumption that there are enough historical data available to assess the past patterns in these data. Each technique will require a different number of observations to get started and, for assessing seasonal patterns, a minimum of four years.

The number of items to be forecast is a factor in the choice of technique. If there are a large number of items to be forecast the forecaster will have to develop a system that is both simple and easy to use, as it may not be practical to use different techniques for all the items. This is known as an automatic or black-box system. On the other hand, if the number of items is small, then the system developed may incorporate subjective information and background knowledge of the items.

In the examples that follow, only univariate techniques are discussed, and the chapter concludes with a section on forecast accuracy.

PRELIMINARY ANALYSIS

It is essential before an assessment of the most appropriate technique is carried out that some form of preliminary analysis of the data is made to evaluate the properties and structure of the data.

This can be carried out by observation of a graph or time-plot of the data, to recognize whether trend or seasonality are present, to look for changes in the structure of the data (perhaps step or slope changes) and to detect the existence of outliers, ie freak or suspect observations. Background information may be required on the nature of these events and, in some circumstances, if it is obvious that a single model will be unable to describe the data pattern, it may be necessary to ignore part of the dataset to ensure the model chosen fits the recent past. In cases where there are freak observations these may have to be adjusted, because such observations will affect the forecast not only for the following period but also for a number of periods into the future.

Having then carried out an initial examination of the data, some assumptions can be made about the pattern of the data that occurred in the past. Effectively the problem is now matching the pattern in the situation with a technique that assumes that pattern. Also, for the purposes of forecasting, this underlying pattern is assumed to be constant over the time horizon for which forecasts are to be made.

SPECIFIC TECHNIQUES

Throughout our discussion of the following techniques it must be remembered that each particular technique has a predefined structure or model, which effectively matches the pattern found in the data and, by its definition, will assume certain characteristics. Our hope is that the model will give a reasonable description of the situation.

There is also, however, another important assumption that the forecaster can make within the scope of the data. If the model is highly stable then this type of model is known as a global model, while a structure that is believed to hold only in the short term is regarded as a local model.

In the following examples, a number of forecasting techniques are used that apply to certain types of data pattern. The first section is concerned with horizontal or stationary data, data that are noisy but exhibit no trend or seasonality; the second section uses data incorporating trend; and the third introduces seasonal patterns. The final section is devoted to a novel technique that deals with data oddities such as step changes and outliers.

A summary of the techniques to be used and the data to which the techniques can be usefully applied is shown in Table 30.1.

Stationary data

The data used in the examples are real information taken from the Taylor Nelson Healthcare Scriptcount database, which records the level of use of prescription products in the UK and in most cases is shown as two-weekly time series.

The first data example covers a two-year period to the end of 1987, measuring the number of prescriptions (in thousands) every two weeks.

Table 30.1 *Summary of techniques and data*

Techniques	Type of Data			Type of Model	
	Stationary	*Trend*	*Seasonal*	*Global*	*Local*
Moving Average	Yes	No	No	No	Yes
Exponential Smoothing	Yes	No	No	No	Yes
Trend Analysis	Yes	Yes	No	Yes	No
Holt's Exponential Smoothing	Yes	Yes	No	No	Yes
Classical Decomposition	Yes	Yes	Yes	Yes	No
Holt-Winters Exponential Smoothing	Yes	Yes	Yes	No	Yes

It shows no movement in terms of trend or seasonal patterns, although there is a marked fall in early 1987, which should merit further attention in a more detailed study. For our purposes, however, the assumption is made that this dataset is reasonably stable or constant and amenable to treatment using the techniques that follow.

Moving averages

The method of moving averages takes a subset of the observations, calculates the average of the subset and uses this as the forecast for the next period. For example, a forecast using a four-period moving average is calculated by summing the values of the present and previous three observations and dividing the result by the number of terms in the moving average (in this case four). This is the forecast for the next period. The methodology here is slightly different from the usual application of moving averages where the average is generally centred around a set of observations.

Notice from Figure 30.1 the differences between using eight and four periods to calculate the moving average. The eight-period moving average is much smoother and, in general, the inclusion of more terms in the average results in a more stable forecast line. In fact, a moving average using the same number of terms as observations will result in the forecast for the next period being the overall data mean!

A compromise must be reached in choosing the length of time period over which the moving average is to be calculated. A longer period will be smoother, as shown on the chart, but it will also be slower to adapt to new variations, so a trade-off must be made. It is worth noting that any variation in the moving average is as much influenced by the period left off the calculation as by the next period included.

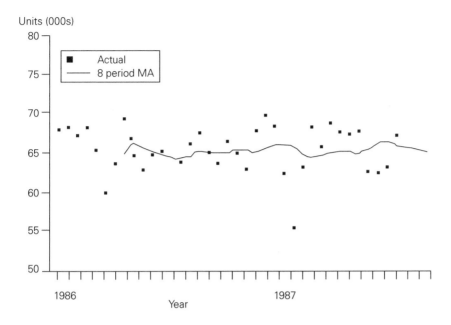

Source: Scriptcount anti-infective drug

Figure 30.1 *Moving averages*

The technique for moving averages is as follows:

Calculation

■ Take M observations (where M is the number of terms in the moving average) including the current observation and calculate their average. Use this average as a forecast for the next period.

Assumptions/recommendations

■ The more observations used in calculating the average, the smoother is the effect, as the average gets closer and closer to the overall mean of the dataset.
■ The method gives equal weight to each of the M values in the data series.
■ Only use the technique when variables change slightly from period to period, ie a horizontal dataset or a slightly wandering mean.
■ Do not use it for trend or seasonal data, or when step or slope changes occur. Its main practical use is to smooth data rather than forecast.

Limitations

- In general, forecasts are for one period in advance.
- It is the forecaster's choice as to how many terms (M) are in the average.
- Exercise caution in using moving averages because of the chance of introducing a new cyclical pattern purely as a result of the averaging process.
- It requires at least M observations to calculate the moving average.

Exponential smoothing

In terms of forecasting, it would seem more reasonable to use a moving average that gives more weight to recent than past data, as the most recent observations surely contain more information about what will happen in the future. Where this is so we need a model that gives a weighting scheme to be applied, which will then give more weight to the most recently observed data points and less to the older values.

This technique is known as exponential smoothing. The weights applied to the data are dependent upon what is known as the smoothing constant or parameter. This parameter takes a value between zero and one and identifies how 'smooth' the forecast will be. What happens to the forecast when different values are used for the smoothing constant? From Figure 30.2 it can be seen that when the smoothing constant is close to one, the forecast responds rapidly to the last data point and is very similar to a moving average with a small number of terms. When the smoothing constant is close to zero, the forecast is slow to respond and shows little adjustment to the new data. This process is similar to a moving average with a large number of terms, but always gives more weight to recent events. This technique provides a robust and widely applicable technique to use with horizontal or stationary data. However, if this technique is used with a data series that exhibits some form of trend, the forecasts produced will consistently under- or overforecast depending upon whether the trend is increasing or falling.

The next section provides some suggestions on techniques that can be used to cater for trends in the data.

The technique for exponential smoothing is as follows:

Calculations

- The new forecast is the old forecast added to the smoothing constant multiplied by the error (the difference between the old forecast and actual observation).
- New forecast = old forecast + (A × error).
- A is the smoothing constant.

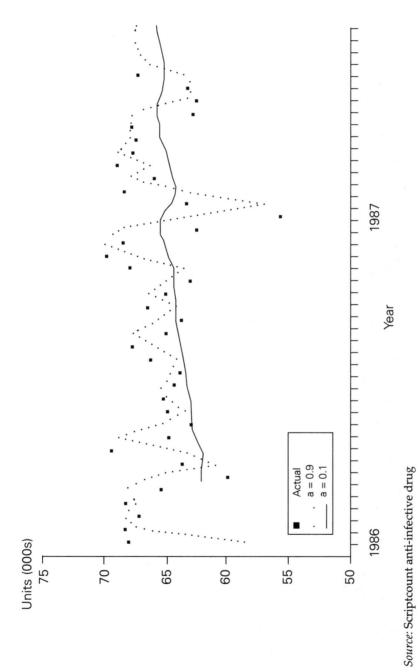

Source: Scriptcount anti-infective drug

Figure 30.2 *Exponential smoothing*

Assumptions/recommendations

■ Decreasing weights are given to the older values.
■ The technique only requires the most recent value, last forecast and smoothing constant to be applied to the data.
■ Data must be stationary or horizontal, and non-seasonal.

Limitations

■ The forecaster must choose the value for the smoothing constant, though many computer packages optimize to find the 'best' parameter.
■ The forecaster must provide an initial forecast.
■ The use of this technique with a trending dataset will give forecasts that are unable to 'catch up' with the trend.
■ Use for short-term forecasts only.

Trending data

The following section reviews two types of model that incorporate trend. Looking at our Scriptcount data example in Figure 30.3, it is clear that the data show a linear trend. Our first impulse is to use a ruler and fit a line through the data by eye. This is known in 'academic' circles as the 'BSTR' (bent see-through ruler) technique.

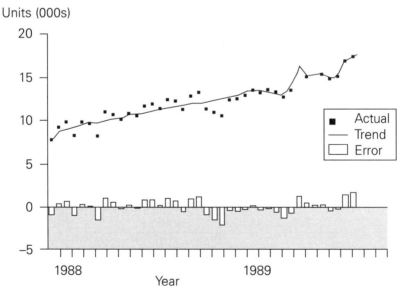

Source: Scriptcount Cardiovascular product

Figure 30.3 *Trend analysis*

This, however, will become tedious if a large number of items are to be forecast and there is no means of ensuring that different users will formulate the same line. How then can we mathematically draw a line through the data? Evidently there are two parameters of interest: the point at which our rule cuts the Y-axis, and the slope of the ruler. In this case, with an upward trend, the slope will be positive, and can be measured as the number of units the Y value increases by when the time index increases by one.

This mathematical line must also be as close as possible to the observations or, put another way, the distance between the line and observations must be small. This is, after all, what we attempt to do 'by eye' with our ruler.

A method that is capable of evaluating our two parameters and is widely available in most computer packages is ordinary least squares. The model can be put in the following form for trend analysis:

DATA = FORECAST + ERROR
FORECAST = LEVEL + SLOPE × TIME

where

DATA are the set of observations;
LEVEL is the point at which the line crosses the Y-axis;
SLOPE is the slope parameter;
TIME is the time index;
ERROR is the difference between the FORECAST and DATA.

In our example dataset, the estimate for level is 8.449 and for slope is 0.176. For example, the forecast for period 10 is: 8.449 + (10 × 0.176), which is 10.209 (thousands of prescriptions).

In this fashion, forecasts for each period can be calculated and projected into the future. Notice, however, that our estimates for both level and slope are fixed and in this case there is some evidence that a local model, where the level and slope are allowed to vary, may be more appropriate. To allow for this Figure 30.4 shows a different approach.

The same model structure is used but, because we have assumed a local model, the level and slope parameters will vary from one time period to the next. This approach is known as Holt's linear exponential smoothing and uses a process similar to the exponential smoothing method already covered.

The technique for trend analysis is as follows:

Calculations

■ The calculation is carried out by ordinary least squares.

Units (000s)

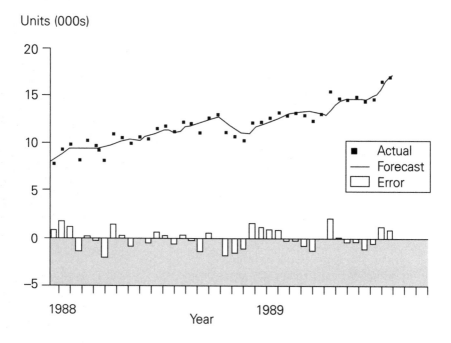

Source: Scriptcount Cardiovascular product

Figure 30.4 *Holt's exponential smoothing*

Assumptions/recommendations

- The model assumes a global trend form.
- It treats all observations with equal weights.
- Accuracy can be closely evaluated using statistical measures.
- It is a widely used tool for short- to medium-term forecasts.
- Do not use it for seasonal data or when changes in data structure occur, such as step or slope changes.

Limitations

- It does not give more weight to the most recent observations.
- The global form may not apply to the dataset.
- It requires a minimum number of observations to fit a stable trend line (10 plus).
- Freak observations distort trend estimation badly.

The technique for Holt's linear exponential smoothing is as follows:

Calculations

■ The new forecast is simply the addition of level and slope. The level and slope parameters are updated in a fashion similar to exponential smoothing:

Level = old level + old slope + A × error
Slope = old slope + A × B × error
Forecast = level + slope
where A and B are smoothing constants

Assumptions/recommendations

■ There are two smoothing constants, one relating to the level (A) and one to the slope (B). Both must lie between zero and one.
■ Decreasing weights are given to the older values.
■ Type of data can be trend or stationary but non-seasonal.
■ The model exhibits simple learning to adjust for step changes.

Limitations

■ Use it for short-term forecasts.
■ The forecaster must select values for smoothing constants.
■ The forecaster must select good initial values for level and slope.

Seasonal data

This section reviews the application of seasonal models where the data show some form of variation during each year that repeats from one year to the next. There are numerous examples of this sort of data in real life, ranging from hay fever medication to sales of turkeys. The form of the seasonal structure may vary but in general the models available are very similar, being composed of a number of different factors. The objective is therefore to break down or decompose the pattern of the data into components that have some meaning.

First, there is the trend factor that reflects the long-term change in the mean level of the data. Secondly, there are the seasonal components, which as already described model the behaviour of the seasons of the year. Finally, there is the remainder, after account has been taken of the first two factors. This is the irregular component and hopefully will be small and random. It is likely, however, that some ups and downs in this component may be explained by other factors affecting the data and so provide a vital source of understanding of the situation, for example short-term supply problems, special competitive activity or the pollen count.

These components can be combined in a number of different ways to form a seasonal structure for our model. For example, an additive model is formulated as:

DATA = TREND + SEASON + RANDOM

and a multiplicative model as:

DATA = TREND × SEASON × RANDOM

The assumption behind the multiplicative model is that the seasonal variation inherent in the data is proportional to the trend factor, eg winter sales always being 50 per cent up on average.

In general, the multiplicative model is more common in the real world and, if an automatic system is to be set up, it may be more practical to use a multiplicative rather than an additive model. An additive model would imply that winter sales of a product were, say, 15,000 units up on the average.

Once again, using the same model structure, two types of method can be used, one assuming that the model is global, where the trend and seasonal components are fixed, and the other assuming a local model, where the parameters are allowed to vary from one period to the next.

The first method is known as classical decomposition (see Figure 30.5). Each step in this method removes the contribution of first, the trend, and then seasonality, until all that remains is the random element.

A second approach is to relax the assumption that the trend and seasonal elements are fixed, and to assume that these only hold for the short term. In this situation the method of estimating the trend and seasonal pattern is very similar to our previous exponential smoothing methods and is known as the Holt-Winters exponential smoothing technique.

Most of the developments made in recent years have been to seek minor adjustments to the basic methodology, which do not affect the structure of the seasonal model. For example, a lot of work has been carried out in the area of estimating the seasonal component by Fourier analysis, which attempts to calculate the seasonality through a combination of sine and cosine functions. This is especially useful in areas where there are a large number of seasons (ie weekly data) and where the seasons are not independent. Usually a small number of sine and cosine waves will cope with a relatively larger number of seasonal terms.

The technique for classical decomposition is as follows:

Calculations

■ There are three steps involved in performing decomposition:
  – First, determine the seasonal factors. Calculate a centred 12-month moving average if the data are monthly. For any other frequency, the

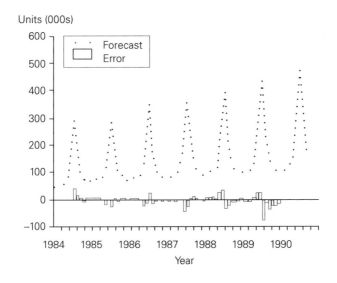

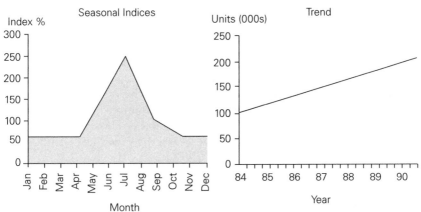

Source: Scriptcount Hayfever product

Figure 30.5 *Classical decomposition*

moving average must use as many terms as there are seasons in the
year. Calculate, for a multiplicative model, the ratio of the actual value
to the moving average, and for an additive model subtract the moving
average from the actual value. This calculation gives the seasonal
factors for the whole set of data. To generate the seasonal factors for
forecasting, average the values for each month.
- Secondly, determine the trend by fitting a trend line through the
moving average already calculated (ie by using trend analysis).
- Thirdly, forecast using either TREND × SEASON or TREND +
SEASON. It will be necessary to evaluate the residuals or irregular

component to check for the existence of a non-random element in the data.

Assumptions/recommendations

■ It is intuitively easy to understand and to calculate.
■ It assumes that trend and seasonal factors are fixed.
■ It is used for short- and medium-term forecasts.
■ More sophisticated versions are used world-wide for deseasonalizing purposes.

Limitations

■ Multiple regression can be used to handle the same sort of decomposition and also include explanatory variables if necessary.

Other types of data

So far the situations in which our various methods have been utilized have been quite regular. What happens when the examination of the structure of the data reveals major discontinuities, freak observations and other data oddities?

First, without manipulation of the data, the techniques covered so far will not be able to handle data such as the final example (see Figure 30.6). This is because the methods can cope when the pattern in the data matches the pattern of the applied technique, but not in the presence of outliers or step and slope changes.

Unfortunately, the choices available are fairly limited. The forecaster may be able to adjust suspect observations or discard data before the discontinuity and then use a projection technique or, if the worst comes to the worst, accept that no projection forecast is likely to be beneficial, and use a subjective estimate based upon the forecaster's own knowledge of the situation.

A novel approach to this sort of data was introduced by Harrison and Stevens in 1971. This method of short-term forecasting was based upon Bayesian principles, which encompass the notion of prior and posterior distributions to describe the model parameters. This means that the forecaster can input his prior ideas on trend or seasonality, and successive data points are used to calculate the posterior distributions for these parameters. The technique produces not only single-figure forecasts but also distributions for trend and seasonality, so giving upper and lower limits to the forecast. The model applied on this dataset is known as the multi-state model, which uses four sub-models, all alert to particular types of data.

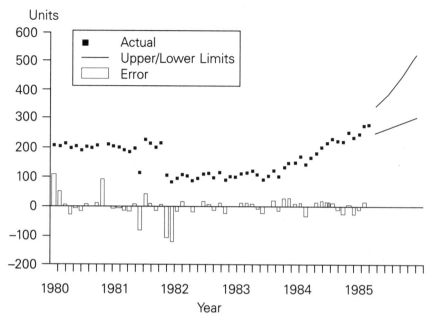

Source: Scriptcount Hayfever product

Figure 30.6 *Bayesian multi-state model*

For instance, in the example shown the data series exhibits two outliers, a step change and then, in the latter part of 1983, a slope change. The model detects both outliers, and once in outlier mode, ignores that data point. For the step change, the model will switch primarily to outlier mode, but once satisfied that the data have moved to a new level, will change to step change mode and update to the new level.

SUMMARY

The univariate techniques presented have all been chosen because of their specific properties when dealing with real data. It is important when using these that the forecaster is aware of both the type of data that the technique is appropriate for and how far into the future the forecasts can be usefully applied.

The forecaster must also be expected to assess the adequacy of the model chosen and how accurate the forecasts are. Inspection of the errors will give a guide to whether there are non-random elements not accounted for by the technique applied. The size and bias of the errors will give a guide to the accuracy of the technique chosen. The following section outlines the degree of accuracy found, when forecasting real data for prescription products.

FORECASTING ACCURACY

How accurate can you expect forecasts to be? Each business sector will exhibit its own level of predictability and the answer will vary depending on the item being forecast. Total market will have different forecasting accuracy from that of aggregate product level or single pack formulations.

The two key parameters estimated in the forecasting models described, namely trend and seasonality, will contribute different effects. Trend is likely to produce bias in forecast because it is a fixed increment to be added for every forecast period projected forward. If it is not estimated correctly it will produce a cumulative forecast error. Additionally, if local trends occur, the forecaster should beware of pushing too far ahead because it is likely that the trend could change again. Seasonality will have more influence on the individual month or period estimation. This contributes to the variability making one month or period higher or lower than it should be, but will compensate in another month or period. Generally speaking, seasonality contributes to the degree of forecast error but will not introduce bias.

Specific results are shown (see Figure 30.7) to give an example of the forecasting accuracy in one business sector at one level of detail. This shows the percentage error of forecast compared with actual for 55 pharmaceutical products. The unit being forecast is retail prescription demand for a four-week total (source: Scriptcount). The technique uses exponential smoothing of trend and level with Fourier analysis for seasonal estimation in a multiplicative model.

At one month ahead (top) 35 per cent of forecasts are within ± 5 per cent of the actual value and 93 per cent within ± 20 per cent. When forecasting periods three months ahead the distribution of results is only slightly less accurate with 31 per cent and 55 per cent within ± 5 and ± 20 per cent respectively. Six months ahead the distribution of results looks quite different, as many forecast errors are positive and showing skewed results. At that point only 70 per cent of results are within ± 20 per cent of actual values with many more in excess of ± 25 per cent error.

The authors are aware that between three and six months ahead significant political initiatives were starting to have the effect of depressing the buoyancy of prescription products. This resulted in many of the forecasts being too optimistic, and is an example of the limitation of the forecasting method used and the need to include judgement where possible.

% of observations

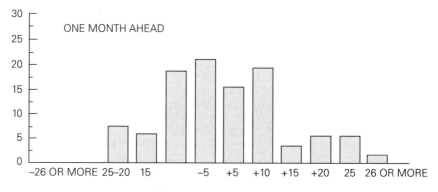

% Difference between actual and forecast

% of observations

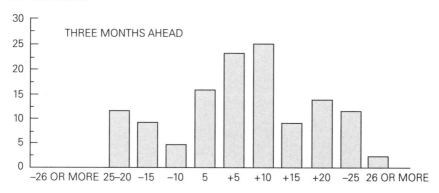

% Difference between actual and forecast

% of observations

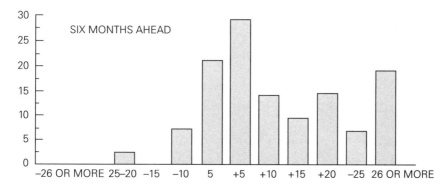

% Difference between actual and forecast

Figure 30.7 *Distribution of forecast error on 55 products*

REFERENCES AND FURTHER READING

Chatfield and Yar (1988) Holt Winters forecasting: some practical issues, *The Statistician*, **37**

Harrison and Stevens (1971) A Bayesian approach to short-term forecasting, *Operations Research Quarterly*, **22**

Harrison and Stevens (1976) Bayesian forecasting *Journal of the Royal Statistical Society*, Series B, **38**

SECTION 5

PRESENTING RESULTS

Introduction

The most effective way of presenting data is to present them before a report is written. The reasons for this relate to being able to understand the information that has been collected, and to determine the initial complications of the research results.

A good report is a short report. It is one that is written in the language of the potential reader in respect of jargon, terminology and industry-related information that the reader is used to. It is one that reports all the findings of the research clearly, gives management feedback on the problems and issues being researched, and provides actions on which to take decisions.

31

Presentations and Report Writing

Peter Bartram

BACKGROUND

'Consider your verdict,' the King said to the jury.
'Not yet, not yet!' the Rabbit hastily interrupted. 'There's a great deal
to come before that!'
Alice's Adventures in Wonderland
Lewis Carroll

Although there are still exceptions to the general trend, there can be little doubt that over the last 25 years or so there have been major changes – and improvements – in the way that market research results are delivered to those who commission them.

When the industry was closer to its infancy, there was inevitably a greater emphasis on developing and justifying the techniques, and on reassuring sceptical clients who were new to the experience that the results could be trusted.

Many leading researchers emerged from, or were heavily influenced by, the disciplines of academic life. As a result there was seen to be a need to produce a treatise in which, following the scientific method, the reader must be made to read through the detailed evidence before the final conclusions were reached. At the same time, the processes of analysis, while meticulous in their detail, were slow, laborious and inflexible. And the emphasis was largely on paper communication, with relatively few market researchers delivering their results in person, and in a group meeting.

While this style of reporting is professionally sound and still has appropriate applications today, for most clients and purposes it could hardly be described as a market-driven, user-friendly approach. Consequently, as the market research industry has matured over the years, there has been a need for a shift of emphasis in reporting procedures. And it can be affirmed that, aided by new technology, and without any significant loss in adherence to technical disciplines, this has largely been achieved.

Computer analysis is faster and more flexible, so that massive volumes of standard cross-tabulations need no longer be produced, and immediate answers to spur-of-the-moment questions can be obtained from equipment on the researcher's own desk and instantly disseminated world-wide. Tape-recording, video and computer equipment is now easier to carry and to use for analysis and presentational purposes. Instead of presentations being done – if at all – after the delivery of a detailed report, they are usually delivered beforehand, and have become the principal forum at which collective decisions on research results are taken. And, more often than formerly, the report is relegated to the status of being an afterthought, placed on file as a reference document for the future.

Research presentations all too often used to be the final fence at which researchers demolished the credibility of their own work. Instead they have now become so much better in terms of both technique and skill, with more information being communicated pictorially by charts and diagrams rather than solely by words and numbers. And reports are usually prepared nowadays with the main summaries placed at the front rather than at the back, on the understanding that this is where the most important and busiest readers want them, and the supporting detailed evidence can be studied by those who wish to read further.

In short (and fully recognizing the many exceptions to the general trend), there has been a shift from an emphasis on technique to an emphasis on application and use. There has been a shift from an academic to a journalistic style, in which the headlines are followed by the supporting detail; and there has been a shift from written to oral communication. In effect, the market research industry has applied to its own reporting procedures the recommendation it so often makes to its own clients: it has moved from a production-oriented to a market-oriented approach.

THE PRESENTATION

The Red Queen said to Alice: 'Always speak the Truth – think before
you speak – and write it down afterwards.'
Through the Looking-Glass
Lewis Carroll

Although most research presenters nowadays prepare printed or electronic
copies of their charts for members of their audience to take away, the
presentation essentially remains a performance: it is fleetingly fixed in time,
engages more of the senses than the written word (ear and eye at least),
and its effectiveness is crucially determined by the personal qualities
displayed by the researcher.

This often makes it a nervous, hiding-to-nothing game in which disasters
are so much more memorable than successes. How many of us can
remember market research (or other) presentations where these happened?

- The presenter talked for far too long.
- The slides or charts were illegible or too complicated.
- The presenter took for granted the technical knowledge of the audience.
- The presenter talked through his hat about the client's business.
- The presenter could not or would not explain the meaning and implic-
ations of the results being shown.
- The senior client executive who was present fell asleep, picked a fight
or walked out before the end.
- The presenter turned up late.
- The equipment was not ready, broke down or displayed jumbled garbage.

It has to be said that these things do not happen as often as they used to,
because more researchers have now become practised in the skills of
presentation. But when things do go wrong – usually as a result of compl-
acency, poor preparation, poor delivery or mismanagement of people –
then it is not forgotten. Least of all is it forgotten by the most vulnerable
person in the room on that day – the research buyer who chose, briefed
and introduced the presenting researcher to his or her management.

Sometimes the problem arises because the market researcher is innately
a different kind of person from the marketing or general management
people in the typical research presentation audience. Although it seems
less true than it used to be, the person who chooses market research as a
career may be of a more precise, introverted or analytical turn of mind
than the more open, extrovert marketing person who is impatient with
detail and anxious to identify the action to be taken.

With such a disposition, a researcher will spend many more days than
the client would wish to pay for, in polishing up a report that may not

really be needed at all, while spending a few hurried hours preparing a presentation that is both dreaded and unrehearsed.

Half the battle for success in delivering a successful presentation is won in the preparation beforehand. This is achieved in two main areas. First is knowing the audience and its expectations. How many are they and how senior, and how well acquainted are they with market research? What are the political crosscurrents that lie behind your project, and what options do they have in acting upon your results? Second is knowing your research material in detail, pruning it ruthlessly and building a storyline and structure for the presentation. If you do this you will be able to field questions fluently, and you will not outstay your welcome. In brief, one needs to tell them what you are going to say, say it and then tell them what you have said. Or, nearly as briefly, one should remember to rehearse it, keep it short, keep it simple – and take nothing for granted.

A more detailed checklist of points to verify in the preparation and delivery of the successful presentation can be identified in the guidelines advocated by the UK Association of Users of Research Agencies. With only minor amendments to suit the purposes of this volume, they are as follows:

1. **Plan it together** The client and agency researchers should discuss the format and content of the presentation before it is prepared, and whenever possible send a draft copy so the conclusions can be agreed before it is finalized.
2. **Probe the background** The research presenter should always fully probe for available details of the business background to the research in hand.
3. **Check back to the objectives** Refer back to the objectives of the research as set out in the proposal.
4. **Check the equipment** Always indicate well in advance what visual aids or other facilities you will need. Verify the size and layout of the room, and your access to backup equipment.
5. **Anticipate the audience** Identify ahead of time exactly who will be attending and, if possible, try to find out their background and concerns.
6. **Simplify it** Edit your material rigorously; many more research presentations are too complex than are too simple. As a rule, do not show more than 25 numbers at once; highlight the ones that matter; and do indicate the message they are meant to convey.
7. **Rehearse it** Be sure to rehearse it; and time it, speaking slowly. Allow plenty of time (at least 33 per cent of the total) for questions and discussion. The typical full-blown research presentation lasts about 90 minutes but many have to be shorter; and at all events remember to keep to your allotted time.
8. **Arrive early** On the day, arrive early. For the research company, two of you attending is optimum, three maximum; and use your best presenter, whatever his or her seniority.

9. **Establish who's who** The research buyer should properly introduce the research company executives to the client executives and vice versa. Note the names and roles of the leading client executives present.

10. **Maintain timing discipline** Check again at the start of the presentation how much time is available, and whether anyone of importance will be leaving early: get the basic message over before he or she departs. Establish also whether questions will be taken during, or only after the presentation itself; in most presentations the former is preferred (and hard to prevent anyway).

11. **Consider documentary support** Client and agency should agree whether copies of the charts, or a hand-out summary will be provided, and whether this is to be done at the start, or after the presentation. If the former is agreed, make sure it is recognized that everyone is to concentrate on the same chart together: if they race ahead, you have lost your audience.

12. **Establish your credentials** Say who you are and where you are from, remind your audience of the objectives and reassure them that your findings are dependable by showing what you were set to do in the project (ie sample, timings, etc) and what you did do.

13. **Make it legible and clear** Use specially designed large typefaces, at best with colour and the latest moving graphics. Except in the most extreme or informal circumstances nowadays hand-drawn charts are simply not acceptable. Keep your charts large and simple; use graphs or diagrams where possible rather than numbers; avoid straight photocopying from the report.

14. **Summarize** Be sure to end with a clear, concise summary, remembering that the average member of your audience is unlikely to absorb and retain more than six points from the presentation. Although opinions differ (and for the report the opposite is recommended nowadays), it is usually best to work up to your conclusions rather than to reveal them at the start.

15. **Prepare recommendations** Always prepare, and be ready to present, your recommendations from the research; but make it clear that they are separate from the findings themselves.

16. **Agree the way forward** The research buyer should ensure the meeting closes with agreement on follow-up actions.

17. **Obtain feedback** Later, follow up any points raised and obtain feedback from the audience on reactions to the presentation.

For presentations to an *international* audience some additional considerations need to be kept in mind. Those whose mother tongue is not the same as the speaker's will rely on visual images and the written word more than the spoken word. To help them with this, the delivery of the presentation needs to be taken at a slower pace (without any appearance of being patronizing) and, where possible, simple wording should be used.

English speakers are particularly bad at this, rattling on as though their own country is the centre of the universe, using unexplained abbreviations (such as ITV, NRS, GPO; or in the USA, IRS, ARF, etc) and topical jokes or allusions drawn from national entertainment media.

In presentations to foreign audiences it is also important to recognize who in the client organization is in charge, and to watch out for body language and other audience clues – jangling worry beads are a sure sign of frustration or boredom. For remote teleconferencing presentations beamed to several locations, it is worth checking at intervals that all audience participants are still with you; and of course in your presentation it is especially important to make sure you are adequately aware of relevant cultural, regulatory and environmental differences.

To a significant degree the improvements that have been achieved in the standard of market research presentations have resulted from the widening range of presentation methods available. However, the main methods of the last 20 years such as flip charts, display boards, overhead projector transparencies and 35-millimetre slides are nowadays beginning to look distinctly outdated. Modern projectors allow you to work directly from your portable PC, and therefore anything you can achieve on your PC can be displayed on the big screen. Last-minute amendments can be made, even in the taxi on the way to the presentation, and copies can easily be e-mailed to the client beforehand.

A range of software programs exists of which PowerPoint, Excel, Harvard Graphics, Freelance and (for chart layouts rather than graphic data displays) PageMaker are currently among the most widely used. However no one package answers all needs, and during the lifetime of this book doubtless other new packages will move to the forefront.

LCD projectors, plasma display screens and other equipment are obtainable widely, even for short-term rental, and are nowadays reliable. But, as with the software you use, it is always sensible to check in advance that your equipment, and the particular version you are using, is compatible in the presentation room. With the latest technology, wonderful effects including cascading, colour images, 3-D and even moving photography can be incorporated, but the consequences of equipment failure or incompatibility are more likely to be irrecoverable and disastrous: always keep a simple paper copy of the presentation in you back pocket or handbag.

The increasing emphasis on the visual display of information has focused attention on the forms of graph than can be used to depict market research results. Much valuable analytic work in this area has been done by Yves Marbeau of DataPlus in Lyon.

For the preparation of charts he sets out some simple guidelines, which, somewhat paraphrased, include:

- Optimize the visual simplicity – even to the extent of following advice from John Cleese to 'put as many words as you would use on a T shirt', and no more.
- Structure the data so the main message can be read at a glance. This is typically done by grouping items in descending order, downwards and sideways, to create the essential 'diagonalization' effect, rather than leaving them, say, in questionnaire order.
- It is better to incorporate the key into the graph itself than to set it out separately.
- Use large typefaces that can be seen at the back of the room – a minimum 20 points in Arial or Helvetica typeface.
- Lower-case letters are easier to read than block capitals.
- Where possible, use both colours and pattern effects to differentiate elements in the graph (the latter to ensure the message is still clear in any subsequent black-and-white photocopies).
- Avoid junk graphs cluttered with distractions.
- Avoid three-dimensional effects (they can be misleading) and pie charts (which are not visually efficient in conveying proportions or comparisons).
- In Arabic countries consider reversing your graph to make it read right to left; in Asia, consider top-to-bottom layout.

In fitting their design to their purpose, Marbeau advocates that one should consider graphs as being of three kinds:

1. juxtaposing, most appropriate for *describing*;
2. cumulating, best for *analysing* and making comparisons;
3. combining, best for *explaining* and communicating complex structures and networks.

These basic kinds of graph can be extended to the 10 shown in Figure 31.1, which Marbeau subdivides into 'the good, the bad and the ugly', of which the three in the lower left corner are least likely to be good, clear and appropriate.

These graphic forms are of the kind that more and more market researchers are using to enhance their presentations so that clients are no longer furrowing their brows at a forest of numbers: the essence of the modern market research presentation is variety in the use of numbers, words and pictures, and variety in the kinds of technology used to produce them. And not least, through the better training and skills that exist in the market research industry, market research presentations are being received more willingly and used more widely.

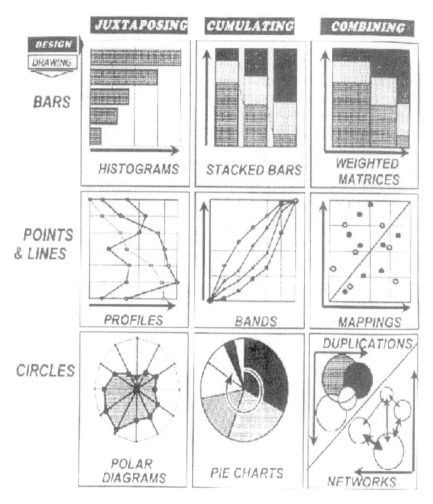

Figure 31.1 *The 10 basic types of graphs*

THE REPORT

'Let the jury consider their verdict,' the King said, for about the twentieth time that day.
'No, no!' said the Queen. 'Sentence first – verdict afterwards.'
Alice's Adventures in Wonderland
Lewis Carroll

While it is true that research presentation has become much more important in recent years, it must none the less be acknowledged that for many projects the end product upon which the market researcher is judged is still the written interpretative report on the findings. This is especially true of work for less commercially oriented clients such as local or national government departments and academic or cultural institutions.

Before matters of style and content are considered, the structure of the report must be settled and all the necessary preparations made. Although there are differences according to whether the project is continuous or *ad hoc*, qualitative or quantitative, or for an individual client or many, the typical market research report nowadays will comprise seven sections:

1. **Introduction** This describes the business or environmental background to the research, and perhaps explains why the research came to be commissioned.
2. **Objectives** They give a clear description of the purposes the research was commissioned for, and possibly itemize the key management decisions it was designed to assist. For some types of project, such as continuous studies, or for supplementary reports, it may also be appropriate to describe the intended purpose of the report itself.
3. **Research method** This describes the population the research was designed to cover (that is, its 'universe'), how and when the data were collected, the number of interviews targeted and achieved, whether any data weighting was involved, whether any respondent incentives were used and the names of any organizations or individuals to whom significant aspects of the project were subcontracted. This section should usually be kept short, at four pages or less; further technical details, such as a listing of sampling points or other matters required by the Market Research Society or ESOMAR Codes of Conduct, can be placed in the appendices at the back of the report.
4. **Summary** This usually comes next, comprising a brief description of the highlights from the findings and a set of conclusions. Before compiling these, the researcher should stand back from the data, examine the objectives of the research once again, discuss the business realities with the client and identify the actions that should most appropriately follow from the research. This section needs to be written after considerable reflection, as it is the part of the report most likely to be scrutinized by the most important decision-makers in the client organization: it is a self-defeating shame if, as happens all too often, it is written in a hurry by a mentally exhausted researcher with a deadline to meet. Note that while it can be discursive in scope, the summary need not lack precision: in quantitative studies, exact percentages should still be quoted rather than obscured in approximations such as 'one in seven said this or that'.
5. **Findings** These comprise a description, in words and figurative extracts, of the main results to emerge from the research. This section will comprise the main bulk of the typical report, and its requirements will

be discussed more fully later. Its content and layout can be varied according to the researcher's (or, better still, the client's) tastes, or to the technical complexities of the project. Among the options available are:

- to describe in words what the numbers say, putting the appropriate tables, charts or extracts into a separate section at the back; if this is done, the text should provide proper indexing references to the tables;
- to describe the findings in words, interleaved with mini-tables, or charts taken from the presentation, highlighting relevant data and cross-analyses. For qualitative reports, verbatim quotations will be used to illustrate the points being made in the main text. It is usually best to provide any full set of data tabulations (or, if required in a qualitative study, a set of full transcripts) in a separate volume, as few clients nowadays are keen to carry around a document of more than about 75 pages;
- to provide a left-and-right format, in which each left-hand page describes in words the data displayed in the table or chart on the right-hand page that faces it. This is a neat format that facilitates more elaborate data extracts, but it can fall apart somewhat if the amount of text or the size of the table needs to exceed the one-page rule in too many cases. Here again, it usually makes sense, and avoids the appearance of repetition, if the full data tabulations are provided in a separate volume.

6. **Data tabulations** For the reasons suggested above – and especially if the data run to more than, say, 50 pages – this section can be provided separately. Whichever is done, it is important to ensure that the tables are preceded by a list of key definitions – for instance, of the cross-break categories, which, especially in crowded tables, can be cryptically ambiguous to anyone wishing to refer to the research at a later date. And of course the tables should carry proper details of both weighted and unweighted bases.

7. **Appendices** In accordance with the relevant Code of Conduct, these should contain any information not already provided in the 'Research Method' section at the front of the report, including:

- the survey universe (actual if different from intended);
- the size and nature of the sample, both achieved and intended;
- any weighting methods used, the cellular values and the differences in profile resulting from them;
- a statement of the fieldwork response rates achieved, with discussion of any possible bias due to non-response;
- the nature of any respondent incentives offered;
- the dates and geographical coverage of fieldwork; and, if requested by the client, a detailed list of the sampling points used and the times of day and/or days of the week when fieldwork was carried out;
- field force(s) involved at any stage;

- subcontractors used for major parts of the research;
- (in qualitative work) the method of recruitment;
- (in desk research) the sources used and their dates.

Other items that should be provided to the client in these appendices if they have not been provided separately are:

- a copy of the questionnaire (or, in the case of multi-client surveys, the relevant part of the questionnaire), or any similar document such as the discussion guide;
- any relevant extract from the interviewers' instructions;
- any show cards or other materials that have been shown to respondents in the interview or discussion;
- where relevant, weighted and unweighted bases (clearly distinguished) from all major conventional tables.

Apart from the decisions on the report's structure, there is a great deal of other preparatory thought and work that needs to be undertaken before the actual writing can begin. It is important to go back to first principles and study again the client's brief for the research, and in particular the objectives it was required to meet: too many research reports lose sight of these, and become a mindless question-by-question logging of answers obtained. Similarly (and especially if no presentation or personal contact has preceded the report), it is important to talk to the client in order to gain a clear understanding of the marketing or management background to the research, and of the level of familiarity with the conventions of research that exist among the intended recipients of the report. In this way one can avoid committing howlers such as:

■ drawing conclusions or making recommendations that are at variance with cost or competitive realities, legal or regulatory restraints, operational feasibility or recent events in the market-place;
■ reporting findings in a manner that reveals that the researcher's expectations are the opposite of the client management's expectations: for instance, it undermines credibility to say 'only 20 per cent of customers were dissatisfied with the service received' if such a figure frightens the life out of a client who had previously thought the proportion was about 3 per cent;
■ reporting independently checkable facts as pure gospel: most clients know their own business environment, and one must be wary of saying, for instance, that 100,000 people have opened an account/used the product/made complaints, when internal records say 'it ain't necessarily so'. This applies equally to published statistics from government or other sources; and it is wise to discuss all these various sources with the client before report writing begins.

The final act of preparation must be to ensure that you are handling a set of data that is technically sound; or if it is not sound in any way, to make sure that you understand the extent to which the findings must be subject to reservations or doubts. If significant, these should be referred to somewhere in the introductory sections of the report. In brief, this means that you must check:

- **Response rates** If they are low (as they often are in postal surveys, for instance), has anything been done, and should anything be done, to weight the sample so that it more fully reflects the characteristics of the survey universe? If this is not possible, what biases are likely to have resulted?
- **Weighting** What effect has the weighting had on the 'effective' sample size (that is, the reduced sample size to which, as a result of the weighting process, any statistical significance testing should be applied)? And what is the effect on the results obtained in certain subsample groups? If it has caused changes at variance with expectations, one must be wary: small numbers of interviews can sometimes be weighted too heavily and turn the weighting process into 'a cure that is worse than the disease'.
- **Whole counts** If this has not been done already, it is wise to check through the whole counts using a copy of the questionnaire: this often reveals slippages, transpositions or filtering errors that are not so evident in the final computer tabulations.
- **Cross-tabulations** The final check required is to ensure that the cross-breaks one has requested are truly defined as they should be. The easiest way to do this is to go through the tabulations to the part of the questionnaire from which each cross-break is derived, and ensure that they match up as they should.

Having checked that you are handling dependable data, and if the introductory sections have already been prepared, you are then ready to look at the results themselves.

The first 10 minutes of doing this (whether in preparing a report or a presentation) can often be described as the most exciting of all the processes in a survey research project. Suddenly all is revealed, and the facts come tumbling out of the data so fast that it is hard to keep pace with the insights obtained. By searching out the key questions in relation to the objectives, 95 per cent of the results needed from the survey can often be identified in those 10 minutes. For this reason it is well worth keeping a notepad to hand so that fleeting thoughts can be captured as they occur: you will find they can be lost for ever if you try to remember them later. After that, the descriptive reporting contained in the 'findings' section of the report can proceed.

It rarely makes sense to report these in questionnaire order, as it is better to structure the sequence in accordance with the various objectives of the research or in line with the client's operational perceptions by looking separately, for instance, at competition, customer profiles, distribution methods and corporate image, regardless of where they surface in the survey interview.

Altogether the aim of the 'findings' section of the report should be to tell a story that builds to a complete picture through a linked line of argument, related entirely to the objectives of the research. This means that it is not necessary to report the answers to every question: you should report only those facts that contribute to an understanding of issues related to the objectives. Likewise, a deadpan recitation of facts will not provide as much enlightenment as a tapestry of cross-referenced information that builds up a rounded picture. This means that answers to one question should be compared with answers to another (for instance, open-ended and closed questions on the same subject).

Typically, in any single part of the report on a quantitative project the following sequence might be adopted:

1. Say what respondents were asked.
2. Report the answers obtained, in words.
3. Show a brief chart or tabular extract with a key crossbreak, if useful.
4. Add an analytical comment on subgroups not shown.
5. Stand back a little from the immediate data in order to explain the implications in relation to other findings and for the market-place as a whole.

In presenting data extracts in the findings you should again try to make life easy for the reader: a list of side headings should usually be placed in descending order of their incidence in the results, with 'Others', 'None' and 'Don't know' answers at the bottom. In trend data tables, the columns across should be shown in date sequence. Helpful 'net-coverage' summary lines should be included (eg for readership data, a line reading 'Any daily newspaper' or, for a list of holiday destinations, a line for 'Any EU country'). If the table extracts are short and simple, and explanations in the text take care of any opportunities for misinterpretation, then it is best to leave them uncluttered. But, if their exact meaning is in any doubt, they should properly be accompanied by:

■ a heading;
■ the question asked, verbatim;
■ identification of the bases used for percentaging – their definition and (unweighted) size.

Other aspects of data analysis are covered more fully in Chapter 24, but it is worth briefly referring here to some of the interpretation issues that arise in report preparation:

- Like 'the dog that did not bark in the night', it can be just as important to report low percentages as high ones: for instance, the fact that few people give as a reason for buying a product the main benefit mentioned in its advertising may be an important finding.
- The smaller the subgroup sample sizes, and the more dubious the data collection, the more likely it is that surprising 'facts' will emerge. In your keenness to rationalize or to see a pattern in the cross-analyses, keep in mind the hazards of significance testing, and do not lose sight of the overall picture.
- Unless the sample size is massive (say, greater than 10,000), do not give an unwarranted impression that the data are more accurate than they are, by adding numbers after the decimal point. Opinions differ as to the sample size below which it is spurious to report the results in percentages, but most researchers would prefer to quote actual numbers of interviews when the base total falls below 50.
- If you wish to report the results from questions asked of a survey subgroup, you should only do so if you have already explained the size and nature of that subgroup. To avoid doubt and confusion it is usually safest to change the base for analysis as little as possible: in a typical survey one might have various sections, each based on 'all interviewed', 'all users' or 'all non-users', but there will need to be a good justification for further complications than these.
- For reporting survey findings, the past tense is perhaps most appropriate while for the summary and conclusions, describing current market realities, the present tense will tend to have more impact. Opinions do differ on this issue but, whichever is chosen, in either section it is confusing if the two tenses are mixed.

Of course, many of the things that need to be said here are applicable to all kinds of report, not just those related to market research. The value and virtues of proper preparation, logical structure, clear expression and a sense of purpose based upon an understanding of the objectives and of the reader are evident in any kind of research-based discipline. Among the best sources of help and advice on clear expression is still *The Complete Plain Words* by Sir Ernest Gowers (revised by Sir Bruce Fraser) (1973) whose simple purpose, using witty and appropriate illustrations, is 'to help people to choose and arrange words in conveying their ideas to others'. Another relevant source is the 'Style sheet' prepared by *The Economist*, which quotes George Orwell's six rules:

1. Never use a metaphor or simile you are used to seeing.
2. Use short words rather than long ones.
3. If you can cut a word, do so.
4. Use the active tense not the passive tense, wherever possible.
5. Never use jargon if an ordinary word will do.
6. Break any of these rules rather than say anything barbarous.

The Economist also advises its journalists (and anyone else) to 'avoid being pompous, arrogant, pleased with yourself, too chatty, and too free with slang or Americanisms'. This last admonition may no longer be relevant, especially among an international readership, but there is no doubt that stylistic individuality needs to be tailored to the impression you want to convey.

Closer to the difficulties of expression that need to be overcome in market research reports is the 'fog factor'. This test of clarity, recommended by Professor Ehrenberg, is a simplified variation of Gunning's Fog Index (1982). For this we count the words of three or more syllables and the number of sentences on about half a page of writing. We then divide the one by the other. A piece with a fog factor of two or three remains easy to read. If it goes up to four or five, it becomes heavy going; and much academic or research writing earns a score of eight or more. Notwithstanding the intricacies of the subject, the aim must be to keep the reader without losing precision in meaning – and especially if the report is aimed at an international readership. (Looking back, the previous three paragraphs – admittedly aided by George Orwell – earn a score of four, which suggests that there is always a need for improvement!)

More than anything else therefore, report writing requires precision of thought and expression, and an awareness of the pitfalls that can occur between what is intended and what is understood. In market research reports, some of these pitfalls arise from words that are used in an insufficiently defined manner, such as:

■ 'more' (or 'less') – it begs the question 'than what?' The researcher must supply the answer, eg 'than in the last wave' or 'than any other subgroup' or 'than any other answer given';
■ the 'majority' – this can only mean 'more than 50 per cent'. It does not necessarily mean 'the most widely given answer'; and it is not the same as a plurality, which is less than 50 per cent, but more than other available answers, collectively or individually.

Altogether it should not be forgotten that without two or more comparable surveys at differing points in time, one cannot say any activity is increasing or decreasing: the one-off survey provides only a snapshot and it is wrong, for instance, to suggest from it that 'there is increasing awareness or interest in buying Brand X'. Other sources of imprecision or confusion include the following:

■ **Means and medians** In many survey reports, the mean is given and it provides a much higher value than the median. This happens in the typical market where 20 per cent of the purchasers account for 80 per cent of the sales. Unless this is explained carefully the client can be beguiled into thinking that his or her average customer is buying a much greater volume than is the case.

- **Grossed-up population estimates** Many clients fasten on to these and use them in a manner that intimates a far greater accuracy than is justified. The researcher must be very careful to express such estimates in very round-number terms; and if in doubt should consult a statistician.
- **Causal correlations** Very rarely can the researcher say that one result is caused by another. There may be a correlation, but one cannot usually say which is the chicken and which is the egg; and not least it may be true that other factors may affect both of the correlated dimensions. To be precise, the researcher should note the correlation and its implications, but without an empirical basis for explaining the causation, the interpretation should go no further.
- **Purchasers' purchases; buyers' buying occasions; buyers, users** This area of definition is full of pitfalls and the researcher must be careful to describe both the groups and the activities referred to, with great precision.
- **Facts and claims** In many areas of interpretation, the researcher can be impeded by the difficulty of designing the perfect questionnaire; and this and other reservations about the accuracy of survey research (which arise not least from the imperatives of sampling theory) make it foolhardy to present findings as incontestable and error-free facts. This particularly happens in questions where matters of prestige or embarrassment are involved, such as 'Do you use any form of deodorant?' Rather than report the results directly, it is wise to insert the words 'claim to' in a sentence saying, for instance, '37 per cent use a deodorant.'

And so, having negotiated these pitfalls and compiled the findings from the research, we come to the summary. As indicated earlier, it is best to stand back a little at this point, consult the client's objectives once again, and ruminate upon the main conclusions to be drawn. At best, it is also wise to discuss the practicability of your conclusions with the client before committing yourself to them.

In this summary section, it is usually best to keep to the same section-alization as was adopted in the findings and, as each point is made, to provide a reference to the part of the report that is being summarized. This section of the report should be kept short, usually occupying not more than four pages of close text.

In the conclusions, which should be separate, the researcher should directly address the business issues raised by the client in the objectives, and should use all his or her experience to provide guidance on the implications of the findings: that is to say, where they are ambiguous or conflict, to offer a judgement on the best conclusions to draw and, while being careful to avoid claiming an unwarranted degree of knowledge of all the business issues involved, to offer recommendations. Very often market researchers are reluctant to do this, but in most cases clients will say it is a reluctance that should be overcome, as they welcome the fresh ideas and opinions of an outsider who, in effect, is the representative of the customer or potential customer.

The final and very necessary act of report preparation is to get the corrections done and the appearances right. This may seem trivial, but to the client, and to the subsequent reputation of the research organization, it can be vitally important. If you can, have a separate person provide a second opinion, especially on the summary, or employ an eagle-eyed editor for checking and proofing, and ensure that the look of the report on the printed page is tidy and not too cluttered or crowded. Most reports are typed in one-and-a-half spacing, and most avoid wall-to-wall print, so the client has margins wide enough for annotated comments. Most have a contents page at the front, so the reader can easily find particular sections when required.

To summarize, the guidelines that have been described in this chapter have shown the reasons why some reports fail to satisfy their clients, or fail to meet the standards to be expected of professional market researchers. Among the reasons most commonly observed are a failure to:

- relate the findings to the original objectives of the research;
- pitch the report at the technical level appropriate to the client personnel responsible for using the results;
- write in a clear style, with precision;
- take account of a technical flaw in the data collection process;
- consult the client at all stages and identify his or her needs;
- understand the client's business and the market in which he or she is striving to succeed.

However, it seems evident that over the last two decades an increasing proportion of research reports and presentations have succeeded in avoiding these pitfalls. The growth of the industry is testimony to the fact that they have met the needs of clients, and have provided them with a confidence that survey research can be relied on for the future.

REFERENCES AND FURTHER READING

AURA (1985) *Market Research Presentation Guidelines*, Association of Users of Research Agencies, London

Bartram, P (1984) The communication of results: the neglected art in market research? Proceedings of the Market Research Society Conference

Bertin, J (1981) *Graphics and Graphic Information Processing*, Walter de Gruyter, New York

Carlton-Ashton, J (1984) Making the best use of an overhead projector, Booklet published by Astra Pharmaceuticals Ltd and the BIM Foundation Ltd

Ehrenberg, A S C (1981) The problem of numeracy, *The American Statistician*, **35** (2), May

Ehrenberg, A S C (1982) *A Primer in Data Reduction and Introductory Statistics Textbook*, John Wiley, Chichester

Ehrenberg, A S C (1982) Writing technical papers or reports, *The American Statistician*, **36** (4), November

Gowers, Sir Ernest (1973) *The Complete Plain Words*, rev Sir Bruce Fraser, HMSO, London

Halpern, R S and Nelson, E H (1983) Research findings and the creative process: bridging the gap, Proceedings of the seminar on effective advertising: can research help? ESOMAR, Monte Carlo

Jay, A and Jay, R (1996) *Effective Presentation: How to be a top class presenter*, The Institute of Management/Pitman Publishing, London

Lutz, R R (1949) *Graphic Presentation Simplified*, Funk & Wagnalls, New York, with *Modern Industry Magazine*, New York

Macnamara, J (1996) *Modern Presenter's Handbook*, Prentice Hall, Sydney

Marbeau, Y (1990) You only present once: kiss, or be killed! Proceedings of the seminar on how to cope with data overload, ESOMAR, Paris

Marbeau, Y (1998) The communication of research results: presenting, reporting, synthesising, in *Market and Opinion Research Handbook*, ESOMAR

May, John (1982) *How to Make Effective Business Presentations*, McGraw-Hill, London

Sussams, J E (1993) *How to Write Effective Reports*, Gower, Aldershot

Tufte, E (1985) *The Visual Display of Quantitative Information*, Graphic Press, Cheshire, Connecticut

Glossary

This glossary is made up of extracts from the *Dictionary of Market Research*, published by, and obtainable from, the Incorporated Society of British Advertisers (tel: 020 7499 7502) and the Market Research Society (tel: 020 7490 4911).

ad hoc Applied to single surveys designed for a specific purpose as opposed to continuous, regularly repeated or syndicated surveys.

advertising research Any research into advertising except media research, particularly creative research, pre-tests of advertisements and evaluation of advertising campaigns.

age groups The age groups most often used in British surveys of adults are those of the National Readership Survey (up to 19, 20–24, 25–34, 35–44, 45–54, 55–64, 65 and over) or broader groups based on these.

agency Market research companies are often referred to as research agencies.

aided recall A means of helping people to remember things by reminding them of associated events or by prompting.

analysis The summarizing of data in a way that is intended to make them more readily comprehensible.

analysis of variance A method of allocating the overall variation of a sample statistic among several variables, to show the strength and statistical significance of the associations with each of these variables.

animatic A representation on film or video of a television advertisement, using a sequence of drawings or simple cartoon animation. Used for advertisement pre-testing to avoid the production costs of a finished commercial.

arithmetic mean The sum of the observed values of a statistic divided by the number of observations.

ascription of adjectives A method of measuring brand images, by showing a list of brands and asking to which of them a particular adjective or adjectival phrase applies.

association The psychological technique of free or spontaneous association is used in qualitative research. It consists of eliciting the words or thoughts inspired by a number of stimuli, which might for example comprise pictures or possible names for a new product.

attitude An attitude, as a basic psychological concept, is a learned predisposition to respond in a consistently favourable or unfavourable manner with respect to a given object.

attribute A difference between people, households, etc of a qualitative rather than a quantitative kind, eg sex, region – or between brands, eg name, packaging material, colour. Also used to refer to the individual descriptions that comprise an image battery, even where these are presented in the form of scales.

audience share The percentage of the total viewing audience viewing a particular television channel.

Audit Bureau of Circulation The ABC validates circulation claims for newspapers and magazines by collecting sales returns in a set format and carrying out spot checks of publishers' internal auditing procedures.

automatic interaction detection A method of dividing a sample into groups based on analysis of variance, in such a way as to maximize the discriminating power of the groups for some dependent variable. The dependent variable might be for example the frequency of purchase of a product. The sample is divided progressively into parts, using demographic or other independent variables to define these parts. At each stage the program searches among the independent variables for the split that maximizes the between-group variance and minimizes the within-group variance for the dependent variable. Each group is subdivided until further splits become statistically insignificant, or sample sizes become too small. This method produces a hierarchy of variables that are significant predictors. It has become a popular form of multivariate analysis for market research purposes, especially for the selection and definition of target groups.

average issue readership The average number of people who see an issue of a periodical publication.

awareness Brand awareness and awareness of advertising are often monitored by means of tracking studies. Unprompted or spontaneous brand awareness is measured by questions such as 'Which brands of . . . can you think of?' Prompted awareness or recognition is measured by showing a list of brands and asking, 'Which of these . . . have you heard of?'

back-check A check by a supervisor or by the field office that an interview has been properly carried out, by telephoning or writing to a proportion of the respondents, or sometimes by means of a personal visit.

base The base number for percentaging, on a typical market research table, appears at the top of each column of percentages. Where both unweighted and weighted bases are shown, the unweighted base is the number of respondents in the subsample, and the weighted base is the number actually used for percentaging.

Bayesian statistics An approach to decision-making that combines previously estimated probabilities with the information derived from a survey or experiment.

before/after test A survey that is carried out before an event, usually some kind of advertising or promotion, and repeated afterwards, in order to detect and measure its effects.

behaviour What people do as opposed to what they think. In a marketing context, behavioural research, behavioural segmentation and behavioural theory are concerned with people's buying and consuming activities.

bias An aspect of survey design that causes the expected value of an estimate derived from the survey to differ from its true value.

bipolar Scales with two ends such as 'sweet–sour' may be described as bipolar, whereas a monopolar scale would establish the perceived degree of sweetness, eg from 'extremely sweet' to 'not sweet at all'.

bivariate Bivariate data consist of observed pairs of values of two variables or attributes, from which it is possible to evaluate the relationship between them.

blind test A product test in which the identity of the brand is not revealed. The reactions obtained, when compared with reactions to the branded product, provide a measure of the effects of branding.

blink rate Hidden cameras have been used to record the speed at which people blink while looking at advertisements, packs, etc, in the belief that a slower blink rate indicates a greater openness to suggestion.

Box-Jenkins A method of statistical forecasting, based on analysis of time series.

bracket code A code that represents two or more answers to a question, eg a single code used for all answers in the range 25–34 to a question enquiring about the respondent's age.

brand A product or service that has been given an identity; it has a brand name and the added value of a brand image.

brand image The set of associations that a brand has acquired for an individual.

brand positioning The position of brands on a map, usually in two dimensions, which represents important factors influencing choice. These factors may include for example price, product attributes, user characteristics and brand images.

brand switching Changes in the brand purchased by a consumer within a product field, eg as recorded by consumer panels.

break(down) A subgroup used in analysis. These groups are often based on classification data, eg a breakdown by sex would comprise subgroups of men and of women.

brief(ing) 1. A research brief is a statement from the sponsor setting out the objectives and background of a study, and perhaps the method, timing, etc, so that the researcher can plan accordingly. 2. Briefing of interviewers prior to a survey is intended to ensure that they understand fully the task to be undertaken.

Broadcasters' Audience Research Board Since 1983, BARB has measured television audiences and viewers' reactions to television programmes on behalf of the BBC and the ITCA. The audience measurement system replaced the former JICTAR contract.

Business Statistics Office One of the main parts of the Government Statistical Service, the BSO collects and publishes a wide variety of statistics on behalf of the UK government.

buying intentions Questions about the likelihood of buying a product during a future period.

buy-response Questions as to whether a consumer would be willing to buy a product at a number of different prices form the basis of the Gabor-Granger method of pricing research. These questions are used to plot a 'buy-response curve', which relates the percentage willing to buy the product, to the price.

call-back 1. A further attempt to contact a pre-selected respondent, telephone number, etc, or to secure co-operation, where the first attempt failed. 2. A second interview with the same respondent in the course of a single survey. 3. A call made by a supervisor to check that an interview has been carried out correctly.

canonical analysis An extension of multiple regression to deal with two or more dependent variables.

cartoon test A projective technique in which respondents are asked to fill in 'speech balloons' in a comic-strip representation of a situation relating to the topic of enquiry.

census Enumeration of all the individuals in a population.

central location Research carried out by a team of interviewers working at or from a single centre, eg hall tests, telephone interviewing.

Central Statistics Office The CSO co-ordinates the collection of UK government statistics by the Business Statistics Office and the Office of Population Censuses and Surveys.

Chi square(d) A statistical test as to whether a sample distribution conforms sufficiently to some other distribution. In market research, it is most often used to test a contingency table for the significance of any association between the two characteristics upon which the table is based.

classification In market research this relates to a group of questions and observations, usually placed at the end of an interview. These tend to be of fairly standard form, and cover for example age, sex, marital status, household composition, status within the household (as head of household or housewife), social grade, terminal education age, tenure of home.

clinic Research to aid product development, in which a group of respondents are invited to provide opinions, and modifications are made to the product before a further group is invited.

closed question A question that has a limited number of logical answers (eg 'yes' and 'no'), as opposed to an open or open-ended question.

cluster A group of neighbouring individuals. A geographical cluster comprises people, households, etc in a relatively small area. Also used to denote a group of people with similar attitudes or characteristics, or a group of brands that are perceived to be similar to one another.

cluster analysis An approach to multivariate analysis, which aims to identify groups of individuals that are relatively similar to one other, and dissimilar to individuals in other groups.

cluster sampling A form of multi-stage sampling in which the final stage is the interviewing of all individuals within the selected group, such as everyone at a selected address.

clustering/clustered sampling Almost all samples of individuals for commercial face-to-face interviews embody clustering to some degree. Instead of the individuals being spread evenly over the area occupied by the population, they are concentrated into a number of neighbouring groups or clusters. It is a consequence of multi-stage sampling, and is done in order to reduce costs.

code A symbol used to classify data for the purpose of analysis.

Code of Conduct The Code of Conduct of the Market Research Society consists of a set of principles and rules with which their members undertake to comply.

coding The process of allocating codes, especially where open-ended questions require that this is done after fieldwork has finished.

coding frame A set of codes used to categorize answers, usually to a single question, sometimes to several questions taken together.

computer-assisted telephone interviewing Telephone interviewing conducted with the aid of a computer. The computer displays to the interviewer the question that is to be asked, together with pre-coded answers (if any).

concept test A study intended to obtain reactions to an idea for an advertisement or a product, before investing in production.

confidence limits The values of a parameter that form the upper and lower boundaries of a confidence interval.

conjoint measurement A method of evaluating consumer preferences among product concepts that vary in respect of several attributes, based on asking people to rank a number of contrasting combinations in order from the most to the least preferred.

consumer 1. The ultimate user of a product, as opposed to the purchaser. 2. More generally, a person or household that uses or buys goods and services, as distinct from the producer and distributor.

consumer panel A sample of individuals whose purchases, product usage and/or media consumption, etc are recorded over a period.

contact Somebody contacted in the course of a survey, but who has not necessarily completed an interview.

contact sheet A record of the contacts and attempted contacts made by an interviewer.

continuous research Research that is undertaken on a continuing basis, or is regularly repeated at frequent intervals, as opposed to *ad hoc* surveys. Examples include retail audits, consumer panels and tracking studies.

continuous scale A type of diagrammatic or graphic rating scale that does not restrict the respondent to any specific number of discrete response categories.

control group A group of individuals who provide a standard of comparison in a test. They are exposed to no test stimuli, or to stimuli for which the results are known.

Copland formula A method of estimating the cover or reach of a poster campaign in a town. The formula involves the number of 'average' sites used, and two parameters, one of which is a function of the population size.

copy test A test of advertising copy, intended to discover how well it succeeds in communicating and how consumers react to it.

corporate image The image of an enterprise as a whole rather than of the particular goods or services that it supplies.

correlation The interdependence between attributes or variables, particularly the relationship between the values or ranks of two variables.

cover(age) The cover, coverage or reach of a single advertisement is the percentage of the target audience to whom it is exposed.

creative research Research applied to the creation (usually) of advertisements. Embraces advertising pre-tests, communication tests, concept tests, copy tests, etc.

creativity groups 1. Extended group discussions in which a variety of projective techniques are employed. 2. Groups using brainstorming and similar methods for product development purposes.

cross-tab(ulation) A two-dimensional table based on answers to two of the questions included in a survey, eg brands used by frequency of product use.

data fusion The combination of partial information from separate surveys that have been carried out using independent samples drawn from the same population to form a single database.

data protection The Data Protection Act 1984 regulates the maintenance and use of automatically processed personal information.

database A set of computerized data available for analysis.

debrief An informal verbal report by a qualitative researcher, or by an interviewer following completion of pilot interviews.

Delphi method A method of forecasting which derives a consensus view from a group of experts.

demographics Demographic variables, eg sex, age, marital status and social grade, normally comprise a large part of the classification data obtained in market research interviews.

depth interview An informal face-to-face interview, which is only loosely structured, and appears more as a conversation than as a question-and-answer session.

desk research As opposed to the collection of primary data via field research, desk research is based on the use of secondary data, eg directories, lists, statistics, reports of past surveys, and published information generally.

diadic See **paired comparison**.

diagrammatic scale A type of rating scale, which is distinguished from numerical and from verbal scales, and is also known as a graphic scale or spatial scale.

diary A means by which members of panels may record their behaviour over a period of time, eg purchases, consumption, television viewing, journeys.

dichotomous question A question to which there are only two possible answers (apart from 'don't know', 'no preference', etc).

direct question A question asked directly of the respondent about his own behaviour, opinions, etc, as opposed to an indirect question. Most questions used in structured questionnaires are direct.

distribution check An observational survey of a sample of retail outlets, which measures the presence or otherwise of specified products, brands and pack sizes. Prices and display may also be recorded.

editing Procedures for tidying up survey data. These begin with inspections of returned questionnaires to ensure that they conform to sampling requirements and that key questions have been answered.

electoral register The annual Register of Electors, which is based on returns made in October and published in February, is in Britain the sampling frame most commonly used for random samples (except for telephone surveys).

establishment survey A survey to establish (usually) the proportion of households possessing certain kinds of appliance, etc.

exploratory research Research undertaken where little is already known about the subject, often as a preliminary to a survey. Relatively quick and cheap methods are usually employed, eg desk research, group discussions, omnibus surveys, and street or telephone interviews on a small scale.

exponential smoothing A method of smoothing a time series and preparing a short-term projection. Each projected value that produces the smoothed curve is a weighted average of all observations for previous points in time, the weights forming a geometric series that diminishes as the time recedes.

exposure A single opportunity for a member of the target audience to see an advertisement.

extended groups Group discussions lasting several hours, often employing projective and other techniques.

F test Also known as the F-ratio or variance-ratio test, this will show whether two or more samples with different means could plausibly derive from the same population.

face-to-face interview This fully descriptive term is to be preferred to the term personal interview, which may sometimes be taken to include both face-to-face and telephone interviews.

factor analysis A branch of multivariate analysis based on the correlation coefficient, used mainly to investigate the structure of attitudes.

field force The interviewers and supervisory staff employed by or available to a company, usually a market research company.

field research As opposed to desk research, the collection of primary data from external sources by means of surveys, observation and experiment.

filter An instruction printed on a questionnaire as to which questions should be asked next, depending on previous answers.

Fishbein model A model of the relationships between behavioural intentions on the one hand, and beliefs and attitudes on the other.

five-bar gates A manual method of counting classified data.

forecast The expected magnitude of some quantity or the estimated probability of an event at a future time.

frequency The number of occurrences of some particular kind of event, eg answers to a question.

Gabor-Granger method A method of pricing research, used for new products and variants of or improvements to existing products. Respondents are shown for example a test pack, and asked whether they would be willing to buy it at each of a randomized set of prices.

geodemographics A method of classifying households based on multivariate analysis of data from the Census of Population.

grossing up The scaling-up of the results of a survey, experiment, test market, etc to the whole population or market.

group discussion (also known as focus group) One of the basic methods of qualitative research, often used in exploratory work and when the subject matter involves social activities, habits and status.

hall test A test for which people are taken to some fixed location, often a public hall.

hand tab(ulation) Sorting questionnaires, and counting and tabulating the answers manually rather than by computer.

head of household That member of a household who either owns the accommodation occupied by the household or is responsible for the rent, or, if the accommodation is occupied rent-free, the person who is responsible for the household having it rent-free. If, however, this person is a married woman whose husband is also a member of the household, then the husband counts as the head of the household.

hole count A term deriving from the use of punch cards in data analysis, meaning a simple count of all the codes present in all of the records, without any breakdowns.

home audit A panel of households, used for regular measurement of product purchases and in some cases consumption. Data may be collected by means of diaries, interviewers and dustbin checks.

hot decking This technique requires the survey to be sorted into an order so that respondents with similar answers on a range of key variables are placed together.

household A private household consists of one or more people living together, whose food and other household expenses are usually managed as one unit.

hypothesis Any supposition, whether or not based on evidence, or an assumption made as a basis for reasoning.

image People's perceptions or impressions of a product, service, company, person, etc, however these may have been formed, and however much they may reflect reality.

incentive An inducement to co-operate in a market research study.

indirect question A question that seeks the respondent's views about other people's behaviour or attitudes, used in qualitative research as a projective technique to uncover ideas that the respondent might otherwise be reluctant to reveal.

in-home test A product test, usually, conducted in participants' homes rather than at some central location, hall, store, etc.

in-house research Research conducted by the organization that wants the information, rather than by a research agency, etc acting on its behalf.

ink blot test The Rorschach and Holtzman ink blot tests, more widely used in clinical work than in market or social research, are projective tests in which the subject is asked to describe what he or she sees in a number of haphazard shapes.

interlocking quotas Quotas that specify the numbers of interviews required in each cell of a matrix defined by the specified characteristics, eg a matrix defined by sex, age and social grade.

interview A contact with an informant, or sometimes a group of informants, in order to obtain information for a research project.

interviewer instructions Directions to the interviewer printed on the questionnaire, including for example filters or skips. They are usually distinguished from the questions by the use of capitals, or sometimes by bold-face or italic type.

Interviewer Quality Control Scheme Established independently in 1986, the IQCS assumed the function of verifying the quality of fieldwork that had been one of the purposes of the former Interviewer Card Scheme of the Market Research Society.

Joint Industry Committee for National Readership Surveys JICNARS represents the Press Research Council, IPA and ISBA, and controls the National Readership Survey.

judgement sample Technically, any non-random sample can be described as a judgement or purposive sample. Statistical theory relating to random sampling cannot properly be employed to calculate confidence limits for estimates derived from judgement samples.

Kish grid/box A table for use by interviewers in random sample surveys to select one person from a household. The procedure gives an approximately equal chance of selection to each member of the household.

laboratory test market Any kind of consumer research or simulation aimed at forecasting the sales of a new product, short of actually selling it in the normal way, is occasionally described as a laboratory test market.

large sample For the purpose of applying standard statistical tests, a sample is described as large where the sampling distribution is normal, or approximately so. This is usually taken to mean a sample size of at least 30, and preferably 50 or more.

lifestyle A lifestyle is a way of life for a community or an individual, expressed particularly in activities, interests and opinions, and to some degree in the products and brands consumed. Various lifestyle classifications have been devised for commercial use.

Likert scale A type of verbal rating scale in which respondents are asked to indicate the extent of their agreement or disagreement with a series of statements, eg for a number of brands. Also called an agree/disagree scale.

mapping Rules or formulae by which the elements in one set can each be made to correspond to a single element in a second set.

market map A diagram that shows the relative positions of brands in terms of the most important brand characteristics, sometimes used to summarize the findings of attitude research.

market research Market research has sometimes been distinguished from marketing research, to mean the collection of data about markets by means of surveys.

Market Research Society The MRS was founded in 1946, and is the incorporated UK professional body for those using survey techniques for market, social and economic research. The Society aims to promote and protect the interests of the profession, and to maintain and improve standards of competence.

market share The proportion of a market accounted for by a particular brand or supplier, either by volume or by value, or sometimes in terms of the number of consumers.

marketing The management function responsible for identifying, anticipating and satisfying consumer requirements profitably.

marketing mix The set of choices made by an organization in respect of those marketing factors that it can control. Important categories in the marketing mix are the so-called four Ps, namely product, price, place and promotion.

mean The arithmetic mean. Sometimes refers to other kinds of average.

media May refer to any means of communication. In an advertising context, includes independent television and radio, newspapers and magazines, poster sites, movie theatres and other means by which advertising is communicated.

media research Research into readership and media audiences.

media schedule A plan for an advertising campaign setting out the media to be used, when and how often the advertisement is to appear and other such details.

median The middle of a set of numbers, half of the numbers being larger and half being smaller.

mode The most frequently occurring value in a set of observations.

moderator The leader of a group discussion.

monadic A monadic product test is one in which each person tests just one product, as distinct from comparative tests, eg diadic and triadic tests.

monopolar An attitude scale is monopolar, as opposed to bipolar, where it measures one quality only.

motivation research Small-scale studies aimed at discovering reasons for people's behaviour.

moving average For a time series, a series of averages such that each covers the same number of successive periods.

multi-client research Also termed syndicated research, this describes studies for which the costs and the findings are shared amongst a number of clients.

multi-phase sampling A survey in which some information is collected from the whole sample, and additional information is collected from subsamples, whether at the same time or later.

multiple-choice question A closed question with more than two possible answers apart from 'don't know', sometimes termed a cafeteria question.

multiple regression A mathematical model in which a dependent variable is represented as a linear function of so-called independent or predicated variables.

multi-stage sampling A sample that is drawn in stages. The units sampled at each stage are each regarded as being composed of a number of units of the next stage, until the final sampling units are reached, ie the people who are actually interviewed.

multivariate Multivariate data comprise observations for each of which three or more variate values are recorded. Multivariate statistical methods are those that simultaneously examine the relationships among a number of variables.

National Readership Survey A continuous readership survey established in 1954 by the Institute of Practitioners in Advertising, and since 1968 conducted under the aegis of the Joint Industry Committee for National Readership Surveys.

nested sampling See **multi-stage sampling**.

niche A small and specialized market segment that is capable of being profitably exploited.

non-response That part of a pre-selected sample of named individuals, or of any random sample, from which no response is obtained.

normal distribution Also known as the normal curve and the Gaussian distribution. A statistical frequency distribution that is of particular importance in sampling theory, since it is a close approximation to the sampling distributions of many statistics derived from reasonably large samples. It is used to make statements about the confidence limits that may be attached to estimates derived from random samples, and for tests of statistical significance.

normative Normative beliefs and statements, as opposed to positive beliefs and statements, are those that concern value judgements. They express opinions about what ought to be.

null hypothesis The central hypothesis in a test of statistical significance.

numerical scale Any scale that is represented by numbers, as distinguished from diagrammatic and from verbal scales.

objective A market research proposal incorporates a statement of the information objectives of the project, and these may be explicitly related to marketing objectives.

observation The alternative to questioning as a way of obtaining primary data.

occupation The basis of classification by social grade and of other social status scales.

omnibus survey A survey that covers a number of topics, usually for different clients.

open-ended question As opposed to a pre-coded question, one where the answer is recorded verbatim, or as fully as practicable, and the answers are coded at a later stage.

opinion poll A survey of opinions about political, social and other issues of public interest, especially as a basis for forecasting voting behaviour.

opportunity to see A single impact, exposure or opportunity to see an advertisement is effectively defined by the method of audience measurement.

optimization analysis In sensory evaluation, optimization analysis can be carried out when sufficient data points are collected on formula variables in a controlled research design.

ordinal scale Ordinal numbers express precedence (first, second, third, etc) and an ordinal scale is one that produces such a ranking.

Osgood scale See **semantic differential**.

outdoor advertising A term covering posters, supersites, signs, facias, advertisements on vehicles and in general all advertising that appears in public places.

Outdoor Site Classification and Audience Research OSCAR was the UK poster audience research system, launched in October 1985 by the Outdoor Advertising Association.

overclaim A tendency for respondents to say that they have done something more often, have consumed more of something, etc than is in fact the case.

pack test Any kind of market research to evaluate a package design, in terms of for example its functional efficiency, its visual impact at the point of sale, the image it conveys of the product and its influence on sales.

paired comparison A product test, also known as a diadic test, in which people are asked to compare two products.

panel A sample of people, households or retail outlets, or sometimes of other kinds of organization, from which information is obtained on more than one occasion.

penetration The proportion of a population or of a subgroup that has a certain characteristic.

peoplemeter An audimeter with provision for recording whether individuals are present.

personal interview Usually taken to mean an interview carried out face to face between an interviewer and a respondent.

pilot A pilot survey is a small-scale replica of a main survey, carried out beforehand in order to reveal the problems likely to be encountered, or to help in the design of the main survey.

placement test A product test in which samples of the product are given to people to try in their own homes, or wherever the product is normally used.

poll A sample survey in which political opinions form the subject matter.

population The whole of the material from which a sample may be taken.

postal survey Any survey carried out by post, using a self-completion questionnaire or diary. A mail survey in US usage.

poster research Research to measure audiences for outdoor advertising.

pre-coded question A question for which the respondent is constrained to choose one or more from a set of allowable answers, or where the interviewer is similarly constrained in recording the answer given.

preference test A product test in which consumers are asked to compare a number of trial products, and to express their preferences.

pre/post Refers to market research conducted before some event, such as a product launch or advertising campaign, and repeated afterwards.

preselected sample A sample in which the individuals who are to be interviewed have been selected prior to fieldwork, as distinguished from field sampling in which the interviewer makes the final selection.

pre-test As opposed to post-test, a test of something before it has been exposed to the public, particularly advertising and promotional material.

pricing research Any kind of research that aims to show how demand for a product or service will vary with its price.

primary data As opposed to secondary data, primary data are those collected at source.

probability A basic concept that expresses the likelihood or chance that something will happen.

probe Any non-directive stimulus that an interviewer uses in order to obtain an answer from an informant, or to encourage elucidation of the original answer, or to seek additional detail.

product test Any research in which consumers, or potential consumers, are invited to try out a product.

profile A description of a group of people, in terms of their sex, age and other demographics, and possibly their behaviour and attitudes.

projective techniques Methods used in qualitative research to overcome barriers to communication between the informant and the interviewer.

prompt As distinct from a probe, this term covers any method used to suggest possible answers to a question.

prompt card A card that lists the possible answers to a question.

proportional sample Where the sample size from each stratum of a stratified sample is proportional to the number in the population within that stratum.

proposal(s) A plan for a market research study.

psychodrawing A projective technique that requires people to express themselves non-verbally, by making a drawing that reflects their feelings about a product or brand.

psychographics Also termed psychometrics, the segmentation or classification of people into groups that are primarily of a psychological character.

qualitative research A body of research techniques that can primarily be distinguished from quantitative methods because they do not attempt to make measurements. Instead, they seek insights through a less structured, more flexible approach.

quality control In a market research project, formal checks to ensure that the work is properly carried out.

quantitative research Any research that seeks to make measurements.

questionnaire A list of questions that normally includes instructions as to its use, and provides for the recording of answers and administrative details, as well as showing the actual questions.

quota A statement of the number and types of people that an interviewer is required to interview.

quota sample A form of non-random or purposive sampling widely use in market research.

random sample In market research, a random or probability sample is usually regarded as one in which each individual has a known (and non-zero) chance of inclusion, ie a calculable a priori selection probability.

random walk A method of sampling addresses in urban areas. Starting addresses are first selected by random methods. Beginning at one of these addresses, an interviewer follows a predetermined route, making calls at regular intervals.

ranking question A question that asks the respondent to place items in order.

rating scale A scale used by a respondent when answering a question.

readership research Surveys that aim to estimate the numbers and characteristics of people who read a newspaper or magazine.

recall Recall studies and questions are those that seek to establish what someone can remember.

recruiting Finding suitable people to take part in group discussions, panels, etc.

refusal rate The number of people who refuse to be interviewed, as a proportion either of the number selected for the sample, or of the number of contacts.

repertory grid (Kelly's) A method of exploratory research used to elicit the ideas that someone has about for example different brands in a product field.

response rate The number of adequately completed interviews, questionnaires, etc obtained from a survey, expressed as a percentage of the number of eligible individuals.

retail audit A method of obtaining information about the movement of consumer products into and out of retail outlets. It uses a panel of shops or other kinds of retail outlet. Audits are carried out at regular intervals such as every four weeks or two months.

round robin An experimental design for product testing by the method of paired comparisons, in which each product is tested against every other product.

sample A part or subset of a population sample size. The number of units in a sample.

sample survey A survey using a sample, as distinct from a census.

sampling error An estimate derived from a sample is usually different from the true value for the population as a whole. The term standard error is often used to refer to sampling error.

score A numerical value assigned to an observation, eg an answer given in response to a rating scale.

screening A brief interview for the purpose of locating individuals with certain characteristics who are needed for a survey.

segment A part of a market or population.

segmentation Division of a market into parts, each of which has identifiable characteristics of actual or potential economic interest. Most often segmentation is in terms either of characteristics of the product or service, or of purchaser/user characteristics.

self-completion A self-completion questionnaire is one that is completed by the informant rather than by an interviewer.

semantic differential A commonly used attitude scaling technique, also known as Osgood scales. It is a bipolar diagrammatic rating scale.

semi-structured An interview or questionnaire in which many or even all of the questions may have been specified in advance, but the questions are typically of open or open-ended form, and there is extensive use of probing techniques.

sensory evaluation This is a research technique to assist technical, research and development management design better products. Data are mapped to show where the subject being researched stands against consumer preferences and in comparison with competition.

significance test Analysis of sample data, to show whether or not they support a given hypothesis about the parent population(s).

simulated test market See **laboratory test market**.

SMART (salient multi-attribute research technique) This technique takes the view that a better way to measure interest in a service company's change is in terms of improvements. The aim of the analysis is specialized since it concentrates on identifying areas of highest cost/benefit in service areas.

social grade (or socioeconomic class) The traditional socioeconomic classification system used by the National Readership Survey, and generally for market research in the UK. The social grade of an informant has been based on the occupation or former occupation of the head of the family unit or, in certain circumstances, eg where the head of the family unit is retired or unemployed and has a low income, it may be based on the occupation of the chief wage earner. Usually this person is also the head of the household.

	New structure	Old structure
Class 1a	Large employers, higher manager. Company director. Senior police/ fire/prison/military officer. Newspaper editor. Football manager (with squad of 25 plus). Restaurateur	A: Professional CLASS 1
Class 1b	Professionals. Doctor. Solicitor. Engineer. Teacher. Airline pilot	
Class 2	Associate professionals. Journalist. Nurse/Midwife. Actor/Musician. Military NCO. Junior police/fire/ prison officer. Lower managers (fewer than 25 staff)	B: Managerial/ technical CLASS 2
Class 3	Intermediate occupations. Secretary. Air stewardess. Driving instructor. Footballer (employee sportsman). Telephone operator	C1: Skilled (non-manual) CLASS 3

Class 4	Small employees/managers, non-professional self-employed. Publican. Plumber. Golfer/tennis player (self-employed sportsman). Farm owner/manager (fewer than 25 employees)	C2: Skilled (manual) CLASS 3
Class 5	Lower supervisors, craft and related workers. Electrician. Mechanic. Train driver. Building site/factory foreman. Bus inspector	D: Partly skilled CLASS 4
Class 6	Semi-routine occupations. Traffic warden. Caretaker. Gardener. Supermarket shelf-stacker. Assembly-line worker	
Class 7	Routine occupation. Cleaner. Waiter/waitress/bar staff. Messenger/courier. Road-worker. Docker	E: Unskilled CLASS 5
Class 8	Excluded. Long-term unemployed. Never worked. Long-term sick	Other CLASS 6

Standard Industrial Classification A classification of industrial establishments.

Standard Region One of the 10 regions into which Great Britain is divided according to the Registrar General's system.

storyboard A set of drawings together with a script and a description of sound effects, which sets out the action in a television commercial.

stratification A technique used in sampling, to ensure that the sample is representative in terms of the factor(s) used for stratification. The population is first divided into a number of subgroups or strata, eg by geographical area. The required numbers are then sampled from each stratum.

street interview A brief interview conducted in the street or other public place, usually employing a quota sample.

structured A structured questionnaire sets out precisely the wording of the questions and the order in which they are to be asked.

t-test A test of statistical significance, based on the use of tables of Student's t-distribution. This describes the sampling distribution of the mean for small samples, ie where the sample size is less than 30 or so. The t-test may be used to compute confidence intervals, to test whether an observed sample mean differs significantly from some expected value and to test the difference between two sample means.

tachistoscope A device that permits brief glimpses of stimulus material, the exposures being controllable in small steps from .01 second or less.

time series A set of sequential values that are dependent on time, ie statistics of quantitative observations of some kind that relate to different periods of or moments in time.

topic guide A list of the topics to be covered in a depth interview or group discussion.

trade-off analysis A research method aimed at discovering the most attractive combinations of attributes for a product or service. Price may be included as one of the attributes, represented at a number of levels. See also **conjoint measurement**.

traffic count Observation of the flow of vehicles or people past a point or along a route, used in for example poster audience research and transport planning.

variance A statistical measure of the variability or dispersion of a set of numbers. It is the arithmetic mean of the squared differences between each number and the mean of all the numbers.

variate A variable that has an associated frequency distribution, eg all the quantities measured in a survey, whether facts or opinions, can be described as variates.

verbal (rating) scale Any kind of scale for the measurement of attitudes or behaviour in which the permissible answers are expressed verbally, as distinguished from diagrammatic or numerical scales.

visual aid Anything that is shown to someone as an aid to communication. In market research the term is applied to the prompt cards, etc used in interviews.

weighted sample A sample to which post-weighting has been applied, ie weighting after fieldwork.

weighting A process that assigns numerical coefficients (weights or weighting factors) to each of the elements in a dataset, in order to provide them with a desired degree of importance relative to one another. Post-weighting is commonly used in market research to correct any imbalances in the demographic profile of a sample.

Index